Bats, Balls, & Burnouts

A Life of Sports, Marketing, and Mayhem

by Bob Wilber

Bats, Balls, and Burnouts
A Life of Sports, Marketing, and Mayhem
All Rights Reserved.
Copyright © 2017 Bob Wilber
v3.0

The opinions expressed in this manuscript are solely the opinions of the author and do not represent the opinions or thoughts of the publisher. The author has represented and warranted full ownership and/or legal right to publish all the materials in this book.

This book may not be reproduced, transmitted, or stored in whole or in part by any means, including graphic, electronic, or mechanical without the express written consent of the publisher except in the case of brief quotations embodied in critical articles and reviews.

Outskirts Press, Inc.
http://www.outskirtspress.com

ISBN: 978-1-4787-7572-0

Cover Design © 2017 Todd Myers
Front cover photo courtesy of Mark J. Rebilas
Back cover photos courtesy of Mark J. Rebilas and Southern Illinois University - Edwardsville Sports Information Department
All rights reserved - used with permission.

Outskirts Press and the "OP" logo are trademarks belonging to Outskirts Press, Inc.

PRINTED IN THE UNITED STATES OF AMERICA

More praise for "Bats, Balls, & Burnouts"

"Being raised in a sports family was simply good fortune for Bob Wilber. Being able to write about it in such a compelling way is pure skill. Whether it's home runs, soccer goals, 300 mph Funny Cars, or the days and characters that connect all of those subjects, *Bats, Balls, & Burnouts* is a great read." -Dave St. Peter, President and CEO, Minnesota Twins

"Bob Wilber's life can be summed up by the phrase, 'Well, that didn't go as planned.' But it did go to some very interesting places for a guy who was never afraid to take a leap of faith. *Bats, Balls, & Burnouts* takes the reader on the journey." -Alan Reinhart, NHRA Public Address Announcer

"*Bats, Balls, & Burnouts* isn't just for sports fans; this book is for anyone who loves a good story. Bob Wilber draws you into each tale with a deft weaving of words and depictions of larger-than-life characters. A delightful, fun, and touching look behind-the-scenes. Loved it!" –Kelly Topolinski, Motorsports Public Relations, WinLight Communications

"Bob Wilber is a storyteller's storyteller. He has lived his life inside the locker rooms, on the fields and in the pressrooms with some of the most colorful athletes of this generation." -Elon Werner, Director of Public Relations, John Force Racing

"I was introduced to Bob Wilber and his story telling via his NHRA blog. I've been captivated by his humor, perspective, and unique ability to tell a story in a way that makes you feel as if you are experiencing it in person. *Bats, Balls, & Burnouts* draws you into his life while giving you a visceral experience in which you can feel the pine tar, hear the crack of the bat, and smell the burning rubber." -Buck Hujabre, Stage Actor "Jersey Boys"

"What an adventure. What a life. What a fun read. Bob Wilber is a great raconteur and he weaves together the wonderful TRUE story of his life and times. His love for baseball, soccer, and drag racing comes through easily and clearly. Chapter after chapter, you'll look forward to each of his incredible adventures and get a unique view of the sports world from a true insider."
-Pat Caporali, Senior Manager - Media Relations, INDYCAR

"Bob Wilber provides an insider's view of three professional sports—baseball, soccer and drag racing. As someone who played pro baseball and scouted prospects after his playing days, Wilber offers an engaging and humorous look into two aspects of the game that we seldom read about: the day-to-day life of minor leaguers and the unsung scouts who discover the talent we watch on major league baseball fields. His energetic "plow forward" approach to his many endeavors shines in his storytelling." -Thom Henninger, author of *Tony Oliva - The Life and Times of a Minnesota Twins Legend*

"Bob Wilber's indoor soccer stories are vivid, and bring back a lot of great memories from my playing days. His ability to write about baseball, drag racing, sports marketing, and life in general make those subjects just as riveting. *Bats, Balls, & Burnouts* is a great read for anyone."
-Greg Villa, former professional soccer player (outdoor and indoor) and former member of the U.S. Men's National Team

*Dedicated to my loving, talented, and
inspiring wife, Barbara Doyle.
This would never have happened without you.*

*In eternal memory of Del and Taffy Wilber.
I will always be "the luckiest kid in the world"*

Foreword

By Del Worsham

Bob and I were lucky. We both had the same passion, and that was drag racing.

Drag racing is a crazy sport. There seems to be a place for everybody. Whether you're doing P.R. and sponsorship work like Bob was, or if you want to be a driver or a mechanic — there's a spot out there for you if you love drag racing and work at it hard enough. Bob found his niche with us, and we ended up becoming the best of friends.

We spent an ungodly amount of time together. I met my wife not long after Bob and I became friends, and he was the best man at my wedding. I even knew Bob before he met his wife, Barbara. Basically, you could say I grew up knowing Bob. I learned a lot about myself and racing from Bob — about being professional, how to win and definitely how to lose.

When we lost the sponsorship and it all came to an end, we all were fortunate. We found jobs within days, and we went on to be successful in our own ways after that. But I'm sure that in our time together, I learned to be a man from Bob.

Bob's a special individual, in that no matter what he does he's successful at it. Whatever he decides to do, he does it well.

Now that he's starting a new part of his life, away from drag racing, I hope he goes on to be happy. I hope he's happy with what he's accomplished and that he has no regrets.

I'm thankful for everything he taught me.

— Del Worsham and his father, Chuck, are drag racers. Starting in 1991, when he was named NHRA Rookie of the Year as a 21-year old, Del drove family-owned Funny Cars for nearly two decades. Bob Wilber joined the Worsham organization in 1997 when CSK Auto began sponsoring the team, and he worked closely with the Worshams for 12 years, until CSK was acquired by another auto parts retailer. After Del won a total of 22 races with his family, he joined Alan Johnson's team in 2009, where he won the 2011 NHRA Top Fuel championship. In 2015, driving for drag racing legend Connie Kalitta, Del also won the Funny Car title — joining Kenny Bernstein and Gary Scelzi as the only drivers to claim championships in both NHRA nitro classes. At the end of the 2016 season, Del announced he was leaving Kalitta Motorsports to once again campaign a Funny Car with his father.

Foreword

By Pete Delkus

Bob and I played together for the Sauget Wizards, a semipro baseball team just across the river from St. Louis. And eventually, when I got a minor league contract, Bob became my agent, landing me a deal for shoes and other equipment. He became my best friend and adviser.

But my best memories of Bob have nothing to do with baseball.

We lived together a couple of winters, and Bob was the greatest roommate ever. I looked up to him. He's so damned smart and a hell of a writer. I wanted to emulate his qualities.

He was heavily into music — Pink Floyd, Genesis, bands like that. One time I had my girlfriend over, and I tried to impress her by playing Pink Floyd. We've been married 25 years now, but a couple years ago she asked me, "What were you thinking, playing Pink Floyd?" And I said, "It's Bob's fault."

I'm from a little town outside St. Louis. My father worked for the street department. Mom worked in a cafeteria. But one summer, when I was playing minor league ball in Tennessee — coincidentally, in a little town where Bob had also played — I drove to Virginia and Bob showed me around Washington, D.C. He opened my eyes to a world that had only existed in books.

He gave me that longing to want to travel and see the world. He shaped who I am.

Bob has no idea of the impact he's had on my life. Forget baseball. It's Bob who made me the person I became.

He's given his best to so many people, unknowingly, as they crossed his path. I don't know about Karma, but I believe good things come to people who do good things. And I believe good things will continue to come to Bob. *Bats, Balls, & Burnouts* contains the stories behind all of that Karma. He was born to write this book.

- *Pete Delkus and Bob Wilber attended the same college, played collegiate baseball for the same program, and graduated with the same degree. They did that, however, nine years apart. They met in the mid-1980s while both played for a semipro baseball team near St. Louis, and a deep and lasting friendship quickly developed. After a stellar professional baseball career in the Minnesota Twins organization, Pete became an award-winning television weather forecaster, first in Orlando, then in Cincinnati. In 2005 he became the chief meteorologist at WFAA in Dallas. Through 2016, he had won 11 Emmy Awards.*

Table of Contents

1	A Most Uncommon Childhood	1
2	The Sixties	10
3	Becoming A Junior Billiken	22
4	Four Epic Summers	31
5	Growing Up Wilber	43
6	College As A Cougar	50
7	Paintsville?	75
8	Young, Dumb, And Having Fun	101
9	Living The Dream	108
10	A Quick Change Of Plans	130
11	Pitching Can Take You Places	152
12	Learn From Your Mistakes	161
13	Pretending To Be A Scout	165
14	Beating The Bushes	187
15	Got Sneakers?	199
16	Suits And Ties	209
17	A Ballplayer And A Storm	233
18	Moving Too Fast	245
19	Escape	259
20	Hello New Jersey	279
21	More Soccer Balls	288
22	A Most Interesting Indy Experience	307
23	The Dream Comes True	318
24	Winning Is Good	337
25	A Watershed Year	356
26	The Hits Keep On Comin'	372
27	The Highest Highs	388
28	End Of An Era	399

29	A Fresh New Challenge	420
30	New Races, New Places	434
31	Aches And Pains	453
32	Got Wilk? Know The Man	473
33	A Life-Altering Decision	487
Epilogue		507
Photographic Evidence		511

A Most Uncommon Childhood

What are your earliest memories? How old were you? Where were you?

I was three, and would soon turn four on June 19, 1960. We were not at home in Kirkwood, Missouri. Instead, we were spending the summer in Charleston, West Virginia in a stately home that had once belonged to the mayor.

I have earlier memories, but they are merely snippets of toddlerhood. I can recall, for instance, when I was small enough to push off of one end of the half-filled bathtub with my little feet and actually "swim" to the other end. It was not a big tub. I was a little guy.

In 1960, though, the memories solidified. It was the summer I figured out that being a Wilber was a little different, even unique, in comparison to the families who lived around us and the kids with whom we would share classrooms. It was also the first summer I became aware of baseball.

Big Del Wilber, my father, had played in the major leagues for the Cardinals, Phillies, and Red Sox before I was born. In 1960, when I celebrated that fourth birthday, he was the manager of the Charleston Senators, the Triple-A affiliate of the Washington Senators who would move to Minnesota a year later and become the Twins. My sister Mary and I were not yet of school age, but once sister Cindy and brother Rick were set free by Sister Gertrude Marie at Mary Queen of Peace, we packed up the family car and our mom, Taffy, drove us to Charleston. My oldest brother, Del Jr., stayed behind to finish his baseball season as a 15-year old who was already a prospect (both on the diamond and on the gridiron) and whose name was quite familiar to all the pro scouts around the St. Louis area. Del would join us later in the summer.

Our car was a Vauxhall, and we called it "The Box." It had the latest features for a late-50s model, including the cutting-edge MRA safety system. MRA stood for Mom's Right Arm, and it deployed automatically whenever an abrupt stop was made, pinning us to the large bench seat in front. In addition, to cut down on contusions or other bruises (and instead go straight to cracked skulls), the Vauxhall featured a shiny steel dashboard.

We rented the massive home on Virginia Street, just a block away from the Kanawha River and only a mile or so from Watt Powell Park, where the Senators played. It had a large open front porch, a grand piano in the living room, and more space and historic charm than any of us were accustomed to in our split-level contemporary back in Kirkwood, where five kids and two parents shared three entire bedrooms. To us, the Charleston house was a mansion. For our dog Zorro, it was territory and he took it upon himself to mark his abode on a daily basis by pooping under the piano before anyone could take him for a walk. These are the things a three-year-old remembers.

I also vividly remember going to the ballgames, although I don't recall much of the action on the field. I was small enough to fit neatly onto my mother's lap in our grandstand seats and I could peer off into the darkness to spot my father in the third-base coach's box. That was Dad. We were in Charleston. Little Bobby Wilber began to realize that something different was unfolding.

The 1960 Senators team featured a number of soon-to-be stars for the Twins, but at the time they were simply prospects for Washington — players like Jim Kaat, Zoilo Versalles (whom we all called Zorro because we couldn't pronounce his name and, well, we already had a dog with that moniker), Don Mincher, Sandy Valdespino, Charlie James, Garland Shifflett (remember that name), and Jim Delsing. Delsing was 34 years old that summer and had already put in parts of 10 seasons in the big leagues, including a successful stint with the St. Louis Browns. Like the Wilber clan and many other baseball families, the Delsings put down roots in St. Louis and our paths would intersect many times over the coming years. Sports are sort of like that. 10 years before I was born my father made his Major League debut with the St. Louis Cardinals. That's when the Wilbers put down St. Louis roots of their own.

My sister Cindy became good friends with Jim's daughter Kim Delsing, and they were part of the inaugural group of usherettes at Busch Stadium in St. Louis when they were teens. Having attractive young ladies showing fans to their box seats was a real innovation in the hip 60s — and quite an improvement over the elderly and often crusty old men in blue suits who traditionally acted as ushers. It was also a development of which our mother was a part, when she worked for the Cardinals' front office.

Jim's son Jay Delsing went on to a successful professional golf career and we all followed his progress on the PGA tour. Daughter Moochie Delsing married one of my baseball teammates from high school and college, Tim Twellman, who was a fine ballplayer but an outstanding soccer player. Tim went on to a terrific pro soccer career and he and Moochie can be just as proud of their son Taylor, who played on many incarnations of the U.S. national team and was a certified star in Major League Soccer. Taylor now does color commentary on national television broadcasts during World Cups and qualifying.

It's Jim Delsing himself, however, who takes the family cake for one of the most memorable pinch-running assignments in Major League history.

Browns' owner and legendary promoter Bill Veeck signed three-foot-seven Eddie Gaedel and sent him to the plate with a toy bat Aug. 19, 1951, to pinch hit against the Detroit Tigers. When Gaedel walked on four straight pitches, Manager Zack Taylor sent Delsing in to run for him. Delsing is reported to have proudly stated, with tongue firmly planted in cheek, "Roger Maris may have hit 61 (home runs), but I ran for a midget." Yes, he did. And he played for the 1960 Charleston Senators on the back side of his baseball career.

On game nights at Watt Powell Park I'd curl up on my mom's lap and stare at the roof over the grandstand. It was a cozy little brick and steel ballpark, like others scattered around the high minors back then. It may have held 5,000 people but to the toddler version of me Watt Powell was as enormous as Yankee Stadium. At three, of course, I had never seen Yankee Stadium but perspective is everything at that age.

Under the grandstand roof hung pendant lights with gumdrop-shaped shades, painted white on the underside to give the low-power bulbs an assist, and green on top, complete with layers of dust and the requisite bird droppings. They created a sort of murky half-light throughout the grandstands and they mesmerized me. At that young age, I was unaware that Watt Powell's playing surface featured an odd "corner" in centerfield rather than the typical curved outfield wall. The wall simply followed the contours of the block upon which the ballpark sat, so it came to a point 420 feet from home plate. You'd think I'd remember that, but it's those pendant lights that represent my most vivid memories of Watt Powell Park.

I do recall one bit of in-game action on a night when Dad went out to the mound to change pitchers and my mom pointed that out to me. I said, "I see Daddy, out there on that bump in the field." That got big laughs, and the unexpected feedback from my siblings and mother were no doubt directly related to the start of my comedy career.

If the Senators won, the club shot off fireworks after the final out. I hated them (the fireworks, not the team) because they scared me. So, while I was just learning the game I was already not a big fan of Senators' victories despite the fact my dad's job pretty much depended on them. It was all about me, then.

I did enjoy going into the clubhouse before and after games getting to know the stars of the team who loomed above me like giants. They had nicknames like "Kitty" and "Zorro" and "Minch" and they adopted me as a sort of mascot. I learned in later years that any smart ballplayer would naturally be pretty nice to the manager's son. I led a charmed life, even at three.

Before the season ended, Zorro (Zoilo) presented me with his Rawlings Trap-Eze fielder's glove. It was a man's glove on a little boy's hand, and I cherished it and kept it for years. That would be a rare thing for a kid who grew up with a house full of baseball possessions, most of which simply faded away over time or, in the case of so many valuable baseball cards, ended up between the spokes of my bike. I treasured that six-finger glove with Zoilo's name on it — my first "real" glove. All those that came before it were simply cheap children's replica mitts. Just after turning four, I had the real thing. That's a good memory to have.

One afternoon before a home game, Dad took me with him to a Charleston television station where he was scheduled to be interviewed. It was just another indication that he was something special, and I clearly remember sitting off to the side as the interviewer talked to him live on the air about the Senators. There were small monitors everywhere and a big boom microphone towering over the cameras and the men operating them. After "being a good boy" for as long as possible, I finally slid over ever so carefully to photobomb the scene. I was a ham, even then. And Big Del thought it was pretty hilarious. Once again, there I was getting laughs. Kitty, Zorro, and Minch heard all about it in the clubhouse that night.

Once we got back from Charleston at the end of that summer, I was aware I no longer had any more winters of scheduled freedom. It was time for nursery school which meant no more winter days scribbling and playing with Mary. Our favorite made-up games were "train," in which we'd line up dining room chairs to simulate a train car, and "elevator," in which we'd stand (for some reason) on the wooden frames of our large living room windows and pretend to go up and down. We accessorized our make-believe elevators by carving floor numbers in the blond wood frames with a pencil. Those numbers were still there when we finally sold the house in the late '90s. We were proud of our work. It had staying power.

I was cognizant that my freedom was about to end and decades of school would follow. Decades! I wasn't even half a decade old, and I wasn't crazy about the thought.

I also noticed something else happening around the house. After the Washington Senators moved to Minnesota to become the Twins, Big Del switched from being the Triple-A manager to being the club's top scout. And Minnesota Twins "stuff" was soon everywhere. Stationery, ash trays, pens, and a TC hat for me. I've said for years that I'm relatively certain I was the only kid in suburban St. Louis who grew up with a TC hat on his head, and my love affair with the Twins continues to this day.

When my joyous freedom was finally scheduled to end with half-days at nursery school, I was carted off like a prisoner to a little one-room building tucked (hidden, perhaps?) behind a bigger school building. I felt like I was being incarcerated. So I did what any four-year-old with a plan would do. I cried. All day. Nonstop.

The woman in charge of said prison kindly asked my mother to keep me at home. The master plan had worked! I had earned another year of freedom, and since Mary was by then in kindergarten, I had the house to myself. At the age of four, I was officially a drop-out, and proud of it.

It was also becoming clear that I was not going to be a particularly healthy young guy. Right around this time doctor visits became more regular as I struggled with chronic asthma and allergies. Specialists were found (thank you Dr. Hampton and Dr. Harrison, may you both rest in peace) and a lengthy list of meds were prescribed. Before I was six, I was getting a shot once a week and taking at least four different liquid prescriptions.

I was a sick kid. Quite sick and quite often. It got so bad that we kept a vial of adrenalin in the refrigerator in case the asthma put me at risk of heart stoppages. And when the asthma wasn't afflicting me, the allergies were pretty non-stop. I grew up with a constantly runny nose and puffy eyes, but compared to the wheezing and difficult breathing I accepted that as a decent alternative. Every day, I took a spoonful of "red medicine" that was laced with so much sugar and cherry flavoring the cap would crust over long before the bottle was empty. If things took a turn for the worse, the next level was a foul-tasting brown medicine we called "Witch's Brew." Good times. Until I turned 10, I spent far too much time at the bedroom window watching other kids having fun outside while I was confined to my room.

The best part of being sick is when it's over. After each bout of asthma or flare-up of allergies, or even just normal kid illnesses like sore throats and the flu, Mom would reward me with a trip to Steak 'n Shake after I started feeling better. Steak 'n Shake still holds a prominent place in my life, and I always feel just a little bit better when I eat there. Steakburger please, with onions, pickles, and relish.

At five I did go to school, and this time I accepted my fate. But I simply couldn't concentrate on what the fine sisters (complete with classic flowing black and white habits) were teaching me when it came to math and science. Reading was fun, art class was my favorite, and man, did I love recess. Our kickball games were epic.

During late spring in first grade, something happened that changed my life forever. There was no first-grade baseball team, but with my last name being Wilber (and with my dad still well-known as an ex-Cardinal) the volunteer coaches put me on the second-grade team.

There was no T-ball then. They lined us up, told us to take the field, and we were playing baseball. At least we thought we were. I have no idea what we were actually doing, but I was out there playing the game my father had taught me, on a real field instead of in the backyard.

The location was Schall School in Rock Hill, Mo. We were the Mary Queen of Peace team, but MQP had only an asphalt playground, so for eight years we played at a variety of other schools and fields around Kirkwood, Webster Groves, Warson Woods, and Rock Hill. Not a single home game in eight years. We should've organized a work stoppage!

My mom was at my first practice. I'd say the odds are enormous that Big Del was off on a scouting trip, as he almost always was from February to November. I was standing in the outfield trying to pay attention when a coach decided to hit the most important fly ball of my life. I assume he was just hitting one to the outfield to give us something to chase, but he hit it right to me. And then he yelled for me to move. And then Taffy screamed "GET OUT OF THE WAY!" I calmly raised my glove and caught it. It didn't surprise me in the least. I was born to play the game.

Today, I have no idea what most of my internet passwords are. I have a really hard time remembering my wife's phone number, and if I don't take a list to the grocery store there is a 99 percent chance I will return home without the single most important item I went to get. But — and this is important — at 60 years of age I vividly remember catching my first fly ball, and that was roughly 54 years ago. I can still remember the field at Schall School, which no longer exists. I can still remember the chain-link backstop, and in my mind I can still see that ball coming right to me. I think that's pretty much indicative of my entire life. See the ball, catch the ball. It's pretty simple.

Surprisingly, I was not unanimously and immediately inducted into some sort of MQP Hall of Fame in honor of my feat, but I was instantly recognized as the best player on the team. And, even though I missed 61 days of school due to illness in first grade, the nuns somehow let me move on to second grade. I don't know if being Del and Taffy Wilber's youngest child had anything to do with that, but I'm actually a little surprised I could even read.

Those grade school baseball seasons all melt into a long stream of diamonds and bases now, and as the years went on I morphed into a pretty good third baseman. We were enormously terrible for a few years, but once fifth grade happened my teammates all started getting better, as did I. I was generally the best kid on the team although by no means the healthiest or most athletic. I had a runny nose and an inhaler in my pocket, but I could play.

And just now, for the first time, I realized how special those MQP years were. Most of us got to play together for six or seven years. We grew up and developed together as players until we were finally pretty good and winning a lot of games. Even if my nose was still runny.

Playing baseball for MQP was only a small part of my childhood "career," though. While those seasons seemed long enough, I'm relatively sure they couldn't have featured more than 10 or 12 games each. The rest of each summer was spent at Fred's Field.

On Woodleaf Court, if you walked down to the circle at the end of the cul-de-sac you could cut through the side yards between the Hoffs' house and Drew Copley's place. Back there, you'd encounter a half-acre of woods lined with well trampled paths. At the top end of those woods lay a downed chain-link fence we could easily step over, and then we were standing on hallowed ground. Fred's Field — in all its quirky glory.

With an endless supply of bats and balls (thanks to my very accommodating father) we were never short of equipment but we were always short of the number of players needed for a full diamond, and the nearest one of those was just far enough away (about six blocks) to make it undesirable. So, after Scott Priesmeyer, Timmy Meehan, Bobby Stryler, the Reilly brothers, and Scott Youngstrom had screeched to a halt in front of the house on their banana-seat bikes, we'd grab our gear (with gloves neatly strapped over the handle of a bat we carried like a rifle, over one shoulder) and head down to the circle, through the woods, and onto the field.

And it's worth noting that this Fred's Field group was completely separate from my MQP friends and teammates. Our parents sent us to a private catholic school but not the one in Kirkwood (St. Peter's). Instead, they sent us to MQP, which was two and a half miles away in Webster Groves. It was sixth or seventh grade before I was even allowed to ride my bike over to Webster to see my classmates.

The Fred's Field gang was from the surrounding neighborhood, although none of them ever lived on Woodleaf Court. All of us, though, lived in an area of no more than a half-mile radius, and since I had most of the equipment and our house was closest to Fred's Field, our driveway was the meeting place every summer morning. No phone calls. No emails. No announcements. Everyone would simply gather.

The naming of Fred's Field (usually shortened to just "Fred's") predated us, and no one really knew its origin. It was a large, rectangular field, perfectly designed for our endless autumn games of touch football, but its shape forced us to create new versions of baseball — versions that stayed with me for years. And all for good reason, because you didn't want to lose the baseballs you'd brought along or break any windows.

Home plate was at the back of what would be one end zone for football, just beyond the woods through which we had all just trudged. There was an old wooden backstop there, so this was meant to be a ball field, but its netting was long since torn and tattered. It couldn't stop anything, but it gave a purpose to that end of the field.

A row of pine trees lined the left side in a straight line, protecting the backyards of the houses on Drury Lane. It was another cul-de-sac like Woodleaf, abutting it circle-to-circle, but a good 25 feet higher in elevation, which made for great bike riding when descending the steep, grassy side-yard that separated the two streets. Down the right side of Fred's Field was a gentle slope leading to an upper level, where a large greenhouse sat, acting like a magnet for errant balls. Hit the ball to where left field should be, and you'd be crawling between trees and then climbing a fence to retrieve it, barring the existence of any angry dogs. Hit it to the right, and the sound of broken glass would generally end the game. Better to flee and live to play another day.

The bases were, by necessity, a tightened and stretched diamond shape rather than a perfect square, and they were nothing more than raw dirt patches in the grass. At the far end of the field sat two swing sets and a slide, and behind them the backyard of the family home inhabited by the Hartmans, the people who owned the whole parcel. Once we grew large enough to hit a fly ball as far as the swings, that became the de facto outfield wall and balls hit that far were deemed to be "automatic" home runs. It took us a few summers to get there, but in the meantime we all developed swings that would almost always hit the ball straight up the middle. I didn't become a pull hitter until I was well into my 20s, no doubt thanks to Fred's Field.

We could play full games of baseball with as few as four guys, utilizing the popular "imaginary man" on the base paths, who would invisibly move up as many bases as the hitter could reach. Frankly, the most players we could squeeze onto Fred's Field was no more than four per team, and we'd start the proceedings with a discussion of the rules for that game. It was creative, it was improvisational, and it was baseball. With no supervision, no coaching, and no umpires, we were left to our own devices, forced to cooperate and innovate if we wanted to play. With no video games or computers to distract us, we simply headed up to Fred's Field and played for hours, or at least until my sister Cindy whistled loudly enough for all of us to know it was finally dinner time. We just played.

We knew that someday we would outgrow Fred's Field, but the specter of losing our sanctuary was something of which we never spoke. It was the great beyond and we wanted nothing to do with it, but then it happened.

It was Memorial Day weekend at the end of the school year in sixth grade, and the Hartman family was having a picnic in their yard, out beyond the swings, while we organized our first makeshift game of the year, picking teams and agreeing on the rules. The unspoken knowledge that we were outgrowing Fred's clung to us that day, as we were all beginning to look less like little kids and a more like adolescents. We knew that once we could routinely hit balls as far as the Hartmans' yard, it would be over. Leave it to me to win the game that day with a towering walk-off blast that landed not by the swings, not on the slide, but clear over all of that, right in the middle of their picnic. It was a walk-off for eternity. We never played there again. Our days at Fred's Field were over. My days as a straight-away hitter were not, however.

I know for a fact that my swing, and the sickening sound of that ball landing at the feet of no less than a dozen Hartman family members, represented the last day of baseball for all the other neighborhood kids with whom I routinely played. They didn't play for their school teams and since we now had no private place to play, it was over for them, but not for me. My Fred's Field era ended, but my real baseball career continued. It was rite of passage to have played there, and a joy.

Fred's Field is long gone. The Hartmans sold the parcel to a developer, who built a subdivision there. Our home plate is now someone's backyard.

Throughout the "Great Era of Fred's Field," I also became more emotionally aware of how much I missed my dad. Taffy would take Mary and me with her to meet him at Union Station or Delmar Station when he'd come home by train, and as the '60s progressed we started making more trips to Lambert Field to meet his plane. He was a baseball scout. There were games and prospects to see. That was his job.

Oh, how we loved the winters when he'd be off the road and home with us, working a winter job, usually at Casey's Sporting Goods in downtown Kirkwood. Many nights he'd come home for dinner and then go back until closing time, and he'd often take me with him. I was the best soccer ball inflator ever. I loved those nights and the cold ride back home in the car, when I'd lay on the backseat and stare out of the rear window, trying to piece together a mental map of where we were by the turns we'd taken. I loved having Dad around.

As I progressed through grade school Taffy went to work for KMOX Radio, a CBS-owned station that beamed its programming all over the Midwest and, on certain clear nights, all over North America. They owned the rights to Cardinals broadcasts, with Jack Buck and Harry Caray filling endless summer nights with their broadcasting prowess. Baseball fans all over the Midwest, South, and even the Rocky Mountain region became Cardinals fans because KMOX came through loud and clear.

Her show on KMOX was "Taffy On The Town," and it was entertainment-based, featuring a lot of light interviews with actors, musicians, and other celebrities as they'd come through St. Louis on tour. Her tools of the trade included a microphone and a bulky reel-to-reel tape recorder in a heavy metal briefcase. I hauled that thing around for many years, as her helper.

Mary and I would accompany Taffy to the St. Louis Muny Opera, and we'd sit quietly nearby backstage as she'd interview the likes of Carol Channing, Tony Randall, Jack Klugman, or Zero Mostel. Some other kids had fathers who were baseball men and former big leaguers, and we knew them. The Schoendienst kids, the Marion kids, the Delsing kids, the Musial family, and many more. We even knew Bob Gibson's kids. But those children didn't have mothers who were radio personalities.

Mary and I also got used to running around the old KMOX studio building behind the long-gone St. Louis Arena on Hampton Avenue. We had the run of the place (including the snack room!) and were quickly taught to always make sure the "On Air" light was not illuminated before walking through any closed door.

What a surreal thing it was to be headed to school, or church on Sunday, and hear a pre-taped "Taffy On The Town" show come on the car radio. There was her voice, coming from the speaker, and yet there she was, driving the car and grinding its gears.

All of those unusual things, though, didn't preclude us from desperately wanting the same stuff the other kids wanted, even those other kids on our Woodleaf Court cul-de-sac. We wanted candy, junk food, games, and while Mary wanted dolls I wanted Revell model kits of famous hot rods, dragsters, and muscle cars. I was a terrible model builder, but following the instructions went a long way in teaching me what a manifold, a cylinder head, or a set of header pipes would look like in real life. Same exact thing, only twenty-four times bigger.

And we all wanted Farotto's Pizza. Farotto's unique "St. Louis Style" pizza (ultra-thin crust cut into squares, with a taste unique to the area thanks to the local use of Provel cheese) and their toasted ravioli were an unmatched joy to consume.

I still know the number (962-0048) because it was scrawled on the kitchen wall right next to the yellow phone with the 10-foot coiled cord that was always in knots. We'd get the word that Farotto's was for dinner and I'd excitedly make the call. Mom or Dad would drive us the mile or so down Manchester Road, and I could walk in there without any announcement. Just a kid with some money in his hand. As soon as I'd enter the door, someone behind the counter would yell "Pizza for Wilber!" And that remained true all the way through college. It was "our place," and I still make a pilgrimage there at least once a year.

The summer after eighth grade (and graduation from MQP) was a turning point, physically and emotionally. Thanks in no small part to the fact I'd been sick for most of my life, I was still a very scrawny kid. I was about to turn 14 and I was probably five-foot-six and 125 pounds, with lead weights in my pockets.

At that point, though, some of the other kids were growing fast and sprouting facial hair at the same time. I was still very much a kid and they were growing into young men. We had one baseball practice before our season was to begin and it took me mere minutes to discover that, for the first time ever, I was not the best player there.

And during batting practice someone threw a curveball. Nothing would ever be quite the same. Ever.

I also knew I'd only have time for one game that year, because right after that we were loading up Taffy's Camaro and heading for the Washington, D.C. I put the uniform on and arrived at the appointed field (yet another away game) to see what appeared to be the actual St. Louis Cardinals on the other bench. If some of my MQP teammates had matured a bit early, this group from St. Peter's had skipped right past puberty into manhood.

I was overmatched. I was disheartened. And I was really confused. But a great adventure was just beginning.

The Sixties

Whenever I'm in my car and the Sirius-XM Satellite Radio is on, the odds are pretty good that you'll find me listening to some hard rock with an edge to it. But, it's not wholly impossible that when I'm flipping favorite channels I'll settle in on what I think is the most unique collection of music currently beaming down from the sky. The channel is called '60s on 6.

Just think about the 1960s, in terms of music alone. We started the decade with acts like Connie Francis, Brenda Lee, and the Everly Brothers topping the Billboard charts. Music hadn't changed much in decades and big bands were not only popular, they were still packing them in at the clubs.

Then, on February 9, 1964, Ed Sullivan hosted a group of four lads from Liverpool on his variety show, and nothing was ever quite the same. I remember, because I had made up a handwritten note card that stated (in my scrawled penmanship) "Reserved To See The Beatles on Ed Sullivan Tonight" and taped it to the television set.

In 1969, at the end of the same decade that began with Perry Como and Annette Funicello, we had Woodstock. Think about that circuitous road from 1960. How can one decade see so much change after so little had happened since the invention of the record player? And if music was in upheaval, the social scene was also exploding, and not in many good ways.

What a decade in which to grow up. And I got to see it all.

The early part of the decade, for me, was a procession of nuns and school, day after day and week after week. Also, there was that part about being sick a lot. The two were not mutually exclusive. You haven't lived life to its bitter fullness until a cute little fifth-grade girl smiles at you and in response a large snot bubble comes out of your left nostril, causing her to scream "Eeeeewwwww" and never speak to you again.

We'd finish our final day each year at MQP with a Mass, celebrated by Monsignor O'Toole, and when he'd stand before us and utter the words "The Mass is ended. Go in peace," it was all we could do to restrain ourselves until we got out of our pews and through the heavy church doors. Then came a sprint to the school bus while tearing off the blue tie every MQP boy wore, often ripping it to shreds before even taking a seat.

Every summer contained the same three benchmarks for how much more fun we had in store or how little time we had left. My birthday was June 19, and at that point we were just getting started. My sister Mary's birthday was July 25, and by then the big see-saw was starting to tilt down toward that dreaded march back to the bus stop, the wearing of uniforms, and the endless classes. Cindy's birthday was August 17, and by then we were in full panic mode. There was no way to slow the days until that first day of school arrived.

The summer of 1963 was a big one, because for seven-year-old me the sleeping arrangements in our three-bedroom split-level were about to change forever. Del Jr. graduated from St. Louis University High in June, and that fall he headed off to West Lafayette, Indiana, to attend Purdue University on a football scholarship. With one less male in the house, I finally got my own permanent bedroom, although I shared it with brother Rick for a while and Zorro the dog for a good long time.

We made quite a few trips to West Lafayette, always passing the statue in downtown Terre Haute that featured a plaque stating, "Don't Spit On The Monument," then staying at the Morris Bryant Motel, not too far from campus.

Del joined the Sigma Chi fraternity, and I clearly recall our visits to the big stately mansion full of clean-cut and dapper young men in suits and ties. It was a different world.

Del's roommate was also a quarterback, and as fate would have it, Del would be his backup for the entirety of his time on the football team, needing to face the unfortunate circumstance of having shown up on campus the same time a superior QB also arrived. They became great friends, though, and one fall Del brought his fraternity brother and roomie back to Kirkwood to spend a holiday. Big Del had an assignment for Del Jr. when he got there, and that was to paint the exterior of the house, which featured a bit of a split-level "Brady Bunch" design that came to a point about 30 feet off the ground.

When brother Del left the house to run some errands, Big Del took the initiative. As Del Jr. pulled into the driveway later that afternoon, he was stunned and horrified to see Dad standing on the ground, supervising the work of his roommate who was on the top step of the ladder, reaching precariously to get his brush to the highest point. As Del tells it, his initial petrified thought was the image of a newspaper headline. It read "All-American Bob Griese Falls off Ladder - Wilber Scholarship Revoked"

At some juncture during every summer, we'd make our annual trip to Wamplers Lake in the Irish Hills of south-central Michigan. My father was born and raised in south Detroit, in Lincoln Park and Allen Park, and during his childhood his folks would take him and his brother Don out to Wamplers to enjoy the rough-hewn charm. That tradition was passed down to us, and our Uncle Don and Aunt Pat would often bring their kids (Michelle, Karen, Donna, and Donn) at the same time we'd be there with our grandparents.

The cottage we nearly always rented was rustic in every sense of the word, considering it didn't technically have a bathroom with actual plumbing until a few years after we started staying there. The cottage even had a name. It was King Tut, and it could actually become quite charming after we'd arrive and spend the entire first day with mops and buckets, trying to get the wooden shack as immaculate as possible. It maintained the ability, however, to always smell like dust. I sneezed a lot.

The first time I was allowed to go to Wamplers and King Tut was in the mid-'60s, and once our parents dropped us off it officially became the first time I'd ever been away from home without them. Just me, Mary, our cousins, and our grandparents. It was idyllic.

We shared three bedrooms upstairs, with rough wooden floors and walls, but the walls only extended up about seven feet, leaving the rafters and the rest of the upper area open. Each door was held closed by a hook. There was a TV in the living room, but there were no stations that could reach it via the rabbit-ears, so we had nothing to do but relax, play, and have fun.

We were a block from the lake with its clear water and sandy bottom, and had the use of a long dock. Someone had a pontoon boat tied to the end of the dock, and I remember we all knew it was OK for us to jump onto that and dive into the lake, but I don't recall ever actually knowing who owned it.

There was a general store (originally a stately old home or possibly a resort hotel from the 1920s) with wooden floors covered in sawdust, but for real groceries you had to drive into Brooklyn, about 15 miles away. At the Wamplers Lake general store, you could buy candy, taffy, and Archie comic books. We read every one of them.

We'd take our goodies back to King Tut, which had an enclosed front porch with a rocking chair and a glider, and would spend many afternoons out there, reading our comics and chewing on long sheets of taffy wrapped in wax paper. Grandad (my father's father) was in charge of pancake breakfasts almost every day. Our grandmother Edna Wilber, but always "Edna Ma" to us, was in charge of comic relief. She was a wonderful woman who just happened to look a lot like my father wearing a wig.

Once the sun began to set, we'd take a leisurely walk around Shoreline Drive to a pool hall and pavilion, where we could play pinball, spin records on the jukebox, and have childhood fun unlike much of anything we now seem to value as adults. Touring rock bands, including Creedence Clearwater Revival, Bob Seger, and Three Dog Night would stop and play in the pavilion, as they worked their way around Michigan. When the pool hall closed for the night (it seemed like midnight to us, but it had to have been no later than 10 p.m.), we walked back to King Tut under the bare yellow lightbulbs that, in theory, were designed to not attract bugs. We'd go to bed, sleep like little angels, and get up to do it all over again the next day.

Up on Route 12, there was a fun-house called Mystery Hill, where by tilting the walls and sloping the floors they could create the illusion that up was down and water ran uphill. A mile or two down the road, the "Prehistoric Forest" was an amusement park with only one ride; a tram that would take us through a maze of fake dinosaurs and miniature jungle mountains. To make the ride totally accurate, they gave us toy machine guns to shoot the tyrannosaurus rex.

Not far from King Tut was a miniature golf course and a real golf course, and over the years it was a rite of passage to graduate from mini-golf to the real links. As far as I'm aware, the real course — Greenbriar — is still there. If it is, I guarantee I'd still recognize some of the holes, especially the final one, where we teed off in a marsh amid tall reeds and had to get the ball up in the air in a hurry, because the fairway went straight uphill to the clubhouse.

There was extended family from Allen Park at the lake almost every summer, inhabiting other cottages near King Tut. They'd be there for a week and then not seen for another year, or longer. It was a totally different world, and it was priceless.

In 2008, when the NHRA racing tour was in Norwalk, Ohio, I flew in and out of Detroit for the race and booked my return flight late on Monday night so I could drive out to Wamplers (which, when we were young, we all pronounced something like "Wompers," for reasons unknown) to see if any of it was still there. It was. King Tut looked relatively the same, only better, and the glider was still on the porch. The pool hall remained, although it was shuttered. The dock was refurbished, but a pontoon boat was still tied to the end of it. I made a side trip into Brooklyn and that little town was still in a time warp, as well. It was one of the more nostalgic days of my adulthood. You could, indeed, go home again — if home was Wamplers Lake.

Our parents would eventually pick us up at Wamplers, and we'd say goodbye to our real cousins and half-maybe-cousins for another year, barring a funeral during the winter, and of course there were a few of those, including Grandad and Edna Ma. And when we'd get home it would be time for Cindy's birthday, and that could only mean that our freedom was expiring, once again. School beckoned.

I'll acknowledge it's more than slightly noticeable here I was not a big fan of elementary school. It didn't have much to do with Mary Queen of Peace, I don't think, and public schools would've likely been just as unappealing to me. The nuns were strict and the curriculum was challenging, but I was a good kid who rarely got into trouble. The only time I was sent to the principal's office by my teacher was when two other boys in my class got into a shoving match, and one pushed the other into a bookcase. Just as the entire wooden case with three shelves full of books was tipping over, I reached over to hold it up. At that exact moment, in walked our teacher, Mrs. Clough, who only saw what I was doing and not how it had happened. I was quickly sent to see Sister Ann, our principal, and I calmly told her what had occurred. She sent me back to class and explained my obviously sincere story to Mrs. Clough, who never smiled at me again.

When I look back, I think I was just a free spirit who didn't like being confined to a desk and forced to learn things I doubted I'd ever need in life, including — but not limited to — long division. Nothing much has changed, in that regard.

Another method for marking the passing of the super slow-motion time created by school was to pay attention to the sports we watched and the sports we played. We weren't, after all, simply a one-dimensional sports family, although baseball was always central to our lives. We played basketball in the driveway and football in the street and up at Fred's Field. Our parents took us to St. Louis Football Cardinals games regularly and it was common for us to go to Busch Stadium and sit in the empty baseball radio booth rather than in actual seats. We could even do that without a ticket or the need to go through a turnstile. We'd just enter through the baseball front office and take the elevator to the broadcast level.

I absolutely had a favorite player on those Cardinal football teams. My mother was raised in San Antonio, and she named me Robert Joseph for a reason. I was Bobby Joe and I still have some distant relatives who call me that. Number 40 for the Big Red was a phenomenal wide receiver named Bobby Joe Conrad — hence his position in my personal rankings as "Favorite Player." One year, there was a present under the Christmas tree that looked an awful lot like a framed photograph, and the tag had my name on it. It was a photo of Bobby Joe Conrad, autographed "From one Bobby Joe to another, Bobby Joe Conrad." I still have it.

At that same time, in the mid-60s, the NHL finally expanded and the St. Louis Blues came to town, taking up residence in the old St. Louis Arena. Dad made hockey fans out of us by purchasing two season tickets behind the north goal, and many winter nights were spent in those yellow "Arena Circle" seats, watching Red Berenson, Noel Picard, Barclay Plager, Jacques Plante, Glenn Hall, and my favorite player with the blue note on his chest, Timmy Ecclestone.

The NHL did something pretty creative when it doubled in size by adding six expansion teams in 1967. It put all the new teams, including the Blues, in the Western Division while leaving the "Original Six" in the East. That, at least, gave the new teams a fighting chance and despite finishing in third place, the Blues did manage to defeat the Philadelphia Flyers in the first round of the playoffs and the Minnesota North Stars in the second, before being swept by the Montreal Canadiens in the Stanley Cup final.

As for motorsports, which would eventually become my passion and my career when I neared the age of 40, the only real annual rite was listening to the Indy 500 on the radio with my dad. I loved that it was a marathon of a race, but every second of it was edge-of-your seat stuff. Back then, the 500 was tape-delayed on television until after the race was completed, and in 1968 Dad and I made sure to keep all the radios and TVs off all day so we could watch as if it were happening live.

We sat down in the living room with potato chips and onion dip, and turned the TV on right before the time slot. As the TV warmed up (that was an actual thing, then) an anchor man was doing a promo for the 10 o'clock news that night, and he said, "It's going to be a beautiful Memorial Day evening in the St. Louis area, the Cardinals shut out the Giants 6-0 today, and Bobby Unser won the Indy 500."

We looked at each other in silence for a few seconds, and then burst into laughter. A great father/son moment thanks to the worst news promo ever.

In terms of drag racing, I loved watching it whenever "Big Daddy" Don Garlits or Shirley Muldowney would pop up on "Wide World of Sports" but I never attended a race until I worked in the industry.

For three straight years in the mid-1960s, I'd make an autumn pilgrimage to Florida where my dad was managing the Minnesota Twins team in the Florida Fall Instructional League. I wasn't quite old enough to fly down there by myself, but mom was always eager to spend a week in the Sunshine State and I was equally eager to shag fly balls and be the batboy for these Twins squads for seven days.

Some future stars were on those teams, and I got to know them all. Graig Nettles, Pat Kelly, and Rick Renick all made appearances in Bradenton during those years, but when I was 11 years old I made a personal connection with the biggest prospect of them all.

During batting practice on my first day in town, my dad put me out in right field because most of the hitters were right-handed and they wouldn't be hitting anything hard my way.

One finally did bloop a ball toward me, and I managed to corral it without too much trouble. But then I made a memorable mistake — I heaved it back toward the mound instead of to the player manning the bucket behind second base. And I hit the young prospect playing second base square on the back of the head. Rod Carew never even turned around. He just gathered up the next grounder hit his way as if nothing had happened.

Somehow, I managed not to bean any more Twins during my week in Bradenton, and I came to the sad realization that it was time to go home and get back to school.

By sixth grade, as we were becoming the "big kids" in school, I stumbled onto a comedic and artistic genius who inspired me and made me laugh. Larry Eberle was one of 13 kids in his family, although I'll admit that number is an educated guess on my part, and I'm also not certain Larry was ever really sure how many siblings he had.

Our sixth-grade teacher was Mrs. Luna, a generous, caring, larger-than-life woman who always looked like she should be wearing an apron and making spaghetti sauce. The best thing about Mrs. Luna was that she recognized something in both Larry and me that other MQP teachers had either overlooked or willfully dismissed, and she brought out our joy and creativity by making us her pet students. For the first time in my life, I enjoyed school. Larry and I were paired off for nearly every assignment, and we hit it off in a grand and almost mind-melding way.

We'd spend many sleep-over nights at each other's houses every month. We'd buy multiple Revell models but throw the instructions away and put all the parts in one pile, to see who could end up with the most humorous or unique "FrankenCar" within a couple of hours. We'd spin the globe and stop it with our fingers, and wherever that spot on the planet was we'd give ourselves a solid minute to come up with a humorous (and fictitious) story about how that country or state was named. We almost never stopped laughing.

In eighth grade, just a few months after we had stayed up late to listen to NASA Mission Control as the Apollo 11 Lunar Excursion Module landed on the moon, followed by the viewing of grainy television images of Neil Armstrong and Buzz Aldrin as they descended from the LEM to walk on the lunar surface, we went to my basement and built a replica of the Command Module out of chicken wire and Reynold's Wrap. My dad took a look and walked away, shaking his head.

Our plan was to replicate a lunar mission by staying in there for at least 48 hours, eating Space Food Sticks, wearing what we had that approximated astronaut apparel, and donning fake communicators that wrapped from behind our ears to in front of our mouths (wire hangers bent to shape and covered in black electrical tape.) We "took off" and headed for the moon with a rudimentary control panel we'd made with fancy flashing lights, and a cassette of pre-recorded communications from Houston. I'm pretty sure we only made it about 12 hours, but we sure had fun.

We went back to the drawing board to see if we could figure out how to build a Lunar Module that could disengage from the Command Module and roll away across the basement floor (roller skates were including in the rough design) while we also began lobbying friends to take a couple of days out of their lives to act us Mission Control for us, communicating with walkie-talkies. None of that happened, but our brains were really engaged and our creativity was exploding.

Larry was an artistic prodigy, as well. When we were 12, he drew caricatures of every member of the Wilber family, and they were better than most you'd ever sit for at an amusement park or shopping mall. They were pure genius.

When we were finally old enough to be allowed out on the back streets, we'd not only pedal our bikes back and forth to each other's homes (a two-and-a-half-mile ride), we'd also cover just about every block of Kirkwood, Glendale, and Webster Groves on day-long rides. We knew the regulars at the candy shop, bakery, and drug stores by sight if not by name, and in those blissful days we rarely had a care more serious than what our next great adventure would be or how many gumballs we could buy with the change in our pockets.

With MQP friends Tom Ward, Mike Fitzsimmons, and Patrick O'Malley, we formed a movie company called Wardoeblerfitz Film Productions, and as such we made five films with a Super 8 camera and an editing unit. When Patrick decided major motion pictures weren't for him, the company name was shortened to Wardeblerfitz. The entertainment biz can be cruel.

In 1967 and 1968, my mother worked in the St. Louis Cardinals' front office and during those summers she'd often come home to Kirkwood for lunch and then take Larry and me back downtown to Busch Stadium. We were 11 and 12 those two World Series summers, and we were allowed to roam all over the city until it was time to head back to Busch Stadium and wave at the receptionist in the lobby of the Cardinals' offices as we marched inside. We had the run of the place.

On those downtown afternoons, we'd usually head straight for the Gateway Arch and the Mississippi River. Taffy would make sure we had enough quarters and dollars with us to go up and down inside the Arch as often as we pleased, when we weren't visiting the moored riverboats and an old Navy minesweeper down on the Muddy Mississippi. We took the tram to the top of the Arch so often we finally started going up one at a time, so the other could lay on the grass and look up to find his counterpart in one of the tiny rectangular windows, 630 feet above. Yes, you can spot your buddy doing that. And then we'd go sit in our box seats right behind home plate to watch Bob Gibson, Lou Brock, Orlando Cepeda, Roger Maris and the rest of the Redbirds dominate the National League.

At that age, of course, you're also starting to notice not all the girls had cooties. Some were actually kinda, sorta, almost cute.

Larry and I decided we were funnier and better looking as a team than as individuals and until eighth grade was over we rarely, if ever, flirted with girls alone. Instead, we acted as each other's de facto agent, helping overcome our own shyness by representing each other. It was a flawless plan with the exception of the part in which we were still 12 or 13 and couldn't actually make things like "dates" happen. We needed support and we got it from my mother and her best friend, Barbara Janes.

Taffy and Barbara were very close and we were constantly shuttling between the Janeses' home and ours, for formal parties or casual get-togethers. Barbara had three daughters — Sally (who was the same age as Larry and me), Lisa, and Susan. For some reason, counter to all intuition and the hormones that were beginning to take over, Sally and I simply became best friends. Like my relationship with Larry, she and I realized the best approach was to be buddies and try to help each other meet new people, and it worked.

The first boy I introduced Sally to was Larry, of course, and we quickly began to call ourselves "The Mod Squad." I think I was the Pete Cochran character. We stayed good buddies for a long time, and a lot of other characters passed through our lives when we'd be sledding down the giant hill by the Janeses' manse or making up new games to play (or, better yet, finding and sharing new albums to listen to) in their big home. It was so large it had a billiards room, a library, a study, and more bedrooms than I'd ever seen under one roof. Plus a boat in the garage and an acre of prime St. Louis County real estate. It wasn't a bad place for a young boy to hang out.

Sally went to public schools, which worked out great for all of us. Larry and I had already determined that flirting with the seventh- or eighth-grade girls at MQP was just a distraction, because it couldn't be much more than flirting and we both had a hard enough time concentrating on what the teachers were telling us. Sally and her friends went to school somewhere else. It was a perfectly symbiotic relationship.

As eighth grade at MQP neared its end, Sally was in junior high and when her yearbook arrived we flipped through it to see if I thought any of her female classmates were cute. I spotted Sue Hinds and pointed to her. One weekend later, Sally invited Sue over to her house and I came over with Larry. The Mod Squad had instantly morphed into The Mod Quad.

Taffy and her friend Barbara — Sally's mom — were great, making sure we had the space to pursue the typical whims of young teens, knowing all along that we could generally be trusted and were good kids. It worked. It was also riotously fun and liberating.

That entire spring of 1970, I also knew what was coming in the summer and it was not going to be a repeat of the same summer routines or the games in the street we'd enjoyed our entire young lives. We were, instead, going away. All the way to Washington, D.C.

Back then, Big Del had to work winter jobs to pay the bills because baseball scouts were poorly compensated and he had never been a big enough star to have made huge money in the big leagues. Also, at just over nine years in the Majors he was not eligible for a full pension. You needed 10 years of service time for that. Even with Taffy working, we were just getting by and I can recall some stress around the dinner table as they wrestled with how to pay tuition, a mortgage, and our other bills.

One of dad's good buddies from his playing days with the Boston Red Sox was Ted Williams, and in 1970 Ted was entering his second season as the manager of the Washington Senators (the new Senators, who had quickly replaced the previous franchise that moved to Minnesota to become the Twins). Ted convinced Dad to leave the Twins organization to take over as bullpen coach for the Senators, and since coaches earn service time just like players, that would get Dad over the 10-year mark and make our lives a lot better.

Early in the spring, Dad had me fly up to Cleveland to meet him and the team for a few days during a road trip, with the games being played in the ridiculously cavernous Cleveland Municipal Stadium. Getting to meet a few of the big-leaguers in the dugout and being allowed into the visitors' clubhouse was fun, but once game-time rolled around I took my spot in the broadcast booth with the Senators' radio guys, Shelby Whitfield and Ron Menchine. I sat silently on the right side of the booth for three games in three days, listening in as Shelby began almost every new inning with the same apt description of the Cleveland weather, saying (in his perfect radio voice) "It's a cold, blustery afternoon here at Cleveland Municipal Stadium." The radio man was being diplomatic. It was freezing, wet, and windy.

By the third day, after having said nothing more than hello to these two radio professionals each day, I heard the producer count them down and back into action in what, by then, had become a familiar routine for me, the silent observer. And when he said "You're on," Shelby

Whitfield said, "Hello again, everybody, this is Bobby Wilber reporting to you live and in-person from the broadcast booth for your Washington Senators…"

My eyes must have bulged out of my head as I whipped around to stare at him, aghast at what I'd just heard. And then the producer, smiling and laughing, said "OK, Shelby, for real this time. In five, four, three, two, one… You're on." They'd been dreaming up that little plan for three days and they got me good.

I headed back home to tell those tales to Larry and my other friends, even as our departure from Missouri drew near. We were heading to Washington as soon as the school year ended, and all of this was happening just as I was about to turn 14 while I had the undivided attention of Sue Hinds, who was cute and did not have cooties.

Taffy took Larry and me over to the Janeses' house just days before we were due to leave. It was a stunning spring evening, and Larry and I escorted Sally and Sue on a walk, arm in arm or hand in hand, with our thoughts swirling. We found an open field just as dusk turned to night. All four of us were utterly and completely silent, not willing to break the mood, but we all knew why we were there and no words were needed. Under the stars on that magnificent night, Sue Hinds permanently took her place as the first girl I ever kissed. Larry and Sally kissed as well.

Sue and I were sure we were madly and permanently in love. It had to be. There was no other option, even if I was due to leave for the entire summer just days later. The word "conflicted" doesn't even come close to describing how I felt.

The undeniable truth was that I didn't have much choice. I had quickly courted a young lady I'd picked out of a yearbook, and within weeks I'd climbed the Mount Everest of securing my first kiss. We had stars in our eyes, but Mom had the maps out and we were ordered to pack our things. We did just that. I even took my record collection.

The logistics, however, were a bit daunting. Once the Vauxhall was out of our lives and Taffy needed her own wheels to get herself to work, we discovered she liked fast cars and for a solid five years we had a Chevy Camaro in the driveway. That was cool, but this trip wasn't really meant for a Camaro, with a mom, two kids, a cat, a dog, and enough baggage to get us through the summer. Not to mention my aforementioned record collection.

Taffy would have to drive the entire way, from St. Louis to Washington, D.C., while I would sit in the front passenger seat with all the maps and hotel brochures, even going so far as to imitate fighter pilots by securing the various maps to my pant legs via rubber bands. The word "nerd" comes to mind. I also had our Siamese cat, named Monkey, on my lap. Mary shared the backseat (if that miniature space could actually be referred to as a backseat) with a cooler, a few bags, and our German Shepherd, Turk. The mini-trunk in the hot-rod Camaro RS somehow held our belongings, and we had 848 miles to go. Plus, and this was critical, I was leaving Sue Hinds behind. Before we reached Indiana I was hatching plans to somehow, some way, get back to Kirkwood to be with the one I loved so dearly.

We spent one night in a hotel, in Columbus, Ohio, and finished that grind of a trip the next day, arriving in Washington, D.C. exhausted (those sporty bucket seats were cool, but our butts really hurt) and covered in cat and dog hair.

The Senators were on the road when we arrived, and it would be a week before they (and our dad) would return. Big Del had been sharing an apartment with a local guy at 4545

MacArthur Blvd., not too far from Georgetown University where our sister Cindy was going to school.

It was a nondescript apartment, and there was a strange guy living there. And did I mention that Sue Hinds was back in St. Louis?

I did have Sue's home address and I was firing off letters every day. She answered each one immediately, and we shared (in cursive, on school paper, with Bic ballpoint pens) how much we desperately wanted to be together.

It was already a hot summer in D.C. when we got there and Mary and I had to find ways to pass the time with Turk, who was not supposed to be in the apartment. We spent what seemed to be endless hours at the small park and tennis court across Q Street, while also going for short walks to a small grocery store near Foxhall Road. Then we discovered the walking trails at Glover Archibald Park. Both of us enjoyed the long trails through the woods as an alternative to sitting on the concrete steps behind the apartment, as did Turk.

And then the planet Earth exploded. Sue Hinds sent me yet another daily letter, but this one included the shattering news that her father had taken a new job and they'd be moving to Rhode Island almost immediately. I would never see her again. And the letters stopped coming almost immediately.

Finally, mercifully, the Senators returned and we drove out to National Airport to meet them. A few of the players remembered me from the road trip to Cleveland but I was far more interested in seeing my father. It was great to have him back with us, and it was the first time in my young life where Dad was back in a big league uniform and I was there to be a part of it. I'd waited my whole life to see him in the big leagues. I never did get to see him play, but the coaching gig with the Senators was good enough for me.

Our first order of family business was to rent a real house. We found one in Bethesda, Maryland, on Hoover Street, just behind Suburban Hospital. It was a classic two-story colonial with plenty of space, so at least we each got our own bedroom. I even found an old record player in the attic (where technically we were not allowed to go) and I could spin my favorite LPs on it every day.

The next day, Dad took me to RFK Stadium. Sue who? I only vaguely remembered her.

I would be going to the ballpark every day with Dad whenever the club was in town. We arrived at the players' parking lot in the early afternoon and used the private entrance into the stadium, then headed down the institutional gray stairway to the bowels of the place where a quick turn to the left took us directly to the home clubhouse.

There was Bazooka bubblegum everywhere. Buckets of it! Cartons of it! Tables covered in it! There were 25 Major League ballplayers, as well, and their uniforms and lockers and the guy called Teddy Ballgame in his office, but my, oh my, there was a lot of Bazooka.

Once early batting practice started on that first day, Big Del escorted me down the tunnel and out into the bright afternoon daylight, with RFK's gigantic, swooping grandstands towering over us. Dad introduced me to Nellie Fox, a legend as a player but by then a coach who was never seen without a giant wad of Red Man chewing tobacco in his cheek. Nellie kindly patted me on the head and said, "Now, you and the other kids head way out into the outfield. It's not safe for you here on the infield." I had never actually considered that.

The sound made by a wooden bat firmly making contact with a baseball, in an empty stadium, is memorable. I loved it then and I still love it now, and it's one of the few sounds I can close my eyes and hear in my head to this day. The first few fly balls that came my way after making that sound were majestic and awe-inspiring. They nearly disappeared as tiny white dots against the deep blue sky, and when they descended I was certain I was going to catch them. And one by one they landed with a thud, five feet behind me on the manicured field.

It took a while, but I finally got a handle on catching the mammoth fly balls hit by honest-to-goodness Major League stars, including the gentle giant Frank Howard, who towered over everyone and once said his worst fear as a ballplayer was that he might one day hit a pitcher with a line drive and kill him. The first time I heard the ball come off his bat during batting practice I was thankful Nellie Fox had told me to stay off the infield.

I also quickly began to develop as a shagger of those fly balls; learning even on the first day how to take a direct route to where I thought they were going to land and then look back up into the sky to find them.

After a ball had been corralled, of course, it had to be thrown back in toward a pitcher who was manning the bucket behind second-base. My throws started off as soft looping tosses that barely made it. By midsummer, they wouldn't look like that. By midsummer, I was catching everything and throwing like a young man. I was also loving every minute of it.

When the team would go on the road, Mary and I would again be left to our own devices, but Taffy had a few things planned for us. Trips to the monuments and museums, of course, but also a weekend (with Barbara Janes, no less) in Ocean City. On a couple of other weekends, Cindy would take us to Assateague Island for romps in the surf. We had our share of fun.

The Senators' bench coach was a guy named Joe Camacho. His two sons, Mike and Tommy, were also there for the summer so we all got to know each other when our mouths were not so full of Bazooka we couldn't talk. After batting practice we'd head up to a block of box seats reserved for the wives and families of the players and coaches, and we'd occasionally watch the games when we weren't busy driving the ushers crazy by throwing peanut shells or begging Taffy for money so that we could stop the vendor who shouted "Pizza, pizza, HOT PIZZA!"

After the games, those of us who were both kids and male could go into the clubhouse, but only if the Senators had won (so it didn't happen all that often). When the final out was made the Camacho boys and I would sprint up the stairs, down the concourse, into the player's entrance foyer, then down the stairway to the underground concourse and straight into the clubhouse to join our dads and the happy ballplayers. And more Bazooka. What was that girl's name again? Sue something?

One night, all went according to plan and as another rare victory was secured the three of us took off on our sprint. Nothing seemed much different until we came to the clubhouse doors and two large gentlemen in nifty black suits, and with earpieces in their ears, came out. They were surprised to see us, and immediately pinned us to the wall. We could barely breathe, much less see, but between their massive shoulders I spotted President Richard Nixon walking by, smiling after having seen the win. The two Secret Service men never spoke to us, but they gave us a seriously quizzical look I'll never forget. Somehow, these three young boys had gotten inside the security perimeter, and I'm probably still on a "watch list" somewhere.

Later in the summer, when the team left town for a lengthy road trip, Taffy scheduled our annual trip to Wamplers Lake and Mike Camacho came with us, ostensibly to be my buddy and play catch with me in front of the King Tut cottage, but more realistically because and he and Mary had a budding romance going.

Remember the lawn game called Jarts? It was that ingenious game that utilized lethal weapons, with which kids like us could have hours of fun. It was soon legislated out of business in that specific form, and to this day I hear grumblers complaining about how "the government took Jarts away from us, like they were dangerous or something. Back then, we could play with heavy steel rods that had points on the end of them, and we came out OK." Yeah, well … about that.

We were playing in front of King Tut one evening, with the original Jarts, when one impaled Mike Camacho right in the foot. He was hobbled for a few days, but he was lucky it wasn't worse. Giving kids heavy metal darts to throw around in the dark while barefoot was about as wise as handing us bows and arrows.

Finally, we headed back to D.C. and the team came back from the road. And Big Del had gotten the 90 days of service time he'd lacked for the full pension, so the Senators thought he'd be better utilized as a scout. My ticket to incredible afternoons at RFK Stadium seemed lost, but by then I'd gotten to know the equipment manager and most of the staff and players, so it was quickly arranged that the equipment guy would pick me up each day, as I stood on a corner of busy Old Georgetown Road, and I'd go to the ballpark with him. Nothing had changed, other than the fact my father was no longer at his locker.

It had been a phenomenal summer doing something I loved, running around the outfield in a Major League stadium, sitting in the clubhouse next to catcher Paul Casanova who befriended me and gave me one of his bats to take home. It was a model C222, which had a tapered handle instead of a knob. In college and the minor leagues, I would go on to use a Louisville Slugger model U1, a slightly different bat but very similar to the C222 "Cazzie" had given me.

I got to know a bunch of big leaguers. I got to hear Frank Howard's bat make contact with a thrown ball, creating a sound that was similar to that made by a rifle as it echoed around the empty cavernous stadium.

That summer started with the heartbreak of leaving Sue Hinds in St. Louis, and it ended with Mary's heartbreak having to say goodbye to Mike Camacho. There was a certain finality and logic to it all, but neither of us understood that at the time.

Becoming A Junior Billiken

For a lot of kids, progressing from one public school to the next is usually just a matter of geography. After elementary school, it's off to your appointed middle school in a bigger building with a bunch of new kids. When you're done there, you move up to senior high in an even bigger building with more new kids.

For me and my siblings, going to a private school did a couple of things. It cut out the "middle man," since Mary Queen of Peace was K through 8, and after that we went straight to high school — which created the need for what was essentially a trial-run for something four years down the road, when it would be necessary to pick a college. After MQP, we needed to select the private high school we'd be attending.

My sisters both attended St. Joseph's Academy, not too far from our home in the west St. Louis suburbs. It was an all-girls institution, and there were a wide variety of all-girls or all-boys schools to choose from. They chose St. Joe's.

My brothers before me both chose St. Louis U. High down in the city, right across Highway 40 from Forest Park. That highway is known as I-64 now, but to anyone from our era it will always be Highway 40. Both brothers were quarterbacks for the Junior Billikens football team, and both earned Big 10 football scholarships, with Del heading off to Purdue, where he was the backup for his roommate, the house painter. As it turned out, Del was a better baseball player anyway and when the Philadelphia Phillies took him in the eighth round of the first-ever Major League draft, he left football behind. Rick ventured north to become a Golden

Gopher at the University of Minnesota, but lasted only one frozen year there before transferring to Manatee Junior College in Bradenton, Florida.

I knew all along that I wanted to be the third Wilber boy to go to SLUH, but there was this pesky detail involving an entrance exam. Every year as many as 500 boys would make the decision to hand over their education to the Jesuits, but every year SLUH would only have room for 225 new freshmen. Hence, the weeding-out process provided by a competitive entrance exam.

Now picture this. It's the middle of eighth grade at MQP and our teachers have begun the process of walking us through the selection of our prospective high schools. Dear sweet Mrs. Clough, who never smiled at me again after wrongfully framing me for the "falling bookcase scandal" asked me where I planned to go. I said, "St. Louis U. High." She replied, with a slight laugh, "Oh, my gosh. You'll never get in there. Not a chance. You need to go to John F. Kennedy." JFK was a brand new co-ed catholic high school which had just opened in the suburbs. They would, apparently, take just about anyone. Even me.

I dug in my heels and dialed up whatever confidence I had, though, and filled out the application for a seat in the SLUH auditorium, where I'd take the exam. If I failed, JFK would still take me. The public school kids in my neighborhood just went to Kirkwood High.

And I got in. Was it because my test score was one of the 225 best? I have no idea.

Was it because my brothers had each been outstanding quarterbacks? I suspect that might've had something to do with it.

Did I plan to play football? At 5-foot-6 and a solid 125 pounds, I did not.

Somehow I fooled them, though, and I was a Junior Bill whether I was going to play football or not. I took it as a very good sign when they did not retroactively expel me the day they discovered I neither looked much like Del Wilber Jr. or Rick Wilber, nor did I throw footballs as well as they did.

The transition from the nuns at MQP to the Jesuits at SLUH was startling. Jesuits, whether ordained priests or "scholastics" (priests in training who went by "Mister" instead of "Father") made up about half of the faculty. Boys made up 100 percent of the student body.

For the previous nine years, boys and girls had shared my classrooms at MQP while the nuns there worked tirelessly at the impossible task of segregating us. Sister Agnes Marie once split the classroom in half, with girls on the left and boys on the right, and we were warned to not even look at each other. No, that didn't work either.

At SLUH, on our first day of school, the Jesuits announced that they'd be hosting a freshman dance Friday night in the auditorium and to make it more fun they'd reached out to the principals at Nerinx Hall, St. Joe's, Visitation, Ursuline Academy, and St. Elizabeth Academy (each an all-girls school) to make sure all the first-year ladies at those institutions knew they were invited. The Jesuits actually invited girls to come meet us. I was flabbergasted.

I understand exactly why the affair was scheduled. It was the Jesuits letting us know that we were beginning the transition from boys to young men, and they had every intention of treating us like young men.

High school is a challenging but rewarding time full of many such transitions. We entered as kids. We left as men. In four short years, the change was startling and usually unnerving. Confidence was lost and gained repeatedly, but by the time you'd walk out on stage to receive your diploma from St. Louis U. High you had become a man. A young and still naive version of the man you would ultimately become, but a man nonetheless.

For me, the hardest part of that freshman year was the schoolwork itself. I could tell immediately the curriculum at SLUH was built to weed out those who couldn't survive. Having never been a whiz at math or science, I knew I'd have to buckle down. But even so, in the first two quarters of that opening year I struggled to make C's. And that just deflated me. Maybe Mrs. Clough was right.

In the third quarter, I nearly gave up. Even English class lost me when instead of learning how to write we were taught how to read Dickens. "A Tale of Two Cities" lost my interest early and I tried to fake my way through it. When my report card arrived in March, I was barely able to summon the courage to show it to my parents. My grade-point average of 1.6 was just a tick above the line that automatically would flunk a boy out.

I met with counselors, we arranged for a tutor, and I tried to improve my study skills, but I had a long way to go. The nagging thought that maybe I should've just gone to JFK would simply not go away. Father Hagan, our freshman counselor, flatly told me that I didn't have a chance and I should enjoy my final quarter at SLUH because it would clearly be my last.

Taffy would drop me off in the early morning, about 90 minutes before the bell, and I'd sit in the cafeteria with a senior tutor who would attempt to walk me through the algebra that was stumping me. And I improved to a 2.3 GPA in that quarter. Somehow, I'd survived. Barely, but survival at that point was pretty much a black-and-white issue. I either did or I didn't. And I did.

For some reason, they allowed me play baseball while I was making all these efforts to stay in school. Maybe it was all just part of Father Hagan's willingness to let me have some fun before they kicked me out.

At MQP I had to play on the second-grade team as a first-grader. At SLUH, I'd have to make the sophomore squad, the B team, as a freshman if I wanted to play my favorite game.

Then I got sick on the first day of tryouts.

I missed a couple of valuable days of school and critical practices but I convinced Coach Highberger to allow me to try out on the third day. While the rest of the aspiring group took batting practice, he took me over to another field in Forest Park and he hit me some fly balls. The experience of that previous summer at RFK Stadium with the Washington Senators paid immediate dividends.

Coach Highberger hit a few routine flies. I could've caught them behind my back, but I made all the plays with the requisite two hands. Then he started to hit them farther, and I caught those too. Finally, he tried to hit them all the way out of Forest Park but I'd track them down as well, catching them going back and to either side, often leaping to backhand them on a flat-out sprint. Finally he yelled, "Come on in."

He said, "Well, son, you can catch the ball. Better than anyone here, as a matter of fact. Let's see if you can hit" and then he had me grab a bat. It was just routine batting practice, but I think it was almost immediately clear that as much as I was ahead of the curve as an outfielder, I was as far behind it as a hitter. That entire summer in Washington was spent in the outfield, learning to catch Major League fly balls. I took not one single swing with a bat.

I made that B Team, but played sparingly on a roster that featured quite a few solid sophomores. I still had a long way to go, both physically as a growing boy and as a hitter, but I made the team and somehow stayed in school.

I'm proud to say that, thanks to the largesse of many of us in the alumni group, SLUH now has first-class athletic facilities for all team sports. But in the early '70s we had no baseball field, nor did we have a home football field, a swimming pool, or a soccer field, but that didn't stop nearly every sports team in the school from competing for state championships and winning many. Our home baseball field was one of the six open diamonds in Forest Park, with no outfield fences, all-dirt infields and outfield surfaces that were as smooth as a rock quarry.

To get to practice, the older guys could drive up Oakland Avenue and cross Highway 40 on Hampton Avenue. The rest of us walked but there was an interesting shortcut involved. An old tunnel ran under Highway 40 just a few blocks west of school, and we could cut through there just like I had once trudged through the woods beyond the cul-de-sac to get to Fred's Field. When you came out of the tunnel, you were right next to the ballfields in Forest Park.

As a freshman, catching the fly balls hit by other youngsters was too easy. Catching any rolling balls out in the outfield, however, was a different story. At RFK, they smoothly rolled right to you like an eight-ball on a billiards table. In Forest Park, they might change directions eight times as they pinballed over divots, rocks, or heavy clumps of crabgrass, and the worst and most unexpected bounce would invariably be the last one before the ball reached you. I took them off the wrists, chest, chin, and once off an ear. I felt fortunate that last one didn't hit me square in the nose. I learned to kneel down and corral them, even if that took extra time, because the time spent kneeling was far less damaging to the score than the time spent running after the ones that got away.

Mom drove me to school every morning for three years. I had a driver's license by my junior year, but I didn't have my own car — a powder-blue VW Beetle — until I was a senior, so for three long years my mother dropped me off at school and we never spoke a word on any of those trips. I have no idea why. I loved my mother, and she loved me, but for three years we simply sat in silence for 12 miles until I got out of the car and said goodbye. I still don't get it, other than I assume we shared a trait of not being morning people.

For those same three years many of us utilized a special method of transportation in order to get home, and it would stun most students and parents today. In a metro area of 2.5 million people linked by superhighways, we hitchhiked. We would walk across the Kingshighway Boulevard overpass to position ourselves on the westbound Highway 40 on-ramp and we'd stick out our thumbs. One by one cars would stop and pick up as many smartly-dressed Junior Billikens as they could and almost invariably the drivers would not just take us as far as they were going but would instead take us right to our homes. Never once did I feel threatened or worried in any way. OK maybe once or twice but here I am, still amongst the living.

If the weather was not cooperating we could walk a couple of blocks south to Manchester Road and ride the city bus to get home. It cost 25 cents and, since Manchester Road is a main thoroughfare that stretches well out beyond Kirkwood, I could ride one bus until I was a half-mile from home. At that point I'd pull on the white cord to let the driver know I needed to get off at the corner of Manchester and Woodlawn right next to Harris Market where we did all our grocery shopping.

The third option for getting home was one we practiced with varying degrees of success. Once you got to know the guys who lived near you, you'd pass in the hall between classes and ask "Do you have a ride?" in the hope someone's father or mother was picking them up and space was available in the backseat. That worked maybe once a week and I'll never forget the time Bob Klostermeyer said he did indeed have a ride and yes I could jump in. His father then drove us straight to their house, a mile and a half from my home. Bob's dad parked in their driveway, shut the car off, and went inside. He never said a word. Bob just shook his head, rolled his eyes, and then followed his father through the front door. I walked home remembering to never again ask Bob Klostermeyer if he had a ride.

I had only a few options for rides, since most of the student body lived in different parts of the St. Louis area. The guys who made up the majority of SLUH's student body were from the southside of town, including the historic district known as The Hill. Located south of SLUH and not much more than a mile away, The Hill was home to generations of Italian immigrants who put down roots in this neighborhood full of small brick homes on tree-lined streets, and many families opened neighborhood restaurants.

I had several classmates from The Hill and the surrounding south side, with authentic Italian names ranging from Derio Gambaro to Ricky Randazzo, Michael Castellano, Johnny Iovaldi, Nick Riggio, and Mark Aiazzi. Of course, I also shared classes with guys like David Sulkowski, Mike McDonnell, Kevin Coughlin, Mike L'Ecuyer, Jim Saint Vrain, and Paul Makarewicz. Also Wally Weiprecht and more than 200 other young men from varying ethnic backgrounds, but the guys from The Hill held a bit of an unofficial and unspoken special place in the SLUH pecking order.

At SLUH, despite our lack of athletic facilities (we did have an actual gym, so the basketball teams could enjoy home cooking) we partially made up for it in another way. We had a rec room in the basement of the main building —- the Backer Memorial — but it wasn't your normal recreation hall with a few ping-pong tables. Instead, it was filled with dozens of pool tables, a double row of vending machines, and dedicated smoking areas for juniors and seniors.

Much like I'm still surprised by how I never developed into a better basketball player considering the endless hours I spent shooting hoops in our driveway at home, I'm as equally perplexed as to why I was never much more than an average pool shark. We played pool almost every day, at least until we were seniors and were too cool to fraternize with the underclassmen. The rec room was just another example of the Jesuits treating us like young men instead of children.

I made a few real friends that first year with guys I had never met before I became a Junior Billiken. Bob Mitchell and I remained good friends all the way through school, Bill Signaigo and I hit it off as well, after connecting the dots to discover that when my sister Cindy had dated a SLUH boy named Ed Signaigo that was his big brother dating my big sister. Bill, Bob, and I lived far enough apart to need rides to see each other outside of school, but we did that enough to have some good clean fun. And listen to Moody Blues albums, one after another, all afternoon. And play touch football.

I'm also now painfully aware that my slight build at the time, and my hope to be a successful athlete among a group of guys who mostly seemed bigger and more mature, brought out a certain cockiness that I can only assume was a result of some kind of peacock syndrome. I flashed my snazzy colors to try to look bigger, better, or more successful than I was. Some guys would shrink into the corners when feeling inadequate. I tried to fake it and I know it came across as pure brashness from a guy who really didn't have much to be brash about, other than his famous parents. There were lessons that had to be learned but I was bullheaded enough to make those painful lessons take a long time. I'm probably still learning them.

During my sophomore year I made the varsity baseball team. Once again, I was playing with and against guys who were bigger, stronger, and more mature, so while my defense kept me on the team my hitting kept me mostly on the bench. And, for a kid who overcame his shyness and feelings of inferiority by acting cocky, being a sophomore on the varsity fed right into that behavior.

Part of being sure of yourself involved looking good on the field and our baggy baseball uniforms made that a challenge. I had an asset at home to take on that challenge, though, and it was my sister Mary and her sewing skills. Each year, she'd take in my pants until they fit snugly.

In addition, the Washington Senators back then had been wearing white adidas spikes, with red and blue stripes. Having a couple pairs of those at my disposal made the guy with the tailored pants look even flashier. I suspect I could've just had Mary embroider "LOOK AT ME!" on my jersey but we somehow never thought of that.

Each year, though, I did get slightly better and I learned a little more about humility and friendship. And each year, I started to mature a little bit more physically. On top of that, I finally found the classes at which I could succeed and A's and B's started to pop up on my report cards more often than the earlier C's and D's, although right through my junior year I needed additional tutoring as the math and science went from being "not really my thing" to "really not a thing I can even comprehend." But, thanks in part to some incredible instructors, I made it.

By 1973, my junior year, my grades were up and my baseball was better. I wasn't leading the world as a hitter, but I was starting to at least get the hang of it, and I know I was a better teammate. What surprised me, as a junior, was that I had no idea just how good my arm was. We'd take infield practice before games, with coach Joe Vitale hitting a series of balls to each outfielder so we could make throws to second base, third base, and home plate. I simply caught those balls and threw them back in as hard as I could. Simple deal. I never really stopped to analyze what my teammates' throws looked like in comparison to mine.

One day, after infield, our second baseman asked me, "Why do you throw so damn hard?" and I was actually a little taken aback by that. I said, "I have no idea. I just throw the ball. I'm not trying to throw it harder than anyone else." He said, "Well, you do." I don't think the tight pants and white shoes had anything to do with that.

The biggest distraction, by this time, was a problem as old as mankind. We were maturing, and by this point there was absolutely no debate about the fact girls did not have cooties.

My first high school girlfriend, and I mean a real girlfriend I actually went on dates with, to real movies and real pizza parlors, lived not far from where I had gone to grade school and her name was Linda. We met on a charter bus heading to Columbia, Missouri, to watch the SLUH varsity football team take on Hickman High, and although she had a massive crush on one of the SLUH players (who, of course, was devastatingly handsome and a man among boys), I was smitten.

We quickly discovered that Linda lived right across Elm Avenue from a girl named Susie, who had been a classmate and good friend of mine at MQP. That was my "in," I think, and I worked hard at the whole "wooing" process for weeks. Linda had her driver's license months before I did, so when we did graduate to real dates we were in the uncomfortable position of having her drive us around. Before the first of those dates, she demurely asked me, "You're not going to slide over and sit right next to me, are you?" I hadn't even thought of that. Things got better once I had a license.

Our golden love affair didn't last that long, but Linda eventually found one that did. One of my classmates at SLUH was a very handsome young man and a very intelligent one, as well. After college, Don and Linda got married and they are still a happy couple to this day, with kids and grandkids.

I also noticed, while dating Linda, that girls really liked guys who played music. I, unfortunately, played no instruments other than the steering wheel.

During our junior year one of my SLUH classmates who had also gone to MQP with me, Art Ruprecht, saved up his money until he had enough to buy a basic set of Slingerland drums. We were both music freaks, trading and loaning albums back and forth as we discovered new sounds and new albums by Cream, Steppenwolf, Badfinger, or Alice Cooper, so I was enamored with Art's descriptions of how he'd put those records on his stereo and attempt to learn the drum parts, night after night, week after week, down in his basement, until he could play along with the LP.

Once he felt he was good enough, he invited a couple of our SLUH classmates who played guitars to come over to his house to "jam" to whatever songs they all knew in common. I tagged along to watch.

It was the first time I'd ever sat in a room with three guys who played their instruments well enough for recognizable songs to be heard. I started singing along a little bit, and before you knew it we had a couple of Derek and the Dominos songs down well enough for them to be listenable.

We decided to become a band. And since we all had grown out our hair, what with it being 1973 and all, we already looked the part.

As I recall, we debated the merits of a few creative names and somehow settled on Barnaby Rudge.

At the same time, the Wilber family had transformed the garage at our Woodleaf Court home into a walk-out family room, and that became our practice studio. I'm sure the neighbors enjoyed that immensely.

We also wanted to play in front of real people but had no idea how to make that happen, so we scheduled a party at Art's house. For a week, the guys left all their gear set up in our refurbished garage (complete with lime-green shag carpet and the requisite beanbag chair) and every night we'd try to get through a playlist of about 15 songs.

We had one microphone and no P.A. system, so I'd have to plug into one of the guys' amplifiers to be heard and, since the amps were behind us in terms of where people would be sitting when we played at the party, that caused a feedback problem. If I faced forward and sang, the shrill feedback from the amps would bring everything to a halt. So, I had to sing facing sideways and sometimes backwards. Considering how I looked at the time, that might have actually been a good thing.

We played some Jethro Tull and I discovered my voice was actually very well suited for covering the vocal stylings of Ian Anderson. We sang in the same range and I could nearly duplicate his sound. I also did pretty well on the two or three Moody Blues songs we'd learned despite the fact we had no keyboard player and no bass guitar. I'm not sure how we did that but it worked. At least to our ears it did.

On the flip side, the guys wanted to play some stuff by the Rolling Stones and The Who and it was quickly obvious to all of us that I didn't have a prayer of sounding like either Mick Jagger or Roger Daltrey. That didn't dissuade us from attempting it but I knew it was ugly.

We played our gig in Art's basement in front of a dozen or so friends, and let's just say our career as a band both started and ended that night. I believe Art is still a drummer and the other guys still play, but the lead singer brought the whole band down to his level and that was it for me. It was (sort of) fun while it lasted.

Meanwhile, away from my one-week stint as a singer, Mary and I were doing our best to hook each other up with friends from our schools but we were cursed with a birth order that made it difficult. None of her senior friends wanted to date a dweeby junior and most of my friends were too intimidated to date a girl a year older.

When our attempts at introductions failed, we basically resorted to hanging out with each other. It's a good thing Mary and I got along so well — and still do — because we were, in effect, going on dates, to movies, to concerts, and out to eat with each other most of the time. Some days we'd simply hop into her little Austin Healey Sprite (which was so small you didn't really get in it as much as you put it on) and we'd go for long drives in the country. Both of us still like to do that.

One night, we were out in the Austin Healey after dark when we got pulled over by a police officer on Old Warson Road. He strode around the car and finally asked me to get out and I, of course, did just what he asked. Fortunately, I was wearing my SLUH letterman's jacket that night and upon seeing that he said, "We had a report of some kids in a very small car causing trouble. Do you go to St. Louis U. High?" I replied in the affirmative and he said "You two be careful. You can be on your way now." SLUH boys were, after all, trustworthy.

Mary and I managed to make the go-out-with-a-friend thing work a few times, and I dated her friend Kerstin exclusively for a bit more than a year. I had a driver's license by then and Taffy would let me drive the family Impala on our dates. But for some reason, Kerstin's mother really disliked me, and that was always difficult for us. By my senior year, Kerstin was a freshman at St. Louis University, and that made it mostly impossible. High school can be tough, when it comes to romances.

During my senior year, Taffy and a few other important civic leaders in St. Louis came up with a concept for a new senior class called "The Student and the System." The idea was for select students from a variety of high schools to come together at one campus, once a week, for a full afternoon. Guest speakers, including business executives, politicians, and others in high places, would drop in to give us a hint as to what we'd be getting into once we graduated.

It was decided SLUH would be the gathering spot for the class and, with that decision being made, Taffy Wilber's son could be in it. This was a great fit, because the Jesuits had, by then, figured out I was a whiz at things like creative writing, geography, civics, and physical education, but we were all wasting precious time by even attempting to put me through any additional math or science classes. Because SLUH's curriculum was so stout we were all technically qualified to graduate, in the eyes of the state of Missouri and the Board of Education, early in our senior year. So, without math or science classes to weigh me down, I had plenty of free time on my hands. We discovered I had a natural talent for study halls as well, and for much of my senior year I even acted as a teaching assistant for freshman creative writing. I had finally found my niche at SLUH.

The "Student and the System" class met weekly in a SLUH classroom, with boys and girls coming in from public and private schools, and for the first time (and maybe the last time) girls were sitting at our desks at St. Louis U. High. It was a revelation for many of us. Probably also a distraction, just as it had been at MQP.

One of those girls was a brilliant young lady from Webster Groves High. Nancy and I got to know each other, went on a daytime date, graduated to real dates, and fell hopelessly in love. And I mean the part about it being "hopeless" quite literally.

After our senior year, I'd be heading off with Bob Mitchell on a great western trek and at the end of that summer she'd be leaving for George Washington University in Washington, D.C. In addition, her parents we moving to Wichita, Kansas. Somehow, some way, we made this work as a real romance for a year and a half. Long-distance phone calls were too expensive for flat-broke college kids so we kept those to a minimum and wrote a lot of letters. Stacks and stacks of letters. It was, of course destined to eventually fizzle out.

Nancy is now a world-renowned chemical scientist. No, really. And she is still known as the mysterious "Nancy DC" to many of my college friends and roommates, who all collectively only saw her for one or two days a year.

That senior spring, I was named captain of the baseball team and I still threw the ball hard. I hit a little better, even winning one game for us with an RBI single off of a hard-throwing righthander who was striking everyone out. Bob Klostermeyer (himself, not his dad) drove me home after that game and as I hopped out of his car he said, "Way to go, Wilbs. You won that game for us."

That's why you work hard to play the game..

It was good to be catching up to the rest of the guys in terms of maturity and it was good to be a contributor to the team on offense as well as defense. And on top of all of that it was good to be a decent student. When Father Bailey said goodbye to me at the end of the year, he professed to be stumped by how low my class ranking was. He said, "How can that be, Bob? For the last two yours you've been a fantastic student. One of my favorites."

"You should've seen my freshman year, Father. I never dug out of that hole," I replied.

Four Epic Summers

Those four years of high school at SLUH were full of the pains of simply being a teenager, the struggles with difficult classes, and the process of physically maturing as both a young man and a baseball player, but they also featured four fantastic summers. They were, to put it succinctly, epic.

The first two were set in Denver, the second two in Spokane, but all four included a great deal of quality time with my dad. Again, my decision to forego American Legion baseball or some other kind of summer ball certainly negatively affected my progress as a hitter but I wouldn't change the experiences, the travel, and the rich characters I met, for anything.

I actually do not remember the moment when Big Del told us the Washington Senators were once again reassigning him. Instead of continuing as a scout for the club, they'd named him manager of their Triple-A affiliate in the American Association, the Denver Bears, which meant he'd be heading out for spring training in February and not coming home until September or October. Factoring in how stressful my freshman year was, especially in terms of grades, I suspect it's not too surprising that this news is now lost in the fog of time.

Once I survived that shaky first year at SLUH, plans were hatched for me to spend much of the summer with Dad, both in Denver for homestands and on the road with the team. I was going to be a bat boy, meaning I'd have my own locker in the clubhouse and I'd be in uniform every night. My job involved some highly technical duties, those being not just the retrieval of the bats left at home plate by the hitters but also the delivery of fresh baseballs to the home plate umpire throughout the game, as well as the gathering of baseballs that were fouled back into the screen. It was a tough job and involved a steep learning curve.

Fortunately, there were already four "real" bat boys there, so the interloper whose father was the manager had some peers and mentors from which to learn.

In June 1971, I got on a plane at Lambert Airport in St. Louis and when I disembarked at Stapleton Airport in Denver, Dad was there to greet me. I was both nervous and excited about what was ahead.

As Big Del drove westward on I-70, I beheld the Rocky Mountains for the first time. I had never seen mountains before. It was June, they were snowcapped, and I was in awe. They seemed too large to be real, but I'd researched Denver in our encyclopedias at home. I didn't like reading Dickens but I liked learning about far-off places and, right up until that moment in the car, Denver qualified as a far-off place. The mountains looked just like they did in the book. I was ready to move permanently but the fun hadn't even started.

I'd been with my dad to many minor league ballparks, including a number of Triple-A parks ranging from Watt Powell in Charleston when I was three years old to Rosenblatt Stadium in Omaha when I was about 10. But nothing at any level of baseball other than Major League parks prepared me for Mile High Stadium.

Mile High was beginning a major transformation then, with the growing popularity of the Denver Broncos creating the urgent need for more seats. It already had the familiar multi-decked grandstand running from the right field corner to just behind home plate but that's where it stopped in 1971. Only a smaller lower deck ran toward the left field corner. Out in right field were the "south stands" atop which the iconic white "bucking bronco" statue would one day stand.

When football season began, all of left field and much of center field would be covered by a hastily-built temporary grandstand that would run parallel to the right-field foul line and the other huge grandstand, creating the rectangular shape needed for football. And once those stands were built, baseball couldn't be played there. That would be an important thing in just a few months.

After a quick stop at the Continental Denver Motel, our "home" for the summer, we parked behind the south stands and walked in through a gate in the outfield fence. It was early afternoon and no players had arrived, but the groundskeepers were busy mowing and watering while they moved the batting cage into place. Instead of heading down the line toward the home dugout we made a right on the warning track until we came to a door with a sign that read "Bears Den." We entered, heading underneath the south stands into what was the biggest clubhouse I'd ever seen.

With Mile High also being the Broncos' home, the baseball clubhouse had to do double duty as the football locker room, and with football teams being more than twice the size of baseball clubs (by number of players and by height and weight) the Bears had the good fortune of being able to use the Broncos facilities as their own. I'd been in low minor league clubhouses with Dad and thus had seen plenty of rooms similar to the clubhouse most people would be familiar with thanks to the movie "Bull Durham" but this was not one of those. Forty-five large open lockers lined three of the walls in the main room and still left enough space for a peninsula of 10 lockers in the middle.

The trainer's room featured four tables and all the latest in gadgets — including an UltraSound machine and both hot and cold whirlpools. The shower room was so large I'm fairly certain it could've accommodated the entire Bears team. Dad had his own office and next to it was his own private locker room and shower. I was dazzled, but I still had people to meet.

The four bat boys were good guys and all about my age. If they resented having me crash their summer-long party, they never let on. I did look a little different than them, though, because the team only had four batboy uniforms.

The Bears were still wearing cotton uniforms so I brought along a pair of white baseball pants from home, which were actually a little off-white. They didn't have a small enough jersey for me, either, so I had to find the smallest one in the equipment room and I absolutely swam in it. I was fairly self conscious about the fact I was wearing mismatched pants and a grown-man's jersey but I was having too much fun to dwell on it.

That 1971 Bears team was a good one and, unlike Triple-A baseball today, it was a mix of veterans from a different era combined with upcoming prospects who were one small step from big league stardom. The vets included pitcher Garland Shifflett. You might recall I suggested remembering his name in the earlier chapter about the Charleston Senators. He played for Big Del on that club, when I was four, and then again 11 years later in Denver. It was full circle for "Shifty," whose first year of pro ball was 1955, the year before I was born. Cisco Carlos was in his 10th season of minor league ball, Dick Nen had already played six years in the big leagues but the big first baseman was back in Triple-A to contribute and end his career. Lou Klimchock had earned his way to the big leagues at the age of 18, back in 1958, but he was in Denver too.

The younger players were an impressive group as well, led by 20-year-old Jeff Burroughs. Tom Grieve was roaming the outfield with grace and hitting for power. Jim Mason was showing why he would soon be a fine Major League shortstop who would play for the Yankees in the World Series just a few years later. Lenny Randle was his own highlight reel at second base, well before he became famous as the Seattle Mariner who attempted to (illegally) blow a slow roller foul while on his hands and knees as it trickled down the line at the Kingdome. That effort still makes blooper shows to this day.

Jackie Brown, Jimmy Driscoll (whom my father called Danno due to his remarkable resemblance to James MacArthur, the actor from "Hawaii Five-O"), Bill Fahey, Rich Donnelly, Tommy Ragland, and Larry Biittner rounded out most of the regular lineup, but then there was Richie Scheinblum. I had never heard of Richie before I got to Denver, but I've never forgotten the year he had as he almost single-handedly carried the Bears to the American Association championship. He had been up and down between the minors and the big leagues with the Cleveland Indians but in 1971 with the Denver Bears he put it all together, batting .388 with 25 home runs and 108 RBI. He was a machine, and he actually hit .300 the next year for the Kansas City Royals before once again fading from the limelight. I was there to see his career year, and it was special.

The thin air in Denver has always made baseball a slightly different game, as the ball flies farther and curveballs break less. It could be a nightmarish park for pitchers, but Mile High tried to make up for it with enormous outfield dimensions. At that time, before the late '70s construction of a grandstand that "floated" hydraulically to transform the stadium from football to baseball, the outfield walls at Mile High were a startling distance from the plate — 348 feet down the left field line, 420 in center, and 365 at the right field foul pole. Still, the ball went a long way.

The main scoreboard at the time was in left-center field, at a point where the wall was roughly 380 feet from home plate. The scoreboard stood approximately 100 feet high, and was topped by a bank of loudspeakers for the public address system. Jeff Burroughs hit those speakers one night. Had they not been in the way, it is estimated that the ball would've landed in Salina, Kansas. That's just an estimate, of course, but in reality it's hard to think that ball wouldn't have landed at least 550 feet from home. Maybe more.

I traveled with the team too, and that experience was thrilling for the 15-year-old version of me. Omaha, Des Moines, Indianapolis, Wichita, and Evansville were regular stops that summer and each had its own charm. Those road trips also provided some key lessons in independence for a young guy, as I'd spend the days wandering around each downtown exploring these strange cities then meet my dad at the team hotel for a bite to eat before heading to yet another ballpark on the 4 o'clock bus, where I could roam around and sort out all the mysteries (and good snacks!) each park had to offer. At the hotel, on the bus, and at the park I became closer to a few of the players, who either took a liking to me, felt sorry for me, or just thought paying attention to me was a good way to impress the manager. Any of those options were fine.

We mostly traveled by plane, and after I arrived in Denver it wasn't long before I was introduced to the sheer terror of flying on Aspen Airways. Rather than flying commercial, the Bears chartered a plane from Aspen and the DC-3 tail-dragger was a prime example of the term "a bucket of bolts."

Coming back to Denver from Indianapolis that summer, we departed late at night and were battling thunderstorms for hours, bouncing around the skies like a Phil Niekro knuckleball on a windy day, dipping and swaying and nearly tipping over, it seemed. No one was comfortable but no one was talking either. All we could hear was the sound of Black Sabbath's "Paranoid" album blaring from Jeff Burroughs' tape deck. To this day when I hear "Iron Man" I'm back on that plane, in the dark, with lightning flashing outside the windows. The eight-track tape played over and over (this was well before the days of iPods or even the Sony Walkman, so we could all hear the music in the dark rumbling airplane) and frankly I think Jeff was the only one to sleep through it.

Hours later, word filtered back to my dad, from the cockpit, that we were short on fuel and would need to land somewhere. And we needed to arrive at that somewhere soon. The pilots picked Hutchinson, Kansas, as the target. Although the airport there was closed for the night, they radioed ahead to get the runway lights turned on and the fuel truck ready. We bounced to a landing at 3:30 a.m. and when Black Sabbath stopped playing, Burroughs announced, "That wasn't too bad. Glad we're home!" No one said a word; they all just waited for the classic stupefied double-take he was about to exhibit as he stepped off the plane and saw not Stapleton Airport or the Denver skyline, but a one-room terminal. At least the levity of that moment broke up the real terror we'd been living through for the last few hours.

That was the last time the Denver Bears flew on Aspen Airways. The team flew commercial from that point forward.

My biggest learning curve that summer was linguistic, as I quickly learned to decipher and participate in dugout banter. Having just left behind the time in my life when chatter consisted mostly of "Hey batter, batter, batter … Swing!" I was unaccustomed to the foreign language that ruled the professional dugout. Like adapting in a foreign land, though, I immersed myself in it in order to pick up its words, cadence, and nuance, and I left there in late August fully conversant in baseballese.

All the phrases were typically shouted in a high register to make them more noticeable in a noisy ballpark and they were yelled quickly in a choppy cadence, with all of the sounds running together. There was little chirping aimed at the other teams, as most of it was simply a rote series of condensed words meant to signify a player's support for his teammates and his interest level in the game. Chatter can range from the obviously false variety all the way to the most impassioned sort of support, but mostly it falls somewhere in the middle.

As for the language of chatter, "Ah-now" was short for "C'mon now." "Ee-go" was the condensed version of "Here we go." Put them together, and you could hear "Ee-go Jimmy, ah-now" which of course meant you were rooting for Jimmy Driscoll, as in "Here we go, Jimmy. C'mon now." It was not an easy language to learn. There were also whole new terms to absorb, including the favorite "hang out a rope," which seemed nonsensical the first time I heard it (shouted as "Ah-now Jimmy, ee-go hang outta rope"). A "rope" is a well-hit line drive, which traces its way into the outfield like a frozen rope. Hence, "Ee-go, hang outta rope." It's a fun language once you learn it.

There was so much for kid like me to learn and we won't even get into my quick grasp of the profane language ballplayers use in routine conversation, although I can say that more than one Denver Bear said goodbye to me at the end of that summer by reminding me that "Pass the f***ing salt" would probably not be appropriate back at the Wilber dinner table.

Another bit of baseballese I picked up had to do with my father. The manager is the skipper, so on just about every team he's called "Skip" by his players. It didn't take me long to not only adapt to that but to bring it home to my siblings as well. Beginning right around then, all of us switched from calling them Dad and Mom to referring to them strictly as Skip and Taffy.

That 1971 Bears team was in first place every day of the season, and when the playoffs began (after I had returned home) they faced the Indianapolis Indians for the American Association title. With football season looming the Bears had a hard deadline to vacate Mile High, so when the series stretched to a sixth game, with the Bears down three games to two, a most unusual solution was planned. Game six would be played at Mile High on September 9. If the Bears won (and they did) game seven would then be played immediately, as the second game of a double-header. And the Bears won that one, too.

Back then there was an actual thing called the Junior World Series, which pitted the American Association champs against the champions of the International League. In 1971, that would be the powerful Rochester Red Wings featuring future Baltimore Orioles stars Bobby Grich and Don Baylor.

Since Mile High was already beginning its transformation to a football stadium, though, all seven games would potentially be played in Rochester and of course that's how it worked out. The teams alternated being the "home" or "away" teams on the appropriate dates, but the series did go seven games, all played in upstate New York, and in the end it was Rochester winning the final game for the championship.

Over the winter, the Senators moved from Washington, D.C., to Arlington, Texas, becoming the Texas Rangers. When I returned the next summer, the players were the same, Denver was the same, but the Bears' big league affiliation had changed.

It was exciting to learn that the Bears had updated to new double-knit uniforms that second summer, so I finally had one that fit like it was mine and that fact, by itself, raised my self-esteem. We again made the Continental Denver Motel our home and by then I was as well-versed at ordering room service as any 45-year old businessman.

I also had a driver's license, although it came with a father who sweated every time I got behind the wheel. With my 16th birthday happening on June 19, it was very much worth it for me to stay home until then, so I could take a shot at having a license when I got to Denver. On my birthday, Taffy took me to the license office for my written test. And I managed to fail it.

Of course, the questions I missed were easy and I had simply rushed through the written portion in a hurry, thinking I had it covered. Just like in school, my lack of focus had cost me dearly. You had to wait 24 hours to try again and it was a long and disappointing wait.

The next day, I passed the written test and absolutely aced the driving portion, even the parallel parking segment that trips up most people. I did that after having never taken driver's education in school. My folks let me drive the family Impala around the tiny Woodleaf Court cul-de-sac whenever I wanted, and my sister Mary took me to an empty parking lot at a shopping mall to practice there one day. That was the entire extent of my driving experience. And they handed me a license and sent me out into the world, if by "world" you meant Denver for the next two months.

There were some new players in 1972, and some new batboys I needed to both help and befriend. There were also 16-year-old girls in the stands, both at home and on the road, and it was instantly noticeable to me that my presence on the actual playing field, along with the full Denver Bears uniform I was wearing, somehow made me the focus of attention for a larger-than-normal group of flirty young girls. Lesson learned, right then and there: Girls like guys in uniforms.

I'll also admit that I was there to have fun and enjoy the summer as the manager's kid, and I wasn't all that interested in cleaning dirty spikes or helping with the laundry. I did pick up bats and retrieve balls during the games, of course, because that was important work and I could continue to improve my nearly fluent baseballese chatter right there in the dugout with the pros, but real bat boys do a lot more than that.

At the time, the Eagles had just struck gold with their first big hit "Take It Easy" and once that song started being played and sung in the clubhouse the other bat boys had a nickname for me. Under the brim of my hat they wrote "Take It Easy" with a marker. I wasn't offended in the least.

Pete Mackanin, Bill Madlock, and Steve Greenberg made their Triple-A debuts as Bears that second year and I have to say this about the three of them: Pete Mackanin was the funniest baseball player I ever met and he was enormously gracious, as well. When I was in college he was playing for the Montreal Expos and whenever they would come to St. Louis he would always take time to meet outside the ballpark after the games, to catch up on my life. Bill Madlock was a great guy and fond of pranks that were always funny except when the hotfoot was given to me, catching the shoelaces on my spikes on fire. That got huge laughs. Steve Greenberg was simply the most intelligent baseball player I ever had the pleasure of knowing. He played his college ball at Yale, and in his 20s he retired from the game to get his law degree from UCLA. He's also the son of Hall of Famer Hank Greenberg, so he's got that going for him as well. Three terrific guys.

The 1972 team was also not as good, and the pure unadulterated fun of hanging around such a successful group the year before transformed into far too many nights that ended with me sharing a hotel room with a frustrated father, eating room-service club sandwiches that didn't taste quite as good.

Win or lose, however, the characters in the clubhouse, on the plane, and in the dugout were rich beyond fiction. There was pitcher Jan Dukes, whose quirky sense of humor made him a favorite among his teammates. It was Dukes who calmly stood outside getting drenched during a typical Denver afternoon thundershower, before he turned toward his teammates, who were staring at him incredulously through the open clubhouse door as he deadpanned, "Reminds me of rain…" It was also Jan Dukes who married a beautiful woman who, apparently, spoke not a single word of English.

There was the day it not only rained during batting practice but also hailed quite considerably. And since the Bears clubhouse was in right field, under the south grandstand, players who were on the field had the option of ducking for cover in the dugout or making a mad sprint for the clubhouse. Those who ran for the safety of the clubhouse were beaten there by burly first-baseman Dick Nen, who ran inside, turned around, grabbed the handle of the door, and refused to let anyone else enter, stranding them in a pelting hail storm while laughing like a maniac.

There was a night when the club wasn't playing well and the umpires' calls all seemed to go the wrong way, until finally Skip had had enough. After another bad call at first, he charged out of the dugout and lit into that umpire unlike anything I'd ever seen out of him. At home, he rarely raised his voice. On this night, out on the field, he was screaming at the inept umpire while just inches from his face. He finally played a favorite card for all arguing managers, by picking up the base and tossing it. Somehow, he didn't get thrown out.

As he came back to the dugout I was honestly a bit scared. I'd never seen him that far off the hook in my entire life and I wasn't sure if the anger was going to carry over once he was back on the bench. Then, as he passed by while I was kneeling on the on-deck circle, he winked and said "That ought to fire 'em up." Perhaps that was the actual night when I learned the meaning of the word "ruse."

I had the time of my life those two summers in Denver, roaming around Mile High, making friends, picking up bats, and winking at girls. I was also becoming a much better player, although my brief chances to hit in the cage continued to seriously limit my growth as a hitter. My outfield play, conversely, was continuing to grow by significant leaps and serious bounds and I could hold my own in terms of range and arm strength with just about any of the players on the team, who seemed so much older but who, in many cases, were only five or six years my senior.

And, oh by the way, I loved Denver. Still do.

That second summer ended with the entire Bears team descending on our house on Woodleaf Court in Kirkwood. The team had played a series in Evansville, Indiana, and Skip arranged for us to take the bus to St. Louis so the Bears could fly home to Denver from Lambert Airport the next morning. We left Evansville around 11 p.m. and rode through the night, with me spending hours playing "Password" in the back with Bobby Jones, my favorite player on that team, and a couple of other guys.

Somewhere around 3 a.m. the big Greyhound made the sharp left turn onto Woodleaf, and Mary and Taffy were waiting with coffee and donuts in the middle of the night. Some of the guys shot hoops outside, others crashed on the couches, and some slept on the floor, but as far as I know we didn't disturb the neighbors on the one night an entire professional baseball team visited the Wilber house. When the bus pulled away, I waved goodbye and was, once again, just another high school goofball. I did have some good stories to tell, though.

During the winter of 1972-73, it became apparent the Texas Rangers were not going to renew their agreement with the Denver Bears and a new home was needed for the Triple-A team. Knowing I'd be spending the summer wherever they landed I had a keen interest in this process, and for a few months it looked as though Portland, Oregon, was the target. I'd never been there but the photos of Mount Hood sure looked gorgeous in my trusty encyclopedia. Unfortunately, that deal fell through. But just before spring training in 1973, the news came that Spokane, Washington, would be the new Rangers' Triple-A team and that my dad would now be managing the Spokane Indians in the Pacific Coast League.

Based on my research in the encyclopedia, Spokane didn't look nearly as beautiful or interesting as either Denver or Portland. And, at 17, I was finally too old (in my mind) to be a bat boy, so my first summer in Spokane was going to be another learning experience.

Upon arriving, I found Spokane beautiful in its own way. In place of the snowcapped Rockies there were pine-covered hills and smaller mountains. Our home there was the Davenport Hotel, a classic from an earlier era just a few blocks from the Spokane River, which bisects the city with a rumbling waterfall right in the heart of downtown. Having grown up near the Mississippi River, which meanders like a muddy conveyor belt down to the Gulf of Mexico, I'd never seen anything like it.

The ballpark, however, was a big step down from Mile High.

Fairgrounds Park sat on the eastern edge of Spokane, in the middle of an industrial area crisscrossed by railroad tracks. It was, for that era, a standard minor league ballpark, with about 4,000 seats, a cramped and dingy clubhouse, and a few small concession stands. I quickly learned it could be a bit of a lonely place, as well. The Indians' owner was running the franchise on a shoestring and it appeared that not a piece of that shoestring was dedicated to promotions or advertising.

In return, the citizens of Spokane did their part by ignoring the club. Let's put it this way: Had they instituted a "Guess the Attendance" promotion on any given night it would've been easy for any fan to simply count the souls in the park, and it wouldn't have taken long. Crowds of 400 to 600 (those are hundreds, not a typo) were sadly not uncommon.

Since I wasn't going to be a bat boy anymore, I needed to find something to do and I managed to accomplish that in a variety of ways. I decided to actually do some work, for once, so I helped the clubhouse attendants do laundry, replace it in the lockers, and shine shoes. When the first homestand ended, and they handed me well over $100 as my share of the tips the players had turned in, I was shocked. Apparently, in the real world, when you work, people will pay you for it!

Secondly, since the shoestring budget also precluded anything more than a part-time groundskeeper, I decided to teach myself the ropes in terms of dragging the infield, patching the divots on the pitcher's mound, and creating better batter's boxes for the players, who loudly let it be known that they thought the dirt there was no better than what they'd played on in Little League. I dug the boxes out, carried wheelbarrows full of fresh clay in from the bullpen, tamped it down mightily, and then doused the entire home plate area with copious amounts of water. Just as I was convinced I'd turned the corner, and that as soon as the wet soil dried it would be far better and more secure, it started to rain.

I quickly covered the area with the round home plate tarp, and prayed it would stop in time for me to pull the tarp off and let it dry. I was consumed with the thought of the manager's kid causing a professional baseball game to be postponed because he'd flooded the batter's boxes. It was a stressful few hours.

The rain did stop, although not until BP had been cancelled, so the tarp came off only about an hour before the game. I held my breath as the first batters dug in, and when no one disappeared into a swamp of quicksand I thought I might be OK. The players had no idea I'd taken on this project earlier in the day, so later that night when I heard them commenting on how great the boxes were, and how much better the footing was, I got a slight nod from the big guy. I was a proud son.

During the games I was stuck in a bit of a nebulous world, too old to pick up bats but yet not a player. For a few days I tried sitting in the radio booth during play but that was too boring, so Skip said, "Why don't you just suit up and sit in the bullpen? Maybe you can even warm up a few guys." Now that was a capital idea.

So, for the rest of that summer as a 17-year-old I wore a nicely fitting Indians uniform (No. 1 on the back, for the record), took a regular round of batting practice with one of the groups, shagged fly balls to my heart's content, and then hung out in the 'pen during the games.

Warming up pitchers was a scary proposition (these guys threw *hard*), but they accepted me and I felt like one of them. In Denver I had felt like a little kid among men but this was different — and better. I also got to be the guy who played catch with the nearest outfielder between innings, which — in my mind — was almost like being in the game. After all, that ball I was throwing was headed out there, inside the lines, and I was being trusted with getting it to the outfielder without overthrowing him. It felt like one degree of separation from the real thing.

I can't be sure if there were any NCAA regulations I was breaking before I even got to college, being in uniform and on the road with a minor league team, but here's hoping the statute of limitations has run out on that.

I only went on a few road trips that summer, mostly to Tacoma and Eugene. It was cool to arrive in those clubhouses and see my locker, with "B. WILBER" written on white tape at the top and with my uniform and equipment neatly put away inside. The little ballpark in Eugene was my favorite, with its classic old grandstands that seemed to be right on top of you. Six years later, when I was playing for the Medford A's in the Northwest League, we played in the same park against the Eugene Emeralds, and that made it the only ballpark I had ever visited with one of my dad's teams and then later played in myself as a pro. I even pitched there one night, but that's another story.

That 1973 Spokane club was really good, with some holdovers from the Denver roster — guys like Bill Madlock, Steve Greenberg, Pete Mackanin, and Lenny Randle, as well as some newcomers like Rick Waits, Pete Broberg, and Don Stanhouse. They could hit, they could catch, and they could pitch, and when you have that combination you're going to win a lot of games. That they did, all the way to the PCL championship.

After they defeated Tucson for the crown, Dad and a few of his players who were September call-ups headed to Arlington where Big Del was scheduled to meet with the Rangers' brass to discuss his guys. Instead, he arrived at the stadium to discover that manager Whitey Herzog had been fired and that a No. 45 jersey with "Rangers" on the front and "Wilber" on the back was hanging in the manager's office, ready to be worn that night as the club took on the Oakland A's. He was told, at the time, that he'd be the interim manager for the rest of September and that "we'd see about next year" over the winter.

Skip used a number of his Spokane players that night and they beat the A's 10-8 with a dramatic comeback to establish his Major League record at 1-0 as a manager. What shocked him was the state of affairs in the clubhouse after the game, where all the players were looking at their feet and avoiding eye contact. He also noticed a complete lack of media in the room so he asked someone what was going on. The sheepish reply was "Everyone's upstairs. They're introducing Billy Martin as the new manager, effective immediately." Del Wilber ended his big league managing career undefeated and I spent one day as a senior in high school knowing I was the son of a big league skipper. It was fun while it lasted.

The next summer, 1974, was the final episode in my string of extraordinarily fortunate years with Dad, and it became one of the most memorable.

The team was again in Spokane. During the early spring I concocted a plan to combine another summer of baseball with a high school graduation present and we quickly worked out the details as to how I would meet up with the team on the road in early June. The trick was, I'd be doing it by car.

Bob Mitchell got the clearance from his folks as well and he became my traveling partner for the escapade. We packed up my Volkswagen Beetle, added my sister Cindy (who needed a lift to Lake Tahoe) and hit the road with wide eyes and more than a little uneasiness. Mitch and I had both traveled quite a bit, but this was different. There were no adults involved — OK, I guess Cindy was technically an adult, but she was really not a lot older than us and just my sister — we were going to be a long way from our homes in St. Louis, and we were going to be gone a long time.

The drive west was awe-inspiring once we got past Kansas. The mountains, the valleys, and the endless expanses of land were like nothing we'd ever seen.

Fortunately, Mitch and I shared nearly identical musical tastes. That would be a key component if you're going to spend a little more than a month traveling with someone driving thousands of miles, so our eight-track collection of Yes and Queen tapes got a non-stop workout.

After dropping off Cindy we had only a short drive to Sacramento, where the Indians were beginning a four-day series with the Solons at the most ridiculous baseball field ever conceived (with a nod to the Coliseum in Los Angeles, when it hosted the newly arrived Dodgers). Hughes Stadium was built for football and track & field, so to wedge a ballpark in they had to put home plate in one corner of the end zone, which made the left field wall all of about 233 feet from the plate. That would be roughly 100 feet too short for anything approaching normal baseball. They put up a 40-foot screen, a sort of see-through Green Monster, but it was still ridiculously easy to hit a ball out of there. For the rest of that summer, any time an Indians player would hit a pop-up to short left field, multiple guys would yell "That's outta here in Sacramento."

After our arrival in Sacramento, Skip pulled me aside and said, "You're in group four during BP, so get your hacks in. And you're in right field during infield practice, every day. I want to see that arm." During BP, I actually got jammed on one pitch and hit a ball that cleared the screen. That's exactly how easy it was. When it came time to take that first round of infield, I was honestly worried about being able to throw the ball within reach of the designated fielders at second, third, and home — so much so, I aimed the ball and "short-armed" it, drawing the criticism of a certain father of mine who said, "Starting tomorrow, just air it out. Throw it as hard as you can and trust yourself." I did, and it was the most marvelous fun an 18-year old could have.

Within days, I could hear the whispers as the players would mutter "Watch this" when it was my turn to throw. Within a week it was spoken out loud. Bobby Jones and Donny Castle were the first outfielders to say it, telling me, "You do realize you have a better arm than any of us, right?" No, actually, I didn't. I was just throwing it as hard as I could to the correct base, just like I did in high school. They spent a few days convincing me and once they did I knew I was no longer a kid and that playing professional baseball was no longer a wild dream. As an outfielder, I was there. Hitting? OK, that needed some work.

After the series in Sacramento, Mitch and I left the VW at the team hotel and got on the bus with the Indians, heading for San Francisco. From there, a long flight to Honolulu and a seven-day series with the Hawaii Islanders. We were on our way to paradise!

We hit Waikiki, we sampled the fresh pineapple, we roamed the streets and sat out by the pool. We did all things Hawaiian and late each afternoon we got on the bus with the team and went to the ballgames, where I continued to show Dad my arm, night after night. To call it sublime would do it an injustice.

One day, Skip rented a car and took us for a drive up to Hanauma Bay and Pali Lookout, where we drove through steaming rainforests and stood at the side of the road in an attempt to make our brains process the tropical beauty of Oahu.

Once we'd finished all the games at the old wooden ballpark in Honolulu, and had eaten all the fresh pineapple in the visitors' clubhouse, we flew back to San Francisco on a red-eye, arriving just before dawn. Mitch and I rode along in the bus as far as Sacramento, where the team dropped us off before heading to the airport for a flight to Tacoma.

Having slept only a little on the flight, we weren't exactly at the top of our form but we drove north as long as we could stay awake, finally stopping late that afternoon in Grant's Pass, Oregon (not too far from where I'd later play as a pro, in Medford). We were exhausted, and after checking into a motel we took a moment to sit on the beds in the room before finding something to eat. Then, just for a minute, we laid back on top of those beds. In what seemed like just a few more minutes, I awoke to see the sun setting outside our window and I figured it was time for us to actually skip dinner and just go to bed and get some sleep, but then I realized I was looking to the east. It was the next morning and the sun was coming up. We had been too tired to drive that far and made a pact to never again push it that hard just to put another 100 miles behind us.

We finished the drive the next day, met the team at the Tacoma motel, and did it all over again for the next three days, although by that point Mitch was starting to lose interest because — well, because he wasn't a baseball player and he was getting a little bored.

But the summer wasn't over yet and a real honest-to-goodness World's Fair — Expo '74 — was spread out along the Spokane Falls only blocks from the Davenport. Could two guys have a better summer after their final year of high school? I think the answer to that question would be a resounding "No."

For decades, I always thought we spent several days at the fair, seeing our first IMAX movie, touring all the pavilions, and enjoying the spectacle of it all. Turns out, when I recently saw Mitch at a class reunion he clearly remembered that we only spent one day there, trying to cram it all in before we went to the ballpark. I guess we saw so much it just felt like multiple trips.

We'd spend our afternoons at the ballpark during the Indians' homestand, with me trying to find ways to keep Mitch from losing his mind because we were there at 2 for a 7 o'clock game. I invented dozens of versions of competitive ways to play catch, just to keep him engaged, but he eventually took to sitting in the empty grandstands and reading. Hey, we were still friends and I did my best. He gave me credit for that.

Finally, in mid-July, it was time to go home. Of course, we still had roughly 1,800 miles of driving to do but we handled that without incident, stayed buddies, and finished the summer having memorized all the lyrics to every song on "Queen II" and "Close To The Edge." The Indians used the enormous motivation of having had Mitch and me with them for a while to win their second consecutive Pacific Coast League championship.

Skip managed the Indians one more year, although this time without winning another Pacific Coast League crown, but by then I had summer ball to play so I stayed behind to work on my game. Those five unforgettable summers with Dad and his teams, in Washington, D.C., Denver, and Spokane were priceless, and they were over.

That last summer in Spokane was really the ultimate swan song — a great adventure and another spectacular season with my father, the man who meant more to me than anyone. It was the end of my youth and the start of my own baseball career.

Growing Up Wilber

It's a common question. After sharing a few stories about the Wilbers with friends over dinner or a glass of wine, I'm often asked, "What was it like growing up in your family?"

It's a simple inquiry but a difficult one to boil into bite-sized answers. And, when it comes to the natural comparison most people want to make to their own upbringings, it's a totally impossible mission for me to accomplish. It's the only family, and the only upbringing, I've ever known. I have no idea what it would've been like to be raised as the son of a bank teller and a stay-at-home mom. Or a construction worker. Or an engine builder. Or an astronaut.

When I was growing up all of my school or neighborhood friends were from much more standard households, and I spent many nights in their homes on sleep-overs. They all seemed to have "normal" American experiences and, in almost all cases, they lived in warm, inviting, and wonderful homes filled with loving parents and families. In many ways I enjoyed being at their houses every bit as much as I liked being home, because by association I was able to experience a variety of different family situations. But, although they seemed nice enough, they weren't my families and those weren't my parents.

I think the significance of having parents who were loving and concerned while they were also often away from home is the most peculiar thing about growing up as a Wilber, especially for my sister Mary and me coming through the Wilber experience as "Irish Twins" at the tail-end of the process. By then, Skip and Taffy were still working hard and were gone a lot but they were clearly also winding down the parenting job and they regularly used Cindy, Rick, or Del Jr. to do some babysitting that often looked more like surrogate parenting.

I'm 11 years younger than Del Jr. When I was 7, he was heading off to Purdue. I was 10 when Rick left for Minnesota. My memories of them at the house on Woodleaf Court are from the distant perspective of being a little kid when they were young men.

Cindy was just five years older than me, so as Mary and I reached the upper levels of elementary school at MQP, Cindy was in high school. Those years were unique in terms of the Wilber family dynamic because Taffy was working full-time, Skip was gone almost full-time, and although Mary and I weren't literally raised by wolves we certainly helped raise ourselves with a lot of help from Cindy. And we all turned out OK.

Mary and I both still have personality traits that reflect that hands-off upbringing. We're independent thinkers, we learned early on how to make decisions and take matters into our own hands, and neither one of us has much of a tendency to look for instruction or approval. We just do things. Sometimes we do the wrong things but we don't wait around a lot for permission. We have to ask for forgiveness every now and then but it's a path we were destined to follow.

Taffy was never a great cook, although until we were midway through grade school she gave it her best effort. Her Tex-Mex "Frito Pie" was our favorite. I think I was probably in sixth grade — that year at MQP when so many important things seemed to happen — when Taffy presented a main course of pork chops to Cindy, Mary, and me at the dinner table. They couldn't have been any more like rubber if they had NHL logos on them.

Cindy proclaimed, at that point, that she would take over the cooking duties going forward and Taffy put up nary an ounce of fight.

We ate a lot better while Cindy was in charge, including a lot of freshly made entrees like lasagna and grilled hamburgers that were delicious for us but which surely played a major part in her decision, shortly thereafter, to live the rest of her life as a healthy and happy vegetarian. Cindy really treated us wonderfully and she was an incredibly supportive sister at a time when I was at my goofiest. She pushed me to try new things and gave me nothing but positive reinforcement when I did.

Mary was my sidekick, my best friend, and my protector, as well. We played together, fought a little, and challenged each other throughout elementary school. We still have an almost telepathic ability to know exactly what the other is thinking and there's no one else in the family I can have conversations with that are so natural and easy. And we're not even actual twins.

While I dreamed of following in my father's footsteps from the time I caught that first fly ball at Schall School, it was my mother who cleared the trail for me and who also kept me on it with as few digressions as possible. I grew up listening to her on the radio, helped her tape interviews, hung out in her office at Busch Stadium before and during Cardinal games, and later rode silently in the car to SLUH each morning when she was on her way to work in public relations. I had no idea what a talented writer she was, however, until I was 15 and she came up with the idea of a Wilber family book.

Her concept was for each of us to write a chapter or three, providing our personal recollections about what it was like to be Wilber kids. She planned to write about being our mom and she'd then help Skip write about his paternal role. It was a brilliant concept and it planted the seeds that grew into this book, 45 years later, but there was one problem with taking it from a concept to a reality — no one other than Taffy and me contributed.

As a high school math failure who was learning to love the use of the creative word, I provided a couple chapters. My initial piece was about the first summer in Denver and it was a joy to write, especially given that the summer of 1971 had just happened. Not a lot of research — as in absolutely no research — was necessary.

I showed it to Taffy and she loved it. She shared with me much of what she had written, with more than a few of those pieces having been typed secretly over the years. Her work was brilliant, and I suddenly realized what a talent she was. We motivated and pushed each other to write more but we never had enough material to put a book together.

And then, being the talented PR person she was, she pitched my Denver Bears piece to a local St. Louis sports magazine. They edited and chopped it nearly to death, to the point where I felt the finished product made no sense, but the more important news was that they published it. At the age of 15 my one-page edited version of that bat boy summer in Denver was in print, in *St. Louis Fan* magazine. That fact remained on my resume' for at least a decade.

In 2013, when *National Dragster* magazine offered me a position as a columnist, writing "Behind The Ropes" to give readers a peek into my world, I'd come full circle and was being regularly published again. Thanks, Mom!

Throughout the '60s, Dad would pass through our lives like a flash of lightning, from February to October. He'd arrive home with a suitcase full of dirty clothes — and hopefully an "airport gift" for Mary and me — and he'd leave a couple of days later on his next scouting trip. The routine went on throughout the decade and we cherished our time with him, but we always felt slightly disappointed that those rare summer days when he was with us were his few moments of rest. He traveled constantly, looking at ballplayers and rating their abilities, and when he'd come home to his wife and whichever kids were still in the house, we fought for his attention while he tried to recharge his batteries.

Once 1970 rolled around, and he was back on the field as a coach and then a manager, he'd head to Florida for spring training in late winter and would be gone until October. That made those monthly two-day visits as a scout seem like a luxury, in comparison.

When evaluating his youngest son on the baseball field, he was even more hands-off and that was something I wrestled with from the time I was 12 and starting to become a pretty good player. He rarely coached me at all, instead preferring to make subtle comments based on how he had approached the game when he played. I, of course, knew exactly what was best for me and I usually debated those points about stances, swings, and base-running until he'd finally say, "OK, do it your way."

Some dads who were athletes in their younger years take the fun out of it for their kids. They demand perfection, constantly critique and criticize play, and give little positive feedback. Skip was guilty of none of those things. When I played well, he gave me a few pointers to take it to the next level. If I quit a sport (12-year-old junior football comes to mind) he never yelled or made me feel overly guilty but he would always make a comment along the lines of "If you quit, you'll never have a chance. I don't want to hear you tell me you can't do something, but if you tell me you don't like doing something, like playing football, I won't argue with you."

Growing up, we also managed to go on our fair share of family vacations, usually with Skip at the wheel as we'd combine his need to be somewhere for baseball with our desire to see the country. As our tour guide and chief entertainer he was stunningly adept at surprising us with his uncanny memory of, seemingly, every road in America. We'd be in the middle of nowhere in Alabama, cruising along a two-lane road in those pre-Interstate days, and as we'd approach a curve he'd say, "Wait until you see the barn up here," and once we'd make the turn we'd all gasp in astonishment at a dilapidated structure that featured the word "Taffy" painted above the weathered doors.

One of his favorite games was to spot roadside mileage signs and turn the numbers into a sports score. If the sign listed "Effingham 48" above "Terre Haute 116" he'd say "Those kids from Effingham must not be able to shoot the ball or play defense." He kept us entertained.

We also traveled by train a few times. On a cold late-winter day we'd leave for Union Station in St. Louis to head for St. Petersburg and the warm sunshine of spring training in Florida, and at the age of six or seven those overnight train trips were almost too exciting for me to bear. I counted the days waiting to go, and at that age a day is still a relatively large portion of your life, so the anticipation was off the charts.

We'd arrive at Union Station on the fateful departure day, hearing the cacophony of sounds in the echo-filled main terminal building where public announcements of arrivals and departures battled to be heard over the moving of heavy equipment and the chatter of travelers, and we'd peer at the trains through the round windows in the swinging doors that would allow us onto the platform next to our train once we'd hear the call "All aboard!" Finally, thankfully, excitedly, we'd walk down our appointed platform to board the steaming and hissing monster that would transport us to Florida. I can remember sitting in a seat by the window as the massive collection of locomotives and cars chugged out of the giant shed behind Union Station, and even then my youthful brain had enough cognitive ability to think, "This is really happening! I'm really on this train! The day has finally come. I can't believe it." We'd share a few cozy sleeper rooms, roam the cars during the daylight hours, eat on fine china in the dining car, and possibly have more fun than kids should be allowed to enjoy.

When we'd get to St. Pete we would take up residence at the Edgewater Beach Motel, just blocks from Al Lang Field, and we'd attempt to mix in a bit of the homework we'd brought with us while we concentrated mostly on playing at the beach or touring the city. At night, we'd get to eat like the big kids at Skip's favorite St. Pete dining spots. We'd hop in Tim McCarver's car for a ride to the ballpark, or hang out with Mike Shannon while Taffy and Skip were otherwise momentarily detained, and we thought nothing more of that than any kid would think of being around their dad's cohorts from work. Apparently, though, these are not exactly like the vacations many of my friends experienced.

When the Kansas City Royals came into existence in 1969 their first game in KC was an exhibition game against the Cardinals at old Municipal Stadium, and Skip gave Mary and me a treat by taking us along. We got to walk on the field, say hello to the players and the Royals' executives, and then watch the game from our box seats. After seven innings (the automatic time of departure for Skip) we went back to the aptly named Downtowner Motor Inn in downtown Kansas City, and as the three of us were watching the sports segment of the late local news the announcer began an intro about a new innovation in baseball that allowed teams to take batting practice in a whole new way. In a completely calm voice, Skip said, "I'm about to be on TV. Watch this."

True enough, they cut away to a video segment that had been shot at the Florida Fall Instructional League the previous autumn and there was Dad in his Twins uniform showing how the new-fangled "Jugs" pitching machine worked, with its rotating tires taking the place of the mechanical arm we'd all known as the "Iron Mike." We never knew he'd done that segment and he never let on until that day six months later when he, Mary, and I were relaxing on the two double beds in a Kansas City motel room. It was classic Big Del.

In many ways, though, I was a typical kid. From the age of five until I was 12, Christmas held a place of such importance in my life I could barely stand the excitement and Dad was a major part of that. It was winter, so he was home and that was reason enough for it to be a wonderful part of every year, but the tree in the living room and the presents beneath it were a gravitational pull that kept me transfixed for weeks.

The Christmas cards would start to arrive in early December and when the first ones hit the mailbox Big Del would give Mary and me the greatest work assignment ever. He'd send us to the darkest and dampest recesses of the basement to find the Christmas lights, then he'd have us untangle them and check all the bulbs. Just doing that — and seeing those colorful lights sparkle across the floor when we plugged them in — was enough to drive me crazy with Christmas anticipation.

He'd take the two of us with him to pick out a tree and invariably he'd want it to "rest" in the garage for a night before we put it up. Are you kidding me? It was about to be Christmas in the Wilber house and our tree had to spend the night in the garage? All part of Dad's master plan, I assume.

The next day we'd set it up and decorate it, always going extremely heavy on the silver tinsel. The Christmas cards would continue to arrive and Dad enjoyed displaying them all in the living room above the fireplace. When your Christmas cards come from families named Musial, Williams, Marion, Schoendienst, and Piersall, that's a good thing to do.

Christmas Eve, when it was a Wilber tradition to allow each of us to open one present, I was completely and utterly beside myself with excitement and anticipation. On that one night I had no problem agreeing to my parents' suggestion that I go to bed early but I also had no chance of falling asleep. I remember those Christmas Eves as marathons of insomnia, but at some point I'd nod off until 6 a.m. when I'd leap out of bed and sneak silently down the stairs.

Most of our presents would be wrapped and under the tree for weeks but Mom and Dad would keep a few bigger and more important gifts safely hidden away so that they could be put on display near the tree at some point during the night when I was wrestling with sleeplessness. The feeling of silently tiptoeing down the stairs into the still-dark living room, well before sunrise, to find a new bicycle in the middle of the floor was akin to what I suspect a prospector must experience when he finds the motherlode of a gold vein. Mind blown.

One year they gave me a mechanical battleship on wheels, called Battle Wagon, and it not only drove itself around the room it also fired miniature shells from its forward-mounted big guns. I was absolutely nuts over it and I shot those spring-loaded shells around the house for a while until, later in the day, I noticed they were gone. When I asked where the shells were, Mom simply said "I guess you lost them" and that kept me confused for hours, or days, or a decade. I suspect "lost" was another word for "we threw them away" but it took me a while to figure that out.

Skip loved being the master of ceremonies on Christmas morning, once we'd finally convince him and Taffy to actually get up and join us. He'd ration the presents to us one at a time and laugh heartily like only the Big Guy could at our giddy glee and overt excitement. It was one day a year, and it always ended too quickly, but there was no better feeling than to be rabid with Christmas excitement as we tore into our presents with both Mom and Dad in the room. With a fire going. Near a real tree. On Christmas Day.

Once I got to be 13, as the youngest Wilber kid, Christmas began to change. The rest of my siblings were too old and too cool to care while I tried to keep the traditions alive as long as I could, assigning myself the chore of untangling and checking the lights then decorating the tree. But, the big hidden presents stopped appearing, the Christmas cards never quite got displayed with such pride, and the holiday became just another mark on the calendar. I miss those days, when Christmas meant everything and my heart could barely contain the thrill of waking up that morning.

Our parents were not perfect. Not by any definition. They both smoked until I was well out of college but both finally quit on different days and never looked back. Taffy used Nicorette gum to get her over the hump but Skip simply quit. He got up one day and quit.

Dad loved his Cabin Still bourbon (or as he referred to it, "Stab 'n Kill") and we learned at a young age to not just pick up any glass of Coke and take a gulp, lest we find out the hard way that it had been heavily spiked. When the Stab 'n Kill became a more serious issue later in life, impacting Mary and me the most because we were still at home to experience it, he declined treatment for a long time. Skip had a couple of falls when he was too deeply into it but in the end he showed his great knack for simply willing himself to do something important. He just quit.

We were also not rich, which surprised most of my friends both at the time and later in life, who figured that the family of a former Major League catcher and his radio-personality wife must be well off. The most he ever made in the big leagues was about $9,600 a year. Those winter jobs when he was working at Casey's Sporting goods, or selling cars, or even the off-seasons before I was born when he, Stan "The Man" Musial, Red Schoendienst, Dick Sisler, and other Redbirds would sell Christmas trees, were evidence enough that the vast majority of ballplayers at the time were not overly well-compensated. The owners owned more than just the teams and the players in those days. They also owned all the leverage. Later, as a scout, he made even less.

Most of what passed for luxury items in our modest but modern split-level home were actually annual gifts from the Topps Bubble Gum Company, who always remained loyal to and appreciative of the players who granted them the right to sell their baseball cards. From the sets of knives we used for decades to our first color television, the source of those prized possessions was almost always Topps.

The appliances in our narrow galley kitchen were also bargains. To make each dollar go a bit further Skip bought our refrigerators and ranges from a discount "scratch and dent" outlet store in Kirkwood. Every major appliance we ever had looked, quite literally, like it had fallen off the back of a truck. It's possible they did.

Skip and Taffy scraped by with what they could earn, saved what little was left over, and sent us to the best schools without even thinking about the alternative.

They produced five children who grew up to own businesses, play professional sports, write books, poetry, blogs, and magazine columns, and (without my help) raise a gaggle of grandkids Taffy and Skip adored.

It wasn't always pretty, and at times it was downright ugly, but it was the ride of a lifetime. I miss my parents every single day, and even now I'll catch myself needing to do some research over some small detail only to remind myself, for the millionth time, that I can't call either one of them for help with the answer.

I'm proud to be their youngest boy, and I always will be.

College As A Cougar

When our senior year at SLUH got underway the most important decision in most of our lives was finally in front of us. There were colleges out there, and deciding where to apply and what the next step in our collective education would be was on everyone's mind. Yes, even mine.

At a prep school like SLUH, roughly 99 percent of every graduating class goes on to college and most of us had at least a semester's worth of advanced-placement credits to take with us. The big difference between me and my classmates was that I was looking for a baseball scholarship at a school that also offered a degree in communications while they were sitting around the dining room table with their parents flipping through brochures asking questions like, "Harvard or Yale?" OK, it's just as possible the decision was between Dartmouth and Princeton or even the two stellar local options of Washington U. and St. Louis U. and many guys applied to both of those. A large number did stick with the program and simply matriculate from being Junior Billikens to just plain grown-up Billikens at SLU, dropping the H as they moved on. I wasn't one of them.

I was contacted by the baseball coach at Valparaiso University in northern Indiana, but they didn't offer scholarships or a communications major. Had I eventually ended up with no four-year option a variety of local junior colleges, many of which had fantastic baseball programs, would've been my choice in order to get a foothold in college while I played baseball at a high level. But then I learned more about Southern Illinois University-Edwardsville.

SIUE was a new school, having opened the core part of its Edwardsville campus just nine years earlier, and that campus was full of strikingly modern architecture. I had been there for concerts at the legendary Mississippi River Festival and was enamored with what I had seen — especially after spending four years at SLUH in a classroom building that opened in 1924. Plus, Edwardsville was roughly a 50-minute drive from Kirkwood, making it close enough to get home for a free meal or the use of the laundry but just far enough away to give me the feeling of being out there on my own, away from the parents.

SIUE also had a fine baseball program, although at the time it was still a Division II school in the NCAA hierarchy, as the "little brother" campus to SIU-Carbondale and its well-known Saluki athletic program. By the time I was investigating SIUE the Cougars had already sent some baseball players on to professional careers, including John "Champ" Summers who would play 10 years in the big leagues, and it was obvious that their program was solid. Then, to top it off, I discovered their highly respected Mass Communications Department and its television/radio broadcasting major. Case closed, choice made, drop the confetti.

All I needed to do was get the attention of Roy Lee, the head coach of the Cougar baseball team.

Roy had been at the SIUE baseball helm since the program was instituted in 1968 but before that he'd also been the manager of the Springfield Caps, a summer team in the highly regarded Central Illinois Collegiate League. Two of his players in the mid-1960s were named Del. One was Del Unser, who went on to play 15 years in the big leagues, and the other was another fine player who just happened to be my big brother, Del Wilber, Jr.

I asked both my SLUH coach, Joe Vitale, and Big Del to reach out to Roy to see if I could earn an interview. They both obliged and succeeded.

It was autumn during the early part of my senior year at SLUH in 1973, and I had put on my best interview clothes to impress the man for whom I was hoping to play my college ball. We met at his office near campus, if by "office" you mean farmhouse. With the school still early in its initial construction phase, the baseball office was actually an old tract home on a sprawling river bluff property that had been residential plots and farmland before eventually becoming part of SIUE's massive geographic footprint. Roy's private office was a former bedroom. And a small bedroom, at that.

We met, we discussed hitting, fielding, and base running, and finally Roy said, "I talked to your coach at St. Louis U. High and he said the same thing your dad told me. They both insisted that the day you get here you'll be the finest outfielder who ever played at SIUE. And, they both insisted it would take me all four of your years here to turn you into a good hitter. I'm the coach who can do that for you if you listen to me and put in the work. So, I'm going to offer you a substantial partial scholarship and I'm going to challenge you to earn a full ride before your sophomore year. You'll play on the JV as a freshman, but I'll keep my eye on you."

We shook hands and I officially committed, therefore cementing my college plans before many of my SLUH classmates.

In midsummer of '74, when I returned from our grand western United States escapade, I was due at SIUE just days later for a three-day freshman orientation program where they would show us around campus, help us get registered for the fall quarter, and give us a taste of on-campus housing by putting us in the Tower Lake Apartments, which at the time were the only option when it came to on-campus residences.

Back then, Tower Lake operated like any other suburban apartment complex. Every two-story building featured eight corner units, each fully furnished with two bedrooms, a dining room, a living room, a bathroom, and a full kitchen. Men and women didn't share units but they did share buildings, and I thought the entire approach was far superior to the ridiculously cramped dorm rooms and single-gender dormitory buildings I'd seen at other schools when visiting friends or siblings. It was a "grown-up" way to start college.

I went over to meet with Coach Lee before classes started in September so he could see my class schedule and check on my address at Tower Lake. When he saw where I'd been assigned, and the names of the other three guys in the unit, he said, "Oh, yeah — this guy is a basketball player, this guy runs track, and this third guy must be a wrestler."

I discovered it was more like this: This guy was a country boy who snored and would share my bedroom. Those other two were from a nearby farm town and it appeared they were only at SIUE to drink beer. They were also sophomores.

So the roommate with whom I shared a bedroom had nothing in common with me and he snored like all of the Three Stooges at once. My other two roomies made a habit of going out at least five nights a week and would come in after 1 a.m. reeling from a long night of Budweiser consumption, usually stumbling in after I had moved to the living-room sofa to get away from the individual in the lower bunk in my bedroom. It was not an ideal situation.

Meanwhile, I got to meet the rest of my junior varsity baseball teammates and discovered that Steve Novak, Kent "Cornpone" Wells, and Carl Grubb had all been put in a unit together, according to plan, along with the equipment manager. Someone seemed to have forgotten to put me in with other athletes when it came time to establish Tower Lake roommates.

I tried to make the best of it, but after one 10-week quarter of sleepless nights, I got Coach Lee to OK a move for me. I left the snoring machine and the night owls to move in with Robin Pauls, a great guy from Marion, Illinois, who was also a fine third baseman on the JV and who, like me, was in a bad situation in terms of his Tower Lake apartment. His other two roommates were also strange people, but sharing a bedroom with Robin made it easy for us to basically just ignore the other two guys who, thankfully, were always gone from Friday morning until Monday.

For the record, my original snoring roommate left SIUE after that year and the other two, who seemed determined to prop up Budweiser sales in the region, flunked out. Not going to class will cause that.

Before I fled the insanity of my initial apartment, though, I listened as my roommate from the lower bunk complained miserably about his "ridiculously impossible Algebra 101" class. He showed me his textbook and it was instantly familiar. It was the same book I had wrestled with as a freshman at SLUH. Prep school fast-track, indeed. At SIUE no math classes ever appeared on my registration forms, while I satisfied the general studies math and science requirement by taking two quarters of geology, which I quite liked. Rocks were way better than cosines or tangents.

The biggest adjustment for me, in terms of school, was comprehending that I loved learning. Instead of feeling like my instructors were force-feeding me ridiculously complicated stuff I'd never again need, I realized my college teachers were simply offering me the opportunity to widen my horizons and learn new things. I had a ravenous appetite for what they were serving and I raced through my classes with pure joy, practically giddy each time I entered a classroom at my beautiful new campus.

After my freshman fall quarter, when my first college grades arrived, I saw I had earned four A's and a B. I also saw a small note in the upper right hand corner of the card. It said "Dean's List" and it would say that every quarter until I graduated. I was becoming a better baseball player, but I was already a better student.

On the field, I fit in perfectly with my JV teammates who actually seemed to look up to me a tiny bit, and when we had our uniforms distributed in the early spring they all agreed that I should wear the jersey with the number one on the back. After four years of SLUH baseball where it generally was concluded that I'd get nothing and I'd like it, it was a stunning revelation to not just be one of the guys but to also be respected for what I could do on and off the field — and to (gasp!) actually be a little popular. This collegiate thing was an entirely new world for the youngest Wilber kid.

When the season started, I discovered something else. I could hit.

We only had 15 games on our schedule, some against other JV teams at nearby four-year schools and others against the varsity squads at much smaller schools, but rain erased a couple of those and we ended up playing just 13 games. We meshed as a group and became a pretty good team that had a lot of fun. I had hoped my hitting abilities would be miraculously better once I got to college, and indeed the miracle seemed to occur. I hit .357 and led the team in doubles.

I also think I confirmed the words spoken by my father and my high school coach with my defensive play, although I was stunned to see that one of my teammates was a little better than me in a number of ways. Don Lange was the fastest player on the team, he was the one guy to outhit me (with an incredible .466 average) and he was the first guy I ever played with who actually had a better arm than I did. He was the total package. And then he blew out his shoulder in a varsity game the next year and was never the same.

The most significant revelation for me was how easy outfield play could be when the field upon which you were playing was not in Forest Park. The outfield grass on both the JV field and the varsity field at SIUE was as smooth as any of the professional fields I'd been running around on the prior five summers, and the ball rolled straight to my glove with rarely a bobble or a funny hop. When Coach Lee came out into the outfield one day during JV batting practice, he said "So what do you think about all of this, Bobby?" I replied, "Coach, this is a dream come true. These guys are great, school is great, and these fields are phenomenal."

Once the JV season had ended and spring quarter was over, we were informed SIUE would be part of the inaugural season for the Missouri-Illinois Collegiate Baseball Instructional League and I was invited to be part of a roster that would be heavily populated with varsity teammates.

My best buddies at the time, Steve Novak from Michigan City, Indiana, and Cornpone Wells from Flora, Illinois, were going back home for the summer, and Robin Pauls had decided to transfer to a junior college closer to home, but I enrolled in a couple of summer classes and eagerly accepted a backup role on the summer team. I was a little nervous around the varsity guys but it was nothing like I'd felt at SLUH, where it was as if I was a little kid around men. I had an inkling that I fit in as a teammate and I was eager to prove that I fit in as a player.

At our second game, I got the start in center field. In my first at-bat, I hit a 15-hopper up the middle that managed to elude the gloves of the pitcher, the shortstop, and the second-baseman, for what we'd call "a line drive in the box score." I was 1-for-1 playing at a new level of competition, and I really never looked back.

It's funny how that first hit changes things. As long as I played the game, and I played until I was almost 40, that first hit each season was the most stressful one. Go 0-for-4 in the opener and you start to press. Break your bat and flare a Texas League bloop hit into right in your first at-bat, and you relax and start having fun. I had fun all summer.

Nearing the end of the summer season, our school newspaper, The Daily Alestle, ran a feature story on the team and as part of that they staged a photo with the club's four best hitters, all holding bats in front like samurai swords. The caption read, "Pictured from left to right are SIU-Edwardsville's top four hitters in the summer league. John Urban (.357), Jack Scarborough (.472), Bill Lee (.319), and Bob Wilber (.309)." I was the lone person in the photo who had just completed his JV season as a freshman.

When the summer ended Coach Lee informed me that I had, indeed, accomplished the first challenge he'd issued me when I interviewed with him in the tract house. I had earned a full scholarship, which covered tuition, books, rent at Tower Lake, and meals in the cafeteria. I dashed home to Kirkwood with the paperwork in hand and informed my mother, who actually cried. We hugged, she shed more tears, and I was a very proud son.

When classes began again in late September, things started to fall into a nice rhythm. We were no longer wide-eyed freshmen learning our way around the campus and its buildings and we were all much more comfortable with the school, the team, and each other. Plus, and it was a big plus, Coach Lee got our apartment situation squared mostly away.

He succeeded in having me placed with Novak and Wells, although we did start the school year with another guy from the track team sharing a room with me, after Carl Grubb also left SIUE. That was fine for a while but then my roomie decided to pledge a fraternity and the frat guys took it upon themselves to initiate him by making his life miserable, which in turn made our lives miserable. They'd bang on the front door in the middle of the night to "kidnap" him for abuse and they'd often barge right in despite our protestations. Eventually, it was unworkable and we asked for another change.

There was a new freshman baseball player on the JV that year and we'd gotten to know him during fall practices. He was from Findlay, Ohio, and his name was Tom Hill. Not Tom. Not Hill. Absolutely not Tommy. Just Tom Hill. Always both names.

Tom Hill was a good ballplayer, but more than that he was a genius. He immediately put himself on a fast track to graduate early but he also planned to do that with a double-major in two technical fields. If his majors weren't engineering and calculus they were something along those lines.

In addition to being book smart Tom Hill was also brilliant with his hands. He could build anything, he restored vintage Corvettes, and he created pencil sketches of Corvettes (his favorite car) that were so ultra-realistic you could hold them in your hands and swear they were photographs. A few years later he got hold of a set of plans for the legendary Bose 901 stereo speakers and he built me a pair that were so far superior to anything coming out of a factory it was breathtaking. So, basically, Tom Hill was just a regular buffoon like the rest of us. Except for the whole genius part.

SIUE finally completed the construction of an entirely new part of Tower Lake, creatively named "Tower Lake — Phase Two." The four of us were the first residents in our new apartment and we all finally felt fully at home. We ate at school a lot, but we also weren't opposed to using the kitchen and Steve made a cinnamon crumb-cake that should have been sold in a bakery. Life was good.

One additional milestone during our sophomore year was that we were all becoming 19-year-olds. At the time, in Illinois, you could buy beer or wine at 19 but you had to wait until you were 21 to drink hard liquor, so the local bars and clubs would check our IDs and then issue either wristbands or hand stamps to those who were old enough for the hard stuff. That was OK with us. None of us were really big-time drinkers at that point. I don't think I went out for beers more than two or three times that year, although one such occasion was a night out at a fabulous club called The Granary, which was actually an old grain silo.

My high school buddy Bob Mitchell came over for one night, with his older brother, and we headed to The Granary to see a band I knew they'd love. Faustus was a great band and in addition to some seriously mad musical skills they also favored most of the same music Mitch and I liked. We consumed many beers as we listened to every set and that night this neophyte drinker was introduced to bed spins. I didn't drink for months after that, although later in my college career I corrected that oversight on a weekly basis.

Between classes we gathered around a huge round table in the middle of the massive cafeteria in the student union. That was our table, handed down to all of us by the guys who had graduated the year before, and no one else ever attempted to sit there. Throughout each day there would always be a baseball presence around that table. You could arrive at any time, grab a bite to eat, and share some fun conversation with a buddy or four.

The food in "the caf," as we called the huge cafeteria, wasn't exactly five-star cuisine but it was serviceable and every Monday morning those of us on full scholarship got a weekly booklet of meal tickets that would usually last us all the way until Tuesday.

One item on the menu was creatively called "Chopped Steak" and, of course, it was really just a hamburger on a plate without a bun with a little au-jus poured over it and a small cherry tomato in the middle, held in place by a wooden toothpick featuring festive bright green or red plastic frills at the non-pointy end. I usually worked my way through the salad bar or got a sub sandwich but a lot of guys chose the chopped steak on a daily basis and something had to be done with all of those toothpicks. Putting them in the trash receptacle made no sense whatsoever.

As it turned out, with the frilly "feathers" on one end they made perfect little darts and the straw from your soft drink made a perfect dart gun. I sat at that table for a full month before I saw one of my teammates take his toothpick, insert it into his straw, hold the straw to his mouth, and with a blast of breath shoot the toothpick straight up. And when my eyes followed the mini-dart I saw a marvelous thing. There were hundreds, maybe thousands, of toothpicks stuck into the ceiling. A veritable forest of toothpicks. And they stretched all over the huge dropped ceiling, making it obvious that it was not a habit afflicting solely the baseball team.

As my sophomore year progressed it became clear I needed a new car. My trusty VW Beetle, which had 75,000 original miles on it, now tended to stall at idle. I had become adept at "two-footing" the pedals — keeping the clutch depressed at stoplights while I simultaneously planted the heel of my right foot on the brake and used the toes from that foot to feather the throttle — just to keep it running.

Mom and Dad had bought me the VW, but they weren't going to provide me a second car. That would be setting a bad precedent. I needed a job.

Taffy got me an interview with the St. Louis Usher Service, the folks who supplied the ushers at both Busch Stadium and the St. Louis Arena, and I was hired. Taffy's help was key because the usher jobs were hard to land unless you knew someone on the inside. She did and I got the job, which came with a pair of navy blue polyester slacks complete with a red stripe down the outside of each leg, a red tie, a white shirt, and an overly bright, practically luminescent royal-blue jacket with an engraved name tag. As ushers, we were meant to stand out in a crowd and there was no missing us in those outfits.

I worked Cardinals games at Busch in the fall and when winter rolled around I worked Blues hockey, St. Louis U. college basketball, Spirits of St. Louis ABA basketball, and other special events at The Arena like the Ice Capades and the Harlem Globetrotters. I actually took the job seriously, too, and went to work each night planning on being the best usher in the house. Considering the slackers I was surrounded by that was not a high bar to clear.

I wasn't a big fan of working the hockey games because the best sections at The Arena were earned by seniority and I was almost always assigned the seats that actually hung from the roof behind each goal. Plus, hockey games take a long time and the fans can be a little rowdy.

I loved working the Spirits games, though, because I was big fan of the team, and since the older ushers didn't want to work that much I quickly became a senior guy at those events, often working the best seats in the house right behind the bench. I could hear Moses Malone, Marvin Barnes, Caldwell Jones, and the rest of the Spirits talking on the bench and on the court. And I took care of "my people" in the section, earning a few tips along the way.

The money from my ushering job gave me a solid $150 a month to put toward a car and I traded my VW in on one of the first Triumph TR-7 models sold in St. Louis. It was British Racing Green (of course) with a snazzy silver stripe down each side, and its modern wedge design made it look like a doorstop rolling down the road. It was fun to drive but it was a mechanical nightmare, with a gearbox that didn't sync and a seemingly endless list of problems that kept it in the shop for almost half the first year I owned it. But — and this was key — I looked absolutely bitchin' driving that car around Edwardsville.

Around the same time, I met a cute little blonde at school. She was from the tiny central Illinois town of Dieterich, with a population of roughly 350. Her name was Nancy, and while my relationship with Nancy DC was already winding down with us both entering our second year of college while being separated by 850 miles, it didn't take long for my roomies to dub my new date Nancy AC, to keep them straight. I have no idea if this adorable and funny girl took an interest in me because of my TR-7, although I think it was likely.

And finally, in terms of seismic shifts, in that second year I was fully immersed in my TV/radio studies. As a real college major it was not "deejay school" in any way, but a very serious approach to all phases of the broadcasting industry and we not only learned how to work the mixing board and edit tape, we also learned to produce shows, write scripts, and navigate the legal and business sides of the broadcast world. It was fascinating stuff and I was a natural at everything up to but possibly not including the legal classes.

The only potential stumbling block came in the form of class schedules. Dr. John Regnell was the head of the department and once I was on the fast-track in my major he became my adviser, in terms of which classes I would take each quarter. When we met late in the fall quarter of my sophomore year, he showed me a schedule for winter that included two afternoon classes each week and I had to dial up my courage enough to say, "I'm sorry, Doctor. During winter and spring quarters I can't have any classes after 1 o'clock."

With more than just a bit of agitation, he replied, "Bob, are you here to get a fantastic education or are we just supposed to bend over backwards to make sure you have it all just the way you want it?"

For the first time at Edwardsville, I felt the pangs of potential failure that were once so common at SLUH. I said, "Doctor, I'm here to get the best education possible, but I'm also here on a full scholarship to play baseball and we practice or play games every afternoon. I have to keep that clear. I owe that to the baseball team."

I could see the agitation abate in his face, and he said, "That's a completely different story. You should've told me that first. No problem, Bob. We'll make it work. And congratulations on the scholarship." Crisis averted.

When winter quarter began, after the New Year holiday, I got my first taste of full-time varsity ball and an odd taste it was. SIUE now has state-of-the-art athletic facilities but when I was a student we had no gymnasium, forcing us to find off-site indoor spaces where we could practice while waiting for the snow to melt. Sophomore year, that meant driving to the north side of Edwardsville to take over a recently shuttered elementary school. There was still chalk at each chalkboard.

The little grade-school gymnasium was barely big enough for a few pitchers and catchers to work out but if the catchers squatted down and leaned their backs against one wall the pitchers had just enough space to reach back and throw the heat, with their knuckles just missing the cinder-block wall behind them. In real-estate terms you would describe the abandoned school as "cozy" and the one thing it didn't have room for was a batting cage. We wouldn't be able to swing the bats in earnest until we could get outside.

I made the team but did not make the traveling squad for the spring trip to a tournament in Galveston, Texas. That was a disappointment but understandable considering the cost involved with taking an extra sophomore on a long road trip like that, so I worked out with the JV and got myself as prepared as possible. Thankfully, the weather warmed and we were able to get outside and hit the ball.

Making the varsity as a sophomore was pretty much a replay of what I'd gone through in high school. I was proud to have done it and eager to play but I could tell it was going to be a challenge. I focused on getting the most out of pre-game workouts, knowing that almost every day those drills would likely be my only chance to play.

In the end, I acquitted myself fairly well. I still remember my first varsity hit, a solid knock into left field at home against Missouri Baptist. Later in the game, with the first one out of the way, I got another hit. They would represent two-thirds of my hit total on the season. I played in 10 games, went 3-for-14, and hit .214, but I was already being trusted to take the field as a late-inning defensive replacement. I didn't make an error all year.

After I started going on road trips, I watched as our team methodically tore apart a variety of talented opponents and in the end we finished 31-20. That earned us a slot in the regionals and we waltzed right through that to punch our ticket to Springfield, Illinois, and the NCAA

Division II World Series. In the second game of that regional we beat Valparaiso, the only other school that had shown any interest in recruiting me. I definitely made the right choice.

Unfortunately for me and a couple of other guys the post-season rosters were more limited than the regular season, so while we got to enjoy the week at the Series, we couldn't play and couldn't even be in uniform once the first pitch was thrown. It was a downer of a way to finish what had been a fun season but the real downer came in the final two games. We were undefeated in the double-elimination tournament, having beaten Florida Southern, Livingston, and Southeast Missouri, and our final opponent was Cal Poly Pomona, which had already lost a game. They'd have to beat us twice to win the Series, and I'm sure you can see where I'm going with this.

In the first game a new buddy of mine, Stan Osterbur, pitched a whale of a ball game but we lost 6-5. We were that close to being crowned national champions. We came back the next night and the wheels came off. The 17-3 drubbing couldn't end soon enough. Our 75-mile bus ride back to school was a very quiet trip.

For right fielder Mike Brown and first baseman Bill Lee, that World Series had been a bit of a coming-out party. Brownie was a year ahead of me and there was no question he was the best player on a good team. He could hit, he could hit with power, he played solid defense, he had a cannon for an arm, and he could run pretty well. He was also a great guy and we sometimes roomed together on road trips. A few scouts had seen him play during the season but in Springfield they were out in force and he put on a good show. They would all be following him the next year, when he was a senior.

If Bill's last name sounds familiar it's because he was, indeed, Coach Lee's son. I've played with a lot of coach's sons and it's not even a contest in terms of which one was the best guy and the best teammate. He was always one of the most popular guys on the team, a real leader on the field and in the dugout, and while Bill had hit well all year he also won games for us at first base with his glove. In Springfield, with all the right people watching, he sprayed long balls all over Lanphier Park.

After the loss, and the dreary ride home, the Atlanta Braves came calling and they signed Bill to a minor league contract with their Gulf Coast League affiliate. He played again the next year with an independent team in Beeville, Texas but 1976 was his one summer with the Braves and he'll always have that fact to remember. Today, he is the commissioner of the Frontier League, an independent minor league in the midwest.

It took us all a while to get over the meltdown at the Series but in my case the grief was eased a little when Coach Lee informed me the summer league would again be happening and I'd be a key part of it if I wanted to play. Oh, yeah, I wanted to play.

I learned a few things that summer. Apparently a lot of my success or failure on a baseball field was strictly between my ears. During summer league the competition was still good but the pressure was off, and I excelled beyond even my wildest hopes. During that summer, in 1976, I basically carried the team. I was catching everything in the outfield while also hitting in the middle of the order and it was 20 games of hot shots off my bat. After a 4-for-5 game at Missouri Baptist, teammate Dave Schaake said the words all hitters love to hear: "Heck, the out you made was the hardest-hit ball all day. Everything you hit right now is a rocket."

According to the semi-official stats kept randomly by our equipment manager, I led the team in almost every offensive category that summer, hitting .425 with eight doubles, two triples, one home run, 13 runs batted in, and I even managed to compile eight stolen bases just to be flashy. When actual NCAA wins or losses were not on the table, the game seemed easy.

Skip made it over to Edwardsville for a game late in the summer and I had another one of those afternoons where everything I hit was a rope, including a line-drive off the pitcher's knee that caromed all the way into our dugout. I was worried about the kid but he seemed to shake it off well enough and I remember thinking I was happy it had hit his knee and not his face.

Skip gave me a pat on the back and a smile, then chatted with Coach Lee for a few minutes before heading back to Kirkwood and his scouting work. Afterward, Coach Lee approached me with a sly grin and he said, "Your dad just told me something good. He said he thinks you're finally getting it and that a pro career might just be realistic in a couple of years. Good work, Bobby. Keep it up, son."

Although he didn't say it directly to me, that would be the first time my dad ever spoke in somewhat certain terms about my chances of playing pro ball.

When fall quarter rolled around to begin my junior year, Steve, Cornpone, Tom Hill and I again shared a Tower Lake apartment, one that backed to a parking area with some thick woods beyond. At the corner of the parking lot was a large industrial dumpster for Tower Lake residents to use as a trash receptacle, and that dumpster soon became a doorbell.

Our assistant coach on the team was Bob Hughes, a former minor-leaguer in the Los Angeles Dodgers system who had his career demolished by a landmine in Vietnam. He barely survived that explosion and before being put under anesthesia on the operating table he managed to convince the medics to make every attempt to save his legs, which they did, but his professional career was basically over.

He was an extremely bright, brutally sarcastic, and spontaneously hilarious guy, and we all appreciated his guidance and loved having him with us. He was a valued part of our team and on many overnight bus rides a small number of us would huddle in the dark with him as he retold vivid stories about his time in Vietnam, complete with real-life illustrations on his heavily scarred legs as he showed us where tiny bits of shrapnel were still working their way to the surface even then. It horrified us, but it established a bond between all of us that was rock solid.

Coach Hughes was always looking for the next outlandish thing and at the time he was driving an old beat-up Ford Falcon. When he'd come over to our apartment, instead of parking the car and walking up to the door he'd just ram the Falcon into the dumpster head-on, making a huge racket, and those of us in the living room would barely look up. Someone would simply say, "Coach Hughes is here."

Bob Hughes changed our lives in many ways, but most noticeably he changed our vocabulary. He was a devoted fan of grisly horror movies and he was the one who introduced all of us to the word "heinous." For Hughes, the more heinous the movie the better. We all seemed to absorb "heinous" into our vocabularies at once and our lingo took the next big leap when Hughes arrived one night at the "Pink Palace," a rental home annually inhabited by baseball players. He entered the kitchen and spotted a door no one ever used. Behind it was a staircase to the basement.

He slowly opened the creaky door, peered down into the musty darkness, and said, "What's down there?"

Someone said, "That's the basement." Hughes then asked what it was like. "We don't know," one of us admitted. "We never go down there."

Hughes turned his head with a devilish grin and, using his best melodramatic movie-commercial voice, said "The most heinous movie ever made… BASEMENT!" And thus a new language was born.

Within days the rest of the baseball team and I were tagging other things, places, and people as the most heinous movies ever made. If a meal was bad, someone would say "Most heinous movie ever made… PIZZA KING!" If anyone ever said anything odd enough to make us shake our heads, that person would then be dubbed a heinous movie. Over time, we shortened it and people we thought were odd or crazy would simply be movies, as in "That guy is such a movie." Finally, the words could be dropped altogether by mimicking the action of cranking an old-style movie camera. This all evolved within weeks, or possibly just days.

I would spend many more years in many more dugouts with Bob Hughes as we both played nearly a decade on the semipro Sauget Wizards, with him leading the way as player/manager. One of the richest characters in the game, he spent 19 successful seasons as head coach at St. Louis University while also throwing daily batting practice for the St. Louis Cardinals — all while playing for and managing the Wizards.

Coach Hughes also befriended Jim Greenwald, who had played at SIUE just before I arrived. Jim signed with the Minnesota Twins after his senior year in 1974, playing a season in their organization. By the time we were all Cougars, he was back in the area playing ball on various semi-pro teams and embracing his role as full-time sidekick to Bobby. When we'd say the words "Hughes and Greenie" it was as if we were talking about one entity.

Greenie would play with me on the Wizards, too. I've known a lot of funny guys in the game of baseball but no two were ever a more hilarious tag-team than Hughes and Greenie. I relished rain delays, when we'd be stuck in the dugout and those two would hold court while the rest of us doubled over in laughter. No two guys ever loved the game any more than they did.

Junior year was going to be big on many fronts — I was first on the depth chart in center field and I'd progressed so rapidly in my major that my advisers were creating new classes out of thin air for me and Jim Keegan, a classmate from the Chicago area who had multiple gifts when it came to broadcasting and humor. Jim was, by far, my best non-baseball friend at SIUE and by that fall we were fairly well recognized as the two stars of the Communications Department.

My only setback academically was realizing I wouldn't have the credit hours I needed to graduate on time. By my junior year, even though it was obvious I wasn't going to get my diploma on schedule, I committed to finishing my degree no matter how long it took.

You must be a full-time student to be eligible to play NCAA sports and that applies in two ways. You have to accumulate a minimum amount of credit hours over the course of each year and you have to be enrolled as a full-time student during your season. It didn't take us long to realize the trick would be scheduling a heavy load of classes in the fall, then scaling back a little in winter, before finally registering for nothing more than a standard load of hours during the peak baseball quarter in the spring.

Taking a couple of classes each summer helped me stay ahead of the minimum number of necessary hours and I really liked the relaxed feeling on campus, when only about 2,500 students would be enrolled instead of the 12,000 who attended during the other three quarters. The fact you could stroll around campus in shorts and flip-flops, as opposed to dashing through the biting winds of deep winter, almost felt like a vacation.

Junior year also brought with it a slightly more routine after-hours social life for us, and beer was at the center of it. We knew all the athletes from the other sports, although the baseball and basketball players got along the best while (thankfully) the wrestlers took it upon themselves to be our guardians when we'd be out at night. We knew the soccer players and were good friends with a few of them, but the tennis guys were a bit detached. SIUE had terrific soccer, wrestling, and tennis programs, as in top-notch even among Division I schools, and the tennis guys were really something special.

Robert Seguso and Ken Flach were the stars on the team and one look at the pro careers they both enjoyed would illustrate why. As a doubles team they won both Wimbledon and the U.S. Open after coming out of SIU-Edwardsville.

Theirs was a different world and I don't ever remember seeing any tennis players at our regular haunts, which included a little bar named Spanky's, a restaurant/bar named Rusty's, The Granary, and a real honest-to-goodness disco called The Encounter, which was inside the lobby of the local Holiday Inn. And yes, it was just like "Saturday Night Fever." And yes, we could all dance.

Once winter quarter came around, Coach Lee again had to find indoor training facilities and this time he was able to rent space in another elementary school with the key difference being that this particular school was still operating. We had to schedule our winter practices to begin at 3:30, but even then a large number of little kids would stick around to watch the college guys train. We'd do our running in the hallways, we'd set up a batting cage in the gym so that we could actually take BP, and the pitchers and catchers would line up three wide to get their throwing in. You needed to have your head on swivel in that little gym, because baseballs were flying everywhere.

When you're working out indoors right up until the bus leaves for the spring trip, it's almost impossible to be ready to play. Taking grounders on the gym floor leaves you unprepared for any sort of rocky infield and for outfielders like me it was impossible to "stretch out" our arms doing any long-toss. That's a pretty critical thing for an outfielder and we'd all get sore arms once we got outside and started throwing more than 60 feet.

In addition to the guys I'd arrived on campus with we added a few new junior college transfers in 1977. Two of them, Lance McCord and James "Oscar" Noffke, would become my close friends, although when I first met Lance I thought he was crazy and far too much of a party guy. I'm sure, in response, he thought I was a boring, antisocial prude.

Our first game on the spring trip was in Atlanta, at Mercer College. We won, I made a running and leaping catch in left-center, and we spent the night there before heading to Statesboro, Georgia, the next day, where we'd play a very good Georgia Southern team. We also learned that a huge and very popular disco was within walking distance of the Days Inn where we were staying, so a large group of us headed over there after dark. We had some fun and then got back to our rooms before curfew. All of us but Lance, who was too busy dancing with and attempting to woo a local girl to get back anywhere close to on-time.

When Lance missed curfew, co-captains Dave Schaake and Mike Brown took it up themselves to let him know they didn't approve of a rookie being so irresponsible. His sentence was to ride from Atlanta to Statesboro in the bathroom of the bus. The rest of us also got the message, and my initial assessment of Lance remained unchanged. I was, after all, very serious about school, just as serious about baseball, and at the time I was only minimally interested in late-night escapades.

We finished that road trip with a 4-4 record, which included a hard-fought but close loss to the University of South Carolina Gamecocks, and by the time we headed home I'd cemented my place in centerfield. I was also hitting .392.

We got back to SIUE and played North Central College from Chicago in a two-game set on our field. Somehow, Skip was home at the time and he came over to watch me play. I had a couple of hits in the first game, including a triple into the gap on the first pitch after I was spun-out and knocked down by a fastball right under my chin, but in the second game I hit three hard shots right down the third-base line and with each one I was certain I'd hit at least a double. One by one they were gobbled up by the third-baseman, who picked that day to do his best Brooks Robinson impersonation. And the doubts started creeping into my head. "Those should've been hits. Instead I went 0-for-4. When will I get my next hit?"

I scuffled along picking up a knock every now and then, but pretty quickly the doubts became more like panic and I went into a hitless skid that got worse by the day. I'm not sure of the exact number of hitless at-bats I managed to string together, but it was over 20 and before long my batting average was on an express-lane route to .200 territory. And these weren't unlucky outs like the three at-bats against North Central. During the epic slump, I don't think I hit one ball hard. It got so bad I'd leave our field in my car and drive the wrong way on purpose, needing to get away and clear my head. An hour later, I'd finally compose myself enough to head home.

Finally, mercifully, on a road trip against University of Evansville I dribbled a seeing-eye roller into left field and the weight of a Steinway grand piano was lifted off my back.

I plugged along and got my average back up into the low .200s, kept playing good defense, and tried to convince my doubting brain that I was better than this. It's all between the ears, right?

In late spring we ventured up I-70 to play Eastern Illinois University in a pair of doubleheaders scheduled for Saturday and Sunday, and it rained on us torrentially all the way there Friday afternoon. And it rained all night. And it rained all day Saturday. It was a simple formula: We didn't see any way we'd play on Sunday, the Holiday Inn in Charleston, Illinois, had a bar, and that bar sold beer. It seemed like a natural progression for a group like us. There was a solo musician in the bar, playing soft ballads on his guitar, and there was a bartender who was more than willing to keep the beer flowing as the rain continued pelting the windows. Right before midnight, when the bar was set to close, we were requesting songs from the singer but he didn't seem too interested in covering tunes by Black Sabbath or Alice Cooper. We were ever so disappointed.

We wobbled back to our rooms, with the rain still pouring, and went to bed.

At 7 o'clock the next morning, there was knock on our door and it was Coach Lee with the "good" news that not only had the rain stopped, but the field was in fine shape and we were going to play. Through our headaches we processed that information and then he told us that we were not only playing the regularly scheduled Sunday double-header, but we'd be playing three games in one day. We were stunned at the news, but we had a tripleheader to play.

We lost the first game but won the next two and a young skinny centerfielder wearing number five on his SIUE jersey hit his first official college home run. My headache was gone, as well.

Later in the spring, we made the same type of trek to Western Illinois University in Macomb, and we managed to play all four games just as intended, on the correct days and just two at a time. I was really feeling confident out in the outfield by then and I was roaming all over the place to catch everything I could get to, no matter where my other outfielders were. After I ranged almost all the way to left field to catch one towering fly ball to end an inning, Coach Lee stopped our left-fielder Mike Liay in front of our dugout, with the whole team watching, and he said "Liay, if you want to make any put-outs in this game you're going to have to call Wilber off. He'll steal your outs, he'll steal your wallet, heck he might even steal your girlfriend if you don't call him off." Everyone laughed, including me, but in my brain that was just a challenge. I'd always catch everything I could get to.

As a group, we strung together enough wins to earn a spot in the NCAA Division II Regionals, and once again we would host those games. That made eight straight regional appearances for the SIUE Cougars, and two straight for guys like Steve Novak, Cornpone Wells, Mike Brown, Stan Osterbur, Greg McBride, Dave Schaake, and Bob Wilber.

We beat Northern Kentucky in the first game, then Wright State in the second. We had to play Northern Kentucky again to stamp our ticket back to Springfield and for that game Taffy came over to watch me play. She was not well at the time and my siblings and I were worried about her. She sat mostly in the car, but the friend who had driven her over would go get her each time I came up to bat. Taffy picked a heck of a day to come watch her boy play baseball.

"The zone" is a weird place that only a few lucky athletes get to visit. Tennis players and golfers talk about it the most, when without warning the game slows down and the shots come easily. Every crosscourt backhand is a winner and every putt falls in the cup.

In baseball, I'd heard guys talk about being in the zone and how the pitches seem to slow down while the ball seems to grow in size, but I had never experienced it. To me, the pitches were in warp-drive and the ball looked like an aspirin tablet. Until that day.

I came up in the middle innings and watched the Northern Kentucky starter's first pitch float right down the middle like volleyball. Strike one. I stepped out of the box and thought about this for a second, even calling a quick timeout to contemplate my approach. My brain was rattled and I thought, "This is just ridiculous. If I try to kill this guy's slop I'll only get myself out. Just wait for it and take a nice easy swing."

Another comically slow fastball headed home and I put the easiest, most compact swing possible on the ball. Line shot into left field for a solid hit. I then came around to score and put us in the lead.

The next time up, late in the game, Taffy's friend went to get her out of the car and I faced the same pitcher once again, wondering on my way to the plate why their coach had left this bum in.

Same deal. Same super slo-mo experience. Same easy swing. This time a fly ball into the gap toward the 375-foot sign. I dug hard for first, thinking it had a chance to get down for a double and yet, when I rounded first, my disbelieving eyes could not comprehend why the left-fielder was standing at the fence watching the ball I'd just hit sail over it for a home run. Taffy cried. And we won.

I told the guys later that I was surprised by how bad that pitcher was and all I saw was puzzled faces. I said, "Man, that was like BP," and saw heads shaking. Finally, someone said, "Are you nuts? That guy was throwing bullets. That was as good of stuff as we've seen all year."

I had visited the zone. But, there's one problem with the zone. You can't make reservations to visit. You can't force your way inside. The zone will invite you to spend a little time there, but only when it wants to. It's a marvelous place when you do get to visit.

After the game, we all visited another sort of zone experience with our yard party outside the Pink Palace, complete with kiddie pool full of beer and a group of ballplayers who mostly just smiled at each other before taking another sip.

What I felt that night, out in the front yard, was beyond any emotion I'd known in my life. It was pure, unfiltered and unbridled joy. It was striking to feel it and to realize I'd never experienced anything like it before, but it was so real and pure I'll never forget it. I'd crushed two balls off a guy everyone else thought was throwing gas. I'd hit a home run. My mom was there, and this momma's boy did everything but share those tears with her as he rounded the bases. And we won. I was surrounded by great friends who had gone on this 1977 journey as a group, and we'd fought hard to get to where we were and where we were going. There's really nothing quite like that.

We headed to Springfield and checked into our rooms at the Holiday Inn before getting back on the bus to attend the NCAA banquet, where all the participating teams would gather for a buffet dinner and a few speeches. I wore the most glorious beige leisure suit in fashion history, complete with enormous lapels and a pseudo-silk shirt with the image of a large feathery bird printed on the front. Also platform soles on my brown shoes. I fit right in.

When the World Series began, Coach Lee made a tactical mistake that he later admitted was our undoing. He held back our two best pitchers, Jerry Deml and Stan Osterbur, and had two other guys start the first two games in the double-elimination tournament. The belief was that our third and fourth-best pitchers could handle those opponents and the idea was to have Deml and Osterbur ready for the championship games. Stan was my roomie on road trips most of the year and we were again sharing a room at the Holiday Inn. He was simultaneously thrilled that Roy wanted him to bring home the trophy but he was puzzled by the risk.

Sure enough, we led University of Missouri-St. Louis deep into game one, but lost the lead and the game. Two days later we did the same thing against Delta State University, from Mississippi, leading for most of the game but finally losing it. Just like that, before we could even understand it, we were eliminated in two straight games. And our two best pitchers never threw a pitch.

When Stan and I got back to the room he was inconsolable. I wasn't sure how to help him. There were many scouts in attendance; it was his chance to show his stuff and possibly get drafted by a Major League team, yet he never threw a pitch. It was a horribly emotional night in our room but it wouldn't be the last one we'd share.

I had collected four hits in the two games, and in the end my average had somehow climbed back to a respectable .264, but all I could think about was Stan's overwhelming sadness and my own frustration about the awful slump that had robbed me of at least 100 points and possibly cost the team a few games. It was not a good day.

Earlier in the spring my dad had taken on a new role with an old employer when the Minnesota Twins named him the manager of their Triple-A club in Tacoma. I didn't expect that to impact me, since I assumed I'd be staying in Edwardsville for more summer ball, but once Skip got out to the Pacific Northwest he learned about a good college summer team in the Seattle-Tacoma area called the Cheney Studs. They were sponsored by Louisiana Pacific lumber, so that would be "studs" as in 2x4's, not a description of the players themselves. Had the latter been the case, I wouldn't have even earned a tryout.

Once he looked into the Studs a little more and heard the team was mostly populated by guys from the University of Washington, Washington State, and other fine programs, he asked me if I'd want to come out there with him for the summer. I could work out with the Tacoma Twins on off-days and play with the Studs all around the Sea-Tac region. That sounded like a pretty fun adventure.

As soon as the quarter was over at SIUE, I took my first summer off from extra classes and flew out to Sea-Tac airport. The next day Skip drove me up to Edmonds Community College, the Studs' home field, and I met the manager, Fred Shull. Bill Waag, who went on to a fine minor league career in the Pittsburgh organization, was there as well and both of us went through some drills as our tryout.

I made the team, although the club already had five good outfielders and I wasn't going to get to play all the time.

I headed back to Tacoma to move into the house where Skip was living, which just happened to be owned and inhabited by the Tacoma Twins' head groundskeeper and his wife. At least I got my own bedroom.

Two things I remember vividly about that house was that it had an unobstructed view of Mount Rainier, the sight of which I never stopped appreciating, and it had cable TV. It was the first house I'd ever been in with cable, and the groundskeeper had sprung the few extra bucks to add a fledgling new network by the name of HBO to his channel listings.

You might find this hard to believe now, but when HBO launched they didn't have enough programming to keep movies or shows running 24 hours per day so they staggered their programming with gaps in the schedule. To fill those gaps they ran canned videos of nature, parks, and oceans. I know this because the homeowners figured they were paying for this channel so they left it on all the time.

Just days after I arrived in Tacoma I turned 21 and Skip asked me what I wanted to drink. Considering he was still in his Cabin Still heyday, that's what I had, mixed with a Coke. I honestly would've rather just had a beer, but I had been drinking those legally in college and when your old man asks you to have a drink with him on your 21st birthday, you drink what he pours.

On the field, despite having just finished my college season at the Division II World Series, I got off to a rough start with the Studs. As was usually the case, my outfield play was just fine but I didn't get any hits in my first few games and the pressure started to mount.

I'll give Fred Shull credit for his diligence when it came to making sure all six outfielders got to play as often as possible. It would've been easy to just sit me on the bench but we all rotated in and out of the line-up on a game-by-game basis, if not during games, and we all got along just fine.

Our home games were in Edmonds but we played all over the Seattle area. I got some instant training in learning my way around the city while we played in ballparks in Kent, Auburn, Bellevue, and as far north as Everett. We even had a two-day road trip to Portland, Oregon, on the schedule, riding in a bus and staying in a motel while we played in a tournament.

I got a few hits here and there but it was a letdown from how well I was hitting at the end of the SIUE season and I knew I could do better. It was also an interesting experience to be playing in the Puget Sound area. The scenery was unlike any I'd seen before and the weather wasn't exactly conducive to baseball. It rained. A lot. But it almost never poured and I don't recall ever having a game cancelled due to weather. Most of the fields we played on had a high percentage of sand or finely ground gravel on the infield, so that rain would soak right through. I remember standing in centerfield, during early July, with rain dripping off the brim of my hat while we had a fire going in 55-gallon drum in the dugout. I asked myself, "What exactly am I doing here?"

On the Studs off-days, I went to Cheney Stadium, the home of the Twins, and worked out with the team. These workouts were more specific than just shagging flies and taking BP. Skip put together a schedule of drills I would do with young outfield prospect Hosken Powell. We'd go out to centerfield and have a coach hit fungoes over our heads, making us spot the ball and then turn and run to the place where we thought it would land. The trick was to always know where the unforgiving wall was, and to make that split-second decision between leaping for the ball or stopping to take the carom.

Hosken was only a year older than me, but he was already in Triple-A and on his way to the big leagues, so it was fun to do the same drills with such a talented and nice guy.

It was a fun clubhouse in Tacoma, with guys like Willie Norwood, Randy Bass, Sal Butera, and Gary Ward on the roster, but the team wasn't playing particularly well and the Twins wanted to make a change. To do that, they fired Skip and made the team's first-baseman the player/manager. That would be Tom Kelly, who went on to manage the Minnesota Twins from 1986 to 2001.

Dad took it fine enough and he knew the team wasn't playing up to its potential, but I could tell at the house that night this was no ordinary dismissal. He knew it was over. He'd gotten his one day as a skipper in the big leagues but then was passed over for other such jobs despite his success at Denver and Spokane. The Twins gave him one more shot, but he failed to get the team where the big club wanted them to be. His managing days were officially in the past.

He asked me if I wanted to stay and finish out the season with the Studs or head back home with him. I had a game the next night, at our home field in Edmonds, so I made the decision to play that game and inform the team I was leaving. Of course, with the pressure off I went 3-for-4 and rocketed a home run well over the left field fence. I can remember our hitting coach shaking his head and smiling before he said, "All you had to do was relax, Bob. You've been pressing so hard it was tough to watch, but tonight you just played and look how it turned out."

Other than simply not wanting to stay in Seattle without my dad, the other reason I was quick to decide to go home was the first phone call I'd made after Skip got fired. I called Coach Lee at SIUE and asked him what he thought I should do. He said he'd think about it and make a few calls for me, and an hour later he called back to tell me the Danville Roosters, in the Central Illinois Collegiate League, had just lost an outfielder and the spot was mine if I wanted it. Yes, the same CICL my brother Del and his buddy Del Unser played in during the mid-60s, for a manager in Springfield by the name of Roy Lee. Full circle, once again.

At the time, the CICL was considered a top-three summer collegiate league, on a par with the Cape Cod League and the Alaskan League. It was good place to play.

And, in retrospect, apparently it's completely possible to go from being a Stud to a Rooster with one phone call. I told Roy I was on my way, Skip booked our flight (in first class on a TWA 747) and we headed back to St. Louis.

Once I got to Kirkwood I called the owner of the Danville Roosters to sort out where I was going and when I should be there. The answers were "Danville Stadium" just off I-74 and "as soon as you can get here." I packed my gear and as many clothes as I had with me and off I went, once again plowing forward without taking a moment to consider what I was doing.

I'd never been to Danville before but it was easy to find. It was about a four-hour drive from St. Louis. I passed a Little League field one exit short of where I was going and had a pang of fear about that dump being our home field but at the exit I headed north and there was a classic, and fairly large, old minor league ballpark just ahead. It was still only about 2 o'clock when I got there, so I waited in my car for the first players to arrive. We had a game that night.

When the first car full of guys pulled in I introduced myself and one of them said, "We're here early, so we'll have to jump the fence. We do it all the time." Indeed, the six-foot-high chain-link fence was in our way and the gate was padlocked, so over the top we went and one of the guys was nice enough to hoist my duffel bag to me after I got inside.

We headed into the clubhouse and over the course of the next hour I grabbed a uniform, with my trusty number five on the back, and a locker. The other guys filed in, our manager arrived, we exchanged pleasantries, and I met the owner, who wrote me a check to cover my travel expenses. As I met the guys, I was impressed and possibly a bit intimidated to hear where they went to school. We were mostly juniors, although Mike Hurdle had just finished his freshman year at Texas A&M making him the youngest guy on the roster. We had players from the University of Texas, Louisiana State, the University of New Orleans, Florida Southern, Vanderbilt, and Miami of Ohio, and without a doubt it was the most talented group of guys with whom I'd ever shared a dugout.

The team didn't have a pair of pants that really fit me and the pair I was given were at least two sizes too big, so that made me feel horribly self-conscious and out of place. As the infamous Dick Stuart once said when he played in the big leagues, "I add 20 points to my average if I know I look bitchin' out there," and I had always felt the same way — hence my request to my sister Mary to take in my pants every year in high school. I had no option that night in Danville.

I started as the DH that night, and all I could think about were two things: My baggy pants and how hard the pitcher from the Springfield Caps was throwing. I struck out four times. I honestly expected the manager or the team owner to kindly inform me that my services were no longer needed once the game was over, and I would've understood completely. They didn't, and I stayed.

I headed back into the clubhouse and wasn't exactly sure where I was going to go next. Once again it was that whole thing about just plowing forward without thinking about pesky details. I had enough money for a couple of nights in a motel but players in the CICL were responsible for their own housing so I knew I'd have to sort something out quickly. And then two guys in the clubhouse asked "You need a place to stay?" I said I did and they both shook my hand and told me to follow them to the boarding house where they were living on the other side of town. A bunch of the Roosters lived there, along with a dozen Iranian students who attended Danville Community College. It sounded like an interesting mix.

Both guys were pitchers and Ricky Kittrell, from Vanderbilt, had bunk beds in his room but no roommate. His buddy was Andy McGaffigan from Florida Southern. The same Andy McGaffigan who would go on to pitch 11 years in the big leagues. They couldn't have been nicer and the three of us would spend the rest of the summer together.

Once we got to the boarding house I also discovered that players were not just responsible for their housing, they also needed to bring their own sheets, pillows, and blankets. No one had clued me in to that fact but between Ricky and Andy they found me enough stuff to get through the first night.

I only had a sheet though, no blanket, and it was a little chilly when we woke up the next morning. Ricky was heading out to run some errands early that day, and he quietly put his blanket over me as he left the room. Seriously.

The trick was to figure out what I'd do for the next three days. The Roosters had an odd gap in the schedule and some of the guys were heading home or elsewhere for the break, but I felt Kirkwood was too far away. I'm sure there was also some fear that if I left town they might not let me come back so I just hung out and explored Danville, buying some sheets and blankets and food for the fridge.

I also discovered that the Danville newspaper covered the Roosters like a pro team, with front-page stories in the Sports section and full box scores. That was not only cool, it also motivated me to hurry up and get some hits so I could read the stories and be proud of them, instead of embarrassed.

Perhaps most crucial of all, I found a seamstress and had my pants taken in. I desperately needed to look bitchin' out there.

I got two hits in the next game, another in the game after that, and then I basically caught fire. I ended up hitting .363 for Danville, playing against some seriously stout competition on an outstanding team, and I got to know a great group of guys as we traveled the state to play other CICL clubs in Charleston, Mattoon, Springfield, Macomb, Bloomington, Peoria, and Galesburg.

We actually drew pretty big crowds at home, as well, with as many as 2,000 noisy fans packing the place on any given night, and the rallying sound on the P.A. was, of course, that of a rooster. Cock-a-doodle-doooo!

Just about every player on that team went on to play pro ball, and Andy was not the only pitcher to make it to the big leagues. He was actually the second-best pitcher on the Danville club. Charlie Liebrandt was a Rooster that summer, and he went on to star in the Major

Leagues for 14 years with the Reds, Royals, and Braves. The whole team was talented and they were all great guys, as well. What a rich experience it was.

Having played with guys that good, and having done more than just hold my own after my rough first night in baggy pants, it slowly began to sink in that I wasn't that far off from their talent level. I could play the same game they were playing, if I could just translate these summer league abilities to my in-season stats with the SIUE Cougars. I had one more chance at SIUE.

Word had also filtered back about what a fine half-season I had in Danville and both the Sports Information Director and the Sports Editor of the Daily Alestle wanted to interview me. The stories were picked up in a few publications, and the headline in one paper boldly said "Del's Kid" above a photo of me rounding third.

Upon my return to school after that eventful summer that stretched from Puget Sound to central Illinois, I made one big decision that had nothing to do with baseball or classes. I decided to leave the Tower Lake group and get my own apartment.

I loved those guys, and enjoyed my three years living at Tower Lake, but sharing an apartment with three other people, no matter how big or comfortable the place is, means sharing everything. From the bathroom to the television, every aspect of home life had to accommodate four guys, and at Tower Lake we'd always have to share a bedroom with one other guy who, more than likely, snored at least a little bit. I felt a strong pull to see what it was like to live by myself.

I found a one-bedroom place on the east side of Edwardsville, putting me a solid 10 minutes from campus and by "place" I mean in reality it was simply a trailer dressed up to look like a permanent structure. It was dinky but it was mine and once I moved in I found myself enjoying the privacy. I still hung out with all the guys at school, around the lunch table, and my classes were getting to be more and more creative as my advisers kept Jim Keegan and me on a unique path, so there was plenty of social interaction each day. At night, I'd meet up with the guys at The Granary (which was walking distance from my apartment) or Spanky's or any of our other haunts, and it was not uncommon for Lance or someone else to come crash at my place after a few beers, but typically I was there alone and I liked it.

We also had a new ballplayer enter our inner circle. He was a freshman named Bob Ricker and when we met him he was short, skinny, and he wore glasses, so we thought he looked just like Radar O'Reilly from "M*A*S*H." After those first few days when we welcomed him to the baseball table in the cafeteria, he would never again be Bob to anyone. He would always be Radar. Also from that point forward, Lance, Radar, Oscar Noffke and I would become the tightest of friends.

Radar took the nickname in stride but I think it motivated him to discover the weight room and he worked out like a man on a mission. Within a year he had created a whole new physique, although he was still short and we continued to call him Radar. He wasn't the most gifted ballplayer but he willed himself to be a good one. It was remarkable to watch.

Keegan and I continued to flourish in the Communications Department. By my senior year, the advisers were creating classes they simply called Colloquium 101 or Colloquium 102, and our assignments were to take the 10-week quarter and create something. We had no actual classes but the faculty provided us time in the studio and support from master control, and they let us do whatever we wanted. I wrote, directed, and produced a science fiction movie one quarter and I "hired" Jim to be the voice of the on-board computer in the spaceship set I had built myself. At other times, he and I would produce and be the on-screen talent for a fictitious TV sports talk show. We could sit in those chairs and just go once the cameras were on, ad-libbing all we wanted about St. Louis or Chicago sports, and somehow we managed to get former St. Louis Football Cardinals quarterback Tim Van Galder to come to Edwardsville to be our guest one day, despite the fact our "show" was only carried by closed circuit on campus.

I was also part of an actual movie which the TV/R department was hired to produce. It was about "close encounters of the third kind" before the film with that very name was made, and we managed to get the UFO/alien expert who coined the term, Dr. J. Allen Hynek, to not only be our technical adviser but to also appear in the film. There was a lot of pressure to make it look like a professional production and my job was to be the lead camera operator. Trying to put smooth slow transitions on tape was nerve-wracking but it was a thrill at the same time.

We wrapped production on time and then the movie simply disappeared. I don't think it was abducted by aliens but I did hear a rumor that Steven Spielberg, who was getting ready to make that blockbuster film, bought it and destroyed it so that there would be no confusion as to who produced what. I have no idea if that rumor was true, but it made us all feel better.

Going into fall baseball practice, I'm not sure if any of us quite understood how much talent we'd lost after the 1977 season. Mike Brown, Dave Schaake, Stan Osterbur, and Jerry Deml were all big reasons we made it back to the Division II World Series, and we didn't really have anyone on the roster to fill those roles. But, having been to the postseason for two consecutive years I think the one thing we were not lacking was confidence. We all just assumed we'd be good.

During Christmas break, I also decided the little trailer apartment was too small, too cold, and too far from all my buddies. I ended my lease and spent a few nights with Oscar, Lance, and a few other guys at the Pink Palace and I immediately knew that we should live together.

My brother Rick owned a home in town, across the street from a local ballpark, but he was working in Mankato, Minnesota, and he had a tenant in the house. When he discovered how badly she was taking care of the place, as in not taking any care of it at all, he threw her out and offered the house to Lance, Radar, pitcher Larry Donaldson, and me. Oscar stayed with the group in the Pink Palace. We spent days cleaning up the filthy house but when we were done we had ourselves a real home. It was an older two-story white frame house and we dubbed it The White House. Of course we did. Lance and Radar shared an upstairs bedroom, I took the master bedroom next to them, and Larry took the downstairs room.

It was a comfortable place in every way and we had a great time living together. We put my stereo in the front sitting room and that became our de facto private disco. The Bee Gees and "Saturday Night Fever" were all the rage then, and on many nights we'd leave one of our favorite haunts and head back to The White House with a few girls to have some serious "dance-off" competitions. It's hard to fathom now but we really got into that, throwing our best John Travolta moves and arguing over the ridiculous scores we gave each other.

After another late winter working out inside the same grade school it was time for our spring trip to open the season and we had not yet been outdoors. We boarded our standard bus, which had brown shag carpet on all the walls and the ceiling, plus four couches, a table in the back for playing cards, and a few regular seats up front, and we headed for Columbia, South Carolina, to once again take on the Gamecocks. It all started with one really bad omen for me. We bused as far as Knoxville the first day and spent the night at the Admiral Benbow Motel then got up in the morning to board the bus again for the trip to Columbia. We hauled our luggage and duffel bags down to the lobby and when the bus pulled up we loaded everything in the baggage compartments. Or so I thought.

Later that day, we arrived in Columbia and headed straight for our hotel there. We disembarked and each reached into the lower-level compartments to get our bags. My suitcase was there, but my duffel bag was not. I was stupefied, horrified, and completely confused. Somehow, in my typical absent-minded way, I'd failed to put my duffel bag on the bus. We were set to play the powerhouse Gamecocks the next day and I had no equipment.

We called the Admiral Benbow Motel and the clerk there verified that one red SIUE duffel bag had been left in the lobby and it featured the number five on the side. Yep, that would be mine.

Our equipment manager seemed to think he could arrange for the bag to get to Columbia in the morning, before our game, but when the flight arrived from Knoxville my bag was not on it. A quick call provided the truly sickening news that it would not arrive until the next morning, which meant I couldn't play. To be fair, I'm pretty sure we could've rounded up enough spare stuff for me to suit up but I think Coach Lee's decision to keep me in a warm-up suit on the bench was proof of exactly how much he considered me to be an idiot. I certainly felt like one.

We lost that game 8-0, but the other bad news for me was that my benching allowed me to try something I'd only done once or twice in the past. I put a wad of Levi Garrett chewing tobacco in my mouth. First-time neophytes in the world of chewing tobacco, whether it's the leafy kind like Levi Garrett or the finely chopped "snuff" like Skoal, usually get very light-headed from the nicotine, if not even a little nauseous. When I tried it once at practice that had happened to me. I'd therefore never tried it again, because I knew I couldn't play feeling like that. On that day, in that warm-up suit, with no chance to play, I gave it another shot. I would reach my 40th birthday before I quit. Bad omen, bad decision.

My bag arrived the next day and I played, driving in a run in what turned out to be a nail-biter of a loss, 3-2 in 12 innings. The runner I drove in was Lance McCord and that was noteworthy as well. Lance was a good all-around athlete who played football, basketball, and baseball at a high level in high school. He had a great arm as a pitcher. But his problem wasn't velocity, it was control — when he'd start missing the strike zone he'd attempt to throw the ball right through the catcher, only to see his control get worse.

During workouts the previous fall, Coach Lee tried putting Lance at third base and he acquitted himself quite well there. He was a decent fielder and even though he hadn't hit much since he'd been in college, he had some pop in his bat. As a result, Coach Lee announced Lance would be the Cougars' starting third baseman in the spring of 1978. He also named Lance and me co-captains. Then we started 0-2 with one missing duffel bag and a bunch of question marks.

We lost to little Newberry College before beating West Virginia State, then headed to Western Carolina University.

Although Western Carolina was on spring break some students remained on campus and for some brilliant reason we didn't stay in a hotel. The athletic department there provided accommodations in a dorm — an all-girls dorm.

The high-rise building was probably only about one-third full, but that still meant there were more females in the building than SIUE Cougars and the trouble allegedly started the second we got off the bus. To this day I think we were framed for something no one on our team actually did but with our rooms being on the first floor and with strict instructions that we were not to go upstairs, it was only minutes before someone reported that two guys in red hats had already been seen snooping around the higher floors. Within minutes there was a law enforcement officer there.

Being co-captains, Lance and I were the team representatives and frankly we were both confused as to how it was even possible for any of our guys to have done that within, quite literally, a minute after our arrival. The sheriff was straight from a Burt Reynolds movie, with a thick southern drawl, and as he pinned this transgression on SIUE ballplayers he looked me right in the eye and said, "Son, you don't want to know what the inside of a southern jail looks like, so you better just 'fess up and we'll put this behind us." I don't think we ever actually 'fessed up, but we agreed to have a team meeting and tighten the rope a bit on our road-weary group.

We also had two new assistant coaches with us in 1978, by the familiar names of Bill Lee and Stan Osterbur. They had plenty to offer in the way of advice, we knew they could also keep us loose with their senses of humor, and they both wanted to stay in shape in the hope they could land another free-agent professional contract before the summer. To us, though, it was like they'd never left.

We lost to Western Carolina and made the long trip back to Edwardsville with a sterling record of 1-4. As per usual for me, I had again gotten off to a hot start and I came home hitting around .400, somehow.

Basically from that point forward we collectively had the worst possible season. Only two guys on the team, both rookies, hit worth a darn and they, Tony Pugh and Tommy Carroll, carried us to whatever wins we could muster. As a team, we didn't hit well, we didn't field well, and we pitched pretty lousy too.

Not too long after we got back we went over to the north side of St. Louis to play University of Missouri-St. Louis and I knew then that this season might be a lost cause. We'd always handled UMSL pretty well but this time they handed us two heartbreaking losses. To make matters far worse, one of their hitters smashed a rocket right at Steve Novak at first base but it took a wickedly bad hop and came up to hit him in the nose. It was the most sickening sound I'd ever heard on a baseball field.

Steve went down in a heap and the first guys to reach him all took a look and recoiled at the sight. The ball had obliterated his nose, smashed his sinuses, and broken some bones. There was blood everywhere, and he was lucky he was still able to see. Steve went to the hospital but the rest of us had to keep playing and there was no joy in it for any of us. There wasn't much joy from that point forward.

Steve was a mess and it was going to be a tough few weeks for him. The doctors did the best they could with his nose, and packed his sinuses with gauze, but he'd never again breathe the same. Weeks later, he was cleared to play but only if he wore a plastic mask over his eyes and nose. He was miserable and so were we.

I never went through a protracted slump that year but I cooled off and never really got going again. The experiment with Lance at third base never really got going either, although he did hit one home run. Before long he was back in the bullpen or on the bench and we consistently underperformed as a group. We also had three road trips completely rained out in advance. Each time, we'd be ready to get on the bus (or in one case on the Amtrak train) when the phone call would come telling us the weather was so bad at our destination we weren't even going. The whole season was like that. Nothing went as planned and we all only got worse as we went along.

We finished the season in Tulsa, Oklahoma, with two games against Oral Roberts University at their spectacular stadium. It was, by far, the nicest ballpark we'd ever played in and Coach Lee had been harping at us all week about not getting intimidated. We really didn't, but it was pretty obvious our coach wanted us to appear as polished as the opposition. He watched Oral Roberts take infield practice, doing all sorts of complicated drills that had multiple baseballs flying in all directions, and he decided we were going to do that, too. We had, of course, never done anything like that and frankly we were lucky we didn't kill anyone that evening. We had baseballs going everywhere.

Coach Lee did put Lance back at third base there and early in the game he made a brilliant stop of a hard smash and then whirled around to throw a bullet right to Novak at first base. Steve caught the throw for the out and he turned to Oscar at second base, saying "He should've been there all year."

An inning later an Oral Roberts hitter tapped a big one hopper right to Lance and he had all sorts of time to make the throw. That was probably the reason why he fired the ball across the diamond and we all watched it sail and rise until it passed over Novak's head on its way to the grandstand, where it kept rising before it nicked the railing at the top and flew completely out of the ballpark. He threw the ball completely out of the stadium. I looked to my left at Bill Stolte playing right field, and Bill had his hands on his knees as he laughed. He finally had to put his glove over his face but he couldn't stop laughing. That pretty much summed up our entire 1978 season and at the end of that second game against Oral Roberts all of us who were seniors knew our college careers were over. We finished 12-20 and frankly we weren't even that good.

My disappointment was overwhelming. I didn't know if I'd ever play another game and I was certain my chances of getting drafted by a Major League club, in early June, had circled the drain and disappeared.

I went back to school to wrap up that spring quarter, my final one on scholarship, and looking at my accumulation of credit hours it was clear I still needed at least two more quarters to earn my degree. In addition, my advisers we about to run out of new ideas for Jim Keegan and me so I was faced with taking some additional freshman-level general studies courses just to pick up the hours.

Before the quarter ended, however, Coach Lee decided he wanted to get a jump on the next season with an intrasquad game and he invited all of us who were seniors to play. Perhaps it was his way of helping us get back out there to forget about the terrible season we'd had. I learned something in that game.

Aluminum bats were taking over college baseball but I had continued to use wood. I thought it would help prepare me for my 20-year big league career and, at the same time, impress the scouts. In the intrasquad game I picked up an aluminum bat and in my first at-bat hit what I figured was a short fly ball to left-center. It didn't even feel all that good upon contact, like it had jammed me a little. Imagine my surprise when I rounded first and saw it clang off the top of the wall at the 375 mark.

It struck me right then that impressing the scouts could've been done with more impact had I just used aluminum. The difference between metal and wood was stunning. That only added to my depression and my certain belief that above everything else I was an idiot.

Nothing was quite as much fun as it had been. Seeing the dream die was crushing. I'd been focused on it since that first fly ball at Schall School and it appeared to have thudded home to a halt, dead on arrival. For many of us, that was all we could face.

As a group spanning my four years at SIUE I'd had the privilege of playing with a great group of athletes but I was more impressed by the types of men they were. For the most part, we all did well.

Dave Schaake became a high-level business executive. Infielder Kevin Pesko ended up as a bank president. Steve Novak went to work in the sports apparel business and eventually was in charge of national sales for Tehama, a golf apparel company owned by Clint Eastwood. Oscar Noffke returned home to tiny Strasburg, Illinois to teach at the same school he'd attended. Radar Ricker opened a successful State Farm Insurance office in nearby Maryville.

Lance McCord took his accounting degree and turned it into a career in finance, working for IBM for a while (a move that would change my life) before becoming a CFO.

Tom Hill graduated early with his double-major and went to work for General Motors. He'd spend the next four decades doing important design and management work for the Chevy Corvette. It was a job he was destined to do.

One player who became a key part of the unit despite being a few years behind us, which meant he never did actually play on the varsity with our group, was Fernando Aguirre. At the lunch table, he delighted us by teaching us all how to say, "Me gusto los legumbres!" That would translate to "I like vegetables." Fernando did "pretty well" in business. When he retired, he did so as the CEO of Chiquita Brands.

With only one or two exceptions, every guy from those teams did very well in life. This one, too.

Whatever my next adventure would be, I knew I had to keep plowing forward.

Paintsville?

After we finished that dismal senior baseball season, I faced the reality that my diamond dream was likely over. I started mapping out my courses to finish my degree and it looked like I'd have to pay tuition for two or three more quarters to get it done, then I'd put my tapes together and start the search for a television or radio job.

Just as I was formulating those plans Skip stepped in yet again. He called a colleague, the general manager of the Detroit Tigers, Bill LaJoie. Later, Skip said he'd told LaJoie something like this: "Bill, Bob can play. I don't know what happened over there this season because the whole team stunk the joint up, but he can play. Heck, he ripped the cover off the ball in the CICL last year, hitting as good as a bunch of guys who will all go in the early rounds in this draft, and playing the outfield better than a lot of guys who played for me in Triple-A. I don't think he got worse and he wasn't hurt, so maybe the whole bunch of them over there just played terrible. I know he can play, and the Novak kid can play too. You ought to give them both the opportunity."

I didn't know for sure that it was going to happen but on the day after the draft the Tigers sent me a certified letter containing a contract for Class-A Bristol, in the Appalachian League. I figured I'd better sign it before anyone could change their minds but I was well aware that this particular moment was one I'd been focused on since I was five.

The dream was not dead yet and I felt like just gotten a reprieve that I couldn't pass up. I owed it to my father to make the most of it, whether I was good enough or not.

They also sent a contract just like mine to Steve Novak but Nove just didn't have it in him. He was tired, he was still hurt, and I'm sure he was as depressed as the rest of us about how it all ended. He turned down the contract and never played another game. Years later he told me, "That was a really rash decision I regret. I should've gone with you and played, just for the experience of being a pro, but I was so over it I couldn't do it. I was just too over it."

I signed that first professional baseball contract in the living room of our Kirkwood home on a sunny afternoon in early June 1978. I remember being tempted to do it in a hurry so I could immediately mail it back, but the simple act of taking my time, soaking in the experience while staring, over and over, at my name typed neatly at the top of it, was a great moment — a moment to savor. Further down the lengthy document, in the area marked for compensation, the typewritten numbers and words were "$500 per month" and "$500 signing bonus." The bonus was a one-time deal, but the salary stretched on for an entire summer, in twice-monthly payments, minus taxes. It wasn't a lot of money — it was basically no money — but it was more than I ever made as an usher and it was compensation for playing baseball, which is a great gig if you can get it. It was a contract to a dream.

A few days later I packed as many casual summer clothes as I could into a suitcase and filled a spare duffel bag with all my baseball gear. I then taped three Louisville Sluggers together, all my favorite U1 model, and Taffy took me to the airport. Skip was out on the road doing his job, but that was the norm and I was used to it. And, once again, with little forethought and almost no dread, I was plowing forward.

After a stop in Knoxville I changed planes and headed for the tiny Tri-Cities Airport near Bristol, Tennessee. My printed instructions told me to gather my belongings and hail a taxi. I was to tell the driver to take me to the EconoLodge Motel, and I was to ask for a receipt after I paid the man.

Driving down the main drag we passed some light towers and the driver said, in a classic Appalachian drawl, "I guess you're here to play for the Tigers, huh?" After I answered in the affirmative he added "Well, that's where you're gonna be playin', right over yonder" pointing to the lights.

He dropped me off at the EconoLodge and handed me my receipt (I'd get that money back in cash once I arrived at the ballpark the next day) before I headed into the lobby. We would all be two-to-a-room for a week, after which all the players would need to find their own accommodations, so the clerk asked me if I had any preferences in terms of a roomie. I actually didn't know who any of my teammates were going to be but I scanned the list she handed me and recognized the name Judson Thigpen. He'd pitched at Delta State for the team that beat us in the '77 Division II World Series. I pointed at his name.

She gave me a key and I headed up the staircase for the outdoor hallway, counting off the room numbers as I went. About halfway down I came to the door that matched the number etched on the green plastic diamond-shaped key fob, and I knocked, just to be polite.

Judson came to the door, I introduced myself, and within seconds I knew I'd picked a good guy with which to start this epic journey. We got up to speed on Delta State and SIUE then started to pick through the many "one degree of separation" people we knew in common. We never spoke of being nervous or being excited. We were just two ballplayers in a room.

After a while, we sat back on our beds and watched numerous episodes of The Three Stooges on a television that featured rabbit ears and a dial. We grabbed a bite at a diner across the street and then, somehow, went to bed. I don't recall if we actually went to sleep, but we went to bed. We had to be at the ballpark at 8 the next morning.

We gathered in the cramped clubhouse, took physicals, were assigned lockers (the green metal high-school kind, complete with clanging doors) and got our uniforms. After that, they herded us out into the outfield and had us take a seat on the grass. Manager Joe Lewis, an old-school baseball man not unlike my father, introduced himself and the coaches, then he gave us the lowdown on what was about to happen.

We'd have a week of "camp" before the Appalachian League season started, and for the first couple of days we'd simply be doing drills and taking batting practice. There were specific ways of doing things "the Tiger way" and we'd be learning those things first. As outfielders we learned how to charge a rolling base-hit and time our arrival so as to catch it with our left foot forward. If you did that just right you could make just one crossover crow-hop step with your right foot to be in a perfect throwing position. I got the hang of it quickly but some of the guys really struggled to "unlearn" the way they'd been naturally catching and throwing the ball for years.

During BP I changed my stance a little by raising my hands to about shoulder height, and I still don't understand that impulsive decision. I'd been hitting with my hands low for eight years, and my timing trigger was to raise them and pull the bat back as the pitcher began his delivery. When coaches would question my odd hand placement (and they regularly did) I'd say "My deal is that when he starts his delivery and he turns his back on me, that's when I turn my back a little on him and bring the bat back. Plus, I'm just more comfortable this way." I must have been slightly intimidated in Bristol, because without any thought I simply switched to a more universally accepted stance and swing. It's about trusting in yourself, Wilber.

I did OK, though. I wasn't the best player there, by any measure, but I fit in just fine and I was a smoother and more talented player than at least half of the guys. I'll admit to worrying mightily that, in pro ball, all my teammates would be playing at a level I couldn't reach, but that wasn't the case and it never would be. Once you get to the pros the difference between the average guys and the future big league stars usually wasn't that noticeable.

For the record, the Tigers' No. 1 pick in the 1978 draft wasn't there. They didn't bother sending Kirk Gibson to Bristol. They sent him right to Lakeland in the advanced Class-A Florida State League.

Just one position player from that Bristol team ended up making it to the big leagues — outfielder Bruce Fields. Bruce hit only .201 that year, but he had a terrific set of tools, a great work ethic, and a fantastic personality. The pitching was just a little too much for him that summer.

John Martin, Dave Rucker, and Bruce Robbins all went on to pitch in the majors. It was a challenge to hit off those guys in BP but it wasn't as if I had stepped into the box to face Randy Johnson in his prime. They were good pitchers, but I'd seen the same level of talent in college.

On the fourth day we finally had an intra-squad game to start the process of getting game-ready. I started in left field. I'll admit I was more than a little nervous.

I handled the few balls that came my way, as I always expected to do, and in my first at-bat I swung and missed at two fastballs. But then, anticipating a breaking ball on the next pitch, I dribbled a roller through the infield for a hit. It didn't officially count, of course, since it wasn't a real game, but it felt great to get it.

In my next at-bat I came up with the bases loaded. On the mound was right-hander Tim Justus, and I'd already heard the whispers about his velocity and control. He could just flat bring the heat but he was all over the place, and that's a combination that makes hitters very uncomfortable. Scouts call it being "effectively wild" because one 96-mph heater under the chin or near the ribs will make a guy back off a little in the box.

When Justus threw his first pitch I got a hint of what big league velocity might look like. Unlike those magical at-bats against Northern Kentucky in the NCAA Regional, I was clearly not in the zone on this day because I heard the ball go by me more than I saw it. It was the hardest pitch I'd ever stood that close to and like all great fastballs it buzzed as it went by. The pop in the catcher's mitt didn't sound like anything I'd ever heard before.

I stepped out of the box and collected my thoughts, reminding myself that this is what I'd dreamed of doing since I caught that first ball at Schall School. This guy might be wild but if taking one on the ribs or elbow was the price, it was worth it to stay in there and drive my left shoulder toward the ball, keeping my swing short and compact.

I fouled the next one off, barely. He threw a couple balls then at 2-2 I fouled a fastball over the first-base dugout. Then another. And finally another, but this one was straight back. When you foul a good fastball straight back you've caught up to it. Your bat was right on it, in terms of velocity, but you got under it a little and that's not surprising when the ball is coming in at 96 mph.

I never worried about Justus throwing a breaking ball or a change-up. He was straight out of high school and he threw bullets. It was his minor league debut, just as mine, and I figured he'd only come with the heat. If he threw me something off-speed, I'd tip my hat to him. I'd be so far out in front of something slow I'd probably miss it by two feet.

In came another fastball and I finally got one on the barrel. I knew I'd hit it well and I even had the presence of mind to actually wait on it a little to take it to right, since it was on the outside part of the plate. I wasn't halfway to first when I saw the right fielder stop, look up, and watch the ball clear the fence and the hill behind it, eventually landing on a road. I had just hit a grand-slam home run in my first game as a pro. As I circled the bases my teammates on the other squad all shook my hand. I couldn't wait to call home.

After the game, as we all shook hands once again and headed for the showers, I heard my name being called by the skipper, Joe Lewis. He asked me, Buddy Slemp, and Dan O'Connor to step aside. He then introduced us to Hoot Evers, another one of my dad's contemporaries from the old days, who was farm system director for the Detroit organization. I had no clue what this was about but I was deeply nervous. How could they release a guy who just hit a grand slam off Tim Justus? How could they release a guy before the season started? These sorts of thoughts whirled around in my head as I stood there with two teammates I didn't yet know.

Hoot looked at us and said, "I want you three guys to know that we're optioning you to Paintsville, Kentucky, here in the same league. It's what we call a co-op team, and along with the Orioles, White Sox, and Twins, we're each sending a few players there so that you can play more and develop faster. You would have to play behind a lot of high draft picks here, guys we have a lot of money invested in. We think it's better that the three of you go up there to Paintsville and get more action."

Looking at me, he said "Bob, we made this decision before today and before we saw your grand slam. You impressed us with all facets of your game. You'll be fine in this league, as will you Buddy and Dan, so get your gear together and get on up to Paintsville. We'll keep an eye on you and we'll look forward to seeing you when we play up there or when you come down here to play us. All the best to you guys. Make us proud."

With that, Hoot turned and walked away and the three of us blankly stared at each other, not sure what to say. We had no idea where Paintsville was but fortunately Dan (whom we quickly began calling OC) and Buddy had both driven to Bristol, so at least we had transportation. We found a map, located Paintsville (after practically needing a magnifying glass to read the small print) and decided on our travel plans for the next day. Plow forward, I guess.

The co-op team concept wasn't common back then, and as far as I know it doesn't exist at all now, but it meant one thing to the three of us. Bristol, in the short-season Appalachian League, was the lowest rung on the Tigers' organizational ladder. It was a "rookie league" in every sense because almost all of us were making our pro debuts. It was as low as you could ever be in the Detroit farm system, and yet somehow we'd managed to get sent down from there.

The next morning, we loaded up and climbed in the cars. I got in with Buddy for one reason: He had played his college ball at Oral Roberts, and even though it seemed then (and still seems now) like a lot had happened and many months had passed since the time we embarrassed ourselves at their ballpark to wrap up the 1978 SIUE season, it had only been about a month, if that. I figured we'd at least have something to talk about.

With map in hand we headed north, mostly along Highway 23. We had plotted out the best route and set our sights on a few landmark towns to make sure we were going the right way. No GPS units on the dashboard then — just paper maps and dead reckoning.

We drove up through Kingsport and into the state of Kentucky, then further north to Pikeville, our first checkpoint. From there, we made a left, then a right as we headed for Prestonsburg and Paintsville.

We saw tiny villages with small wooden shacks and smoking chimneys, and little towns, each with a short Main Street lined with small shops. The folks we interacted with were straight from central casting, and little boys in overalls with straw hats and a single long blade of grass dangling from their mouths were a common sight. Before cable TV and the intrusion of national retail chains this part of Appalachia could be considered a fully cut-off part of the country. It's likely none of these kids knew what a Big Mac was.

After about five hours, when we arrived in Paintsville (population roughly 4,500) we followed the directions we'd been given to get to WSIP, the only radio station in town. WSIP was owned by Paul Fyffe and it was Paul who had bestowed this professional minor league team upon his hometown. He was the owner of the Paintsville Hilanders and we were about to become his three newest players.

We met Paul at the station and all immediately felt relieved to be a part of such a classy gentleman's operation. He was kind, honest, humble, and excited to be launching this team. He took the time to ask each of us where we were from, where we'd gone to school, and what our families were like. In our few days at Bristol we'd not only never met the owner, we didn't know who the owner of the team was. We met Paul before we met anyone else in Paintsville.

Paul had even taken the time to set up bank accounts for us at the Paintsville Bank and he arranged to have our paychecks deposited there every two weeks. The man thought of everything.

Our new manager, Ron "Yank" Mihal, came into the room and we introduced ourselves to him. Ron had never managed professionally, so in that regard we were all in the same boat. We had never played professionally, either.

We discussed what positions we played and when I told him I was an outfielder I could see him grimace. He said "We have more outfielders than we need. Can you play third base?" At that point, my tendency to say whatever popped into my head finally bit me. I said, "Well, only if you want to get me killed." Yank clearly did not like that answer. I thought, for a brief second, that I should laugh it off and say "I'm just kidding. Of course I'll play third" but the truth was I really didn't want to play there. I hadn't played on the infield since seventh grade. Trying to play third seemed like an express-lane trip to the stop where you get released.

They had new contracts waiting for us, as well as copies of the forms that indicated our original Bristol contracts had been optioned to Paintsville. The term "optioned" means the Major League club could recall us and reassign us whenever they wanted and we still were the property of the Detroit Tigers. They basically had loaned us to the Paintsville club.

Paul informed us that he'd already found lodging for Buddy, OC, and me so we headed through charming downtown Paintsville and up the hill overlooking it to a stately old white frame home. We met the owner, an elderly woman of modest means, and she took us up the exterior back stairs to see the apartment that would be our home. It featured one bedroom, a living room, a kitchen with an eat-in table, and a full bathroom. The two biggest problems seemed to be the fact it had no air conditioning and the bathroom included a bathtub, but no shower.

Buddy offered to make the living room his sleeping quarters and OC and I then moved into the bedroom to choose which single bed we wanted. He, wisely, went first and chose the little bed by the window. I got the one over by the wall. There was an electric fan in the window but OC — certain it would fall in the middle of the night and quite possibly chop off his legs — turned it off. We all woke up drenched in sweat, but OC would not agree to keep it running overnight, nor did he think it was a good idea to trade beds with me. We simply had to deal with it.

We learned a lot the next day. We learned OC had arrived in the Appalachian League still suffering from a thumb injury he'd sustained before being signed. He was a catcher and it was on his throwing hand, so that was bad. But what was worse was that the injury made it impossible to swing a bat. After the trainer took a look at him, he was told he could not participate in any baseball activities until further notice and that night he followed orders and laid on the living room floor with his hand dunked in a bowl of ice-water. That was the extent of the team's high-tech approach to rehabbing him from his injury. He seemed pretty down about it, which I fully understood.

Buddy was a utility player and it looked as if he could play any position on the field, which was a good thing. Having not said anything about third base possibly getting him killed, he was slated to play there a lot, while the plan was that he'd also play an equal amount at shortstop and some in the outfield. We liked each other and had Oral Roberts-SIUE stories to share but our personalities were different and we never really became very close.

The next day, at a field in a city park that was serving as our practice facility while a small grounds crew got Johnson Central Park ready for play, we met our new teammates.

Vince Bienek, Tom Kokos, Mark Platel, and Kevin Hickey were the property of the White Sox, so they were in the same situation. Bienek, an outfielder, had been a teammate of Buddy's at Oral Roberts and he and I hit it off quickly. He was from Southern California, and he was funny, daring, and a heck of a player. Kokos was a utility player like Buddy and they each were told they'd play quite a bit at third. Platel was big, tall pitcher who, in my memory, spoke not one word all summer. I'm sure he did, but not to me. Hickey was a story unto himself.

Kevin was from the south side of Chicago. He grew up in tough neighborhoods where gunfire was not uncommon and he had a bit of an edge to him, although it was overshadowed by his outgoing personality. What made him unique was that he'd never played organized baseball at any level. He'd played some softball but not baseball.

Every year the White Sox would hold a massive "cattle call" at a city park. Like many aspiring kids who thought they could use the tryout as a launchpad to stardom, Kevin took a chance and went to the park that day. In sneakers, he picked up a baseball on the mound and threw left-handed, which at least gave the scouts a reason to watch. They weren't expecting much but what they saw got their attention. This kid who grew up just a couple of miles from Comiskey Park, and who had never played baseball, threw his fastball in the mid-90s. He was the only player out of the bunch who got as much as a conversation, much less a contract. And now he was with us in Paintsville.

Chino Cadahia, Jose Rodriguez, and Chris Geason were all the property of the Twins. Chino was a portly catcher from Miami, although what he lacked in physique he made up for with hard work and a powerful bat. He was also a great guy with constant smile, and I could tell on that first day that he was going to be a team leader. Jose spoke only basic English with a thick Spanish accent, so Chino was by his side most of the time. Jose was an outgoing, reed-thin shortstop, always with a wide grin on his face, while Chris was the outlier in the Twins group. He was a pitcher, and a very handsome one at that, but he had a look on his face that belied the truth. He was disappointed to have been sent to Paintsville and he didn't look like he wanted to be there. I recall him coming out of his shell eventually but he didn't pitch much.

From the Orioles we had Stan Hendrickson, a lanky first baseman from the mean streets of Philly. We could tell he was a good guy when we met him and since our first game was going to be on the road in Bluefield, West Virginia, against the Bluefield Orioles, he'd be the first of us to play against the team to which he was originally assigned.

The Cardinals and Braves, who also had teams in the Appalachian League, had declined to send any players to Paintsville, so the rest of the roster — roughly 24 additional players over the course of the summer — was made up of undrafted and unaffiliated free agents. Yank had been scouring the colleges in the Virginias and Carolinas to find these guys and in terms of talent they ranged from outstanding to nearly inept. It looked like a stretch to call it a co-op team but we were all there and we quickly banded together.

In 1978, the league consisted of the Bristol Tigers, Elizabethton Twins, Johnson City Cardinals, Kingsport Braves, Bluefield Orioles, and us, the Paintsville Hilanders tucked neatly away in the coal mining hills of eastern Kentucky.

At that initial practice in the city park we also got our first glimpse of Yank as an instructor. Many of the guys had already been there a few days and they had tried to clue us in, but none of us new guys got the point, or maybe we just didn't want to get the point. The drills were as simple as things we'd done in grade school, and during the first drill Yank hit us each some routine fly balls. We casually caught them. OK, we nonchalantly caught them, just like we did in school. He did not like that. Not one bit.

We were told that we should catch every ball with two hands whether it was practice or not, and that showboating would not be tolerated. I think the veins on his neck were bulging a bit and I'm sure most of his ire was aimed at three of us — Roy Dixon (a talented free agent from North Carolina State who had been surprisingly overlooked in the draft), Vince Bienek, and me.

And if Yank thought we were showboating with one-handed catches, I'm not sure what he would've thought had we really let it all hang out. All three of us were good enough outfielders to perfect all sorts of ways of amusing ourselves during batting practice. Behind-the-back catches were routine, including one where you could stand there watching the ball until it almost hit you in the head and then you'd simply bend over and catch the ball at the belt, behind you. Or, you could act like you didn't see the ball at all and then deftly catch it when it was just inches away. Snatch catches, where you'd snag the ball as you snapped your glove down? Easy. Holding your glove up and letting the fly ball hit right in the palm, but never closing the glove so the ball would fall out and you'd catch it with your bare hand at your waist? Oh, yeah. Basket catches with your glove casually positioned right next to your thigh? Sure. We could all showboat, but we decided to cool it until Yank calmed down during the season.

The next morning we gathered at WSIP to individually cut some promotional "liners" for the station to run in support of the team. The guys all said their names and where they were from, then said "Come on out to Johnson Central Park to see us play," or variations thereof. Some were pretty good but most were pretty painful to listen to. When it was my turn I dialed up my best "professional radio guy" voice and smoothly ad-libbed the script. I said "Hello, Paintsville, this is Bob Wilber from Southern Illinois University, and I'm now a proud member of YOUR Paintsville Hilanders. I hope you'll come out to see us play this summer, at Johnson Central Park."

I looked up, through the glass separating me from the control room, and what I saw looked like something out of a sitcom. At least a dozen faces were staring at me with wide-open eyes, many only peeking around the side of the window frame. I hadn't told anyone I majored in this stuff in college. Paul asked me, right after that, if I wanted to do some sports reporting or have a show at the station. I told him that sounded like fun, and we ought to talk about it.

We then headed out to survey our new park, or what there was of it.

As the home field for Johnson Central High School in the little burg of Paintsville, you might imagine that it was not the most spacious or modern ballpark in the minor leagues. In terms of seats, there was one grandstand with individual stadium seats right behind home plate and I'd suspect the capacity there was roughly 250 to 300. A fully enclosed press box stretched across the top. There were also two other grandstands behind the first and third-base lines but those were bleachers and I can't imagine they could hold more than 200 apiece, and only if everyone sat in the smallest possible spot. I've seen various websites and archived newspaper articles that list Johnson Central Park's capacity as ranging from 1,200 to 5,000. There's no way. Being very generous, I might be able to peg the ballpark's capacity at around 700. Maybe 750, tops. We never would know, since we never filled the place.

To pack Johnson Central Park to capacity, roughly one seventh of the town's population would have to attend a game on the same night. Obviously that never happened. Imagine if one seventh of the greater St. Louis area attempted to attend a Cardinals game at Busch Stadium on the same evening. That would be roughly 357,000 people. The ratios stay the same so even drawing 600 would be unlikely in Paintsville.

We were a little taken aback by its size when we got there but we were happy when we ventured inside the home clubhouse. Paul Fyffe had done a fine job in there. From the dugout we had to walk through an open spot next to the grandstand into a hallway. On the right was Yank's office. On the left was the clubhouse. Located under the third-base stands, it was one long room with all the lockers down the right-side wall. At the end, a shower room. Seems simple enough, but after having spent a few days in the Bristol clubhouse, which was not much bigger and featured those narrow metal high-school lockers, the sight of real pro lockers brought smiles to our faces.

Paul had hired carpenters to build them, and they'd done a fine job. They were open lockers with a large area for hanging clothes, a floor area for spikes, and a top shelf for spare gloves, hats, and miscellaneous things, including blow dryers and tobacco.

When we entered the room we were happily surprised to see nameplates on each locker, with our names and numbers meticulously painted on them. At the end of the room, right next to the showers, I found WILBER 5. Not only was my name on my locker, but somehow either Paul had found out that I'd worn the number five at SIUE and he arranged to have me wear it as a pro, or it was the most incredible coincidence ever. Knowing the kind of man he was, I've always suspected the former.

The first order of business, after acclimating ourselves to the surroundings, was to try on our uniforms — white for home games and powder blue for the road. Again, I don't really know if it was pure luck or some fine research but my uniform fit perfectly. Tight pants were the norm then and mine fit like a second skin. And that big five on the back sure looked good.

Our home unis had a script "Hilanders" across the front and they also featured a bat-swinging ballplayer in a kilt on one sleeve. I suspected that was some sort of connection to the Scottish Highlands and our slightly adjusted spelling created the Hilanders. So we had a guy in a skirt on our sleeves. We thought that was pretty cool.

Our road jerseys followed a great baseball tradition, in that they simply had PAINTSVILLE arched across the front in block print. They were pretty cool, too.

Then we went out onto the field.

Johnson Central Park was OK but it was nothing like SIUE or the Bristol playing surface. The left field wall was probably six inches to a foot higher than home plate, so the left fielder would always have the advantage of playing downhill.

The outfield grass was decent but it was immediately obvious we'd all have to be on alert for bad hops. My philosophy ever since playing on those terrible fields at Forest Park was that if I was going to play 300 feet from home plate I'd have no excuse for not catching any ball I could get to. You might have to play it safe and drop to one knee but you almost always had plenty of time to watch the ball and field it.

The infield, though, was not a pretty sight. The dirt was hard and featured quite an array of rocks and pebbles — enough that the infielders were shaking their heads that first day and looking a little fearful. I was thinking my earlier comment about not wanting to get killed at third now might look a little more legitimate. Right then, the infielders took it upon themselves to start picking up rocks.

Then there were the lights. We were there in the middle of the afternoon on that first day, but one look at the light towers told us all we needed to know. Utilizing standard baseball sarcasm I said to Roy Dixon, "Well, look at it this way. The lights might be pretty small, but at least there's only a few of them!"

Before we left to all go get some lunch (sorry, no clubhouse catering in Paintsville) our P.A. announcer came down to meet us, one by one. As he did so he asked us if we had any nicknames he could use during the games. I told him I was The Hawk, because that was the nickname semi-officially handed to me in college and, more important, I felt relatively certain that I did indeed roam the outfield like a hawk, if a hawk could wear a glove and understand the rules of baseball. Vince Bienek, in all seriousness, said, "I'm the Bronze Fox" and I decided right then that Vince and I were working at the same humor level and we'd be buddies.

That night we returned to the park and played an intrasquad game to get acclimated to the lights, if by that you mean we turned the bulbs on and played baseball while also attempting to actually see in the dark. It was pretty dim out there but we'd all grown up playing under bad lights at some point, so we were somewhat accustomed to it. As bad as poor lights are, the truth is they are at their worst early in the game. Once you acclimate to them it feels like it gets brighter.

I came up in the middle innings and Kevin Hickey was throwing his lefthanded heat. If seeing a Tim Justus fastball in the middle of the afternoon was hard, seeing Kevin's pitches under the Paintsville lights seemed truly daunting, but I got one on the barrel and drove a ball into the right-field corner. I legged it out for a triple, sliding into third just ahead of the throw. And I felt pretty good about myself. Actually, back then before I pulled or strained a number of leg muscles numerous times, I could get around the bases pretty well. The triple was good but it didn't surprise me.

And, of course, both my grand slam off of Justus and my triple off of Hickey were in practice games. There was pressure to perform, of course, but they were practice games. They didn't count. Some parts of my success never really changed.

After the game Paul and Yank asked us all what we thought and our comments were mostly about the rocky infield and the lights. Paul told us he'd work on that. When we came back from our first road trip, a couple of days later, he had indeed made some improvements but before we'd see those we needed to get on the bus the next day and head to Bluefield.

The Appalachian League schedule-makers had done us no favors. We were slated to bus down to Bluefield the day before the opener, then play the game on a Friday night. After the game, we'd get back on the bus and drive back to Paintsville to play three more games against the same Orioles, with a Saturday night game followed by a Sunday afternoon doubleheader.

Our ride to Bluefield was a quiet one. We barely knew each other, we were all a bit nervous, and most of us were far from home in a remote part of the country we'd never seen. We looked out the windows a lot.

One player on that bus had seen those hills and highways before. He was actually from Paintsville and starred on the high school team there, in multiple sports. Bill Mike Runyon (the pair of first names sounded authentically Appalachian to the rest of us) was signed as a free agent, so he was literally right at home.

In Bluefield we checked into a motel on the day before a game for the only time all year, just to make sure we got a good night's sleep. The next day we all collectively went stir crazy until the bus left for the ballpark at 4. We were so amped up to begin our honest-to-goodness professional careers we could barely stand it. When the door on that charter bus opened, in the motel parking lot, we scampered aboard like fourth-graders going on a field trip to the zoo.

We went to the park in our street clothes because Yank had been told by the Orioles we'd have a full visitors clubhouse to use, right behind our dugout. As we arrived at the ballpark, we carried our duffel bags in with our heads on swivels, taking in the sights of a much more impressive minor league facility with a large covered grandstand, impressive light towers with real lights, and roomy dugouts. The field looked fantastic and all of us were struck by what had to be the best and biggest natural "batter's eye" backdrop out beyond centerfield — a large Appalachian hill, covered in green trees. Some fields have no backdrop at all to help the hitters pick up the white ball as it leaves the pitcher's hand. Some have 10-foot high green fences. In Bluefield, they arranged to move a small mountain into place beyond center field. OK, maybe the mountain was there first but it was the best backdrop I'd ever seen and it's probably still the best, all these years later.

We nervously got dressed in our new blue road uniforms. We headed out for batting practice and while each group was hitting the rest of us stretched and jogged in the outfield. When BP was over Yank posted the lineup card in the dugout. The name Wilber was listed on the card but in the lower section, under the heading "Reserves." It was my first professional game after a lifetime of waiting for this moment and one of our starting outfielders was from the group of unaffiliated free agents Yank had signed to round out the team. It was a disappointment, for sure, but it was Roy Dixon and I thought he was pretty fantastic, so I kept my chin up and played the role of a good teammate on the bench.

It didn't take long for us to cringe and shake our heads at the poor Orioles' shortstop. He was tall and a little uncoordinated, as if he'd gone through a rapid growth spurt and he didn't quite know how to corral those arms and legs. Balls rolled through his legs, or up his arms, and at the plate he seemed totally lost. He had just graduated from high school and it sure seemed like the Orioles were throwing him to the wolves.

We were actually making comments in the dugout about him, saying, "That poor kid shouldn't be out there. He's completely overmatched. Poor guy is gonna get hurt."

As it turned out, that poor guy got a little better as the season went on, although he did end up striking out 46 times in 239 at-bats while committing a whopping 32 errors in 62 games. His batting average was a respectable but not especially impressive .264, but of his 63 hits, all but eight were singles. He hit no home runs and one triple. Those are the sorts of numbers that could get a guy released, but the Orioles trotted him out there every day. In the end, he made it. He made it to the big leagues and to the Hall of Fame. His name was Cal Ripken Jr.

Future Baltimore stars John Shelby, Larry Sheets, and Mike Boddicker were on that Bluefield team as well, but I only know that from research. We all remember the gangly "poor kid" at shortstop from memory.

My photographic memory did not store the result of that game so I don't know if we won or lost, but I do know what we discovered when we went to the clubhouse to shower. Before the game we'd tested the showers to make sure they operated and that they actually provided hot water. They did on both counts. We were pleased.

After the game we discovered one pesky fact. When the Orioles were showering over in their home clubhouse, all the water went there. When we turned ours on, only a slow dribble of cold water came out.

We had no choice but to clean up in the sinks and get on the bus for what would be our first dark ride home. After rocking back and forth in our seats for about five hours as the driver negotiated those winding coal roads, we arrived at Johnson Central Park just before dawn. We had our home opener to play in a little over 12 hours.

On the road we rarely left the park before 10:30 after a night game and by then we were starved. But, in those little towns in that part of the country, it was nearly impossible to find any restaurants open.

Every trip back to the motel or back home after a getaway game featured a full-on team effort to spy any place that might serve food. Before long we took to sarcastically shouting out every business we passed. "There's a Mobil station" might be followed by "Hey, there's a library. Oh, never mind. It's closed." Somehow we seemed to manage to find a place most nights and when that place would be a Bonanza or Sizzler steakhouse we were the happiest guys in the league.

One night, a few weeks later in Bluefield, we found one of those places still open and because of the shower issue we were all still in uniform. As we headed through the serving line with our trays, one of the girls working the cash register asked, "Are you guys all baseball players?" To which one of our guys replied, "Gosh, no. Why do you ask?"

Those getaway days had their own special qualities. Check-out time at the motel was usually noon, but our bus wouldn't leave for the ballpark until 4 at the earliest. Rather than pay another night's charges for all of our rooms, the team would hold three rooms and pay for a late checkout on those. One of the rooms was for Yank, the pitching coach, and the trainer. We had the option of piling into one of the other two rooms with a dozen other guys to vie for bed space and fight over the TV channel, or we could walk around until it was time for the bus to leave. Before long, many of us decided to make getaway days our haircut days. It was a way to kill some time.

Roy Dixon and Vince Bienek got a lot of the innings in the outfield, and I had no real problem with that. They were both good players, and Vince was one of the best all-around athletes with whom I'd ever shared a dugout. Roy was fast, had a great arm, and could run down anything in the outfield. When the three of us played together not much got between us and runners were ill-advised to attempt to take an extra base.

Another unaffiliated guy, Eddie Gates from East Carolina State, was the fourth regular outfielder, and a number of other guys slid into and out of the lineup as we went along.

Opening night, as a full team that had just played its first game on a short but tiring road trip, we started to click. Chemistry can't really be predicted or forced. Either you all get along and enjoy playing together or you don't. Just a few days into our time together, we all knew we were going to be a tight bunch and we all liked each other a lot.

Our home opener was also against Bluefield, of course, although they waited until the next morning to follow our bus tracks up to Paintsville. I don't recall how Cal Ripken did that night but I can assume the rocky infield did him no favors. In that regard, we were all pleased to see Paul had brought in a group of laborers while we were gone and they'd worked their way from first to third picking up as many rocks and pebbles as they could. The field was still hard as concrete, but it was better.

I did start that game, in left. I got another one of my patented dribbler hits through the hole and went 1-for-4, meaning I was officially hitting .250 and my name would forever be listed in the Appalachian League records. It was a small sample size, but it was pretty accurate for most of the season.

Our groundskeeper was a short barrel-chested guy who went by the name of Bear, because he kind of looked like one. In Appalachia, however, one must understand that Bear is pronounced almost exactly like Bar, and we all adapted to that so as not to offend him or have him ignore us altogether.

Bear was very pleased to point out to us the park's two new lights. Two. But they were very big. One was on the tower behind first and its counterpart had been added to the tower behind third. As it turned out, they were indeed very bright and they improved the conditions quite a bit but later I asked Bear why we only got two of them. He said "Cuz they're so bright you'd be blinded like lookin' at the sun if we had more." And he sincerely meant that.

Before I got my hit in the opener I walked to the plate to hear our P.A. guy say, "Now batting, number five, playing left field, THE HAWK, Bob Wilber." All I could do was nod and smile. When Vince came up he got the same treatment, with "The Bronze Fox" inserted between his position and name. Some guys would've been embarrassed but that's why Vince and I got along so well. We never asked the announcer to stop doing that.

Before the opener, that afternoon, Paul had hosted the entire team at a banquet with various Paintsville business leaders. It was quite a nice affair, actually, and the best part of it was seeing how proud Paul was — of us and of himself. He had brought professional baseball to this little burg in the hills and he was the toast of the town for having done so. All over Paintsville, cars were adorned with bumper stickers that proudly proclaimed "PAINTSVILLE HAS PRO BASEBALL."

Quickly, however, that first season of pro ball began to turn into just another string of home games and road trips and we all fell into a rhythm. The motels and the ballparks would become familiar, the early-morning arrivals back in Paintsville routine.

After we'd played those three home games against the Orioles in two days it was already time to go on the road again. I was starting to understand why it might be better to play for one of the teams in the Tri-Cities, where you could sleep in your own bed most nights and riding the bus meant a 20-minute commute to the other ballpark. The truth is, though, that longer road trips build valuable chemistry if the chemistry is good. If it's not, road trips can tear a team apart. It was good, and we all got into the flow.

That next trip was one I was looking forward to because it was a four-game set in Bristol. Buddy was looking forward to it as well but OC was still on the disabled list with his painful thumb.

I started two of the four games. One night we were tied in the top of the ninth and I came up with the bases loaded. I hit a smash up the middle to score two runs and we held on in the bottom of the inning for the win.

After the game the Bristol radio guys asked me to come up to the booth for an interview. They knew I was the property of the Tigers and they were eager to ask me how it felt to beat the team that owned me. The play-by-play guy asked me, "What were you thinking when you came up with the bases loaded, here in Bristol against the Tigers?" I said, "I was thinking of hitting a grand slam."

Their eyes widened and they nervously laughed a little, as if they couldn't believe I'd make such an audacious comment, so I suspected they didn't know the backstory.

When I got to the visitors clubhouse, which in Bristol did indeed have hot water, everyone was out of the shower and ready to get on the bus. It may have been an irrational thought on my part but I recall hurrying like crazy to make sure they wouldn't leave me behind. And then we called out the names of every gas station and drug store we passed as we searched for food.

Joe Lewis and the Tigers coaching staff were great to me that week, taking the time to come over when we were taking batting practice to give me some tips. One coach had watched me take my leadoff from first one night and saw I had crossed my left foot in front of my right. He said, "Never do that. As you move up the ladder the pitchers get smarter, and if they notice that you're crossing your feet to get a lead, they'll wait for that moment to throw over. You'll be dead meat with your feet crossed." How could I get that far in baseball, with so many good coaches, and yet never hear that advice? You can always learn something new.

One thing we learned — the hard way — had to do with the fact Paintsville was in a dry county. The nearest cold beer was an hour away, and I have no idea where you'd find hard liquor. It's likely you'd need a "source" for that sort of thing and the product would probably come in a mason jar. When the four-game series in Bristol ended, we established a new routine for road trips. After the final game the first stop the bus would make was a liquor store. We'd stock up on beer for the homestand and maybe even enjoy one on the bus to help us wind down for the long ride home.

Yank, meanwhile, was holding onto the reins tightly, with rules so strict most of us felt like we were back in high school. The way I see it, baseball is a game. It's supposed to be fun. Players at that level either need to have the maturity to make the experience fun, within reasonable bounds, or develop that maturity quickly.

After a few weeks, we asked for a meeting with Paul and expressed our frustrations. He listened earnestly and spoke to Yank, who then relaxed the rules. And, since we lacked a pitching coach, he hired Mark Connor from the University of Tennessee to join us in that capacity. We were 9-19 when we met with Paul and we finished the season 33-36. We went 24-17 after the meeting.

As the summer progressed the trips became a blur but the team continued to gel, and while we were never in serious contention to win the championship we could hang in there against anyone in the league. We were also getting to know each other a lot better and real friendships were being developed.

At SIUE I had discovered a knack for doing a pretty good impersonation of Jackie Stewart, the legendary Formula 1 driver who, by then, was doing color commentary on TV during the Indy 500 and the few F1 races that were televised. His Scottish brogue and his excited and energized delivery were unmistakable and I often did my best Jackie Stewart at parties or during batting practice. On one early road trip with the Hilanders, I let it slip that I did a pretty good version of his commentary and all the guys begged to hear it. Right there on the bus, rolling down the road, I did a full minute of classic Jackie, complete with thick Scottish comments about Emerson Fittipaldi, Niki Lauda, and the six-wheel Elf Tyrrell car that was all the rage back then. It brought the house down. Maybe it just brought the bus down, but it was greeted with applause and laughter, and those two things had always been something I loved to create. Still do.

After that, any time we'd be on the bus after a win, whether it was a long ride back to Paintsville or a short hop back to the motel, I'd be sitting in my seat and after a few minutes I'd hear the requests, but none of them were spoken in words. The guys would start to quietly make a noise like a Formula 1 car passing by and then slowly ramp up the volume until it sounded like our entire bus was full of race cars. "Zzzzhhoooom" came the calls and that was my cue to celebrate our win with 15-seconds of Jackie Stewart.

Around this time, early in the season, two things happened almost simultaneously that were each pretty momentous for me and a couple of SIUE alums. A few days earlier, I'd been talking to our new pitching coach, Mark Connor, and he was moaning about a our lack of left-handed depth on the staff. We had one left-handed starter, one middle reliever who saw little action, and Kevin Hickey as our closer. That was it.

So I told Mark, "Hey, I know a really good lefty who can start, go long relief, or do anything you want. He's a bulldog, too, and he wants the ball. I've seem him shut down some great teams. His name is Stan Osterbur and if you want to sign him I can get him here." Mark talked it over with Yank and they came back to me and said, "Get him here as soon as you can." I've rarely been more excited about calling a buddy. Within 24 hours, two SIUE Cougars would be on the same team in Paintsville, but there'd also be one more in the league.

Lance McCord had gone to a Minnesota Twins tryout camp in St. Louis, as a pitcher, and they not only signed him, they sent him to Elizabethton — just in time for the Hilanders' first road trip there. I was thrilled for both Stan and Lance. OK, I was thrilled for all three of us. I thought it was pretty mind-boggling that we'd all be there during the summer of '78. I hoped the SIUE Athletic Department was proud of us, as well.

Stan got there as fast as he could, in time for our trip to Elizabethton. He moved in with Buddy, OC, and me but that meant we were really one too many for the elderly woman's upstairs apartment. We decided to put off that move until we got back from the road trip.

There was only one on-field problem. Stan hadn't been throwing much and he needed to get his arm in shape. He threw bullpen sessions with Mark Connor to try to get his command and velocity back and Yank then had the bright idea to use him as slave labor to throw batting practice every day. After about a week of that Stan was nearly over it but he hung in there.

When we got to Elizabethton the three former Cougars met outside the clubhouses in right field and we made the remarkable (but not surprising) mistake of not asking anyone to take a photo of us. The evidence we were all there together is simply in the record books. What were we thinking? Maybe we were all just so excited to be there we looked right past the obvious.

I started in right that night and got a hit early in the game. I knew Lance was also a bit out of shape and he hadn't pitched too much that spring anyway, thanks to Roy's decision to make him a third-baseman. I told many of my teammates "If you go up there and never swing, there's decent chance he can't throw three strikes before he throws four balls" but no one took me up on it once Lance entered the game in the middle innings.

I was pumped up to face him for the first time ever and then Yank pulled me out of the game. I couldn't believe it. I should've just kept my mouth shut about the two of us being teammates and roommates, because once Yank knew that fact he assumed I'd press too much. Heck, I pressed too much all the time. Having Lance on the mound wouldn't have made it any different. I wonder if he would've drilled me in the ribs just to say hello in pro ball.

The next night, Eddie Gates was in the game in right field. Eddie was a really nice guy and a fine hitter but his head was a little noticeable in terms of its size and shape. Within days the guys took to calling him "Box Head."

During the middle innings, Eddie was stranded on second when the third out was made and in those situations it's normal for a player who plays defense on the same side of the field to bring the base-runner's glove and hat out to him, so he wouldn't have to run to the dugout to get his gear and then turn around and run back out to his position. That's why we all had our names and numbers written prominently on our gloves, in Magic Marker. My gloves all said "WILB 5."

Stan Loy was our regular second baseman and he was a very funny guy. Since he was playing second, and Eddie was standing there waiting for his gear, Stan grabbed Eddie's glove but put aside his hat. He reached over the railing into the grandstand and picked up an empty popcorn box and ran toward Eddie, who wasn't paying attention. Those of us in the dugout were holding our breath and trying not to laugh too early.

As Stan approached, he handed Eddie his glove and then handed him the box. Eddie "Box Head" Gates had his gear, and he laughed right along with us. Had the dugout floor not been covered in heinous amounts of tobacco juice, we would've been rolling on it in convulsive laughter. Seconds later, Stan Hendrickson arrived with his real hat but that was a moment for the Baseball Humor Hall of Fame, if there were such a thing.

After the four-day Elizabethton trip we made our requisite stop at a liquor store and headed north to Paintsville, where we'd face the Johnson City Cardinals in a four-game series. We won a couple and lost a couple before getting back on the bus and heading to Bluefield, with its mountainous backdrop and Cal Ripken at short. In the first game I hit a towering fly ball to dead center and originally I didn't think I'd hit it that solidly, but the center fielder ran back and made a leaping catch at the 405 mark to take a professional home run away from me. If I'd just pulled the ball 10 feet to the left my career stats would be different.

Once again, back on the bus for another overnight ride to return to another homestand, this time against my boys on the Bristol Tigers. In the opener, I was in left field under those sketchy Paintsville lights and a young catcher came up. He hit a fly ball deep into the darkness to my right and I cruised over to where I was sure it would land, but he'd been out if front of it a little and with side-spin it kept drifting. So I kept cruising and it kept drifting, sailing a little deeper. As this was happening, I felt a pang of embarrassment because any good outfielder knows to see the ball, judge where it's going to land, and sprint there to be ready. It was still drifting on me as it came down and even though I knew I was going to catch it I also knew I'd have to leap and backhand it to make that happen. So I leaped.

I saw the ball enter the webbing of my Rawlings glove and then saw my arm hit the top of the outfield wall right at my elbow. I quickly pulled my hand back inside the park to officially rob that kid of his first professional home run and as I did so I actually heard two little boys yelling, beyond the fence, with one of them saying "He caught it!" before I even had time to pull my arm back into the park. We had no warning track at our ball yard, so while I knew I was close to the fence I wasn't completely sure where it was and that's probably a good thing.

Our outfield fence was wooden and I had been extremely lucky to hit right in the middle of one of the boards instead of plowing into one of the metal posts. The plywood cushioned my impact, and then like a vertical trampoline it tossed me gently to the ground. I immediately hopped up and held my glove up high, to show the umpires I'd caught it.

Even if I had sprinted to the spot I still would've needed to leap and catch the ball. But arriving, jumping, and backhanding the ball just as I hit the fence was remarkable. It could've gone wrong many more ways than it could've gone right but it all worked out and I got a full round of high-fives coming off the field. Yank said, "Bobby, that was a Major League catch. Way to go, man."

All of those years with Skip's teams, roaming those big outfields, once again came in handy.

Being back in Paintsville, my roomies and I were procrastinating about finding a new place and part of the delay was the realization that we were most likely going to have to find two new places. There weren't that many rental properties in Paintsville that could accommodate four guys. But then, the decision was made for us. The accomplice was Buddy.

We rarely used the bathtub, and we'd even gotten used to driving out to the ballpark to take showers if any of us wanted one. Since we showered before we left the park each night and could take one before getting dressed for BP, it wasn't like we were smelly and dirty all the time.

During the homestand against Bristol, though, Buddy decided to take a bath and he started the water. A half-hour later, he remembered he'd done that. We had a flood on our hands.

All it took to get us out of the upper apartment at the elderly woman's house was some serious damage to her ceiling below. Decision made, but I don't know who paid for that damage. Was it the woman's insurance or was it Paul Fyffe? I know it wasn't Buddy. My guess is that Paul handled it quietly. That would've been very much like him.

I'm not sure where Buddy and OC went but Paul found an interesting place for Stan and me. It was a small studio apartment on the second floor above an old shuttered drug store, a few blocks east of downtown Paintsville. It was just one room, plus a bathroom, but at least the bathroom had a shower. We could finally spread out in terms of sleeping arrangements and didn't have to worry about a fan chopping off OC's legs. It was all we needed.

The oddity didn't end with the room being above a long-closed drug store where we entered through a creaky back door and then went up a dark wooden staircase to an equally dark narrow hall, lit by a single bulb hanging from an exposed electrical cord. It continued with the entry door to the apartment. The knob did not have a built-in lock and there was no deadbolt. What we had was a heavy padlock and latches on both sides of the door. When we'd leave for the ballpark we'd put the lock on the outside. When we'd go to bed we'd put it on the inside. I'm not sure the crime rate in Paintsville even warranted a lock and the most valuable items in our place would've been our clothes, but we felt better locking ourselves in at night.

One night in Paintsville, Max Patkin, the "Clown Prince of Baseball," was in town to do his schtick during the game. I'd seen Max many times when I was spending summers with my dad's teams and his act in the coach's box would always have me laughing hysterically. Years later, it was great to see him honored with a cameo in the hit movie "Bull Durham."

I said hello to Max before the game and we shared more than a few laughs telling stories about Big Del Wilber. Max was a genuinely nice man and for decades he toured the country doing his baseball comedy act in ballparks ranging from Mile-High Stadium to Johnson Central Park, all during real games and often with him performing while coaching at first or third. It had to be a tough and lonely life but the fact teams and managers would let him do his act during the game was, perhaps, the ultimate sign of respect.

When I came to bat for the first time that night, with Max keeping the crowd laughing from the third-base coach's box while Yank vacated and moved to first, I walked to the plate and heard him yell loudly enough for all to hear, "You should'a seen the schnozz on this kid's dad. His nose came in the room two seconds before he did." I called time-out, tipped my hat, and did a deep bow in his direction. All those years with my dad. All those years watching Max. All those years wanting to be a professional. I'm not sure if having Max rib my dad in a game in which I was playing was the single greatest honor I had felt up until that point, but it had to be close. It warmed my heart.

During a midsummer homestand Paul again brought up the possibility doing some on-air work at WSIP. I definitely wanted to, although the open slots for doing "live" local news were always in the early morning.

Professional baseball players are not typically morning people. When your job happens from about 3 in the afternoon to at least 11 p.m. and you get home still wound-up from the adrenalin of the game, you tend to fall asleep well after midnight. Sometimes hours after midnight. So you sleep until almost noon, on most days. Some guys slept even later than that and it was not a huge surprise if, on a road trip, the bus had to be held after our scheduled 4 o'clock departure because a pair of guys were still sleeping. Getting up at 7:30 a.m. to go on the radio was a challenge but I wanted to do it.

Paul gave me free rein to run the sports segments during the morning shows and I'd scour the teletype to find stories I wanted to use. I imagine there were some local residents who wondered why they were hearing a new voice while getting results from Formula 1 races instead of local sports news, but that was me. I was trying to widen their horizons.

Within a few weeks, we shifted to more of a call-in format, informally known as "Talk To The Hawk," and that was delightful on many levels. We decided to do it one day a week during homestands, so as much as I remember it as a long-running series that probably means we did the show no more than four or five times and by the second show it was clear I'd have to be on my toes when the calls came in.

There were certainly a large percentage of calls from local listeners but at least once per show I'd get a call from one my Hilander teammates and it was my challenge to figure out who it was before I gave my answer.

They'd try to disguise their voices but it was the pointed questions that tipped me off.

"Hey, Hawk. I'm a big fan and I was wondering what you thought of Yank Mihal's decision to play Buddy Slemp in left field instead of you last night. You've been hot lately. Were you mad at him, and do you think he's a good manager?"

The length of the question provided me about 15 seconds to decipher both voice and inflection, and if I got it right I could expose the imposter with a coded answer.

"Well, you know what, he's the manager and that's always his call. We have 25 guys on this team and we all want to play. I want to play every night but that's not going to happen. My buddy Roy Dixon was just telling me the other day that he thinks Yank is the best manager in all of baseball. That he's a true genius. Whatever Roy says, I agree with because Roy is a genius himself."

That was the weekly challenge.

And the mystery caller was right. By late July I was heating up. At one point, I played in 10 straight games and we won most of them. I didn't have access to our stats, which seems an impossible thing today, but my dad did get the weekly print-outs for all of minor league baseball and he kept close tabs on me. Just as August was starting, we talked on the phone and he said, "Hey, you're hitting .283 right now. Keep this up and you'll make it to .300 for the season. That will make you a real prospect for Detroit."

While that was great news I couldn't help but feel the first pangs of, "Why did you have to go and tell me that?" I didn't fall off a cliff like I had often done in college, but it was in my head and I did all I could to forget about numbers and just have one good at-bat after another. One pitch at a time.

Then the Twins released Lance. I got a short letter from him, and the postmark was Highland, Illinois, where his parents lived. That's all I needed to see, and the letter was just a few sentences long. "They let me go. It was fun while it lasted," was the gist of it.

Right after that, Elizabethton came to town in early August, to wrap up our longest homestand of the season — two games against Bristol, three against Johnson City, and then four against the Twins. Looking back at the schedule, I'm stunned to see we had a day off in there, on a Thursday, but I remember what I did that night when I didn't have to go the park and play. Kevin Hickey and I drove down to Prestonsburg and watched a movie. It was "Grease."

During the Elizabethton series, we'd been rained out in one game of the series already and to make that up we were playing a doubleheader under the lights. We'd won the first game behind the masterful shutout pitching of Billy Ray Sorrell, a big, strong kid from North Carolina whom Yank had signed to a free-agent contract. My pal Vince Bienek had a good game and third baseman Steve Chandler went deep twice to propel us to a 5-0 win.

Doubleheaders, in the minors, feature games that are seven innings each, so when we came to bat in the bottom of the ninth in the nightcap, we were already deep into extras. I was 1-for-3 with a walk.

Frank Williams, our third baseman, led off with a double and was then balked to third by the Twins closer — a guy who would go on to Major League greatness and fame. His name was Jesse Orosco. Old number five was due up next.

Jesse threw serious heat, even before he got to the bigs. Fortunately, for me, he had not yet grown confident in the slider that would make him a Major League star who would accumulate 144 saves over a masterful 24-year career.

If we could score a run in the bottom of the ninth we'd creep to within four games of the Twins for first place in the standings. And I was up.

I spent one an entire game in "the zone" during college. This at-bat against Jesse, with the game on the line, was a different kind of trip to the zone because I worked my way there at the plate.

Jesse threw left-handed and very hard. On this night he was also up in the strike zone pretty consistently, with a fastball that almost looked like it was rising on the way to the plate. Such a thing is an illusion. Tim Justus threw a fastball that seemed to rise but none do, unless they're thrown from a submarine delivery or they're fast-pitch softball pitches released down near the ground, or they're plastic Wiffle Balls. Thanks to gravity, all overhand pitches sink on their way to the plate and pitchers often use grips and spins to make them sink even more. When a hurler throws particularly hard, though, the backspin on a fastball is able to counteract some of the gravity-induced sink, and that difference fools the hitter into thinking the ball is rising. It's an illusion based on the comparison to a more normal pitch.

With that in mind, and with Jesse's stuff keeping his pitches at the belt or higher, it became a matter of catching up to him.

I swung and missed. I fouled one off, much like I had against Justus that day nearly two months earlier. And then I fouled another, and another, and another. In total, I took a ball or two but managed to foul off eight or nine pitches. And then I hit one right on the sweet spot and lined a rope into right center. Game over. It was the only walk-off hit of my pro career and it was more memorable because it came against such a highly respected opponent.

When I saw Jesse's first pitch that night, it was too fast for me. With each pitch I saw it a little better; the velocity seemed to slow down and the ball looked bigger. By the time I hit the game-winner Jesse Orosco was hittable, despite still throwing the same mid-90s heat with which he had started. Zone visited. Game won.

As a result my walk-off made a winner out of pitcher Pete Conaty, an unaffiliated guy from East Carolina. He earned the W that by going the distance and scattering five hits. He was a fine pitcher and I was surprised he went undrafted. Our paths would cross again a few years later.

The next day I was in the lineup and I singled to left in my first at-bat. Taking my lead (and not crossing my feet) I saw Yank, over in the third-base coach's box, giving me the sign to steal second. As soon as the pitcher began his delivery I took off and I knew I had gotten a great jump. Just looking at the second-baseman's body language, I also knew I had it stolen. Then, just as I began to launch myself into a classic feet-first slide, I felt something terribly odd in the back of my right leg. It felt as if a huge rubber band had stretched right up to, but not quite beyond, the breaking point. I'd never felt that sensation before. I was, however, safe at second.

It didn't hurt to stand up but I knew something bad had happened. Our trainer came out and neither one of us was smart enough to know, immediately, that it was a pulled hamstring. I brought my right heel up behind my leg, grabbed it with my hand, and pulled it up even further. No pain. Of course there was no pain. Had I pulled a quad that stretch would've hurt like hell, but doing it only shortened the hamstring muscle. Had I tried to bend over and touch my toes, well that would've been a different story. I said I was OK and our trainer believed me. I'm not sure who was the bigger dummy. We'll call it a tie.

Sure enough, the next hitter put a ball in play and I took off for third. Within one step I knew I was actually hurt. Very much hurt. Injured, actually. Getting hit by a pitch hurts.

Seriously pulling a hamstring so badly you can't come close to running is being injured. I hobbled to third and caught my breath. Yank asked if I was all right and the only thought going through my head was, "He's not taking me out. I may never get back in."

The next batter hit a gapper into right-center, allowing me to jog home a bit wobbly. I went straight into the dugout, dropped my pants to my knees while hiding behind two other guys so Yank couldn't see me, and told the trainer "Tape this up as tight as you can get it. Cut off my circulation if you have to. I'm playing."

Somehow I got through that game, but the next day it was clear I'd be on the bench a while. Our trainer quickly learned how to masterfully tape a hamstring pull and each day would start with me on the training table on my back, with my right leg bent at the knee. He'd apply those cross-layered wraps of athletic tape until I was a mummy from knee to hip and he'd do it so tightly I could barely straighten my leg when I got off the table.

We headed to Kingsport the next day and once we got to the ballpark Stan became my personal trainer. At SIUE we had a sports-medicine guy who was a maniac about hard work after an injury. He wouldn't even give the soccer players a day to rest after blowing out a muscle or twisting a knee, and he'd have them doing hard resistance training the same day. We all knew the drills and exercises, which required a buddy, and Stan got after it with relish.

I'd get taped, and we'd go out to the visitors dugout while everyone else took BP. I'd lay on the bench on my stomach and we'd do some of the most painful resistance training I'd ever done, with me lifting my lower leg while he pushed against it and then the opposite with me trying to lower my leg while he pushed against it. Finally, we'd do the "negative" version of resistance, with him trying to lift or lower my leg while I resisted. Then I'd flip over and we'd do it all again with me on my back. That first day had me in tears, but I needed it.

With Stan's help I was able to jog again within five days and able to run hard within eight, but I wasn't quite game ready. In a game, instant bursts of speed are needed and they also present the most danger to hamstrings. A week is a good chunk of rookie-level season but I was making progress and Stan helped me keep after it. I kept the leg wrapped and taped for most of the remainder of the season, though, and as it turned out I would actually never quite run as well again, nor would I play quite as often as I continued to work to get stronger. It had been about 12 days between games for me and it was the first time I'd ever missed a stretch of games because of an injury. Ever.

Later in life, when I was nearing 40 and finally quit playing, I'd pulled each hamstring many times and I could never risk going flat-out. It's a good thing I became a power hitter later in my semi-pro career. You only have to jog when you hit them over the fence.

Stan got to pitch on that road trip and I clued in all the guys about his bulldog demeanor on the mound and that it fired him up to hear his teammates yelling his SIUE nickname "The Count." "C'mon, Count, go right at 'em. C'mon, Count!"

He didn't get hit hard but he had the sort of bad baseball luck all pitchers know well, when every ball that's hit finds a hole, and that just added to my misery. I hadn't gotten back on the field yet and my best friend had spent weeks throwing batting practice just to earn his chance, but the rust hadn't worn off and the guys in this league were better contact hitters than he'd ever faced.

The last three weeks of August were broken up with a series of four-game trips. Four on the road, back on the bus. Four at home, back on the bus. I know we had the toughest bus rides in the league, although Bluefield had it nearly as bad. The rest of those teams, in the Tri-Cities, complained about the two entire times they had to make the ride to Paintsville and back. We did it, in the opposite direction, every week.

During those long rides we passed the paperback version of "The Amityville Horror" around the bus and each guy who got it would invariably spend an entire trip reading it cover to cover, gripped by the suspense. If, like me, they chose to read it in the dark bus when we headed back home after a getaway game, they could bank on a couple of teammates patiently waiting many hours before jumping in front of them to scare them to death. I was 75 percent done with that scary book, deep in the middle of the night, when two sets of hands instantly appeared in front of my face from the row behind me. Well played, boys. My heart rate must've hit 150.

I finally got back in the lineup feeling about 90 percent healthy, but was never again on the field as regularly as when I was hot in late July and early August. Playing full-time allows a hitter to get in a groove and part-time playing does just the opposite. My 1-for-3s and 2-for-4s turned into 1-for-4s and 0-for-3s and the average sank to around .260 instead of climbing to .300, as Skip had hoped.

On our final trip to Bristol, playing against my Detroit club one more time, Yank put me in the starting lineup at shortstop. I'd been taking ground balls there during BP, but the brutal truth was that while I was a heck of an outfielder, as a shortstop my best attribute was still that I was a heck of an outfielder. Earlier in the month Lenny Faedo, the shortstop for Elizabethton who would later play very well in Minnesota, watched me take infield practice at short one night and his comment was "Um, you're not actually a shortstop, are you?" I told him his powers of observation were astounding.

I technically made an error that night against the Tigers, trying to turn a double-play, but I rushed the transfer of the ball from my glove to my hand after the toss from Eddie Gates and that allowed the batter to be safe at first. It wasn't an error in the scorebook, because the scoring rules state that a double-play can never be assumed. The ruling was that I had completed the force play at second but I'd failed to make the throw. So, my career records show I never made an error at short, but in my mind they are wrong. I should've made that play.

In the bottom of the ninth we were tied with two outs and a runner on second, and the hitter knocked a hard ground ball up the middle. The runner was off with the swing and I ran hard to my left in the hope I could at least knock the ball down. Somehow, surprising even myself, I not only got to it but I also fielded it cleanly and then I relied on a lifetime of watching baseball in order to do my best impression of a real shortstop saving the game. I caught it, straightened up while spinning around counter-clockwise, ready to throw, and when I saw the runner digging for home trying to end the game I fired an absolute strike to Chino at the plate and he tagged him out. My outfielder's arm strength came in handy on that one.

We scored in the top of the 10th and held on to win the game. I got to do the post-game radio interview again, and by this time I had learned not to worry the bus might not wait for me. And Joe Lewis, the Bristol manager, patted me on the butt and said "You stole that one from us, kid."

It was all going well enough. The hamstring was better, I was hitting OK, and then I got jammed at the plate and broke one of my U1 bats. Much to my horror, when I went to the rack to get another, I discovered it had been my last one. There were 11 games left.

Not only would the club not spend the money to buy any extra bats, they couldn't have gotten to us in time anyway. The team had bought us each a small supply of bats to start the season and counting the three I brought on the plane I had six or eight to work with. Most of the other guys were hoarding their last bat or two as well but for most of them it was an interchangeable thing, since they all used more standard models. I had gotten comfortable with the weight and feel of the U1 in college and I liked that it had a flared end at the bottom, instead of a knob. For the rest of the season I'd have to beg to borrow other guys' bats or simply use the random generic pieces of junk that were left in the bat bag.

You wouldn't think it would make that much of a difference, but it does. In baseball, just putting on some other guy's glove feels enormously strange because we all broke our gloves in to precisely fit our own hands. Put on another guy's glove and your first thought would be, "Wow. How the hell can he even play with this?" And he'd think the same thing if he put on yours.

Bats are the same way. You find a model you like, you find the length and weight you want, and it becomes a natural extension of your hands. You don't even think about it being a piece of cylindrical wood. And now all of my natural extensions were gone. What was left in the bag was a small assortment of gigantic pieces of lumber nobody on the team wanted to swing.

Then, when we got back home again for our second-to last homestand, the club released Stan.

When we'd been eliminated from the 1977 NCAA Division II World Series, without Stan or Jerry Deml ever getting a chance to pitch, what followed was one emotional night in our motel room. When grown guys, especially dedicated athletes, face the loss of their dreams, you can't help but bare your soul a bit to let it out. It's akin to a grieving process.

I had helped get Stan a second chance in Paintsville, and he worked his butt off to take advantage of it. But there we were, in our studio apartment above the former drug store, sitting at the end of our twin beds looking at each other. It was deja vu, and I was as devastated as he was. He wasn't just a teammate, he was my friend. It was a tough night. Early the next morning, Stan quickly loaded his car and headed home. He'd never play another inning as a pro. That's how suddenly it can end.

I was the only SIUE Cougar left in the Appalachian League.

Stan's departure was a loss in more ways than one because now I had no wheels and no way to get to the ballpark. I'm sure you'll be able to guess who stepped forward to help me.

Not long after Stan left, there was a knock on my padlocked door. Paul Fyffe was standing there, holding a set of car keys. He said, "Here you go, Bob. Give me a ride back to the radio station and then keep this car for the rest of this homestand and for the next one."

Paul Fyffe didn't own any junker cars. This was a very nice sedan with power everything and when I dropped him off at WSIP he said "Oh, check under the driver's seat when you get back to your apartment." I did just that, and there was a bottle of moonshine tucked away under there. I don't think I dared drink it, but the thought was worth a million beers right then.

We hit the road again, then came back home for our final homestand and our last hurrah in front of some of the nicest and most supportive fans I've ever known. Our final home game before the last road trip was "Fan Appreciation Night" and after the game all of the fans came out onto the field to say goodbye to us. There were many hugs, and many people were crying. They were that sad to see us leave. I think more than a few of us had a couple of tears in our eyes too.

To wrap up the season we headed back to Elizabethton and Johnson City for a seven-day road trip. Those of us who were flying home would head to the Tri-Cities airport the day after the last game against the Cardinals. Everybody else would take one last bus ride to get back to their cars.

Tom Bloemke, a pitcher who joined us just before Stan was let go, became my new roomie on the road and while I hadn't played college ball with him and didn't consider him one of the best friends I'd ever made in the game, we hit it off immediately. Tom was also from Missouri, so we had a lot in common, and it was a good way to ease the pain of losing Stan.

Going into the last 11 games, I was hitting .256 and I still hoped to climb it back up to .270 or .275. But, using bats so heavy the great Bambino himself would've passed them over, I struggled to make contact. I got one more hit in my last few games and after being as high as .283 in midseason, I finished at .219 with one double and nine walks.

I ended up playing 31 games in the outfield, mostly in left. I threw out two runners, made only three errors, and of all the guys who played regularly in the outfield I had the highest fielding percentage, at .957. I also played two games at shortstop without an error and — you're not going to believe this — I played one game at third. And I'm still alive to write this book!

I'll never know if having a few more U1s in the rack would've helped me avoid that late tailspin but I do know the lack of those favored bats definitely hurt me. Each time I'd head to the plate I felt like I was either swinging a tree limb or the leg off a grand piano. Being confident is everything when you're a hitter. Feeling uncomfortable, whether it's your bat, your glove, your spikes, or even your baggy pants, creates just enough chatter in your head to make you lose focus.

And no one will ever know how things might've gone had I not stolen second base against the Twins that day and blown out my hamstring. Had I played in just half of the games I spent rehabbing with Stan, I would likely have gotten 24 more at-bats. That's a lot when you only get 104 plate appearances on the season. We'll never know.

We finished our final game against the Johnson City Cardinals, a team that had the same "birds on the bat" logo on their jerseys as my father had worn in the 1940s. We lost, and it was over. It was a hollow feeling, and no one spoke much on the way back to the motel. Those who did, whispered. And there was no Jackie Stewart imitation on the bus.

Bloemke and I left our Kingsport motel in a cab the next morning and caught a flight to St. Louis. I was eager to get home but I really didn't want to leave.

It was a summer of amazing highs and painful lows. But above all else it was a chance to live the dream I'd been chasing forever. Every time I arrived at the ballpark and put on the uniform, I reminded myself just how lucky I was. Being able to play for a man like Paul Fyffe took it to a new level.

How can you not cherish a summer in such a fine place, with such great guys? How can you not treasure sitting down for lunch at Wilma's Cafe in Paintsville and having a young boy walk across the room with a napkin and a pen, saying, "You'da Hawk, ain'tcha?" I was indeed The Hawk, and I took the extra time to sign all of my autographs Bob "The Hawk" Wilber.

We all made $500 a month that summer. All rookie-level players made the same salary. The high draft picks simply got bonus checks with the decimal point in a different place than it was on mine. But even though I only grossed about $2,000 that summer, I went home with more than $1,200 of it. That's partly due to the joy of calling Paintsville home, where the restaurants discounted our food or, at times, comped it altogether. We were their team. We were their boys. They took great care of us.

I remember it all as if it just happened. It was 38 years ago.

I think I did Skip proud.

A lot of guys on that club, who all ended up being trusted teammates and friends, made themselves proud as well.

Kevin Hickey, the lefty who had never before played baseball, made it all the way to the White Sox. He pitched six years in the big leagues as a reliever.

Chino Cadahia put together a remarkable minor league career, finally getting as high as Triple-A for the Twins. He then went on to a long and successful coaching career, finally making it to "the show" as a bench coach for the Braves and Royals.

Roy Dixon proved he should've been drafted, and the Tigers purchased his contract from Paintsville. We'd be seeing each other in spring training.

Roy and I could keep each other entertained effortlessly. It became one of our favorite routines to find a watering hole after road games and spend hours doing renditions of Johnny Carson's memorable "Carnac The Magnificent" character. We'd hold an invisible envelope to our foreheads and, after much deep thought, would foretell the answers to the three questions within. Then we'd pretend to tear open the envelope, blow into it, and pull out an equally invisible note card. To take it to the next level the supposed "questions" on the card not only needed to be funny, they also needed to rhyme.

I broke the game with the all-time winner one night, at a night spot in Kingsport. I pretended to hold the envelope to my head and said, "Taking a chance. Putting on a front. And a rock quarry." Roy played the Ed McMahon foil to my Carnac, by repeating those answers back just so I could impersonate the standard Carson double-take and leer. After miming the act of opening the envelope, I said "What are: Off on a lark, whistling in the dark, and Johnson Central Park?"

In addition to that, Roy came to Paintsville with a nickname established by his teammates at NC State, who spotted his Charlie Brown-like face and dubbed him "Pie." Instead of putting his number on the knob of his bat, Roy wrote the symbol for Pi. Roy Dixon was a funny guy.

Vince "The Bronze Fox" Bienek was on his way to what I was sure would be a big league career, but he tore up an ankle just a couple of years later in Double-A ball, and was never the same on the field.

Our great owner, Paul Fyffe, made enough of a splash with his co-op Hilanders that the Yankees sent their rookie-level team to Paintsville the next year. They were enormously successful. And a month after I returned home I received a package in the mail from Paul. It was my white home uniform jersey. The one with the number five on the back. Paul Fyffe defined the term "class act."

Mark Connor, the pitching coach brought in after our summit meeting with Paul, used his first job as a launching pad for an illustrious career. He not only was a calming influence on Yank, which made things better for everyone, he was a terrific instructor and mentor for the pitching staff.

When the Yankees made the decision to move their rookie affiliate to Paintsville the next year they hired Mark as a scout, and after one year on the road they made him the pitching coach for their Class-A team. He moved up the ladder quickly, and by 1984 he was the bullpen coach for the New York Yankees. In New York. At Yankee Stadium. He'd come a long way from Johnson Central Park.

Mark then headed back to his alma mater at the University of Tennessee for a couple of years, as the head coach, but the allure of pro ball was too strong and he returned to the Yankees in 1990. He would coach in the big leagues for a long time and he'd do it very well, having that same calming influence on his pitchers wherever he went, whether that meant he was wearing the uniform of the Arizona Diamondbacks, the Toronto Blue Jays, the Baltimore Orioles, or the Texas Rangers. He's still with the Rangers, although now he fills a front-office role as special assistant to the GM.

The whole thing was amazing. We played for a phenomenal owner, in front of devoted fans, in a fantastic little town we'd never heard of. We became fast friends who avoided rifts and never had to put up with any clubhouse troublemakers. We played for a skipper who could drive us a little crazy but that only made our bond as players all the stronger.

We rode the bus more than any other team in the league and we found ways to not just enjoy that, but to embrace it. We also learned how to sleep on those overnight rides back to Paintsville, when you couldn't worry about invading another guy's personal space. Someone else's shoulder often made a good resting spot for your head and the favor would be returned in kind on another night.

We loved each other. We loved the game. We battled injuries, we were constantly nicked up and bleeding from our skinned knees and thighs, the "strawberries" one earns when sliding on an infield as hard as concrete, but we gave it everything we had every night.

We all grew up a lot. And we laughed. We laughed a lot. We laughed without constraint. Because baseball is a game. It's supposed to be fun.

Young, Dumb, And Having Fun

As soon as I returned to St. Louis after the 1978 season had ended I called my dad for a bit of an informal "debriefing" about how things had gone. He seemed fairly positive about all of it and he definitely thought the hamstring injury and the lack of bats on the final road trip had negatively affected what had actually been a pretty solid year.

Then he asked me if I was going to be a part of the Fall Instructional League in Florida, which would start up in just a few weeks and last about a month. I actually had no idea if the Tigers were going to invite me but as he put it "If you don't hear from them, and you want to go, you should let them know that." On the spot, I made up my mind. I said "You know what? I'm tired. That's the most games I've played and most buses I've ridden in my life, combining SIUE and Paintsville. Plus, I want to go back to school and get another full quarter of classes in."

He totally understood that, and said, "I've always thought a guy's first year of pro ball is the hardest adjustment he'll ever have to make, especially in a bus league. There's a game every day and long overnight rides, and you do get tired. Go back to school, take a month off from workouts, but be ready to play the day you arrive in spring training next year."

I called Lance and Radar to see what their thoughts were about a place to live. They'd both be full-time students that fall as well, and we all knew we'd want to live together again, so we started looking. At the complex where I had my one-bedroom apartment a year before they also offered two-bedroom townhouse lofts that were really nice, but Radar said he'd checked on that and they were 100 percent leased. I thought maybe it would help that I'd lived there so

I gave them a call. "Well that's a different story, since you're a former resident. We'll slide you to the top of the waiting list," the manager said.

Less than a week later they let us know that a unit had opened up and we were set. Lance and Radar took the upstairs bedroom. But then Lance informed me that one of the SIUE basketball players, Mike "Pootie" Miller, who was also done with his scholarship but back at school to finish up his degree, was looking for a place as well. I knew Pootie a little and he seemed like a great guy, so I was happy to share a room with him. By the third week in September, we were all moved in.

We didn't have much in the way of furniture, just a ratty old couch, a TV, our mattresses, an old floppy chair for the loft, and my stereo, but what else do college guys need? Well, as it turned out we apparently needed two more things. During the first week we were there Lance changed everything in an epic new form of Monty Pythonesque tomfoolery. He brought to the apartment a full-size replica of the Venus de Milo statue. And it was gold. And Radar said "Why do we want that? Its arms are broken off." I'm still unaware of the original home of said Venus although I can guarantee that it did not come from the Louvre.

In addition to Venus, Lance also provided a framed print of a famous oil painting which represented 100 percent of our wall art. It was a portrait of explorer Amerigo Vespucci, or someone very much like him. We chose to believe it was good old Amerigo, although we also chose to call him Americus because that sounded cooler.

Back in our bedroom, both Pootie and I just threw single mattresses on the floor. I'm not sure I could get out of bed in the morning if I tried that now, but it was the norm when we were young and indestructible.

There was also a sliding door in our bedroom, facing the back, and train tracks ran no more than 50 yards away. At first, we worried about the noise but within days, the trains didn't really bother us. To this day, the clackity-clack of trains and the blaring blast of the horns are soothing to me, not annoying.

And then Radar found a door somewhere. Possibly he found it in his dad's garage. It was standard contractor's grade, unpainted, it had never been hung or used as an actual door, and it had the round hole where the knob would go, but he envisioned it horizontally and he said to Lance "Hey, if we get a couple of saw horses we can put this door on them and have a big enough desk for both of us to study in our room at the same time!"

Initially, Lance gave him a nod as if he thought that such a thing was a capital idea, but within seconds they both cracked up, simultaneously realizing how ridiculous that thought was. For weeks, they'd both sarcastically say, "We can study in our room at the same time!" and burst out laughing. Hey, it was a good idea. For some people. Like, maybe calculus majors.

That's how it was for Lance. He's enormously smart, and he was an accounting major, but I almost never saw him studying. He was bright enough to simply go to class, ace the tests, and move on.

Radar was a physical education major and from time to time I do recall him bringing anatomy or physiology books home to get ready for a test, but none of us really sat in our rooms and studied. In my major, most of the work was practical and done in the studio, followed by writing term papers or scripts. So, I had to do a lot of work outside the classroom but almost none of it was memorization or test prep. I loved to write, so it never really felt like work to me.

Pootie was, indeed, a fantastic roommate. He was as nice as he could be, polite, and very tall. Lance used to laugh at him when he'd watch TV lying on the living room floor. He'd say, "Pootie, your feet are next to the front door and your head is almost in the kitchen. Be taller!"

Plus, Pootie went home to his family and girlfriend in Peoria every weekend. In a lot of ways, he was the perfect roomie.

Away from our classes, we did field an intramural team in the SIUE Flag Football League for the second year in a row, and we once again dominated. We didn't totally run the table by going unscored upon, like we had the prior year, but we won the championship and had a great time doing it. Our usual Thursday night hangout, Spanky's, even "sponsored" us with free jerseys, which made us the only team in the league that didn't have to wear the smelly mesh jerseys the refs handed out before every game.

Our games were scheduled on Friday afternoons, and the biggest challenge every week was getting our 6-foot 8-inch roomie to commit to playing. All week long Pootie would say, "I don't know, guys. I like to go home."

We'd keep working on him every day, all week. I'd say 50 percent of the time we'd win him over and he'd delay his trip back home by a few hours, and then Kent Hendrickson could simply throw lob passes into the air and wait for Pootie to catch them. The other half of the time the gravitational pull of mom and his Peoria girlfriend were just too strong, and they won out over silly football games.

Radar and I liked to tape up our ankles and like some football players we'd do that on the outside of our shoes. It's called "spatting up" because the tape looks like formal spats over your black shoes. With our games being at 3 on Friday afternoons, Radar would be anxiously saying "Are you taped yet?" by 10:30 in the morning. Then he'd follow up with, "I'm already spatted. I can't wait to play." We did have our fun.

Lance's biggest issue was the cold. Once it got late into the quarter near the end of the intramural season, it could get down into the 20s or even the teens on game day. He'd spend all day saying, "I'm not playing in this," then he'd show up and grab five touchdown passes.

I mostly played free safety and some wide receiver but I also helped the team quite a bit as our punter. For some bizarre reason, ever since I played one season of junior football as a 10-year-old on the Kirkwood Cardinals, I discovered that my favorite aspect of football was kicking.

As a kid, I had very real aspirations about being a kicker and punter but I also really didn't much want to play actual football. There just wasn't much of a market for kicking specialists at that age, and once I got to SLUH I was told they didn't use them either. If I wanted to kick and punt, I'd have to play a position. So I never played organized football again until we played the intramural flag version of the game at SIUE.

By then, I had developed a heck of a leg as a punter and would regularly hit tight spirals 40 to 50 yards. We didn't actually get to fourth down very often but whenever we did I could almost always pin the other team right back on their goal line. It was fun, and I enjoyed the punts as much as I did the interceptions and run-backs as a safety.

Socially, that fall of 1978 was no different than the year before. We'd hit The Granary, Spanky's, Rusty's, and The Encounter on their appointed nights, sometimes venturing as far afield as a place called Off Broadway, in Lance's hometown of Highland. Off Broadway was aptly named, since it was a small brick building a half block off Broadway Avenue in Highland, and inside it was simply one small room. A deejay was set-up in the far left corner and a wooden dance floor took up about half the floor space, surrounded by tables and chairs in a dark room. The dance floor couldn't have been more than 15x15, and the "disco lights" were nothing more than strings of Christmas bulbs with a few spot-lights thrown in. Yes, there was also the required disco mirror-ball spinning above the dancing area. And boy could we dance. And boy we were proud of our moves. Stayin' alive, stayin' alive, ah-ah-ah-ah, stayin' alive!

By then, I owned a little red Ford Fiesta. I'd had enough of my super-sexy but super-awful TR-7, and the reliability and affordability of the little front-wheel drive hatchback built by Ford's European factories and imported to the U.S., was what interested me. That little car was undefeated and unscored upon when it came to snowy roads. It had just the right combination of weight and displacement to plow through anything. One night, when some other friend's car wouldn't start on a cold night in a heavy snowstorm, we somehow piled six people into my Fiesta. We never even spun the tires, although since I was busy concentrating on the road I'm still not sure how we got six adults in there for the 20-minute drive back to Edwardsville.

Wednesday night at The Granary was SIUE night, and we all got in free with our student ID cards, so that's the night you'd find the place packed with fellow Cougars. Faustus often played on Wednesdays, but we considered them such a great live band we'd even go there on other nights when you'd have to pay a cover charge. The odd thing about being there on a Friday or Saturday night was that it felt strangely different. It was usually not as crowded, and (gasp!) there were people there from St. Louis and other surrounding towns. Actual strangers in what we considered "our place."

As for Spanky's, we usually only went there on Thursday nights because it was dollar pitcher and dime draft night. Looking back on that little three-room bar the most inconceivable thing now is that, somehow, the fire marshal never happened to be passing by on a Thursday. It was packed, and by packed I mean wall-to-wall in the most literal sense. You could spot a buddy 15 feet away and it would take you 15 minutes to wade through the crowd and meet halfway.,

The thing that made Spanky's special was its communal feel. It didn't offer live music, like The Granary. You could find a couple pool tables and a foosball table in the back room for entertainment, but that was it. But on Thursdays we all seemed to know each other, with the baseball, basketball, wrestling, and soccer teams frequenting the place, along with cheerleaders, reporters from the school paper, and other students.

Once you got there and bought a pitcher for a buck or a draft for a dime, that was it. For three hours you'd laugh with your friends and everyone always seemed to be filling up someone else's glass.

Best of all, when we won the flag football championship and had a team photo taken in our Spanky's jerseys, they proudly framed and displayed it. We thought that was off-the-hook cool.

Rusty's was the classy joint we frequented on Friday nights, even going early for appetizers and happy hour. It was probably the nicest restaurant in Edwardsville, and the bar side of Rusty's was always a mix of SIUE students and locals.

Rather than stand and mingle, like we did on Thursdays at Spanky's, we sat around tables in comfortable chairs. And, of course, there was a dance floor. In the late '70s, there was a local zoning ordinance that required a dance floor. OK, I made that up, but it sure seemed that way.

The Encounter was inside the Holiday Inn out by Interstate 270, right at the Edwardsville exit. If Rusty's was classy, The Encounter seemed to take it to the next level. You could, conceivably, even take a date to The Encounter, but we weren't collectively that big on dates, or as Lance called them "desert fruits," as in "I actually have a desert fruit tonight. If it's terrible, I'll see you at The Encounter as soon as I can get there." As a disco, it was Off Broadway on "Saturday Night Fever" steroids, with great lights, a big dance floor, stellar deejays, and fantastic sound.

In the early days of October in the '78 fall quarter I received two wonderful pieces of mail. One was from Rawlings Sporting Goods, letting me know they were offering me a glove contract for the 1979 season. With the contract, I would receive two new Rawlings gloves per year, along with a pair of spikes, and all the undershirts and batting gloves I'd need.

Just as important, I also got a letter and contract from Hillerich & Bradsby, the fine folks who had been making the Louisville Slugger since Babe Ruth was hitting with a massive 40-ounce bat and Ty Cobb was choking up with his famous split grip. The letter stated that H&B would be offering me a contract as well and the cool thing was that my autograph would be branded on the bats. You've arrived at some sort of important juncture in your life when a Louisville Slugger has not just your name in block print (we all got those in Paintsville) but your actual authentic legible autograph on it.

We worked out the specifics of my favored U1 model, including length and weight, and I ordered the cupped-end version of the bat, wherein a scoop of the wood is carved out of the end of the barrel. Why? For one thing, it looks cool. Then there's science. Hard dense wood hits the ball farther but it also makes the bat much heavier. So, if I wanted a 32.5-ounce bat, they could make it out of a 33.5-ounce piece of wood and then scoop an ounce out of the end of the barrel. And, let's be honest, it did look cool. That's always important.

I had to sign my autograph legibly six times and send those back to them so they could choose which one would work best, and I had to check the box denoting whether I wanted a set of golf clubs or $250 as payment for my rights. Everyone else with a bat contract chose the golf clubs. I chose the money. I was still a broke college kid who had only gotten a $500 bonus to sign.

A few weeks later a long cardboard box from Louisville showed up at our apartment. Inside were my first two Bob Wilber autographed bats, sent to me by Hillerich & Bradsby as keepsakes and a welcome to the Louisville Slugger family. I'd be lying if I played it cool and said I didn't stare at them and hold them in my hands for hours. It was yet another big moment on the road meandering toward my dream.

I went through dozens of those U1s the next year but I still have two in my possession. One of them hangs on my office wall below a Del Wilber autographed model, with which he hit three home runs on three swings one night in late August 1951. With those three homers, he drove in all three runs in the game, and the Phillies beat the Reds 3-0. We called it his "Perfect Day" and it surely was. Dad's bat hangs higher than mine on the wall. For good reason.

I also spoke with a rep from Hillerich & Bradsby just a few years ago and he was happy to inform me that they have kept a record of every personalized bat they've ever made, including the model, weight, length, and the original autograph they had used for each contracted player. My name is, therefore, still stored at their headquarters in Louisville, should I ever need some new ones made. I probably won't be playing much ball anymore, but that's good to know. Just one less thing to worry about.

During the Christmas break our roomie situation changed again. Pootie graduated and Radar moved back home with his parents because his father informed him that living near campus with us was bad for him. Or, as Lance called it, Radar's dad implemented the "no-more-fun-of-any-kind doctrine."

Meanwhile, Oscar made the move to join Lance and me in the apartment and to make it even more fun he brought his girlfriend, Theresa Natta. So, Lance moved into my room while Oscar and T Natta (her appointed name to us) took the upstairs bedroom.

T Natta fit in perfectly, for the same reason she and Oscar seemed to be a very good match. She not only got our sense of humor she could deal in the currency just as well as any of us. She was also just starting out as a hair stylist then, so in lieu of rent we charged her one haircut each, per month. It was a perfectly fine arrangement and much fun was had by all, although Lance insists to this day that T Natta still owes him her share of the last month's utilities. With fines and interest compounded over the years, she now owes him $4.5 million. That's a lot of haircuts.

It was a cold and snowy winter in that part of the world and the year was capped off by a major blizzard just after Christmas, which was then followed by a plunge into subzero temperatures. The power went out all over the Edwardsville area when the heavy snow turned to ice and started taking down power lines. In our sarcastic terminology it could be said, "Well, it might be heinously freezing cold but at least our electric furnace doesn't work."

For days we moved everything out of the freezer and into a snowbank right outside the sliding door in my bedroom.

The power outage stretched on for nearly a week and with each passing night our apartment got colder and colder. We had been planning to host a major New Year's Eve party and the only good reason we had to keep that plan in place was that we knew a wall-to-wall crowd would at least warm the place up for one night.

We had candles burning everywhere and we did indeed have a houseful of guests for the party, which featured no music because we had no power. And then, as if by some form of divine intervention, the power returned about 10:30 p.m. People cheered. And then, around 11:30, the power went back off. People groaned and we decided to move the party to Tower Lake, where the power had been on for a couple of days. Oh, the lengths to which we would go when a party must continue.

When classes reconvened after New Year's Day I plotted my course with a specific eye toward the middle of March. Not only would that be the end of the quarter, and spring break, it would also be precisely when I'd need to be in Florida for spring training. My reporting date in Lakeland was a day or two before the quarter technically ended, so I had to carefully work with all of my instructors and professors to make sure I could take any finals or turn in any term papers early.

I had chosen to graduate with a minor in the field of study broadly defined as "communications" which featured all sorts of interesting and not very challenging courses about the ways we communicate. It did not include classes that taught us how to write ridiculously long run-on sentences. That gift comes naturally to me.

We studied wolves in one class because of their specific means of communicating with each other and the social strata they must institute for the good of the pack. Those alpha males were an interesting bunch. And then there were the classes where we studied communications via alternative methods, as opposed to actually speaking. Facial expressions often say much more than the words you might be uttering, and a good detective knows that reading your eyes is far more valuable and foolproof than listening to what you might be saying. Did you also know that if two photos of the same person's face are lined up side-by-side the vast majority of people will think the one with larger dilated pupils is more attractive, as compared to the same photo with small pupils? That fact alone is proof that college is valuable.

All of it was good and my grades stayed in Dean's List territory throughout the winter. But it would be incorrect to state that my focus was totally on school. I was much more intent on spring training.

I did not want to show up in Florida out of shape, because just taking the time to get my arm ready for action would put me well behind the guys who were coming from warmer climates. So I needed a place to work out.

At the conclusion of our senior season Roy Lee had decided to retire. He was replaced by Gary "Bo" Collins as head coach and Bo had no problem with me working out with his new team. I could take batting practice, get my throwing in, and run and stretch with the guys whenever my schedule allowed. Also, by that time, Bob Hughes had also moved on, becoming head coach at Jefferson Community College south of St. Louis. I had a standing invite to work out there, as well, and actually preferred that despite the 45-minute drive. Bob's facilities were fairly standard for a junior college, but SIUE was still practicing in a grade school. I drove down to Jefferson at least three days a week as spring training approached.

I took my classes. I got in shape. And I counted the days until it was time to head south. I'd been waiting my entire life for this moment.

Living The Dream

On January 23, 1979, I received the certified letter I'd been waiting for all winter. It was my contract. The Detroit Tigers still had me on the Bristol roster but the cover letter made it clear that I'd have every opportunity to make the Lakeland team out of spring training. That would be fairly important, because a 22-year-old in his second year of pro ball didn't stand much of a chance to continue playing if the best he could do was Bristol.

Lakeland was in the Florida State League, which was a big step up from the Appalachian circuit, but I was confident I could make the leap. Perhaps *hopeful* is a better description of how I felt. It's hard to say because I was once again going to be playing with and against guys at the next level, and I had no idea how much more advanced the competition would be.

I was also momentarily pleased to see that I'd gotten a small raise to $600 per month. The pleasure was fleeting, however, after I learned that Major League Baseball had upped the minimum pay in Class A to $600 and therefore the raise had been mandated, as opposed to earned.

I'd been going to spring training in Florida since my early childhood. I'd ridden trains to get there, I'd sat wide-eyed in the backseat of the Wilber family car, and I'd even flown a time or two. I'd hung out with the St. Louis Cardinals in St. Petersburg, the Minnesota Twins in Orlando, and the Texas Rangers in Plant City. I even shagged fly balls and picked up bats. And all of that was because I was Del Wilber's kid.

This time, I'd be driving my Ford Fiesta and I'd be headed for Tiger Town, the complex in Lakeland that would play host to all the Detroit minor league teams. Next to the complex was Joker Marchant Stadium, spring training home of the big club.

In terms of proximity we'd be working out across one small parking lot, roughly 200 yards, from Lou Whitaker, Alan Trammell, Ron LeFlore and the other big leaguers. In reality, we would be a million miles away. I knew that but my mind wasn't focused on the big leagues during that cold January day in Edwardsville. It was focused on getting there and making the Lakeland team. I could see no logical reason why the Tigers would hold me another year in Bristol.

Edwardsville is roughly 1,000 miles from Lakeland. Back in '79, the Interstate highway route between the two towns was nearly done, but there still were spots in Kentucky, Tennessee, and Georgia where it had gaps and two-lane roads were the way to bridge those sections. All told, it was probably a 20-hour trip.

I'd driven it nonstop with a co-driver in the past but I wasn't going to do that this time. I wanted to arrive bright-eyed and fresh, not worn out from the road, so my plan was to drive to just shy of Chattanooga, Tennessee on the first day, where a Holiday Inn was perched just a few miles from Lookout Mountain. Then, on Day Two, rather than push it all the way to Lakeland I'd just drive to Valdosta, Georgia, about 350 miles south. That would leave me just 230 miles to go on the third day. I'd be pulling into Tiger Town by lunch time.

As the days ticked by, the most memorable and enjoyable class that quarter covered TV news. It met just once a week, but each class was four hours long. We'd arrive in the studio at 12 noon (or earlier if we wanted to) and Dr. Kamil Winter would give us an overview of what he expected by that afternoon. Then all 10 of us would tuck ourselves into a small "newsroom" and get to work. We'd scour the wires for stories, assign different parts of the show to various people, write the stories, edit them, and put them into some sort of order while other classmates were working on graphics and video. By 2 we'd have the show put together and Dr. Winter would play the role of executive news editor, going over what we had and pushing us to make it better.

By pure chance, I was assigned the anchor duty the first week and I brought a coat and tie to complete the look. By 3:15 we were at our stations, with classmates handling the cameras, the lights, the graphics packages, and the floor direction. I was joined onstage by two cohorts doing weather and sports. It was just like the real thing, except with fewer people watching.

At precisely 3:30 we'd go on the air to a small group of closed-circuit TVs in the building. And at that point I got my first dose of what real television news people hide so well. When you're reading the news from sheets of paper (no teleprompters for us) while trying to keep it interesting and coherent, directors are almost constantly talking in your earpiece, often shouting directions. It's a difficult thing to master.

In addition, Dr. Winter had a few mishaps up his sleeve for each news show. Lights would go out, cameras would fail, graphics packages would disappear, one of our microphones would cease to function, and somehow he once even managed to mess up our scripts so that each of us had our stories in a different order. He was one devilish master but he was weeding out the pretenders from the contenders. After that first show, he told us all (in his thick Czech accent that made my name sound like "Mistah Vilba") what we'd done well and what we had botched. And he added, "I think also that Mr. Wilber will be our anchor for all the shows this quarter. Mr. Wilber, you have what we call charisma. But please don't wink at the camera again when you sign off." And I thought the wink was awesome.

By the ninth week we were clicking as a unit and despite Dr. Winter's technical hurdles — and his propensity for yelling at us in our earpieces at the worst possible times — we got better and better. I loved it. I felt the stress of starting with nothing and delivering a show just a few hours later, and I relished it.

I had to miss the final show, though, because of that pesky little detail that had been locked into the front of my brain since January. I would be leaving for spring training, and someone else would have to anchor that final half-hour of news. Before I left, Dr. Winter told me I'd get an A for the course and he added "Mr. Wilber, you can do this. You can be a star at this. When you're done playing those baseball games, come back here and see me." It was an honor to hear those words from a professor who brought out the best in me.

It had also become clear that I was still five classes short of my degree, so I'd be headed back to SIUE again in the fall. For a kid who detested school as much as I once did, it was not lost on me that I actually looked forward to another quarter of college.

Finally, the week for which I'd been waiting my entire life arrived. Before I finished my final news show and turned in my term papers I made a quick trip to downtown St. Louis and the world headquarters for Rawlings Sporting Goods. I went in empty-handed but came out with two new gloves, each a Pro-B model. In addition to the two new fielder's gloves I left with a box of batting gloves, three new baseball undershirts with black sleeves, and a new pair of spikes.

For most of my life, when I did wear Rawlings spikes they were big old bulky things, with thick leather soles. They felt like clogs but they were all we knew at the time. At SIUE we discovered the new sleek and streamlined shoes adidas and Puma were making and we all made the switch. They fit better and had plastic soles that were much lighter than the old leather ones.

By 1979 Rawlings had finally made the transition and I eagerly picked out a pair. I was nearly ready to go. I did, however, still need to begin breaking in my new gloves.

Today, baseball gloves can be bought off the shelf at a fine sporting-goods store and used the next day. Back then, when dinosaurs roamed in the outfield, it could take months to break in a glove. When you got them they were so stiff you could barely move the thumb and little finger toward each other, much less touch them together. There were also precious few shortcuts for breaking them in, so it was a laborious process.

I always had at least four broken-in gloves in my duffel bag so the method going forward would be to spend at least 15 minutes per day playing catch with the new gloves to start the break-in. I'd always have at least two gloves that were my "gamers" and in perfect condition, while I'd also keep a couple of slightly worn gloves as emergency back-ups, and the new gloves would go into rotation for at least six months before they were ready for game action.

And, for the record, almost all the guys I've ever played with called them gloves. Catchers and first-basemen wore mitts. Everyone else wore gloves.

Then the day arrived. I'm not sure how much I slept the night before but I was packed and the car was loaded before I went to bed. My official Detroit Tigers duffel bag — with my name neatly painted in flowing script on the bottom of one end — nearly filled the rear of the Fiesta but somehow I fit a large suitcase and all my U1 bats in there as well. I was nervous, excited, a little worried about the trip, and eager to go. And yes, of course I still have that duffle bag.

I'd already said goodbye to my friends and roomies and 37 years later I can still remember backing my car out of the drive and then manually shifting it as I drove down the street. I was on my way.

The first day was uneventful. I drove through southern Illinois, then a bit of western Kentucky, then down through Nashville. After that it was a straight shot to Monteagle, a steep peak. I pulled off I-24 near Lookout Mountain after a funny little segment where the highway dips into Georgia for just a few miles. There's actually a "Welcome To Georgia" sign followed almost immediately by a "Welcome To Tennessee" sign just minutes later. I always thought the Tennessee one should say "Welcome Back" or "You Couldn't Stay Away, Could You?"

Back then, I always stayed in Holiday Inns — for two reasons. My dad had always stayed in Holiday Inns when possible and the company was the first to launch an integrated reservations system. If you went to the lobby of any Holiday Inn, you could ask the desk agent to book your reservations at other Holiday Inns in America via their Holidex machine. I have no idea how it worked, but it did. Holiday Inn would always get a lot of business from me.

Like most of the Holiday Inns at the time, the one I stayed in that night near Chattanooga was two stories with outdoor walkways. I got my key with the classic green plastic fob and went to my room. Day one was complete, but only after I called my mom to let her know I was there.

Bright and early the next morning, after a breakfast of scrambled eggs and bacon, I was on my way again, needing only to traverse Georgia from north to south including the always interesting bisection of Atlanta. That's 350 miles of Georgia with a sprawling and congested big city in the middle, so any time you would make that trip you knew it could take six hours, eight hours, or more depending on what Atlanta put in your way. I took my time and made it in about six, stopping at the Valdosta Holiday Inn around 3 p.m. I pulled off the road, checked into my room, and had Steak 'n Shake for dinner.

The next morning I was back on the road by 9 and crossing the Florida state line just minutes later. And there were palm trees! It was finally getting very real.

Lakeland is pretty much right in the center of Florida and since I-75 veers west to reach Tampa, the shortest route is to leave the interstate and follow Highway 98 in order to arrive in Lakeland from the north. As I approached I-4, the east-west interstate that connects Tampa to Daytona, I saw something that made the hair on my arms stand up. It was the massive light towers of Joker Marchant Stadium, leading me like a beacon when I was still five miles away.

I turned down the road that borders the western side of Tiger Town, pulled into the driveway by the main business office, took a deep breath and went inside.

I signed everything the woman behind the desk put in front of me. She handed me the itinerary and my ID card.

As I grabbed my suitcase and began to walk over to the dorm I heard a familiar voice, yelling "Hey, Hawk!" It was Roy Dixon, and a happier pie-shaped face I could not have seen. He had gotten into town the night before and was, therefore, at the complex as soon as they opened the office. Roy gave me a basic tour, pointing out the clubhouse, the dining hall, and the dorm, and off I went to find my room.

Every bedroom in the three-story U-shaped Tiger Town dorm featured two twin beds and a few other necessities. The roommate pairings were alphabetical so my new roomie would be

Jim Wilfong, from La Verne, California. He was indeed the brother of Rob Wilfong who was in his third year with the Minnesota Twins. Jim seemed like a nice guy and, as I found out that night, he did not snore. That's all the info I needed in order to rank him high in the roommate standings.

After introducing myself to Jim, I headed over to the clubhouse.

We had about 120 players in camp on that first day. The Evansville guys, who made up the Triple-A team, had the first group of lockers while the Double-A guys on the Montgomery roster, the Lakeland players, and the group slated to be on the Bristol team filled the rest of the cavernous room. Other than the Triple-A guys, the rest of us seemed randomly sprinkled throughout the place.

I checked in and received a uniform, which fit and had a five on the back, and was shown to my locker — where I quickly unpacked my duffel bag just so I could stand back and stare. The equipment managers had already written my name with a Magic Marker on a piece of white athletic tape across the top of the locker. I was, to use a technical term, giddy.

That first day was nothing more than orientation and meetings and we got to talk with all the coaches and managers a bit. I also introduced myself to a few of the guys who had lockers near mine, just to be friendly, but getting to know all 120 players was either going to take a long time or not happen at all. Finally, it was time for our first dinner together.

Tiger Town and Marchant Stadium sit on the site of a former World War II air base and a couple of the roads in the complex were easy to spot as former runways. A few of the hangars still existed, as well, and our dining room was actually the original mess hall for the base. Instead of any aircraft or war insignias it now had a large Old-English D painted on the wall above the serving line. The rules for the cafeteria were simple: One trip through the line and no wearing of hats. Other than that, have at it.

I managed to track down Dan O'Connor and Judson Thigpen after dinner and minute by minute I seemed to feel more at home. Did I mention I was in spring training? In Florida? With the Detroit Tigers?

When my new roomie and I returned to our dorm room we noticed something different in the central TV lounge. On each floor, a large bulletin board was attached to the wall in front of the stairway. It was the first thing you'd see when you arrived on your level. Earlier that day it had nothing pinned to it. That evening, there was a single piece of paper with typewritten information tacked to the center of the board and across the top of the board was a horizontal sign that stated, in bold print, "CHECK THIS BOARD EVERY MORNING."

The sheet in the middle was the hour-by-hour schedule for the next day. A new one would appear there every morning and later in camp another much more stressful sheet would begin to appear every morning, when players began to be released.

For the first week we'd just be doing drills and taking batting practice, although later in the week we did graduate to intrasquad games in the afternoon. We arose early, worked hard, ate well, and slept as quickly as we could to get up and do it again.

We would need to be dressed and ready to go at 8:30 each morning. Breakfast was not mandatory but it was certainly recommended, so guys would start filtering into the dining hall by 6:30. Then we'd take a casual walk to the clubhouse and begin the slow process of getting dressed. I don't recall anyone ever missing the 8:30 announcement directing us to the complex for stretching and exercises.

Tiger Town featured four full-size diamonds in a cloverleaf shape, all surrounding a central viewing tower where scouts, coaches, and managers could keep an eye on the minor league teams. We also had two batting cages with ancient "Iron Mike" pitching machines and a practice infield off to the side. In addition, the bullpens and practice mounds made it possible for up to 16 pitchers to get their throwing in at any given time. Tiger Town, like all spring training camps, was a beehive of activity. There was no time to waste.

Every workout was orchestrated, starting with the 8:30 announcement that would always come over the loudspeakers as, "Good morning, gentlemen. It's a beautiful day in Tiger Town. Let's get to work. Run, do not walk, to the field you are assigned to and start your stretching."

Each day, we'd start our stretching with the head and neck and slowly limber up and stretch out those muscles, working down through the shoulders, back, lower back, hips, thighs, hamstrings, groin muscles, calves, and ankles. It was exactly the same, every day. I still remember those drills.

And every day I'd think, "Why can't someone figure out a way to get really loose, and really stretched out, so that it lasted more than 24 hours?" It was a tedious way to begin each morning.

On that first day, before the 8:30 announcement, I got a piece of great news. The four different rosters were posted in the central part of the clubhouse and my name was on the sheet that had the word "LAKELAND" across the top. That was a heck of a good way to start my first camp.

As we got dressed one thing was instantly noticeable. We all had the exact same uniforms. They were road gray with the Old English D on the left chest, all double-knit pullover shirts and pants with a navy-blue waistband. And since all 120 of us were wearing them at least five or six guys in camp would be wearing the same number, whatever that was. I was one of six guys wearing the big five on his back.

After getting suited up, the last thing we'd pass on the way out of the doors to hit the field was a table of important supplies. There were tubes of eye black to cut down on the glare, a variety of sunscreens, and tubes of zinc oxide, that creamy white stuff most of us put on our noses. We didn't care how we looked but we all cared enough to know we didn't want to miss time because of bad sunburns. After the lather-up station was another table but this one was not so healthy. It was completely covered in all manner of chewing tobacco and bubble gum. The tobacco companies shipped dozens of cases to each organization during spring training and the season, and it was always available. We never paid for any of it then, but most of us paid a lot for it, for many years, after our careers were over.

On that first day we also met with the Lakeland manager, another old-school guy from my father's era. His name was Fred Hatfield but most everyone called him either Hat or the universal Skip. I don't recall too many people calling him Fred.

Hat played nearly 10 years in the big leagues, much of it during the same time as my dad. They obviously knew each other and as far as I'd ever heard from my dad they got along just fine.

During our meeting I felt a little subconscious snub from him, although I tried to pass it off by rationalizing he wasn't exactly the most outgoing or friendly guy in camp and it was clear he was going to run this team his way. It was a bit of a grouchy way, at that.

After morning drills we'd break for lunch which we'd eat on a long covered patio attached to the clubhouse. We'd grab sandwiches and drinks and plop down on picnic tables, or take our food back to our lockers. An hour later, we were back on the fields.

I always wore batting gloves on both hands, but if you haven't swung a bat much over the winter you can almost bank on having blisters after the first day. Band-Aids were handed out freely, as were tubes of a substance called New-Skin. It was actually a glue you could put on blisters to harden them. By the end of the first week, if you were lucky, the blisters turned to callouses.

Arms had to be cared for, as well. Throwing a baseball overhand is one of the most unnatural and damaging physical acts a young man can perform. Just about everything involved in the standard overhand throw is designed to get the ball from Point A to Point B as rapidly as possible, but the shoulder and the elbow were never really designed for it, hence the staggering number of rotator cuff and elbow surgeries we see every year. Tommy John was a fine pitcher during his career but I'd imagine most young players for the last 20 years only associate his name with elbow ligament replacement.

So, we'd spend days building up our arms and getting stronger before playing any games. We'd also do a lot of running, to get the legs in shape. And by a lot of running I mean a lot of running — both wind-sprints and distance laps around the entire complex. After all, why spend all that time stretching in the morning if you weren't going to run?

The days during that first week ended around 3, and we'd all head for the showers. With 120 guys in the room, that process would take a while, but no one was in a hurry. Dinner wasn't until 6.

That total number of 120 also contained a dark side. Nearly the entire Bristol team from the year before was in camp in addition to the four of us from the Paintsville Hilanders. Some Triple-A guys from the year before were over in the big league camp and many of them would be coming back, forcing other players further down the ladder. To compound the problem, in a few months after the 1979 June draft, a new roster of players for Bristol would be signed, just like we had a year earlier. There wouldn't be room for everyone. Before spring training ended, roughly 30 guys would have to be cut. I didn't want to think about it.

We always had a few hours to relax on our own before dinner, then we'd all walk across the yard from the dorm to the dining hall for our meal. The food was generally tasty and there was plenty of it, although the trends toward good nutrition had not exactly caught on yet, back in those dark days. We ate a lot of hamburgers, hot dogs, and white-bread sandwiches, but one night each week we'd have steak and potatoes. Nobody skipped that meal.

After just a few days it all became a routine. Check the bulletin board in the morning, eat breakfast, head to the clubhouse to get dressed, and be ready to "run, not walk" to our assigned fields at 8:30. Then drills until lunch, which would be followed by more drills and copious amounts of batting practice, during which there could only be one guy hitting. The rest of the group would be catching the balls that were hit and throwing them back in. Those Band-Aids and the New-Skin were coming in handy for a lot of guys.

A few days into it we played some intrasquad games in the afternoon. Generally, Evansville would play Montgomery, to keep the competition level somewhat equal, so that left Lakeland and Bristol to square off on another diamond. To me, those games were most interesting from a talent evaluation viewpoint. Were the Triple-A and Double-A guys that much better? Some were clearly older and a little bigger than most of us, but it wasn't a night-versus-day thing. I think the area in which those guys really stood out was infield defense. They gobbled up everything and they turned the double-play like big leaguers, while also doing so with a bit of flair. At our level, everything was a lot more methodical.

Hustling from field to field I found myself much more focused on the work than socializing. We all seemed to get along just fine but the looming threat of cuts affected everyone. I mostly socialized with Roy and OC and I shared a room with a guy who didn't snore.

In the dorm, there was a speaker system on each floor so that the older gentlemen who manned the front desk could page people. Only players were allowed beyond the lobby and apparently one pitcher by the name of Roger Weaver had a lot of friends who came to see him. One of the volunteers at the front desk was an older man with a thick Boston accent. At least once per day, between the end of workouts and and the start of dinner, we'd hear what sounded like "Rajah Weavah, Rajah Weavah, you have a guest in the lobby." I didn't even know Roger Weaver, but within a week I felt like I did.

We also learned on the first day that we had a midnight curfew, and to enforce it they didn't have to do bed checks — they simply locked the doors. Any player who missed curfew had to ring the bell to be let in. I never once came close to missing curfew.

Finally, after a week that felt like a month, things got more interesting. We began our actual schedule of spring games against other teams. In addition to that Hat told me I'd also be taking some grounders and getting some work in at first base, a position I had never played. I hadn't thought to grab a first-baseman's mitt when I was at Rawlings, but the Tigers had an old (as in prehistoric) mitt in the supply room and that went in my locker. For a few days I'd just be taking some grounders during practice while learning some of the fundamentals of the position from our coaches. In the games, I'd play center field.

That first morning the games began felt instantly different. Instead of drills all morning, we'd do our normal stretching and running, and then take a long round of BP. If we were playing a road game our departure time from Tiger Town was denoted, and meals were worked in around that schedule. We'd be making trips over to Winter Haven (15 miles east) to play the Class-A affiliate of the Red Sox, or to Tampa (about 40 miles west) to play a minor league club in the Reds camp. On many other days, those clubs would come to Tiger Town to play us. We saw a lot of those guys.

We also played the Bristol squad a lot and it was not uncommon for the staff to move guys around from team to team, just to fill needs. The big league team would often grab guys from the complex to give the veterans a break and that would cause ripples all up and down the system.

For road games, two Tiger teams would make the same trip on the same bus. I got to know a few guys on the Montgomery team fairly well just from those bus rides. They didn't seem much different than us.

On the first trip over to Winter Haven I was playing center and had hit a nice single my first time up to record my first hit of the spring. I was officially batting 1.000. When I came up the next time, I drilled a fastball into the left-center gap for a stand-up double. When I got to third after a wild pitch, Hat said, "Attaboy. Couldn't have hit that one better myself." I remember thinking, "I wonder if he means back during his playing days or now?"

Once we got on the bus, still in uniforms covered in sweat and dirt, I was seated next to an outfielder from the Montgomery team and he asked me how I'd done. When I said "2 for 3 with a double" he shook my hand and say "Way to go, man." That felt more than just pretty good.

Back at Tiger Town I heard the bus driver hit the air horn a couple of times as we pulled in. I asked the guy next to me what that was about and he said, "If either of us comes back here as a winner, we let the camp know." Pretty cool deal, and it was all starting to feel like a place I belonged.

A few days later, when we rode over to Tampa to play the Reds, I played first base. I was basically petrified. I'd been getting used to it in practice and during our infield routine before games, and I knew I could make all the throws and catch the throws that came my way, but corralling those grounders was all new to me. In practice they hit them fairly hard but they weren't rockets. In the games they often came at you exactly like rockets. I took my fair share off the wrist or off the heel of the glove, but I took pride in always knocking the ball down. Nothing scared me more than having one go right through my legs, and that fear was a great motivator.

The daily routines were so ingrained by the end of two weeks it was all subconscious. It was also just as I had dreamt it would be.

One day, one of the big leaguers came over to get some additional running in. He was a pitcher with a sore arm and he'd been trying to rehab it and get better for much of the last two years. It wasn't going well. But, the floppy blond hair was instantly recognizable and Mark "The Bird" Fidrych spent the entire afternoon with us over there, talking to everyone between long laps around the outfield.

By then, the big club was starting to play a few night games in the stadium and we all had free access to those. One evening, when they were playing the Philadelphia Phillies, we went over a bit early for BP and I spotted a familiar face playing catch in front of the visitors dugout. It was Pete Mackanin, who had always been so gracious to me on my dad's teams.

I shouted his name and his eyes lit up. He ran over to the railing and shook my hand, saying, "Hey, Bob! What are you doing here? Are you on spring break?" I took some great delight in telling him that I was actually playing for the Tigers. He thought that was cool but I could also see a little funny look in his eyes as he did the math. If his former batboy from Triple-A was now in spring training with the Tigers, he had to be getting up there in years. Indeed, Pete was starting his seventh year in the big leagues and he would only play two more. He was 28. An actual veteran in a young man's game. Today, he's the manager of the Phillies.

As our games rolled on I'd have my typical mini-streaks of hot hitting followed by a cold front of 0-for-3s, but I was doing as well as most of the guys on the Lakeland squad. Roy wasn't hitting much but the Tigers clearly liked his athleticism and he covered the outfield like a gazelle. One day, when the Lakeland and Bristol clubs were playing each other instead of traveling, Roy was in center for Bristol and I hit a mammoth shot into the left-center gap. The four fields in the complex now have permanent fences but in 1979 they had no fences at all. When the ball left my bat I could instantly feel that I'd crushed it, but Roy had all the room in the world to track it down and he did that, leaping and backhanding it probably 410 feet from home plate. My own buddy took a home run away from me, but that's the nature of the spring training beast. I would've done the same to him.

And then the big toe on my right foot began to hurt. It was hardly noticeable at first, then it gradually grew a little worse each day and it was turning red and getting quite swollen. When the pain got so bad I couldn't run, I headed to the training room to have the docs look at it. They immediately diagnosed it as a massively ingrown toenail which I'd also allowed to become infected. They told me to lay on the table and grip the sides, because they were going to have to dig it out. With no painkillers.

As they prepped their sharp shiny objects, a small crowd began to gather. Everyone loves a little ghoulish doctoring when it's someone else on the table. And when the lead trainer poked a very sharp hooked needle into my toe I literally saw stars and thought I might pass out. My groan only drew a bigger crowd. I've suffered my share of injuries and I've been drilled in the elbow by 90-mph fastballs but nothing hurt more than that moment when the hook went into my toe. Absolutely nothing.

It may have only taken them two or three minutes to cut it open and dig out the nail, but it seemed like an hour. I was drenched in a cold sweat. We still had the infection to take care of, though, so I was informed I would not suit up for two full days, and then they'd reevaluate. They might as well have cut my foot off, at that point. I was devastated.

I limped back to my locker in flip-flops, slowly took off my uniform, and then got back into my street clothes. And all my Tiger teammates headed out to play. It was reminiscent of those childhood years when sickness kept me confined to my room while everyone else played "kick the can" out in the street.

Hat saw me and spat out, "What's wrong with you?" in a General George Patton sort of voice, and when I told him it looked like he'd bitten into a lemon. He said, "A toenail?" with the sort of disgust usually reserved for an overbearing father who was disappointed in his son's lack of toughness. I told him about the infection and that the trainers were worried about that and that I was not allowed to play even though I'd be more than happy to suit up right then and there and charge right out the door, but he just spun and walked away shaking his head. Much like Mrs. Clough back in seventh grade at MQP, he never smiled at me again.

They cleared me on the third day but the toe was still terribly painful, and under the bandage was a significant open wound. So I did what any guy with a glove and shoe contract would do. I cut out a piece of my shoe right over my big toe. I realized fouling a ball off that toe would probably kill me, but I had to try something. And the next day I called Rawlings and told them the story before I asked if I could order another pair of spikes. Their rep, it turned out, was coming to Tiger Town in a couple of days and he'd bring them to me. For the time being, I'd wear the pair with one square-inch of leather missing above my big toe.

The third day also brought some bad news. When I checked the bulletin board in the morning I saw the lineups for the various clubs and noticed I'd be starting that day in left field. For Bristol. They'd moved Roy up to Lakeland and moved me down to Bristol. I instantly had a pain in my gut to go with the one in my toe.

The Bristol staff welcomed me warmly, though, and that made the transition a little better. I wasn't back to full-speed running at that point, so for a couple of days I just took BP and got my throwing in. Finally, with my new shoes in my locker and my cut-out shoe on my foot, I started playing again. The Bristol coaching staff was 180-degrees different, in a very good way. They were full of optimism and motivation and they complimented everything we did in the proper way while taking the time to stop and correct us when things went haywire. It was a better atmosphere, but it was Bristol.

I did just fine with the Bristol guys. Although I was one of the two or three best players on that roster, that meant nothing to me. If I didn't work my way off that roster and back onto the Lakeland team I'd be driving back home by the end of camp. And the first cuts of the spring were looming.

One day, when we were playing an intrasquad game, the big league team sent over one of their starting pitchers so he could in get some extra work. He had been dealing with a tight arm and the staff wanted to take a look at him before putting him back in any big league game action. That was cool to be a part of but what was cooler still was the fact he came in to pitch during an inning when I was due up, so I got to hit off him in front of all the execs and the major league staff. By then, in both college and pro ball, I'd already faced a number of guys who would later pitch in the big leagues but this was the first time I was facing a guy already there — a guy with a real Detroit uniform on and his name on the back (although that name is lost in the fog of time). I was amped up but I also understood the importance of the moment. If I could do something good in this one at-bat, a lot of important people would witness it.

I battled like crazy, fouling off a bunch of pitches and working the count to 3-and-2. I probably made the guy throw 10 pitches before he busted me with a change-up unlike anything I'd ever seen. With the same arm action as his fastball, it came in 15 miles per hour slower and the bottom fell out of it. I tipped it, but the catcher held on for the strikeout. So close, but that's how baseball works.

The next day, I got up at 6 like I did every morning and there on the bulletin board were all the same itineraries and notes, but there was a new sheet as well and it scared me to death. It listed six or eight names and the players listed were instructed to report to the office immediately. Judson Thigpen was one of them. I wasn't.

I saw Judson in the dining hall after he'd gotten the news from the camp coordinators, but he brushed past me without saying a word. His locker was empty by the time we got over to the clubhouse after breakfast. Yes, it's every bit the horror you might imagine it to be. Guys refer to the moment as "dying" and I understand why.

There was roughly one week left in camp and I was still on the Bristol roster. The next morning, my roomie got the axe. Jim Wilfong would not be joining his brother in the big leagues. There was no trace of him after breakfast. I'd have a room to myself from that point forward.

With no roomie to disturb I'd wake up earlier and earlier every morning and sneak down the tiled hallway in my socks to peer at the sheet in the darkness. I wanted to know my fate while everyone else was still asleep. And every morning I saw friends and teammates on that heartless list, but never mine.

By the final days of camp, when I was running full speed again and back to wearing full shoes (thank you, Rawlings!) I was getting up as early as 4:30 to check the bulletin board. I don't know who tacked the list up each morning and I don't know what time they did it, but I know it was earlier than 4:30 a.m.

Each morning, more names. Each morning, more dreams died. Some of the names were guys I really thought could play and the Triple-A and Double-A guys were not spared on the sheet at all. The final day of camp finally arrived and one last sheet would greet me in the darkness. My name was not on it.

Also on the board were the final rosters for all four minor league clubs. The Bristol guys would simply remain at Tiger Town for what is called "Extended Spring Training" and they'd continue to play games and work out until June. They weren't safe, though. There would likely be a few more cuts before and after the draft in early June. The Montgomery and Evansville rosters were listed along with instructions for their travel to their home cities for the summer. The Lakeland team would stay right there and move their gear into the big league clubhouse at Marchant Stadium over the next couple of days. There was only one problem. My name wasn't on any roster.

In the darkness, I figured I was just reading it wrong, or not seeing it, but I scanned Bristol and Lakeland 10 times and saw no Bob Wilber on either list. Heck, I checked Montgomery as well, just to see if by some miracle I'd skipped Lakeland altogether and had instead been assigned to the Double-A Southern League. Nope.

I went back to my room and got dressed. I sat on my bed until 7 trying to remain calm while all the possibilities danced through my head. None of them made any sense. I hadn't been cut, but I couldn't find my name on a final roster.

Finally, I built up enough courage to walk over to the executive offices and as I approached I saw the Detroit general manager, Bill LaJoie. Without hesitation I said, "Good morning, Mister LaJoie. I'm a little confused. I didn't see my name on any roster." He actually looked a bit confused himself, as well as a little agitated, and he said "That must be a clerical error. You'll be staying right here. You're on the Lakeland roster. Sorry for the confusion, Bob."

My first feeling was relief. Enormous relief. My second feeling was still one of confusion, because the look on LaJoie's face said far more than the simpler answer of a clerical error. To this day I wonder if Fred Hatfield wanted me released but others above him in camp overruled him. From that point forward, Hatfield's grumpy attitude toward me only got worse.

We had two days off to find apartments and once I was certain I was on the Lakeland team I tracked down Roy and OC and we all agreed to live together. Three Paintsville boys were movin' on up to Lakeland.

Roy quickly found a really nice apartment near Florida Southern College, about 12 minutes from the ballpark. It was still full of the prior tenant's rental furniture, so I called the company to see if we could just take over the payments and keep everything. We could do that but we needed to come to their office in Tampa to write a check and sign the papers. Roy and I made the trip in my Fiesta.

We also all had to go to the Lakeland Tigers' business office in downtown Lakeland, to sign new contracts. That would be a good thing, because it meant we'd finally start getting paid. In spring training our housing and our meals were all provided, but we didn't get a salary. Now that the season was starting those big after-tax checks for roughly $240 every two weeks would start rolling in.

Once we were settled it was time to get back out to Marchant Stadium to move into our spacious new clubhouse. The benefit of playing in the Florida State League was that all the teams would play their 137-game seasons in ballparks that doubled as spring training homes for their Major League clubs. Our lockers were huge, the room was gigantic, and all the facilities were top-notch.

On the first day we got our home and away uniforms and immediately appreciated that we had two different looks. We had orange and white hats and orange socks at home, with white uniforms that had a script "Tigers" on a slant across the front, and on the road we wore gray unis with navy blue hats and navy blue socks. To us, that was first-class all the way.

Our socks were stirrups, of course. Nobody was wearing soccer socks back then, and in bit of a throwback our stirrups were very short. Only about two inches of white sanitary hose showed on the front and back, and we were prohibited from altering them. We did, though, work pretty diligently at stretching them a little. Just a bit.

Two unfortunate things happened to me as we filled our lockers and got our uniforms. The team had only three sets of pants my size, and there were four of us who wore that size. Since the other three guys were draft picks and considered major prospects, you can guess which one of the four got the pants that were one size too big. Considering how important it was for me to look bitchin' out there, that was just short of a crushing blow.

In addition, one of those three other guys also wanted the number five on his back and considering it was Howard Johnson, who would go on to a fine career with the Tigers and the Mets, there was no question about that one either. I wore number three.

Then, Hat came out into the room to give us a little talk, but all I remember was that he stopped by my locker after he was done and said, "Follow me to my office." Gulp. Here we go again.

Hat informed me that we had 28 players in the room but it was a strict league rule that we could not have more than 25 guys dressed for games. A pitcher named James Wheeler and I would start the year on the inactive list, and another pitcher was already on the long-term disabled list. We could work out during all the pregame stuff, but we'd have to put our street clothes back on and sit in the seats for the games. My immediate thought was, "You gotta be kidding me," but I only said, "Yes, sir." Let's just say that after all my years around professional baseball teams, I was a little skeptical of this supposed strict league rule.

We had a workout that night, getting used to the same lights the Detroit Tigers played under during the spring (lights that bore no resemblance to the candles we played beneath at Paintsville) and opened the season the next night in Daytona Beach, against the Astros.

In 1979 the Florida State League consisted of two divisions. Our division, the North, was made up of the Winter Haven Red Sox, the Tampa Tarpons (Reds), the Dunedin Blue Jays, the St. Petersburg Cardinals, and our Lakeland Tigers. The South was made up of the Fort Lauderdale Yankees, the West Palm Beach Expos, the Fort Myers Royals, the Miami Orioles, and the Daytona Beach Astros.

Because of the distances the Astros played a hybrid schedule, as if they were in the North and the South at the same time, but in the standings they were in the South. The rest of the teams in the two divisions each made just one long road trip through all the towns in the other division. Our trip was scheduled for late in the summer.

To open the season we loaded our bags into a first-class bus painted in Tigers colors with "Lakeland Tigers Professional Baseball Club" in big letters on each side. We made the trip up to Daytona Beach, got dressed in a fine visitors' clubhouse, then did our pre-game drills. I decided right then that I'd throw from left field during infield practice, then sprint to first base and take a couple of rounds of infield there, as well. If Hat didn't want to speak with me, he'd at least have to admire my determination. After that, Wheeler and I took showers and sat in the grandstand. I hated it.

As I recall, we opened the season with two games in Daytona Beach but we bused back to Lakeland after each one. And so it began wherein we all developed a quick distaste for games against the Astros. One-hour bus rides were easy. Even two-hour rides were nothing, but anything over three or four hours was a grind. Eight to 10-hour rides can be easier than a four-hour trip, because your brain accepts the challenge and you're ready for it.

To play the Astros we not only had to get to the Atlantic Ocean, we had to battle our way past Disney World and through Orlando. It could easily take three hours or longer to get to their park or back home, depending on how many wrecks on I-4 brought traffic to a standstill. That could mean leaving our park at noon and not getting back until 1 in the morning. It was no fun, and most of us didn't know each other that well yet, so there wasn't much camaraderie on the bus.

In the Appalachian League we all figured our jobs were safe for the whole season and probably until spring training. We pulled for each other. In Lakeland, we'd all just witnessed the anguish of guys getting released on a daily basis and everyone developed a look-out-for-yourself mentality to survive. I made a few good friends on that team, but it was nothing like the chemistry we had in Paintsville. Roy and OC were carryovers, and of course we lived together, but it took a while for me to connect with other guys in the clubhouse.

When we finished those two games with the Astros we returned for our home opener and quickly discovered an almost-universal fact about the Florida State League: Not too many people really cared we were there.

Starting our Class-A season just days after Major League spring training, I suspect the letdown for the locals was enormous. Looking at our "crowds" both at home and on the road it was clear a lot of people in Lakeland, or Tampa, or Dunedin, clearly didn't care the teams were around. St. Pete, however, featured a fine downtown stadium the retirees could walk to and they packed them in pretty well.

Our roster included the Tigers' first-round draft pick from 1977 but arm woes kept him on the shelf for much of his career. Kevin Richards was a nice enough guy but three years of being hurt had worn on him and most of the time he kept to himself. He was the guy on the disabled list, so also inactive, but I noticed during our home opener that he was staying in uniform and would be sitting in the dugout during the game.

I marched into Hat's office and said, "Look, Skip. I'm staying in uniform. It's hard enough not being active, but it's useless for me to sit in the seats." He rebutted me with the "official league rule" statement but I had an answer for him. I said, "Well, apparently that rule doesn't apply to number-one picks, because Kevin has stayed in uniform both games so far." He grumbled, looked unhappy, and said, "All right. Go ahead." One small victory in a difficult battle.

I still had one more critical problem. My pants remained too big. After a couple of games I asked the equipment guy if I could take my pants to a local tailor and have them taken in a little. He just shrugged his shoulders and said, "Sure. You gotta pay for it though." It was worth every penny.

I found a couple of local ladies who did such things, and by the next night I had form-fitting pants that looked totally bitchin'. My self-esteem finally began to improve.

And I also noticed another major challenge. It was going to be extremely important for me to take pregame practice and BP seriously. I could tell my skills were getting a little soft not playing in games, so I began getting to the ballpark earlier and working much harder.

We had a batting cage with a pitching machine next to the clubhouse, out in the right-field corner at Marchant Stadium, and I'd come out as early as 1 to fill the hopper full of balls and crank the machine up to its fastest speed. It probably only got the ball up there in the low 80s, though, so I began moving closer and closer to the machine, until it was only 50 feet away instead of 60, and then even 45 feet away instead of 50. And every day I'd hit hundreds of pitches before doing extra running in the outfield.

Once BP started, I took my position in one of the corner outfield spots, and played each ball hit to me like it was the real thing. My manager just grumbled at me and never smiled, so I had to do something to stay sane.

I was getting to know Howard Johnson pretty well and we got along great. He was four years younger, just 19 at the time, and while his natural athletic skills were phenomenal he needed a lot of polish to take his game to the next level. During BP the coaches would hit Ho-Jo hundreds of ground balls at third, so I took advantage of that by taking my spot at first. That way, he could fire them across the diamond to me to work on his throws as well. The kid had an amazing arm and it gave me a chance to work on that part of fielding at my new position.

He'd get frustrated at times, having made a big leap from his freshman year in junior college to high A-ball, and he sometimes needed to have his spirits picked up. He thought I was funny and he'd often sit next to me in the dugout during games, saying, "Make me laugh, Wilb. Make me laugh" if he was having a particularly rough night.

Howard Bailey was a left-handed starting pitcher from Michigan and he and I quickly realized we hit it off pretty well, too. We'd even frequent the local bars after home games once in a while, with our two favorites being the bar inside the Holiday Inn out by the interstate and a little pool hall called The Hu Ke Lau, just down the road from my apartment.

I discovered the cutthroat attitude at this level made it better to be friends with guys who played a different position. It was easier to root for those guys and care about how they did. The rest of us were simply focused on survival.

Roy was the obvious exception to that rule, and while I was still inactive he wasn't cracking the lineup very often either, so we could pull for each other. OC, frustratingly, was still not 100 percent healthy coming off the thumb injury that kept him sidelined for most of the year in Paintsville.

John Crawford was a talented catcher but he was a unique guy in a position the rest of us couldn't fathom. Like Judson Thigpen, he'd also been drafted out of Delta State University and had played against me in the NCAA Division II World Series. He was assigned directly to Lakeland in '78, so he was back for a second year. He was a fine player and a nice guy but he'd had enough and wanted to go home. The Tigers would certainly let him do that but if he quit he'd have to pay his own travel costs. If they released him, they'd pay to send him home. He demanded his release and the Tigers refused. For a month, he played for us on the Lakeland team while not wanting to be there. I don't recall who won that stalemate but it surely confused the rest of us. We were dying to stay and he was dying to leave.

The league's setup created a blur of games and bus rides, since there was only one real road trip on the schedule. We'd commute to all the other towns in our division, as well as Daytona

Beach, usually playing single home games between trips to St. Pete, Dunedin, Winter Haven, or Tampa. I much preferred the home games because I could go to the park as early as I wanted and get in my extra work.

The Daytona rides never got any better and I recall telling Roy one morning, on the day of a scheduled trip, that I almost wished I was hurt — then I wouldn't have to make that awful bumper-to-bumper trip.

Finally, due to a couple of injuries suffered by other guys, I was activated. But I still didn't play for a week. Everything began to feel like a waste of time.

Then, in front of another fine crowd at Al Lang Stadium in St. Pete while playing the team that had the birds on the bat embroidered on their jerseys, our big first-baseman Mike Wright argued with the umpire after he was called out to end an inning. The argument escalated and Mike blew his stack. He got ejected from the game and stormed through the dugout into the clubhouse while I looked on, dumbfounded. It was the most emotion I'd seen from anyone on the team all year. But it wasn't surprising that it was coming from Mike because the Tigers had drafted him out of Vanderbilt, where he had also played three years as the Commodores' starting quarterback. Football is a game fueled by emotion.

And then I heard Hat's voice from the other end of the dugout.

He said, "Wilber, you're at first base." I hadn't even thought of that. My first Florida State League action was going to be at a position I'd only just started learning. I hopped up the steps and trotted out there, still carrying the prehistoric old mitt the Tigers had given me in camp.

And because trouble always finds the new guy, the first hitter grounded out (I caught the throw just fine) but the next singled and the third hitter popped a bloop into right. The runner took off from first, assuming it would fall for a hit, but I hung by the bag to see if it would be caught and sure enough our right-fielder, Cliff Wilder, made a running shoestring catch and fired the ball to me, trying to double up the runner to end the inning. His throw was a bit short but I dug it out of the dirt like I knew what I was doing. What I didn't do quite so well was keep my right foot on the base. I knew I'd pulled it off a split-second before I caught the ball and I had a just a blink of a moment to sarcastically think, "Oh, that's gonna go over great with Hat," but then I heard the umpire yell "He's out!" and I calmly trotted off the field and dropped the ball on the mound as I passed it. The same umpire blew two calls in one inning. One cost Mike Wright an ejection and a fine, the other helped me not look like a fool.

In the next half-inning, I came up to bat. The Cardinals pitcher was a knuckleballer and I'd faced him in Johnson City the year before. When his knuckler was working it wobbled and darted so much it wasn't just hard to hit, it was hard to catch. My theory on knuckleballs was to be aggressive at the plate. He wasn't going to throw it by me so I moved well forward in the batter's box and as soon as I'd see one that looked like a strike, I'd hack at it.

His first pitch was indeed a knuckler but it basically didn't break and I hit it right on the button. Line drive, base hit. In my first at-bat.

Before it was time to go back on the field I walked back up into the clubhouse and found Mike Wright still stewing in there. I quietly said "Hey man, do you think I could borrow your first-baseman's mitt? This thing they gave me is horrible." He smiled, laughed a little, and said "No problem, Wilb. Good luck out there." and he tossed it to me.

As it turned out, I would be 1-for-1 and batting 1.000 for another 10 games. It was enormously frustrating and I had a number of teammates sit next to me in the dugout on various nights, saying things like, "What's going on? Why aren't you playing? You look like a good player to me." I didn't have an answer for them.

Maybe it was our apartment that was at fault. Frankly, for three guys making up almost one-eighth of the Lakeland roster we weren't doing much. OC was still not fully recovered from the bad thumb he'd had since we met, and he had only a couple of plate appearances on the season. Roy was playing more than us but it wasn't going that well for him, either. He'd played in only a handful of games and was hitting well under .200, so as a group we would often reconvene after a game in the apartment and wonder aloud, "What the heck are we all doing here?" I'm not sure any of us really knew. It was a frustrating way to make $600 a month.

About a week and a half after my appearance in St. Pete we made the bus ride over to Dunedin to play the Blue Jays. To that point in the Toronto Blue Jays' short history the big league expansion franchise had been awful, losing over 100 games each season. The fruits of their scouting labor were beginning to bloom, however, in Dunedin. Future big-league stars Luis Leal and Dave Stieb were on the team as dominant pitchers, while Geno Petralli and Fred Manrique stood out as position players who would make a solid mark someday soon in Toronto, as well. But one outfielder didn't just stand out. He was one of those rare talents who bore very little resemblance to the rest of us. He was Lloyd Moseby.

I played against a lot of guys who went on to successful Major League careers, including the klutzy teenager in Bluefield named Ripken. Usually, they were clearly more talented than a typical Class-A player but Moseby was different. He looked like a big-leaguer, a proverbial man among boys. He was far different than the rest of us.

Lloyd was 19 years old that summer. He was 6-foot-3, 200 pounds, and all muscle. He was the classic five-tool player who could hit, hit with power, run, field, and throw. When he came to the plate, you paid attention.

One night, earlier in the season at Marchant Stadium in Lakeland, Lloyd got into a fastball and hit it a ton. Had it not hit the lights on one of the massive towers in right field, NASA might still be tracking it.

I was looking forward to watching him again that night after we made the 90-minute drive over to the small beachside community of Dunedin, just north of Clearwater. When we arrived in the visitors clubhouse I was aware of Hat having a chat with one of our regular outfielders. Soon after he came over to my locker and said, "Listen, he can't go tonight. You're in right field."

I was actually starting.

But, just to keep me grounded, I overheard two pitchers having a conversation about the situation and one of them said, "Roberson can't go tonight. Who the heck is going to play right field? One of us?" The other pitcher said "Maybe. No, wait — Wilber is an outfielder!" Yes, as a matter of fact, I was. Or at least I used to be. And hey, pal, I was still hitting 1.000 after that scalding rope I laced off the knuckleballer.

On the mound for the Blue Jays that night was Luis Leal. The same side-arm-throwing Luis Leal who would make his big league debut the next season and pitch six successful years in the American League.

Also on that Dunedin team was a huge right-handed pitcher by the name of Nick Baltz, who had been a senior at SIUE when I was a freshman. We only played against each other in practice, and Nick was a 6-foot-6 dominating presence, so I spoke to him in reverential tones when he was a Cougar. He originally signed with the Expos after college and pitched one year in the Florida State League for them, but was let go. He then pitched a year for an independent team in Baton Rouge before landing in Beeville, Texas, with Stan Osterbur and Bill Lee in 1977, making that quite a little SIUE reunion down there among the tumbleweeds.

After going 12-5 in Beeville, Nick caught the eye of the Blue Jays and he spent the next three years in their organization. In 1979, on this night, he was in Dunedin and sitting in the bullpen, located in the corner down the right field line. Right next to me. He verbally rode me like a rented mule all night but it was all in good fun and it kept me loose. I think that was his plan, actually.

It was a little odd to be out there to start the game. It was just as odd to feel how odd it felt. In some ways it felt like the first day of camp because I was thinking too much and not doing things instinctively, but when a runner on first tried to get all the way to third on a single to right, and my throw nailed him by five feet, it felt like baseball again.

At the plate, I knew Leal would be a handful, and he struck me out my first time up. His delivery was odd, as he spun around during his windup, showing the entire back of his uniform to any hitter, then whirled and threw what began appearing to be an overhand pitch but which ended up being almost a side-arm delivery. He had good velocity and a lot of sink on his fastball. He threw what we called a "heavy" fastball because even if you hit it square, it still seemed to knock the bat back in your hands.

In the fourth inning I came up with one out and the bases loaded. Yes, the importance of this at-bat was not lost on me. If I could put the ball in play off a tough pitcher and drive in a run, I might, just possibly, get to play some more. I went up there looking for his fastball and I got one. I crushed it. Directly to the shortstop.

It was a hard shot that would've gone through for a hit if it had been two feet to the left or right, but it went right to him on one short hop and after a flip to second and a relay to first they had a double play and were out of the inning. I had nothing. I went 0-for-4 that night, but it felt good to get back out there and I knew I'd hit a couple of balls hard. Sometimes they go right at the wrong guys.

After the game we got on the bus still in uniform. OC sat next to me and he said, "How did that feel?" I pointed to the dirt on my pants and replied, "It feels good to be dirty. I just wish that ball would've gone through."

And there's the rub. If you're playing regularly, the next chance for that ball to go through would come the next day. I had no idea when my next chance would come. I assumed it wouldn't be soon.

A few days later, we had a doubleheader scheduled in Lakeland and a circus broke out. Literally.

Before the first game a representative from Ringling Brothers came into our clubhouse and told us that one of their tightrope walkers was going to walk a wire between the two huge light towers in right field, and that they'd need some players to hold ropes that would steady the wire. I wanted absolutely no part of it, and as I was plotting my escape to get out of the room he said "Actually, I think we're going to need all of you." Wonderful.

The wire looked to be 1,000 feet in the air. It was probably about 120 and the towers were at least 125 feet apart. Five long ropes were looped over the top of the wire, and four of us would be holding each rope, with each group placing two guys in right field and two outside the outfield wall. I'd be on the playing-field side and my partner on the rope would be Howard Johnson.

When the walker took his first step we could feel the vibration travel down the ropes and right into our hands. To keep it tight, we each wrapped the rope around our wrists once and we leaned back to put some weight on it. As the walker stepped over the looped rope we were holding, I could honestly feel a man's life in my hands. I couldn't wait for him to get to the other side. Ho-Jo and I said nothing to each other. Nobody did.

The walker finally got to the other side and I exhaled. And then he turned around to go back in the other direction. He pulled out all the tricks on the return walk, standing on one foot, sitting on the wire, spinning around twice. I wanted nothing more in the entire world than for that guy, carrying his long pole, to just plain stop it.

When he got to our rope again, Ho-Jo whispered "Wilb, I think I'm gonna jiggle our rope a little." I whispered, "Ho-Jo, if you do that you'll kill the guy. And then you'll die too, because I'll kill you." Mercifully, it was soon over and nobody died.

A night or two later, just to keep the fun at a fevered pitch, we rode over to St. Pete to play the Cardinals again. I didn't play. But — and this was a big but — Kevin Richards pitched. Yes, the same Kevin Richards who'd been hurt for three years and who didn't take off his uniform for games our first week. Being a bit rusty, he was wild and hit a guy. I know he didn't mean to but the Cardinals were all chirping lustily from their dugout.

In the next half-inning the Cardinals' pitcher hit one of our guys. And we started shouting threats from our dugout. When Kevin then purposefully plunked a Cardinal in the next inning, all hell broke loose and both teams raced toward the mound. We had a full-tilt bench-clearing brawl on our hands.

I'm proud to say I was the first guy to the top step of the dugout and on the field but what I saw out there bore little resemblance to the few baseball fights I'd been in previously, where most of what happened was two guys rolled around in the dirt while everyone else paired off with a member of the other team and did the old "Hold me back" routine. In St. Pete that night, by the time I crossed the third-base line every Cardinal I saw had absolute hatred in their eyes and once we all got out there by the mound you needed a second set of eyeballs in the back of your head, because haymakers were being thrown from all directions.

I made a quick decision to run straight at someone in a Cardinals uniform who was about my size and I tackled him. On the way to the ground I said, "Just stay down. If you try to get up we're both going to get hit." That actually worked. For a minute, while order was restored by the umpires, this anonymous Cardinal and I held each other back. I'm not afraid to admit I was terrified when I arrived in the middle of that donnybrook, but I survived it.

We got back to Lakeland to play the Blue Jays again and the word quickly spread that Dave Miller was in town from Detroit. Dave was the head of minor league operations for the organization and he was in Florida to look at our struggling club.

That night, something unique happened. In the sixth inning, Hat came down to me on the bench and said, "Get loose. You'll finish the game in right field." It was the only time I'd appear in a game because the manager had made the decision to insert me. Nobody was hurt and nobody had been thrown out of the game.

As I trotted out there I could see Dave Miller sitting well down the line, all by himself. I wasn't so much nervous as I was disoriented. It was my first appearance at Marchant Stadium and we were under the lights. It had been so long since I'd been out there for a night game I wasn't exactly sure where I should be and the outfield looked enormous. These are things that had been natural to me for many years but on that night it all felt strange. Fortunately, the balls that did come my way were easy plays and I handled them fine.

At the plate I got one at-bat and this time I think I fully realized my career was on the line, with Dave Miller in the seats. I battled my butt off against a hard-throwing right-hander, and I finally hit a ball fairly hard but the third-baseman made a nice backhanded play and threw me out. I was 1-for-6 on the year. Six entire at-bats. That equates to a .167 average, though the sample size was miniscule. Put it this way: Had any one of those hard-hit balls made it through, I would've been hitting .333. I'll admit I was relieved Dave Miller wasn't waiting at my locker after the game.

The next day we had a road game in Winter Haven and it was pay day. Unlike Paul Fyffe in Paintsville, who deposited our checks directly into the bank, the owner in Lakeland brought them to the ballpark on the appointed day and handed them out. Before we got on the bus Hat told us the owner was running late and we'd get our checks when we returned. So I got on the bus.

For some reason I chose to sit in the bullpen that night after it was clear that I, shockingly, would not be playing. Our pitching coach, Billy Moffett, was out there with our relievers and I liked Billy a lot. He'd pitched for the Cardinals when I was growing up and he knew my parents fairly well.

Early in the game I tried to keep things loose out there with a few patented one-liners but I got the impression Billy was either distracted or worried about something else. He barely acknowledged me when I spoke. It just felt odd.

We finished the game and got back on the bus still in uniform and when we got back to Marchant Stadium to shower, Billy came over to my locker and said, "Hat needs to see you in his office."

Like many before me, it was my turn to die.

I went in and closed the door. Hat said, "We don't think you can play at the Major League level and we don't think it's worth anyone's time or money to send you to Bristol, so the big club has made the decision to release you. We knew that before the game but the paycheck thing got us a little messed up and you were on the bus. I wasn't going to pull you off the bus in front of everyone to do this. Do you have anything you want to say?"

I had a million things I wanted to say. I also knew none of them would make a difference. I just said "Nope" and walked out.

There's a horrible silence in the room when someone comes out of the manager's office because all of the other guys know why he was in there. This time it was me. Everyone just looked at their feet and mumbled in muffled tones. I didn't even take a shower. I just got dressed and left.

Out in the parking lot, OC and Roy were waiting for me and they both looked as crushed as I did. As it turned out, the Grim Reaper would be coming for both of them within a week or so. OC's career would offer him one more shot in 1980, in Visalia of the California League, but he only played in 35 games and hit just .119 in 84 at-bats. Roy hit just .143 in Lakeland before the Tigers let him go and then he went out to Bakersfield to finish the summer playing for Yank Mihal again. Out there he hit just .123 to end his career.

That's the mystery that is baseball. Roy Dixon could play. He was good. He was as fine an outfielder as any I'd ever played with but in Lakeland and Bakersfield it all went away. Dan O'Connor was a real prospect when the Tigers signed him. He was big and strong, he could hit, and he was a fine catcher. He was good, but fate conspired to make all that meaningless. The same thing happened to me.

Baseball can humble you in a hurry.

The technical "cause" of my release had to do with the Tigers' first-round draft pick just days before. They'd selected Rick Leach, out of the University of Michigan. Leach had been a heck of a quarterback for the Wolverines, but he was an even better baseball player and the Tigers decided to put him right into the Florida State League, just like they'd done with Kirk Gibson the year before. Somebody on the Lakeland club had to go in order to make room for Leach. That someone was me. I suspect it was Dave Miller who told Hat to put me in the game that night and it would've been Dave who made the decision. I just wish I could've made the decision a much more difficult one to make.

We went back to the apartment and I called my folks. Skip was pretty upset at the way the team had mishandled me since the first week of spring training but it was me talking him back from the ledge instead of the other way around. I said, "Hey, if I'd played better, Hat wouldn't have had a choice in the matter. I didn't play well enough and I was an idiot on top of it. I should never have let that ingrown toenail get so bad and get so infected. That happened right during the most important part of spring training. I just ignored it, and that was me just being stupid."

I found it interesting that I wasn't going to miss too many of the guys on that team. We had almost zero chemistry and unlike Paintsville, where we bonded as brothers, most of the guys in the Lakeland clubhouse were just players. We were much more mercenaries than teammates.

That's not to say we didn't have fun. Baseball players are, almost by nature, funny guys. We could crack each other up easily, the banter was always loose and easy, and it's generally that way with just about any team, at any level. We were just a group of funny guys together in a clubhouse, or on a bus, or in the dugout. Very few of those guys felt like brothers to me. Maybe that was because I was so rarely in the trenches with them.

I'd miss Howard Bailey and he'd soon be in the big leagues. I'd miss Ho-Jo and he'd not only soon be in the big leagues, he'd also soon be in the World Series. If you've ever seen the classic footage of Mookie Wilson's dribbler going right between poor Bill Buckner's legs, allowing Ray Knight of the Mets to score the improbable winning run in Game Six against the Red Sox, it's Howard Johnson who meets Knight at the plate to give him a hug. Beyond those guys and my roomies, I didn't feel much of anything.

There's a lot of hard work that goes into every day of the season and it's a grind well beyond what most fans know, but it's all worth it when you get to play. When you don't, all you get is the grind.

My strong feeling that baseball is a game and should be fun was put to the test in Lakeland. It hadn't been much fun at all because I hadn't played in many games. I doubt it was a ton of fun for a lot of the Lakeland boys that year. The team finished 50-87 and in last place, 29 games out of first.

I wasn't in a huge hurry to get home, so I went out to the park early the next morning and cleaned out my locker. That afternoon I actually smiled a bit when the team got on the bus for another dreaded ride to Daytona Beach. I didn't have to be injured to miss that ride — I just had to be unemployed.

Then I loaded up the Fiesta and hit the road, heading north. I stopped in Atlanta for the night (at a Holiday Inn, of course) and drove to Kirkwood the next day. I pulled into the driveway just before dusk on that June evening and the next chapter presented itself to me when my mother came running out of the front door to meet me. Her words stunned me beyond measure. It was time to plow forward, yet again.

A Quick Change Of Plans

I had 1,000 miles and a lot of time to reflect on things as I drove north and I had no good reason to think anything other than my lifelong dream was finally dead. The Lakeland experience had sapped most of my confidence.

When I came to a halt in the driveway on Woodleaf Court, I leaned back in my seat and took a deep breath. Then I saw my mother bolting out the front door and down the front steps, yelling something I couldn't quite make out.

I opened my car door just as she approached the front fender and I finally understood what she was saying.

She was shouting, "You're an Oakland A! You're an Oakland A!"

The most articulate response I could formulate at the moment was "What?"

She breathlessly tried to explain but either her words were jumbled or my brain was too fried to process it, so I calmly said, "Let's go inside, and you can tell me all about it."

We sat at the dining room table and she told me in one long rambling sentence that the Oakland A's had called, and that they wanted me to go somewhere up in the Pacific Northwest, she couldn't remember exactly the name of the team, but that they wanted me there right away. That was about it for details, as far as Taffy could remember.

As it turns out, there's a background story.

Charlie Finley still owned the Oakland A's, although that worried the commissioner's office. After winning three straight World Series titles in the early 1970s, Finley saw the dawn of the free agency era looming and surmised that salaries were going to skyrocket. Being a notoriously frugal man he immediately began to dismantle an A's team that had dominated baseball and he did so by selling off his stars before they could leave as free agents. Reggie Jackson, Catfish Hunter, Sal Bando, Joe Rudi, and many others were literally dumped in a fire sale, while Commissioner Bowie Kuhn butted heads with Finley every step of the way trying to stop the insanity by invoking the "best interests of baseball" clause.

Despite Kuhn's efforts, Finley was winning the battle to demolish his own franchise. In Finley's mind, if he couldn't keep the lid on salaries with free agency becoming a reality he'd go out trying to embarrass the commissioner who was letting free agency happen. It was a war of egos.

Even in their championship years the A's were never a threat to lead the American League in attendance, and once the stars left town the fans deserted the team altogether. To make it worse, with the club in a classic financial death spiral, Finley kept cutting costs as the income dried up. For a month, in 1978, he hired the campus radio-station at the University of California-Berkeley to satisfy Major League Baseball's insistence that all clubs have broadcasting outlets. Two college students did the play-by-play for what must've been a wonderful 30-day span but the station had a signal that only covered the campus and it did not even reach the Oakland Coliseum.

With no stars, no promotions, and effectively no radio, the A's basically disappeared from the sports radar screen in the Bay Area. On April 17, 1979, when I was in Lakeland marveling at playing in front of 550 fans or less at Marchant Stadium, the Oakland A's played a Major League Baseball game in front of about 250 souls in their 50,000-seat stadium. To be fair, 653 tickets had been sold for the game but first baseman Dave Revering took the time to count the crowd a few times and each time the total number ranged from 235 to 265. The official attendance, in the box score, reflects the number of tickets sold but the A's players universally agreed upon the 250 figure. They said they could hear individual conversations in the stands. It's easy to understand why the players started to refer to their home park as the Oakland Mausoleum.

With attendance and enthusiasm nearly nonexistent Finley kept working toward his quest of imploding the franchise by stripping the organization of its staff. By '79 the A's front office consisted of six employees, one of whom was Finley who had named himself general manager while another was a local teenager by the name of Stanley Burrell. Stanley originally joined the club when Finley saw him selling baseballs in the parking lot while dancing to a boombox, and he told the lad he wanted that energy and passion on display inside the park as a bat boy. Players began to call him "Little Hammer" because he looked like a young version of the real Hammer, Hank Aaron.

While still a teen, he would be given the title of executive vice president but his role was actually to be Finley's eyes and ears. That was necessary because Finley had become a full-time absentee owner, preferring not to be anywhere near what few baseball fans were left in Oakland. Stanley Burrell later changed his name to MC Hammer. Yes, that MC Hammer. Can't touch this. Or make it up.

Finley also decided scouts were a waste of money so the A's only reviewed information gathered from independent scouting services, then weighed those recommendations against the pesky need for signing bonuses. It made no sense for Oakland to draft top-notch talent because Finley would never part with the money necessary to sign such players.

When the 1979 June draft was completed the A's managed to sign their second pick, pitcher Mark Ferguson, their 15th pick, pitcher Keith Call, and their 34th and final pick, catcher John Pignotti. That was it. Outfielder Oscar Burnett, their sixth-round pick, wanted to sign but was attempting to negotiate. They had just three draft picks signed and a fourth on the hook, but they also had a club in the Class-A short-season Northwest League that needed to be stocked with living and breathing young men and that team would open its season in days.

The Medford A's, based in Medford, Oregon, were that Class-A team at the bottom of the organizational chart for the team that ranked at the bottom of every metric in baseball. All Finley really wanted to do was dump the A's and walk away but his battle with Bowie Kuhn was personal and, as retribution, he intended to embarrass Major League Baseball. Even so, he had to maintain a minimum farm system and that meant the Medford A's needed players.

Finley did three things. First, he compiled a list of free-agent college players who were good enough to have earned attention from the scouting services but who had gone undrafted, and he sent out feelers to many of them. Second, he re-assigned a handful of players to Medford from the organization's advanced Class-A club, the Modesto A's in the California League. Third, he called in some to help to scour the wire for names of recently released Class-A players who had a pulse and could walk, talk, and chew gum, and who also might be willing to play in the Northwest League. My last name caught someone's eye (I have never known exactly who it was) and a call was made to the front office in Detroit, where word apparently was passed along that my lack of playing time in Lakeland was not totally due to an utter lack of talent. The manager of the Medford team, Rich Morales, then called our home in Kirkwood. I was somewhere north of Atlanta, driving home.

My mother had taken the call and in those days prior to cell phones she had to wait nearly 24 hours to tell me the news. Knowing her son well, she had promised Morales that I would sign and that she'd make sure I got out there in a hurry. It's a good thing I drove home in two days.

That night, after I arrived home, I got a call from a woman who was the administrative assistant to Charlie Finley. She sounded about as excited to hold that position as one might imagine, but at least she had the details I required. I needed to be in Medford the next day and my flight to Portland, which would connect to a flight to Medford, left Lambert Airport in St. Louis at 6 in the morning. I barely had time to do my laundry.

After driving 1,000 miles in two days and then not sleeping much that night thanks to a whirling mass of wonder, excitement, confusion, and anxiety, combined with a 4 a.m. alarm and the fact I was on the sofa, I was exhausted when I got on the plane. I was still in that state when I walked down the steps from the small prop-driven puddle-jumper that had taken me from Portland to Medford. Once again it was time to just keep plowing forward, although I was having a hard time keeping my eyes open.

My instructions were to take a taxi to the old Medford Hotel in the center of the city and once there I learned my roommate for the next couple of days was already in the room. He was John Pignotti, Oakland's final pick in the draft, from Claremont College in California and he had beaten me to Medford by a day.

I rode a lurching elevator up a few floors, wandered down the musty hallway, and knocked on the door to our room. John seemed like a nice guy and after a few minutes of pleasantries he said, "You look beat. Why don't you take a nap while I go out and look for an apartment. If I can find one, and you want to room with me, we can do that. We have to be out of this place by tomorrow." Sounded fine to me.

It was roughly 11 a.m. when I put my head on the pillow. Just 24 hours earlier I had been driving through Tennessee on my way home. Baseball players will go to enormous lengths to keep their careers alive, usually without much deep analytical thought but almost always with a great deal of desperation. Players like John Crawford in Lakeland, who wanted to go home but couldn't get the Tigers to release him, were extremely rare. The rest of us would have to be told to go home, often repeatedly.

I awoke when John came back to the room a few hours later and told me he had two critical pieces of news. I collected myself and remembered where I was, why I was there, and who he might be, and then attempted to listen carefully. First, he had found an apartment, although it was basically just a large studio. Secondly, we needed to head out to the ballpark to sign our contracts because our season would start the next night.

We went straight to Miles Field, out on the south edge of town, and as we walked in I smiled. It was a classic old minor-league park with a nice covered grandstand which, combined with some bleachers, held about 3,000 fans. As groggy as I was, I also had been looking around as John drove us through Medford and I liked what I saw. There was a huge lumber facility across the road from the ballpark and the smell of freshly cut trees wafted through the air.

As we entered through a side gate, a handsome man with an A's cap on walked toward us, stuck out his hand and said, "Hi, guys. I'm Rich Morales. I'll be your manager." When I told him my name he smiled broadly, then said "I'm really glad you're here, Bob. If you didn't make it by noon tomorrow we were going to have to sign someone off the street to have 18 guys on the roster. That's the league minimum. You'll be starting in left field tomorrow night."

All of this sounded great to me and the fact my contract was for $700 per month was even better. We met Doug Emmans, the team owner, when we signed and he was excited to get the season started. "This town is buzzing about the team," he said. "They haven't had a club to root for since 1971. You're going to love playing here." It felt like an alternate universe where my services were wanted, the owner was excited, and the manager planned to play me.

Rich then gave us a quick tour of the park. I was familiar with my new skipper because I remembered him from his playing days with the White Sox. He was a slick-fielding infielder who couldn't hit a lick, which is easy for me to say. Of all the non-pitchers who had played Major League ball since 1930, with 1,000 or more at-bats, only two guys (Ray Oyler and Mike Ryan) had lower career batting averages than Rich's .195 mark. He was a friendly outgoing guy making his managerial debut with us. What a treat that would be for everyone involved.

As part of our tour, Rich then took us to the clubhouse. After spending the last couple of months in Lakeland, in a spacious clubhouse made for big-leaguers, I was in for a bit of a shock when we entered the small building behind the third-base dugout. Roughly a third of the building was a concession stand. The rest was what approximated a clubhouse.

It was one small room, rectangular in shape, certainly no bigger than 15 x 20, and there were no lockers. Behind a corner was a bathroom and a few showers.

Around the edge of the main room ran a wooden bench attached to the cinderblock walls. Above the bench, all around the room at a height of about six feet, a series of 2 x 4s were bolted to the wall and nails were pounded into the wood to act as hooks. Morales pointed to a spot on the bench, and said, "That's your spot, Bob. And those are your three nails." Still fatigued after traveling by car and plane diagonally from one corner of the country to another, I wasn't sure if I wanted to laugh or cry, but I was heavily leaning toward laughing. Plow forward!

We unpacked our duffel bags, stuffed them under the bench to mark our territory as others had, and told our new skipper we'd see him early tomorrow. "Get here as early as you can," he said. "These uniforms are relics and it might take us a while to find stuff for everyone." We were in for an adventure.

As we walked back out to the car I saw an old rusted pile of junk that vaguely reminded me of a bus. "Wow, look at that old thing," I said. "Yeah," John said. "That's our bus." I was sure he was kidding. He wasn't.

The bus looked prehistoric and it was indeed (I learned soon thereafter) a 1940s-era former Greyhound. It had tiny little windows, a small windshield, and a pair of split windows in the back. John said Doug Emmans had bought it for the grand sum of $1,500.

John also suggested I take a look inside and what I saw had me shaking my head even harder. The interior looked completely original and the dust was so thick I couldn't see out of the windshield. This heap looked more like a barn find than a working vehicle, and I had an inkling this was going to be fun — if by "fun" you meant not fun at all.

I hadn't yet bothered to look to see what other towns made up the rest of the league, so while John drove us back toward town I looked at a schedule we'd picked up in the owner's office.

The Northwest League was split into two divisions. The North was made up of the Bellingham Mariners, the Victoria Mussels, the Walla Walla Padres, and the Gray's Harbor Mets. The good news was we'd only make one trip to each of those towns. The bad news was I had only heard of Bellingham and Walla Walla. I had no idea where Gray's Harbor or Victoria were. John didn't know where Gray's Harbor was either but he said "I'm pretty sure Victoria is in British Columbia, on an island." He was correct. And Victoria was nearly 600 miles from Medford. We'd be going there, apparently, on a bus that looked like a vintage movie prop.

In the South we were joined by the Central Oregon Phillies (based in Bend, Oregon), the Salem Senators, and the Eugene Emeralds. All four teams were Oregon-based, with Salem, Eugene, and Medford all on I-5, so that sounded easy enough. Bend, however, was in the middle of the state. We'd be playing those three teams a lot and our schedule had us playing 72 total games, at home and on the road, in the next 73 days.

Our first stop after leaving the ballpark was the apartment John had found that morning and after signing our lease I got to check it out. It was sort of a studio, in that a half-wall separated the living area and kitchen from the lone queen bed, and it was fully furnished, but there was only that one bed. John said "Don't worry about it. You take the bed, and I'll go buy an air mattress or sleep on the sofa."

The unit was in a nice complex made up of three buildings in a U shape, with a pool and hot tub situated in the middle, surrounded by a grassy lawn. It looked like it was going to be a fine place to stay and when we pulled in I noticed a couple of cars with Oakland A's bumper stickers on them. A bunch of guys were sitting around the pool, so we went out there to meet them.

They seemed like really good guys and one of them was Mark Ferguson, the A's pick in the second round of the draft just days before, while another was Keith Call, the 15th pick. Those two and Pignotti represented three quarters of the draft picks the A's would be able to sign. Oscar Burnett was still negotiating with Finley and wasn't in town yet. I didn't like his chances of getting what he wanted.

I met a pitcher that day named Craig Harris who had actually been drafted in 1977 in the first round by the A's, as the 17th overall pick in the draft. He'd signed out of high school and had done so before Finley had declared all-out war against Kuhn, so he got a sizable bonus. The unfortunate thing for Craig, whom everyone called Harry, was that he'd suffered from arm problems since he signed and here he was back in Medford in 1979, his third year in the Oakland organization. I guess if we had one big name on the team, it would've been Harry.

We weren't going to be able to officially move into the apartment until the next day, which gave us some time to take care of a few details. We found a bank a block away and opened checking accounts so that when we got paid twice a month we had a place to put our riches. We bought sheets, towels, and pillows, and John (whom I was already calling Pig, for short) bought an air mattress.

The next stop was a local sporting goods store to see if we could find white spikes. We were, after all, now playing for the A's so the white shoes were part of the uniform. I was lucky enough to find a pair of adidas in my size, but the three stripes on each side were also white and I wanted green stripes. So, I bought a couple of green Magic Markers and later that night I customized my new kicks.

I also called Rawlings to see if they'd consider sending me a first-baseman's mitt. Despite the fact I had already claimed 100 percent of my contracted goods, they agreed to expedite one to Medford. "Maybe we can just put it against next year's allotment," the rep said. I could only hope.

In the morning, Pig and I officially got our apartment keys and unloaded the few personal items we had then had lunch before heading out to Miles Field. Most of the guys were already there and I worked my way around the room introducing myself.

Then we got our uniforms. Rich was right. They were relics.

The Lakeland Tigers and Paintsville Hilanders had supplied their players with new custom-designed unis but the Medford A's were continuing an old tradition: They used hand-me-downs.

For opening night we wore all-white A's uniforms that had been passed down from the big leagues, to Double-A, to A-ball, and finally to short-season A-ball in Medford. My pants had at least four names written inside the waistband, with all of them crossed out but the most recent. The only one left legible was the last name Nottle. They had belonged to a career minor-leaguer named Ed Nottle and he had worn them in 1978 when he managed the A's club in the Northwest League. That club, however, was in Bend. I figured I had the best pair of pants in the clubhouse if they had belonged to the skipper the year before, and as if fate was smiling on me, one of the prior recipients of those pants actually had them taken in to make them tighter!

The problems with our jerseys were many. Some had missing numbers, others were stained, and the only reason we had enough to go around was because we didn't yet have a full roster of 25 guys. In addition, we didn't have road uniforms and those are pretty essential since all home teams wore white. Rich had implored Doug Emmans to buy us a new set and he did, but they weren't in yet. They would be Kelly Green so we could wear them at home or on the road, and we'd wear the white pants all the time.

Then we met Mike Altobelli, who had just arrived from Chicago after going undrafted out of the University of St. Francis. With that introduction the summer of 1979 took a huge leap forward. Pig met him first as we all strolled around our new ballpark hours before BP. Within minutes we were all best buddies and "Alto" agreed to also move into the apartment with us, to split the rent three ways. Somehow, the two Italians insisted I keep the queen bed and said they would sleep in the living room. Seemed silly to me but they refused any other option. They said it was because I was the veteran and they were rookies, so who was I to argue?

We were all antsy to get on the field and play our opener but Morales wanted us to sit tight so that we could have a meeting. We were in a new town, with a new team, around new teammates, and in a new league, so we had plenty to talk about. We established some rudimentary signs for the night, while Rich added that we'd get a little more complex with them as we went along. For the opener, he just wanted to be able to signal when to steal or when to bunt.

We went over a number of small issues like that and then Rich wrapped up the meeting by looking at all of us, seated on our communal bench under our nails, saying, "Listen. I better not see or hear anyone acting in the least bit cocky this whole summer. Basically, all this team is made up of is a bunch of guys nobody else wanted. We're nothing more than a team of free agents who just happen to be wearing four-year-old Oakland A's uniforms. Now let's get to work."

We hit the field and starting batting practice but it only took a minute for all of us to recognize the next great problem involved with being the stepchildren in the Oakland organization. The netting on our batting cage was so torn, frayed, patched, and full of holes, it was useless.

The whole idea of using a cage for BP is to keep foul balls and errant pitches in a confined area, while it also allows each group of hitters to collectively stand very nearby while one guy hits. After one player gets his 15 swings the next hitter can jump right in. With balls flying right through this thing, we all had to stand way back to avoid getting clobbered. Rich promised he'd get the owner to buy a new net for the cage, to go with our new jerseys, but the way things were shaping up I began to wonder if the lights at Miles Field would actually come on when someone flipped the switch.

The lights did come on. We had a nice introduction before the game, with each of us shaking hands with the owner, Doug, before taking our places on the third-base line, and we looked around at a near-capacity crowd in the stands.

On the other side of the field were the Central Oregon Phillies, who had arrived in a spacious and modern tour bus with Phillies' logos all over it. When I saw it pull in, I looked longingly in its direction. It was a Lamborghini compared to our Yugo.

Once the national anthem was played it was time to take the field. I ran out to left both excited and nervous, glad to still be playing the game but wondering how I'd do considering I had played almost not at all for the prior two and a half months. I had six entire at-bats in Lakeland, and had played about half my defensive innings at first base.

Once Mark Tolli threw his first pitch, the realization hit me like a slap to the side of the cranium. I was in Medford, Oregon. I was playing in the Oakland A's organization. I was surrounded by guys I had not met until just a day earlier. I was still getting paid to play baseball.

I shook my head to clear the thoughts and focus on the game. Sometimes, when you plow forward it takes a while for reality to sink in.

Our centerfielder was Bobby Garrett, a 5-foot 8-inch guy from Cal State Fullerton with blazing speed, and in right field we had Dan Randle from Hayward, California. Both of those guys could really run. I figured we had a chance to be a pretty good defensive outfield if I was going to be the guy who covered the least amount of ground.

In my first at-bat, I did what I so often seemed to do by hitting a seeing-eye 15-hopper up the middle for a hit. The first one was out of the way. During my next at-bat I hit the living hell out of the ball, crushing what I thought was a sure double to left center. I hadn't hit a ball that hard in a long time and it felt deliciously good. Then the left-fielder for the Phillies, who was also a professional and didn't care how good it felt for me, made a spectacular diving catch to rob me. I finished the night 1-for-3 and quite happy, despite our loss.

After the game, we headed back to our benches and nails in our cozy clubhouse and as I got undressed I did exactly what I'd done in Paintsville and Lakeland after every game. I threw my uniform and my other clothes, including our green stirrup socks and bright yellow sanitaries, on the floor. And one of the guys said, "Uh, we have to wash our own stuff here. They don't do it for us." I had not even noticed we didn't have a clubhouse attendant.

The next night, I went 2-for-3 with two hard hit line drives and I managed to score a run by barreling into the catcher and jarring the ball loose from his glove. It was fun to be playing again. And, I was no longer feeling that out-of-body "Where am I?" sensation. Plus, we won that game. Life was starting to feel good again.

A noteworthy thing about the Phillies was their middle-infield combo. Their second baseman was Carl Linhart and I actually knew him a little. He was from Granite City, Illinois, which is just west of Edwardsville. We never played with each other but we knew enough people in common to say hello and catch up during the two-game series. At shortstop for the Phils was a guy who certainly did seem pretty good then but I don't think anyone in Medford for the home opener would've predicted that he would play 23 years in the Major Leagues, finishing his career when he was 43 and seemingly the owner of the Fountain of Youth. He was Julio Franco.

Then we went on the road in our movie-prop bus. And, just to add to the fun, instead of hiring a bus driver, the team had somehow conned our radio play-by-play guy into driving it. Seriously.

Much to my surprise, after we had boarded the bus at 8 a.m. for the drive up to Salem to take on the Senators, the smoke-belching behemoth actually started.

And, on that first bus ride we learned two new things.

One, Craig Harris had a boombox and he brought it with him on the bus. He would do so all summer but the only 8-track tape he wanted to play was Carole King's "Tapestry" album. If the No. 1 draft pick on the team wanted to play Carole King, we were all going to listen to Carole King.

Two, Harry had decided, after years of going by his nickname he now wanted to be called Craig, to change his luck. So, of course, no one ever called him anything but Harry. If anyone would ask him a question, like "Hey Harry, what time is it?" he'd start the answer with "Craig, man." So what time was it? "Craig, man. It's 1:30."

On that first short trip for three games in Salem our skipper created an alphabetical rooming list, so I shared a motel room with pitcher Robert Wood. I was getting to know Mike

Altobelli better by the day, though, and we were becoming great friends in a real hurry so we put in a request and for the rest of the season we roomed together both at home and on the road. There are guys you meet in the game and bond with immediately. Alto was one of those guys. Alto was, perhaps, THE guy.

I played one of the three games in Salem, and got another single so I was, by then, somewhere in the neighborhood of 4-for-12, which is a good neighborhood. As in .333 good. When we returned to Medford to play the Senators at our place, Rich let us get our rest the first day but then called for early batting practice the day after that, since we were still running behind in terms of how much practice we'd had since hastily convening in southern Oregon.

We got two pieces of good news. First, our new green jerseys were in so we'd all look considerably better beginning that first night back at home. And second, Doug had kept his word and had installed a new net on the batting cage.

But, my baseball career was about to take yet another brutal turn for the worse.

Rich had found a pitching machine somewhere so rather than wear out his arm or one belonging to someone else, he fired it up for BP. The first group included Bobby Garrett, catcher Frank Kneuer, Dan Randle, and me. Garrett would get his cuts first and I would jump in second.

As Rich began to feed balls to the machine he discovered it was shooting pitches that would be up in my eyes if I had been the one hitting. With Garrett in the batter's box the pitches were almost over his head. Rich tried to adjust the machine but it was not only refusing to budge it was also electrically shocking him every time he tried. And the pitches stayed up where Garrett couldn't reach them. Finally, Rich made one more attempt to aim the pitches lower but again the pitch was high and Bobby Garrett took the biggest and wildest swing he could, practically coming out of his shoes to do it, and at the end of the swing he let his bat go out of frustration.

I was standing no more than five feet behind him.

At that moment we discovered one nasty fact. When they had installed the new netting, they secured it to the top and back of the cage, but no one had bothered to secure it down the sides.

I saw Bobby Garrett swing and then immediately saw a Louisville Slugger just inches from my face. I can still see it to this day. I heard it hit me more than I felt it, and as soon as it made its impact across my mouth and right cheek I knew I was hurt. I also looked down and saw the ground coming straight up to hit me.

The bat hit me in the mouth pretty hard and I can recall thinking, "Oh, great. I'm going to look like Daffy Duck for the next month." But then I put my tongue against my two front teeth and I could tell it was worse than that. They were both broken, with one missing the bottom half and the other missing a sizable chip off the bottom, about two-thirds the way down, and they were so loose I'm sure I could've spit them out like a hockey player.

I put my hand to my mouth to see if I was bleeding and when I pulled my hand away the palm of my white batting glove was soaked with bright red blood. Kneuer, whom we were already calling "Baloosh" because of his resemblance to John Belushi, was the first to my side and he did a bit of a recoil when he saw where the blood was coming from. It wasn't my mouth. It was my cheek just below my right eye. "Hold on, man. You're opened up pretty good," Baloosh said. "Just lay still."

You know it's ugly when everyone is running around you in circles but no one really knows what to do. I suggested that someone find me a towel. In a hurry.

I got the towel and held it to my face and by then Rich and our trainer, Charlie Saad, had decided to take me straight to the emergency room at the Rogue Valley Regional Medical Center, a couple miles away. I wasn't even woozy, really, so we walked to Rich's car and off we went, with me still in uniform (fortunately, I wasn't wearing my nice new green jersey for early BP) and my spikes on. And Rich began to drive like he thought I was about to die.

With my broken and loose teeth, and with my bloody towel still held to my face, I calmly lisped "Hey Skip. I'm going to be OK. I'd rather not die in an accident on the way to the hospital."

Apparently my humor calmed him down and we got there safely, pulling up to the ER door. I got out and click-clacked my way inside as my spikes hit the tile floor. After one look by the receptionist the staff leaped into action, putting me on a gurney and wheeling me into an exam room. "Hey, go back to practice," I told Rich. "Just promise me that someone will come back here to get me after you guys are done," although it sounded more like, "Hey, go back to pwacktith."

Rich waited for the ER doctor to arrive, and after taking a look the doc said, "Yeah, he's going to be here for a few hours. You can go back to the ballpark if you want."

I was on my back with the doctor prodding around below my right eye, and he kept saying "Does this hurt?" each time he'd move his fingers. It really didn't, though. My mouth was what hurt.

"For that bat to slice you open like this, it had to hit you really hard," the doctor said. "You're opened up right down to your cheekbone. We'll go take some x-rays, because I can't believe it didn't shatter your cheekbone and I don't want to risk having any floating bone chips that close to your eye."

Off we went to the x-ray room and when they put me on the table under the machine they had me lay on my left side initially. I found out then I was still bleeding pretty badly because it was puddling up on surface of the table.

We rolled back to the ER and awaited the results, and when they came in the doctor said, "Nah, we've got to do this again. I don't see anything but I still don't believe you didn't break something."

Back to x-ray, back on the newly cleaned table, and then back to the ER after round two. This time, the doctor admitted that he'd been wrong and my cheekbone was incredibly strong.

"OK, Bob. We're going to stitch you up and I think, considering what you do for a living, I should use my patented 'Rawlings' stitch pattern on your cheek," the doctor said. "You'll look like a baseball for the rest of your life."

When I looked at him warily, he said, "I'm just kidding. We're going to use what we call a running subcuticular stitch, all below the surface. I'll do some dissolvable sutures down deep, and then the subcuticular row near the top to close you up completely. I'll do my best to keep you handsome."

To prep me for this fun they put a sheet over my face that featured a hole right above my wound. To numb me up, though, he was going to have to give me a shot of novocaine. He said, "This is going to pinch quite a bit," which is a doctor's way of saying this is going to make your head explode.

He took a hypodermic needle and stuck it into the bottom of the wound.

There was a nurse in the room. She was standing by the table near my right knee and she was a relatively large woman. When that needle went into my face, without any conscious thought my right leg and my adidas-clad right foot reflexively jumped off the table and hit her basically in the chest. I apologized as best I could with broken teeth and a sheet over my face but all she said was, "I'm going to take his shoes off," as if I couldn't hear her.

I have no idea how long it took for him to stitch me up but I finally felt them putting a bandage over my cheek before they wheeled me into a recovery room. I think all the adrenalin then exited my system and I felt utterly exhausted. An hour later, our trainer Charlie arrived.

Charlie had to adapt to how things were done in Medford, as well, because he had been the Chicago White Sox trainer for many years. Morales had played for the ChiSox then, and by the time Rich got the Medford gig Charlie was no longer with Chicago, so Rich talked him into coming along.

Charlie told me in the car how worried he'd been that I might lose my eye. I found that funny, because all I really worried about was my teeth. I hadn't allowed myself to even think how easily I could've been blinded had that bat rotated slightly faster. He got me back to the clubhouse and I finally had my first chance to look in a mirror. It wasn't pretty.

My front teeth were jagged and all of my teeth across the top and bottom were so loose I could move them back and forth just by touching them, although the pain quickly dissuaded me from doing that. I also discovered that one of my top front teeth had impacted the tooth below it, chipping a piece of that one off, as well.

The white bandage had already soaked through with dark red blood that would soon turn a sickly brown, and although I didn't yet have a black eye I knew one was coming.

By the time Charlie and I got to the ballpark the game was about to start and I joined the guys in the dugout for a while before going up to the radio booth. Baloosh was the first one to see me and he ran over saying, "I can't believe you're walking around. I can't believe you're alive. Dude, you were sliced open all the way to the bone. I could see your cheek bone. Your cheek was opened up like this," and he made a sideways V with his first two fingers.

I had actually met a nice young lady during our first homestand and once she and I chatted a bit after the opener we made plans to have a date when the club got back to Medford. As fate would have it, on the very day of my injury some of the guys had rented the party room at the apartment complex and we were going to have a little soiree that night after we got back. And that young lady and I were scheduled to attend as our first date.

While I was in the dugout, I saw her approaching the fence and when she saw me she looked crestfallen. "This is just how it always goes for me," she said. "I heard on the radio that one of the A's got hit by a bat and was hurt pretty bad during practice today and of course it just had to be you. Unbelievable."

She never asked "How are you?" We did have the get-together after the game, and she did come along, but 15 minutes into it she'd had enough of the guy with the bloody bandage and the rapidly swelling and discolored eye. I never heard from her again. The poor thing. That's just how it goes for her.

As for me, the next morning was brutal. By then the pain had really set in and my black eye was incredible, with shades of purple, red, yellow, and green blending into an overall mess as it swelled enough to shut my eye. With my left eye, I stared at the bathroom mirror in disbelief.

I'd been ignored by my manager in Lakeland, wasting 10 weeks of my life and career for reasons I never understood. I drove 1,000 miles to get home, fairly well convinced that my so-called career was over. I got a break and immediately flew to the Pacific Northwest to start over again, discovering I had a manager who was a great guy and happy to play me. I met Mike Altobelli and had a new best friend within days. And then I got hit in the face by a bat thrown in anger by my own teammate. And for the record, Bobby Garrett never apologized. I don't think he was being rude, I think he just didn't know how to do it or didn't know what to say.

I felt absolutely helpless and such a long, long way from home.

We had another home game or two before a road trip to Eugene was on the schedule. I hung out in the radio booth and helped our play-by-play guy with the production for those games and then finally the team left for Eugene and I didn't go. "Stay put and rest," Rich said. "You don't need to ride in that bus just to watch us play."

I was really sad that the trip was to Eugene because I was looking forward to seeing it. I hadn't been there since I traveled with my dad's Spokane Indians and I was eager to play in that great ballpark. Instead, I had to stay home. By myself.

I didn't have a car, I couldn't let anything solid touch my teeth, and the bandage was really getting pretty gross. All I could do was watch TV for three interminable days and when I was hungry I'd walk a few blocks to Denny's for breakfast, where scrambled eggs worked if I made sure the fork made no contact with my teeth. Then there was Taco Bell for lunch or dinner so that I could get a couple of burritos and eat the center out of them with that ultra-clever Taco Bell contraption, the plastic spork.

I was miserable.

Once the team got back to town Rich said he wanted me in uniform on the bench. I had never actually been put on the disabled list and despite the fact it didn't feel like my teeth were getting much better and my bandage was still hideous, I might be able to pinch-run if he needed me. I was all for that.

I was in a better mood just being in uniform. Before the game, pitcher Don Van Marter joined Alto and me signing autographs at the fence, and I instinctively wrote Bob "The Hawk" Wilber on a baseball. When Van Marter took the same ball from the young fan he started cracking up. I had kind of forgotten that no one in Medford knew anything about The Hawk.

I told him that was my nickname in the Appalachian League the year before and everyone there thought it was cool. He laughed and said "Well, you're never going to live it down here."

Van Marter spread the word and from that point forward guys on the team would insert the word "Hawk" into anything. We were the Medford Hawk A's. We played at Miles Hawk Field. But the best of all was Van Marter himself becoming Don Hawk Van Hawk Marter. Those laughs could not have come at a better time.

A few days later it was time to head back to the hospital to have the top layer of subcuticular stitches taken out and it would be the first time I'd actually see the wound, making me the final member of the Medford A's to know what it looked like.

The doctor who had fixed me up took off the bandage and I looked in the mirror. All I could see was a thin red line, as if it had been written on my face in ballpoint ink, and two black knots of thread at either end of it. He clipped off one of the knots with surgical scissors and then pulled on the other end. I could feel it snaking its way out of my cheek and within a second he had the long black string of thread out of my face.

This random emergency room doctor had done an absolutely brilliant job.

When I got to the ballpark the guys were amazed. Baloosh couldn't stop shaking his head, comedically looking at me, looking away, then looking back saying, "No way. Absolutely no way. I saw your cheekbone. You can barely tell it ever happened." Then he'd make the sideways V with his fingers and say, "It was like this. I saw your cheekbone. No way."

I still have the scar but 37 years later I have to point it out to people, and some can't see it at all. They just take my word for it.

It's important to note that I'd been in Medford for barely a couple weeks. We were mostly strangers when we arrived but baseball has a way of making friends out of strangers. These guys were already my brothers, and as certified underdogs we were much more like the Paintsville Hilanders than we were like the Lakeland Tigers. From Day One, we were a tight bunch of misfits.

Once the stitches were out I was fully cleared to play but there remained a problem. My teeth were still killing me, so I'd barely been able to eat and an already skinny version of me was now practically malnourished. Milk shakes didn't help because sucking something thick through a straw was so painful it felt like my teeth were falling out. I was subsisting on scrambled eggs and the insides of Taco Bell burritos.

I took BP that first day and could barely swing the bat. It was pretty awful.

We soon went on the road again up to Bend to play the Phillies. We got there fine, in the clown bus, and when we pulled into the motel parking lot and picked up our keys at the front desk, Alto noticed a cafe across the road. It had a sign that said "Buffalo Burgers and Milk Shakes" so we had no choice but to try it out. Despite the fact I had to cut up the burger with a knife so I could eat it carefully with a fork while I "drank" my shake with a spoon, it was fabulous and I finally had the ability to get some protein into me.

We'd play in Bend two or three more times that summer and by the second trip Alto and I had perfected our method of picking up our keys, dropping off our bags in our room, and running across the road to eat. After we'd pay our bill, we would walk out the front door and pass a dozen teammates still waiting to be seated in the tiny place. They obviously did not share our priorities.

On the trip back to Medford after our final night-game in Bend the bus made itself the center of attention. Somewhere on a two-lane road in the forest, it quit running. We pulled over to the side of the road and it was dead.

With no signs of life anywhere near us on this dark night all we could do was wait, in the hope someone would come along. When a car did, Rich jumped out and waved them down. He had a conversation with the driver and his wife and came back aboard the darkened bus. "This couple lives just outside of Medford," he said. "If anyone wants a ride with them you can go," and by the time the word "go" was out of his mouth, Alto and I were off the bus.

So we hopped in a car in the middle of the night with two perfect strangers in the center of nowhere. What could possibly go wrong?

Nothing did. The driver kept his promise to Rich by stopping at the first pay phone and calling for a wrecker, then he and his wife drove us to our apartment. About half the team got home that way and the other half waited it until daylight, when a service truck got there and managed to get the bus to run.

It would be the first of many such escapades and they never happened anywhere but remote locations in the dead of night.

And my teeth still hurt, although they were firming up a little bit and feeling slightly less awful.

We worked our way back to Eugene not long after that and I finally got to dress in the same clubhouse the Spokane Indians had used and play in the same classic ballpark. It was a bit spine-tingling for Del Wilber's son. It had only been six years since I'd been there, hanging out with the Spokane club, but it seemed like a lifetime.

Rich was sliding me back into the lineup more and more but what magic I had conjured up when I arrived in Medford was gone. I was still weak and my timing was horribly off at the plate. The hits stopped coming, and by that I mean they stopped almost completely. I don't think I got more than three or four additional hits the rest of the way although one of them was a triple at Salem that would've been a home run in any other park in the league, and Rich ribbed me a little at third saying "If you were in better shape, you would've gotten an inside-the-park dinger, Meat." It was little solace to the guy who had started out so well in his new home.

In July, we heard from teammates Shaun Lacey and Dan Randle that they were living with the radio guy, who had gone through a divorce and had plenty of room. To make it more enticing, he let them stay there for free. Alto and I were eager to keep a little bit more of our tiny paychecks, so we moved out of the apartment and over to the duplex.

Around the same time, Oscar Burnett was finally with us and the team had also signed Pete Slattery, a pitcher from Boston. Along with power-hitting Terry Harper, another great guy, they came along with us to spend the rest of the season doing something that approximated camping-out, but indoors.

When the radio guy got divorced his former wife took almost all the furniture. Lacey and Randle had two single beds in the dank basement but the rest of us slept on the floor in the living room. It wasn't exactly the glamorous life of professional baseball we'd all envisioned but hey, the price was right. The first rule of minor league baseball is, "If it's free, it's for me."

Though the main level had no furniture it did have the radio guy's deejay set-up and his record collection. It was a fantastic stereo, and every night we'd come back from the park and wind down by listening to music that ranged from obscure to classic.

One of the obscure albums was by a band called Crack The Sky and none of us had ever heard of them. Apparently they were regionally popular around West Virginia and Pennsylvania, but their album had found its way into the record collection of a DJ in Oregon.

To make it slightly more challenging to get into their music the album was a "live" recording of them playing their most popular songs, but of course we'd never heard any of the tracks before. It turned out Dan Randle and I had similar musical taste and he and I both took a serious liking to this technically talented band playing music with which we were unfamiliar. We'd lay on the floor in what had been the dining room, and play the grooves out of that album.

My favorite song, played over and over in the darkness late at night, had lyrics that went:

Maybe I can fool everybody tonight.
Maybe I can make everybody believe in me.
Maybe I can fool everybody,
And fool myself if I'm really lucky.

The song resonated with me, as I tried to grapple with the year I was having.

Around that time, the A's set me up with a series of dentist appointments to get my two front teeth capped. The pain from how loose they'd been had subsided enormously by then but three weeks of procedures to have two root-canals and the caps installed kept me entertained. Actually, the root canals were the least painful part because I got novocaine for those. On the days when he did the fittings with my new caps, he didn't bother with the pain killer. He used a sharp pointed hook and then forced me to bite down on a small wooden block as hard as I could, to push the caps up and into place. Those days were capable of inducing cold sweats.

At least I was getting back to normal but I wasn't hitting worth a darn.

And then, because the injury had taken its toll on my overall fitness I tweaked my hamstring again and my right shoulder began to kill me. This was all adding up to be an adventure unlike any I had imagined when my mom told me I was an Oakland A.

As miserable as I could have let myself become I made a conscious decision to be positive and relish every day of life in the Northwest League. I may have been hurt and I may have been half the player I knew I could be but I was no dummy. I figured this was the end of my career and by the end of the winter I'd be putting tapes together to get a real job somewhere in broadcasting. One thing that made me feel better about that, and very confident, was that I knew I could do baseball play-by-play as well as any radio guy who had done our games. I could not, however, drive a bus.

With my positive attitude and my decision to make the most of it, I survived. And with Alto as my best buddy on the team I laughed a lot. We were inseparable and we cracked each other up. I think some of our teammates thought we were nuts. One night in Bend, where our motel had outdoor hallways and a lot of the guys left their doors open until it was time to go to sleep, I left our room to buy a soda out of the machine. As soon as I got outside Alto yelled, as loud as he could, "I love you, Bobby Wilber!" I yelled back "And I love you, Michael Altobelli!"

Passing the next room, I looked inside and saw Rich Morales. He just shook his head, laughed, and said "You two are somethin' else."

Pete Slattery was a great guy, as well, despite the fact we mimicked his Boston accent relentlessly. His girlfriend back home was named Barb. He pronounced that Bahb. I'd say "Pete, what's your girlfriend's name?" and he'd say "Bahb." Then I'd say "And what's my name?" and he'd say "Bahb." This kept us occupied for many hours on long bus rides.

Playing within our division was merely a nuisance in terms of bus rides. The trips to Eugene, Salem, and Bend were all manageable when the smoking old heap didn't break down. About midseason, though, we finally found out just how tough the league could be for the guys with the worst bus who were based in the town that was farthest south.

We had a four-game series in Walla Walla and needed to leave at 6 a.m. in order to make the nine-hour drive. We arrived at our hotel around 3 in the afternoon and left for the ballpark an hour later. I don't remember the score from that night, but I'm assuming it wasn't pretty.

I played the next night and in my first at-bat the pitcher drilled me in the left elbow with a fastball. It was as if this entire season was quickly becoming a dark comedy. Charlie came out to see me as I trotted to first and he asked if I was OK. I can't imagine that he expected me to say anything other than, "Oh yeah, I'm good," and that's exactly what I said. So he froze my elbow with ethyl chloride spray.

My hamstring was feeling a little better, and the pitcher had a very slow delivery, so on the second pitch I took off for second. The throw beat the slower version of me by just a hair, but the second-baseman never even came close to putting the tag on me and yet the umpire yelled "Yer out!"

I knew the ump since we saw his crew quite a bit, and I liked the guy. But I screamed at him, "He's gotta tag me Roy. He didn't even try. You have to be better than that. I'm trying to survive out here. Be better!"

He just walked away. A couple of innings later, I came up again and after I tapped my bat on the plate with my left hand I attempted to pick the bat up and put it on my shoulder, but my left elbow would not cooperate. I quickly put my right hand on the handle and did it that way. Three pitches later I struck out. It's hard to hit when you're healthy. It's about impossible when your left arm doesn't work.

After the game the ump I'd argued with came up to me and said, "You were right. I was lazy and called you out because the ball beat you, but he never tagged you. I'm sorry, Bob. I'm trying to survive out here, too." We nodded at each other, shook hands, and silently gave each other a very empathetic look.

After the final game in Walla Walla, against the Padres, we got on the bus for the nine-hour drive through the night. You can probably imagine where this is going. Somewhere in northern Oregon well after midnight, the bus quit on us again. Many of the guys had dozed off already but I was in my typical wide-awake state on bus rides and I could tell the motor was not cooperating.

It was a moonless night and pitch-black out there on a two-lane highway near the Columbia River. Most of the guys stayed on the bus but a few of us got out to wander around and see if we could spot any signs of life in the darkness. Finally, a car came by and Rich sent the radio guy with that person, to get to the next town and find us a replacement bus. Or cars. Or vans. Or anything that would get us back to Medford.

As the sky began to brighten in the east we could start to make out the topography. What we had thought was a lake was actually a field and to our left was a large hill. We were probably about 30 miles east of an Oregon town uniquely called The Dalles and all we could do was wait. Then our radio guy showed up, riding in a school bus.

He had gotten a ride to The Dalles and had found this bright yellow school bus. And it came complete with a driver. There was only one hitch. It was a bus for elementary school kids. The seats were tiny.

The bus also had no storage space so all of our gear would have to go inside with us. We made the most of that by filling many of the seats with duffel bags and then laying on top of them. We then bounced on down the road with the windows open.

A few hours later we stopped for fuel and food in Bend. On road trips, we were given about $8 a day in meal money and every time we went on the road we'd get that all at once on the first day. I was out of money and in 1979 if you didn't have any cash and were on the road, you were truly out of money.

We all entered a McDonald's as the bus driver filled the fuel tank and I stood far to the back, assuming (or hoping) I could at least scarf a few fries from someone. Finally, the lady behind the counter looked at me and said, "And what would you like?"

"I'm sorry. I'm out of money, so I'm not getting anything," I said. And she replied, "But what would you LIKE? It's on me." I can't imagine how brutal I must have looked to get a free lunch out of it.

We arrived back at Miles Field at 6:30 p.m. and the Eugene Emeralds were already there. We played at 7. We got creamed. And the next day our bus was back in its parking spot outside the ballpark. Perhaps it was actually a zombie bus. Every time it seemed to be dead, it came back to life.

After a short homestand we went out on the road for one of the longest trips I'd ever been on with any team. We would play two in Eugene, then head to Gray's Harbor to play the Mets. By then we'd discovered where Gray's Harbor was. It was near the coast in Aberdeen, Washington.

Gray's Harbor was the name of the body of water next to Aberdeen and it was also the name of the county. When we got there we also discovered that the name Gray's Harbor was 100 percent accurate. Coastal fog and rain plagued us the entire time we were there, but we played through it.

Olympic Stadium in Aberdeen was bizarre. An old wooden structure, it was designed to be two legs of a huge square, as if it had been originally built for polo or some other sport that needed twice the space of a football or baseball field. The old grandstand ran from just behind home plate to the right-field corner, and then all the way out to dead center, coming to an end probably 450 feet from home. A temporary fence both shortened the distance in center and ran over to the left-field line.

In addition to the wonderfully soggy weather, it was a quiet place. The players and coaches outnumbered the fans every night in a park that could easily hold 8,000.

The weather apparently made us cranky because we were riding the home-plate umpire all night one game, letting him know in no uncertain terms that we thought he was technically incompetent and that he'd be wise to find a new line of work. Finally he'd had enough and he marched over to our dugout and stared right at us. He pointed at individual A's as he went down the line saying, "You're OK. You shut up. You're OK. You're on the edge. You're OK." Then, finally, "And you, you are OUTTA HERE!" And he threw Keith Call, the starting pitcher from the day before, out of the game. Keith had to go sit in the bus as his punishment.

Keith Call was the quietest guy on the team. He rarely spoke, and he absolutely had not been yelling at the umpire. When he got tossed, that only made the rest of us scream louder. Finally, Rich stood up and yelled "Everybody sit down and shut up."

When things quieted down he added, in hushed tones, "You guys are idiots. He threw Keith out because he pitched last night. He wanted to make a statement but he didn't cost me a useful player. Get it?" We got it. And we felt like what he'd called us. We were idiots.

From Gray's Harbor we headed further north to Bellingham, well above Seattle near the Canadian border. We played four games there, against the Mariners, and Alto and I were happy to discover a bar and disco across the street from our hotel. The first night we were there with Baloosh and a few other guys and the place ran a freestyle disco dancing contest. Alto, of course, won.

In the bar area they had a first-generation video console. It was a football game. You played against another guy and there was a track ball in front of each player. To make your players move on the screen, you rolled the track ball as fast as you could. The game was a riot, and Alto and I played it a number of times that night.

The next evening in the dugout, we decided we would play a full NFL-length contest when we got back there after our game. We'd need about $10 in quarters to do that, and frankly we were more fired up about the video football game than the one the Medford A's were playing.

I was in the lineup that night and during my second at-bat I was called out on strikes on a pitch that was a foot outside. I turned and stared at the umpire, then slowly dropped my bat and then my helmet on the plate. This is what we call "showing up the umpire" and it's an especially bad thing to do in front of paying customers.

The ump took off his mask and said, "Pick that up." I said, "I don't have to. And on top of that you're terrible."

The witty back-and-forth went on for another 10 or 15 seconds and I knew what was next. He was going to throw me out of the game and that would mark the first time such a thing had ever happened in my life. I was almost looking forward to it.

And then the bat boy ran out and picked up my bat and helmet. The umpire and I just stared at each other until he finally said, "Let's make this easy. Go sit down."

After the game, once the bus got to the hotel Alto and I ran to the video machine as fast as we could. We played four 15-minute quarters, rolling those track balls furiously. The next day, during BP we both discovered our forearms hurt so much it was painful to swing. We decided it was probably a good idea to not tell Rich what we'd done to get so sore.

And then we wrapped up the road trip with four games in Victoria, British Columbia. We'd have to get to Victoria on a ferry boat, and while we were parked in line at the dock to drive aboard with our favorite bus, other busloads of young school students were arriving in beautiful modern tour buses to join us. I looked to my left and saw a bus full of Girl Scouts staring at us and pointing. They were laughing at our bus.

The ferry ride was something magical and many of us had never done anything like it. We were able to get off the bus and walk around the boat, buying snacks with our American dollars and then getting Canadian money in return. We stood at the railings and were transfixed by the scenery as the boat navigated between endless pine-covered islands to make its way to Victoria over the course of an hour or so. To a man, we thought that boat ride was a highlight of the summer. To me, it was hard to fathom that the scenery was real. It looked too beautiful to be natural.

After four games in Victoria, which was also one of the most beautiful cities we'd ever seen, we had a solid 13- or 14-hour ride back to Medford. That was brutal. We played the Salem Senators a few of hours after we got back and basically handed them a freebie. We were strong young men, professional athletes in the best shape of our lives, but we were worn down. We were barely able to function, thanks to the bus rides, the cheap food, our accommodations, and the stress of what we were trying to accomplish. It was simply overwhelming.

Our pitching staff was falling apart, specifically in the bullpen. Rich had trotted nearly everyone out there that first night against Salem just to try to stop the bleeding, but each new pitcher got ripped just as badly as the guy before him.

After the game as we sat at our nails almost too tired to get undressed, Rich walked over to me and asked, "Have you ever pitched?"

Despite being worn out both physically and mentally my brain could fire just enough neurons to look back through the years and ascertain that, yes, I had pitched before. Why, it was just as recently as fourth grade.

I said, "Yeah. Sure!"

"Well, I hope I don't have to use you," Rich said, "but if we get ripped again I might run you out there to give these guys a break."

The next day my mom arrived in Medford. We'd talked on the phone about my facial and dental injuries and she had decided to come out and take a look for herself. The way my season was going, this was likely to be my last hurrah and if we wanted to file any claims against the A's for negligence, with regard to the untied net on the cage, she wanted to be a part of that and see me with her own eyes. After all, my college degree would have the word "television" in it.

She was relieved to see I looked better than she had anticipated and we even had time for a check-up with the doctor to let him take a look. Then we picked up Alto and Keith Call to give them a ride to the ballpark. "Hello, Mrs. Wilber," Keith quietly said, but Alto put on his best authentic Italian accent, spread his arms wide, and said, "Mama! You raised a good boy here. You did good. You did real good!" Then he gave her a bear hug.

That night, as if it had been scripted, the Salem team ripped our staff again. The Senators got three in the second, three more in fourth, one in the fifth, and then hung a 10-spot on the board in the sixth.

Rich actually put Oscar Burnett in the game at that point and he succeeded in throwing a fresh can of gasoline on the already roaring fire. Oscar gave up seven earned runs in an inning and two-thirds. He is forever listed in the record books as having a career earned run average (ERA) of 31.50. That's 31 and a half. The decimal point is in the correct place.

Rich looked at me while Oscar was imploding and said, "You're next, Chief. Go warm up. And hurry."

When my shoulder wasn't throbbing I still had my good arm as an outfielder and I could regularly hit the catcher's mitt with a one-hop throw from 300 feet away. What Rich did not know was that, like most position players, I had messed around from time to time on the mound and I found I couldn't throw consistent strikes from just 60 feet 6 inches away. But, during those summers with my dad and the Denver Bears, I did discover one important thing that would come into play that night in Medford. If I dropped my arm-angle down and threw submarine style, like Kent Tekulve or Dan Quisenberry, I could throw strikes all day and the ball had a ton of sink. If I aimed for the catcher's mitt at the belt, the ball would drop well below the knees as it crossed the plate.

I hustled out to the bullpen before Oscar's uniform caught on fire and Pig warmed me up. It was the first time I'd ever warmed up in a bullpen to actually enter a baseball game. And my mom was there.

Finally, Rich couldn't stand to watch anymore and he went out to get Oscar. He pointed to me in the bullpen and brought me in. As he handed me the ball on the mound, with the score 24-5 and the bases loaded, he said, "Hold 'em right there," and smiled. I actually laughed a little.

Baloosh trotted back to the plate to catch my eight warm-up tosses and he looked to be about a mile away. My first negative thought was, "Gosh, I hope I can throw this close enough to him so he can catch it" but then I relaxed and threw my first warm-up. It went straight into his glove.

After those eight tosses (I hesitate to classify them as pitches) I took a peek into the dugout and saw Rich staring at me in some form of disbelief, with his head cocked to the side and his arms folded. I'm sure he thought I was going to just heave it up there as hard as I could, and yet there I was throwing from way down below at about 75 mph.

Then a real live professional hitter took his spot in the batter's box. He looked at my first submarine pitcher for strike one. He fouled off another. Then Baloosh put down two fingers for a curve. I hadn't really thought about how I was going to throw one of those from that angle, but I slung it up there with sort of a frisbee action and the hitter just stared at it. Strike three.

I had to put my glove over my mouth as I walked to the dugout because I was grinning from ear to ear and possibly laughing a little. And I saw my mom, who was standing and applauding.

I went back out there for the ninth and did walk a guy and hit another, but with two outs I got ahead of the hitter with a couple of sinking strikes and then Baloosh trotted out to talk to me. He said "Just once, straight over the top."

I took my stretch and tried to make my delivery look the same but at the last second I threw it straight overhand as hard as I could. Swing and a miss, another strikeout. My ERA was 0.00 after my first professional outing. Sadly, our big comeback in the bottom of the ninth only netted two runs and the final was a footballish 24-7. The 742 fans who were in attendance seemed like 10,000 to me.

After the game Rich had a big smile on his face as he said, "You shocked me with that stuff, but you got 'em out. Way to go, Wilby."

Taffy and I went out to eat at the Red Lion Hotel, where she was staying, and I just kept shaking my head and saying, "I can't believe I just pitched." It didn't seem real, but it was. Taffy answered, "Yes, you did. You were great. And I love your roommate."

The next day, Rich and I had a chat and I agreed with him that it would be in everyone's best interest if I spent the rest of the season as a pitcher, although I'd always be available to pinch hit or go in for late-game defense. From that point forward I was a reliever and when I wasn't doing that, I was a late-inning sub in the outfield. To make myself more useful when I wasn't doing either of those things, I'd coach first-base.

I came in a week later up in Eugene in front of a crowd of 1,478 paying customers. I pitched two innings and gave up one hit. I struck out two. The one hit was an eye-opener, though. I got a sinker up a little and a good professional baseball player mashed it to left-center. My initial thought was, "Wow, so that's what a home run looks like from this perspective," but it was just a double into the gap. I decided right then that, if I had a choice, I'd prefer to never see what a home run looked like from that perspective.

A few days later, we were home against the Bellingham Mariners and poor Robert Wood got exactly one out in the first inning before giving up five runs. Then Steve Marlow came in and he coughed up three more runs while only getting one out. We were down 8-0 and yet we still only had two outs on the board in the first inning. Rich rushed my roomie Pete Slattery out there and he managed to get that final out in the first and then pitch two more innings without giving up any more. During the third, Rich looked at me and said, "You're up, and I'm going to ask you to finish this. Take one for the team, no matter how bad it gets. Can you do that?" I said I'd give it my best.

That night against the Mariners I pitched six innings, gave up 10 hits but only four earned runs and I struck out two. Three more runs did score, but on errors by the defense so they were unearned and didn't impact my stats. During one stretch which included the fifth, sixth, and seventh innings, I put zeroes on the board and even threw a couple of guys out at first myself after cleanly fielding come-backers. In the bottom of the ninth, down 15-6, our guys actually put a heck of a rally together but our seven-run inning came up just short of getting me the win. We lost 15-13.

I was mad about giving up so many hits and giving up my first runs but Rich met me in the dugout and said, "Great job, Wilby. Great job."

We finished the season with one last road trip to Eugene and a few of the guys decided to take bus matters into their own hands. They sneaked out to the ballpark before dawn and stripped all the wiring out of the engine, then at 8 a.m. they acted just as surprised as the rest of us when it wouldn't make a sound. Our owner quickly arranged to charter an actual Greyhound bus for us and we rode up to Eugene in style. I wasn't a big fan of what those guys did but I enjoyed the ride.

We checked into our hotel and went to our rooms to rest. Then, around 4 we began to pop out of our rooms to head to the ballpark. And there sat the old bus, practically mocking us by its very presence.

That night we had a small lead going into the ninth and Rich had me warming up to get the save, but before he could get me in the game the Emeralds won in walk-off fashion. I was honored he had thought of me in a crucial situation.

Somewhat fittingly our final game of the year was rained out, so we actually "only" played 71 games instead of the scheduled 72. Our record was 33-38. My final stats as a pitcher showed 10 innings pitched, 12 hits, 4 earned runs, and six strikeouts. My ERA was a solid 3.60, and that would keep you employed if you could do it all year.

Rich and I had a chance to chat thanks to the rain-out and we discussed my potential future as a pitcher. It was only then that I admitted my ever-so-slight bending of the truth when I told him I had pitched before, and that I was strictly making it up as I went along during the 10 innings I did pitch. I had no clue what I was doing.

When he reflected on that, he paused and then said, "Well, we need to get you to spring training as a pitcher and have you work with a real pitching coach. All I could do was run you out there but if a pitching coach can work with you, I think you have a chance to actually do this."

As lousy as I felt about most of the season, dating back to Tiger Town, it felt good to hear that and it gave me a glimmer of hope about the future — just a glimmer, but without the pitching success there would have been no hope whatsoever. It was something.

Then, on that dreary day in Eugene, we loaded our bags, boarded the monstrosity and rode back to Medford one more time, listening to Carole King on Harry's boombox. (Craig, man.)

On the bus, we reminisced about the season and shared a few more laughs. Most of the laughs came from a litany of "most commonly asked questions" we heard from fans at the ballpark.

One was, "How do you guys stand these ridiculous bus rides?" We usually replied, "Well, at least we're in a beautiful part of the country," and that was true. Slattery finally had enough, though, and the last time someone gave the routine answer he shouted, "Bull! It doesn't matter how beautiful it is if it's 3 o'clock in the morning and you've just finally fallen asleep and someone elbows you in the ribs and says 'Look, it's the Space Needle'."

For the record, the two other most common questions we heard from fans had been these: "When's your next game?" Answer: "Tomorrow."

"When are you guys going to be pros?" Answer: "We already are." The postscript to that answer should've been "But not for long."

When we pulled back into Miles Field that final time, we said our goodbyes.

Alto and I were best friends of the highest order. Pete Slattery still called his girlfriend and me by the same distorted Bostonian name of "Bahb." Harp, Slats, Lace, Oscar, and Danny had been great roomies, as well, on that living room floor. Rich Morales had been a great skipper and a truly good guy. Baloosh looked at me and made the V with his fingers one final time, then gave me a hug.

On the year, the Medford A's drew a total of 34,656 fans to Miles Field, for an average of just under 1,000 per game. It was the most people I'd ever played before at home games. And, on more than a few nights, we got word in Medford that we'd outdrawn the big club when they'd also played at home that night. Things were sometimes tough in Medford, but they were downright awful in Oakland

We'd competed against some guys who were going to be stars, including that Julio Franco cat who would play in the big leagues until he was nearly eligible for AARP benefits. Jim Presley had been on the Bellingham team, and he ended up playing eight years in the show, with most of those being just down I-5 in Seattle. Mark Parent eventually went from the Walla Walla Padres to the team in San Diego. As for the Medford A's, we mostly all just went home.

Frankly, I was glad 1979 was over. But it wasn't quite over yet.

Pitching Can Take You Places

My flight home to St. Louis was a muddled mess of emotions. Whereas I was mostly devastated about both the injury and the way things had subsequently gone on the field after my up-close-and-personal introduction to a flying Louisville Slugger, the pitching experience had given me cause for hope.

It was a strange hope, but it was hope. I knew I'd been ad-libbing it on the mound but even so I'd sent six professional baseball players trudging back to the dugout after striking out on whatever nonsense I was throwing. Six K's in 10 innings. A lot of guys who have worked at their craft on the mound for their entire lives would like to do that in the pros.

I was as much mystified as excited. Maybe pitching wasn't really that hard. Maybe my funky delivery was just strange enough to do that one most important thing a pitcher can do. Maybe it made hitters uncomfortable.

In my last appearance on the mound I had been messing around with a pure side-arm delivery, because I could get far more velocity on the ball that way. The problem was, it was really straight. It was also a four-seam fastball and I wasn't yet smart enough to know that a four-seamer from the side tended to be straight, although it might move in a little to a right-handed hitter. After I used it to strike out one poor soul, he approached me during BP the next day to say, "Man, that was really some bad-ass stuff you were throwing. It felt like the pitch was starting out behind me. Good luck the rest of the way." I remember shaking my head when he walked away. I was thinking, "Really?"

Sitting on the plane reflecting of all these things provided no clarity. It did, however, help me make a decision to reach out to Lance as soon as I got home. He could be the pitching coach I didn't have in Medford and if we could find a way to make the sidearm pitch sink, we might be onto something.

Once I got home, and had a nice lunch with Skip and Taffy, I immediately called Lance to catch up on things and run the pitching concept by him. We agreed to live together again, just the two of us this time in a grown-up apartment with actual furniture and no Venus de Milo, and he was thrilled with the pitching idea as long as I'd agree to catch him after he'd caught my stuff each day. He hadn't quite given up on the dream yet, either.

Lance had finished his degree and taken an accounting job with Pepsi-Cola at its plant in St. Louis, which was only about a mile from SLUH near Forest Park. With his need to be close to the center of the city combined with my need to be somewhat close to SIUE, we chose a spot in-between.

For years, when we'd head out to the west side of St. Louis for any reason, most of which were entertainment related, we'd take I-270 around the north side of the city to avoid downtown traffic. Just after crossing the Mississippi heading westbound you'd pass an apartment complex called Raintree, and its billboard overlooking the highway said, "If you lived at Raintree, you'd be home now."

Advertising works. We chose Raintree. He could be at Pepsi in 15 to 20 minutes and I could be on campus in the same amount of time. Mission No. 1 had been accomplished.

We then found a variety of ballfields with mounds to use for our pitching sessions, which we'd hold two or three times a week during September while it was still warm.

On the first day, using my new first-baseman's mitt as the entirety of our catching gear (no, we didn't own a mask, either) I simply showed Lance my delivery and so-called arsenal of pitches.

He immediately saw some things that were causing my body to be a little ahead of my arm. I was using a big leg kick, like a right-handed version of Steve Carlton, and by the time I got my arm back and ready to come forward with the pitch my body had already gotten there. We made that tweak and it all felt a bit smoother.

The problem was velocity. If I threw submarine I had much better sink and slightly better control. The issue was the speed. Throwing from down under, I don't think I was hitting much more than 75 mph. In comparison, the best submarine pitcher in baseball, Dan Quisenberry of the Kansas City Royals, was generally around 82 mph. Also, it's really hard to throw a curveball from there because the spin tends to make a submarine pitch just hang out over the plate like a Frisbee, rather than actually curve. Hanging curveballs usually end up a long way away, once they finally come down.

When I showed him my sidearm delivery he said it picked up 10 mph immediately, but it was straight as a string. I was under the misconception that a four-seam fastball would run or sink more because it had four seams cutting through the air, and thanks to science it's those raised seams interacting with the air that make a baseball move. That was, apparently, not the case when you're throwing sidearm.

Lance showed me how to place my finger tips just over the seams at the point where they come closest together on the ball, and the first time I threw one with that grip with only those two seams cutting through the air, the pitch stayed relatively fast but it ran down and in toward a right-handed hitter. It was a "there-you-go" moment and the best part was I could throw an effective curve from that arm slot, too. The curve would do just the opposite of the fastball, as it would run down and away.

For nearly three weeks we met when we could, and I'd dial up my courage to catch his stuff after he'd caught mine. Lance threw hard and it was also not impossible for him to throw a 90-mph heater in the dirt. No catcher's mitt, no mask, no chest protector, and no shin guards. We were dedicated but I'm not going to say we were very smart.

Fortunately, we both got through those weeks without anything too bad happening. And wow, we broke-in that new first baseman's mitt to perfection. Once it arrived in Medford I'd already gotten hurt so I just stuffed it in my duffel bag and let it sit there. After two weeks of catching each other it was in prime shape.

But I wasn't back in St. Louis just to work on my pitching. I needed to make progress on my degree. I could really load up on classes and finish by Christmas or I could take a more reasonable amount and get done by March. I chose the latter option. Classes would start the last Monday in September. I had three classes on my schedule, with two of them meeting at night.

Once we'd completed six or seven pitching sessions I called my dad. I told Skip that I was starting to get the hang of this deal, with Lance's help, and that I wanted to throw for him so that he could be honest with me about my chances. He happily agreed to do that and we set it up for a couple days later using the mound at Meramec Community College, a few miles from the house in Kirkwood.

Lance and I got loose, then he took his spot behind the plate and I started pumping them in there. Skip stood right behind the cage, watching intently. I fired two-seamers that had heavy life and snapped off a few curves that had bite in the opposite direction. It probably lasted no more than 15 minutes.

Afterward, Skip was relatively effusive in his praise. Over the years he'd mastered the art of being diplomatic with his youngest son, in terms of my baseball skills. When I'd get on a hot streak he'd vociferously praise my hitting. When the hits dried up he'd try to encourage me and point out things I could work on. He never once said, "Sorry, you just can't hit and you're never going to."

On this day, after he'd seen me pitch, he had a look on his face I'd never before seen. He prefaced his remarks with one of his go-to lines, "Well, I'll be go to hell," and then said, "You can do this. You need a little more velocity, but more repetition can do that for you. The fastball is good, and the curve is coming along. Lance has to keep working with you on the release point for that, so that you're not telegraphing the curve with a higher release. The only thing I can tell you is that you should work on a change-up. With three pitches, you'll get a lot of people out."

I couldn't help smiling, and I vowed to work on that change-up although I'd already been dabbling with it a little. We didn't have much time, though. It was getting to be late September.

A few days later, Skip once again did what Skip always did best. I dropped by the house to pick up a few things on the day Lance and I were moving into our new apartment, and he said, "Hey, Oakland ends the season in Kansas City this weekend. I talked to Lee Stange and he said if we want to come over on Saturday we can meet at the Marriott and he can talk about pitching with you. And bring Lance along, too. We'll have lunch and you can pick his brain."

Lee Stange had pitched in the big leagues for 10 years; the first four with the Minnesota Twins right after they moved to the Twin Cities. I remembered him most from those days, since Skip was working for the Twins then. In the 1970s Stange transitioned to coaching and was the pitching coach for the Red Sox, Twins, and finally the Oakland A's. Lance and I were pumped to meet the man and see what bits of magic he could impart to us.

Early on the morning of Saturday, September 29, Lance and I drove to Woodleaf Court and picked up our traveling partner for the day. It's about a three and a half hour drive from Kirkwood to the ballpark in Kansas City, which was then known as Royals Stadium (it became Kauffman Stadium in 1993.) We were supposed to meet Stange for lunch at the Marriott, across I-70 from the stadium, but we got there a little early. As in maybe 11 a.m. Possibly 10:30. We weren't supposed to meet him until 1. This is what you call being "Del Wilber early," and it's a trait I absorbed from the big guy.

We walked into the lobby and couldn't help but spot various A's as they wandered around, all dressed to the nines and clearly big-leaguers. I sensed an immediate feeling of inadequacy wash over me. I'd been around ballplayers my whole life, more than a few of whom had ended up in the Hall of Fame, and I never felt anything but completely at ease around them. This was different. As a kid I was just hanging around my father's colleagues. On this day, in this hotel lobby, I was an aspiring pitcher with a ludicrous dream of transitioning to the mound at the age of 23. I felt like an imposter surrounded by these guys who had worked so hard to get the big leagues at their chosen positions.

And then I calmed my own nerves by remembering these were the Oakland A's. On this late September day, as they closed out a season during which my Medford A's had many times drawn bigger crowds at Miles Field than they had at the Coliseum, their record stood at 53-107. Once I digested those thoughts the players didn't seem quite as intimidating.

Somehow, despite our nerves, we managed to kill the time until Stange arrived for our late lunch. It was nearing 2 p.m. Lance and I introduced ourselves and I said, "We're thrilled to be here, and Lance and I are both honored that you'd take some time to talk pitching with us."

"Well," Stange said, "let's go over to the ballpark and see what ya got."

I hadn't exactly expected to hear him say that.

I said, "Well, that's incredible but we didn't bring our gear with us."

"We'll be fine," he said. "The guys will loan you whatever you need. We'll get you decked out."

Talk about plowing forward. I'm not sure of another moment in my life where the chance to change absolutely everything presented itself with so little warning.

At the ballpark we walked through a set of glass doors and down a hallway to the visitors clubhouse. At Royals Stadium. In Kansas City. Us. We opened the door and did our best to look calm.

It was a big square room with large lockers lining the four walls. A few couches, tables, and chairs filled the middle. On the front of each locker a fresh green Oakland A's jersey on a hanger was dangling from a hook, with the number on the back facing out. It was a sea of Kelly green. Even though it was the second-to-last day of the season, and the A's had already lost 107 games, there were a surprising number of players already in the clubhouse.

Stange sought out the equipment manager and asked him to help us get some gear together while he got dressed. With the equipment guy's assistance, Lance and I circled the room and sought shoes, pants, and gloves. Mike Norris gave me a spare uniform with a nice pair of form-fitting pants, while Rick Langford loaned me a glove and a pair of white adidas spikes with green stripes. The equipment manager went to his case of extra supplies and got us undershirts, thigh-length underwear, yellow sanitaries, and green stirrups. I asked the bat boy if I could borrow his hat. The nice young man obliged.

Once we were dressed, wearing mix-and-match gear from a number of guys, Lee introduced us to the catcher who would be working with us in the bullpen. The second we walked in the room I had wondered who that would be, because catching two guys like us before game 161 could not possibly be considered a treat. The answer was Mike Heath, a stud of an athlete who began his career as a shortstop but made it to the big leagues as a catcher. He was only a year older than us but after having been drafted out of high school in the second round of the 1973 draft, by the Yankees, he was already a well-known and highly respected player.

We met Mike and he could not have been more gracious. In typical baseball fashion we connected the one-degree-of-separation dots quickly, noting that Mike had played in the Yankees organization with a former SIUE alum Dennis Werth.

Finally, when everyone was ready, Heath patted me on the back and said to both of us "Let's go out there and have some fun. Whattaya say?"

I simply said, "Followin' you, big guy."

Plow forward, indeed.

We exited the clubhouse and entered a long tunnel, which connected directly to the end of the dugout. Like so many other tunnels I'd been through with my dad it was long, dim, and it sloped downward. It was basically a long square concrete tube, with rubber runners on the floor and a few recessed lights in the ceiling. At the end, I could see there was a door because the small slits all around its edges were lit up from the afternoon sun.

As if this surprise visit was something I did every day, I opened the door and squinted at the bright sun and an impossibly blue sky. I looked to my left and saw my father holding court with some A's coaches on the bench, and I hopped up the steps to stand on the field. As I passed Skip he winked and said, "Show them what you've shown me. Don't hold back."

With the visitors being on the third-base side I headed for the bullpen beyond the left field fence. I passed the Royals third baseman, who was fielding ground balls hit by a coach, and he made eye contact. George Brett said, "How's it goin' man?"

It was going fine.

Lance and I jogged out to the bullpen to get our blood moving after the morning drive and the interminable wait in the Marriott lobby. When we got to the chain-link portion of the outfield wall, which separated the bullpen from the playing field, we opened the door and strode right in. Then we did some stretching before we began to throw.

Originally, Royals Stadium had an artificial playing surface. It was nearly all synthetic turf with the only organic substances being the dirt on the mound, and at home plate, and in the sliding pits at each base. The bullpens, however, were different. They featured real grass and it was magnificent.

The Royals groundskeeper was George Toma, whose name is legend to anyone associated with athletic fields. With the playing surface being artificial, he and his crew were kept busy keeping it clean but they were not challenged to keep it growing. Having George Toma as the head groundskeeper in an artificial-surface stadium was somewhat akin to hiring Van Gogh to paint the exterior of your house with a roller and a can of gray latex.

Toma and his crew clearly relished the chance to make the bullpens special. As Lance and I stretched to get loose I marveled at this patch of green grass. Every blade stood straight up. Every blade was precisely the same height. The color was brilliant, and completely uniform.

And then I walked over to the mound. Being in the bullpen, where two pitchers often need to warm up at once, it was a rectangle rather than a circle. It was perfect. I almost felt as if the spikes on my shoes were defiling such a pristine place.

Heath and Stange arrived just moments later and I began the warm-up process by playing catch with my catcher, who stood behind home without his mask on. I ramped up the velocity as quickly as I could, subconsciously trying to make this as little of a bother as possible for the big league player I was throwing to, and then I said, "I'm ready."

Heath put on his mask and crouched behind the plate. I dug a little bit of dirt out from in front of the pitching rubber, which was so perfectly smooth and level to the dirt I had never had any experience putting my right foot on such a thing. I wound up and threw my first fastball.

Stange immediately said, "Oh, a sidewinder huh? OK, here's my first tip. Right-handers aren't going to like you much, so make it even worse by moving all the way over to the far right side of the rubber."

That made sense. Although it only made sense on a mound like this. In a place called the Major Leagues. The mound in Medford was typical for that level of professional ball but I don't think it would've been possible to stand over on the right side of the rubber at Miles Field. There were too many ruts and holes to deal with, especially the rut where all the other pitchers were landing with their front foot. On this mound, on this day, I could have thrown barefoot from any place I wanted. It was a world with which I was wholly unfamiliar.

I threw a few more and they were moving nicely. Heath even had to swipe at one backhanded when it dove down and in more than he expected, and I heard him say "Whoa!" to himself. Stange then said, "OK, let's work on your windup. You've got a pretty high leg kick and you're bringing your two hands down behind your knee when you do it. That's wasted motion and it's making your arm lag behind your body. Just bring your knee up then start to bend over at the waist. At the same time, spin a little to your right to add some torque to your delivery and help get your arm going, and drop your hands over both sides of your knee. When your hands get to the bottom, keep the flow going and just pull your throwing hand out of your glove to take it behind you."

I did just as he said. And threw the single best fastball I'd ever thrown. At that precise moment the orchestra stopped randomly warming up and the symphony began. It was all there.

I marveled at how different it felt and I also had time to ponder that if he thought my arm was lagging behind my body now, he should've seen me three weeks earlier. My arm might've shown up at the stadium an hour after I did.

With the new windup the fastball was faster, the sink was heavier, and my location was more consistent. Heath said "Nice pitch" a few times as I worked. I then spun a few curves and they were effective as well. I even mixed in a few of the newfangled change-ups I'd been working on.

Not a single ball in the dirt. Not a single pitch that wasn't a strike. It was incredible. The memory of Baloosh running out to the mound and saying, "Just once, right over the top," seemed like ancient history. It had happened less than two months earlier.

After about 15 minutes, we wrapped it up. Lance then took the hill and began his warm-up tosses while Stange came over and chatted with me.

"So you haven't always been a pitcher, huh?" he asked.

"Well," I said, "actually I began pitching in Medford about seven or eight weeks ago. Before that, it was fourth grade."

He laughed and said, "Look, I'm not going to blow smoke or lie to you. It seems like a longshot at your age but I've never really seen anything quite like it out of a guy who just started pitching a couple of months ago. Every other outfielder I've seen turn into a pitcher did it because he could rare back and throw hard. You're doing something at a different level and I think this is worth a solid shot."

He continued by saying, "You need some intense coaching, and just here in 15 minutes you did everything I told you to do and you got better. I'm going to recommend that the club bring you to the big league camp as a non-roster player for spring training, just so we can work with you. That will be your best chance to get up to speed in a hurry."

I probably didn't hear that last sentence. My brain was still processing the idea that I had just heard the words "big league camp."

I was stunned.

Stange patted me on the shoulder and said, "Great job, Bob. I'm glad you came over here today to have this chance. Let's see if we can make it pay off." I just said, "Yes, sir. And thank you!"

Lance then did his session, making Heath's mitt pop in a way my pseudo-fastball had not. He threw his 15 minutes and Stange said, "You throw harder than half my staff. Of course, looking at us that's not saying much, but we'll see if I can get you a try-out in the spring. Stay in shape, son."

We all shook hands, with Lance and I thanking Stange and Heath profusely. Heath was all smiles, but even better was the way he treated us — like teammates, like equals, with no sense our bullpen session had been beneath him.

It all felt ... rewarding. And oddly peaceful.

We took our time walking back in, staring up at the enormous grandstands and the Stadium Club restaurant with its huge windows overlooking the field. The blue table cloths with white napkins folded to look like crowns caught my eye. I looked out at the unique pointed ends of the upper deck in that magnificently designed stadium, remembering how a few years earlier I'd gone out to sit in the last seat in the front row of that deck, just so I could spot that seat whenever the Royals would be on TV. And then we headed back up the tunnel to the clubhouse. By then, the place was packed with players and pregame rituals were happening everywhere.

I looked around to absorb it all and commit it to memory, including the fact infielder Rob Picciolo appeared to have two dozen pairs of white spikes in his locker. I had one pair that summer in Medford. And I shined them myself. We were standing in a zone we had always aspired to visit, and it wasn't lost on me just how much I continued to love this game. I loved it desperately. I knew I always would. The hair on my arms was standing straight up.

I also didn't want to be in the way of the real players as they got ready to play the second-to-last game of the year. I gave Rick Langford his spikes and glove, with a thank you, and Mike Norris saw me and said, "How'd it go?" I said it went great, and he said "Happy to help. Just throw that stuff in the bin. I have another uniform."

Just throw that stuff in the bin. More words we never heard in Medford.

I was in a hurry to get out of everyone's way but Lance was taking his time, totally soaking it all in. He even decided to shave at the long line of sinks, after he showered. It was all part of the experience and I totally got that. Considering my upbringing, Lance and I had different perspectives standing there in a big league clubhouse full of big league players, who were wearing Oakland A's uniforms as they were about to play the Kansas City Royals. I got that. I appreciated it. And I wanted him to remember it all.

We finally made our way outside and Skip was waiting there. He said, "Lee told me both of you guys did great. I'm proud of you."

We decided to stick around for a few innings of the game and took our seats right behind home plate, in the best box-seats in the park. Mike Morgan was on the mound for the A's.

Morgan was actually three years younger than us but he'd signed out of high school and had been placed right on the big league roster in '78. He'd made his big league debut right after the draft at the age of 18. As we watched, he pitched eight innings, gave up 11 hits, and six earned runs. He struck out three and walked five. He took the loss as the Royals won 6-2, and it dropped his record to 2-10 on the year.

We drove home in the darkness and my head was spinning. It was so surreal I wasn't sure how to comprehend it. We flippantly use the term "unbelievable" in daily conversation and without much thought, but what had just happened to me, or what I had caused to happen, was unbelievable.

Within days it was getting too cold to throw outside and Lance and I didn't have much access to indoor mounds. It was time to give our arms a break for the winter.

We got into our rhythm in our new grown-up apartment with nice rented furniture, my classes started at SIUE and October turned to November. Then I found a receipt for a certified letter in our mailbox. The lump in my throat was matched only by the pain in my gut. Contracts come in January. Releases got sent out in the fall.

I didn't want to go to the Post Office, but I did. And sure enough, contrary to all of my hopes, the clerk had me sign for an envelope that bore the Oakland A's logo in the upper left corner. Inside the envelope was my unconditional release. I stood there and shook my head for a minute, trying to figure out if the whole thing had been an elaborate charade. Or possibly a dream.

I had Stange's phone number and I gave him a call. I told him what had happened and he said "I'm really sorry, Bob. I'm in the same boat. They let the whole staff go this week."

Good old Charlie Finley had struck again. In his latest cost-cutting move, he fired his entire Major League staff and let go a large number of minor-leaguers. Stange never had a chance to attend the team's winter meetings to file his report on me.

I thought briefly about trying to line-up some tryouts in the spring but the rational side of me knew how fruitless that would be. Who would even take the time to look at a 23-year-old outfielder who wanted to pitch but had already been released twice?

It was in improbable story, and the only way it would've come to fruition was with Lee Stange and the Oakland A's, after that one day. It could not have possibly gone any better, and yet it didn't happen. Maybe it wasn't improbable. Maybe it was impossible.

I had lunch with Taffy and Skip in Kirkwood, and Skip just shook his head. "I've never been more proud of what you've done," he said. "You did everything possible to make this pay off after a very tough year. Don't ever forget a minute of it."

I haven't.

I was 23. I had played college and professional ball and had my share of memorable moments. I played with and against a number of guys who went on to big league greatness. And I pitched for roughly eight weeks. The last pitch I threw in my career was to Mike Heath, at Royals Stadium.

How could anyone forget a minute of that?

Learn From Your Mistakes

My unexpected release from the A's was difficult to handle. I was forced to acknowledge the dream that began with catching my first fly ball at Schall School was finally and officially over. In addition my patented "plow forward" mentality had suffered a deep bruise and I wasn't sure how to heal it. Up to that point, I had maintained the ability to just keep going because I knew things would work out in the end. This time, when it all looked the rosiest and even my wildest dream was seemingly within reach, it was yanked away so ruthlessly I was shaken by the finality of it.

As disappointing as it was, I didn't hide in a dark corner or cry about it. I had to keep going and there were plenty of important things on my agenda. Dr. Winter was certainly happy to see me when I got back to school, and the concept of heading off to the broadcasting world wasn't one I totally opposed.

Plus, Taffy and I decided to sue the Oakland A's.

It was clear that negligence was involved with the batting cage fiasco, but as long as I was still a member of the organization I wasn't going to go after any compensation. Once I was no longer employed by Charlie Finley I figured I might as well press the issue to see if any monetary award could be secured. I'd certainly gone through my share of pain and suffering.

My sister Cindy lived in the Bay Area and she knew an injury lawyer. Once he heard the details he said, "I don't know how much we can get, but I'm willing to put the hours in just to make Finley pay you something." He made it clear that he, and many others in the region, would love to make Finley compensate someone for something, no matter the amount.

In the end, about two months later, I accepted a check for $3,600 after hearing from the lawyer, who said he didn't think there was much more to squeeze out of the A's. It wasn't much, but it was enough to finally close the door and move on.

It was also a time of transition in terms of maturity. In our nicely furnished suburban St. Louis apartment Lance and I were evolving into actual adults, and in his case the evolution was accelerated by his full-time job. My three classes kept me busy enough and with two of them being night classes we found the days of Spanky's, The Granary, and our other Edwardsville haunts behind us. Lance and I still went out on weekends, usually in the St. Louis suburbs, but our non-stop socializing was over.

All my classes were electives. One, a 10-week night course, involved the reading and analysis of classic books.

In that class with me was a journalism student who had, at one point, covered the SIUE baseball team for the school newspaper. His name was Bill Plaschke. Bill went on to work for the Los Angeles Times, where his beat was also baseball but by then he was covering an outfit known as the Dodgers. He became an award-winning columnist and author and now appears as an expert commentator on ESPN.

It was Bill who, during a discussion, announced to the class one night the only problem with Cornelius Ryan's "A Bridge Too Far" was that its title was inaccurate. He said it should've been called "A Book Too Long."

Before the fall quarter ended I huddled with Dr. Winter and other members of the Mass Communications Department, developing a plan to put audition tapes together over the winter quarter. They were kind enough to allow me to reserve time in both the radio and television studios. Dr. Winter again reminded me not to wink at the camera when I signed off.

To finish my degree during the winter I once again had only three classes on my schedule, leaving me plenty of time to get those tapes done. And again, two of the classes met at night with one being Detective Fiction, in which we read and analyzed the styles of such great writers as Dashiell Hammett, Raymond Chandler, and Agatha Christie. For 10 weeks, all we did was read a book per week and then discuss the ways the writers had woven their webs of clues and red herrings. What became quickly obvious was that writers couldn't just sit down and ad-lib a detective novel. It all had be plotted out, with complicated timelines and charts. Just like this book. OK, maybe not.

I also needed one general studies course to satisfy my requirements and as a sixth-year senior I chose freshman psychology. My plan, which in retrospect was not particularly brilliant, was to only go to class for tests and take them without studying. I challenged myself to get a B via common sense alone. I did that, but an A would've been easy in the entry-level class.

Finally, my last class for my minor in communications was another in the study of nonverbal communication. Did you know that we all tend to blink more rapidly when we're lying? It's true. I went to college for six years to learn stuff like that.

In the dead of winter my dad went to the baseball winter meetings in Toronto, and when he came back he asked me a question I had never really anticipated. He asked me if I wanted to be a scout. Not a Boy Scout. A professional baseball scout.

In Toronto he had been talking with Pat Gillick, the general manager of the Blue Jays, and Pat had asked about me. He knew Big Del's youngest had been playing minor league ball but he was not aware I'd been released. When he learned of that detail he asked Skip if I'd be interested in joining the organization, which was just entering its fourth year of existence as an expansion franchise.

Skip told Gillick he wasn't sure, and that I might be burned out on the game altogether, but he'd run it past me. Either way, it was a gracious offer from one longtime baseball man to another, all to benefit a son.

For much of the game's history baseball scouts were generally like my dad. They were older guys who had played or managed and who could still spot prospects using nothing more than their eyes and a stopwatch. Sabermetrics, analytics, and other ways of judging not just talent, but also value, were decades away. It was still as old-school as it had been when the first scout saw Lou Gehrig. That would be a man by the name of Paul Krichell, by the way.

In 1980 things were beginning to change in the scouting world, and they would change rapidly. The Blue Jays planned to be on the cutting edge of those changes.

By then, the signing bonuses awarded to high draft picks were getting so large — well up into seven figures — that forward-thinkers like Gillick believed it would be wise to hire scouts who were younger, more energetic, more analytical, and better able to handle the lonely life on the road.

As surprised as I was by the offer it only took me a few minutes to weigh the options of staying in the game I loved versus joining something that more accurately resembled the real world. I chose baseball.

A week later I met with one of the team's senior-level scouts, at the St. Louis airport, for an interview and apparently I did pretty well. I was offered a full-time job as a scouting supervisor who would cover a number of states in the midwest. My annual salary was an astonishing $8,600.

Still just 23, I was the youngest full-time scout in Major League Baseball. The broadcasting tapes were never finished.

The plan was to finish my classes and get my degree, then take off with one of the team's established scouts for a few weeks to learn the ropes. I recall honestly thinking, "Well, how hard can scouting be?" The plow-forward mentality was back.

But if the plow-forward mentality could bring great things to my life, it could also lead to mistakes.

Just a few weeks before my college education was due to end I met a nice young lady in one of my night classes. My thinking was that college was where you met your wife, so with just a few weeks left I had better hurry up and get serious. She was sweet, attractive, and she laughed at my jokes. What's not to love?

Her name was Kathie and she was from a tiny town in eastern Illinois just a few miles south of Danville, not far from the Roosters' stadium. I was up-front about having accepted the scouting job and that, within weeks, I'd be hitting the road. From that first day with the Blue Jays until early November I would be almost constantly in cheap roadside motels but we both never really stopped to think about that.

We went on a few dates before I left and I managed to get back to the St. Louis area a few times during the summer. For some illogical reason we both decided getting married was the best thing to do. And we figured we ought to do it just as soon as possible.

To add to the fun, by that point the Blue Jays had told me they'd be transferring me to California, right after the new year. Even that didn't dissuade us.

Once we started planning the wedding I think we both realized getting married so quickly might not be the best idea but, like many kids at that point, we felt as if we were swept up in a wedding for everyone else instead of for us. We still hardly knew each other but the machine had us in its gears and there seemed to be no better option than just going through with it. So we got married.

My travel schedule was brutal and there's no way I was anything but a lousy husband because of it. It's hard to be a good and caring partner when you're never there. I called home every night. I hardly ever went out with friends or other scouts. I never once raised my voice to her. But I was constantly gone, chasing prospects all over my multi-state area where high school and college baseball games were more important to me than my new marriage. Considering how I grew up, with a father who did exactly the same thing, I can now see that such an eventuality might've been impossible for me to avoid.

After four years of scouting I left baseball for good, but my next job and the one after that both demanded backbreaking travel. I was still never home.

And despite all of that, we never once had an argument. That's a reflection of her personality. She was the gracious hostess, the devoted wife, and the keeper of the household. I was basically just gone. I was a husband in absentia.

I was unhappy, and I assumed she was as well. This wasn't the blissful marriage we'd seen in the movies. We didn't have much joy, nor did either one of us feel much love.

I moved out. Within a few weeks she began dating the man with whom she would get remarried and start a family, and they soon moved to Florida. This time, she got the right guy. It just wasn't me. I still wish both of us would've realized that before we took the plunge.

Her family was wonderful. Her dedication to making the marriage work was remarkable. I'm eternally sorry for having put her through such loneliness, but I'm thrilled she found her soulmate and made a wonderful life for herself, her husband, and her kids.

Back in the late winter of 1980 I couldn't see any of that. I was afraid scouting would consume me so much I'd never meet the right woman. I was too dumb to realize the right thing has to happen for its own reasons and can't be forced. Bottom line — I was simply too immature to be a better husband.

It took me a long time to fix all of those shortcomings and I suffered through as many slumps in my relationships and personal life as I had in the batter's box.

I still wonder how or if that part of my life could've been different, or better, but as painful as some of the mistakes were, I wouldn't change them. These dominoes had to fall in a certain order. My maturation had to happen at its own rate. There were still many disappointments ahead of me, waiting in the weeds, but I believed there was something out there that would change my life for the better. I just had to hang on and find it.

In the meantime, there were a lot of baseball games to watch.

Pretending To Be A Scout

In early March 1980, with my degree in hand, I packed as many scout-worthy clothes as possible into an old-school Samsonite suitcase and hit the road. I had no idea what I was in for and no clue how to really do it but I'd been accompanying my father on scouting trips for much of my life and I figured I was fully capable of faking it until I could make it work.

To get started, I actually had to board a puddle-jumper at Lambert Airport in St. Louis and fly down to Carbondale, Illinois. Carbondale was home to SIUE's sister school, Southern Illinois University-Carbondale. SIUC was clearly the big sister in the family, though, with a much larger campus and enrollment. As illustrations of its loftier status, the Carbondale campus usually was referred to as just SIU, and its sports teams — the Salukis — played in Division I. To this day, when people ask me where I went to college, if I say I graduated from Southern Illinois the response will be, "Oh, you were a Saluki!" There remains a lot of explaining to do.

Carbondale is only 100 miles from St. Louis but I needed to fly because I would not yet be in charge of my own scouting itinerary. I would spend the first month or so with Don Welke, who was the Toronto scouting supervisor for a large portion of the Midwest. As his apprentice I'd be learning from one of the best and I'd eventually take over a number of his states.

Don picked me up at the tiny Carbondale airport and we headed directly to SIU to watch the Salukis play a home game. I had with me a stopwatch, a pen, and a Blue Book to make the costume complete.

The Baseball Blue Book was a small binder that was published and distributed annually to scouts and front-office personnel. In it were reams of information we can now find with a few clicks on our smartphones, but back then those names, numbers, addresses, and schedules were critical bits of information to have at your printed disposal.

Throughout my childhood I'd seen the routine. Each year, when the new Blue Book arrived, Skip would empty the contents of the prior year's edition and replace those pages with appropriately sized and three-hole punched baseball scorecards and blank scouting reports. Nearly all the scouts did the same, recycling their old Blue Book to serve a new purpose each spring, and those 6 x 9-inch blue binders were the most visible indicators that scouts were at a game.

As we walked into the SIU ballpark it hit me that I felt like a pretender. It was as if I'd dressed up as a scout for Halloween but the other attendees at the party were men I'd known for years as my father's colleagues. I was plowing forward, once again, but this time there was a bit of "why am I doing this?" involved in the transition.

I said hello to Don Lenhardt, a longtime baseball man from my dad's era I'd known since my early childhood. He was 58. I was 23. It still felt like I was Del's kid and he was just one of Dad's scouting buddies. It was not a wholly comfortable situation for me and watching the game I realized the biggest problem I was going to need to overcome was that I still wanted to be playing. Many of the players on the field that day were only two or three years younger than me. Just two years earlier in the spring of 1978, I'd been on that field playing for the Cougars as we took on the Salukis.

The plow-forward theory does create its own inertia, though, because once I stepped off that little plane and joined Don for a month on the road, there was no turning back unless I fled in the middle of the night. All I could do was ride in the passenger's seat, watch ball games, keep notes, and check into and out of hotels and motels all around Illinois and Indiana.

It was our responsibility to pay for our expenses wherever we went, and then we would file a weekly expense report for reimbursement. While I was traveling with Don he'd pay for both of us, but I had to watch what he did because all that paperwork was something I'd have to do myself as soon as I was on my own.

As for the motels we'd be staying in, the Blue Jays didn't have a firm limit on rates but there was a highly recommended guideline. Anything over $29 per night was frowned upon, but many Holiday Inn locations honored a special baseball rate of $19 per night so I was right at home.

Welke was an interesting character and he was clearly the right choice as a babysitter for the youngest full-time scout in Major League Baseball. He was a family man, quiet, and serious about his work. He was also a bit of a rarity in the scouting ranks, as he had not played or coached the game professionally.

We rarely talked about what he looked for in a player. Instead, Don taught me the mechanics of the job, especially how to organize trips to visit the greatest number of schools in the most efficient manner. To that end he actually used me as his administrative assistant, asking me to use a four-color pen to fill in his master calendar.

We needed to see high schools, junior colleges, and four-year universities, and earlier in the winter he'd sent a letter to every coach in the area, asking for their schedules. It was my job to take all of those schedules and write the dates into Don's calendar in the appropriate colors. For the first few weeks it felt like I was far more a secretary than a baseball scout, but the truth was I would need to know this stuff and do it on my own in short order.

I realized my life had quickly changed. I'd been living with, playing with, and riding on buses with guys my age since I arrived at college. We shared experiences and had similar senses of humor and we kept ourselves entertained.

Now, riding in a car all over the Midwest with a baseball scout 14 years my senior who was buttoned-down and quite serious, I felt as if I'd landed on an alien planet after just having said goodbye to my friends on Earth. It was an adjustment I'd have to make if I was going to do this for a living.

Don and I also experienced one of the most difficult aspects of scouting in the Midwest. It was a cranky and unreliable thing called the weather.

Rain-outs throw a scout's entire schedule off, especially if you're attempting to see a specific pitcher. Once the weather would go bad at one school there were a lot of quick adjustments that had to be made to avoid wasting time. Don would scour his master calendar for the next stop, and off we'd go, hoping the rain we were driving in would stop by the time we got to our new target. Smartphones with weather apps would've really come in handy back then.

We planned on seeing a prospect at Notre Dame one day and as we pulled into South Bend it began to snow. We walked into the athletic department to meet with the head coach and he let us know that the early springtime white stuff was forecast to come down all day, and they'd likely not play. When Don and I left the building to walk 100 yards back to his car it was an absolute blizzard and the flakes were both huge and wet. By the time we got to his sedan, both of us were covered from head to toe. We looked to two living snowmen and for the first time we shared a belly-laugh together. I said, "I'm beginning to think it would be a lot easier to be a basketball scout, where all the games are indoors." Wiping the snow off his sleeves he replied, "But what would be the fun in that?"

We headed for Chicago but again the weather was the biggest challenge. Don and I checked into his favorite Chicago motel (under $29 per night) on North Avenue, near Elmwood Park. We then plotted out the next five days with trips planned for a variety of high schools, the local colleges, and other stops both in the suburbs and deep in the city.

Don also had an "associate scout" in Chicago, an unpaid volunteer who fed him information and covered back-up games for him. Way back in the day, those guys were called "bird dogs" but by 1980 the more formal term was preferred. The only way they got paid was if a player they recommended ended up signing with the team. Mostly they did it for the love of the game.

His guy in Chicago was an older gentleman, in his 70s, who had been around the game his whole life. We visited his small brick home on Chicago's north side and made plans for me to head out to Northern Illinois University, in DeKalb, with him the next day.

It was a sunny day the next morning but when I walked out of my motel room I knew I had not packed nearly enough warm clothing for this gig. It was barely 30 degrees and the wind was whipping. In Chicago. Go figure. By the time we got to NIU, about 90 minutes later, the windchill factor had to be no more than 20.

There were a number of other scouts there, and it was so fiercely cold the head coach for Northern Illinois invited us to sit in their dugout. I considered it a matter of survival.

Frankly, I don't recall seeing anyone who qualified as a prospect in that game and even if a player could have been marginally classified as such it would've been difficult to tell watching them trying to perform in those conditions. To me, it was a frigid waste of time. But I learned another thing that day.

To many of the longtime scouts the games were social affairs. They'd known each other for decades, in most cases, and while they were looking for prospects they were also happy to socialize, smoke cigars, and tell old stories.

Despite the fact it was miserable and despite the fact there were no prospects to be seen not one scout left early, and that included my chauffeur. Part of that was the camaraderie but another important part was a respect issue for the NIU coach. It would be one thing to sneak out of the bleachers to warm up in your car for a bit, but getting up and walking out of his dugout in the third inning would not only be disrespectful, it would be insulting. That was a chilly lesson to learn. This scouting stuff was a lot more complicated than I originally thought.

Finally, after a little more than a month of rain, snow, and cold, I was free to go and spend the rest of the spring scouting on my own. Pat Gillick, the Toronto general manager, gave me the following words of critical advice: "I want you to keep it simple. Scout these guys for tools we can't teach. We can't make your arm much better if you don't throw well. We can't make you run much faster if you're slow. We can work on your swing and we can work on your glove, so look for speed and arm strength as a starting point. Those are the tools we look for. Use your stopwatch and time every player from home to first. Always get there early for infield practice, to see their arms. If you see guys with natural ability in terms of those tools, write them up and get a report to us."

In a matter of a minute, Pat Gillick had summarized just about everything a guy really needed to know about scouting. That's one reason why he's in the Baseball Hall of Fame today. He knew the game, but more important, he knew how to communicate what he was after.

I flew home to St. Louis and the first order of business was vehicular. I needed a new car. My Fiesta was done and it wasn't comfortable or spacious enough for months on the road.

Lance had played on the Elizabethton team with a pitcher named Barry Jenkins. Both of them had been released before the season ended but Lance and Barry had hit it off and were friends. Barry also lived in St. Louis and quickly landed a job as a regional sales manager for Chrysler. Lance introduced me to him, and 24 hours later Barry was delivering a nearly new Chrysler Cordoba to the driveway on Woodleaf Court. Sadly, it had cloth seats not fine Corinthian leather (cue Ricardo Montalban.) It had also been an executive car and had only 6,000 miles on it, so he sold it to me for $3,600. I had my ride, and it was stylish, so it was time to hit the road but only after one additional detail was completed. I also needed a credit card. I'd never had one of my own.

I applied for an American Express card but that would take a month to be approved. So, Taffy took me up to Commerce Bank in Kirkwood and she co-signed an application for a new MasterCard. It had a $500 credit limit. I certainly wouldn't be out there living it up with that and I'd need to pay it in full every month just to have the ability to check in at those $29 motels.

My first trip on my own would take me up through central Illinois and eventually back to Chicago where Toronto's "cross-checker" scout, Al LaMacchia, had joined Don Welke to see a couple of his prospects. Cross-checkers were just what the name implied. Each scout would file his reports and rank the players in his region, and the cross-checkers would then come to look at the top-ranked players with a fresh perspective, to decide exactly where those players fit on a national scale compared to the lists other scouts had submitted. It was a tough job but Al was a tough old guy from my dad's era. The prototypical old-school baseball man. Picture Abe Vigoda with a cigar.

Before I got to Chicago, though, I needed to stop in Lincoln, Illinois, to see a prospect who was an infielder. Don didn't know the kid's name but he'd heard there was player at the local high school who could really play. So I went to take a look.

I showed up at the ballpark early and spotted a coach unloading bats from his trunk. I rolled down my window and introduced myself and then said, "We've heard you have a pretty good infielder here. A real prospect. What's his name, coach?"

The guy said, "Oh yeah. Write his name down right now. He's our shortstop, Greg Bee."

Once the team hit the field for warmups I spotted Bee and thought he was OK, and possibly even pretty good. Decent arm at short, he could run a little, seemed decent fielding the ball. But, the kid at third base really wowed me. He could field everything hit his way, he had a powerful arm, and during the game he showed me he could really swing the bat and run. I remembered Pat Gillick's advice about what to look for.

After the game, so as not to be disrespectful to the coach who had recommended the shortstop, I asked him if he'd send both Greg Bee and the third baseman over to my car so that they could fill out personal information cards.

Both of the guys oohed and aahed over my nice new Cordoba and they eagerly filled out the cards. I wrote a report on the third baseman that night and I'm proud to say I got him right. He went to Eastern Illinois University and then was drafted in 1983 by the Kansas City Royals. He went on to play 12 years in the big leagues. His name was Kevin Seitzer.

As for Greg Bee, the shortstop, I found it more than a little amusing later when I took another look at the Lincoln roster and noticed the last name of the assistant coach I'd spoken with in the parking lot. It was Bee.

Once I got back to Chicago, I met Al LaMacchia and reveled in his humor and brash personality. He reminded me of every scout I'd sat near on trips with my dad and Al even had a few Del Wilber stories to tell.

Al and Don sent me off to see a high school catcher down in the city and as I watched the game I remember thinking he wasn't very good. He didn't throw particularly well, he had a slow bat, and he was a hefty kid who didn't get down the baseline well at all. I wondered why Don and Al had sent me to see him.

When I got back to the motel they knocked on my door and asked me how the kid had looked. I said "Well, the pitcher on the other team didn't have much but he was jamming the hell out of the kid with that junk. He did hit a long home-run over the centerfield fence but it was off a nothing fastball right down the middle. His arm's OK and he handled himself fine behind the plate."

They asked me if he could run and I diplomatically said "Well, he runs OK for a big guy," figuring they'd sent me to see the kid because they liked him. Who was I to question the evaluations of these two esteemed veteran scouts?

Al said, "How do big guys run? Does he get a headstart because he's big? I just want to know if he can run."

I said he couldn't, fearing a disagreement. Al smiled and said "Good. We've seen him and he can hit the ball a long way but he's not a prospect. I wanted you to see him and tell me what you thought. You got it right, but remember the part about running. You can run or you can't. It doesn't matter if you're big or small."

More sage advice. Point taken.

In mid-April I drove out to Columbia, Missouri, to see a pitcher for the Mizzou Tigers. It was my only chance to see the kid and after checking in at the Holiday Inn I watched the news and saw the dire forecast for the next day. It featured a 100 percent chance of rain with a high temp in the mid to upper 30s. Not good.

When I awoke the next morning, I listened carefully to discern if it was raining or not. I didn't hear any rain so I got up and tiptoed to the window to take a peek, as if I was sneaking up on the weather. My reaction to what I saw would be apt for a Saturday morning cartoon show, complete with bulging eyeballs and cowbell sound-effects as I shook my head in disbelief. There was at least a foot of snow on the ground and my car looked like an igloo. The forecast had been slightly wrong in the temperature department and the heavy rain turned into heavy wet snow. I had another thought about being a basketball scout. But what's the fun in that?

I had enough time scouting on my own to see some pretty good players and send in a dozen or so reports that first spring, ranging from guys I thought were big-league prospects to others I simply wrote up so that they'd be in our files and we could keep an eye on them. Teams do that often, tracking guys they think might get better, and to that end sometimes the best advice to a promising high school kid is, "You should go to college and get your education." We could see if those players would improve as they got older. I remembered that period well from my own life.

That first June I also learned another valuable lesson. If you sell cars for a living, and have a very good year, you know you sold a lot of cars and the results are there for everyone to see. Most jobs are like that. If you do your job to the best of your ability, the rewards will come your way.

Baseball scouts know all too well that such a rule doesn't apply to them. You can be the best scout in the world, and outwork every other scout in your region. You can find great prospects and file all the reports accurately. You can nail every guy perfectly in terms of tools and abilities. But then there's that pesky thing called the Major League Draft in early June, where all the MLB clubs take turns choosing players.

Most of the guys I wrote up that first spring were selected. Every one of them was taken by other teams. Pat Gillick was kind enough to call me and let me know that at three different times during the 25 rounds in which the Blue Jays participated, they had one of my players on the board as their next planned selection but other MLB clubs chose those guys before the Jays' turn came up. It was like working all year just to spin the roulette wheel to see if it paid off.

You could see that glass being half-empty and think it had all been a waste of time, but for me as a rookie it was an important first step. I'd just have to keep working hard to get some guys signed in the next draft.

Once the draft was complete and I came up with nothing, it was time to take on another challenge the Blue Jays put before me. They wanted me to travel to Utica, New York to spend a few weeks as a coach for the Utica Blue Jays, their rookie-level affiliate in the New York-Penn League. Many of the players on that team would be picks from the just-completed draft.

The Utica club was also heavily populated with Hispanic players, as the Blue Jays were already well ahead of the curve in terms of scouting the Caribbean and Central America. Of the 31 players who would play in Utica that summer, 14 were Hispanic and most of them were very young. There were seven players on the roster who were only 18 or 19 years old.

My rudimentary Spanish from high school would help me get acquainted a bit when I got there, but I was relieved to see that former Major League infielder Hector Torres would also be in Utica as a coach. I remembered Hector from his nine years in the show, and being a native Spanish speaker he would not only be a great help in the dugout and clubhouse but he'd also be able to help me brush up my Espanol in a hurry.

The manager of the Utica team was Larry Hardy, a former major league pitcher. Larry had signed with the San Diego Padres after they drafted him out of the University of Texas, and he had a fine 10-year career as a pro. I remembered him from 1974, when my buddy Mitch and I traveled to Honolulu with my dad's Spokane Indians. He was pitching for the Hawaii Islanders that summer.

I had the option of flying to Syracuse and taking a cab over to Utica, roughly a one-hour drive, or making a connection in Syracuse to fly to Utica in a twin-engine prop aircraft operated by Empire Airlines. I chose to get to Utica in 15 minutes rather than an hour.

It was a stormy night when I arrived in Syracuse and the sight of that tiny Fairchild Metroliner was a little worrisome as the lightning flashed and the winds swirled. I wasn't sure what I had gotten myself into but I put my head down and dashed out onto the tarmac to climb the stairs and take my seat.

I doubt we flew over to Utica at more than 10,000 feet and the flight was as bumpy as any I'd ever experienced. We dropped, swerved, tilted the wings, and jostled our way 50 miles eastward in the rainy darkness, fluttering around the sky like a runaway kite. As we were descending into Utica we were hitting pockets of air where the plane would drop a considerable distance before the pilots could correct things, and I remember thinking, "If we drop 15 feet like that when we're only 10 feet off the runway, this isn't going to be pretty." That's exactly what we did.

We were bobbing and weaving our way on final approach to the runway when the bottom dropped out again and we slammed down hard on the pavement. I heard a number of groans and grimaces from the few others who were on the plane with me and then we came to a shuddering stop on the taxiway, barely off the main runway. The pilot said, "Folks, sorry about that. We're going to have to wait here for some help. I'm pretty sure we blew out at least three of our four tires on the main landing gear. I can't taxi from here."

They sent a van out to pick us up and I made up my mind right then that I'd take a cab to Syracuse when it was time to leave Utica.

I met Larry and Hector the next day out at the ballpark, a quaint little bandbox named Murnane Field. It was great to be back in uniform again and still being a week shy of my 24th birthday I easily could've passed for one of the players I was there to instruct. Since we gave the players blue uniforms to wear for the first few days, while Larry, Hector, and I wore white, I thought it was a dead giveaway but three different times on that first day I had a player stop me and say "Why did they give you a white uniform?" or "Are you really a coach, or are you a player?"

We spent a week doing drills and working out and since the team seemed to have no firm plan for teaching "the Blue Jay way" I just put into practice what I knew. I put them through their stretching, running, and throwing routines exactly like we had done in Tiger Town the year before. When it was time for me to work with the outfielders I did the same drills to show them how to come in on a ball or go back and find it in the sky. Little did all the rookie Blue Jays know that they actually doing things the Tiger way.

One of the players on the roster was the Jays' 13th-round pick in the draft, out of Texas A&M. He was Mike Hurdle. I already knew Mike well, because we played together on the Danville Roosters in 1977, the summer after my junior year and his freshman year. It seemed like eons had passed since that summer, and much had indeed happened, but it had only been three years and we weren't that different in age.

One night, nearing the end of the first week of workouts, we played an intrasquad game under the lights and Larry asked me if I could pitch. I told him I'd be happy to and I dealt my sidearm stuff up there pretty well for four innings. Behind me, my second baseman was Hector Torres, he of the nine-year big league career that had wrapped up just three years earlier. We were both smiling.

During the fourth inning, Larry came out to the mound and he was met there by our Spanish-speaking catcher and Hector, who translated for him. Larry looked at me and said, "How about you just throw fastballs. They can't hit your curve or change-up, and as much as I want them to see good pitching I also need them to gain some confidence and run the bases a little." From that point forward, for two more innings, the catcher simply put down one finger as his signal before every pitch. To make the charade a little better, I even shook him off a few times, knowing the one finger (the universal signal for a fastball) would be coming right back.

I was pleased to be throwing so well and with such command that the young players couldn't hit me, but it didn't occur to me at the time that instead of saying, "OK, sure," maybe I should've said, "Well, if they can't hit me, don't you think you should sign me?" I probably made the right choice by not saying that. No need to replay the "If you want to get me killed" line I threw at Yank Mihal upon arrival in Paintsville.

After the week of drills we started the season on a wet summer night in upstate New York. I couldn't possibly tell you who we played but Larry did give me two responsibilities for each game. On the lineup card posted in the dugout, it was my job to note who made the last out each half-inning so we'd know who was hitting first the next inning or who we'd be facing first on the other team. And I'd be coaching first base. I thought that was pretty cool, although there wasn't much I could say to many of our players if they made it that far, other than "Bueno."

We then made a road trip to Oneonta to play the Yankees' farm club and that marked my second trip to that small village not far from Cooperstown. My father had taken me there many years before, on one of his scouting trips, and we had a grand old time taking pictures of the Wilber Bank and Wilber Park. Skip even went inside the bank and asked if he could have something with Wilber Bank printed on it and they gave him a money pouch used to carry coins. Sadly, the pouch was empty but yes, when the Wilber clan first came to America from Scotland, many of them settled in Oneonta and the Wilber legacy remains strong there. It was fun to be back.

The Utica Blue Jays team bus stopped at a Burger King in the afternoon, when we arrived in Oneonta, and Hector and I helped the Hispanic guys order their meals. Only a few knew the word "hamburger" in English but the Spanish "hamburguesa" was one I knew. We managed to get everyone fed and it was obvious that some of those guys were really hungry. It's not easy being 18 and finding yourself in a strange land with a language you don't speak. They hadn't been eating much.

And can you guess what happened on our trip back to Utica after that trip? Our bus broke down. Apparently, it was my aura all along.

After a few more weeks my stint in Utica was up and it was time to get back home because I still had a busy scouting summer ahead of me. It was time for what we called "pro coverage" and I'd be on the road pretty much nonstop until September, racking up miles in my Cordoba.

Each Major League team assigns pro coverage to a number of its scouts every summer. It was our job to make sure the big club had a detailed scouting report on every minor league ballplayer in North America, since those guys are often included as extra players (or "players to be named later") in Major League trades. My assignment that first summer was to cover the Class-A Midwest League as well as the Eastern Division of the American Association, the same Triple-A league Big Del Wilber's Denver Bears had been in. To accomplish those two tasks I'd have to clear the Midwest League first, since there is a method to pro coverage. I learned this via more great advice from Pat Gillick.

To see every pitcher and reserve player on a team a scout would need to see the club at least five or six days in a row. So, when I started my Midwest League coverage in Burlington, Iowa I watched the Burlington Bees play a four-game series at home and then followed them to Cedar Rapids to watch them play three more games there. Then, since I'd just seen Cedar Rapids for three games, I followed them to Waterloo and saw them play three more times. Then I followed the Waterloo team. It took me about a month and a half to finish the tour and it felt like it took just as long to fill out all the detailed scouting reports. I remember my dad complaining about all the paperwork scouting entailed and now I was getting a taste of it myself. Detailed reports on every player, on every team, in the league. In pencil.

Once I finished the Midwest League, including ball clubs in the aforementioned towns as well as Clinton, Wausau, Wisconsin Rapids, Quad Cities, and Appleton, it was time to make a quick pit stop at home before finishing my summer in the American Association.

It was an interesting transition to quickly go from the small ballparks of Class-A to the much bigger parks in Triple-A, and it was also interesting to see the obvious difference in the level of play. The Class-A guys were still at least three steps from the big show but the Triple-A guys were only one phone call away. For my coverage I'd have to see every player on the Springfield Redbirds in Illinois, the Iowa Oaks from Des Moines, and the Evansville Triplets and Indianapolis Indians in Indiana. With Des Moines being the outlier in terms of geography, I was fortunate to be able to follow them on a road trip and not have to drive back to the center of Iowa. The Evansville team was still the Triple-A affiliate of the Tigers but none of my Bristol or Lakeland teammates had gotten that far yet. They would in the years to come.

One might think the Triple-A assignment would be more stressful than the Class-A coverage, and in some ways that was true, but the Triple-A scouting reports were actually easier to write. You didn't have to project much to assess the caliber of a guy in Triple-A but the guys in

A-ball had so much more growing and developing to do it could be a real challenge. Imagine if I had been scouting the Appalachian League two years earlier instead of playing in it. I can't guess what my report about Cal Ripken would've contained but I doubt I would have projected him as a big leaguer, much less a Hall of Fame inductee who had smashed Lou Gehrig's "unbreakable" record for consecutive games played.

The guys on the scouting staff who had the most prestigious assignments were the ones doing their pro coverage in the big leagues. They not only filed reports on all the other teams but they also filed scouting reports on how to pitch to specific players. They stayed in big-league hotels, devoured catered meals, and otherwise traveled in style. Not a lot of $29-a-night roadside motels for those guys. Today, those jobs are all specialized and a club might have six or eight scouts watching other teams and noting their tendencies, but back then we had two. Those guys seemed like rock stars to the rest of us.

The best and worst part of pro coverage was that it was exactly like playing in the minor leagues except I sat in the stands, I had no teammates, and I had to drive my own car from town to town. There was an enormous amount of free time every day, in whatever small town or mid-sized city I was in, but I had no buddies to hang with and no chance to burn off energy by going to the park early for extra hitting. There was, however, plenty of time for walking around local malls or watching TV. Plus, there was always paperwork to do. It never ended.

It was common to run into scouts from other organizations who were covering the same teams, sometimes for a week or 10 days, but most of those guys were much older. I stayed mostly to myself that first year and the boredom of each day was unlike anything I'd anticipated when I began scouting. I ate a lot of junk food, stayed in a bunch of lousy motels, and watched tons of minor league baseball. And I had plenty of time to sit there and ponder the concept that I should still be playing instead of pointing a radar gun and operating a stopwatch in the third row behind home plate.

Less than a year earlier I'd left Royals Stadium in Kansas City thinking I would be going to the big-league camp for spring training. Instead, I found myself in Waterloo, Iowa timing batters as they ran from home to first.

The summer finally ended and I spent the next two months covering fall ball at various colleges and junior colleges in my region, but those assignments were just a way to keep us busy compiling notes for future reference. Finally, in late September, it was time for the annual Toronto organizational meetings where all of the scouts and cross-checkers would meet with the big league staff to go over what we'd just done and what we'd be doing the next summer.

It was great to meet the rest of the scouting staff, as well as Pat Gillick and the Major League front office, and I was happy and relieved to see the scout who covered Florida for the Jays. His name was Tim Wilken and we'd met earlier in the summer when we were both assigned to cover a huge amateur tournament in Wichita. Tim was an outgoing and funny guy who got my jokes, but better than that, he was only slightly older than me. For two years, he'd been the youngest scout in baseball before I wrestled that crown from him. It was our new goal to see how often we could work together and keep each other company on the road.

Before the meetings ended we were all treated to an evening at the final game of the Blue Jays' season, at old Exhibition Stadium. I'd never seen anything quite like it.

Exhibition Stadium was the longtime home of the Toronto Argonauts of the Canadian Football League and as such it was in no way suitable for baseball. Before MLB expanded and the Blue Jays arrived in 1977, a redesign was implemented. To avoid the typical pitfall of squeezing a baseball field onto a rectangular football site, they did something different. With a huge permanent grandstand on only one side of the football field they could make sure home plate was a suitable 330-feet from the left field wall. They then built a new one-level grandstand around the field, from the left-field corner to the right-field corner.

The main football grandstand ran from the left-field corner to out beyond center field, but the outfield wall only abutted the front row to the left-center alley. After that, the big grandstand went off on its own toward the far football end zone and, therefore, at least half the seats in that huge seating area were way too far from home and facing the wrong direction.

The scoreboard was in the back of the football end zone but the right field fence cut across the Argonauts' field around the 30-yard line, leaving the scoreboard a full 150 feet behind the fence in a no-man's land reserved for the Argos. Homers hit to right would clear the wall and then bounce and roll all the way down the artificial-surface of the football field, complete with yard lines, until they earned the distinction of being both home runs and touchdowns.

The new baseball grandstands were close to the action, though, and in total they might have matched the capacity of the main football stands. Maybe.

As we sat in the park that night I told Wilken, "This stadium has about 8,000 of the best seats in the Major Leagues, and about 30,000 of the worst." That was the general assessment of the place.

At the meetings I was given my orders to report to Fresno by late winter. The reason for my transfer was a guy named Rich Hacker. Rich was an established and highly regarded scout but he had kids and he lived where I did, in St. Louis. The club wanted to hire him, so Gillick asked if I'd move to California to help the organization. I had no problem with that, and I got a new contract for the unimaginable amount of $13,300 per year.

The team also announced, at the meetings, that for the first time in the club's young existence they would be filling out the scouting staff to include two national directors who would split the country in half and be in charge of all the full-time scouts, allowing Gillick to focus on the big-picture task of building the organization into a winner. My boss, out in California, would be Wayne Morgan, who lived in the town of Morgan Hill, on Morgan Avenue. That is all true. You can't make up trivia that rich.

I made a trip out to Fresno that winter to find a place to live, and then made the drive in yet another new car in early February. I had gotten such a great deal on the Cordoba and it served me well in 1980, but it got lousy fuel mileage and I wanted something a little sportier. I actually got more for it as a trade-in than I had paid and with that I only needed a small loan to switch to a brand-spanking-new Datsun 200SX, a quick little two-door that sipped gas at a fairly efficient rate. This also began a string of years in which I'd be buying new cars annually because regional baseball scouts could have no trouble whatsoever putting 60,000 miles on a car during a calendar year. Your options were to run a car for three years and then basically give it away, or try to get out of it gracefully each year.

My area in 1980 had included parts of six states around the Midwest but in 1981 my area was going to be just the San Joaquin Valley in central California. My boss, Wayne, would cover the San Francisco Bay area, the coast, and much of the northern part of the state, while another scout, Bob Zuk, would cover Los Angeles, San Diego, and the rest of Southern California. Each of us would see more prospects in our limited sections of the state than most of the Toronto scouting staff would see in multiple states. It's California. The kids are good. They play a lot of baseball.

Wayne drove over to see me after I arrived and got moved in and we went to lunch. His first words of advice were, "Don't get fooled by these kids. Everyone does, but try not to get fooled until you really get used to this. These kids can play 200 games a year if they want to, so by the time they're entering high school they look really polished. You're going to think they're all good. Stick to the tools. Make sure they can run and throw, if they're pitchers we want to see 88-89 minimum, and that's before we analyze control and command. These kids are flashy, so don't let the flash blind you."

I said I wouldn't, but within a week I was already succumbing to the dreaded disease of falling in love with flash when there wasn't enough real skill. It was hard not to do that.

Living in Fresno, I was centrally located in my area and could easily get to Bakersfield in the south or Sacramento in the north on Highway 99, the main expressway through the central part of the valley. I would get to know that highway very well.

Right in my town I had Fresno State and Fresno City College, two good programs. Just to the south I had College of the Sequoias in Visalia, Cal State Bakersfield, and Bakersfield City College. To the north, Merced Community College, Sacramento State, Sacramento City College, University of the Pacific in Stockton, and U.C. Davis. And every town on the map had high school baseball teams I needed to see.

The good news was the compact size of my area made it pretty easy to get from point to point rather than have to go off on three-month tours through multiple states, but the driving was just as challenging whether I was staying out in motels or making round trips.

As it turned out, that first spring in Fresno I saw plenty of good baseball but not a lot of great players. The highest-rated player I had in my area was Brian Williams, a senior from South High in Bakersfield, and what a specimen he was. He was 6-2, 190 pounds, and extremely athletic. The first time I saw him play, in a home game at his school, he hit a scorching double in his final at-bat and then ran right out of the ballpark to win the 100-meter dash in a track meet that was taking place right next to the baseball field. He could do it all.

Wayne came to see him and had me throw BP to the young man, and afterward he told me "OK, you're getting it. This kid has at least four tools. He can run, he can hit, I'm not sure about his power yet but he's strong, he can catch the ball, and he could throw it through the side of a battleship if he wanted to. Good job."

I felt good about that but word was spreading about young Mr. Williams and by the next time I saw him there must have been 15 other scouts there. I'd met his mom and we'd discussed what the young man wanted to do, since he could easily earn a college scholarship. His mom told me he wanted to sign, and she was all for that. They were not well off and lived in a rough part of town. He wanted to help his mom and get her a nicer place to live.

Wayne agreed the kid was good enough for any team to pick him in the first 10 rounds of the draft. As it often seemed to go for me, the Dodgers thought so, as well. They drafted Brian Williams in the sixth round. That one really hurt.

Just before that draft, while I was still hoping we'd get young Mr. Williams, I was called over to the Oakland East Bay area to help Wayne and Al LaMacchia work out a solidly built first baseman from a high school in Hayward. We found a field and I threw him BP, just laying them in there overhand, and even my 75-mph straight stuff was tying him up and jamming him. He was so strong and so muscle-bound he had a hard time fluidly swinging the bat. Frankly, I didn't think he had a chance but Wayne and Al liked his physical stature enough to select him in the 22nd round. The handsome young man turned down the offer and instead accepted a full athletic scholarship to play both baseball and football at the University of Southern California. As it turned out, football was his sport. He went on to play 11 stellar years as a linebacker in the NFL before moving into the coaching ranks. I think Jack Del Rio made the right choice to turn down the Blue Jays and go to USC.

I had also met one of the Blue Jays' injured pitchers that summer, a lanky guy named Jay Robertson who had been the club's third-round pick in 1977. Jay was from Sacramento and he was only a year younger than me. We hit it off really well and he asked me to take a look at a buddy of his, who he thought could pitch. The guy's name was Fritz Lund.

We set up a tryout at Sacramento City College and I took a spot behind the screen with my radar gun in hand. I smiled when I saw Fritz's sidearm delivery and the heavy sink on his fastball. I also smiled when I saw him hitting 90-92 mph on the gun. His curve was good and his stuff was nasty. Fritz had been released by the Oakland A's the same time I was although he had been pitching in Modesto that summer, a level higher than Medford.

After the workout the three of us went out for dinner and a couple of beers. I can't overstate how great it felt to be out with a couple of ballplayers my age, having some fun and enjoying each other's company.

We got a huge kick out of the fact we had such similar nicknames for the book "Ball Four" which is widely considered to be the best baseball book ever written. Penned by pitcher Jim Bouton during the 1969 season, it was a daily diary from spring training to the final game with realistic and brutally honest looks at the baseball life both on the field and off. It was considered a bit scandalous at the time because up until then baseball autobiographies were generally ghost-written and whitewashed. Plus, Bouton's early years were with the Yankees, so if providing tell-all tales of the clubhouse and the road weren't bad enough he made it worse by telling those stories about the fabled Yanks, including Mickey Mantle and Whitey Ford. In today's light "Ball Four" is touching, sharply defiant, brilliantly written, and absolutely hilarious. When it was published it was the sort of thing that would cost Bouton his job and a lot of friends.

Lance and I each read "Ball Four" at least 20 times. I could pick it up tonight and read 100 pages before putting it down and it would be just as enjoyable as the first time. We called it "The Bible According To Bouton." Over dinner that night in Sacramento, I mentioned the book and both Fritz and Jay got really excited. Fritz said, "We call it 'The Good Book' and we've each read it a dozen times." Smallish planet, especially the part populated by baseball players.

I called Wayne the next morning and told him about the workout.

"Why don't you call Toronto and see what they think," he said. "It might depend on whether we have any open spots with the Class-A or Double-A clubs, because it doesn't make any sense for him to pitch at a lower level than that."

I called Elliott Wahle, the director of player development for the Blue Jays, and he said, "We might have a need. As it turns out, I'm coming out to see Wayne next week. Can you set up another session with him? I don't think Jay Robertson would steer us wrong."

I did that and we had the workout. Mysteriously, Fritz's fastball on that day was 86 to 88 mph and it didn't sink as much. Afterward, I told Elliot the story about Fritz's first session but all he could go on was what he had seen. We passed. Those pesky Dodgers did not. They signed Fritz and sent him to Lodi, just down the road from his home in Sacramento. What we didn't know at the time was that Fritz's arm was giving out on him and after a couple of games with the Lodi Dodgers he was released. It had still been a fun adventure and I got one great night with a couple of really good guys out of it. That sort of recharged my batteries.

For pro coverage that summer I'd only be handling the Class-A California League, and again I'd have to write a report on every player on every team. I'd have the Fresno Giants right in my backyard and the Visalia Oaks (a Minnesota Twins affiliate) just 40 miles down the road, while the rest of the league consisted of the Modesto A's, the Stockton Ports (Milwaukee Brewers), the Lodi Dodgers, the Redwood Pioneers (a California Angels club in Rohnert Park, just west of Sonoma), the Reno Silver Sox (San Diego Padres), and the San Jose Missions, an independent team managed by none other than Fred Hatfield. I figured he'd probably not be interested in speaking to me.

The first stop on my California League extravaganza was a homecoming as I drove up to Modesto to see some familiar faces on the A's. Mike Altobelli was on that team and when he saw me in the first row during batting practice I thought he was going to run through the backstop to hug me. Also in Modesto, two years after our time together in Medford, were Robert Wood, Mark Ferguson, Terry Harper, Joe Williams, Jim Durrman, and the one and only Don Van Marter, the artist formerly known as Don Hawk Van Hawk Marter.

After BP, they all came over to the screen and we excitedly brought each other up to speed on everything we could think of including my facial scar which was, by then, almost invisible. It was great to see all those guys and it was genuinely heartwarming to share handshakes and hugs with all of them.

Back at the Fresno apartment, which overlooked one of the swimming pools in the complex, I had noticed the same group of athletic looking guys hanging by the pool during the afternoons. I went out to join them one day and I could overhear them talking about baseball and the Fresno Giants. I introduced myself, told them about my past, and within minutes I was part of the gang. Billy Heimach was an infielder for the Giants, Kelly Smith was an outfielder, and Jeff Trax was a pitcher, although he was out for the year with an arm injury. Jeff could've stayed home but he had made the decision that spending the summer with his friends and teammates was better for his state of mind than being back in Michigan by himself. All three of the guys were sharing an apartment one building over from mine.

I'd see them whenever we were all in town and a real friendship began to grow, especially between Jeff and me. Had I been a member of the Fresno Giants I'm sure Jeff and I would've been roomies on the road and at home. We got along that well.

And then, on June 12, the Major League players went on strike.

At first, it was business as usual. I still had the California League to cover and since no one knew how long the strike would last we all stayed out on the road with our expense accounts.

Within a week or two, the Blue Jays began to surmise that the work stoppage was not going to end quickly so they pulled us all off the road to save money. Pat Gillick called and told me to do my best covering the Cal League out of only Fresno and Visalia. And no overnight stays until the strike was over.

There would be entire teams in the league that I'd have no chance to see but as the summer went along I'd end up seeing the Giants and Oaks so many times I felt like I knew all the players personally. As Gillick would say, later in the summer, "If you missed anyone on the Fresno or Visalia teams you ought to be fired." I laughed and agreed with him, saying, "I think I know all their birthdays, girlfriends' names, and shoe sizes I've seen them all so much."

The Visalia team featured a big strong first baseman who was having a mammoth summer. By the end of the season he was hitting .359, with 27 home runs, and 111 RBI. He was truly a man among boys and when the big league rosters expanded (after the strike ended in August) he skipped right past the rest of the Twins' farm system and went straight to the big leagues. That would be Kent Hrbek, and it was a revelation to watch him play that summer.

If Hrbek's numbers in Visalia were startling, Rob Deer's numbers for the Giants were jaw-dropping. The big outfielder "only" hit .286 but his 33 home runs not only led the league, they were also all absolute bombs. He did strike out a lot, 146 times in 135 games, but when he got all of one there were gasps in the ballpark.

Frank Williams was a sidearm-throwing pitcher for the Giants and he was everything I had dreamed of one day being. His stuff was filthy, which means it was slightly better than nasty. Williams went 14-9 as a starter, striking out 170 batters in 187 innings.

Yes, my scouting reports on all three of those guys stated that they'd play in the big leagues. All three did, and did so very well.

As the strike kept going my life became a surreal replay of a typical summer as a kid. I had nothing to do all day until it was time to go see either the Giants or Oaks at night, and the swimming pool was right outside my door. Jeff and I were at the pool every day with the only exception being the 100-degree afternoons we'd spend on the tennis court. When the team went on the road it was just the two of us. When the team was at home, Jeff and I would be out there before noon and then Billy and Kelly would announce their impending arrival by sailing a frisbee over our heads and into the water from their upstairs apartment one building away.

We'd play games in the water like 12-year olds, including judging each other on who could make the most acrobatic horizontal laid-out diving catch of a frisbee, before belly-flopping onto the water.

We were 12. Seriously. We didn't just act like juveniles, we became them. And when Kelly and Billy went on the road with the Giants Jeff and I would hang by the pool all day, then play board games with beers in our hands until late in the night.

It eventually became obvious that Jeff should move out of their apartment and into the spare bedroom in mine. I have no idea how many tampering rules we were breaking, with a Giants player living with a Blue Jays scout, but I think it's too late to punish either one of us now.

When the summer ended we all headed south to Zuma Beach near Malibu, to spend one last day together. It was idyllic. And when it was over we all shared hugs and said our goodbyes and good lucks. I've never seen any of those guys again. But it was a masterpiece of a summer while it lasted.

The apartment complex was downright lonely after the Giants' season ended and my new buddies headed home. I hit the road to cover as many fall games as I could see while the Major League season wrapped up in a mostly confusing and possibly unfair manner.

With a large chunk of the season erased by the strike, MLB decided to crown a champion by splitting the season into two "halves" and instituting a two-round playoff format by pitting the first-half champs against the second-half winner, in each of the four divisions. That certainly created some drama for a fan base that was seriously disappointed by the strike but it also came at a price for fans in St. Louis and Cincinnati.

The Cardinals actually won the most games in the National League East, if you combined the two halves into one whole season. But, they didn't finish either half in first place so they were not in the playoffs. The Reds did the same thing in the NL West, winning the most games but finishing second in both halves. And, honestly, what the heck were the Cincinnati Reds doing in the West anyway?

At the conclusion of the ad-libbed playoffs, two very good teams did earn their way to the World Series. It would be a classic match-up between the New York Yankees and the Los Angeles Dodgers with the Yankees having home-field advantage. The pinstripers would open the series with two games at home.

Once the World Series participants were decided I got a phone call from Pat Gillick, who was attending the Series with a small entourage that included Toronto team president Peter Bavasi, Elliott Wahle, and the newly hired manager of the Blue Jays, Bobby Cox, who would take over the reins in 1982. It was great to hear from Pat but I wasn't sure why he was calling me from New York.

The boss said, "Hey Bob, why don't you come down to L.A. when the Series gets there and join us?" I waited not one split-second to agree.

The team booked a flight for me and reserved a room at the Hyatt Wilshire in L.A. I flew down on Thursday, October 22 to join my colleagues.

The first order of business was a small banquet that night, at Dodger Stadium, and I joined our group in the rental car Pat had secured. It was, much to my bemusement, a station wagon. We had a fine time at the soiree, mingling with a room full of MLB bigwigs including all the Yankees and Dodgers, and when it was time to head back to the Hyatt we all climbed into the wagon to make the drive.

One of the Yankee coaches approached Pat and said, "I've had enough, too. Do you have room in there to give me a ride?" He hopped in and sat next to me.

I put out my hand and said, "Yogi, I'm Bob Wilber. I'm sure you know my dad pretty well."

For the next 20 minutes I got to sit next to Yogi Berra and listen to him tell stories about my father, all of which elicited enormous laughs from everyone in the car.

The next day, Peter went to the ballpark early for some important function team presidents need to deal with as part of their lofty job descriptions, and the rest of us headed down to Dodger Stadium for Game 3 in the station wagon at a more reasonable time. We had two sets of tickets for the game, with Gillick and Cox taking the home-plate box seats while Wahle and I sat behind first base, but the fun began before we ever entered the ballpark.

Dodger Stadium is in Chavez Ravine and its forward-thinking design still looks modern today, 54 years after it opened. One of its innovative features is the placement of parking lots on different levels, achieved by terracing the ravine outside the stadium. The terraced lots made it possible to park on the same level of the stadium as your seats, in many cases.

Like most stadiums surrounded by lots, it also featured various areas of exclusivity in terms of VIP parking. As we approached the ballpark with one of our executives behind the wheel, we drove straight for the Dodgers' small private parking area located next to a VIP gate. As the security guard saw us pulling up in our rented family truckster, he stood to block our way with a hand held straight out in front of him.

Our driver, who shall remain anonymous, flashed the car's headlights twice but the guard only said, "Private lot, and you don't have a pass." Our devious driver said to him, "Mr. Campanis said to flash the lights twice and you'd let us in," referring to Dodger general manager Al Campanis. The guard wrinkled his brow, shook his head a little, weighed his options, and said "OK, park over there."

As we drove on, Bobby Cox asked, "Is that true?" and our driver just laughed and said, "Not even close, but it works every time." OK, his name rhymed with Schillick. Cracked us up.

After the game we returned to the hotel and it was soon a beehive of activity. The Yankees were staying there as well and the lobby was full of familiar faces from the current team and from legendary Yankees' teams of the past. It was a gathering of baseball greatness. We headed, as a group, out to the pool deck and sat around a table having a drink. Then, one of the current Yankee players stopped by to say hello. I introduced myself, and we shared a brief conversation before he moved on to chat with others seated out there on a wonderfully comfortable Los Angeles evening.

I grew up around baseball royalty. As a kid, Stan "The Man" Musial was nothing more than a good friend of the family. On that night, though, it dawned on me that I had just calmly chatted with Reggie Jackson while surrounded by front-office power hitters, as if I did that sort of thing every day. I remember thinking, "I gotta tell Lance, Radar, and Oscar about this trip."

The next day, Peter Bavasi had some meetings at the hotel which would again keep him from riding with the group but this time the rest of them hopped in a taxi and left me behind so I could drive Peter to the stadium when he was free.

As we approached the private parking lot I was only slightly petrified. I took a quick breath, flashed the lights twice, and was motioned straight in. We parked 25 feet from the gate. Bavasi said "How'd you pull that off?" I just smiled and said, "Works every time."

After the game that night, with our entire group reunited, Pat drove us to a tiny Mexican hole-in-the-wall restaurant not far from the stadium. After much delicious Mexican fare and a Margarita or two, things started to loosen up at our table. Eventually, long after the food was gone, various members of the Toronto Blue Jays executive team took turns standing up to address everyone in the restaurant by singing their college fight songs.

When they asked the young scout to join in I had to decline on the basis that Southern Illinois University-Edwardsville did not actually, technically, have a fight song. Not wanting to be the outsider I said, "I'll sing my high school fight song, though. It's better than any of your songs," and launched into "Oh when the Bills, oh when the Bills, oh when the Bills go marching in. How I want to be in that number, when the Bills go marching in. Hey!" There was a round of applause. At least at our table.

The reverie continue within the confines of the car, where future Hall of Fame inductee Bobby Cox and I sat in the back of the wagon with our feet hanging out of the rear window as we drove down Wilshire Boulevard on the way to the hotel.

After the three games in L.A. were over the rest of the group flew to New York for the final two games and I headed back to Fresno for a couple of days before I had to leave on my next adventure. And I was laughing about the fun we'd had.

Before the World Series, Wayne Morgan had called me with definitive word on my assignment for the early part of the post-season. He and I would be doing some additional pro coverage by splitting a league in half. It was the Mexican Pacific Winter League. I wasn't sure what to think of that but I knew I needed to do some research.

The Mexican Pacific League was a winter league for very high-level professional minor leaguers, with most of the teams featuring a couple of older Mexican stars and quite a few young American players. Most of the Americans were Double-A or Triple-A prospects.

With Tijuana and Mexicali in the league, a scout like me could actually stay on the American side of the border and just drive to the games each night. I liked the sound of that. So did Wayne and with his seniority he took those two teams. I'd be heading to places like Mazatlan, Hermosillo, Ciudad Obregon, Guaymas, Los Mochis, and Guasave. I had heard of Mazatlan. I had not heard of any of those other cities and had no idea where they were. Among many other things, I needed a map.

The Toronto travel department took care of all my reservations for flights, rental cars, and hotels, which was a good thing because I wouldn't have known where to start. On the appointed day I flew from Fresno to Los Angeles and then made a connection at LAX to a Mexicana Airlines flight down to Mazatlan. It was dark when we arrived and I stepped off the plane into a different world.

I picked up my Hertz rental car, which actually had an aftermarket tape deck under the dash, and followed the map to my hotel. To get there I drove through darkened neighborhoods on dirt roads, often lit only by the open fires burning in trash bins as chickens, dogs, and children ran around freely. This was most definitely a plow-forward moment.

My hotel in Mazatlan was, though, a resort on the beach so it was very nice and the staff all spoke fluent English. In the morning I ordered huevos con tocino por desayuno. That would be eggs with bacon for breakfast.

I did a little sightseeing that first day and one reason for that was to memorize the route to the stadium. These were not little ballparks. They were substantial concrete and steel stadiums and the teams drew big crowds. That night, I arrived early before the gates opened and flashed my Blue Jays business card at the gate. I found a seat behind home plate and began one vivid experience.

After four nights in Mazatlan I needed to follow that team on the road and my flight the next morning was to Hermosillo, about an hour north in the state of Sonora. What greeted me there was a revelation. I had never been to Mexico prior to this trip and my assumption about the place was based solely on what I had seen on television or in magazines. That meant I only had visions of Mexico City, Acapulco, or Tijuana, and I suspected the rest of the country must look like that with the smaller cities bearing a great resemblance to the mean streets of a border town. Hermosillo, it turned out, looked more like Topeka. It was a nice city of about 700,000, and with it being that large I was taken aback I'd never heard of it.

The ballpark was clean and modern, the streets and shops looked like middle America, and the people were extraordinarily nice to me. I stayed at a Valle Grande Hotel, which appeared to be a substantial chain of nice places in that part of the country. I enjoyed my time there and my Spanish was getting better by the day.

After four days in Hermosillo my itinerary had me flying down to Ciudad Obregon. That was a bit odd because it was only a couple of hours away by car from Hermosillo and Guaymas (another town in the league which I'd be covering) was halfway between. I followed my instructions, though, and got on an Aeromexico flight that lasted about 25 minutes. At 30,000 feet. Our climb to 30,000 was completed just as we arrived over Ciudad Obregon and the pilot then put us in a steep downward spiral until we were safely on the ground. I'd never been on a TWA or American Airlines flight that did that.

At the rental car counter a nice young lady filled out my paperwork and when she was done I asked her how to get to the Valle Grande Hotel in that fine town. Her English wasn't perfect, and her sense of direction was lacking a little, so finally she said, "I'm done with work now. I will ride with you and take you to the Valle Grande. My boyfriend will pick me up there." Seriously.

She directed me to the hotel, in the middle of this city of 450,000 I'd never heard of, and when I pulled into the parking lot at the hotel she got out and waved goodbye. That was some serious customer service. I then went inside and they didn't have a reservation for me. Just before full-on panic set it the clerk told me there was another Valle Grande in town and my reservation must certainly be there. I drove just a few blocks and, yes indeed, I did have a room.

As I made myself comfortable I turned on the television and watched Monday Night Football. The date was November 2, 1981. I know this because it was easy to look up the MNF game between the Denver Broncos and Minnesota Vikings in 1981. I could hear Frank Gifford, Howard Cosell, and Dandy Don Meredith in the background but for the Mexican audience they had their own announcers calling the play-by-play. I remember what teams were playing that night because the announcers came back from every commercial break to let me know I was watching "Los Broncos de Denver, y los Vikingos de Minnesota." I can still recite that sentence in exactly the right tone with an accurate accent. Es verdad.

After four fun-filled days in Ciudad Obregon I was headed for Guaymas, where I'd meet Wayne Morgan. We both drove, from opposite directions, to this wonderful little gem of a town on the Gulf of California and checked in at a fabulous beachside resort. A few other scouts were there as well including Angel Figueroa, a well-known scout who was a Mexican native. Spending a week or more with him would make things all go a lot smoother.

During the days, we'd sightsee and have lunch or dinner at restaurants I never would've gone to by myself and all the food was incredibly good. We ate everything they put in front of us and never got sick, although the best advice we got before we went south of the border was "Just drink beer. Do not EVER drink the water, and don't have any ice in your Coca-Cola if you order one. The beer won't hurt you but the water will lay you low."

We had noticed, at other stadiums, a fairly heavy presence of security guards dressed like military guys, all holding guns of various scary calibers. I wasn't sure if that made me feel safe or scared but I went with the flow and acted as if all was normal because why would it be odd to be at a baseball game with a paramilitary guy standing behind me with an automatic weapon?

A few games and towns later I noticed a complete lack of such security at the ballpark we were visiting, and I asked Angel if that was a good thing. He said, "Not really. They're afraid to come here."

Another custom I was getting used to, when traveling with the my new amigo Angel, was the constant arrival of beers sent to us by fans who spotted us in the seats. He told me, "Always accept it, then stand and wave to the crowd with the back of your hand and nod your head a little, then take a sip. You can set it down after that but you have to take a sip to respect the person who spent his hard-earned money on that cerveza." We'd end up having a dozen nearly full cups of beer under our seats by the end of each game but we took a sip out of each one.

I finally headed, on my own, down to Guasave in Sinaloa, and the drive was interesting. On three different occasions I was stopped at checkpoints by armed "officials" carrying weapons. The only odd thing about these guys was their uniforms, which were usually a collection of various vaguely official-looking pieces of apparel that may or may not have been associated in any way with law enforcement. I was pretty sure one guy, who checked my ID and looked me over for quite a long time, was wearing a Boy Scout shirt.

When I got to the ballpark in Guasave, batting practice was underway but I'd never seen BP beneath only two banks of lights. To save money, I suspect, the team took pregame drills with only the towers behind third and first illuminated. That left the entire outfield covered in gloomy darkness. It was the oddest thing I'd ever seen at a professional baseball game.

When the gates were about to open for the game a security guard told me I had to leave. I attempted to tell him who I was and showed him my Toronto business card, but his job was to make sure no one was in the seats until it was exactly time for the gates to open, so there was no reasoning with him. I asked him where I could find the "gerente general." That would be the general manager. I found the office, found the GM, and we chatted in a combination of broken English and shattered Spanish for a while. He gave me a ticket for a reserved seat behind home plate and when I asked him if he had a roster he said, "Not here. Rosters in the office. I take you there."

I followed him as he walked through the concourse, out into the parking lot, and into his car. He said "Office is downtown" and off we went on dirt roads with the ubiquitous open fires and wandering animals, until we came to a small business district. We pulled up next to a brick storefront and he hopped out and went inside. He came back with a printed roster of his players, and we drove back to the ballpark. The oddities just would not end.

And then, of course, when I found my seat with the ticket he had given me, someone was already sitting there with the same ticket. I found another seat a few rows away.

When the game started I kept my normal notes and scores, and in many ways it was just another ball game — another in an endless procession of ball games. And then I saw a new pitcher for the home team take the mound. I sat up a little straighter as I watched the American fire pitches toward the plate. I pointed the radar gun a little more precisely. I carefully noted his 92- to 94-mph fastballs, all with life and on the corners. His slider was a gem, always low, always away from the hitters' favored zones. I wrote his name carefully. He was Jim Gott.

I was excited about having seen him, but I knew nothing about his career. These days I'd Google him on my iPhone, but in 1981 I had to get back to my room and dig through my stacks of statistical books. As it turned out, he was the property of the Cardinals.

I called Pat Gillick the next day and excitedly told him all about this Jim Gott character I had unearthed. Pat did some digging and he replied, "Well, the Cardinals don't have him on the 40-man roster and he hasn't pitched above Double-A in five seasons but if he's as good as you say, we need to think about taking him in the Rule 5 draft."

The Rule 5 draft happens every winter and it allows clubs to cherry-pick players from other organizations if the player has played a specified number of seasons and is not protected on the 40-man Major League roster. Teams pay $50,000 for any player they select but the player then has to play the entire next season one-level higher than the roster he was on. If he doesn't pan out, and the selecting club changes its mind about him, they can offer him back to his original club for $25,000. The Cardinals had put Gott on their Triple-A roster, assuming no one would put him in the big leagues for the full 1982 season. Pat Gillick was intrigued, though, so he sent a couple of cross-checkers to Mexico to see what I had found. I, meanwhile, needed to get up to Los Mochis for the final week of my trip.

For the only time on the entire Mexican adventure, I stayed in a Holiday Inn. The air conditioning in my room didn't work, the water from the tap was brown, and the cleanliness of my sheets was debatable.

I asked the girl at the desk to have the maintenance man fix my AC and she said he would. By tomorrow. And she said that every day I was there.

On the second day I ate at the hotel for lunch and ordered a club sandwich. The next time I left my room was four days later. I'd been eating every bit of the local Mexican food people had put in front of me and it was all great. Then, it was a club sandwich at a Holiday Inn that introduced me to Montezuma and his greatly feared revenge. It was awful.

My room with no air conditioning, which would be fixed tomorrow, overlooked the pool and each night a mariachi band would serenade the guests. I was in no shape to go to ball games so each night I laid in bed with a fever as the band played Mexican favorites just outside my window. I couldn't escape the thought I was going to die in Los Mochis and no one would find me.

After four days I was finally able to get out of there and I called Gillick to let him know I'd been slaughtered by Montezuma's Revenge. I had only seen the Los Mochis team a couple of games but he told me to head home. I'd done all I could do.

To get home, I flew south to the big city of Guadalajara where I had a room in a modern convention hotel waiting for me. In the cab, heading to the hotel, I marveled at gleaming office buildings and shiny car dealerships along wide boulevards. Not a single open fire or roaming chicken to be seen.

In the morning, it was time to go back to the huge international airport to catch a flight to Tucson. When we landed, I knew I'd just experienced one of the most unique trips of my young life, but it was also really good to be home.

My first year had been an interesting introduction to the scouting profession but 1981 had certainly been incredible. Even now, it's hard to believe all of that happened in one calendar year.

But the fun wasn't over.

Before Christmas, Pat Gillick called once again with some new life-changing news. After one season as a scout for the Blue Jays, St. Louis native Rich Hacker had been offered a new job with his hometown Cardinals and he'd quickly accepted it. With the Cardinals, Rich would be assigned the position of manager for the Johnson City club in the Appalachian League. The Blue Jays needed a new scout for the Midwest region and I lobbied for the job.

I liked Fresno. I enjoyed California. But the allure of being able to move back to my hometown and travel the well-known highways and backroads of a very familiar area was a far greater gravitational pull than anything out west.

After that one phone call I got the word I'd be packing up and moving again, back to St. Louis. That was fine by me.

Before that move, however, I'd have to head to Toronto for our winter organizational meetings, this time held in the deep-freeze of early January in Ontario. At those meetings I had another teachable moment and I realized, once again, just how young and naive I was.

With the entire scouting and player development staff in one conference room at our team hotel, we went over long lists of details, prospects (both hits and misses), and scouting reports. Finally, Gillick said, "And let's talk about Jim Gott." Just as I was about to open my mouth, I heard two voices competing for recognition in the back of the room, shouting over each other to take credit for Gott's "discovery" in Mexico. Grown men. Professional scouts. I was flabbergasted.

I looked at Gillick, who was already looking at me, and his facial expression wasn't so much "Don't worry about it" but more "Are you going to stand up for yourself?" I waited for the two alpha males to verbally beat each other into submission and then calmly raised my hand. Gillick recognized me and I said, "As I told you right after I saw him, Pat, I thought he could pitch in the big leagues right away. I still feel that way, and I think the Cardinals somehow totally missed on this guy. I'm willing to put my job on the line to back up that report. I'm sure the other guys feel the same way."

From the back of the room came the sound of crickets. Pat Gillick smiled at me and nodded his head.

Beating The Bushes

With a January, 1982 moving date set I prepared to pack while also tending to yet another vehicular problem. Like most scouts, I was piling up miles on my personal car at a staggering pace and that left me very much underwater in terms of value.

The Blue Jays graciously gave me enough of a bonus and a raise to make it all happen. I was able to pay off the old car, sell it for what it was worth, and still have a great down payment on a new one. The first thing I did after I arrived in St. Louis was to purchase a new Toyota Celica with a four-speed manual transmission. I was back in business and ready to rack up more miles. And it was a really fun car to drive.

A few things were going to be different in 1982. I'd have a full calendar year to beat the bushes for talent in the Midwest, as opposed to 1980 when I spent most of my time prior to the draft as an apprentice rather than a full-time scout. My area was also shifted geographically to be more L-shaped than east/west, so I'd be traveling the highways and backroads of Minnesota, Iowa, Missouri, southern Illinois, Kentucky, and Tennessee. I'd have a new boss, too, and would now be reporting to the scouting director who handled the eastern half of the country. His name was Bob Engle and he was the scout who originally interviewed me at the St. Louis airport. He and Wayne came at things from slightly different perspectives, though, and I could tell at our annual meetings that Bob could be the sort of guy who might, possibly, rub me the wrong way. I figured I'd almost certainly do that to him, as well. He was confident and opinionated and he didn't mince words. I was young and cocky and sure I had all the answers. Oil, meet water.

I would also be starting my year with a long-distance assignment, as the Blue Jays made me part of a group of northern scouts who would travel to warmer climates to assist our colleagues in the south rather than just wait for the weather to warm up back in our areas. I would head south the first week of February and then work my way back north over the next two months.

I left suburban St. Louis in the dead of winter. I'd eventually find my way to Florida but there was baseball to be seen between the snow and the palm trees, so I picked up some assignments for the scouts who covered Arkansas and Louisiana.

When I arrived in Natchitoches, Louisiana to watch Northwestern State University of Louisiana play a game, I learned many things. First of all, a real Cajun accent is like a foreign language and with Natchitoches being out in the Louisiana countryside it was extraordinarily thick and heavy. I felt bad saying "I'm sorry" or "Pardon me" to the locals every time they'd ask me a question or answer one of mine. Secondly, even though it looks like the town should be pronounced "Natch-i-toe-chis" it's actually "Nack-a-tish," as spoken by the locals. And I don't recall seeing much of anyone there who could play.

I then spent a week on the I-10 corridor in the southern part of the state, visiting schools in Lake Charles, Alexandria, Lafayette, Baton Rouge, and New Orleans. I think I adapted better to Spanish when I was in Mexico than I did to Cajun in "Loozy-Anna." On the day I left "Newollens" for Florida it was still as indecipherable as it had been the day I arrived.

Louisiana State, the University of New Orleans, and Louisiana Tech all had fine baseball programs, and I wrote up more than a few guys on those teams before I departed for the Sunshine State. The Blue Jays actually drafted one of them, Augie Schmidt from UNO, with their No. 1 pick although I wouldn't get credit (or blame) for that. My trip to see him play made me something close to the ninth Blue Jays' scout, cross-checker, or executive to do so because there has to be a complete consensus before you draft someone with your first selection. I thought he was really good, but I didn't have any basis for a comparison against other high-level prospects around the country nor did I really have the experience.

Adding to the importance of the Blue Jays' first pick in 1982 was the slot they held in the opening round. Their initial choice would come before every other MLB team not named the Chicago Cubs, who had the first overall pick and used it to select Shawon Dunston. The Blue Jays picked second and chose Schmidt. Augie Schmidt never played in the big leagues.

Tim Wilken alone had Dwight Gooden, Ron Karkovice, Lance McCullers, Rich Monteleone, and Pat Borders in his area. All went on to terrific Major League careers and Tim was able to nab Borders, out of Lake Wales High, in the sixth round. But to the Blue Jays, Augie Schmidt was the cream of a bountiful crop. Elsewhere in that 1982 draft were Randy Johnson, Bo Jackson, Jimmy Key, Barry Larkin, Will Clark, and many more stars-to-be. They were all chosen after Augie Schmidt. Scouting was an enormously inexact science in those days, and it remains that way today.

While I was in Florida I stayed in Orlando to be centrally located and a number of other Blue Jays scouts were at the same resort, all doing what I was doing. We were there to help my buddy Tim Wilken, who couldn't possibly see and then double-check, all the Florida prospects by himself. In addition to that, many of us northerners could get a jump on teams from our areas if they were down in Florida to play the southern schools or to participate in early-season tournaments while the snow melted back at home. There was so much to do, and so much ground to cover, we had a meeting on the day we all arrived in Orlando just to map out our routes and integrate our coverage. Many days I'd be out on my own, but when it came to big-time prospects we often traveled in pairs or as a pack, to each have our input on potentially high draft picks.

Wilken had seen Gooden, McCullers, and Monteleone enough to have them expertly evaluated. I went with him one day to watch Borders but before we could see him hit a Florida downpour drenched us and ended the game.

The days were full of road trips and the nights were often spent in the resort restaurant or lounge, comparing notes on what we'd seen that day. We didn't always agree but the unwritten rule for the northern scouts was that while we were free to state our opinions, the final call would always be made by the scout in charge of the area. It was his name that would forever be attached to the player.

On one sunny day I was passing through Lakeland on my way to see a high school player in Winter Haven, so I stopped in at Tiger Town. It had been three long and eventful years since I'd been to spring training there — a lifetime ago, it seemed. A nostalgic wave of deja vu washed over me the moment I saw the light towers at Marchant Stadium.

Minor league camp hadn't started yet so all of the big leaguers were over on the Tiger Town complex doing drills and taking BP. Once I saw that I knew I had to park my car and walk in.

I quickly strolled up behind Howard Johnson and said, "Ho-Jo, do I need to make you laugh?" He turned around with a quizzical look but then his face lit up and he said, "Wilb! Make me laugh, Wilb! Make me laugh!" We had a few minutes to chat and catch up on things before it was his turn to jump in the cage. Ho-Jo was just 21 and he would make the big club out of spring training, although he would split time that season between the show and Triple-A. I was glad I took the detour to Tiger Town to see him and say hello.

As things began to warm up at home, most of us plotted our routes back to our own territories. Wilken and I did stretch it out a little though, as he followed me up to the Florida panhandle so we could see a few more games together, still the youngest scouts in baseball. We got adjoining rooms at a motel near Panama City and spent a few days watching games, writing reports, chewing tobacco, and having a few beers. Then I continued north.

Rather than head straight to St. Louis I picked my way back north with a few stops in Tennessee. I watched Middle Tennessee State play a home game in Murfreesboro and I really liked one of their outfielders. When I wrote a report on Ken Gerhart that night it included the highest rating I'd yet given to a player in my area. I thought he could play in the big leagues and so did the Baltimore Orioles, who selected him in the fifth round. While Gerhart only played three seasons in Baltimore, he did indeed play Major League ball.

I also ventured over to Clarksville to see Austin Peay State play a game on the day a pitcher named Keith Gilliam was scheduled to start. When I'd sent out my requests for schedules his coach made mention of him and he let me know that Gilliam (pronounced Gillum) had been drafted by St. Louis the year before but he'd chosen to stay in school.

I watched him pitch and loved his bulldog "go-right-at-'em" attitude on the mound. He wasn't overpowering but he could paint the corners and pitch like a pro. He was also left-handed, which is a good thing. I wasn't sure how high his ceiling was but I knew he could pitch as well as any guys I'd faced in Class-A ball, so I wrote him up as a prospect and sent in the report.

Soon thereafter, I headed to northeastern Kentucky to watch another left-hander. Based on what I'd heard from coaches and other scouts, he was a bit of an enigma. He was pitching for Rowan County High in Morehead and was the ace of the staff. Of course, in remote areas like that being the ace of a high school staff could be something akin to being the best artist in a paint-by-numbers club. What I'd heard was that his father was a college professor who had an interest in kinesiology, and he had his son on a strict throwing program.

When I arrived at the ballpark I met the team's head coach and he told me, "This is Joe's second start this year, and he's going to be throwing exactly at 85 percent, in terms of his velocity."

It was uncanny. First of all, the kid was physically mature beyond his years and his mechanics on the mound were beautiful. I hadn't seen more than a handful of pitchers in my life with a more fluid or graceful delivery. And it seemed like every fastball he threw was exactly 80 mph. He toyed with the kids on the other team and won easily. I was bemused, confused, and enthused. I needed to see this kid again.

Over the next month I'd travel back to eastern Kentucky to see him pitch three more times. I chatted with his dad on the phone and was a little surprised at how coy he was regarding whether or not his boy could be signed out of high school but something about the kid had me hooked. Each game, his coach told the growing audience of scouts that the kid would be throwing at 85 percent, 90 percent, or 95 percent of his best velocity.

Once he got up into the high 80s with his fastball, I didn't care if he could throw harder. He wasn't a thrower to begin with. He was a pitcher. He had impeccable command and he understood the art of keeping hitters off-balance. He changed speeds effortlessly and, in all the games I saw him pitch I never once saw a hitter have a good at-bat.

I had him listed as the No. 1 player in my area, and nobody else was close.

I called Bob Engle and implored him to meet me in Kentucky before the kid's final game. Engle seemed less than enthused but he agreed to fly down. There were at least 20 scouts in the tiny grandstand with a matching number of radar guns pointed at the well-built and handsome young man on the mound. On that afternoon he was right around 88 or 89 mph with his typically wonderful command.

After the game, as most of the scouts mingled in the parking lot to tell lies about what they had just seen, Engle walked over to me and proceeded to dress me down in front of the entire gaggle of scouts. He said, "I don't want him moved down on your list. I want him off your list. Period. You've totally wasted my valuable time and I won't forget it. If he's on your list next week, I'll consider that a termination offense."

He got in his rental car and spun the tires in the gravel. I suspect I've been more embarrassed in my life but I don't recall exactly when.

I was dumbfounded. I was angry. I wanted to crawl in a hole. All I could do was get in my car and calmly drive away. Within a mile, I had made up my mind. This kid was staying on my list. In the top spot. I had to make myself believe it was simply a difference of opinion and I had to stand up for what I believed.

Some players are prospects from the the moment you see them. The vast majority are easily recognized as non-prospects by the time they've taken infield practice. The rest are players you have to project and have faith in. You have to peer into the future to imagine what could be. This kid had to be seen over the course of a month, not just once. And you still had to imagine.

My name was on his report and I was sticking with my belief. If it got me fired, so be it. I was in it to win it, not to cower and hide.

I didn't get fired. The Pittsburgh Pirates thought the high-schooler was good enough to select in the third round as the 60th player taken in the draft. His name was Joe Magrane.

The "signability" issue was real, though, and when the Pirates couldn't convince the Magrane family that his future in pro ball should start immediately Joe accepted a scholarship to the University of Arizona, one of the finest baseball programs in the country. Three years later, after his junior year, the St. Louis Cardinals drafted him in the first round. He would go on to play eight solid years in the big leagues with his best season being 1989 when he went 18-9 for the Redbirds, with an ERA of 2.91 pitching against real Major League baseball players, not high school kids. And he wasn't supposed to be on my draft list at all.

I may not have gotten fired but my relationship with Engle was ruined. As much as he'd shown me up, yelling at me in the parking lot and spraying me with gravel, in the end I'd shown him up by leaving Magrane in my top spot. Magrane proved I was right but in terms of professional relationships I was in a precarious place.

Not long after the parking lot drama I was near St. Louis and I saw on my master calendar that Jefferson County Community College had a home game starting just as I was passing by. I didn't know much about the team, but it was a good junior college program so I figured it was worth a stop.

Late in the game, Jefferson brought in a right-handed pitcher who made me sit up a little straighter in my seat. He was tall and lanky and his fluid delivery was nearly side-arm, creating a lot of heavy sink. On my gun he was hitting 91-92 mph with every fastball. I didn't know if any other scouts were sitting behind me so I turned my radar gun off and simply enjoyed the show. He was dominant.

After the game I asked him to fill out an information card and he happily did so. He said, "I'd love to play professional ball. It's all I've ever dreamed of. I hope someone drafts me because I'll sign for any amount."

I got back home and filed a glowing report on the kid. Along with Gerhart and Magrane he was clearly one of the three best players I'd seen in my territory. So I called Engle to tell him about it. You can imagine how well that went. He said, "Draft a kid nobody else has seen? I don't see that happening."

So, this cocky young scout went over his boss's head. I called Pat Gillick and told him the story. I got in a few Magrane mentions as well. He listened respectfully.

Back then, junior college players had a loophole in the draft rules they could often use to their advantage. If their season ended more than a set amount of days before the draft they had an "open period" in which they were allowed to negotiate and sign as if they were free agents. This kid qualified.

I called Gillick again the next day, stating my case over and over. Finally, on the final day of the open period, he capitulated and said, "OK, Bob. If you can sign him for $1,500 go ahead and do it. I'm putting my trust in you on this one."

It was 6 p.m. and the open period closed at midnight. I called the kid and told him the deal and as excited as he was I could tell there was something else on his mind. He said, "Mr. Wilber, my coach told me that since I won't be 21 until December I'll need my parents to sign my contract, too. Is that true?"

I said it was but I hoped his parents would want to give him the chance to play professional baseball. "Oh, they want that, too, but they're out of town and don't get back until tomorrow," he said.

It was going to be pretty much impossible for the kid to even reach his folks, much less sign a contract. At 11 p.m. when it was clear we couldn't do this, he was very emotional on the phone. All I could say was, "Hey, Mike, I'm going to do all I can to get you drafted next week. You're going to get a chance to play, trust me."

We did draft him. In the 27th round. We also took Keith Gilliam, from Austin Peay, in the 18th round so he was my second drafted player, and I got them both in the same year. Things were looking up until Engle called. He said, "You got your guy, but we drafted a lot of pitchers ahead of him. Some of them probably won't sign but if all of them do we won't have room for him. I'll keep you posted."

I called the kid and brought him up to speed on all of it. He was thrilled to be drafted but distraught that he still might not sign a contract. And, of course, all of those pitchers did sign. We never offered the kid a contract. I recall his raw emotions vividly.

Being drafted, though, helped earn him a scholarship to Oklahoma State, which has an outstanding program. Playing for OSU put him in front of many more scouts. In 1984 the Detroit Tigers took him in the draft. In the fourth round. He finally got to sign his name on the dotted line but not with the Blue Jays.

The kid named Mike was Mike Henneman. He would pitch in the big leagues for 10 years, earning 57 wins and 193 saves, with most of them coming while he was a Tiger.

I had Gilliam to sign so I had to brush off the disappointments of Henneman and Magrane. I called his family home but was told he was at work. His father told me he'd let Keith know that I'd called and that we had drafted him.

Only at that point did I find out what a bad team Austin Peay State had that year, and that Gilliam's record was something well short of pretty. He'd finished the year 2-9 and a wave of fear swept across me. I'd just scouted him that one day, liked what I saw, and never really paid attention to him after that. Had I made a huge mistake? I didn't know but we were all going to find out. In public and on display in real-live professional baseball.

He eagerly signed his contract, thus further negating my ability to sign Henneman, and the Jays sent him to Medicine Hat, Alberta in the Pioneer League. He went 10-2 and at the end of the summer Pat Gillick called me and said, "I think you struck gold with Gilliam, Bob. He can pitch, and I think he'll pitch in the big leagues. Great job." My instincts had been right. His record in college was misleading.

I agreed with Gillick. I thought I had done a great job. I knew I was right in terms of Henneman and Magrane, too. I just had a boss who disagreed with my assessments and it wasn't very comfortable to have such an adversarial relationship with the guy who controlled my employment.

After the draft my summer featured more of the same from the prior years. It was time for pro coverage and in 1982, that meant half the Midwest League and half the American Association. More trips to Cedar Rapids, Waterloo, and Quad Cities, where the annual mayfly hatch was one of the most epic things I'd ever seen.

These tiny insects breed near water and with the ballpark in Quad Cities sitting directly next to the Mississippi River it's a perfect location for massive outbursts of the flying snowflakes. They typically hatch in huge numbers, all at once, and live no more than an hour. They have no way of eating or digesting food so their only purpose in their short little lives is to mate and create millions of offspring.

During a major mayfly event it appears to be snowing horizontally, as they hatch and swarm, and one night in Quad Cities the game had to be halted with both teams running for cover and fans heading for the parking lots as a huge hatch of millions of mayflies enveloped the field. Outside the park, our cars and the entire lot were covered in dead mayflies who had accomplished their only goal. That's what we call taking one for the team.

My American Association coverage featured three of the same teams I'd reported on two years earlier, those being Evansville, Indianapolis, and Iowa, but the Cardinals had moved their Triple-A affiliate from Springfield to Louisville, and that club made huge news. In my opinion, the Louisville Redbirds changed minor league baseball.

Playing at Cardinal Stadium, home to the University of Louisville football team, they packed in the fans from the first game and the local love affair with minor league baseball was a revelation. Crowds of 20,000 to 30,000 were common and by the end of the summer the Redbirds had become the first minor league team in history to draw more than a million customers.

Prior to that first year in Louisville the minors seemed to exist only as a partially subsidized feeder system for Major League Baseball and they rarely were promoted enough to draw substantial crowds. In my career the most people I ever played in front of was between 2,500 and 3,000, and most games drew fewer than 1,000 paying fans. It seemed the collective belief in baseball was that minor league teams could never promote well enough for it to pay off in increased ticket sales, so most owners spent as little as possible and hoped for the best.

When Louisville regularly began filling its large stadium it became apparent the old way of thinking was no longer valid. Within just a few years minor league clubs at every level were spending the money and taking the time to promote themselves. Minor league baseball has never looked back. Now, at every level from independent leagues to Triple-A, large crowds are a common thing. And the Louisville Redbirds started it all.

I also spent that week with another scout who was not a lot older than me, and we sat together every night. When he mentioned the Holiday Inn Priority Club I had no idea what he was talking about. I soon learned.

Holiday Inn was breaking new ground with its Priority Club, as one or the first loyalty programs in the hotel business. To attract new members and sell more rooms they instituted a program that granted points for nights, with many attractive reward targets. There were some rules, including one that stated the most points you could earn for consecutive nights at an individual Holiday Inn was two. My new scouting buddy, whose name I have sadly long forgotten, told me how to work the system.

"In a town like this it's easy," he said. "Every two days I check out and move to another Holiday Inn here in Louisville. After two nights there, I check out and go back to the first place. I'm earning a point every night."

I was intrigued but it sounded like a hassle. Then he said, "They totally messed up with the targets, too. They're way too easy and for guys like us it's a slam dunk to earn the biggest reward. If you get 75 points, it's a free week at any Holiday Inn in the world and two airplane tickets to get there. You can do it in three months if you work at it hard enough. I'm going to win it twice! I'm going to Ireland for one trip, and South Africa for the other."

That changed everything. I joined the Priority Club the next day and started earning points. I would do whatever it took to hit 75.

After my fun-filled week in Louisville it was time to head to Evansville where the Triplets' roster included Howard Johnson, Howard Bailey, Larry Pashnick, and Bruce Robbins, all of whom had been on the Lakeland Tigers with me in 1979. I was really looking forward to seeing those guys so I got to Bosse Field early on my first day in town.

I spotted Howie Bailey first and he came over to the railing with a huge grin on his face. We caught up on three years of news and he yelled at Ho-Jo and the other guys to come over. As a group, we talked and laughed and relived our not so happy time with Fred Hatfield in Lakeland. I was impressed by how well all of them were doing and they were shaking their heads just thinking about me as a scout, now in my third year.

Howie Bailey said, "You're coming over to our apartment tomorrow for lunch. I'll go write down the directions. Be there at noon."

We had much more time to catch up on things that next day and it was as if we were all still teammates. Baseball friendships can last forever.

Howard Bailey had already been to the big leagues once and he would be back in Detroit by the end of that summer. Howard Johnson made the big club out of spring training and would be back with the Tigers that summer as well. Once he got there he'd never play another game in the minors. Larry Pashnick would be called up later that summer as well and he bounced back and forth between MLB and the minors for three more years, ending his career in 1984 with the Twins. Bruce Robbins was a quiet and introspective guy who had run the table back in '79, going from Lakeland to Double-A Montgomery and then on to Detroit. He was the first of that Lakeland team to make it. He'd end up playing parts of two seasons in the show.

And here's a fun fact about Bosse Field, then the home of the Evansville Triplets. Most of the action scenes in "A League Of Their Own" which is in my top five baseball movies, were shot at Bosse Field. Google it. You'll recognize it.

I had one final trip scheduled for a homestand in Indianapolis in order to complete my coverage of the Reds affiliate known as the Indians. With it being my last pro coverage of the summer, I called Lance and asked him to come over from St. Louis and join me. We had a great time for a few days and he pointed out the Indians' second-baseman, a guy named Neil Fiala.

I was familiar with Fiala's name and Lance correctly pointed out he was a St. Louis kid who had gone to SIU-Carbondale, as a Saluki. We were the same age so it's certain I played against him in both high school and college, but I didn't really know him. His path and mine would later not just intersect, they would be interwoven for some fabulous baseball and even better memories.

For the record, my report on Neil Fiala listed him as Triple-A, tops. As Maxwell Smart used to say, I missed it by *that* much. He actually played in five games in the big leagues, two for the Reds and three for his hometown Cardinals. He went a combined 1 for 2 and will forever be etched in the record book as having hit .500 in his major league career.

During that summer one other thing was becoming evident for this St. Louis boy. The Cardinals were pretty good. They had not been to the World Series since my mom worked for them in 1968, but with Ozzie Smith, Tommy Herr, Keith Hernandez, Terry Pendleton, and George Hendrick, they were racking up the wins and making a run for the pennant. Baseball in St. Louis was back to being the biggest thing in town and the buzz around the city was contagious.

I had a couple of weeks at home after my summer coverage concluded, to recharge my travel-weary batteries, and then it was time for my fall assignment. This one would be a little better and more enjoyable than the Mexican Pacific League, not to mention safer in terms of Montezuma's Revenge. My job that fall was to cover part of the Florida Instructional League. When I heard that news my first comment was, "When can I leave?"

The answer was mid-September and it would take me about three weeks to cover the teams I'd been assigned, which did not include a team fielded by the Japanese professional league, although it was always fun to watch those games. It would be three glorious weeks on the Gulf Coast where the water is warm and the sand is soft. It sounded as much like a vacation as it did a business trip.

While it was tempting to do the Holiday Inn hopscotch game the club surprised me by giving me a green light to stay right on the beach in Sarasota. Pat Gillick said, "Have a good time, send me some good reports, and try to keep it under $50 a night." I reserved a cabana room at the Sandcastle Resort just south of Lido Beach. It was heavenly.

I'd be seeing games at the Ed Smith Sports Complex in Sarasota, the Pirate City complex in Bradenton, and the defunct Kansas City Royals Academy, east of Bradenton. The Royals had developed the academy in the 1970s as a residential baseball school working in conjunction with Manatee Junior College, where players were sent to take classes. It featured dorms, meeting rooms, lounges, and a full cafeteria, as well as a complex of playing fields that all had the exact dimensions of Royals Stadium in Kansas City. Although the academy concept failed, the complex remained a first-class baseball facility for many years.

During my first week I saw a number of games at the former academy and I noticed a nice car in the parking late with license plates that read "SABES." That car clearly belonged to one of two very fine pitchers on that Instructional League team. Bret Saberhagen had been drafted that June by the Royals but he did not play that summer. His first appearance as a pro was made that fall in Florida. Also on that team was Mark Gubicza, who would go on to win 132 games in 14-year big-league career. It was a pleasure to sit in the sunshine and watch those guys deal.

The Florida Instructional League featured young highly-regarded prospects still in the minor leagues so the level of play was fantastic. All the games started at 1 p.m., as well, leaving me plenty of time in the late afternoons to hit the beach or find new restaurants. In addition, Sunday was an off-day every week. It was a wonderful way to finish things up at the end of a difficult and tiring year.

When I was at the Ed Smith complex one day, carefully watching a catcher from the Braves organization who really impressed me, I turned around and did a double-take when I saw who was sitting one row behind me on the wooden bleachers. It was Fred Hatfield.

Hat was scouting by then, with his managerial days behind him, and I was stunned when he acted as though we'd been best friends back in Lakeland. "Well, there's my old ball-gamer," he said. "How are you, Mr. Wilber?"

I wasn't sure what to say. I wasn't even sure what to think. All I could do was reply, "I'm fine Hat. Great to see you." It was a bit surreal but I figured the high road was the better path to take so over the course of the next few days I was polite every time I saw him. I never said a single word about Lakeland.

Once I wrapped up my coverage it was time to head north. But that was OK — the Cardinals had won their division and were headed to the playoffs and I'd get home just in time to witness it.

The Blue Jays got me box seats for the home playoff games against Atlanta and after the Cardinals advanced to the World Series, where they would face the Brewers, Pat Gillick was on the phone to me the next day.

The club would generously provide me 12 tickets per game, which stunned me. As Pat said, "It's your home town. We have the tickets and you're going to be swamped with requests, so we'll take care of you."

On the day before the first game I met with Pat and few other members of the staff in a hotel room near the Gateway Arch. Spread out on one of the beds, like bars of gold, were stacks of World Series tickets. It felt as though we might've needed an armed guard out in the hall.

For each home game I got two tickets right behind home plate and five other pairs scattered around Busch Stadium. I had no shortage of friends and family who wanted to use those valuable ducats.

My problem with the box seats was that they were in a place where I'd be surrounded by baseball executives from other organizations. I was there, in the ninth row of section 149, as an official representative of the Toronto Blue Jays. But deep inside, having grown up in St. Louis as the son of a former Cardinal, I was Redbird fan. Sitting where I was, I couldn't cheer. I couldn't even clap! That was about as difficult as not laughing at Robin Williams.

The Cardinals ended up winning the Series, coming from behind in the seventh game. Since the people around me were from other teams they had no real rooting interest in the game and by the seventh inning of game seven, most had left. I was finally free to cheer.

I'd also given a ticket to Oscar for that game and he'd been keeping an eye on my section as the game went along. When he saw all the other baseball people vacate, he sneaked down to the lower level, against the flow, and found me. He took an empty seat next to me and we both cheered lustily when Bruce Sutter struck out Gorman Thomas to end the game. What a great way to wrap up 1982.

We held our organizational meetings in Toronto again that winter. What I learned this time around was two-fold. First, even though my buddies and I felt like professional beer drinkers in college I could not hang with my scouting colleagues on the Blue Jays. On our first night in town we closed down the hotel bar and the Labatt Blue never stopped flowing. We had our first meeting at 8 a.m. the next day and I'm not sure I've ever felt more horrible. The older guys, who drank me under the table the night before, looked totally bright-eyed. I was an amateur among seasoned pros, in that regard.

Secondly, it struck me that I wasn't having much fun. I'd consciously elected to go into scouting because it sounded far more enjoyable and rewarding than broadcasting or anything else in the real world. I began to realize I might have been wrong.

It's a lonely job, for one thing. You work alone and are on the road for months on end staying in lousy hotels and eating terrible food. You see the actual people you work with, as part of your organization, just a few times a year. You run into scouts from other organizations haphazardly, but even that meant little to me. Most of them were my dad's age. I was still just 26. And you watched an awful lot of bad baseball just to hopefully find a gem hidden here or there in the tall grass.

It was beginning to sink in that maybe, just maybe, I needed to find the next great thing. I was smart enough to keep my job, though, while I began to think it all through.

In terms of travel, 1983 would be mostly a replay of the year before — the same southern trip to begin the season, with stops in Louisiana on the way. The same number of weeks in Florida, and yet another long trip back north to my home base in St. Louis. From there, even longer trips throughout my area, getting back home for a day or two each month.

Minnesota would be part of my area for the second straight year and it was quickly becoming my favorite state out of all those I covered. I loved the friendly people (years before I'd ever hear of the concept of "Minnesota nice") and the Twin Cities were a destination I always looked forward to when plotting out my trips. Plus, there were a number of Holiday Inns in Minneapolis and St. Paul.

I was seriously focused on getting to 75 points with the Priority Club and jumping around from Holiday Inn to Holiday Inn was the way to hack the system to make it work. I'm relatively sure the front desk people at those hotels were aware of what many of their loyal customers were doing but no one ever said a word. I'd spend two days at one place, then move across town for another two days. And so it went all spring.

Unfortunately, 1983 was not much of a productive year in my area. There were some mid-level prospects and I wrote up anybody I saw who could play but there was no Magrane, Henneman, or Gilliam to get excited about. I'm sure that was a relief, in Bob Engle's world.

By April, I could tell I was burning out. I'd get up some days and absolutely dread going to another high school or college game. It could be so bad I'd feel physically ill. So, I called my brother Del.

Del was already a huge success in the sports marketing world by that time and he was just starting his new agency, DelWilber+Associates, in Washington, D.C. I told him how I was feeling and how unrewarding all this hard work and backbreaking travel seemed to be. He said, "Give me a couple of days to think about this. I'll call you back."

A couple days later I called him knowing that he'd never track me down in whatever backwater town I was inhabiting, and he said, "I can get you an interview with Wilson Sporting Goods, but the opening they have is in Lansing, Michigan. I can also get you an interview with Converse Shoes, and it sounds like you may be able to stay in St. Louis if you get that job." I thanked him profusely and said I'd be thrilled to do both interviews.

Wilson flew me up to Detroit and I spent a day with their head of sales and marketing along with one of their sales reps for that area. We called on a few sporting goods stores and then went up to the Pontiac Silverdome to meet with the Michigan Panthers, of the United

States Football League. Then the three of us headed to dinner and the two Wilson guys made me an offer. It was, indeed, based in Lansing. I graciously thanked them and asked if I could think it over for a few days.

Before I called them back I flew up to Chicago to interview with Roger Morningstar, a former basketball standout for the Kansas Jayhawks who was then a regional manager for Converse. We met at O'Hare Airport and found a quiet corner. At least as quiet as any corner can be at O'Hare.

My brother Del had given me one great piece of interview advice. He said, "Tell them you're a numbers guy and a results guy. Tell them you love baseball but scouting isn't for you because you can't control your own rate of success. With Converse or Wilson, if you do a good job you'll be rewarded."

I said almost those exact words to Roger Morningstar at the airport and his demeanor changed from a slight bit of interest to laser-like focus on what I was saying.

Two days later Roger called me and said, "I already had a guy picked out for this area. It was a done deal. When the company called and said they'd heard about some guy named Bob Wilber, and that I should interview him, I didn't want to do it. Well, do you want the job? You're the right guy for it."

Technically, the job was something called a "dual rep" since I'd be calling on key retail accounts to sell shoes while also handling all the endorsements and promotions in my area, which would be the state of Illinois south of I-80, meaning everything in the state other than Chicago and its suburbs.

I said yes.

By then, we were finally closing in on the June draft and I had to get my prospects organized, my list constructed, and my final reports filed. And 1983 became my third year out of four wherein I landed exactly zero draft picks. It seemed like a fine time to hang it up.

I called Bob Engle and resigned. He didn't sound too distraught.

Got Sneakers?

I will always consider mid-June in 1983 a significant moment, perhaps even an epoch, in my life. I was finally walking away from baseball, walking away from the dream, and walking into a new career. But one thing didn't change — my career was never about the salary. It was always about the passion.

Much like I plowed forward into the scouting business without a clue as to what it would entail or whether I'd enjoy it, I headed off to the sports apparel and shoe universe assuming it would be a neat thing to do. And, since I loved sports stuff and sneakers, how could it possibly be anything other than fun?

After wrapping up the final details of my scouting career I got on a plane and headed for Boston. At the time Converse had its headquarters in North Reading, just north of Boston, and it had a gentleman there by the name of Bob Geffvert, whose job it was to train new employees and teach them the ins and outs of the shoe biz. I'd be training with him for a week, along with another new hire who would be doing the same job as me, but in Miami.

Bob was an older gentleman and an interesting guy. He'd been in the business quite a while and his approach was clearly old-school at a time when sneakers and other athletic shoes were going through a monstrous transition. Once plain and utilitarian they'd quickly started transitioning to high-tech pieces of engineering that increased performance while also attracting an entirely new customer base who saw them as fashion statements.

Bob was a little behind that curve but he patiently walked us through the current line of shoes and gave us a history lesson on the marquee item produced by the company: The Converse All-Star that bore the name of Chuck Taylor, who was the first "celebrity" endorser in the sports world. He was a basketball player, a salesman, and a bit of an engineer who found ways to improve the original All-Star design and then sold the product as fast as the company could make them, way back in the 1920s.

Bob also trained us a bit as salesmen, trying to teach us a few techniques to overcome objections and close a deal. It was Bob who taught me the single most essential thing in the sales business: "Guys, when the customer says yes, say thank you and then shut up. It doesn't get any better than yes."

We spent a week there learning about vulcanized rubber, insoles, midsoles, slip lasting, full leather versus split leather, and other technical aspects of the shoe business. We learned the product line, which was fairly wide-ranging and on its way to being vast. At the time, in addition to the canvas "Chucks" the company was also a major player in a lot of other sports. The Jimmy Connors and Chris Evert tennis shoe models were dominant, the "Dr. J" leather basketball high-top was the most coveted shoe on the hardwood and the playground, and the Base Stealer was not only a huge favorite in the baseball world, it was in the Hall of Fame. Lou Brock broke Maury Wills' record of 104 stolen bases in 1974 wearing red Base Stealers with the iconic Star & Chevron logo on the sides. The spikes he was wearing when he stole base No. 105 were shipped directly to Cooperstown. Football cleats, for grass and turf, running shoes, track shoes, casual shoes, and other niche sports were all part of the line.

At the time, Converse was undeniably an important player in the business if not the most dominant company in the athletic shoe realm. One could make the case that Converse was a significant part of American history, considering the Chuck Taylor All-Star was introduced in 1917 and had remained the cornerstone of the company since then while always being made in America.

Peeking up over the business horizon, however, were firms by the name of Nike and Reebok, while adidas, Puma, New Balance, and Mizuno were also growing. Times were changing. My timing was either impeccable or horrendous.

During our week of training I noticed the Red Sox were playing a homestand and I asked my training buddy if he wanted to go. I said, "I don't know if I can get good seats or not, but I'm pretty sure I can get us in," and he was excited to do it.

I called the Red Sox front office, and asked to speak to the person who handled tickets for Major League scouts. When I was put through I was honest about it. I said, "This is Bob Wilber, and for the last four years I've been a scout for the Blue Jays. Just a couple of weeks ago, I left the Toronto club to join Converse Shoes and I'm in town at the company headquarters here in North Reading. A colleague of mine and I would like to come to the game tonight but I want you to know I won't be there in any sort of official capacity. Do you think you can just get us in? We don't care where the seats are. We'll stand, if we have to."

The woman on the phone said, "Absolutely Mr. Wilber. Just go to the will call window at Gate B, on Van Ness Street. We'll take care of you."

We drove through the madness that is Boston traffic and parked near Fenway. We went to will call and picked up a small envelope with my name on it. I opened the envelope and pulled out two tickets for seats in the Field Box level, section 45, row A.

Section 45 is directly behind home plate. And we were in the first row. That's a pretty amazing way to watch a ball game at Fenway Park.

Once our training week was over I headed to Chicago to spend a week with Roger Morningstar and a pair of his guys who worked the Chicago area. I initially spent a couple of days with Roger at the company's regional office in suburban Hinsdale, going over the college and professional teams I'd be handling and reviewing their contracts. Then I spent a few days riding with two pure sales guys.

My job as a "dual rep" would require both sales and promotions but the guys I accompanied were strictly salesmen. They called on sporting goods stores, shoe stores, and big department stores. I found it fascinating.

Finally, I was set free to get to work. I had my list of accounts and spent the first week at my home office calling them to introduce myself and set up meetings. Roger wanted me to spend my first month concentrating on the sales side of it but by August I'd be mixing in trips to the University of Illinois, Illinois State, Southern Illinois-Carbondale, Western Illinois, Eastern Illinois, and of course my alma mater. We had Converse shoes on every basketball player at each of those universities.

College players are amateurs, which means they can't be given anything directly nor can they be paid to wear anything. So, the shoe companies court the head coaches. With U of I being the most prestigious school in my region, I'd be getting to know Coach Lou Henson very quickly and I'd make the rounds to see all the other coaches as well.

After decades of Converse being the biggest (and sometimes only) fish in the pond, competition to land contracts with major schools had been heating up in the decade before I joined the company. Puma and adidas had been aggressive with college coaches, driving up the price of admission for everyone, so even back then in 1983 coaches like Henson were getting payments well up into six figures in exchange for the commitment to put Converse shoes on their players. In addition to that, Converse would supply hundreds of pairs of leather high-tops, apparel for all the players and coaches, and travel bags for the team. All so the Star & Chevron logo would be visible on television and from the seats.

As I made my way around Illinois I found myself enjoying the process enormously. I also discovered that my favorite part of the sales side was dealing with the local mom-and-pop sporting goods stores in so many of the little towns that dotted the map. These were real people, running small businesses, and at the time they could already sense the end was near. Big stores and national chains were changing the landscape.

I built some solid relationships with those store owners. The future was inevitable, but I made it my personal commitment to help them succeed and stay in business as long as they could. Within weeks I could feel the excitement begin to build every morning, when I'd look at my appointments in Champaign, Decatur, Salem, Effingham, Springfield, Charleston, Marion, Benton, or Bloomington. It was obvious to me that this wasn't about selling shoes as much as it was about building relationships and trust. I loved it.

I also had two "key accounts" in my area. One was Brown's Sporting goods, a regional chain of big stores with their headquarters in Peoria. Brown's sold nearly as many Converse Shoes as all the mom-and-pop stores combined. I'd be spending a lot of time there, but I really liked the buyer and we quickly connected on a personal level.

The other was Penn-Daniels, a holding company that owned a number of super-discount stores. They could sell a lot of product for me in their "bargain barn" outlets but I wasn't very fired up about working with them. Perhaps I just wasn't greedy enough or maybe I didn't see the value of dumping our goods in bargain-basement discount stores. I knew you wouldn't see any Nike or Reebok shoes on those messy shelves and I didn't think Converse belonged there either, no matter how much they could inflate my numbers. In addition, the buyer there wanted nothing to do with a relationship or trust. He was blunt when he said, "Don't come here without a solid list of close-outs I can buy for nickels on the dollar. That's all I'm interested in."

I quickly adapted to the landscape and taught myself the ropes in terms of product knowledge and presentation skills. And, plotting a course through Illinois on a weekly basis was not a lot different from my scouting trips so that came easy. There were also plenty of Holiday Inns in my area and I was closing in on 75 Priority Club points just a month before the program was going to be altered.

With just two weeks left before it would take far more than 75 points to reach the top level I could see I would end up about six points short, so I decided it made perfect sense to check in and out of a Holiday Inn in St. Louis, on my own dime, every other night for six nights. The cheapest hotel in the area was in Clayton, a bustling city in the west suburbs with tall office buildings and crowded sidewalks. The Holiday Inn was right in the middle of that part of town. I reserved a room there for six different nights spread out over two weeks while I continued to stay in Holiday Inns while out on the road.

After I would check in at the downtown Clayton location I'd take the elevator up to the room to mess up the bed and put a couple of towels on the bathroom floor. I don't know why I was paranoid to the point of thinking anyone might care if I stayed in the room or not, but that ruse seemed important at the time. I also developed a paranoia about being recognized by anyone. They'd have to wonder what I was doing checking in at a local hotel during the afternoon.

Finally, I was at 74 points and I had one last night reserved in Clayton. It was unlikely that anyone had been casing the joint and noticing my arrivals and quick departures for two weeks, but I still worried about it and I wanted to get this last room checked off the list to get my total to 75 points.

And then I pulled up in front of the Holiday Inn and saw its electronic message-board sign over the front door: "WELCOME LOYAL GUEST OF THE DAY — BOB WILBER." Hello, Clayton!

I got my points, I got my confirmation, and later that year I'd take a week off and fly to London, staying at the Holiday Inn on Sloane Street, just a block from Hyde Park. All for free. Thank you, very much, Holiday Inn.

I remember hearing at the time the program cost some executives their jobs. They underestimated the number of people who could rack up 75 points and they missed it by a lot. They started the program with a trade agreement in place, swapping with Pan Am Airlines for free rooms for their flight crews in exchange for free round-trip tickets on their planes but by the time I crossed the finish line and booked my ticket to England, Holiday Inn was buying the airline tickets. The promotion sold a lot of rooms for them but it cost them a lot of money as well.

To this day I'm still a member in good standing of the Holiday Inn Priority Club, but all you can earn these days are free nights for a lot of points.

That winter, we had our annual Converse meetings at the Camelback Resort in Scottsdale, Arizona. I'd finally get to meet the rest of my colleagues.

The Converse sales and promotions staff was heavily populated with former college and pro basketball players. Back then, playing a little in the NBA or in Europe was a dream for most college guys, but if you only were able to do that for a short time you'd still need to be gainfully employed after your playing days were over. What better pool of employees could Converse want than ex-basketball players? The first thing I noticed at the meetings was that I was shorter than almost all of my colleagues and I was a lot shorter than many of them, including my boss Roger who was 6-foot-6. I was the only ex-baseball player on the staff.

Mark Gannon had been a star at the University of Iowa, where big basketball stars are statewide heroes. He handled Iowa for Converse, of course. He was also one of the funniest guys I'd ever met.

Roger had been a big-time player for the Kansas Jayhawks and when he'd travel with Mark to call on sporting goods stores in Iowa, they were legends when they walked in the door.

At the meetings, we were introduced to all the new styles the company would be bringing out in 1984. One of them was a new top-of-the-line basketball shoe called the Star Tech, and it was about as sexy as a basketball shoe could be.

The Dr. J high-top was finally being phased out, and it was about time. It was a simple shoe, basically just a leather version of the Chuck Taylor. The Star Tech, though, was a completely new design and it was a fantastic shoe. There was only one problem.

At the same time Nike was developing a new shoe as well. It was a little something called the Air Jordan. Nothing would ever be the same.

We hadn't seen the Air Jordan, but we'd heard plenty of rumors. Still, we were highly skeptical of the Nike shoe. They hadn't really made a big dent in the basketball world to that point and we didn't take them seriously. A shoe with air in it? Ridiculous. Maybe we were just cocky.

I went back to work after the meetings, totally fired up about the Star Tech and some other new lines we were introducing, including an all-new baseball shoe to replace the Base Stealer. The older shoe was durable, but clunky. I'm not sure how Lou Brock stole 118 bases wearing those boats. The new shoe was sleek and light with a new midsole for cushion. It was fabulous. New football, cheerleading, aerobics, running, and tennis shoes were in my sample bags as well.

My relationships with my clients continued to improve but things were obviously tough for the small operators and at times their sales would be so slow they couldn't put together a minimum order for me, even if they desperately wanted the new products. I did all I could to help them.

In the little town of Benton I had a store account owned and run by a husband and wife, and they were phenomenal people. I looked forward to seeing them every time I was in their area and when their inventory began to stack up, making it impossible for them to order our hot new stuff, I worked out a deal to come down there and do a marathon radio remote for six straight hours.

They needed to clear the old stuff out, so I'd go on the air and say, "The next person to walk in here on this cold winter day wearing a Hawaiian shirt, can have two pairs of Dr. J high-tops for the price of one. Within minutes we were watching a dozen Hawaiian shirts come running through the door. We let them all have the deal.

It was a huge success, and I felt great after helping them blow out the inventory. They immediately placed a big order for Star Techs and our new cheerleading shoe which was taking the cheering world by storm. Everyone was smiling, including the people in the Hawaiian shirts.

By early 1984, I was fully up to speed. I had a company car, a gunmetal gray Plymouth Voyager minivan, and I'd spend my days roaming Illinois. I still lived in St. Louis and Roger had initially wanted me to move to Bloomington or Champaign to be more centrally located. But when I couldn't find a house or apartment I liked or could afford he let me stay home and commute to work each week. I'd hit the road Monday morning and get back home Friday. It became a blur of hotel rooms, presentations, and customer service, while I also transitioned all of my college teams to the Star Tech. The job was enormously energizing, although challenging.

Early in my Converse days, I realized something else — now that I was no longer getting paid to watch baseball games, I could play again.

My former roomie Lance was playing for a team called the Sauget Wizards (pronounced "SO-Zhay"). Rich Sauget, who basically owned the little town just across the river from the Gateway Arch, was a big baseball fan and when he met Bob Hughes and Jim Greenwald, who were both moonlighting as security guards at Rich's nightclub called Oz (hence, Wizards), they began to talk about putting an elite semi-pro team together.

Hughes and Greenie had played pro ball and they knew plenty of guys like Lance and me who had, as well. Rich had the money and the passion, so he built them a nice ballpark with great lights, within view of the Arch. Hughes and Greenie then went to work assembling one of the best non-professional teams in the country. I was honored, and a little nervous, when they asked me to come out and fill in for a few of their final games in 1983.

I hadn't played in four years, but it all came back to me better than I could have imagined. I hit a home run in my first game, my arm was still strong, and I could still cover a lot of ground in the outfield. Both Hughes and Greenie were very complimentary and they asked if I'd join the team full-time in '84. Of course I would.

Neil Fiala, who had played his five games in the big leagues and I'd scouted when he was in Triple-A at Indianapolis, agreed to play as well but only after laughing and saying, "I hate you guys. Now I'm hooked again." In 1984 we had seven guys on the team who had played professionally. The rest were either former college players from good programs or current college guys who needed a summer team. We were in two leagues, although our primary circuit was the Mon-Clair League (short for Monroe and St. Clair, the two Illinois counties where the teams were based.) And, we played enough non-league games to have a schedule that included 70 games in a little over three months, with a double-header every Sunday afternoon. All because we loved playing. We had to love it. Those Sunday afternoon double-dips in July could broil you alive.

One of our best pitchers was still at school at SIUE and like me he was a TV/radio major. He also threw submarine and he got people out at an astounding rate. His name was Pete Delkus, and when Skip came to a few of our games and saw Pete pitch, he raved about him.

Pete was also a truly outstanding guy and we quickly became friends. We shared the quirkiest parts of our mutually goofy senses of sarcastic humor and routinely had each other in stitches. Our relationship would move to a new level in just a couple of years.

I noticed something remarkable after joining the Wizards — in the four years since I'd last played, I'd filled out and gotten stronger. I could hit, and I could hit with power. I was playing the game at a different level and even though I'd made it to high Class-A ball as a pro, the Wizards were the best team I'd ever been a part of.

Despite being on the road every week, I'd book my appointments in a way that gave me time to get back to Sauget (or wherever the Wizards were playing) by game time. When I'd get to the park the guys would say, "Where were you today?" and I'd reply, "Well, three hours ago I was in Urbana meeting with Lou Henson." I don't think I missed a game.

Roger was cool with all of it and he was supportive of my return to the game I loved. As long as I could make my meetings and sell some shoes, I could play all 70 games. I managed to do just that.

The other teams we played were similar to us, in that many of them had some ex-pros or ex-collegiate players on their rosters. It was tough competition and the games were played with energy, dedication, seriousness, and a lot of skill. Life was good, and when I was at the ballpark life was great.

In 1985, while traveling the state to put those Converse shoes on as many feet as possible, I had the best baseball season of my life. I hit .360, clobbered 18 home-runs, and led the team in doubles and RBI. At the end of the season, I was named Most Valuable Player. I still have the trophy.

For dual reps like me Converse also had a dual compensation plan. I earned a salary (far more than I'd ever made scouting) and I had been given a bonus plan based on the promotional side of my job. If I hit my targets in terms of college teams in various sports, I'd get a hefty bonus at the end of the year. To show his support for my reborn baseball career, Roger added a new target to my bonus plan. It read "Sign and outfit one semi-pro baseball team to wear Converse baseball shoes."

The Sauget Wizards were soon decked out. We had blue spikes, duffel bags, and t-shirts for pregame workouts. We were the class of the area. And, man, was it enormous fun.

In addition to the bonus for getting the Wizards into Converse shoes Roger added another custom element for me, just for fun and motivation. At the time, all around the St. Louis area one of the most popular bands was a trio by the name of Sceptre. They were a cover band for all things New Wave and as such played all electronic and synthesized instruments. The female lead singer was surrounded by stacks of keyboards, and across the stage from her another player had a bank of synths and one of those '80s keyboards worn around his neck like a guitar. The drummer played an electronic drum kit as well. They cranked out 80s hits one after another and were extremely talented musicians. Wherever they played, their fans followed, making Sceptre nights a big hit with the club owners.

I saw them at least twice a month back then, and one time when Roger was riding with me for a few days before flying back to Chicago I took him to see Sceptre at a nearby club. Even though it wasn't necessarily his cup of musical tea (he was a big Dan Fogelberg fan) he really enjoyed the show.

On my bonus plan a new entry soon appeared. It read, "Sign one New-Wave band in the St. Louis area to a shoe and apparel program."

Roger Morningstar was a great boss.

In 1985 things were really rolling and I had fantastic relationships with most of my accounts. The relationships were so solid that when one new account, who hadn't even opened his store yet, was robbed and had his entire inventory cleaned out, two other accounts of mine near his town pitched in and sent him enough Converse shoes to open. I paid them back with some comp merchandise and a great deal of thanks.

On the baseball field, I was "raking" as we say when a hitter is so locked in the hits seem to never stop. Bob Hughes had been working with me during batting practice and his instruction took me to a new level as a hitter. Up until then I used the "see ball, hit ball" method, which works great for really talented athletes. For me it meant I was pull happy, trying to hit everything to left field, and once pitchers learned that they never came back into the inner half of the plate. When you're pull happy and get a pitch on the outside corner, you tend to hit dribblers to the third-baseman or one-hoppers back to the pitcher. With Bobby's help I developed a much better eye for pitch recognition, I began to understand pitchers' thinking and have a better idea what they would throw, and I learned how to react quickly enough to spray the ball all over the field. And when they did come in on me, I routinely hit it a long way.

It was fascinating to go through the process at that age. It was different game. I discovered it was as much a thinking man's game as opposed to a purely athletic endeavor, and I was thrilled by it. It was the best year of baseball I ever played. Even better than the MVP season the year before. I was truly playing at a different level.

One afternoon we were playing a game against a St. Louis-based team at Florissant Valley College. My first time up, I hit a bomb straight down the left-field line. Those kinds of fly balls almost always hook foul if a right-handed batter hits them because they have some side-spin on them, so when the home plate umpire yelled "Foul ball" before I'd even gotten out of the box, I didn't argue. But then, as if it was in slow motion, I watched the flight of the long fly and was surprised to see it wasn't actually hooking. I said to the ump, "Wait a sec. Watch it," and sure enough it stayed fair and the umpire overruled himself, saying, "That's a fair ball. Home run." as he circled his finger in the air to signal it. I was still standing at home plate, but I ran the bases quickly to not show anybody up. That was the only time in my baseball career when I got an umpire to overrule his own call.

Our Converse national meetings that year were at the Doral Country Club and Resort in Miami. During the presentation of our new products for 1986 I noticed something and it wasn't something all that good. Instead of completely innovating, the company was starting to imitate a little.

We did introduce a hot new leather high-top called The Weapon and buyers went pretty nuts over it. Larry Bird wore a black and white version for the Celtics while Magic Johnson wore one that was white with purple and yellow accents to match the Lakers' colors. We blew them out when we hit the road after the meetings. The commercial the company shot, with Magic showing up in a limo at Larry's house to play him one-on-one, helped move a lot of shoes, too.

And about Larry Bird, from French Lick, Indiana. Most people are familiar with his country-boy persona and I'm here to tell you that all of it is true. Many NBA players sign their shoes and give them away regularly and Converse was adept at keeping the inventory flowing to the arenas so they could do that and always have more. Larry Bird treated his shoes just like he had in high school. The word around the company, verified by Roger, was that once or twice a season Larry would call headquarters and say "Hey, my left shoe is kind of worn out. I don't need a whole new pair. Can you just send me a left?"

Aside from The Weapon, in terms of running shoes and some other lines, the product managers did their presentations at Doral and occasionally said things like, "This shoe from Reebok is hot, and we've one-upped it." They were imitating other companies' designs, looking for what was already hot. When I heard that I knew things were on a slippery slope.

We did keep innovating with the bread-and-butter basketball line and soon came out with two new high-top shoes for our team accounts. They were pretty expensive and weren't designed as a fashion statement, so we weren't going to sell many of them at retail, but as dual reps we were charged with getting those shoes on as many influential feet as possible. That's when I learned something about college coaches.

I scheduled a meeting with Lou Henson at Illinois and I was really excited to show him the new shoes and explain how they were actually going to help prevent injuries among his players. He smiled at me and changed the subject. So I tried again, and showed him the new features that made the shoes far more stable around the ankle than anything Converse had ever made. Heck, they made the Star Tech look archaic. He just smiled and nodded.

Then I realized that he really didn't care. We were paying him a solid amount of money and his equipment managers were handling whatever shoes we sent. The training staff worried about injuries. I was preaching to the wrong audience. It was one of those eye-opening realizations that changed everything for me, and not necessarily in a good way.

Coach Henson did, however, offer me two tickets to the Illini's home game the next night, when they'd take on Iowa State. Coincidentally, I had a St. Louis neighbor who also was on the road a lot and he happened to be in Champaign-Urbana at the same time, so we went to the game together. The seats weren't bad. They were the first two folding chairs on the floor next to the Iowa State bench. The job did have some nice perks.

And speaking of chairs, the next famous ex-hoops star Roger hired to work in our region was a former Purdue point guard named Steve Reid. Steve rode with me for a week after he started and we had a lot of fun together. He even attended a Sauget Wizards game and cheered me on.

Steve was a dead-eye shooter at Purdue, extremely well-known and popular all around Indiana, which would be his area. He was also famous for something he didn't do, but was a part of.

Most people have seen the video of Indiana Hoosiers coach Bob Knight going ballistic during a game, screaming at the referees while earning technical foul after technical foul. As a Purdue player stepped to the free-throw line to shoot the first technical, Knight grabbed a plastic courtside chair and he flung it all the way across the court where it skidded right in front of the startled shooter at the line. That was Steve Reid.

Our next annual meeting was back at Camelback in Scottsdale and by then I was fully integrated into the Converse family. Still, I couldn't help but notice one important detail among the national team of dual reps. I could work hard, I could earn my full bonus, and I could do good things for the company. I was even popular, among the group. One thing I could never be, however, was a 6-foot-6 ex-basketball player. Those guys made up the vast majority of the dual reps and for good reason. They were great to me and I liked all of them, but when it came time to socialize I was rarely part of their inner circle. I just wasn't one of them and I didn't speak their language.

And business was not going well. As hard as we all worked to keep the orders moving and the coaches happy, Converse was being overrun by Nike and Reebok. Those two companies were so successful and their products so overwhelmingly popular (the Air Jordan did OK, huh?) they were leaving Converse, adidas, and Puma in their dust. All of our numbers were down, and the vibe felt like it was getting desperate.

And then my brother Del called, once again.

He tracked me down at a motel in Galesburg, Illinois, and said, "OK, you've done that job pretty well for a few years now. Do you want to come work here, with me?"

I was kind of stunned. I knew the next great thing had to come along soon but I hadn't expected Del to offer it.

Del is 11 years older than me. When he went off to college at Purdue I was only seven. We were not what you might call extremely close as brothers. I loved him, and I admired him a great deal, but we didn't really know each other that well.

I did tell him I'd be interested, however.

We set up a day of interviews with his vice presidents and booked a ticket to Washington, D.C. to meet his colleagues at their offices in McLean, Virginia.

Another new plow-forward moment was staring me in the face.

I put on my best business attire and headed to Lambert Airport for a 6 a.m. flight to Washington National. Once there, I hopped in a cab and headed to the DelWilber + Associates offices.

I met the staff and interviewed with all of Del's VPs, spending close to an hour with each of them. He'd made it clear to me that nepotism might have gotten me to that point but the vice presidents would make the decision as to whether or not I would work there, and there were other qualified candidates vying for the position.

When my interviews were done I headed back to the airport and flew home. It had been a whirlwind day but I didn't have the job yet.

A week later I'd made the cut to a second round of interviews and I repeated the trip to D.C. in a new jacket I'd bought to make it appear that I had a full business wardrobe. I most certainly did not.

At that second meeting I was apparently a bit cocky. I felt I was the perfect fit and expected everyone to surely see it, so I went in relaxed instead of eager. Del called me at home the next day and said something along the lines of, "What's wrong with you? They all said you acted like you were interviewing them." So, I went back for a third round, tail tucked firmly between my legs. This time, I got the job.

I'd be starting in August which meant I had to do two things I most certainly was not looking forward to. I'd have to call Roger and break the news to the best boss I'd ever had. And I'd have to leave the Wizards before the season was over.

Roger took it OK and wished me well. He then hired Steve Reid's brother to take over my area. The newest Reid and I would talk often for the next month as I helped him learn the ropes by remote control.

Hughes and Greenie, along with the rest of the Wizards, were likewise sad to see me go but happy for me in terms of my sports marketing career. At my final game pitcher Scott Brown presented me with a fabulous cake in the shape of a jersey with my name and number on the back, just like our real Wizards jerseys.

The next morning, it was time to go to work. In a jacket and tie. And wing-tip shoes.

Suits And Ties

I flew to D.C. to start this new stage in my life and career, leaving my worldly belongings behind for a couple of weeks. I needed to find a place to live before I could have the movers pack it all up and put it on the road so I made the initial trip on a Saturday to give myself a chance to get acquainted with the western suburbs. While I was there I inhabited the lower level in charming Bed & Breakfast called Del's house. I knew the proprietor and got the "little brother discount."

When I woke up and showered on Monday for my first day at work, it felt an awful lot like the first day at school and there was no denying a bit of tension and a dose of "Why am I doing this?" as I put a knot in my tie and donned a suit. I had never had to dress up to go to work, unless you call the florescent blue blazer and bright red tie I wore as an usher, during college, dressing up.

My first day was mapped out for me, with an agenda full of meetings with all the vice presidents, the staff, and my colleagues while a tour of the office building was also thrown in during the lunch hour. From 8 a.m. until 5 p.m. it never stopped and then the keeper of the Bed & Breakfast took me home.

There were two VPs working out of the office, Hilary Mark and Brian Redman. Haughton Randolph worked from an office in Connecticut but would soon move to D.C. to join us and Jim Hartley lived on the West Coast, but they were both kind enough to fly in for my first day to discuss the projects I'd be working on. It was all exciting and nerve-wracking at the same time but everyone there seemed talented, dedicated, and gracious. My position, as a project director, meant I was slotted into a nebulous not-quite-management job reporting to the vice presidents while my other young colleagues (all doing the same things) were called project managers. As a group we were crammed into subleased space on the ground floor of another company's building and it was a beehive of activity. The bees, myself included, were a bright bunch of go-getters trying to make names for themselves in the high-powered world of top-level sports marketing.

DW+A had a number of prestigious clients when I arrived and one of the biggest was the National Hockey League. Basically, DW+A acted as the marketing and promotions department for the NHL and Del had brought in Gerry Helper, the former PR guy for the Buffalo Sabres, to be the firm's "inside guy" in the world of sticks and pucks. At any given time as many as six staff members at DW+A might be handling specific duties for the NHL, especially surrounding the All-Star Game, but I wasn't one of them. I'd be focused on other clients.

Another big project, but one I did not work on, was for Audi managing its sponsorship of a major alpine skiing tour. Managing the project required the DW+A rep to go to the top of the mountain and then ski down the course at the end of the day. Since that required real skiing skills and since they also wouldn't allow me to come down on a Flexible Flyer sled, I was out of luck.

IBM was a huge client as well and Del had been talking to them about a significant multi-faceted sponsorship of Major League Baseball. In addition, DW+A represented USA Baseball, the governing body for the U.S.A. national team, which was also the Olympic team every fourth year. Much of my focus, not surprisingly, was going to be the baseball projects although I'd handle some other clients as well.

That first day was a blur of names and unfamiliar faces showing me folders full of projects with which I'd quickly have to get up to speed. The second day was all about work. I had a lot of catching up to do.

One of the first accounts I took on was with U.S.A. Baseball, managing the Chrysler sponsorship DW+A had brought them earlier that year. Because I was a rookie in sports marketing, I couldn't wrap my head around the value of the deal. Sure, we had Chrysler logos on much of what the national team wore but with no television coverage the only thing of value for Chrysler was eyeballs in the stands, and while 3,000 people per game is nothing to sneeze at it wasn't a very strong return for the sponsor. I felt like a dummy on my second day.

I didn't think Chrysler was in it for the sake of philanthropy and the U.S.A. baseball team, made up of amateur college players, was still off the sports radar for most Americans. It would be my job to help fix that. I came up with Chrysler-logo'd batting practice jerseys, wrist bands, and travel bags. It all looked great, but with no TV it could've looked spectacular and it wouldn't have mattered.

It turned out that I was, unfortunately, somewhat correct. The first time we traveled to Detroit to present a summary of the program to the marketing people at Chrysler their response was pretty much a solid "This is all we get for the money?" I couldn't say I disagreed with them. None of us did. Television was the only way to make this a good deal for Chrysler but cable and sports programming were still in their infancy. It would take us a while to put any kind of deal together. We needed them to be patient.

Meanwhile, I was also brought in on the new IBM program. It was a neat concept and helped me get over the feeling-like-a-dummy stuff from the U.S.A. Baseball program. This one I totally got and very much liked. It would also be a ton of work.

One part of the IBM program was called "The IBM Student Pennant Race" and it was aimed at local elementary school students in every Major League market. The theory was to reward hard-working kids who fell into the gap between the straight-A students, who were lauded all the time, and those in danger of flunking out. It would honor students who worked hard, stayed focused, and maximized their learning, while also being a good influence on their classmates. Their teachers would select them.

IBM would then buy all of the selected kids tickets to the predetermined "Student Pennant Race" game and prior to the game they would host the students at a nearby banquet room or gymnasium, with a reception and special gifts. Each team would provide one player as the program's local spokesman and that guy would attend the reception, often in uniform, to meet the kids and give them a motivational speech.

Two other colleagues split the program with me and we divided the MLB teams up, although not equally. There were 26 teams in Major League Baseball then so two of us took nine and the other project manager took eight.

There would be a lot of travel involved, as we flew around to meet with the teams, the local IBM offices, and the school board in every city. I'd never worked in a high-pressure environment like that and the program was so complex we had to keep voluminous notes as well as binders stuffed full of information, for every market.

It was our job to work closely with the schools and teams to make sure we got them all to the reception on a battalion of buses, then to the game, and finally back home again. I'm pretty sure we didn't lose any kids. As in, I'm almost certain we didn't. Like I said, there were a lot of kids. We would've heard about it if we lost one, right?

A second piece of the integrated program was a hospitality element, allowing IBM to host important clients in suites at MLB games. We acted as the liaison, connecting IBM to the teams, securing the suites, ordering the catering, and supplying the tickets, all of which created more binders full of notes and data. My new office was quickly becoming overrun with white binders but the work was invigorating.

The final piece of the overall program was called the "IBM Tale of the Tape" and it was a wildly fun element. It was the first program that allowed all MLB teams to provide a consistent method for determining the distance traveled by home-run balls.

I'd love to tell you how IBM developed a system of radar, lasers, and mainframe computers to instantly and accurately calculate the distance in real time, just as the ball reached the seats. That would be a great story. It wouldn't be true, but it would be a great story.

The real story is that we asked all the teams for blueprints of their stadiums. Then we got out rulers and pencils and plotted distances to a wide variety of seats or landmarks where home runs could land.

It went like this. We knew the distance from home plate to the outfield wall. We also knew how far each row of seats was from the wall (that differs from park to park, and sometimes even from section to section in the same park). It was easy to then map out about 10 seats per section, to give the spotter as many close reference points as possible. If seat 5 in row 10 of section 119 was 345 feet from the plate, and the ball landed in row 12 of that section, seven feet away, it would be a 352-foot home run. And, of course, at stadiums like Wrigley Field and Fenway Park, where home-runs could leave the stadium entirely, we were challenged with coming up with some measurements for balls on Waveland Avenue or Landsdowne Street.

And, across all the ballparks, there were two additional variables.

The first was that we all agreed the distance from home to a landing spot within the stadium would usually not be the distance we'd announce. Different ballparks had different designs, and if you were only measuring from home plate to a specific seat a ball hit into the first row of the upper deck might not show as a much longer distance than one hit into the row directly below it, in the lower deck. That wouldn't make sense to fans, who know upper-deck blasts do, indeed, go farther. So, we'd have to come up with a way to determine where the ball would theoretically land if the grandstands weren't there and it flew unimpeded to the ground.

That led to the second part of the equation. Say three different home runs all landed in the same seat in the second deck above the left-field wall but one was a screaming line drive, another was a routine fly ball, and the third was a towering fly ball, coming almost straight down as it landed. All three of those would hit the same seat but they'd have to be extrapolated into different total distances due to their differing trajectories.

So, with that in mind we'd plot the blueprints and assign three different optional distances for the target seats. It was, indeed, the fine folks at IBM who gave us the formulas for plotting the three distances because, unlike me, they were smart people who understood math. And the three options were actually labeled "Screaming Line Drive," "Routine Fly Ball," and "Towering Fly Ball."

Each Major League team then had to assign a person to sit in the press box and be the spotter. Every one of them used interns for the job.

So let's assume Dave Winfield comes to the plate in Yankee Stadium and he hits a screaming line drive that flies into the 15th row one section away from the foul pole. Hopefully, our college intern was watching. If not, he or she quickly had to ask someone else where the ball went and how it got there. Then, said intern would check the chart, find a target seat about 12 feet from where the ball landed, add or subtract the distance from the nearby target seat, and select the final number by using the "Screaming Line Drive" option.

As quickly as possible, our brave and valiant intern would then rush the number to the public address announcer and the scoreboard operator. Seconds later, the announcer would say "That home run by Dave Winfield was measured at 356 feet, by the IBM Tale of the Tape" while the scoreboard posted the same thing.

The Cardinals were one of my teams, and while I was in St. Louis to meet with them about the Student Pennant Race program I stayed around to watch part of their home game that night. Late in the game I walked back to my downtown hotel where I dialed in KMOX to hear how the game ended. When a Cardinal hit a home run I could hear the crowd and see the fireworks going off from my room, and I laughed when longtime color analyst Mike Shannon said, to Jack Buck and the world, "That home run by Willie McGee traveled a massive 402 feet, according to the IBM Tale of the Tape, Jack. The scientists at IBM came up with this laser-beam that measures these home runs to within an inch or two of how far they actually fly." Oh. I guess that made me, sitting at a table with a ruler, a pencil, and the blueprints of Busch Stadium, a "scientist" at IBM.

The Toronto Blue Jays were another team of mine and on our Student Pennant Race day I met up with Lloyd Moseby, our assigned player whom I had played against in the Florida State League, and we rode in a golf cart to the reception. It was being held across the highway at an outdoor amphitheater. Riding along in the golf cart with us was my former boss, Pat Gillick. He smiled and said, "I knew you had it in you to do a lot of things, other than just watch ballgames. You look good in that suit, too." We did not sing school fight songs.

When we picked up Moseby and Gillick outside the Blue Jays' clubhouse I met Rick Leach, who was now playing for Toronto. I said, "It's a pleasure to meet you, Rick. I was the guy Detroit released so they could send you to Lakeland." He took a step back and looked a little worried, so I said, "Hey, man, I was honored to give my roster spot to a guy as good as you," and he gave me a hug, saying, "Sorry about that. It was out of my control." I'm pretty sure it was out of my control, as well.

The complexity of the IBM program also required us to visit the company's world headquarters in Armonk, N.Y. on a regular basis. Back then IBM had strict rules for business apparel, with all the men wearing dark suits with white shirts and conservative ties. We made sure to dress that way when we traveled to meet with them there (which was hard for me, since I was already "Mr. Paisley Tie" by then) and I recall always being intimidated when we'd arrive. It was a sprawling campus with each large building teeming with like-dressed professionals filling countless offices down endless halls. This whole sports-marketing thing was certainly different than scouting or selling shoes.

With Chrysler, the U.S.A. Baseball program wasn't our only job. We also had a program in place to manage their sponsorship of the Big East basketball conference. That program was handed to me and I was charged with making sure the on-site elements all took place. So each month I'd head out to a campus to make sure the presentation of the Chrysler Coach of the Month Award was handled correctly, both in the arena and on national television. I'd fly in on game day and arrange to meet the local Chrysler person well before the opening tip.

After flying up to LaGuardia Airport one cold winter day, my job was to meet the Chrysler executive at the St. John's University gym, Alumni Hall, to help him present the big, heavy, gold-plated, basketball-shaped trophy to legendary coach Lou Carnesecca. I drove my rental car to the Queens campus, found the gym, and went into the lobby to meet the Chrysler exec an hour before tip-off. Fifty-five minutes later he still hadn't shown.

I huddled with the university's sports information director and we hatched Plan B. He'd find a similar trophy in the office and we'd both try to remember to turn it around so that a non-Chrysler plaque wasn't clearly visible on television. I would stand in for the Chrysler exec to present the trophy to the coach.

Just before tip-off, the network camera focused on the big trophy then zoomed out to show me and Coach Carnesecca supposedly "chatting" as I handed him the trophy. The actual conversation was me saying, "Congratulations, Coach" and him replying, "Thank you. Thanks. Thank you. Thanks a lot. Thank you. Thanks. Thank you" for what seemed an eternity. I then took a seat in the front row as the St. John's and Villanova teams tipped it off. Less than a minute later an exasperated and slightly disheveled Chrysler executive came running into the gym, holding the real trophy. He'd been stuck in Queens traffic for 90 minutes. Thank you. Thanks. Thank you. Thanks a lot.

It was a story I'd enjoy telling Del and the VPs when I got back to the office.

One client we didn't have but that I desperately wanted to add to our list, was the Major Indoor Soccer League. I was brash enough to think I could talk Del into it.

I'd been a big fan of the MISL since 1980 when the St. Louis Steamers came to town and immediately began filling the Arena to the rafters. Standing-room only crowds of more than 18,000 were not rare, and the team took the town by storm.

I thought the sport had the perfect mix of flow and scoring, with a style of play that was just like hockey while it featured typical scores of 10-8 instead of 1-0 or 2-1. To me, as an indoor winter sport hockey didn't have enough scoring, and basketball had far too much. In indoor soccer every goal was big because it could be the one that won the game but you knew going in that you'd probably see the two teams combine to score at least 15 goals. It was always a fun experience. Del was correct, though, when he told me we had enough on our plates without adding another property to our portfolio. Down the road, we'd talk again.

In the meantime, we had another new client to service. M&M Mars came on board, hiring us to do a consulting project to see how they could best promote and reinvigorate the 3 Musketeers brand, and I was assigned to work with Del and Hilary as the project director.

The company's corporate headquarters were in Hackettstown, New Jersey. That's not necessarily an easy place to get to, unless you live in Hackettstown, so when we'd fly to Newark M&M Mars would have a limo waiting for us. At least we'd spend the 90-minute trip riding in style and comfort.

The initial concept for the assignment was to find a sport that was cool, hip, and appealing to a young audience. It needed to be skill-based but not overly violent or macho. It also needed a big audience but it would help if it was an emerging sport so that the price was still affordable.

The first thing we did after that initial meeting was create an exhaustive list of all the sports we could possibly think of, including such diverse pursuits as BMX bike racing all the way to Quick-Draw pistol shooting. Then, over the course of a week or so we met regularly in the conference room and assigned values to each sport, on a sliding scale based on how macho or tough the sport was while also taking into account how cool and hip it was and how much kids liked it. And it had to be affordable.

Del, Hilary, and I met many times to analyze the entire sports universe and finally settled on a group of 20 we'd share with M&M Mars. After getting their input and a few outright vetoes, we whittled it down to 10. Then to five. At that point, we gave them our advice but we let them select the sport they wanted to get into. They chose the MISL.

I was happily surprised by that and I knew I needed to contact the league office in New York City to let them know about it. Within days I was in a meeting with Deputy Commissioner Mitch Burke and Commissioner Bill Kentling, telling them the exciting plans we were putting together. Getting to know Mitch was a pleasure because he and I shared the same passion for the sport and a similar sense of humor. Getting to know Bill was ultimately life-changing. Not many years later, Bill Kentling would put me on a course that would massively alter my life, my career, and eventually even my level of fame. But first we had to put this deal together with the marketing guys in charge of the 3 Musketeers brand.

Del and I were flying up to Newark regularly then riding in the limo out to the quirkiest corporate headquarters I'd ever seen.

The huge building was one gigantic open office. The senior executives were in the middle of the room, acting as the hub on the wheel. The various business units were the spokes. Everyone could see everyone and all the cubicles were nearly identical. It was the craziest thing, but it was very much a part of M&M Mars corporate philosophy of inclusion, transparency, and teamwork.

While we marveled at its design we also were impressed by the fact all of these people were in one room and it really wasn't all that noisy. Later, one of the 3 Musketeers execs told us, "They pump a lot of white noise in here. It's pretty amazing how it muffles everything. If you stay late enough, when they turn it off at night, it's almost jarring how much this place echoes."

When we'd arrive at the building we'd be met and credentialed by the 3 Musketeers team and then they'd take us to a lower level that was full of conference rooms. Obviously, we couldn't meet in their cubicles.

As we massaged and adapted the plan to include signage at all MISL arenas, promotional halftime games for kids, and game program advertising, I kept Kentling and Burke in the loop. Finally, it was time for the top two 3 Musketeers executives to see the sport for themselves.

They flew down to D.C. so Hilary and I could take them to a Baltimore Blast home game. Burke set us up with gift bags and midfield seats just 10 rows from the action. And the place was packed with 10,000 fans. The execs loved the game and the energy, and both Hilary and I were thrilled.

A couple of days later I got the call I was waiting for. 3 Musketeers was officially going to become a primary sponsor of the Major Indoor Soccer League and all its teams.

In mere days the MISL was holding its All-Star game at The Forum in Los Angeles and we made plans to bring the 3 Musketeers execs out to the game to introduce them to league officials and to make a presentation to the teams.

The game was a sellout and the crowd was energized. Everything went just great, until we heard the bad news about the New York Express franchise. They were out of money and out of time. They announced, at the All-Star game, that they were folding the franchise. Effective immediately.

The history of indoor soccer, like many other emerging sports, is littered with folded franchises. It was an upstart game that caught on in some markets, like St. Louis, Baltimore, Kansas City, Dallas, San Diego, and Wichita, while it never gained traction in many others. May you rest in peace, Hartford Hellions, Pittsburgh Spirit, San Francisco Fog, Cincinnati Kids, Los Angeles Lazers, Chicago Horizon, Minnesota Strikers, Cleveland Force, and Memphis Americans.

Upon hearing the news of the Express going out of business, the 3 Musketeers executives said all the right things and told us not to worry. It was a solid plan with a very cool sport and they thought it was wonderfully priced. And then a week went by. And another week.

Not long after that I got the other bookend to the original call I'd been waiting for. This one was the call I never wanted to get. They told us a senior-level executive, who had to sign off on their marketing program, was the roadblock. He never signed off and stated he wouldn't. Stunningly, the entire deal went away with one call.

I'll never know if it was because of the New York Express or if the senior executive simply didn't like soccer. It didn't matter. The plan was dead.

Away from work I was apparently still on the radar of Pete Delkus, my former teammate and stud pitcher on the Sauget Wizards. The 1987 draft had come and gone and Pete had, incomprehensibly, not been selected. He called me at my office in a panic, not believing what had happened, and I said, "Give me a day. I'll call you back tomorrow." I made a series of calls to scouts and scouting directors I was still in touch with and had Pete lined up for in-person tryouts with the Cardinals, Dodgers, Padres, and Royals, all within a week. I also called my dad and told him. Skip then made a phone call to the Minnesota Twins.

He called Jim Rantz, who was the Twins' director of minor league operations, and Jim got general manager Terry Ryan on the phone. Within minutes Ryan told Big Del, "If you say this kid can pitch, Del, then no questions asked. Tell him to be in Elizabethton as soon as he can get there." I was pretty proud of getting Pete some tryouts. Skip made one call and got him a contract. Pete was overjoyed, and he stayed in touch with me as his first pro season went along. He was in for one remarkable ride.

Back at DW+A my brother Del never had a need to prove how adept he was in the world of sports marketing. His success was in plain sight and he could consistently juggle 15 flaming plates while staying focused on every new challenge and need. I'd always been impressed by my brother, but working with him took it to a new level.

Case in point: Del had started conversations with the executives at USF&G, an insurance giant based in nearby Baltimore. The plan was to do something big. The aim was to make a major national statement. The target was a major NCAA football bowl game. The Sugar Bowl.

Del had also brought another vice president on board — Maidie Oliveau, a talented and highly respected attorney from New York City. With the stakes getting bigger and the contracts growing more complex it would be a huge benefit to have an in-house attorney. And it would improve our prestige to have her work out of a new Manhattan office, expanding the DW+A footprint.

Del even asked if I'd be willing to move to New York to work there with Maidie. I didn't mind the rapid pace and skyscraper landscape for meetings or conferences but I couldn't imagine living there. I thought about it for a week but declined. I think Del understood, and in the end no one from our office moved to New York.

Maidie was brought into the USF&G meetings so Del could pursue the next great thing, whatever that might be. I was assigned to it as project director, ostensibly to have someone with a sports background filter through the elements and benefits as discussions moved forward. Madie was an accomplished negotiator and lawyer, but her background was not in sports. It would be my job to make sure USF&G got the value it was paying for.

Maidie and I made only a couple of visits to Baltimore before USF&G officially charged us with the task of negotiating the title rights for the prestigious Sugar Bowl, played annually at the Superdome in New Orleans. Once the plan was official, we'd end up spending quite a bit of time in the Big Easy.

The Fiesta Bowl had been the first bowl game to add a title sponsor to its name, becoming the Sunkist Fiesta Bowl in 1986, so our talks with the Sugar Bowl were a big step onto a truly national stage for DW+A. Many of those trips to New Orleans consisted of lengthy days in smoke-filled board rooms followed by equally lengthy nights at exclusive restaurants, where my dinner entree might, just possibly, include an entire fish with one eyeball staring at me, cooked inside a parchment bag. I'll admit to not even recognizing many of the dishes I was served but like a dutiful marketing man I ate whatever they put in front of me.

The bowl committee was a classic old-boys network of New Orleans executives and with their attention to detail the process seemed to drag out longer than I had imagined possible. Either that or they just liked sitting in steamy rooms full of cigar smoke before heading off to yet another seafood dinner.

Finally, all the contracts were signed and Del and I headed to the Superdome for the big announcement. It all went well, the publicity was astounding, and both USF&G and the Sugar Bowl staff were ecstatic. As we stood at the 50-yard line on the Superdome's artificial turf, surrounded by media members and celebrities, Del looked down at the hole in my black wing-tip shoe and said "OK, now you need to go buy a new pair of shoes." I hadn't even noticed.

I was flying off in a multitude of different directions to stay on top of the IBM project, the Chrysler Big East program, the Chrysler U.S.A. Baseball endeavor, and more. As a staff, we all seemed to be on the go constantly and we were all racking up frequent flyer miles by the thousands, on multiple airlines. Yet, something was missing in my life. I wanted to play baseball.

I contacted the coach at George Mason University, which wasn't too far from my apartment in suburban Reston, and asked him if he knew any semipro teams in the area that could possibly use a guy like me. He gave me the name of an old baseball man who fit the bill, in nearby Fairfax. I called Woody Harris and he invited me to the team's first practice.

The Fairfax team didn't really have a nickname. The jerseys simply said FAIRFAX on the front and that was it. I went to two practices with what seemed like a great bunch of guys and Woody told me I'd made the team. I was happy about that, and it was great to be playing again, but it frankly didn't go over so well at work.

We worked long hours at DW+A, often staying at the office for 12-hour days or longer and usually working at least one day on the weekend. The vice presidents led by example and the young staff followed that example and tried to outdo it. There was literally no time for a life outside the company, but I wanted to make the time.

Del and his VPs couldn't really tell me I was not allowed to play but it was clear they disapproved when I'd "duck out early" at 6:15 after having gotten to work at 7:30 in the morning. To everyone else at the company, I was bailing out. To me, I was feeding my soul.

My response to any mention of not playing was, "The first time I miss a deadline or fail at my assignment because of baseball, just tell me about it and I'll quit the team. The first time." There wasn't really much anyone could say about it after that and no one ever had a reason to tell me I'd failed. I just had to work more efficiently to get everything done and then dash off to wherever we were playing in the Washington metro area.

And the team was really good. Like the Wizards, many of the guys were ex-pros and they all still loved the game. I'd say the average age on the team was around 30, so I fit in right in. The guys all took the games seriously and we worked our butts off to win the majority of them. And, like most baseball teams I played on, the squad was made up of hilarious teammates. Plus, by sheer coincidence the team also featured a former teammate of mine. Pete Conaty, from the Paintsville Hilanders, played for the Fairfax club. Once again, it was a smallish world.

It didn't take long for me to gravitate toward a couple of talented players who perfectly shared my sense of humor. Mark Siciliano and Rich Gill became my best buds on the team.

Mark was new to the Fairfax team as well, after having played his college ball at James Madison University, and he was solid. I'm sure we were drawn to each other because we were the two new guys but we became great friends because our personalities meshed so well.

Rich was a solidly-built infielder who could really play the game. I don't think he played pro ball, and if that was the case it made him the perfect example of how really good players get missed by all the scouts. He and Mark hit it off too and the three of us would spend a lot of time together in the dugout and on the field.

I played well for Fairfax, hitting seven home runs in our 30 or so games that summer. And I busted my butt to get to almost all of them even if it meant driving straight from the airport. I kept all my gear and my uniform in the trunk of my car and it was typical for me to pull into the parking lot and get dressed in the driver's seat.

Much like the guys on the Wizards would always ask "Where were you today?" when I'd get to the park, the Fairfax guys quickly learned about my job and they would say the same, except in response they'd hear "Detroit" or "New York" instead of "Peoria."

In mid-season Woody gave us some big news. The Korean National Team was in the U.S. to train before an international competition, the Intercontinental Cup, and as a warm-up we had been selected to play them at the University of Maryland stadium.

With the game being scheduled for a Saturday afternoon I'm proud to say a large percentage of my coworkers finally relented on the "baseball is bad for business" tenet and attended. Del even brought his wife Kay to the Maryland Terrapins' park, as well as a video camera.

We were rarely ever nervous before a game but this was a team wearing jerseys that said "KOREA" across the front. I had a gaggle of DW+A colleagues among the thousand or so people in the stands and I sure didn't want to look like a buffoon in front of them.

I started in left field, batting seventh. In the bottom of the second the score was 0-0 and the batter ahead of me, Rich Esser, got plunked by a pitch thrown by a Korean hurler who came at hitters with the same submarine delivery I had used in Medford.

I strode to the plate and dug in. I took the first pitch, wanting to see his delivery, and it was ball one. I fouled the next one off. Then ball two. Then a swing and a miss on some high heat. I fouled the next one off, and the pitch after that, but as it came down in the grandstand I heard a bunch of the fans yell "Oh no" or "Ooohhh." Apparently, the foul ball hit a Korean woman right in the head.

There was a delay as she was attended to and a round of applause when she got up and walked to the first aid station under her own power.

The next pitch was a submarine fastball and I crushed it to left. Running to first, I had maybe three steps to enjoy the feeling before it hooked foul. As I walked back to the plate I remember thinking, "If I strike out now, that would really suck."

On the next pitch I got the same fastball and hit it about as well as I could possibly hit a baseball, with one of the shortest and most compact swings I'd ever taken. I knew it was gone when it left my bat. So much so that I simply dropped the bat and started jogging for first. The left-fielder never ran toward the wall. He just stood and watched it clear the fence.

I couldn't remember another time when I'd circled the bases after a homer while hearing the crowd clap and cheer. We never played in front of 1,000 fans in Sauget, and I never hit a homer as a pro. I hit a few in college but the sound was not like what I was hearing as I shook the third-base coach's hand and headed for home.

I hit a double later in the game then threw a strike to the plate to keep a runner from scoring, and we beat the Korean National Team. The final score is lost in the fog of time. I just know we won and I went deep. Woody sent a kid out beyond the fence to get the ball, and he gave it to me. I still have it.

Del brought the video tape into work on Monday and gave it to me with a genuine smile. He said he'd had a great time at the game and the home run was impressive. He and Kay even came to another game before the season was over.

I still have the video and would often watch it when I would not be hitting well, because the swing I took during that at-bat was perfect. On the tape, somewhat hilariously, just after I made contact Del must have been startled by the roar of the crowd because he accidentally turned the camera off. By the time it came back on I was rounding first. I didn't care. The swing was there and my trip around the bases takes place against a soundtrack of cheering fans, many of whom worked with me. It was pretty special.

We finished the season playing in a tournament near Ocean City and we won it. I still have the cheap faux-pewter cup with "Eastern Seaboard Champions" engraved on it.

That same weekend DW+A moved into new and much larger offices in McLean. Such a move, however, was going to be a challenge for me. Every employee was instructed to move all of their office belongings and files over the weekend so that everyone would be ready to work on Monday morning. I would be gone all weekend, playing in the tournament. Fortunately, three of my colleagues offered to move my boxes while I was away.

We were expanding quickly and the new office space was desperately needed. We had new conference rooms, a new break room, larger individual offices, and (gasp!) windows. It was a huge step up for Del and the company. We were clearly major players in the industry.

And then, only a few weeks later, Del began to talk to me about possibly moving to St. Louis. He'd brought in longtime friend and business colleague Larry Albus to open a Midwest office and it seemed like a natural fit for me. I knew Larry fairly well, since the Albus family was close to the Wilbers and the three Albus boys also went to SLUH for high school. I was certainly interested.

I called Woody Harris and told him that it looked likely I would not be back to play for the Fairfax team in '88. He and five of the guys met me for dinner so I could return my uniform and it was great to see them all and wish them well. One more time, I'd joined a group of guys I'd never met for a summer of baseball and we all became friends.

If the St. Louis move was going to happen the transition wasn't going to occur for a number of months but my travel schedule remained insane. I still had all of my other accounts and projects to handle when I heard we'd been officially named the marketing agency for the International Baseball Federation, which had its headquarters in Rome. As in Italy.

The best news was that the Italian Baseball Federation would be hosting the World Baseball Cup in 1988, so Maidie and I needed to head over there for a visit. We were making headway in terms of that elusive television contract we needed for the USA team and this big international tournament would act as a catalyst to get that done.

Our job, on our initial trip to Italy, was to be driven around the northern half of the country so that we could visit all the ballparks where the tournament would be held.

It was a five-day trip with the head of the IBF and Italian Federation acting as our tour guide. Each day, we'd hit another city or two and drive to the ballpark, where I'd get out of the car to take a look. Once I was certain that what I was looking at was an actual baseball stadium worthy of an international competition, I'd click off a few photos and we'd head to the next city.

Aldo Notari was the head of the IBF, and he was a big, gregarious Italian who spoke somewhat solid English. He was also extremely proud that his country and his national federation would be hosting such a prestigious event.

Italy was introduced to baseball after the American armed forces joined the British in pushing the Nazis out of the country during World War II. Baseball is now played around the world, very well in many places, but Italy was the first European country to embrace the sport. The ballparks and small stadiums I was visiting were quite nice.

Our driver was a fine Italian gentleman by the name of Sergio Bernini and the car he drove was a fabulous Lancia Beta. I don't remember half of my internet passwords or what I had for dinner last night but I recall my driver's name and the model car he drove when I visited Italy in 1987.

And you might find this hard to believe. We ate extraordinarily well everywhere we went.

Parma was Aldo's original hometown, and he planned a sumptuous feast for us the first night in the fine hotel at which we were staying. Then Aldo discovered the restaurant had failed to hold its private dining room for us, so he spoke with the hotel manager. The staff emptied the lobby of its furniture and brought in a large dinner table and formal chairs. We ate Italian delicacies and drank Chianti as VIPs in the lobby.

We spent days and nights in Florence, Milan, Grossetto, Turin, Bologna, Modena, and Parma. Much of it was a blur of motorways and ballparks, but Aldo made sure we saw the sights and had a memorable trip.

Finally, Aldo drove us back to Rome, taking us to the Coliseum and too many relics and ruins to count.

Once we were back in the office Maidie and I discovered we had another amazing trip on our mutual agenda. The International Baseball Federation would soon be holding its global meetings in Havana, Cuba. Maidie and I would be attending.

At the time, few Americans could enter Cuba. As marketing reps for the baseball organization, we were allowed. Getting there, however, wasn't easy.

With no formal relations between Cuba and the United States, there was no Cuban embassy at which we could obtain the necessary visas. Czechoslovakia, however, had a Cuban consulate within its embassy and in those Cold War days even a visit to the Czech embassy was a vivid experience. We headed to the area of D.C. known as Embassy Row and parked in front of the imposing building. We knocked on a huge wooden door and were allowed into a long, dark atrium lined with tall columns. The marble floors made our footsteps echo. It felt exactly as if we were in a James Bond movie.

At a large elevated desk, an unsmiling Czech military man with a huge hat looked down upon us, took our passports, and walked away. When he came back, we had our visas.

On the day we needed to fly to Havana we traveled to Miami. That's because the only way an American could get to Havana was to fly on an Eastern Airlines 727 charter and that flight left Miami at 3 a.m. We would fly over to the island in darkness, arrive at Jose Marti' International Airport in darkness, and be driven to the Riviera Hotel in darkness.

The hotel was a throwback to the 1950s when the Mafia ran the island and gambling was king. And it wasn't a throwback in a purposeful retro sense. It was truly a throwback. Nothing had been updated. Nothing was new. Almost nothing worked. Elaborate chandeliers had only two or three illuminated bulbs.

Our rooms were clean so that was good, although I had no handle for hot water in the sink and my mirror was rotted and mildewed. The next morning we arose early and looked out our windows to see a surreal scene; the wide Malecon thoroughfare as it hugged the coast in Havana. We thought we'd flown a 727 to Havana the night before but it appeared we'd been in a time machine. It was still 1956.

Havana was remarkable. It was crumbling, there were long lines outside of grocery stores, and the cars were either 1950s American behemoths or more recent Russian Volga automobiles that barely ran. The black market for '55 Chevy parts was enormous.

We were supposed to be there for four days. On our first day, we met another group of Americans who hailed from Indianapolis. They were there to present an outline of their plans to host the Pan Am Games in Indy. Once we met, we were nearly inseparable.

The Cuban organizers had planned most every minute of our time. While we were told we could come and go as we pleased the truth was we had almost no time to do that. The head of the Indianapolis entourage told Maidie and me, "We went for a walk yesterday, around a few neighborhoods, and got pretty lost. It was time for our dinner with the Cuban people and we didn't know how to get back to the hotel. Then we heard a honk. One of the Cuban advisers waved us over to his car and drove us back here. They were following us the whole time."

At the hotel we discovered the joy of Mojitos made with Cuban rum. They were dangerously delicious. And I was almost sad I didn't smoke cigars because right there in the lobby old Cuban men were hunched over tables making them with the finest Cuban tobacco. We also ate well and on our first night we were escorted to La Bodeguita Cafe, where the walls were covered in autographs and messages and the red beans and rice were to die for. I hope my autograph is still there. I'd like to find out someday.

We came back to the hotel to find invitations in our rooms. The Canadian embassy, which did have formal relations with Cuba, invited us to a reception the next night. I still have the invitation.

On the third day, we attended the baseball conference in a room reminiscent of the United Nations. We wore earpieces to listen to the translations of all of the speeches given in other languages. I learned then, and found it odd, that Madie spoke something like seven languages but not one of them was Spanish.

We did have one afternoon free and our Cuban hosts offered to have a driver take Maidie and me to a beach east of Havana. That sounded like fun so we headed that way and discovered a few things along the way. We'd been told since arriving that it was illegal to use American money in Cuba, yet when we got to the beach and wanted to rent an umbrella Maidie attempted to pay in Cuban currency but the vendor shook his head and pulled out a thick wad of American one-dollar bills. So much for that tip.

We also could not go in the water. There was a hurricane brewing in the Caribbean, and while it was still a day or two away it had the water stirred up into a frothy mess with a terrible rip current. We stuck a toe in and backed away quickly.

That night, after dinner and a show at the historic Nacional Hotel, we were supposed to fly home at 3:30 a.m. on the Eastern 727 but the hurricane was getting close and the flight was cancelled. The hurricane passed to the south of Havana but we still had to hunker down and ride it out and we spent much of that time with the Indy entourage, playing cards in their suite and drinking more of those delicious Mojitos. The next evening we got the go-ahead to be driven back to the airport, in the dark of course, but the storm was still active.

We hadn't seen our passports since they were taken from us at the airport upon arrival, so getting those back was our first goal. They wouldn't give them to us until the plane landed. When it did, they handed us our passports and we quickly dashed out into the wind and rain to run up the steps and get onboard.

There were only a dozen people or so on the big jet with us so boarding went quickly. Not quickly enough for the pilots and flight attendants, however. They were screaming at us, yelling, "Let's go. Hurry up. Get in a seat. HURRY!" They wanted to get out of there before the weather worsened.

As soon as the Cuban ground crew pulled the stairs away, the pilot hit the throttles while the flight attendant was still struggling to close the door. She never did get fully seated before we took off and as soon as we were in the air all 12 of us broke into applause.

We connected to flights back home in Miami, road-weary and still mesmerized by what we had just done.

I got back into the groove and spent the winter flying all over the country. By then, I was known as the guy in the company with the absolute worst luck in terms of airplanes. Basically, if given a choice, no one would fly with me because every plane I was supposed to travel on had an enormous chance of never taking off, or diverting to a different airport, or being so late we missed connections. I was jinxed.

Once, my TWA plane was taxiing to the end of the runway at Washington National, surprisingly right on time, when the pilot ran the nose gear off the asphalt and onto the muddy grass. We had to be towed out.

Another time, as I sat near the jet bridge at Chicago O'Hare waiting to board a 747, I watched as one of the baggage handlers ran his train of luggage carts into one of the engine cowlings, damaging the engine. That initially infuriated me but I had to laugh a little when the guy leapt off the tug and ran away. He just ran away, looking over his shoulder. I wonder how far he got.

And then there was the endless day during which all I did was fly into and out of a string of increasingly smaller airports. My destination was Kansas City. My first flight was delayed, of course, so I missed my Atlanta connection to KC. With the help of our travel agent I then got on a flight to Memphis, where I could connect to a different flight to KC. Except that connection was cancelled. Sitting in Memphis, it was clear I would never make the meeting so I decided to head back to D.C.

All I could do was fly eastward. First to Knoxville, then to Greenville. Finally, a flight to Washington Dulles, with one seat available, took me home. I started at Washington National at 7 a.m. and returned to Dulles, landing near midnight. All for a meeting I never attended.

As we got further into 1988, I got the news that I'd be going back to Italy for the World Cup of Baseball. My primary job was to be the liaison between the Chinese television network and the Belgian production company producing the games. I, of course, spoke not one word of either language.

I flew back to Italy by myself and spent four days in Florence. Fortunately, both the Chinese and Belgian groups had translators with them so we got everything set up and made all the right introductions. The Chinese wanted me to attend that day's game in Grossetto, where the U.S.A. team would be playing, just to make sure everything worked and the Belgians had their cameras pointed in the right direction.

I hadn't planned on leaving Florence and I had no car, so I found Aldo's assistant and asked him how I could get there. He introduced me to two Dutch umpires who were calling the U.S.A. game. I could ride in the back of their car. Sounded fine to me and when we headed outside the hotel it got even finer, if by finer you mean worse. Their car was a Renault 5. Here in the U.S. we knew that model as the Renault Le Car. It was tiny. Possibly microscopic.

I was painfully scrunched into something that qualified as a back seat behind the burly Belgian ump who was driving, but the real pain didn't start until I sneezed. We were roughly five minutes into the two-hour drive. The sneeze pinched a nerve in my lower spine and that caused all the lateral muscles in my lower back to spasm and seize up. And I couldn't move.

When we finally got to the ballpark I wasn't sure I'd be able to get out. I gritted my teeth and somehow extricated myself from the miniature two-door auto, then hobbled like a bent-over old man to the U.S.A. dugout. I'd met the trainer before and I headed straight to him. I don't know what he gave me, but it worked. I felt no pain. I did, however, see elephants playing in the outfield and unicorns running the bases. Whatever it was it was powerful, but at least I could survive the rest of the trip.

Being on my own while the tournament was happening meant I had no tour guides to take me to fabulous Italian restaurants and I spoke so little Italian the thought of even going to a restaurant was a bit intimidating. I found a pizza shop a block from the quaint Florence hotel, where you could order by the slice, and survived on that, pointing at the pepperoni slices and holding up two fingers before handing over the appropriate number of lira.

When it was time to go home I flew out of the Florence airport on an Alitalia flight headed to Paris, where I'd have only a 30-minute connection to catch my TWA flight back to JFK in New York. Fortunately, I'd seen the itinerary before the trip and had decided to have our travel agent formulate a Plan B for me in case I missed that connection.

We were, indeed, late getting out of Florence and when we pulled up to the gate in Paris I saw my TWA 747 being pushed back from the gate. I'd missed it by minutes.

Plan B was a fine one, though. Back then it was possible to actually book multiple flights and get all your money back if you didn't take one so we were constantly double- or triple-booking our flights to have options going both ways. My Plan B had me getting on a British Airways jet and taking that to London, where my travel agent also had reserved a room for me in the Grovesner Hotel at Victoria Station.

I flew to London Heathrow, got on the Tube (London's famous and wonderful subway) and rode it to within a block of the hotel. I even had time to walk around the city and enjoy an afternoon and evening there. In the morning, I was back on the Tube heading to Heathrow where I caught my TWA flight to JFK. And, being in coach, I was thrilled to see a lot of empty seats. So many empty seats I could put the armrests up in the center section of the coach cabin and lay down like it was a bed.

You couldn't possibly book travel plans like that now but we did it all the time back in the 80s.

Upon my return, Del called me into his office and we again spoke of the St. Louis move. I was all for it and within a month the moving vans were taking my stuff back home.

Our office there, with Larry Albus running the place, was just west of where I grew up in Kirkwood, at the intersection of I-270 and Manchester Road — the same Manchester Road that ran from SLUH to just a block north of Woodleaf Court, allowing me to take the city bus home when Bob Klostermeyer's dad couldn't give me a ride (to their house). It was great to be back.

Larry was nothing short of a marvelous boss, as I assumed he would be when he joined the company. Del was a great leader and he'd chosen some dedicated people to be his vice presidents. Larry made it clear, on my first day there, that he'd lead and motivate but I'd be expected to produce stellar work without much meddling. He said, "You're talented. There's not much you do that I can do any better, especially when it comes to writing proposals and presentations, so I'm here to support you and I'll have your back. Feel free, feel creative, and feel like you own it."

That was great to hear.

I got back to St. Louis in April of 1988 and quickly found a funky apartment just a couple of exits north of work. Larry gave me the second-best space in the office, right next to his, and we got to work.

A month later, I called Bob Hughes and told him I had returned and wanted to play for the Wizards again. He was genuinely thrilled and Larry had no qualms. He said, "You know, I heard a tiny bit of grumbling from the McLean office when you played out there last summer. I have no problem with it. Just make sure the work gets done. After the work is done, have a life. Do what you want."

I still had most of the same clients after the shift to St. Louis, but I picked up two new ones and Larry handed them to me as my own personal accounts. The first was Black & Decker and the second was the Minnesota North Stars hockey team.

Black & Decker was looking for a creative way to promote its latest incarnation of the Dustbuster. The new one had a rotating sweeper head on it and it was billed as the best Dustbuster yet. Hilary and Del challenged me to come up with something valuable for them and their advice was to be outlandish.

Within a couple of weeks, I had the Cincinnati Reds, Oakland A's, Atlanta Braves, and Seattle Mariners agreeing to have their batboy clean off home plate every game, during the seventh inning stretch, with the new Dustbuster. The Denver Zephyrs, a Triple-A team, agreed as well.

We also did some Dustbuster giveaway promotions and I flew to Oakland, Cincinnati, Atlanta, and Denver to see it happen in person. It was a little kitschy but it was fun and the crowds seemed to like it. Sports Illustrated liked it enough to publish a small story and include a photo of a batboy doing his sweeping job. Black & Decker was thrilled.

The North Stars had provided Minnesota with a good share of glory playing at the Met Center in suburban Bloomington, but by the mid-80s the wins started to dry up and the crowds thinned considerably. When the 1987-1988 season ended, the North Stars had racked up exactly 19 wins, along with 48 losses and 13 ties.

With a record like that and crowds dwindling, the NHL went looking for help to assist the team with its sponsors who likely wouldn't stick around if they couldn't be convinced there would be value. The league, with its long-term relationship with DW+A, pointed the team in our direction. Del handed the client to Larry who not only appointed me to make it happen, he gave me the freedom to do it how I saw fit.

I got to work in a hurry and we set up a two-day event for one of the final home games of the North Stars' disastrous season. We'd spend one afternoon meeting with current sponsors and then the next day meeting with potential sponsors. That night, we'd host them all in a suite for the game.

There was no PowerPoint in those days. My presentation would look much like a modern one but it would be printed on clear plastic sheets and shown on the wall with an overhead projector.

As I got to work on the individual slides for each presentation I expected my vice president to be heavily involved, if not hovering over me while I worked. Larry, though, said, "Just do it. You have good ideas. When you're done with both presentations, I'll take a look."

Over the course of a week I focused strictly on the North Stars and I then presented Larry with two groups of collated slides, one aimed at keeping what sponsors the team still had and the other designed to bring in a few new ones. We couldn't make the team play any better but we could certainly advise the organization's marketing people on how to give their important partners more value and therefore more return on their investment.

Larry flipped through it and said, "It's great. I'll go up there with you, but you should present this."

We ventured north and stayed at the Marriott hotel just across the street from the Met Center. After we arrived, we spent the remainder of the afternoon with the North Stars' marketing team showing them what we planned to present the next afternoon, and they were all smiles.

Our agenda the next day was to meet in the Marriott banquet room with the team's current sponsors, for lunch at noon. I would then make my presentation at 1. And I woke up feeling terrible. I ached all over, had a dandy sore throat, a runny nose, and I looked like a million bucks, if by that you meant I looked hideous.

Larry and I had breakfast and I said, "Look, I think I need to go back to my room and lie down for a while. If I had to do this presentation right now, I couldn't do it. Hopefully I'll feel better by noon."

I took a couple of aspirins and an antihistamine tablet and put my head on the pillow. I fell back asleep almost instantly and, miraculously, felt much better at 11. I even looked better. I wasn't close to 100 percent but I felt better.

When I made my presentation, showing simple bullet-points on each slide and then ad-libbing to give the sponsors more information, I was happy to see everyone in the room paying close attention. Even the guy in the suit standing in the back of the room. That's where Larry stayed.

There were handshakes all around when I was done and the same thing repeated itself the next day. The presentations worked great, and my boss was happy.

We attended the game that night and the suite was full of important folks, some of whom already backed the team and others who were thinking about. At one point I was sitting in the front row having a great conversation with a couple of nice gentlemen. When we introduced ourselves, one of the men said, "Hi, Bob. Nice to meet you. I'm Jake Leinenkugel." I had no idea what he did for a living. When I asked, he replied, "Well, we own Leinenkugel Brewing in Chippewa Falls. We make Leinenkugel Beer." You never know who you might be sitting next to at a hockey game.

Larry and I headed back to St. Louis knowing we'd done the best we could. We gave the North Stars the blueprint for marketing success. It was up to them to make it work.

During the summer, I enjoyed my work and enjoyed playing for the Wizards again, even more. We had a few new players, but they were great athletes and fun guys to be around. We took the game as seriously as we ever did, and despite the fact guys like Neil Fiala, Bob Hughes, Jim Greenwald, and I were all getting older (I was 32 that summer, and the youngest of the four of us), we still played at a very high level.

The highlight of each summer was a tournament in tiny Valmeyer, Illinois. Valmeyer no longer exists in its original location. It was wiped from the map by the great Mississippi River flood of 1993 and afterward it was relocated and rebuilt on higher ground.

The Valmeyer tournament was played in quaint ballpark in the middle of the original little town. The local team was always good, giving us tough battles throughout each season in the Mon-Clair League. Waterloo was just up the river bluff from Valmeyer and if the Wizards didn't win the tournament title you could just about bank on the Waterloo Buds being the champs. Like us, they were good and kept the core of their team together for many years. Valmeyer, Waterloo, the Wizards, and five other teams would make up the eight-team tournament every summer, right around the 4th of July.

The town always put on a great event in a middle-America, flag-waving, red, white, and blue, apple pie sort of way, and it was not uncommon for us to play in front of many hundreds of fans, who overflowed the grandstands and would often stand down the foul lines. For two days there would be four games each day running from morning until evening. On the final day two teams would square off for the championship. It was truly an honor to play in the Valmeyer Tournament and it was fun to win it a couple of times, even if we did have to play the 9 a.m. game on day two.

In 1988, I was playing well in the tournament and had hit a home run against the Valmeyer club. My second time up, I fouled a ball directly off my left ankle and went down in a heap. It hurt. Like, a lot. It was the most painful foul ball I'd ever hit off my own leg. I managed to line a hit on the next pitch and still remember telling the tall Valmeyer first-baseman how badly it hurt. That was noteworthy because I had never spoken to him before.

A few years ago I found a VHS video of that tournament. I had it transferred to DVD and eagerly watched it, enjoying seeing Hughes, Greenie, Neil, and newer players like Robert Giegling, Jerry Pitchford, and Jeff Junker (pronounced Yunker) on the screen. Giegling and Pitchford were great outfielders and as a trio not much got by us out there, although I was playing first base as much as I was in right field.

Giegling had gotten his college degree in psychology. He was therefore professionally qualified to state, during one game, that the collection of personalities on the Sauget Wizards presented him with a perfect case study.

Junker was tough catcher and a very good one. You had to be tough to catch in the Mon-Clair League. We played multiple night games during each week and a doubleheader every Sunday afternoon. Those twin-bills were hard on catchers, with the summer heat usually hitting 95 degrees with 85 percent humidity.

Junker could be hilarious, as well. In Valmeyer during the tournament he was at the bat rack getting ready to hit when a young fan yelled from the stands, "Hi, number 10!" Junker, calmly looked at the youngster and deadpanned, "Hi, little kid" as he walked to the on-deck circle.

As I watched the video, I came to the point where I was batting and fouled the ball off my ankle. It hurt all over again. And then when I got to first base I could see myself look up at the Valmeyer first-baseman and speak to him. Sometimes my memory is astounding.

We played well all summer. We swept Waterloo at their place, thanks in part to a grand slam I hit in the top of the final inning in the first game. That blast tied the game. We'd been down 8-4 with two outs. As big as my homer was, it was Bob Hughes who hit the winner on the next pitch. The 9-8 win was amazing and I felt like it was one of my biggest baseball thrills.

We stayed hot in the playoffs and faced the Alton team for the championship. When we won, on Alton's field, we mobbed the pitcher on the mound and celebrated just like any Major League team would in the World Series. Then we got in our cars and drove to Sauget where Rich Sauget was waiting for us at his saloon, Pop's. When we walked in, 15 bottles of champagne were lined up on the bar. Very little of it went in our mouths.

Within a month, Rich had ordered and installed a beautiful addition to the highway sign that denoted the Sauget city limits on the off-ramp from the I-70 bridge across the Mississippi. It said "Home of the Sauget Wizards — 1988 Mon-Clair League Champions."

It marked the only time in my life I'd poured championship champagne on teammates and the only time a team I played for was honored by a highway sign. Pretty cool stuff.

John Parke was one of our best pitchers on that team. He was a former Vanderbilt hurler and a good one. Again, another example of a player easily good enough to play minor league ball but all the scouts missed on him.

JP, as we called him, became one of my best friends. Our sarcastic senses of humor were identical. We'd sit in the dugout and deadpan while our teammates shook their heads and smiled.

Earlier that summer, JP had been pitching a no-hitter against the Granite City team at its park. I was in right field and we all knew he had the no-no going but baseball tradition dictates no one was to speak of it. We all knew it, and we were winning the game, but our dugout remained almost totally silent. We figured it was better to just shut up than to accidentally mention the fact JP hadn't given up a hit.

I was nervous in right field. I wanted my buddy to get his no-no and while I'd be thrilled to see him get it with a strikeout, I'm sure all my teammates felt like I did. If the ball came to any of us we'd lay out and put our lives in peril to catch it. With two outs, JP threw a fastball right down the middle. The hitter lined it into left for a hit. JP then struck out the next guy.

In the dugout, we all gave him handshakes and hugs and I asked him, "What happened?" He said, "It was weird. It was like an out-of-body experience. I just threw it right down the middle, because I wanted to hurry up and see how it would all turn out."

Once the championship was behind us we all went back to our normal jobs and lives, but the core group of us made the commitment to work out together over the winter. We loved it that much. Bob Hughes was the head coach at St. Louis University by then so we had access to their batting cage throughout the cold months. We'd gather there almost weekly to keep our hitting strokes sharp and our arms in shape. It was the most dedicated group of baseball players I'd ever been around and we were playing for free.

At work Larry and I toiled away throughout the St. Louis winter. Del even transferred a couple of additional staffers to our office and at one point we had six or seven people filling every inch of office space we had.

I still had the U.S.A. Baseball account and things were getting better in that regard because we were finally able to put a TV deal together with the USA Network. At one of our meetings in the U.S.A. Baseball headquarters in Trenton, New Jersey we were finishing up our discussions and talking about their upcoming season. It wasn't an Olympic year, but the college players they were recruiting to play on the national team were, according to their PR guy Bob Bensch, some of the best who would ever wear the U.S.A. jersey.

I had told them about the Wizards and how dedicated we were, and then on a lark, while being only partially serious, I said, "You know, we're pretty good. You should put us on the schedule."

The hardest part after that was not high-fiving the U.S.A. Baseball staff when they said, "Sure. We can do that." I do, however, imagine my gulp was audible.

When I got back to St. Louis after that meeting I called Hughes and let him know. The date would be June 20 at the U.S.A. team's home stadium in Millington, Tennessee. I got the impression Bobby thought I was kidding. It was more like, "Sure, we are. Uh-huh." Once I convinced him I was serious, his tone changed.

The Wizards had never traveled overnight for a game. We would need to do that to play the U.S.A. team. They booked rooms for us at the Best Western across the highway from the stadium.

The next hardest part was going to be the wait. We were all fired up, and June 20 seemed an awfully long way away.

Work moved along well, Larry remained a fabulous guy to work for, and the weather finally warmed up enough for JP and me to meet regularly, three or four days a week, at an open ball field behind an elementary school. We called it our spring training. We threw, stretching out the distance to get our arms in shape, and more important, we ran a lot. We could hit in the SLU cage but we couldn't run there. Still three weeks before the Wizards first game we were working out diligently to be ready for the season.

We opened in late May and I got off to a tough start. I wasn't hitting particularly well and once I'd fall into a phase like that I tended to forget all the things Hughes had taught me. I started swinging at bad pitches and trying to pull everything. When it's going like that it feels like you go up to the plate with two strikes on you already.

While I worked my way through that and worked with all of my clients at DW+A, I also took on the added responsibility of becoming the PR rep for the Wizards.

I wrote a press release about our upcoming game in Millington and sent printed copies of it to the St. Louis Post-Dispatch and all the neighboring papers in Illinois. The Post and the

Belleville News-Democrat each had a sportswriter call me for an interview and both ran big stories on this unknown band of baseball players who were heading off to take on the U.S.A. team in Tennessee.

I wrote up notes on every Wizards player as well as our full roster, complete with the colleges and pro teams each of us had played for, then sent that to Bob Bensch at the U.S.A. headquarters.

Most of us decided to head down on the morning of June 19 (my birthday, coincidentally) and we checked in at the Best Western by early afternoon. We headed over to the ballpark and met with the U.S.A. staff, who loaded us down with official credentials on lanyards, as well as programs, photos, and other bits of memorabilia. We all stared at the back of the program where the U.S.A. schedule was printed. To see a list of the series they would play against Mexico, Japan, Taiwan, Cuba, Korea, and Canada, was cool. To see the Sauget Wizards listed on June 20 was nothing short of stunning.

I'd brought a video camera with me and with JP and catcher Jim Donohue along for the ride in my car we started taping everything, documentary style. I still have the raw footage, transferred to DVD now, and it continues to crack me up.

U.S.A. was playing a team called Athletes In Action the night before they'd play us, so we all went over to the ballpark to watch. I can't say that the 22-6 shellacking the U.S.A. put on what we thought was a very good A.I.A. team gave us a lot of confidence. We enjoyed the game but we almost wished we hadn't seen it.

Our game would start at 7 p.m. on June 20. By mid-morning we were all pacing around the motel, so we decided to put on some gear and head over to the practice field to at least take some early BP.

After a couple of hours we felt like we'd burned off enough energy to finally relax and we gathered around the pool for a bit. By 4, we couldn't stand it. One by one we'd go back to our rooms and then reappear in uniform. By 4:30 we drove over to the ballpark, beating the home team there by quite a bit.

On the "documentary" video we shot, I rolled taped as JP got out of my car to take some photos of the exterior of the U.S.A. ballpark and just then Hughes and Greenie showed up in their car. As Hughes is taking his equipment out of the trunk the video catches him looking right at me, saying, "We're just early as hell, aren't we?" as he laughed out loud.

We took more BP on the practice field then filed into the ballpark and into our dugout around 5:30. The clock was ticking far too slowly.

On that U.S.A. club were future big leaguers Jeromy Burnitz, Bret Boone, Fernando Vina, Dan Wilson, and Matt Mieske. That night, we'd be facing pitchers Dan Smith (Creighton, followed by the Texas Rangers), Erik Schullstrom (Fresno State, followed by the Minnesota Twins), and Ricky Kimball (Florida State, followed by the Oakland A's minor leagues). By every metric and every measure it was the finest collection of talent the Wizards would ever face. With the exception of our one former big leaguer, Neil Fiala, it was the finest team any of us had ever faced.

We did the full World Series-style pre-game introductions, with both teams lining up on opposite baselines, and my PR work paid off. The P.A. announcer knew where each of us had gone to school and what pro teams some of us had played on. Then they played the national anthem and the game began.

Smith was the first pitcher we faced and he struck out the first Wizard he saw, Dave "Moose" Kassebaum — who, of course, stood about 5-foot-8. One could assume the U.S.A. team collectively yawned and felt like this game would be a repeat of the mauling they'd put on A.I.A. the night before. Neil Fiala came up next and on his second pitch he laced a rocket down the right-field line. It cleared the fence by a good margin but not before it hooked just foul. We didn't score in the top of the first, but Neil's shot did more than just land in foul territory. It put a chink in team U.S.A.'s armor.

We started Joe Mehallow on the mound. Joe was a classic "crafty" lefty who didn't throw hard but worked the corners and changed speeds. When he got us off the field without giving up a run, I think all of us were proud to look at the scoreboard and see it 0-0.

In the top of the second, we got a couple of runners on and I came up with two outs and men at first and second. As I dug in I couldn't help but allow the thought "I wonder what this is going to look like?" to creep into my head. Smith's first pitch was a slider away. I managed to not be over-anxious and took it for a ball. His next pitch was a fastball at the letters. I smashed a line drive right back over his head into center field and Jim Donohue came around to score. The Sauget Wizards led the U.S.A. team 1-0.

Joe Mehallow went three innings, gave up just three hits, and allowed no runs. The crafty lefty even struck out one batter.

My buddy JP came in to pitch in the fourth and he gave up two runs. We got off the field trailing just 2-1, but there's no denying we had to collectively wonder if the turning point had just been reached and that for the rest of our lives we'd only be able to tell our friends and families that we, the Sauget Wizards, had actually led the U.S.A. team for three innings before the wheels fell off and we lost 19-1.

JP settled down, getting us out of the fifth with no further damage. In the top of the sixth I came up again with two more runners on. Schullstrom was pitching. On the first strike I saw, I took a hack. There was only one out and with runners at first and third I figured my long fly to center would at least score one and if it made it to the wall it might score two. I dug hard for first.

When I rounded the base and looked up, I saw the most perplexing thing. The U.S.A. center fielder was stopping short of the wall, in front of the 405-foot mark, watching the ball I'd just hit leave the park. I had just clubbed a three-run homer to dead-center and we were back in front 4-2 going to the bottom of the sixth.

JP pitched another fine inning, leaving the game after three, giving up five hits and two runs. He struck out two.

Scott Brown, who would sign a minor-league contract with the Pittsburgh Pirates not long after this game, came in for us in the seventh and he gave up two runs. We were tied.

In the top of the eighth Jim Donohue came up to face Ricky Kimball and he promptly untied it. He obliterated the first pitch he saw, driving it off the top of the scoreboard above the left-field wall. The crowd was stunned. So was team U.S.A.

We got another run in the top of the ninth on a U.S.A. throwing error and then "Downtown" Scotty Brown got in a little trouble in the bottom of the ninth, giving up a run and putting runners on first and third with one out. The tying run was 90 feet from home. The winning run was on first. I was so nervous I could barely breathe.

Scotty promptly got Matt Mieske to ground into a double play, 6-4-3. Game over. The Sauget Wizards had defeated the U.S.A. team 6-5. We are still the only US-based team to beat the U.S.A. national squad.

We did some interviews on the field after the game, which led to the Memphis Commercial-Appeal running a headline story about us the next morning. The banner header read "USA stunned by semipros from Illinois." The sub-headline said "Wilber, Donohue homers spark Wizards." I still have it.

We signed a few autographs in the parking lot and headed back to the motel. I stopped in at the front desk and said to the clerk, "Hey, we just beat the U.S.A. team and we're going to have a couple of beers around the pool. If any guests complain, just come tell me and we'll take it inside."

She said, "We already heard and don't you worry, sugar. If anyone complains I'm going to tell them to put in earplugs. Ya'll enjoy yourselves, and congratulations!"

I needn't have worried. As a group we sat around a few tables in the dark. We never spoke above a whisper. All we could do was sit there and shake our heads, repeating things like, "I can't believe we just did that," or "I can't believe we beat those guys." After the U.S.A. team sent over a stack of pizzas, showing some great class, we ate a bit and went to our rooms. We were exhausted and proud. I had just enough energy to call Skip and Taffy and tell them about it. I'm pretty sure my mom was crying on the other end of the line.

The St. Louis Post-Dispatch ran a story on the game as well, along with the box score. There was my hitting line in print for eternity: 3 plate appearances, 2 at-bats, 2 hits, 1 home run, 4 RBI, 2 runs scored, and a walk.

When I walked in the DW+A office on Friday, Larry and my colleagues were waiting for me. Everyone in the office stood and clapped and as I looked around I couldn't believe what they'd done. Crepe paper streamers were everywhere, as were balloons. The box score and Post-Dispatch headline, which had been photocopied and enlarged, were both taped up all over the walls. It was about as touched as I've ever been.

I got back to work and kept playing for the Wizards for the rest of the summer. Life was good.

And then, in late July, I got word of a new professional sports development in St. Louis.

The Steamers, who had taken the town by storm in the early 1980s playing brilliant indoor soccer games at The Arena, had followed a typical trend in the sport. The original owner sold the team for a big profit. The second owner didn't have quite the same level of financial resources and he lost enough to sell out for next to nothing. The third owner took a beating as well and the team had folded a year earlier in the spring of '88. The word in local sports circles was that a new expansion franchise was coming to town. The owner would be a rich Yugoslavian businessman who was living in San Jose. I was intrigued.

When the rumors were confirmed and it was announced that the team would begin play in October, as the St. Louis Storm, I walked into Larry's office and said, "Can we talk? I need this to be strictly confidential." He said that would be no problem.

I said, "Larry, I think I want to let the Storm people know that I'd like an interview. I've loved indoor soccer since it came to town and it would be a dream of mine to work for them."

He smiled, and said, "Have you told Del this?" I said I had not. I wanted to see if an interview was even possible before telling Del about the idea. If the Storm wasn't interested in me, no harm and no foul. Larry said, "I'm good friends with the attorney they're using to get the team going. I'll make a call for you, and I'll recommend you."

The new owner was Milan Mandaric. The head coach would be the best coach in MISL history, Don Popovic, also a Yugoslavian. I met both of them in the lobby of the downtown Marriott.

The next day Milan offered me the position of vice president-marketing and promotions, for very good money.

"I think you're general manager material, Bob," Milan said in his thick accent. "But Anheuser-Busch wants one of their men to be the GM so I think we have to go that way if we want their support."

I agreed with the assessment and quickly accepted the position.

I called Del twice that day but he was swamped and never had time to call me back. I knew word would get out quickly and I didn't want him to hear about it from the press or someone else. I faxed him my resignation.

I'm not proud of that. It was an enormously stupid decision based a bit on panic. He called me immediately and he wasn't happy. He told me I should have talked to him first and he was absolutely right. He capped it off by saying, "I can't believe you're going to do this. Your last name is already on the door!"

I'd have to qualify it as a bit of a brotherly falling-out. Del and I continued to speak when necessary but our relationship remained pretty distant for a couple of years. That gave me a pain in my gut because I knew it was my moronic fault. But, knowing that I'd be packing up and heading for work at The Arena in a week made me very excited.

The St. Louis Storm had an owner, a head coach, a VP-marketing, and a nickname. At the time, we didn't own a soccer ball or have any players. And in roughly 10 weeks we'd be opening at home, at The Arena, against the Kansas City Comets.

There was a lot of work to do. And I was off, plowing forward yet again.

A Ballplayer And A Storm

But what about Pete Delkus? After the one call Skip made to the Twins Pete reported as instructed and spent the summer at Elizabethton in the Appalachian League. He had played for the Cougars and gone through SIUE's TV/Radio Mass Communications Department nine years after me. In 1987, also nine years after me, he was in the same Appalachian League in which I had played.

Somehow, even though he was an undrafted pitcher on a staff full of well-compensated draftees, his manager liked what he saw and put Pete on the mound when a game was on the line. Pete came through. He came through all summer.

That season, Pete Delkus appeared in 21 games with his submarine stuff, coming in out of the bullpen. He pitched 37 innings and gave up just 29 hits and 5 earned runs while striking out 44 batters and walking only 7. His ERA was 1.19 which is outstanding at any level.

In 1988 he was promoted to Kenosha, Wisconsin in the Midwest League. His manager there was Ron Gardenhire. Pete did not give up a single earned run in spring training. He did not give one up in April. He put more zeroes on the board in May. He gave up no earned runs in June. Not an earned run in July, either. In August, just before the Kenosha season ended, he finally gave up two earned runs. His astonishing line was 61 games, 33 saves, 68 innings pitched, 43 hits and those two earned runs. He struck out 58 batters and walked 13. His ERA was an otherworldly 0.26, meaning he basically gave up just one earned run for every 27 innings pitched, although the truth was he pitched an amazing five consecutive months without giving up an "earnie." The numbers are basically impossible and yet he did it. And people noticed. He was named Twins Minor League Player of the Year and was awarded the Rolaids Relief Man Award for the minor leagues.

After that season the Twins GM, Terry Ryan, told Pete, "You're going to be a rich young man, very soon."

In 1989 he was again promoted, this time to Orlando in the Double-A Southern League. He pitched 139 innings there, saving 10 games while striking out 63 and walking 28. His ERA was 1.87 in a very tough league.

When he returned to St. Louis after his season in Orlando, I was just starting with the Storm and Pete moved into the second bedroom in my suburban apartment. The Rolaids trophy, which featured a large brass fireman's helmet — because relievers are asked to put out fires — inhabited our living room.

One night we headed to Bogart's in west St. Louis county, a fine establishment with multiple bars and live music. While we were talking I spotted a stunningly gorgeous girl staring at both of us, but mostly at Pete. He was too shy to approach her so I flagged down a young lady selling roses and had her take one to the beautiful young woman across the room. I added, "Tell her it's from him" as I pointed at Pete. The young lass smiled broadly when the rose arrived and came over to say hello. A romance was born. My dad may have gotten Pete signed but I introduced him to his future wife, Jacque.

My friend's life was plowing forward. So was mine.

At the Storm we hit the ground running. We had no choice. Our coach, Don Popovic, went about the business of putting a good indoor soccer team together. I went about the business of assembling and managing a team of young go-getters in the front office.

We needed to quickly create sales and marketing materials then hit the streets and the phones to put them to good use. It was a daunting task and we were starting with nothing. We had roughly 10 weeks to go from zero to success. We needed to create a soccer franchise, brand it, sell it, and promote it. My days were a nonstop stream of meetings, both in-house and around town.

It soon became clear that our general manager was not the guy to handle all of these tasks and within six weeks he was relieved of his duties by our owner, Milan Mandaric. An experienced soccer consultant was brought in to handle the financial and budgetary side of the business, to guide us when we had questions, and to be Milan's eyes and ears in the office. It was on me and my staff, though, to sell the tickets, create the promotions, and bring in the sponsors. The sponsorship part was totally my responsibility.

As for my staff, I inherited a couple of people who'd been contracted by the agency that helped found the franchise, but I needed more. After interviewing a dozen applicants I settled on those who seemed to have the correct fire in their eyes. One of them was my Sauget Wizards teammate John Parke.

I'd helped JP get an internship with the St. Louis Blues the prior winter and I knew him well enough to have a grasp on his enormous creativity and intelligence. He'd be my right hand in the front office, and I needed him — the two of us had a lot on our plates.

We needed to publish a program to sell at our home games but no one on my fledgling staff had ever designed one. John and I took on the task with the help of a local printer, who showed us how to mock up a magazine on blank pieces of paper. That weekend, at my kitchen table, we scribbled penciled notes on each page, denoting what content would go where. In places where bios or stories were needed, I wrote them. We hired a photographer to give us the artwork. A graphic artist created the cover. My sales reps and I had to sell the ads.

Many of the larger ads in the glossy program were part of sponsorship packages, and the first one I sold was to the local office for Steak 'n Shake. I put a proposal together after landing a face-to-face meeting and presented it to the regional marketing manager. I'll admit I was nervous. It was my first marketing meeting for this new team and I wanted to have some early good news for Milan and Don, who were counting on me to make the franchise viable while they spent the money to bring in the best possible players. I pitched my plan, showed the gentleman the price, and he shook my hand, saying, "Great! You have a deal. We're happy to support the team."

Steak 'n Shake's program revolved around an in-game promotion called the "Steak 'n Shake minute." If the Storm were to score a goal during the final minute of the first half or the final minute of the third quarter, everyone in attendance could use their ticket stub to get a free order of fries at any area location within 24 hours. When that happened it would be JP's responsibility to rush up to our office and call all 33 restaurants in the St. Louis area to alert them. He said, "Gosh, I hope we win a lot of games this year, but I sure hope we don't score very often during the Steak 'n Shake minute."

To entertain and inform our fans I needed a public-address announcer. There was nothing wrong with hiring a guy nobody had heard of, as long as he was a good announcer, but I wanted to use the position to give us some instant credibility. I hired Kevin Slaten.

Kevin had been a high-profile television and radio sports commentator in St. Louis for years.

Everyone knew Kevin Slaten. His willingness trudge to The Arena all winter to sit next to the penalty box and do the P.A. announcing was an indicator we were for real. On top of that, Kevin's recognizable voice was perfect for the high-energy cheerleading done by indoor soccer announcers.

On the ticket-sales front I motivated and prodded my staff to sell season tickets one call at a time. It was an inglorious and difficult endeavor but critically necessary. Season tickets and group sales were the foundation of the franchise, as there would be no income from broadcast rights or profit-sharing in the MISL. There was no league-wide broadcasting program in place, and it's hard to share profits when none of the teams make any money. Our target was 5,000 season tickets but that was a number seemingly pulled from thin air by Milan and Don. Looking at our sales rate and the limited time we had it became obvious we'd be extremely fortunate to sell 2,000, and if we did that we'd be in the upper third of the entire league.

Once mid-September rolled around and opening night was just weeks away, a new commission-only intern joined the sales team. Pete Delkus was not necessarily a soccer fan but being so well-known in the area meant he had plenty of valuable contacts, especially in his hometown of Collinsville, Illinois. Plus, he was my roommate. And his addition to the staff gave us a grand total of three former or current Sauget Wizards in the office. No other team in the MISL had even one!

The days were an absolute blur. I'd never been so busy, yet so energized, at any job. I couldn't wait to get to work in the morning and I stayed late on a daily basis. I had so much to do and did much of it myself, but I also had a staff to lead. To make that more of a challenge, I had no formal training in business management so I did the next best thing — I managed my young group as if I was Roger Morningstar, my boss at Converse. I coaxed them, I cheered them on, I was always there when they had questions, and I expected success from every single one of them.

Since they were all working on small salaries boosted by commission on sales, I helped them out in that area as well. I had a solid salary with no commission plan, so when a meeting with Ralston Purina turned into the purchase of 9,000 tickets for a single game I handed the deal to the sales staff so they could earn some much-needed money from it. I did that a number of times on additional deals, knowing it would help them survive while it kept them happy and motivated. It couldn't have been easy hearing a "no thanks" followed by a click on the phone all day so it was important to keep their spirits up.

And although I had no formal training in public relations, I understood its value. We had a modest advertising budget but we could barely make a dent in the busy St. Louis ad scene compared to the other sports franchises in town. We needed that ultra-valuable asset created by public relations. We needed free advertising.

I began by building relationships with all the major television, radio, and print outlets in the area. On the fly, I learned that those organizations were also looking to add value for their advertising clients and if I made the Storm a viable add-on for their sales efforts, all the parties involved could reap the benefits.

One by one the radio stations gave us their support and the newspapers treated us well. We'd rarely be on the front page of the sports section, but we were treated like a professional team in a town full of well-known and historic franchises. It was a good start.

KSD was a rock-format radio station at the time, and while many stations worked closely with us the folks at KSD seemed to adopt us as their pet project. They brought us a three-game sponsorship from Wheaties cereal, which sold some tickets but — more important — got us mentioned on the air a lot, bringing us a great deal of credibility.

Another promotion they delivered to us was with the Missouri Lottery, a big ad buyer at the station. At a selected game in mid-season the Missouri Lottery would provide 5,000 high-quality thermal drinking mugs featuring our logo and those of the Lottery and KSD, to give away. In addition they would also give us 5,000 scratch-off tickets to put inside the mugs. I had a suspicion that game might go pretty well.

We shared the building with the St. Louis Blues and it was necessary to keep those relationships healthy, as well. There was no denying we were the little brother in the family and the Blues staff wasn't all that interested in helping us compete with them but they also made it clear they would never market against us or try to impede us in any way. They did help me save some time by introducing me to various vendors who produced giveaway items for them. I welcomed all the help I could get when it came to saving minutes.

Once our Astroturf floor arrived we decided to use the day the arena staff was going to install it as an open house. The staff laid the floor down over some thermal boards and the hockey ice and we planned to open the doors to let any interested fans in free. My sales staff would roam the aisles and concourses, hoping to sell tickets while showing off available seats. Meanwhile, to keep people entertained, the team would scrimmage on the floor.

I had no idea if the open house would be a bonanza or a complete bust and I feared the latter quite a bit. If we let folks in for free and no one showed up that would not be what I'd consider a very good sign. We got a lot of free help from the radio stations I was working with, hyping it as much as they could.

That Saturday morning we were up in our offices getting ready when a staff member from The Arena came in and said, "We open the doors in two hours. You've already got a parking lot full of cars and they're tailgating out there. Looks like they're having fun already. Good job!" Smiles all around. It was a good day.

The weeks rushed by, and opening night was looming. There would be no stopping the game from happening. We'd either be ready or we wouldn't. We needed music and we needed a dance team. Rusty Hermann, a talented guy who could handle both of those details, dove in and made it all happen. The dance team was terrific and Rusty manned the in-game music himself.

Rusty also brought up the critical subject of intro music. A familiar song would have to be selected as the tune we'd use to bring the players onto the field for pregame introductions, with spotlights on them and smoke pouring from the entry next to the south goal. It had to rock, it had to get people on their feet, and it would sure be nice if it had something to do with our nickname. We chose the "live" version of REO Speedwagon's hit "Ridin' The Storm Out." It was perfect. Rusty also came up with some thunder sound-effects and a couple of strobe lights that would flash in the dark building to make it look as if we actually were riding a storm out as the players took the field.

A day before the opener our game programs arrived and John and I marveled at them. Our scribbles, made at my kitchen table, had morphed into an honest-to-goodness program, full of information and photos. It looked nothing short of big-league and the two of us were legitimately proud of what we'd created by sheer guesswork and intuition. I suspect it also helped to have a talented printing house turn our scribbles into a magazine.

I'd been monitoring individual ticket sales in the office for weeks, leading up to opening night. They'd been pretty strong for a month but in the week leading up to the opener they really started to pick up. I was confident.

When the big day arrived the floor was in place, the dancers were in uniform, and our team was ready to go. The only glitch came when the Storm logos were painted on the field that day and they weren't drying very fast. For much of the afternoon the operations staff at The Arena manned blow-dryers as they attempted to hasten the drying process. They made it with minutes to spare.

Don Popovic had brought in some solid talent and I thought we'd have a chance to win a lot of games. As the marketing guy, of course, I had no input or control over how many goals we scored but I knew a good team would help us sell tickets. Our starting goalkeeper could do that, as well.

Slobo Ilijevski came to America in 1977 from his native Yugoslavia. He hooked on with a few soccer teams but was down to his last few dollars when he landed a tryout with the St. Louis Steamers in 1980 and earned a contract. His sprawling miraculous saves made him a huge fan favorite. When Don then signed him to play for the Storm, Slobo was tireless in terms of promoting the team. Any time I could get him on the radio he graciously jumped at the chance to do the interviews, with his charmingly thick accent.

The rest of the team was a blend of foreign players and Americans with a few St. Louis boys thrown in. St. Louis has been a soccer hotbed since the 1950s and finding local talent for the indoor game was not just a publicity stunt. These guys were good.

We were collectively a nervous wreck the day of the opener. I kept an eye on the ticket computer monitor, smiling as the numbers rang up consistently from outlets all over town. The team arrived. The Kansas City Comets arrived. The Storm was about to become a reality.

We'd brought in searchlights to scan the sky outside The Arena, acting as a beacon for arriving fans while signaling, in Hollywood premiere fashion, that this game was a big deal. We waited. At 6 p.m., one hour before kickoff, the traffic started to back up in front of the building. At 7 p.m., when a singer performed the national anthem, the cars were still coming in.

We put roughly 14,500 people into The Arena that night. We lost the game, and it was an uncommonly low-scoring affair, but our promotions went off just fine, the fans had fun, and as I stood behind the goal and looked at all those people, I felt an enormous rush of pride — not just for myself, but for my staff. I had goosebumps and wasn't too far from shedding a tear. The work had been manic, but the results were there and it all felt so worth it at that moment.

You don't just announce you have an indoor soccer team and hope for the best. You have to work at it, day after day, tirelessly promoting and selling. We'd all put our hearts into it, and 14,500 St. Louis soccer fans thanked us in the best way possible.

We'd have our ups and downs, in terms of attendance, and we finally settled in with an average crowd being in the 6,800 range. Some nights were better, especially when the Blues would be on the road and we'd have the rare opportunity to play on weekend nights, but those Tuesdays in the dark winter months when so much of our most avid demographic was going to bed early on a school night could be pretty tough. It was never much fun to walk into the building to see 3,800 fans sprinkled throughout the 18,000-seat St. Louis Arena.

Yes, the St. Louis Arena. It was a special place. It had been built in 1927 to host the National Dairy Show and its domed wooden roof and steeply pitched seating areas gave spectators views unlike most other indoor venues from that era. In front, where the main lobby and ticket windows were, two large spires framed the building's entrances. Our offices were on the top floors of the east tower.

When the NHL expanded and the St. Louis Blues came to town in 1967 The Arena went through a long series of upgrades and renovations which continued until just before the building closed in 1994. The first renovations included the replacement of the original wooden seats with modern plastic ones and the addition of real NHL hockey glass above the boards, replacing the chicken wire that had been there for the minor-league St. Louis Braves.

It was a massive landmark on the St. Louis landscape sitting directly across the highway from historic Forest Park. It was also full of secret back staircases and cave-like hallways, and all of us enjoyed knowing how to navigate those passageways the public never saw.

The Arena was kept mostly rodent-free by an expert team of feral cats who called the place home. I never saw a mouse the entire time I worked there but also rarely saw the felines. One night, though, I happened upon a pair of them peeking out from a space in the riser upon which the first level of seats were placed. Game nights were good for the cats. Lots of appetizers would be dropped on the floor to go with their mouse entrees.

Many people in St. Louis clearly recall when the place was renamed the Checkerdome for six years in the late '70s and early '80s. The Blues' ownership group wanted out and St. Louis-based Ralston Purina stepped in to buy the team and The Arena. They changed the name to the Checkerdome to promote their checkerboard branding. What many people don't remember is that in the early '80s the Steamers were filling the place to the rafters and indoor soccer games were "it" in St. Louis sports, while the Blues struggled to fill even half the seats. Ralston Purina had, by then, realized their purchase was quite a cash drain and the company announced they had sold the team and it would be moving to Saskatoon, Saskatchewan.

The NHL had no desire to have a team in Saskatoon and they nixed the deal, so Ralston Purina simply walked away and handed the team to the NHL. The league was ready to fold the franchise but just before doing so they found a buyer to keep the Blues in St. Louis — whereupon the building reverted to its historic name, the St. Louis Arena.

It was an honor to call "the old barn" our workplace.

During an early home game we managed to score a goal during the Steak 'n Shake minute. JP dashed to the office and made all the phone calls. The next day the marketing person from the chain called me and said two things. He said, "It went great and we sold a lot of steakburgers to go with those free fries. But, can you do me one favor? Can you have your announcer ask the crowd to please use their ticket stubs at a Steak 'N Shake near their homes? Hundreds of people tried to use them at the Hampton Avenue location, a block from The Arena. They were lined up out the door, onto the sidewalk, and down the road."

We did that starting at the next game. I never got another call so I assume our loyal fans did what we asked them to do.

After our third home game Kevin Slaten gave me a call and dropped a bomb. He'd been offered a prestigious position at a top TV station in Denver and he was accepting it. I needed a new P.A. announcer.

I immediately set up auditions with a number of candidates, including my SIUE buddy Jim Keegan whom I seriously wanted to hire. Jim and I had messed around at school, imitating P.A. announcers, and I knew he had it in him to be the new in-house voice of the Storm.

The Arena sound engineer set us up for the auditions on a weekday afternoon. I had 10 or 12 guys ready to read the various scripts I'd prepared while I also asked them to give me their personal renditions of player introductions and goal calls. Each time, I'd give them an example of what I wanted and ask them to do it. Each time, my reactions ranged from real disappointment to a feeling of, "Not bad, but not what I'm after."

Back in those days indoor soccer was breaking the mold for game presentation and announcing and I wanted to keep pushing that envelope. The other major sports took a keen interest in what we were doing but they publicly mocked us for the pyrotechnics, smoke machines, loud announcers, and the music we played while the game was underway, not just during breaks. They called us a circus. Maybe we were a circus, but the fans seemed to dig what the clowns were doing.

After a full two hours of individual auditions I thanked everyone for coming and told them I'd be in touch. I also thanked the sound guy for helping us make it happen, in an empty arena, and he said, "If you want my opinion, there was one announcer who was better than all the rest of them combined. You should hire that guy to do the job."

I said, "You think so? Which guy was it? I didn't think any of them were right."

He replied, "It was you. Every time you gave them an example of what you wanted, it filled the building. You should do it."

I had honestly not thought of that. During the first three games with Kevin doing the P.A. I hadn't given his work a second thought because I knew he was an experienced pro and he'd be great. I concentrated on our game production and directed my staff almost constantly on our walkie-talkies. I felt like the game couldn't go on without me being in charge of everything. It had, apparently, become my turn to be the micromanager.

I thought about it overnight. The next morning I spoke with Milan and told him my plan. If he was OK with it I would become the new P.A. announcer for the St. Louis Storm. The key thing was I'd have to let loose of the reins a little and show my staff I had confidence in them. They would have to put on the game production without my constant supervision, although I'd keep my walkie-talkie and stay involved as much as I could when my voice wasn't blaring through the speakers.

I knew immediately what I wanted to do with my goal call and couldn't wait to break it out. Goal calls, for the announcer, don't come right after the ball hits the back of the net but rather after the officials give the scorekeeper the exact time of the goal and the name of the player who scored it, which might be 10-15 seconds after the fact. It was a chance to get the crowd revved up again after their initial spontaneous celebration when the goal was scored. I was going to simply stretch out the word Storm until I nearly ran out of breath. "Stoooooooooooooorm goal! Scored by No. 7, Daryl Doran! Assist to No. 21, Fernando Clavijo! Time of the goal, 2 minutes and 25 seconds!"

For my first game I was pumped beyond measure. And we got shut out. Indoor soccer games are almost never shutouts but this one was and I never got to try out my new goal call. After that first night, though, I felt comfortable behind the microphone and I quickly adapted to the delay over the P.A. system, which can throw off a lot of people. You hear your own voice coming through the speakers about a half-second after you begin speaking and the best way to overcome that is to cup one ear with your hand while focusing strictly on what you're saying.

As we moved on my staff proved to me they could make the games work and I proved to myself I could be a first-class announcer. It felt like being part of the game, and in many ways that's exactly what it was.

After pre-game warmups the teams would head to their dressing rooms for a quick break and then it would be time to introduce the players. We always did the visiting team first with the lights on in the building, and I'd do that respectfully but with as little emotion as possible in my voice, introducing the players in numerical order. Once the visitors were introduced it was time for the home team.

After a short pause for effect, the lights would go off. The spotlights would begin to "ballyhoo the house" (an actual term, which meant the four spotlight operators would move their beams wildly in all directions). And I'd find myself beating the table with my pen as if I was warming up to play the drums. I was getting myself pumped up and it always worked.

When the first notes of "Ridin' The Storm Out" hit the speakers, with a synthesizer sounding like a storm siren, I waited for the first guitar chords and got to work. "Ladies and gentlemen. Get on your feet! And welcome... Your... St. Louis... STOOOOOOOOOOOORM!"

To have 8,000 people in the building gave me goosebumps knowing my staff and I had put them there. To get those 8,000 to cheer on my command was exhilarating.

And when our Brazilian forward Claudio DeOliveira put one in the net, I got another chance to show off my lung capacity. I'd stretch out the final "o" in Claudio for as long as five or six seconds, all at top volume, then drop an octave to say his last name in something like a growl. The crowds ate it up.

I loved every day of my job at the Storm but I loved game days the most. We quickly established some routines to make sure we were ready by the time the gates opened, one of which involved taking part of the staff to Ponderosa Steakhouse with me for lunch, where we'd pack on the protein for the long night ahead and go over our notes.

We had a promotion with Eagle Snacks, the former salty-snack division of Anheuser Busch, and it required John and me to select a random section in the arena for each game. We'd look at the ticket sales and the seat maps and pick out a section that looked like it would be full, and two hours before the gates opened we'd take the appropriate number of cases of Eagle Snacks to the usher's room — the same room where I'd checked in each night when I wore the blue blazer years before. The ushers were kind enough to hand them out for us after I announced the winning section.

We'd get our game programs ready and deliver them to the concession people. We'd go over our halftime plans, which generally included a routine by Rusty's dancers, followed by an on-field competition between randomly selected fans, as well as a promotion we did for Trans World Airlines, in which a large plywood sign was attached to the front of the south goal. It had big holes at the bottom and smaller holes up high. Two of those holes were barely bigger than a soccer ball and were in the upper corners. The selected fan got one shot from the penalty spot and he or she could choose to shoot for the easy targets and win a gift bag, or the contestant could take a shot at the upper corners to try to win two TWA tickets for any destination the airline served, anywhere in the world. No one ever won that but a few came close.

At a few games, after the dancers were done with their halftime routine we'd fall back on a go-to gimmick. We'd put two teams of peewee soccer kids out there and let them run around and fall over. The fans always enjoyed that mayhem.

When it came time for the KSD/Missouri Lottery giveaway game, the beautiful thermal mugs showed up early and we put out a call to our Fan Club asking for volunteers to help us stuff them with scratcher tickets. Dozens showed up that afternoon and we managed to get the 5,000 tickets stuffed into 5,000 mugs before we thanked them with pizza. We drew well over 9,000 paid admissions that night.

When we asked the fans to stand and wave if they had a winning scratch-off nearly a thousand did. The Lottery officials had told us, "It's just math. About one in four will win something, even if it's just another ticket, but with 5,000 scratch-offs in the house we're going to have some big winners. It wouldn't be unlikely to have some folks win a thousand dollars."

The next day, Milan came into the office for one of his rare visits. "That was a good crowd," he said. "Do more of those promotions." It wasn't the first time I wondered if he knew how hard this was, but now I was certain. "Do more of those promotions." You bet!

I knew we were doing a good job. I knew my young staffers were working as hard as they could. But by midseason it was becoming obvious that Don had sold Milan on a dream of money-making success despite the fact the business of indoor soccer had no real history of such a thing. Milan was a rich man in the computer business and he had gotten that way because he liked to make money. He had little interest in continually wiring cash into our account to make sure we could meet payroll.

We would've needed to average close to 12,000 paid admissions to break even. How Don convinced Milan that such a number was reasonable is something that borders on being a magic trick. We were right near the middle of the league in terms of average attendance, drawing about 6,800 per game, and that equated to losing money. Milan's money.

As the season went on our hired-gun consultant bore the brunt of Milan's complaints whenever we'd need a new infusion of cash but all of us began to see much more of the owner and his coach. They began to hover over us, grilling us in meetings. It got to be exhausting and distracting and one thing it did not do was motivate my staff to do the impossible. For Don, yelling at his players to get their attention was routine. For Milan, it was clear his business leadership style didn't include such histrionics but he was getting frustrated and he had Don at his side, raising the volume and the level of criticism. All we could do was accept the barbs and keep digging.

To clear our minds, there were other fun distractions to experience while working at The Arena. Big-time rock bands played the venue quite often and we could sneak out of our office and into the dark upper reaches of the seating area, through a secret door, to listen to sound checks in the afternoon.

When my favorite band, Rush, came to play we had three Storm jerseys made up with the last names Lee, Lifeson, and Peart on the back. I didn't get to meet the Geddy, Alex, and Neil, but I got a tour of the backstage area from their road manager and he promised to deliver them to the guys. That night JP and I went down to the home bench behind the boards, and watched the show from there. It was a fantastic concert, but JP was disappointed they didn't play his favorite Rush song, "The Trees."

When a national volleyball tournament came to town I was hired to do the P.A. despite knowing little about the game and its terminology. I brought one of my sales reps, Tisha Vandemore, with me because she'd played high-level collegiate volleyball, and she whispered to me what to say, in the correct lingo, each time a call was made. It was a great experience, speaking softly in a quiet building, and I was paid the enormous sum of $50 to do it.

Our players were constantly making appearances around town. Once, I joined our players as they signed autographs while youth teams played at an indoor soccer facility, and when a team scored and one of the youngsters yelled, "Stoooooooorm GOAL!"

I had joined an elite group of people who have heard themselves being imitated by strangers.

On the home and baseball front, my roomie got some great news in the middle of that winter. The Minnesota Twins had added him to their 40-man Major League roster. That meant he'd be going to the big-league spring training camp and while it was unlikely he'd make the 25-man regular season roster he would be pitching against big leaguers in Florida and he'd be expected to make the Triple-A roster, for the Portland Beavers.

We were both eagerly looking forward to Pete's debut in spring training and then the Major League teams locked out the players before camp started. After all the hard work he'd put in, Pete now had to wait.

The lockout lasted an interminable 32 days and drastically shortened spring training, which normally seems too long. That year, 1990, they would play only a bare minimum number of games.

When the lockout finally ended Pete had to get to Orlando in a hurry. During his final night before departure I made an announcement during a quiet break in the game. I said, "Tonight, the Storm says goodbye and good luck to one of our valued sales reps. Pete Delkus will be leaving tomorrow to attend Major League spring training with the Minnesota Twins, in Orlando. We ask you, Storm fans, to help us wish him the very best!" I was happy to hear Pete get a rousing ovation.

Once spring training started I got daily phone reports from my roomie, including the day he called to say, "We played the Astros today. I faced Terry Puhl and shattered his bat into a dozen pieces." Another time he called just to tell me that the great Kirby Puckett had taken to calling him "Delk" and Kirby would yell out his name in the clubhouse. When Kirby spoke, everyone listened. When Kirby acknowledged you with a nickname, your status was elevated. Pete Delkus. My former Wizard teammate. Pitching against Terry Puhl and breaking his bat. Being recognized as a peer by Kirby Puckett. I was thrilled for my friend. And very proud of him.

As the Storm's season wound down it was clear we'd make the playoffs but the team was not quite winning enough. We'd brought in a few stars, guys like Stan Terlecki and Marcio Leite, and we'd have some great games from time to time, but we finished 24-28 and lost in the first round of the playoffs to the San Diego Sockers.

At our final regular-season home game, which was "Fan Appreciation Night," we staged a post-game promotion that involved an expensive speedboat and about 4,000 paper airplanes.

When the game ended the arena staff removed the south goal and towed the high-priced boat out to the center of the field. The fans in attendance had been encouraged to buy as many sheets of special airplane paper as they wished, for a dollar apiece. All the money went to charity.

First, we contested the initial round of the competition. On my count, everyone threw all the planes they had purchased toward the open speedboat and any planes that landed inside it would earn the thrower a shot at winning the boat in the second round. I counted down, "Three, two, one… Throw!" and it absolutely rained paper airplanes for a solid 30 seconds.

All in all, we had about a dozen planes inside the boat and we announced the names written on them to get the finalists into position. One guy had thrown four of the planes, so he obviously knew how to expertly make and throw a paper airplane. He also knew how to drink a lot of beer.

In the final, the front hatch was opened and the first person who could throw a plane into the open hatch would win the boat. The dealer who supplied the beautiful craft had taken out an insurance policy to cover the cost should anyone win it. He definitely wanted that to happen, since he'd doled out about $2,000 on the policy. Dragging the boat back to his dealership after having purchased the insurance was the last thing he wanted.

Mr. Beerdrinker threw his first plane and just missed. He threw his second and came up well short. He threw his third and fourth but missed again. He then fell back into a seat and passed out. Nobody won the boat but much fun was had. I doubt Mr. Beerdrinker felt very good the next morning.

After we lost to San Diego in the playoffs to end our season we came back to The Arena the following morning to have some meetings and discuss what we'd done right and what we could do better. Your basic post-mortem. It was a Friday.

Milan and Don did not show up that day but their lawyer did. One by one he brought many of my staffers into an office and fired them. I was the final one called in. He gravely looked at me from behind the desk and said, "Milan and Don are not happy to have lost so much money this season, so we're going to go in a different direction. We're letting you go. Do you have anything to say?" I stood and said, "As you were," and walked out. My staff was waiting for me in my office, all with pasty white faces and traces of perspiration. They were all talking at once and I could tell they were desperate for some good news.

All I said was, "Guys, it's Friday afternoon. I'm not sure what any of us are going to do but I do know that it's highly unlikely any of us will land new jobs over the weekend. I suggest we clear out our desks and head to a happy-hour somewhere." That's what we did.

I'd been fired by two Major League Baseball clubs who didn't want me as a player. Now, I could add to the list a professional indoor soccer team that didn't want me in the front office. It was truly depressing, but I knew in my heart I'd done the best I could and I'd done it well. I didn't see how their "new direction" could be any better.

And those flashy game productions with the wild player intros and the rocking music, which were jeered by the other major sports? Have you been to an NHL, NBA, or NFL game lately? They mocked us then. But they copy us now.

We were certainly a trailblazing bunch of clowns.

Moving Too Fast

After our happy-hour excursion on Black Friday I slept in a little the next day. By mid-morning I was lying on the living room sofa listening to music, trying to figure out what had happened. And the phone rang. It was Roger Morningstar. Of course it was.

Roger, who had by then been promoted to a national position with Converse, said, "Hey, man, I know how much you love the work you're doing in the soccer world, so I don't know if this will interest you or not, but I wanted to run it by you. We're going to need a new regional promotions director in the southwest. It covers parts of six states and it involves promotions only, working with NBA, MLB, NFL players, and the NCAA schools. I didn't want to start interviewing until I talked to you but I also don't want you to leave soccer if that's where your heart is."

I had to stifle a laugh. This was just too typical for my life, and too unbelievable to actually be happening. I'd told my Storm staff, the day before, that we should all just relax for a couple of days because none of us were going to get new jobs over the weekend. I guess I was the exception to that rule.

I couldn't lie to Roger. "Well, your timing is fairly amazing," I said. "The soccer team let almost all of us go after the final game. They actually thought they were going to get rich owning the team. Apparently they never heard the line about how you become a millionaire in indoor soccer. You start with 10 million."

Roger said, "Wow, I didn't know that, and I'm sorry to hear it. When did that happen?"

This time I did laugh. I said, "About 18 hours ago."

We talked for another half-hour. Roger explained the position to me and said I'd need to live near the regional office in Irvine, California. If I took the job I'd be living in an expensive part of the country and although I'd absorb a fairly big pay cut in terms of salary, the bonus was an all-or-nothing 100 percent match. If I ticked off every item on the bonus list I'd get a check matching the amount of my annual salary. The hard part was surviving financially for a full year until I made that happen. The good part was that Roger Morningstar would again be my boss and he had a track record of making sure his staff members had the resources and leadership to always earn their bonuses.

It sounded like a dream job, and considering my employment situation at the time it was almost a miracle. The region included Southern California, plus all of Arizona, New Mexico, Nevada, Utah, and Colorado.

All I'd have to do was make sure I had six players each on the L.A. Rams, L.A. Raiders, Denver Broncos, San Diego Chargers, and Phoenix Cardinals. I'd also need two players each on the L.A. Dodgers, Anaheim Angels, and San Diego Padres, while I'd be required to also sign two players each on the L.A. Lakers, L.A. Clippers, Phoenix Suns, Utah Jazz, and Denver Nuggets. In addition to all of that, there were college targets to hit, as well. UCLA, Cal Irvine, Air Force, New Mexico State, Nevada, and a number of other college basketball teams were already wearing Converse, so I'd be in charge of maintaining that.

I told Roger I'd sleep on it and call him in the morning. Within an hour I made up my mind and called him back. I was returning to Converse Shoes. And I was moving to SoCal.

As unlikely as it seemed, I was plowing forward again.

I flew to Orange County to meet with Mike Zinn who would be switching over to a regional sales management job and giving up the promotional gig. He showed me around the office, handed me the files, and gave me a few tips on how to handle the job. I also took one full day to drive around looking at apartments from Anaheim to San Juan Capistrano.

Since I'd be doing as much flying as driving I decided what mattered for housing was proximity to both John Wayne Airport, in Orange County, and the office just south of there.

If I was going to be within 20 or 30 minutes of both the office and the airport, why not live near the beach? I found a two-story, two-bedroom apartment I could barely afford in Dana Point, just a half mile from the ocean, and quickly put a deposit on it.

I definitely needed the large second bedroom. Mike had already told me how one challenge in the job was the actual in-house inventory of shoes I'd need, since the office had no storage space. The company was trying to streamline production processes by making all the shoes they'd need for non-basketball professional athletes in single large batches, so it was incumbent upon the regional reps to stock up with enough shoes to get their contracted athletes through a season.

The unintended consequence of that production method was that it pitted the regional reps against each other in terms of inventory. The quickest guys on the trigger, when the football shoes came out in early summer, might grab so many the next guy couldn't get the inventory he'd need to hit his bonus. Rejoining the company in mid-year would put me at a great disadvantage in that regard and it would take me a while to figure out all the tricks.

After my initial visit to So Cal, my next official function would be a trip to Boston. The company was holding its annual meetings and I'd have a chance to meet my promotional colleagues and see Roger again.

At the meeting it was obvious that we were the rock stars of the company. While the sales guys slogged through multiple days full of tedious meetings, the promotions reps went to side rooms where we sat and talked about how things were going. Then we went to lunch. I was there to listen.

And, at that first meeting on the first day, I sensed something. I was there in body and I was doing my best to pay attention but something was dragging me down. There was a ghost-like presence in the room and I couldn't shake it. It was the specter of the St. Louis Storm.

Much like we all need to go through the step-by-step grieving process when we lose a loved one, it became clear to me we also need to do that after facing a difficult and disappointing job loss. We have to go through the disbelief, the anger, the resentment, and all the other negative feelings before we can handle acceptance and be happy and motivated again.

I had lost a job I absolutely loved and then taken a new job, quite literally, the next morning. I never went through the process. As I sat there at a conference table in Boston, I'm pretty sure I was still in shock.

I heard the guys talking about their athletes and schools and I listened as they complained mightily to Roger, mostly about inventory issues. But instead of soaking it all in I kept seeing soccer balls flying into the back of the net. I thought about being the Storm's P.A. announcer, the fun of the games, and the rewards of leading my staff to what I knew, in my heart, had been a good season under challenging circumstances.

It was more than just a small nagging thing. It weighed heavily on me. I was sitting in a room full of successful former athletes who were now working with prominent pros and celebrity-level college coaches, giving shoes away for a living. Who wouldn't want that job? I was hearing from Roger just how great Magic Johnson was and how much I'd enjoy working with him on a one-on-one basis. Yes, Magic Johnson. I was hearing Roger pump me up with confidence and yet it felt like it was draining right back out of me as fast as it went in.

It worried me. I felt no excitement at all about a job I should've been thrilled to start. I even recall dreading some aspects of it, including the pushy amateur tournament organizers and the college coaches. Plus, the other guys made it clear the company's glory days were in the past. Nike was the king. Deep inside me, there was a familiar "fight or flight" battle going on. The flight side was running neck and neck with the fight. I almost felt like dashing out the door.

After the Boston meetings, where I did my best to keep all these negative feelings hidden and to myself, I commuted out to SoCal for about a month before packing up and moving once again. Converse would pay to move my meager belongings, and I drove my car from St. Louis to Dana Point over the course of three days. I began the trip on my 34th birthday, June 19, 1990.

Mike Zinn took a week to be my guide while he also filled me in on the various quirky people I'd be dealing with. As he put it, "The pro athletes are pretty great. You're going to love working with them. Some of the college coaches are really grateful and easy to work with but some can be a pain, and their egos need stroking all the time. Usually, the toughest people to work with are the guys that run the local amateur basketball tournaments because they have us in a tough spot and they take advantage of it."

He continued, "We're in a pitched battle with Nike and Reebok, especially Nike. They get aligned with these kids when they're still in grade school and then they work over the high school coaches to have their entire team wearing what the prized pupil wants. Then they steer them to a Nike college. It's not like the old days. These tournament organizers just pit us all against each other and demand the world. If we stop fighting these battles, we'll lose the war. But I have to tell you, it's not a fun part of this job. It stinks, actually."

Well, that sure had me fired up.

We then met up with one of those tournament organizers, joining him for lunch at a Perkin's near Pomona. He was everything Mike had said he would be and he never cracked a smile. He just made a series of ridiculous demands. As a stand-alone event, his tournament would never give Converse enough promotional value for what the guy was demanding. But it was a new world in the shoe business and these kids needed to be seen and courted early. We had the shoes. He had the leverage. We didn't have much choice if we wanted to keep Nike's Air Jordans and Reebok's Pumps from running us out of the gym.

Roger flew out for a few days of my training, chiefly to introduce me to coach Jim Harrick and his staff at UCLA, as well as Magic Johnson's agent Lon Rosen, and Magic himself.

At UCLA's beautiful Brentwood campus we entered the athletic department building where we met first with assistant coaches Brad Holland and Mark Gottfried. They seemed like terrific guys and they welcomed me to Bruin basketball. Most of the conversation, though, centered around their star prospect and incoming freshman, Ed O'Bannon.

O'Bannon was a perfect example of the state of the shoe biz at the time. Converse had been tracking him and working with his coaches since he was 14. Getting him to UCLA was a coup, because the star-to-be had offers from all the top schools and he would be staying with the Star & Chevron logo. Theoretically that meant that when he'd go on to NBA stardom, he'd be loyal to the brand.

After the brief chat with the assistants we were ushered in to meet with coach Harrick. I once again sensed that pesky "I'm not a basketball guy" feeling I'd so often felt during parts of my first stint with the company, while Roger and the coach launched into a 20-minute conversation about the game and the players. I knew the words, at least most of them, but I was in no position to join in a debate on which big men could run the floor, or push the pace, or pick and roll. I suspect, if Roger came with me to a baseball clubhouse he'd know what I felt.

Harrick was a big-time coach at a big-time school. He was getting paid big-time money to put Converse shoes on his players. He was doing so at Pauley Pavilion, the same historic floor where John Wooden led the Bruins to 10 NCAA national championships. And, Roger and I were expected to be reverential. Let's just say it wasn't wholly unexpected.

We did have an enjoyable look around and took a walk on the floor at Pauley before we left. In the car, Roger agreed that coaches at this level could be a handful.

Traffic in the Los Angeles and Orange County area, back in 1990, might have been at its worst. Even though the state and municipalities were already adding lanes to the existing network of roads uniquely referred to with various "The" designations, the drive from Irvine up to Brentwood to get to UCLA could take hours, even in the middle of the afternoon. It was something I was going to have to deal with a lot.

Before heading back down to Orange County, battling that incessant traffic on "The 405," Roger and I stopped in Century City. We rode an elevator to a high floor in a large corporate building, then walked down the hall to a nondescript office. Next to the door was a small plaque that read "First Team Marketing." Inside the door was a receptionist who greeted Roger with a smile and a hug. Beyond her was a single, simple, spartan office. Inside the office was Lon Rosen and his client, Earvin "Magic" Johnson.

Lon Rosen had been an intern for the L.A. Lakers while attending school at USC. After getting his degree, he went to work as director of promotions for the Fabulous Forum and the Lakers. While still doing that job, he became Magic Johnson's agent. He had two clients, Magic and Laker legend Jerry West. West's peers often referred to him by a nickname. It was "The Logo" because a silhouette image of Jerry West was used to create the dribbling player in the iconic NBA logo. That's what we call a legacy.

I found it fascinating that Lon Rosen had just the two clients. Every agent I had ever met worked non-stop at collecting new clients while trying to keep the current ones happy, all so they could make a living by taking a percentage of each athlete's paycheck. Lon Rosen's office wasn't flashy. It wasn't even as nice as the Converse office in Irvine. He clearly cared little for the trappings of wealth and success. He preferred to give all of his attention to Magic and Jerry. Lon Rosen had all of his financial eggs in just one Laker basket, and he was going to take very good care of that basket.

We spent an hour there, talking with the two of them about their lives before finally getting to the subject of shoes. Converse was coming out with a new shoe for Magic, and Magic alone, and we had a lot of ground to cover in that regard.

As for Magic himself, he's the same radiant personality you see on TV. He owns the room but not in an overbearing "look-at-me!" way. He's extremely gracious and made me feel I belonged there.

Later that summer The Forum would host one of the largest 3-on-3 tournaments in the country on its vast parking lots and we would debut the sleek new Magic shoe there while also setting up a tent to sell as many pairs as we could. I learned at that initial meeting I'd be in charge of driving a rental truck full of expensive shoes to The Forum, as well as a large inflatable version of the new shoe, and I'd be the one who took the remaining shoes and the cash back to Irvine. If you know where The Forum is, and the neighborhoods you have to drive through to reach it, you can understand, perhaps, why Roger exercised his seniority and designated me as the courier. Still, I lived to tell the tale.

Roger flew back home and I was on my own. My apartment in Dana Point was nice and the drive to the office wasn't bad, since I could make the full distance on backstreets, but the suite had an odd design. Mike's office was next to mine but the wall separating our two spaces had been added after initial construction and it bisected a large window. Somehow, it must have seemed like a good (lazy) idea to stop the wall at the front edge of the window sill, leaving a six-inch gap between the wall and the window, instead of going to the trouble of sealing the wall completely.

As it turned out, Mike and I shared one trait — we were both loud talkers on the telephone. At DW+A, my colleagues were constantly asking me to close my door because there wasn't a spot in the spacious office where my voice could not be heard. If anything, Mike was louder than me. With that open space between our offices, it was a hard place to work. I also didn't like knowing Mike could hear every word of my phone conversations, which would often be between me and clients he had worked with. So I began to work more and more from home.

My first order of business was to meet my pre-existing endorsers on the Angels, Dodgers, and Padres. I went to Anaheim first.

At Anaheim Stadium I entered the front-office lobby and told the receptionist who I was. She called down to the Angels' equipment manager and got the clearance for me to go to the clubhouse. It was still early afternoon, so few players would be there.

I introduced myself to the equipment man, managing to slide in the fact I was a baseball guy myself. He showed me around and let me know I could come to the park any day I wanted, staying in the clubhouse to work with my clients until batting practice was over — although it would always be appreciated if I got to the park just before the players arrived, to be as unobtrusive as possible. I was good with that.

The two players I inherited were outfielder Luis Polonia and infielder Dick Schofield. I'd never met either of them but Schofield and I would have a lot of things to talk about. A Springfield, Illinois, boy, his dad had played for the Cardinals just like mine had. We'd be certain to know a lot of people in common.

About an hour later, after a tour of the dugout and the playing field, both of my guys showed up. They could not have been kinder and Schofield and I had a rollicking conversation about all the people we both knew. I talked to the guys about their shoe supply and promised I'd be back to see them again within a week, with a few new pairs and other gifts.

The Padres were next and I headed down the freeway to see them the following day. My clients there were two pitchers, Mark Grant and Eric Show. The manager of the team was Jack McKeon and I wanted to say hello to him, as well. McKeon had managed the Omaha Royals both years Skip managed the Denver Bears, so the last time I'd seen him I was a 16-year-old batboy.

While I was waiting to see McKeon I chatted with Jack Clark, the slugging first baseman who had played for the Cardinals and I said hello to the one and only Tony Gwynn. I considered it an honor.

Eric Show was polite enough, although he had a sort of brooding intensity about him. He warmed up to me a little more after I told him my story. Grant was a friendly outgoing fellow and grateful for Converse's support. McKeon, an old-school guy if there ever was one, was spectacular. He spoke glowingly of my father and claimed to even remember me as the young batboy with the uniform that was too big. I chuckled and said, "Well, then that's 1971. In '72 we got the new double-knit unis and mine fit like a very tight glove." I was glad I'd had the chance to chat with him.

To finish off that week I'd be heading up to Dodger Stadium, which could be another long trip on the area's most congested freeways. I got there early, just to be safe.

At Anaheim and San Diego I'd been given free rein in the clubhouse. Things were different, though, at Dodger Stadium. After I arrived, the receptionist called down to longtime Dodger equipment man and clubhouse attendant Nobe Kowano. I was ushered into an equipment room down the hall from the clubhouse, deep in the concrete bowels of Dodger Stadium, and told I would not be allowed in the actual room with the players. Instead, Nobe would bring them to me. I had no argument with that and immediately turned the conversation to my dad, figuring Nobe would remember him. His face lit up and our relationship was set in place right there. I was no longer a threat to the peace and tranquility of Dodger Stadium. I was a fellow baseball guy.

My first Dodger player was pitcher Tim Crews. We met in the hallway outside the equipment room and hit it off immediately. He was very much a great guy and before I left the ballpark he not only thanked me profusely for the support, but also said, "Let's get together for lunch one day, when you're up here near the ballpark!"

My other Dodger player, also a pitcher, was brought to me next. I had been waiting for this moment since the day I saw Mike Zinn's players on the Dodgers' roster. When the tall, handsome pitcher arrived, I shook his hand earnestly and said, "Jim, I'm Bob Wilber, your new Converse rep, but our paths have crossed before. I was the Blue Jays scout who spotted you in the Mexican Pacific League."

Jim Gott's handshake turned into a hug as his eyes misted up a little. He was emotional, and that made me the same way. He said, "Oh, my gosh. I never knew and they never told me who spotted me down there first. By the end of the season they were sending in the big guns from Toronto but I never knew how they found out about me. I had told my wife that I was done. Five years in the Cardinals' organization and I couldn't get out of Double-A, and then there I was pitching in Mexico like baseball was the only thing that mattered, and that success was the only thing that mattered. I was done. I was over it. And then the Blue Jays took me in the Rule 5 and all this happened. You changed my life."

He thanked me some more and promised to do all he could do for me and Converse. I knew he would. It was a landmark day in my life to finally meet the man.

Of those six California-based ballplayers, all wearing Converse, only four would live much longer. Sadly, Eric Show was found dead in his room at an addiction-rehab facility four years later. And Tim Crews, that affable Dodger who wanted to have lunch, was tragically killed in a Florida boating accident during spring training in 1993. I was saddened deeply to hear of Show's issues and his demise, but I was shattered when Crews died. We never had that lunch.

The baseball introductions were over, and the relationships were all good. I'd visit each team a couple of additional times that summer because I could drive to see them, but soon I was busily flying and driving all over my region. It was a crazy job.

By late summer, when I had the baseball guys under control, it was about to be time for the NFL camps to open. Six players per team sounded like a lot but with 55-man rosters it wasn't that daunting of a task. What was more than daunting, as in practically impossible, was landing any big-name players at the so-called "skill positions." Quarterbacks, running backs, and wide receivers were on TV a lot and they had some leverage to demand fairly high-priced endorsement deals from the shoe companies. We didn't have that kind of budget. Kickers' feet were the most visible of all and not surprisingly they were the most picky about their shoes, so we had little chance at landing any of them, either. I would focus on special teams players and linemen.

The biggest hurdle was knowing who was actually going to make the team. With such big rosters and with nearly twice as many players attending training camp, even big names would often hear the ominous news, when an assistant would say, "Coach wants to see you in his office. And bring your playbook."

I started hitting training camps as soon as they opened, starting with the L.A. Raiders who used the most bizarre site I'd ever seen. Their camp was in Redondo Beach and it was held at a former elementary school. Seriously. I thought it was ridiculous when the SIUE Cougar baseball team held preseason camp at a grade school and I certainly never thought I'd see an NFL team doing the same thing.

When I called on the Raiders I got my first lesson in what pro football players are all about. They are big. They look scary. They play a violent sport and appear to operate on intimidation. They also could not have been any nicer.

Mike Zinn had much of the starting offensive line in Converse the year before and all of them looked like locks to make the team in 1990. In addition he had a backup running back who also returned kicks, and I'd aim to keep him in our shoes as well. I called the equipment manager ahead of time and asked him to alert those guys that I was coming. Yes, I was a bit nervous.

My guys were, to the best of my recollection, Steve Wright (tackle), Steve Wisniewski (guard), Don Mosebar (center), Max Montoya (guard), Bruce Wilkerson (tackle), and Vance Mueller (running back). When I arrived at the school a monster of a man held the door open for me and we walked into the school's main central hallway together. I asked him where the equipment room was and he said, "Follow me, I'm headed that way."

When we got to "the cage" (a ubiquitous term for the equipment room, in football) I introduced myself to the manager and the huge giant behind me said, "Oh, you're the new Converse guy. I'm Steve Wright. I wore your shoes last year and sure hope you'll have me back."

Steve then took me into the locker room and personally introduced me to all the guys who had Converse deals in 1989. To a man, these tough and violent Raiders who played for a team that promoted how mean and nasty they could be, were absolute gentle giants. Gracious, polite, and extremely thankful.

When I met Vance Mueller, I could see in him everything Zinn had raved about. Vance had been drafted by the Raiders in 1986 out of (get this) Occidental College. He was undersized for an NFL player, at 6-foot and 210 pounds, but he had a heart as big as any and he was absolutely obsessed with outworking everyone around him. He was entering his fifth year in the league and each year he had to be so good the team simply couldn't cut him. As soon as we met we established a real friendship and later that week he and his wife took me to dinner in Redondo.

Until we could get new shoes to the guys they were all going to wear what they had from the last season and they all promised to perform a trick that's no longer allowed by the NFL. They liked to "spat up" with tape around their shoes so we provided them with a flexible stencil of the Star & Chevron. Every one of the guys would spat up for games and then ask the trainer to spray-paint the logo on top of the tape since they'd just covered it up. Good guys.

The rest of my NFL teams were not so ready to go. Many of Mike's guys had been cut. Others would be cut in camp. Still a few more had quit the game due to injuries. I was mostly starting from scratch with the Rams, Chargers, Cardinals, and Broncos.

I visited every camp. I met every equipment manager and did my utmost to establish a rapport with each of them in a short time — all while they were attending to as many as 85 players. It wasn't easy.

What it came down to was the equipment guys themselves. If they were overwhelmed, or not of the mind to really care about Converse shoes, I was going to have a tough time. If they were like the Broncos' guy — who took me under his wing and said, "Look, let's wait until the final cut. All of these guys are looking for shoe deals, and I promise I'll get you six of the best guys who don't have deals yet. I'll call you, and you can ship me the shoes" — then my job was easy.

I went to U.C Irvine to meet with the Rams, the University of Northern Colorado in Greeley to see the Broncos, UC San Diego to meet the Chargers, and University of Northern Arizona in Flagstaff to see the Cardinals, in addition to hanging with Vance Mueller and getting to know Steve Wright in Redondo Beach.

Once all the teams were met and my players were landed, I was immediately introduced to one of the craziest and most frustrating aspects of the job. Not only did Converse ship all the necessary football shoes to us at once to cut down on production and shipping (and Roger looked out for me by making sure I got what I needed) but they also cut costs in another drastic way. All the shoes were white leather, and all the logos on the sides were white felt. We had to "customize" them for each of our teams with bottles of paint and a supply of brushes Converse sent us.

I wish I was kidding. I spent two solid weeks making that happen. I postponed all my out-of-town travel so I could work all day on the phone or visiting local coaches, then grabbed a bite for dinner and sat in my living room during the evenings, with an inverted lid from a cardboard banker's box on my lap while painting the logos on the Broncos' shoes orange, the Raiders' shoes black, the Cardinals' shoes red, and the Rams and Chargers shoes blue. It was insane. And very messy.

At first I was meticulous about finding ways to mask off the logo so that I didn't get any paint on the white shoe leather. Then, I just dove in and went for it, saving the time and learning how to "stay within the lines" as best I could. I kept some white touch-up paint handy for the times I got a little sloppy.

Once each team's complete allotment was done (and keep in mind each player needed multiple pairs of both artificial-turf and grass shoes) I'd box them up and ship them out.

I was 34 years old. I worked with Magic Johnson. I had played professional baseball and scouted for the Toronto Blue Jays. I'd traveled the world for my brother Del's agency, including a rare trip to Cuba. My job title with Converse was impressive and I was working with some amazing athletes. And there I was for 14 straight nights, painting shoe logos until midnight. I had an apartment full of shoes that had to sit out to dry and boxes stacked to the ceiling so I could ship them all out.

I decided, at that moment, that despite how nice the players were it would be OK with me if I never did this again.

Meanwhile, I was making the awful drive from Dana Point to the UCLA campus at least twice a month. Not because I had business to attend to with the coaching staff but because Roger had made it clear that face time with the coach was vital.

I had cases of football shoes that needed to be painted and shipped and professional athletes to sign and service but every 10 days or so I'd have to put that all aside and spend hours in traffic just to sit in the gym or the coach's office and talk. And not about anything important.

Apparently, that wasn't enough. In September, Roger called me to say that Harrick had complained, saying I obviously didn't care about UCLA basketball because he "never" saw me. Roger knew better but we talked at length about how I needed to ramp up the face-to-face sessions, even to the point of driving up there just to hang out in the gym while the team was going through unofficial workouts. If I needed to get an expensive hotel room in Hollywood to do that, he'd approve it.

I never got a hotel room but I did give the coach all the love he wanted. I'd qualify it as an unrequited sort of love.

And then it got worse. Incoming freshman and loyal Converse guy Ed O'Bannon was playing in a one of those unofficial pickup games when he landed awkwardly on a rebound and tore the anterior cruciate ligament in his knee. He had not yet played a game for the Bruins. He hadn't even participated in an official practice. He was out for the year, at the very least, and one of the doctors expressed doubt he'd ever walk normally again, much less play NCAA or NBA basketball. It was awful news, and it further increased my frustration with that one college team.

It was also nearly time for NBA camps to open and I felt overwhelmed. Roger could sense that, and when he had to attend a conference at The Broadmoor Resort in Colorado Springs he asked me to meet him there. We spent a long dinner talking our way through my frustration.

I can say this about the experience. Had my boss not been Roger Morningstar, I would not have stayed in the job past the end of the summer. I was miserable. I was getting swamped by tournament organizers, college coaches, and even high school coaches, all with different demands. I had baseball season wrapping up, football camps ending, and basketball on the horizon. The shoe-painting gig hadn't helped my disposition much, either.

Roger eased me back from the ledge and said, "Let's go to the Air Force Academy tomorrow. I'll introduce you to the head coach, Reggie Minton. He's a great guy."

We went to the beautiful Air Force campus the next day and spent a delightful couple of hours with the coach, then had a fine dinner with him and his wife. I felt better. Maybe there was hope.

The next day we went up to Denver and McNichols Arena to meet with the staff of the Denver Nuggets. Just getting a chance to sit in their locker room and chat for an hour with Dan Issel was another big boost. I'd been a fan of his since the days when his Kentucky Colonels, in the ABA, would regularly beat up on my beloved Spirits of St. Louis. Issel was, by the time I met him, a broadcaster for the Nuggets and our group conversation was stimulating. I felt more charged up than I'd been in weeks, if not months.

The NFL and NBA facets of the job kept me traveling almost constantly that fall. I'd go out on five-day trips and try to see as many players and coaches as possible. I was feeling better about things and getting all of my requisite players signed. I even went to a UCLA football game as the guest of one Jim Harrick. It was fun to sit in the Rose Bowl but it was just as much fun to see my guys on television, in both baseball and football.

Then, while I spent an early autumn afternoon doing paperwork at the Embassy Suites in Scottsdale, Arizona after calling on the Cardinals and the Suns, the phone in my room rang. It was Bill Kentling, the former commissioner of the MISL.

How did Bill Kentling find me at a Scottsdale hotel? I have no idea.

Kentling said, "Son, if you're interested there may be a chance we can go racing together."

I said, "Bill, I don't know anything about racing."

He replied, in the charming country accent he could dial up whenever he needed it, "That's why I called you. I'm not looking for a race fan, son. I'm looking for a marketing guy."

I asked him to tell me more.

"Well, I've got good news and bad news," he said. "The good news is I just took a job as president at a world-class racing facility. The bad news is it's in Topeka, Kansas."

I laughed and said, "I don't care. I'm about over California as it is. I spend half my life stuck in traffic. I've been out there four months and I haven't made one friend or even met my neighbors. Topeka sounds pretty good to me."

The position was general manager for sales and service. Bill described Heartland Park in glowing terms. The multipurpose track was just a little more than a year old but the original staff had done a subpar job of marketing it and the owner had lost far more money than he'd budgeted. He brought Bill on board to right the sinking ship. Bill called me to help, but he cautioned I'd have to interview for the job and he was talking to some other people.

In its first season of operation, the track hosted an International Motor Sports Association sports car race and drew approximately 25,000 for that event. Going forward, it was envisioned that IMSA would be a cornerstone for the venue while the track had also hosted an American Motorcycle Association Superbike race, some smaller road course events, an NHRA divisional meet, and the inaugural AC Delco NHRA Heartland Nationals in 1990. Rather than IMSA carrying the load, the NHRA national event was the only one to turn a solid profit.

After gauging my sincere interest he said, "Well, IMSA is running at Del Mar, down by San Diego, next weekend. I'll set you up with the best passes and set you loose. Let me know what you think when you get back."

I had never been to a professional racing event of any kind. I also had no idea people spent the entire day, or even the entire weekend, at the track to enjoy these endeavors. As if it were a baseball game, I showed up an hour before the race was to start on Sunday. And I thought I was early.

I got my pass and wandered into the sprawling temporary course by the Del Mar horse track. The IMSA cars were fabulous, the drivers were amazing, and I stood directly next to the track with only a waist-high concrete wall separating me from the roaring machines. I did notice one negative as I looked around playing the role of impartial observer.

The very nature of road course racing makes it tough to be a fully involved spectator. I was standing in one of the premier spots in the facility but all I could do was watch the cars go by in a blur. They'd disappear for a while, and then come back by again. I had no idea who was leading or what lap they were on.

Other than that, I was fascinated. I called Bill that night, after the race, and told him it was fantastic. He said we'd set up a date for an interview in a few weeks, in early December. I was definitely interested.

I got back to work, but I'll admit the racing bug had bitten me and I was distracted. And the amateur basketball tournament organizers were at full tilt, cruising like sharks smelling blood in the water.

On a Monday night, after having spent the day in traffic visiting colleges from Fullerton to Azusa, with Pomona in between, I returned home to find 25 messages on my answering machine (the kind with an actual cassette inside it). I listened to the messages, wrote down who I'd want to call back on Tuesday, turned off my phone's ringer and went to bed.

At 9 a.m. the next day, I sat down with a bowl of cereal and saw the answering machine blinking its red eye at me. With a mouthful of Cheerios I stood up to look at the electronic counter on the top of the machine. I had cleared the machine late the night before. It said I now had 32 new messages.

I swallowed my Cheerios and sat down. I stared off into the distance trying to calm myself and focus. It was impossible.

I got up, went out to my car, and headed to the beach. I sat in my car for an hour before I walked out to the shore and sat in the sand. I stared at the horizon, wondering what I was doing and why I was doing it. My heart was absolutely racing and my brain was spinning so far out of control I felt dizzy.

There were fabulous parts of the Converse job but there were aspects of it I clearly was incapable of handling. I was beyond my mental capacity and the numerals on my answering machine had tipped me over the edge.

I went back home and called Roger. I said, "Rog, I can't do this anymore. I can't do it. These tournament vultures and college coaches are eating me alive. I'm sorry, but I can't do it."

Falling back on his best Roger Morningstar management skills he said, "Take the whole week off. Just do me one favor. Write down all the people who left messages and I'll call them all back. Turn your machine off. Go somewhere. Go get a hotel room on a beach or wherever you want. I'll cover it. Just get away and recharge."

I said I would and it was a huge relief to walk away from the relentlessness of the job, but I knew in my heart I was done.

I only went away for one night, staying a mile from home in a hotel room overlooking Dana Point harbor. I made my decision before dinner. I was going home. I'd have to rent my own truck and tow my car but I was going home.

I called Roger and broke the news. He wasn't happy about it. I was leaving at time when a lot of things were still up in the air in terms of college teams and the NBA guys, but he didn't try to talk me out of it. He just said, "I'm really sorry for you. I'm sorry it didn't work out. We'll figure it all out and hire someone new but just do me one favor. We'll be friends forever, but If I call you again and offer you another job, turn me down." He said that to break the tension, but he also meant it.

Roger Morningstar was the best boss I'd ever worked for. He always had my back. I learned to view him as a friend and trusted adviser and nothing mattered more to me than earning his respect. I'd let both of us down.

In retrospect, my lack of a grieving period after the Storm had haunted me during my return to Converse. The disappointment from that debacle sapped my ability do the job at a level I expected. I just couldn't get excited about it.

It was a waste of six months.

I called Kentling and told him what I was doing. He urgently said, "Hey, I'm still interviewing people and I need to interview you. Don't do this because you think you have this job in the bag. You don't."

I said, "I understand that, Bill. It doesn't matter. I'm leaving here as soon as I can get packed up and it'll take me three days to get to St. Louis. I'll crash at my parents' house and I'll call you. As soon as you're free, I'll drive over to Topeka and we can meet. I'm confident you'll give me the job, but even if you don't I'll be OK. I just have to leave here."

It was the closest thing to a complete meltdown I'd experienced. All I could think was that I needed to get home.

1990 was not a good year for me. It wasn't exactly a stellar year for my buddy Pete Delkus either.

We'll never know if it was the condensed version of spring training that did it, but something wasn't right with the pitching arm of a guy who wasn't just good, wasn't just great, but was completely and utterly dominant at three different minor league levels.

He was, for the fourth consecutive year, promoted to a new level after spring training. He would be pitching for the Portland Beavers. In his first few outings, he got pounded. Yes, it was Triple-A, just one step from the big leagues, but Pete Delkus never got pounded. Never. Except in Portland.

His first four or five appearances were totally unlike him, which leads me to believe the shortened spring training left him not quite ready to go. After that, for the next four months he got somewhat close to being back to normal but what he really became was everyone else's normal. For the first time in his career he had an ERA that didn't start with a one or a zero. At 4.18 his ERA was better than the 4.55 team average, but that's what it was. He was actually average. He'd never been average before.

For the first time as a pro, he gave up more hits than innings pitched. He struck out a career low 35, in 90 innings. Something was wrong.

That fall, after the conclusion of the season, he was taken off the 40-man roster. In 1991, he would even be demoted to Double-A Orlando for much of the season. And his elbow was hurting. By the end of that year, it was hurting too much to pitch and Pete underwent surgery to "clean it up." That sounds simple, like taking a shower. It wasn't, and he never pitched again.

He'd done remarkably well for a kid who only got a shot thanks to Del Wilber's phone call. But he came up one step short of the dream. As for Terry Ryan's prediction that Pete would be a wealthy young man in the near future, neither Ryan nor Delkus could know how such a thing might become true.

It did. Just not on a baseball field.

While in Orlando Pete had befriended the sports reporters at WFTV, the ABC affiliate. He even took the time to do an exhausting internship there while also playing baseball in the Southern League — one of the toughest bus-travel circuits in pro sports. When his baseball career ended the station wanted to hire Pete but it didn't have any openings in the sports department. They did, however, offer Pete an entry-level broadcast position as a weather forecaster.

Pete rose through the ranks quickly, while also earning his accreditation as a meteorologist by the National Weather Association and the American Meteorological Society.

He worked in Orlando for four years then moved to the Cincinnati market where he was chief meteorologist at WCPO. In 2005 he joined WFAA in Dallas, the fifth largest television market in the country. He's one of the best weather experts in the U.S. and fabulously popular in the DFW area. After winning 11 Emmy Awards he is, indeed, well compensated for the work he does.

"Bob, they pay me a lot of money to talk about the weather," he once told me. "But I'm working a solid three, sometimes four, hours a day for it." He's never been anything but sarcastically hilarious.

So 1990 didn't go as planned for either one of us. We both survived, but not without some scars. Pete's were physical. Mine were emotional.

I was 34. I'd already done some amazing things but the next hurdle in my life was directly in front of me. I looked forward to decompressing for a while in Kirkwood. I really wanted to see the woman who took care of me when I was sick, who motivated me when I was down, and who encouraged me to develop many of the skills I was still learning to use.

It was time to go home.

Escape

I rented a truck, loaded my possessions, and drove to St. Louis. It was more of a trudge than a drive. I had an interview ahead of me but no guarantee of a job and I had three long days to reflect on what had just happened. All these years later it's easy for me to understand how I could be depressed and unmotivated after pouring my heart into the Storm but at the time all I could do was ponder, helplessly, why I hadn't been able to wipe the slate clean to enjoy a dream job that simply entailed giving shoes away to famous athletes.

When I arrived in St. Louis in mid-November, I rented a storage unit and unloaded my stuff not knowing for sure when I'd be loading it up again for my next move. I hung out in Kirkwood with my folks for a week and almost immediately I began to feel more grounded. Sometimes family is the key.

I dug through memorabilia, scanned every scrapbook and photo album I could find to reestablish those connections to home and family, and day by day I realized I was starting to feel human again. Even starting to feel like "me" again. And I was getting more energized by the day.

I called Bill Kentling and said, "If that interview offer is still on the table, I'll drive over there as soon as you want." We picked a day later that week and I drove west.

Upon arrival in Topeka, after a five-hour drive, I followed Bill's careful directions and headed south after exiting the Kansas Turnpike at Route 75. A few miles down the road I passed Forbes Field, a former Air Force base, and drove through the tiny village of Pauline, where the skyline consisted of one lonely grain elevator. I saw Heartland Park and its state-of-the-art suite tower ahead on the left side of the road but my instructions told me to turn right, heading to a housing development called Montara.

Heartland Park, at the time, was owned by Lario Corporation out of Wichita. Lario had also purchased Montara with plans to renovate and redevelop the former Air Force housing development, but when sales of the newly remodeled homes stalled they were forced to allow rentals and Montara remained stuck in a mixed zone of affordability cursed by a lack of desirability. With most of the homes having been built as modular houses it had a clear "trailer park" vibe to it.

Two of the homes acted as the offices for Heartland Park. They were situated back-to-back sharing an open backyard and connected by a walkway. Bill, who had only recently taken over the track as president, hadn't totally bothered to remodel the units into something more corporate but with desks and chairs filling each place it felt mostly like an office. His office was the master bedroom in the northern home and the marketing and PR staff shared the living room, dining room, and bedroom spaces in the other unit. As much as he'd done to decorate his office with work stuff it still looked like a bedroom. It was one.

Bill showed me around and we dashed through the brisk November air to see the other house and meet the staff before heading back to his office for the official interview. One of his first comments surprised and confounded me, when he said, "Son, what you need right now is a win. Am I right?" I should've been prepared for something like that but I was clearly caught off-guard.

I took a few seconds to compose my thoughts and said, "I don't see it that way, Bill. I know, in my heart, that I did a very good job with the Storm. Our owner and our head coach didn't see it that way and they're certainly not the first to be wrong about such things in the history of indoor soccer, but I've heard from enough players, staff members, league officials, media folks, and heck, the staff at the St. Louis Blues, to know the truth. We did the best we could and it won't be long before they regret the decision to start over. It won't get better for them. As for the Converse deal, it was a great chance to do something exciting but taking the job the morning after being fired and relocating to SoCal within days was the wrong thing to do. I just didn't know it at the time.

"I chose to leave there. I had every endorsement I was supposed to get. My boss had my back and was disappointed I didn't want to stay but the gravitational pull to just get home to the Midwest was too strong for me. Now, I'm charged up and ready to go and I'll feel very much at home here in Topeka. Very much at home."

Bill nodded in a way that meant "good answer," then introduced me to the operations staff. He asked the head of maintenance to give me a tour of the property and the track. We drove back across the highway, unlocked the heavy rolling gate on the north side of the venue, and drove in. We passed under the pedestrian bridge behind the tower and then drove under the tower itself, and out onto the drag strip. It was the first time I'd ever been on a race track.

My guide drove me all around the road course, describing its construction and the official nicknames for many of the turns. The first one, a sharp right at the end of the main straight — which also doubled as the drag strip — was called "Paycheck." He added, "They call it that because if you can't negotiate the turn, you won't get one."

The last three turns on the track, as it passed under another pedestrian bridge to again join the drag strip, were called "Lions, Tigers, and Bears." Oh, my.

What became clear during my tour was this: While the drag strip might not have been an afterthought it was clearly a secondary reason for the facility having been built. There never would've been a Heartland Park if not for an avid sports-car community in the area, which lobbied for the venue and dreamed of packing it with fans for road course races. Since the track was going to have a long front straight anyway, it was simple to have that double as the strip and that led to the inclusion of the grand tower full of suites, timing rooms, announcing studios, and a press box behind the drag strip starting line. I met people working at Heartland Park who had been there since it opened and some of them actually seemed to lament the fact NHRA events filled the seats and generated income. It was supposed to be a mecca for IMSA, the Sports Car Club of America, and other road-racing organizations.

The multipurpose design of the facility brought with it two negative issues for drag racing. The first was having the road course join the strip just ahead of the starting line. Sears Point, in Sonoma, had the same problem at the time. With the road-course cars joining the strip at an angle, they would drive in an arc from the left guard wall to the right before heading down the straight. After thousands of laps, the rubber laid down by the sports cars created an arc-shaped bump on the drag strip.

The second issue was grandstand layout. With the road course needing to work its way through the property and with pit lane needing to be in-between the drag racing surface and the main grandstand, the largest set of seats was a considerable distance from the drag strip. The second-largest, an angled grandstand next to the tower, was much closer but it was behind the starting line looking downtrack. The closest stands, smaller ones atop a small berm on the right side of the track, were actually close to the action and had great sightlines. They were the best drag-racing seats in the house but the problem with them was distance from the pits. Heartland Park is a mammoth place and walking from the right-side stands to the pro pits is more than just a hike. It's a long way, walking behind the tower and over the road course.

Like most things designed by committee, Heartland Park was uniquely constructed to appease many interests. It ended up serving none of the purposes as well as it could have. Think about all those cereal-bowl multi-purpose stadiums built in the 1960s. They could host NFL football and Major League Baseball, but they weren't good football stadiums and they definitely weren't ballparks. Heartland Park was a lot like stadiums called Riverfront, Three Rivers, Fulton County, RFK, and Busch. And it was a lot bigger.

Another challenge with marketing the place was its location. Topeka is the state capital and with a population of a little more than 100,000 it was large enough to have some big city amenities. It was not, however, big enough to support such an expensive track so Heartland Park was going to need to be marketed and promoted heavily in Kansas City, Wichita, and other outlying areas. It couldn't succeed as a local track. It had to be regional. The original marketing staff had not factored that into the equation nearly enough. The track was still relatively unknown in the Kansas City and Wichita areas.

I drove back home after the interview and the tour, turning it over in my mind. I loved being excited. I wanted the job. I figured I wouldn't mind Topeka. I was eager to learn about racing and wanted to lead a new staff in a sales and marketing capacity. It felt right. I hadn't been eager for much of anything in the prior six months.

A few days later, Kentling picked up the phone on his desk and dialed a number. A second later, the phone on the Wilber family's kitchen wall rang. I answered it. When he offered me the job, and let me know the compensation, I accepted immediately. It would be the most money I'd ever made.

We decided I would not start until the new year, since very little business was going to take place during the holidays. I could spend more time with my family and I'd have time to arrange my move and find a place to live.

I made the drive back in mid-December, getting a motel room on Topeka Boulevard this time, and I scoured the town for a residence. I was tired of apartment living but in no position to buy a home, so I scanned the classifieds looking for a house to rent. I found one in a newly-built golf course community. The golf course, called Colly Creek, was owned by a gentleman who also owned the home as an investment. He was happy to rent it to the new general manager of Heartland Park.

It was modest brick ranch backing to an open field. At about 2,100 square feet it was more room than I'd need, but it was mere minutes from the track. It was in a state of some disrepair and needed a thorough deep-cleaning but the owner agreed to discount my rent if I'd do the painting and cleaning myself. I was happy to do that. I was happy, period.

When the holidays were over and I finally went to work at Heartland Park, it was the dead of winter. Within hours, as I shuttled back and forth between the headquarters house and the marketing abode, it became apparent that the elements would play a role in all of our lives. Whether it was brutal cold, searing heat, rain, or snow, we'd all be spending a great deal of time dashing through the shared backyard in order to do business. And in addition to that daily routine, our racing events would need cooperation from the weather, as well.

My office in the marketing house was the master bedroom. Interestingly, my desk was in front of the window, and in order for me to face the door it also faced the closet. The sliding closet doors were mirrors. I'd have the distinct pleasure of staring at myself all day. It was a bit odd.

On my desk was a computer. The closest thing to a computer I'd ever used was an IBM electric typewriter with a floppy disk for a bit of memory, in the Storm office.

My Heartland Park computer was an Apple IIc, featuring an early Mac operating system. I wasn't even sure how to turn it on and I surely didn't feel much confidence when it came to using it. At DW+A our secretaries used bulky IBM desktops with Windows MS-DOS "green screen" software. The monitors displayed everything as green text and confusing code, and doing something as simple as creating a larger bold font for a cover page necessitated the insertion of complicated format codes. To see if the cover page was correct, the only method for doing so was to print it and hope.

On the Mac screen, little folders and documents were displayed in cartoon fashion, but they looked like actual things. That eased my mind a little but I'd still need some lessons and I got them from one of my staff members. Jade Gurss was in charge of public and media relations for the track and while he technically "reported" to me on the organizational chart, I could tell immediately he was more than my equal and we'd collaborate more than I'd manage him. At the time PR was something I knew little about, so it was a relief to have a real pro filling that slot. He was talented, dedicated, and a wonderful guy. He also taught me, in a few hours, how to use my Apple computer. His first piece of critical advice was, "An Apple is designed to do what you want intuitively, but it craves organization. So, don't just litter documents all over your screen. Create folders for your projects and then put the documents in the correct folders. You'll figure it out."

I figured it out. And we got to work.

It was clear to me that Jade was just one part of a team that had some real talent and dedication. Unlike the Storm, where I had to be very hands-on to help underpaid entry-level front-office people exceed their own expectations, Kentling had used a different approach. He convinced ownership to allow him to invest in good people so he could bring in real talent and not have to deal with constant turnover. It was a management style I would always try to emulate.

Our schedule in 1991 would kick off with a "soft opening" in April. We'd hold a local bracket race, where cars ranging from purpose-built dragsters to daily drivers could be matched up with handicapped starts, and we'd do that on a mid-April weekend to work out the kinks and test-run everything from facility management to promotions and advertising.

After that, on our schedule, we had the IMSA race in early May followed by our NHRA divisional meet, an Automobile Racing Club of America stock car race, a Super Chevy Show, a nostalgia road course event, an AMA Superbike weekend, and the biggest event of the year, the AC Delco NHRA Heartland Nationals in the late September. Also thrown in were additional bracket races, a national go-kart championship, and a variety of private events and test sessions.

At our first major staff meeting Bill laid out his vision for taking Heartland Park to a new level. We'd promote ceaselessly, we'd work the media constantly, and we'd aim to over-deliver on every aspect of the shows we were producing.

For the IMSA race we floated ideas for making it a spectacular family event, instead of just a sports car race. Among the ideas that stuck when we threw them against the wall were a petting zoo, wandering clowns and jugglers, mascots from nearby schools and pro teams, and a temporary open-wheel grand prix course on the drag racing staging lanes, utilizing the ultra-cool cars from the Monaco Grand Prix facility in Kansas City. I was very familiar with the Monaco Grand Prix cars, which took go-karting to a new retail level. They actually looked and handled like little Indy cars. There was a franchise in Fresno when I lived there and I spent a fortune making lap after lap in them, driving until my fingers bled.

At our next meeting, in our marketing house, I assigned roles to various staff members in order to make all of the ancillary activities happen and I'll admit I expected to have to remind and cajole them to help them succeed. One week later, every one of them reported the work they had done and they were all well ahead of schedule. In one week, they'd put an event together.

We had souvenir programs to create for every big event and ads to sell within them. On our white dry-erase board we kept a running total of income generated by each staff member, including program ads, on-track signage, sponsorships, and ticket sales. They all did terrific work.

Bill also wanted to take the ARCA race and make it into a bigger show. ARCA was a third-tier stock-car group, with no big-name drivers the general public would recognize. So we changed that. We sent out feelers to Dale Earnhardt, Darrell Waltrip, and Kenny Schrader, and all three accepted our offers. In addition, car owner Rick Hendrick decided to race in our event as well, in the Tide-sponsored car he campaigned. Ricky Rudd drove that car on the NASCAR circuit but Hendrick would drive an ARCA-certified version of it in Topeka. He also planned to bring with him the actual City Chevrolet car from the movie "Days Of Thunder." We arranged for the teams to adapt ARCA-legal cars for their drivers and all of them were painted as precise duplicates of their Winston Cup cars.

For our NHRA divisional we also tossed the generally-accepted rule book in the trash. Most tracks saw those points meets as participant races, or "back-gate" events where income was generated by the fees each racer paid to enter the venue in order to compete. They did not see them as viable spectator races, so they promoted them as an afterthought or not at all. We decided to rewrite that notion by hosting a major Top Fuel match race in conjunction with the meet.

In March, prior to opening the gates for the first time, many of us headed to Gainesville for the NHRA Gatornationals. We wanted to see how a premier race on the tour took place and follow our counterparts around to soak in some of that knowledge by osmosis. It was the first drag race I'd ever attended. I was already the general manager of a major track on the tour, but the 1991 Gatornationals were my first exposure to an NHRA national event.

When we arrived sportsman cars were on the track doing their wheelstands and making what I thought was a lot of noise. I also thought they were going very fast. I had no clue.

I'd been warned about those brutal Top Fuel Dragsters and Funny Cars and had seen them on Wide World of Sports, but no verbal warning would be sufficient when it came to preparing me for what I was about to see, hear, smell, and feel. The first time I watched a nitro Funny Car warm up I thought I was either in heaven or hell. Maybe both at the same time. The fumes were noxious, and bitter, and nearly asphyxiating. But man, oh man, they were cool!

When I watched the first Top Fuel car launch, from a solid 50 yards away, I was certain I could take the noise. With fingers planted firmly in my ears, it was still impossibly loud. But more shocking was the concussion that hit me in the chest and vibrated every ounce of me. It was pure sensory overload and I was completely and utterly addicted. It was clear to me, in just one day, that NHRA Drag Racing was beyond special. It was a thing and an experience unto itself, and nothing in the racing domain could possibly compare to it. That was an assumption I made with very little racing experience. It's one I've maintained and affirmed to this day.

What I had not been warned about were the perils of wearing a white polo shirt to the track. As I watched the first Top Fuel qualifying session from atop the tower, behind the starting line, I was unaware that my white shirt was changing its appearance by the second. At the end of the session, I looked down to see what appeared to be a large quantity of ground pepper all over me. When I attempted to wipe it off, it only stuck more firmly or left long black streaks. The Gainesville staff member who was showing me around laughed, and said, "We call those Goodyear freckles. You'll notice we wear dark shirts. And before you touch your face, you should probably go look in a mirror." I was soaking up knowledge by the minute. If you stand behind Top Fuel cars, even two stories up, you're going to get covered in bits of rubber.

I had another assignment in Gainesville, in addition to the soaking up of knowledge and feeling the impossible power generated by the nitro cars. Kentling had already reached out to former NHRA Top Fuel World Champion Gary Ormsby about being one of the Top Fuel participants in our planned match race. He had sent me to Gainesville to soak it in, but my primary mission was to get our second driver signed for the show. He wanted a popular female and Lori Johns was the ticket, in her Jolly Rancher Top Fueler.

I walked over to Lori's pit area and spotted her signing autographs at the ropes. We headed into her lounge in the trailer and quickly worked out the details regarding the format and the fee. Technically, it would be billed as a "best two out of three" race on the Sunday of the meet, but the plan all along was to make three runs no matter who got to the finish line first during the initial two.

Kentling had said, "Go down there and get me Lori Johns. If you fail, come back on your shield."

I came back standing. Things were falling into place and the fun was about to begin.

We kicked off our promotional season with a full-page ad in the Topeka Capital-Journal, showing our full schedule and ticket information. We also planned quite a few radio advertising campaigns and Bill asked me to search for a good high-energy voice talent. I told him he already had one, in me, but his skeptical look was impossible to miss. I told him I'd have a tape for him the following day.

I wrote a script for our season-opening bracket race and went home that night to record it. I had no studio, and no way of creating a real echo-effect or reverb, so I did the next best thing. I recorded the 30-second spot while talking into an empty metal trash bin. I got the gig.

I'd never actually recorded radio ads before but I was completely familiar with how the studio worked and I quickly got the hang of how to "overlap" my own voice to make the ad more "urgent" and exciting. I'd record one line, then we'd back up the recorder a quarter second and I'd record the next line, talking over myself for just a bit. I was pleased to hear that it sounded like the real thing. I would do all of our radio and TV voice work, all year.

Another key benefit for a guy like me was access to a fleet of company cars provided by track sponsor Chevrolet. We had a Lumina, a Beretta, and a Caprice to use for company business. We also had two Corvettes that would act as our pace cars for road races. And I had a key to the main gate at the track. You can probably see where I'm going with this.

The gravitational pull to get two guys like Jade and me over there to put those cars through their paces on the full 2.5-mile road course was too great to escape. I learned those turns in a hurry, and Jade and I would go over there to learn how to go faster, upshifting and downshifting those six-speed manual gearboxes constantly. It was nothing short of a rush and we did it more than a few times. I don't suspect we fooled any of the other staff members whenever we'd both leave at the same time saying, "We have to go run some errands. In different cars. For about an hour…"

Well before the IMSA race we brought in American driver Tommy Kendall for a press conference. We had enough time the night before to play some pickup basketball with Tommy at a nearby gym and then had a great media turnout for the press conference the next afternoon. Tommy was fantastic. I then had to get going because I needed to visit the track with our local sign maker to check out various spots on the retaining walls where we'd be putting large sponsor decals.

The sign guy and I drove over to the track in one of the 'Vettes and after I opened the gate and closed it behind me, we drove under the tower to cruise down the front straight. Just as I was crossing the starting line on the drag strip, I was stunned to see our other Corvette scream out of the final turn and accelerate away from me. Tommy was driving and Jade was smiling and giggling from the passenger's seat as they flew by.

I turned to the sign guy and said "Are ya in?" He nodded and tightened his seat belt. I put my foot down and ran up through the gears in hot pursuit. I caught Tommy and Jade in a couple of laps, mostly because Tommy let me. Then, coming out of the turn known as "Bears" and onto the front straight, I picked my spot and passed him on the inside.

We made two full laps with me in front of Tommy Kendall. I was more laser-focused on the turns and my shift points than I'd ever been about anything, and the adrenalin was pumping through my veins. By the second lap, I was pretty darn pleased with my own bad self. And then I looked in the rearview mirror.

Tommy was right on my tail, so close I couldn't see his headlights. But he was steering with just his left hand dangling over the top of the wheel, as if he was driving up Topeka Boulevard on his way to lunch at Pat's Pig. He and Jade were in the midst of a casual conversation, probably talking about music. The illusion that I was outracing Tommy Kendall was shattered. Like many illusions, it was fun while it lasted.

I sheepishly pulled into the pits and the sign guy and I got back to our original assignment. Later, I asked Jade if Tommy had said anything or if he had acted mad when I passed him. He said, "No, not really. He thought you did a good job, but he laughed and said you have no idea how much faster you could go. He didn't want to scare you by passing you so we just cruised around the track behind you." They just cruised.

Our initial bracket race went fine and we even sold a few tickets, hot dogs, and beers. It was time to turn our full attention to the IMSA race, the Camel Grand Prix of the Heartland, set for May 5, with practice and qualifying scheduled for May 3 and 4.

We had no electronic ticketing process at Heartland Park, so the only way for us to sell tickets was totally old-school. We had to actually print them all in advance and sell them directly. We opened up a ticket office at the track and one entire wall was filled with printed tickets to various events, stacked in slotted shelves and color coded. It was a cumbersome and slow way to do business, but it's all we had.

We quickly discovered one other thing about the IMSA race. Fans seemed hesitant to purchase their tickets in advance. The property was so massive, with huge earthen berms surrounding much of the road course, an attendee would have no problem getting those general admission tickets on the day of the race and they could then move around freely and enjoy the Grand Prix from a variety of viewpoints as the day went on. We actually promoted the freedom of the berms as an attraction but in terms of ticket sales they worked against us. The motivation to buy a reserved seat in the grandstand, in advance, was not nearly strong enough and that left us in a precarious position. The Topeka weather in May could be all over the board and a good walk-up crowd would be dependent upon good weather.

When the weekend began the conditions were spectacular. For two days of practice and supporting events the skies were a deep blue and the temperature hovered in the wonderful 70s. Our miniature Grand Prix track was being mostly ignored, however, because of the remote location of the drag-racing staging lanes inside the sprawling facility. We learned a lesson there. If people can't see it, they won't try it. The petting zoo was a hit, though, as were the clowns, jugglers, and other entertainers we brought in.

As a form of market research we did "license plate surveys" in the main parking lot each day. We'd drive a golf cart up and down the rows of cars and keep notes as to what states or Kansas counties we saw. No iPad surveys inside the gate. No written questionnaires. We just counted license plates.

Then, before dawn on Sunday morning, I awoke on race day to a horrible sound. It was raining.

Sports car races go on rain or shine, so that wasn't an issue. The issue was walk-up sales. The punch in the gut only got worse when I went outside. It wasn't just raining. It was also about 40 degrees and the wind was howling. Basically, it was miserable.

We learned something else that day, about the psychology of geography. To make the Grand Prix of the Heartland a success it was going to have to draw well from the Kansas City metro area, and we'd done a lot of advertising and PR work there. To a Topeka resident, Kansas City is perceived as nothing more than a short 45-minute drive to the east. It would not be unusual for a Topekan to go to KC for dinner, and they often ventured there for Royals or Chiefs games. To a resident of Kansas City, though, the impression of Topeka was that it was somewhere out near Denver.

With the cold driving rain covering most of Kansas and the KC metro area, any chance of a decent walk-up was doused. We were wet, we were cold, and we took a financial bath as well.

And that's all too bad, because the racing was thrilling. At our main event, IMSA ran two classes at once, with the highly-powered and aerodynamically sexy IMSA GTP (Grand Touring Prototype) cars sharing the track with the slightly lower-powered, but still sexy, Camel Lights class. The rain eventually stopped, the racing was awe-inspiring, and the winners were Chip Robinson in the GTPs while the Camel Lights winner would be one Parker Johnstone. Parker and I would later become good friends when he joined the NHRA broadcast team. On May 5, 1991, however, he was just a happy winner on a miserable day.

Kentling gave us Monday off, to recharge our batteries, and I took that day to do something important. I went to the Topeka Humane Society and looked for a cat.

When I came to a stack of four cages, each with an adorable little black and white kitten inside, I looked at the first one and he stared right back at me. When I bent over to look in the cage below, he reached out and tapped me on the head. By doing that, he adopted me. I named the little Sylvester look-alike Shasta. He would be my companion for the next 16 years.

When we reconvened around the conference table on Tuesday, Kentling made it abundantly clear that the weather had been our downfall. We'd done all we could, but Mother Nature killed us. He also admitted that our venue, for road course races, worked against us in terms of advance sales of reserved seats. Combine that with the fact IMSA charged a huge fee to bless any venue with its presence, and it was financial disaster.

Our next big event was our match race and its concurrent NHRA Division 5 points meet. We held a press conference a few weeks before the event, and again the regional media turned out in good numbers to interview Gary Ormsby.

At the press conference much of the questioning had to do with a certain speed target. Top Fuel cars, at the time, were flirting with the 300 mph mark but no one had yet gotten there. While any times or speeds at the match race would not count as official runs, the media wanted to know if Ormsby thought they could do it. He said, "My crew chief, Lee Beard, would sure love to run 300. It wouldn't count for anything but it would bring us and our sponsor Castrol a lot of attention. If the conditions are conducive, we'll turn all the knobs as far as they'll go."

After the press conference I drove Gary back to the Kansas City airport and when I returned to the office I noticed an odd look on Kentling's face. I asked him what was wrong and he said, "He's not well. There's a certain look to a guy when he seriously ill. Gary is not well at all."

When the weekend arrived I drove to the airport again to pick up Lori Johns, and as we passed a number of sportsman teams pulling their trailers on the Kansas Turnpike, she made a habit of rolling down her window to wave at each one of them. We heard a lot of honks and made a lot of people smile.

Inside the track, the Ormsby and Johns teams were parked right in the middle of the vast Heartland Park pit area, in a location befitting their status as the stars of the show.

Our advance sales had been good and we'd done some heavy TV and radio advertising all over the region in support of the event, but once again we were going to be depending on a good walk-up on Sunday. We'd guaranteed Ormsby and Johns a hefty amount of money and if we wanted to cover that outlay we'd need to draw at least 10,000 fans.

Sunday was, mercifully, a beautiful day. We didn't pack the house, but we put a solid 12,000 people in the seats and we did a little better than just breaking even financially. After the IMSA fiasco, it felt good to look around and see so many smiling faces.

Our two star attractions and their teams were fantastic, although the conditions weren't going to allow anything close to a 300 mph run. Ormsby "won" the first two races, but both teams knew they were coming back for a third. Of course, we had our P.A. announcer play it up as, "Folks, as you know this was billed as a best two out of three event, but both teams have elected to make a third run, just for you GREAT Heartland Park fans." A little showmanship never hurt anybody. It was a fine event from every angle, and although we didn't make the track owner rich with our gate receipts, at least we didn't make him any poorer.

A few days later, Kentling brought us all together to let us know that Gary Ormsby was, indeed, a very sick man. Gary had called him that morning with the news of his cancer. He died on August 28 that year. His final run down a track in his Castrol Top Fuel Dragster was at our match race, at Heartland Park.

Today, the main road into the track is Gary Ormsby Drive.

We held our nostalgia road course race early in the summer and it was one of the more peculiar events I'd ever seen. The public had little interest in it so the crowd on race day was fairly disappointing, but the true oddity of the event was the participants themselves. They were mostly rich, and the nostalgia racing vehicles they were driving were, in some cases, priceless. We had sports cars, Le Mans cars, stock cars, and various other forms of historic road-racing vehicles, and they were mostly being piloted by amateur drivers who were there to get a thrill, but who all universally didn't want to break anything or bump into anyone. It ended up being something like a high-speed parade for three hours, as they drove as fast as they felt was reasonable while giving each other plenty of room.

I wasn't sure what we'd just witnessed, but it was time to get back to work to get ready for this thing called a Super Chevy Show. I had no idea what it would be other than what Kentling told us. "These things are really successful, and they come to town to handle just about everything," he said. "We can just stand back and be of assistance if they need us." That sounded good to me.

The Super Chevy Show was amazing. It featured multiple days of drag racing, although the vast majority of the cars were from the slower sportsman ranks. What was quickly obvious to us was that the racing was secondary. The huge Heartland Park pit area had been transformed by the Super Chevy organization into a massive car show and swap meet. Chevy enthusiasts from all over the Midwest made the trek to watch some racing, peruse the parts for sale, and stare at the incredible show cars. It seemed like 90 percent of them left with something shiny in their hands.

And Kentling had been right. The touring organization took care of everything. We just basically watched and smiled. It was a heck of show.

All along, we'd been multitasking and also getting ready for our ARCA race, and it was looming.

We couldn't bring Earnhardt, Waltrip, or Schrader to Topeka for a press conference so we did the next best thing. We hired a professional video crew to interview the drivers for us, out on the NASCAR tour. And there was no better place to do that than Sears Point Raceway in Sonoma. Like Heartland Park, it was a road course.

When we saw the video they had shot, we were thrilled. All three superstar drivers raved about running in our ARCA race and all claimed to be on board if NASCAR ever wanted to add Heartland Park Topeka to its tour. We very much wanted that to happen and Kentling was gently nudging NASCAR to seriously consider us in future years.

To make a big splash with the media, we had kept the news of Earnhardt, Waltrip, and Schrader to ourselves. When Jade sent out his invites for our press conference, all he hinted was that this announcement would be the biggest piece of news for Heartland Park since it had opened. When lunch was over and the conference started, Bill Kentling simply said hello and then ran the video. There were gasps when Dale Earnhardt, the Intimidator himself in his trademark sunglasses, said, "I'm excited to race at Heartland Park. We hear there might be some NASCAR adventures there in the future, and I hope that's the case. I can't wait to get there."

Waltrip and Schrader were equally as effusive. When the video ended, the attending members of the media actually stood and applauded.

Another big piece of news at the press conference was that we'd signed a high-profile sponsor for the race, which would be officially known as the Wendy's Big Classic 100. Wendy's locations all over the region would promote the race with tent cards on their tables, paper liners on trays, and discount coupons available for all customers.

Our ticket sales looked solid going into race weekend and the weather was good. It was hot, but the sky was blue. On Friday, four transporters arrived and the black No. 3 Goodwrench Chevrolet was unloaded, as were the instantly recognizable No. 17 Western Auto Chevy Waltrip would drive, Schrader's No. 25 Kodiak car, and the No. 5 Tide car Hendrick would pilot.

Interestingly, for Heartland Park staffers like me and for the ARCA racers in attendance, just as much attention was paid to the toy Rick Hendrick had also brought along. It was the No. 46 Chevy Lumina with the name Cole Trickle above the side windows. The car itself was a movie star.

Waltrip, Schrader, and Hendrick spent all day practicing on Saturday, with Schrader bouncing back and forth between his car and Earnhardt's, shaking them both down and getting them set up. Earnhardt himself wouldn't fly in until Sunday morning.

We drew about 17,000 on race day, just about but not quite breaking even after the hefty appearance fees were paid to the NASCAR boys, but Kentling saw the race as an investment. He wanted to prove to Midwest fans and to NASCAR that Heartland Park Topeka was a viable place for the biggest stock-car circuit in the world.

Schrader ended up winning the race in dominating fashion. Waltrip finished ninth after a couple of spins in the "Lions, Tigers, and Bears" set of turns, and Hendrick finished 23rd in the Tide car. Dale Earnhardt lost control early in the race in turn one, a sweeping left-hander on the stock car version of the road course, and his Goodwrench car slid a long way across the grass before hitting the barrier wall hard. He was fine, but he was done for the day. About 30 minutes later, his private jet took off over the track, from Forbes Field, and the pilot tilted the wings to say goodbye.

Immediately after the winner's circle celebrations, Jade Gurss grabbed me and said "TNN will run video of our race tonight if we cut the highlights right now. Can you do the voice-over?" Without hesitation I said yes, and we dashed out of the tower to a satellite uplink trailer parked on the drag racing staging lanes. I scribbled some notes, then watched the video package the crew had just edited together. We had about a minute to make the uplink, so I basically ad-libbed it. We did it in one take. That night, I tuned in to TNN to watch their motorsports news show, and the anchor said, "ARCA took its series road-course racing in Topeka today, and some NASCAR stars joined in the fun. Bob Wilber has the report from Heartland Park." There was the video, there was my voice, and there was my name at the bottom of the screen. And they even spelled it right. It had been an exhilarating day.

Not long after that, however, we got some more bad news. Our friend Tommy Kendall had crashed badly during the IMSA race at Watkins Glen, New York. It was the same Turn 5 that would soon claim the life of NASCAR driver J.D. McDuffie. Tommy's crash had been head-on into the wall, and while he survived it, the injuries were serious. Basically, both of his ankles were crushed. He'd have a long and painful road ahead of him to recover.

We also returned our two white Corvettes to Chevrolet around that time and took delivery of a new one in the bright metallic colors that were so popular at the time. It was green — and fast. I took it on a pair of road trips, driving it to Denver to see the Mile High Nationals at Bandimere Speedway, and to St. Louis to display it at a major festival. While I was there, I drove over to Woodleaf Court to display it in the Wilber family driveway.

My mom was afraid to drive it but her history of loving high-horsepower Camaros had her grinning from ear to ear. I let her sit in the 'Vette and fire it up. When it rumbled to life she was absolutely giddy.

Our next big event would be our AMA Superbike race and Jade was particularly excited about that. He was a big fan of motorcycle road racing, and he knew the names and styles of all the best riders. We brought one of the best, Scott Russell, in for a press conference a few weeks before the event.

There were, however, a lot of things conspiring against the success of the AMA event. For one, it utilized the entire 2.5 mile version of the road track so the need to buy reserved seats in advance was at about the same nearly-nonexistent level as it had been for the IMSA race. Secondly, and possibly more importantly, it was to be held only three weeks before the NHRA AC Delco Heartland Nationals, our biggest event of the year.

We promoted and advertised as well as we could, but by the Monday before the race it was obvious we weren't going to draw many racing fans, as ticket sales barely broke the 2,000 mark. Bill Kentling called us together and said, "There just aren't enough racing fans to go around here, and the ones we have don't have enough money for this race to work, so close to the NHRA event. We're having an outstanding advance sale for NHRA and we'll pack the place for four days. The bikes are lost in the shuffle."

He then said, "So here's what we're gonna do. You guys divide up this list of major companies in the region. Call them, convince them to take 2,000 tickets for free, and ask them to give them to their employees and customers. But, and this is the key, tell them we need for them to say they bought the tickets. If they won't agree to that, we won't give the tickets to them."

The theory was one of creating value. Free tickets were great, and some people would surely use them, but on the day of the race if anything at all came up as a conflict most people would have no qualms about passing up a freebie when more important things were happening. If the companies would make a big deal out of having bought them (utilizing just a slight version of a white lie) more people would be compelled to attend because the tickets had perceived value.

It worked to a degree and we probably did have 9,000 people on the property for the race. They did buy some souvenirs and concessions so every dollar there was one we wouldn't have brought in otherwise, but the AMA race joined the IMSA affair as a serious money loser.

Finally, it was time for the NHRA to come to town.

After having been to Gainesville for the NHRA Gatornationals and Denver for the Mile-High Nationals, I felt I was ready for the epic scope of a national event. I wasn't even close to prepared. Once the AMA race was over and we were three weeks away from the AC Delco Heartland Nationals, our activity ramped up to a fever pitch. It seemed we couldn't work late enough or get in early enough to make it all happen.

We did manage to put tickets on sale via the telephone and we partnered with NHRA to heavily promote the race all over the region in order to make the phone ring. Of course, we didn't exactly have a "call center" to handle the incoming inquiries. Our office administrator and receptionist took the calls as fast as she could, filling out order forms and taking credit card numbers. She was terrific but she was completely overwhelmed.

It was late September and I'd been working at Heartland Park since early January. In all those months, I'd never seen anything like the excitement and interest the NHRA race was creating. It was intense, it was energizing, and it was exhausting.

We had an intern from the University of Kansas helping us out at the time, and her job in the weeks leading up to the race was to visit every business in Topeka that had a sign or message board out front. She'd drop off a flyer that courteously asked those businesses to alter their signs to say "Welcome NHRA racers and fans!" By Monday of race week, it seemed like every business in town had done that.

Almost all NHRA races are regional events, drawing from a wide range of states and often from distant countries. Many are in big markets, where it's tough to break through the clutter created by the major professional sports, and where the media advertising costs are exorbitant. In that regard, we had a real advantage in Topeka.

The advertising was affordable, even in Kansas City and Wichita, and the event itself was the single biggest thing to happen in Topeka all year. The city was proud to host such a big national event and the businesses went out of their way to welcome the visitors. For Topeka, it was as if the Super Bowl was coming to town.

Back then, NHRA used a qualifying format in which one session was held on Thursday, another on Friday, and then two on Saturday. That made it a four-day event, and while that could dilute the attendance on the first two days, we still pulled in big crowds.

By Saturday, we were wall-to-wall. I stood on the walkway on the backside of the tower, with Kentling by my side, and we marveled at what we saw. Incoming cars were backed up to the north on Route 75 as far as we could see. Dust was billowing in the grassy parking lots as the endless stream of vehicles pulled in, one after another. Fans streamed into the facility, jamming every entry gate. It was a roaring success.

I had the freedom to cruise all over the venue, to check on things, help where I could, or just watch. I'd brought Taffy and Skip over to Topeka as well, and they spent two great days attending their first drag race. It was heartwarming to have them there with me, witnessing such a major success.

I also had my camera and the access to go anywhere I wanted, so I spent a couple of qualifying sessions in the staging lanes and trackside, shooting photos of the cars. I was mostly attracted to the Funny Cars, though I liked the Top Fuel and Pro Stock machines as well. I know I was mostly attracted to the Funny Cars because after my 35mm photos were developed and printed, almost all of them were of Funny Cars. And, strangely, a lot of the shots were of the same car. It was the Raybestos-sponsored car driven by Richard Hartman. At least half the shots I took were of young Richard's car. Twenty-four years later, Richard and I would finally work together.

We thought Saturday couldn't be beaten in terms of attendance and excitement. I drove over to the track at dawn on Sunday, coming in a secret back way through Montara, and the line of cars on Route 75 was already out of sight.

The crowd just kept coming, with these avid fans filling every seat in the house and standing 10 deep at the fences. It was, for us, an outrageous success. Kentling and I took our spot on the walkway behind the tower once again, surveying the packed parking lots, and he said, "This can all be yours someday, if you want it."

My instant mental reaction to that compliment surprised me. I'd very much enjoyed my year at Heartland Park. I liked the road course stuff. I'd instantly fallen in love with NHRA Drag Racing. But there were two thoughts already in my head on that glorious Sunday in late September.

I'd seen the stress Bill was under all year, despite his innate ability to appear calm at all times. At that precise point in my life, I really didn't think I'd want that stress and responsibility when millions of someone else's dollars were at stake.

Second, and more important, I'd worked hard with my staff to do everything possible to make the year successful but there was no real winning or losing when it came to running a track. In baseball and soccer, the most energizing and rewarding thing was the winning and losing, as a team, on game nights. At Heartland Park, I had no rooting interest. Even the guy who runs the stadium can still root for his baseball or football team. All we could hope for were big crowds and good weather.

I'd seen the weather dash all of our plans for the IMSA race. That was a loss, and we absorbed it as a team, but it wasn't a loss in the team-sports sense. It was a loss we couldn't surmount no matter what we did. We were destined to lose and there couldn't be a dramatic comeback in the final minute or the late innings. We were the Washington Generals and the weather was the Harlem Globetrotters. The weather always won.

I'd worked hard and had fun, but there was a puzzling emptiness to it. I couldn't escape the fact, though, that this NHRA stuff blew my mind.

I'd gotten to know many of the NHRA drivers and I found them to be engaging and fantastic to work with. I stood near their pits and watched their crews compete as teams. I met their public relations reps in the media center and appreciated how much passion they poured into supporting their teams. I missed that.

I also deeply admired the way NHRA put on its events. The IMSA teams were high-dollar organizations and their approach was to rely on the on-track racing to entertain the fans. They were actors and the track was their stage. When they weren't out there performing, they were out of sight. Even the ARCA guys pushed back when we suggested they emulate the NHRA approach and allow fans to get up close to where they worked on their cars. They looked shocked at such a suggestion, and only said, "Sorry, we don't do it that way." We had to put up fences to keep the fans away from their transporters.

The NHRA was just the opposite. They did everything in their power to give their fans total access. The fully open pit area was something I'd never seen in any sport. It was like a baseball team playing a game while allowing fans to tour the dugout.

The NHRA drivers bought into it, as well. They signed autographs for hours, posed for pictures, and chatted with anyone who wanted to talk. It was, by comparison, incredible to see. I'd been in sports my entire life but I'd never experienced anything like our NHRA national event.

There we were, the former commissioner of the MISL and the former vice president of the St. Louis Storm, two guys who had never dreamed of being in racing, standing on the walkway behind the Heartland Park tower while admiring the immense crowd that was pouring into the track. And right then, I felt the first pang of "there's something better" knocking around in my gut. All I could say to Bill was, "This is pretty amazing. Two indoor soccer guys standing here, watching more people come into this facility this weekend than some of our teams drew in a full season. Amazing."

Pat Austin, a successful Alcohol Funny Car driver, won in Top Fuel that day. He was driving Gary Ormsby's car for tuner Lee Beard. That was an incredibly fitting tribute. The other pro winners were Darrell Alderman in Pro Stock, and Mark Oswald in Funny Car. Oswald was driving the gorgeous In-N-Out Burger car, at a race approximately 1,500 miles from the nearest In-N-Out.

At the end of the day, when the crowd had departed and the media interviews were over, we all shook hands and told each other what a great job we had done. And I felt that pang again. We weren't congratulating each other for winning the trophy. We hadn't won the pennant and poured champagne over each other's heads. We weren't gathered on the mound or in the locker room to celebrate. It had been a long year full of hard work and endless hours, and at the end of it we all shook hands and said, "Good job."

I couldn't escape the inkling, once again, that it might just be another plow-forward moment.

I did nothing for a day other than relax after the hectic national event. And I managed to put those inklings out of my mind for a few more weeks. We had our performance reviews coming up and I didn't want anything to get in the way of that. I was sincerely interested in hearing how Bill would describe my job performance.

When we had that meeting, he was typical Bill Kentling. He was firm, he was direct, he was fair, and he was completely honest. He gave me very high marks for most of the work I'd done but he fairly criticized me for my shortfalls.

One of those shortfalls was budgetary, in that I never paid enough attention to that pesky budget thing he had worked so hard to develop. He said, "It's pretty common for marketing guys to just want to do what they think is right and ignore the accountants. Well, you have to be better than those common guys. This is somebody else's money and we have budgets for everything. I want you to dream this creative stuff up, that's great, but you're not supposed to just go out and do it without making sure the guy who writes the checks is good with it."

I understood that, and he was right.

He also told me that the way I'd led my team created some resentment among the group that worked across the highway at the track. They felt we weren't engaged with them and that we acted better than them because we wore ties and worked inside, while they were over there mowing a hundred acres of grass or working on the facility's wiring. He said, "We don't get to have all of this fun without those guys having the place in top shape and up and running. Without them, we have no stadium, no ballpark. There were some times you pitched proposals that had elements in them those guys would have to take care of for you, and you never asked them before you pitched it. You just told them about it later."

Again, he was right on target and I was the one who set that tone in our marketing house. To us, we were the behind-the-scenes stars of the show, who came up with the sponsor packages and ticket promotions. And I was the voice of the track on TV and radio. It's no wonder there was some resentment from the crew that actually gave our events a place to happen. Lessons well learned from a great boss. A life lesson learned, really.

There were a few other criticisms, about my style and approach, including my maturity in a number of ways.

"Overall you did a great job," Bill said. "Other than the IMSA and AMA races, we hit every ball pretty hard. We reached a number of goals I'd established for next year, a full year early. Had it not been for the IMSA and AMA disasters, we'd have come damn close to breaking even. We can all get better but you did a fine job in a lot of ways. We have an obligation to the owners, though, to stop the bleeding. We need to cut out the sure money-losing events, and tighten our belts around here. It's going to be hard."

And the very next day, my landlord informed me that he wanted to put the house on the market. The golf course was failing, the housing market wasn't getting any better, and he didn't have the luxury of owning four houses in addition to the one he lived in. Spectacular.

I looked around for a new place, but once again the plow-forward guy in my brain saw all of these challenges as a sign that it was once again time. My heart wasn't even in the house search.

Bill and I were flying out to San Diego for the IMSA banquet and that gave us a lot of time to talk at great length about all of the things on both of our minds. Before that trip was over we mutually came to the conclusion that the next great thing must be out there and I should go look for it. Plus, if belts were going to be tightened, a good place to start was the large salary he was paying me. My staff members had picked up some great experience, by then, and it wasn't completely necessary to have a high-priced general manager watching over them.

He graciously offered me an outstanding severance package, and even allowed me to keep working out of my office in the other house for as many months as I'd need, while I searched for the next great thing.

Out in San Diego, it was time to put our tuxedos on and attend the IMSA banquet before we'd fly home the next morning. Tommy Kendall attended, in a wheelchair that supported both of his legs and protected his ankles, and he was the absolute center of attention. Bill's compassionate conversation with Tommy nearly brought me to tears. I think it brought both of them to tears, as well.

After dinner, as the actual banquet ceremony was about to begin, IMSA showed a video of the season's highlights, race by race. Each new scene started with a static shot of the race track itself, with the name of the location on the screen. Daytona, West Palm Beach, Sebring, Del Mar, Watkins Glen, Laguna Seca, Lime Rock, and others were all cheered for loudly when they were shown. When Heartland Park came on the screen, with the word "Topeka" below it, the entire room booed. Loudly. I initially assumed they were booing the lousy weather we'd had, but it felt like a real slap at Topeka and it seemed clear the room full of sports car people didn't like our town. The rest of the people at our round table were visibly uncomfortable. Bill was rightfully furious, and we stormed out. IMSA would never again have to bear the burden of a trip to Kansas.

After we got back Bill put the word out for me, to NHRA and the other track owners, and within days I had calls from Houston Raceway Park and NHRA headquarters. While it might have been an adventure to go run the Houston track, it would've been a replay of what I'd just done. The only thing it would accomplish was moving me from Kansas to Texas, and that wasn't what I was looking to do. I declined the interview.

I couldn't, in good conscience, decline the generous offer to attend the Winternationals in February to meet with the NHRA media relations folks, led by Denny Darnell. I put that on my calendar while I pondered other options and talked to all of my most trusted advisers. Unfortunately, the MISL was in the early stages of its death throes so going back to indoor soccer at that point in time was probably not an option. After Heartland Park and things like the AC Delco Heartland Nationals, it would've seemed like a step backward, anyway.

I toyed with a number of options over the next month, and even considered doing some freelance work in the PR realm. I'd come to Topeka knowing very little about that part of the sports world but I learned a lot just watching Jade Gurss. I knew I could write, and someone could teach me the styles I'd need to perfect. I figured I could do that if I had to, but February was coming and NHRA sent me a ticket to fly to SoCal for the week.

I arrived on the Monday night of race week. I spent Tuesday at NHRA headquarters and Denny Darnell's initial assignment was for me to write a press release announcing a new major sponsorship the organization had landed. Honestly, the hardest part of that test was figuring out how to work the desktop computer and its archaic operating system. I actually needed some quick tutoring on that, because it looked nothing like my Apple II.

Writing the press release was easy and Denny used it "as is" for the announcement. He then gave me Wednesday off to drive around the area and investigate housing options.

"Sticker shock" wouldn't quite describe the magnitude of my wide-eyed amazement at what it would cost to rent a small one-bedroom apartment more than 20 miles east of the track on the congested 10 Freeway. I knew there was no way I could afford anything near Pomona or Glendora, after having heard what Denny said about compensation. It was roughly half of what I'd made in Topeka in a part of the country that was, at least, three times more expensive. It was nothing short of scary and mind-boggling. How could all these millions of people afford to live in this place?

I worked the race for all four days, putting out pit notes and interacting with the reporters who were there. When it ended I even wrote up small bio stories about the winners and submitted those to the press.

I flew home the next day and stewed on it the whole way back to Topeka. It was time to vacate the house, it was time to start getting paid again, and it was probably time to go back to St. Louis if something else didn't happen.

I ruled out the NHRA job. Considering all the pros and cons what leapt out at me the most was that it didn't solve the problem of winning and losing. It was just like working for the track, in that it was an impartial role working all year at a bunch of "neutral site" games. I said no. I think Denny Darnell knew that was coming. He did, graciously, pay me for the work I did during the race week.

I landed a consulting gig with the YMCA of St. Louis, helping them part time, and I headed home. That was enough to pay the bills while I continued my new career search, hoping to find a full-time gig for an NHRA team. That was my new goal in life.

While I did that, I realized I had more than enough free time to rejoin the Wizards. Bob Hughes and Jim Greenwald, the founders of the team, had moved on to bigger things. Neil Fiala was no longer playing either, and most of the guys on the team were strangers to me but they looked pretty good. As in, really good.

Neil's brother Rick Fiala was managing the team and he'd approached it in a different way than Hughes had. Bob's philosophy was that it was best to find 14 or 15 really dedicated players, so that everyone would get to play a lot. Rick didn't like having to sweat out whether or not nine guys would show up for every game so he put an 18-man roster together. When we'd all show up, a lot of guys would sit. That wasn't a lot of fun. We weren't there to "make it" anywhere. We all wanted to play.

In early summer Rick got a coaching offer that was too good to pass up and he accepted it. I was named the new manager of the Sauget Wizards. I would be a player/manager but my first priority was managing the team.

I moved some guys around to what seemed like odd positions, because my initial impression had been that a lot of guys were playing positions they wanted to play but those were not necessarily positions for which they were best suited. We won my first game as skipper.

We won again, and again, and again. I ended up being 13-0 as a manager before we finally lost. My dad came to a number of games and I could tell he was proud of me, once again following in his footsteps. Before long I put my own play at the bottom of the priority list and I concentrated solely on managing. I loved the strategy, both in making out a lineup and in making in-game decisions. It was more fun than I ever dreamed it would be.

I was named manager of one of the two All-Star teams and was also elected to play in the game, although I deferred on that part. I was too busy making sure all of my pitchers got an inning and everyone else got in. I was having a fantastic time but my career search was still ongoing.

I didn't want to settle. I wanted to stay in drag racing if I could, but the things that weren't right with the track job needed to be corrected. I put some more feelers out and got one nibble.

There was a guy in New Jersey who was having some success doing marketing and PR for two top professional NHRA drivers. He had a real job consulting for the east-coast electronics chain Nobody Beats The Wiz, a new sponsor he'd just brought to Funny Car star Chuck Etchells, but he moonlighted with Motorsports Marketing Inc. (MMI) out of the basement of his suburban home.

Bill Griffith was his name and he called me a few days later. We talked at length about what he was doing and what sort of help he needed and although his New Jersey bluster was a little off-putting to me, there was no denying his success as an upstart marketing guy on drag racing's biggest stage. He'd gotten Etchells his first primary sponsor, he was working on other things for Top Fuel and Funny Car driver Mike Dunn, and he had some other smaller clients paying him monthly retainers as well. This was exactly the sort of job I was looking for. We'd be representing actual drag racing drivers and organizations. They would be teams we could root for. We'd all be winning and losing together. And someone else could worry about selling the tickets.

What he desperately needed was a communicator and writer to take over the PR part of his new business. He could pitch deals all day and all night, and he had a solid track record for closing a lot of them, but he was at heart a salesman. He didn't write very well or tell compelling stories that would get his sponsors and his drivers in the paper or on TV. I could do that.

Over the phone, we stayed in touch while I once again put all of my stuff in storage back in St. Louis. I flew out to Newark a few weeks later and we went to one of the many major match races put on at historic Old Bridge Township Raceway Park in Englishtown. The odd thing was, Bill never officially interviewed me and he never asked me to show him any examples of my work. He just wanted to meet me to see if we were compatible. I hadn't really thought of that.

About a week later he called again to tell me I was one of two people he was considering for the job. There was a woman in Kentucky, who was "really good" as he put it, but she was hesitant to move to New Jersey and he was hesitant to have her work from home. He made it clear that if I wanted the job, there'd be a move in my future.

We both considered it for a few more days. I'll admit the thought, "Boy, I'd like nothing more than to move to New Jersey if I could" had never really crossed my mind. I didn't dislike the place, and I thought Raceway Park was a cool track, but the hustle and bustle in-your-face lifestyle didn't suit my much more laid-back Midwestern style very well. We decided to meet one more time so I could see his house in Wyckoff and the basement we'd be working in, while I could also check out the housing options.

Wyckoff was a pleasant surprise, almost to the point of being a shock. I was expecting Newark. Instead, it looked a lot like Kirkwood with beautiful homes on tree-lined suburban streets. It still, however, had a legitimate New Jersey vibe to it.

His basement was just as expected. There were a few desks scattered around, no windows, and one young man, Jim Algeo, acting as his assistant.

I stayed in a hotel on Route 17, just a few miles from Bill's house, and from my window I could see the Empire State Building. It sure felt like I was a very long way from home. I spent the next day with a local rental expert Bill knew, and we checked out four or five rental properties in Wyckoff and Ramsey so that I could live just a few minutes from work.

The rentals we saw weren't going to cut it. One was a studio in a building that hadn't been renovated since I was born. The monthly-rent figure blew my mind. Another was a slightly larger apartment but it was on the second floor over an old retail store that had been closed and shuttered for six years. No, thank you.

Finally, I took another day and widened my search to areas further afield. I stumbled onto a nice condo complex in the quaint little village of Harriman, N.Y., just north of the state line, and I inquired in the management office as to what they would cost. That figure was frankly four times what I could afford and probably 10 times what any bank would lend me, so I asked him if he knew if any of the condos were for rent. He said yes and sent me to one where the owner was having an open house. It was at the top of the hill with gorgeous views for miles. As I walked up the stairs to look at the unit, the owner and a couple were coming down. The owner said, "They beat you to it. It's no longer available." Just when things were looking so bright.

I then passed another building with a "FOR RENT" sign in the window, and quickly drove to a nearby pay phone to call the number scrawled at the bottom of it. The woman who answered the phone actually owned five condos in the complex and she rented out four of them. As of that day she had a two-bedroom unit available, also with views as far as the Hudson River. I snagged it before anyone else could.

Then I called Bill Griffith and took the job.

I was moving to New Jersey. Plow forward, right?

Hello New Jersey

On my first day at work, Bill Griffith gave me a key to his front door. He also showed me to my desk down in the basement. It came complete with a wooden dining-room chair for me to sit on. No pad, no swivel, no arms.

The desk contained some blank paper, paper clips, and a stapler. There was not a computer in sight. There was a copier and a postage machine, with a FAX being the most sophisticated piece of equipment in the room.

Bill explained how it all worked, saying, "I use a typing service. I hand-write press releases and FAX them to a woman across town. She and her daughter type them up and FAX them back for corrections. We do that two or three times until it's done."

I shook my head just to see if a cowbell sound-effect could be heard. There was only silence.

"Wow, how long does it take you to write a press release and then finally get it out?" I asked.

His answer was, "Usually about a week."

It was archaic, even by the still mostly archaic standards of 1992.

After attempting to write in this manner one time, I made a small request — I asked Bill if he'd buy me an electric typewriter. At least that way I'd be able to write the original much quicker. His face puckered up like he'd bitten into something he thought was a tangerine, only to discover it was a lemon.

He acceded, but only after I got my first lesson in the New York/New Jersey tradition of "having a guy."

I told Bill I'd go to an office supply store and find the best deal on a typewriter. The volume of his voice tripled and his New Jersey accent ramped up to 100 percent, as he shouted, "Don't ever do that. Do not EVER do that. I got a guy who can get stuff like this cheap. I'll call my guy."

His guy got us a 10-year old IBM Selectric. I'm sure it was a heck of a deal.

During my first week on the job I learned many things. I'd arrive in the morning and unlock the front door to enter the Griffith home. To get to the basement, I had to pass through the eat-in kitchen where Bill's wife would be seated in her nightgown feeding Cheerios to their toddler son, who had many of those Cheerios stuck to his face. I'd say "Good morning!" and head downstairs into the dungeon (office).

Within a couple of days I could tell I wasn't digging this particular work space. It felt like I was 9 years old again, turning the Wilber basement into a play office, and wearing my best school clothes to feel like a real businessman. I also understood I'd have to get over that. This was the job I wanted. This was working for a team. No one ever told me it would be easy or luxurious.

Bill, as it turned out, was a little bit in-your-face but that's not exactly uncommon in that part of the country. During my first week he was on the phone with our key client, Chuck Etchells, the owner/driver of the Nobody Beats The Wiz Funny Car who had just won the NHRA national event down the turnpike in Englishtown. As the conversation progressed it began to escalate. I was, basically, aghast at the tone.

The next day I caught Bill at a good time and said, "Look. We're really different. Maybe you can light a bit of a fire in me but I think I also can show you how to not fly off the handle like that. It can't be a good thing to be screaming at your client."

He looked puzzled.

"So you're saying maybe we can balance each other out because you don't like the screaming and yelling," he said.

"Nobody likes screaming and yelling, Bill," I replied.

He shot back, "Well, I'm not going to walk on eggshells around here because you're not a screamer and you don't like it."

"Bill," I said, "being polite and calm isn't walking on eggshells. It's just the right thing to do. We're professionals here."

The key word must've been "professionals" because he immediately calmed down and said, "You're right. You're absolutely right. We can be good for each other. I see what you're saying."

We both made a concerted effort to bring our best qualities to the work and minimize our negative tendencies. Bill taught me about management and negotiation, while I brought my communications and writing skills to the table. As a team we were better than just the simple sum of our parts.

Englishtown had been the final race before the famed NHRA Western Swing, featuring a trio of races in Denver, Sonoma, and Seattle on consecutive weekends. There was only one problem. Etchells, the tour's most recent winner, had never planned on hauling his car and transporter all around the United States. He had decided, before the season started, to skip the Western Swing.

The Western Swing held almost no importance to Nobody Beats The Wiz, since they only had stores in the eastern part of the country. They had signed off on the idea to skip the Swing. But now, with Etchells coming off a win and climbing in the points, it seemed like a much better idea to go to Denver. He decided to make the trek to the mountains, with his own equipment, and he won there, as well. Two wins in a row for our team but Sonoma and Seattle were next.

Rather than haul all of his stuff the rest of the way, Chuck and Bill struck a deal to use Johnny West's car and trailer for the next two races. The change kept Chuck on the tour and in the points hunt, but he wouldn't get past the second round in California or Washington.

Bill Kentling then called me, sarcastically saying, "Wait. You're representing a guy who just won two races in a row and he wasn't even going to go to the two after that?" I acknowledged it seemed odd, but the sponsorship wasn't that substantial and he didn't want to spend the money. It worked out OK in the end.

After the Swing it was time for me to attend my first race as part of MMI, representing our driver. It would be the first time I'd attend an event in-person as part of a team and that's what I had wanted to do since I left Heartland Park. I'd be heading to Brainerd, in central Minnesota.

I went in a day earlier than Bill and checked into the room we'd be sharing at the quaint Chaparral Bunkhouse Motel in Brainerd, a small town that could also be described as quaint. Or rustic. When I got to track the next day I entered a facility that could be called both of those things, times four. Nestled in the woods in the midst of many of Minnesota's most beautiful lakes, Brainerd International Raceway was — and still is — one of a kind. I quickly discovered I loved Brainerd. I still do.

I also discovered I loved being part of a team, even if I was just the assistant to the guy who handled the marketing. Bill and I stood by the fence and watched each qualifying session and every round of racing, cheering for our guy to do well and win rounds. We were cheering. I had never done that at a drag race. It felt good.

A few months later Bill and I drove to Newark International Airport and flew to California for the Winston Finals.

Early on Sunday evening, under a moonlit sky on a Ponoma track that seemed to stretch to oblivion, Chuck beat Freddie Nealy to win his third race of the year. I got my Winston winner's hat and joined the team next to the car in the Winner's Circle for photos. And, I had no idea how hard it was to do that. After all, I'd only been working with this team for about five months, and my driver had won three times. This stuff must be easy, right? Yes, I still have the hat.

Just days before we had left for Pomona the phone rang in our office and it was actually for me. I recognized the voice and the accent instantly. It was affirmation calling, if by affirmation you mean Don Popovic. The Storm coach was calling me from his office at the St. Louis Arena.

Don said, in his thick Yugoslavian accent, "You were the best we ever had. Milan and I didn't know it at the time but it became obvious after we made the changes. We need you back. Will you come back and run this team as the GM?"

I'd been keeping up on the state of MISL. It wasn't pretty. The league was down to just a handful of teams and all of them were hanging by the last tattered thread. It wouldn't take much for the last four walls of the house of cards to collapse. As much as I loved the sport, loved the town, and loved the team, it was not an option.

I thanked Don for calling and told him I appreciated his candor and honesty. I then added that I'd just gotten into my new position in drag racing and I wanted to give it a shot. Normally, it would've been very much like me to say yes without any thought, move back to St. Louis just months after I'd left, and have the league cease to function within days. For once, I was smart enough to say no.

At MMI, one of our clients was Al Hanna, a former Funny Car competitor on the East Coast who was, by then, touring with his jet Funny Car making exhibition runs at match races. When Al brought out a new car, with a different style of air intake, I wrote a creative press release about it and National Dragster magazine ran it in its entirety. I had landed quotes or snippets in the magazine before, but that was the first full feature I'd done that ended up in print. Creating something out of thin air and having an editor like it enough to print every word of it was pretty cool. And cooler still was the knowledge the story was about a car and driver in an exhibition class.

Bill was also working closely with Mike Dunn, who was a Top Fuel driver at the time. Bill and Mike were pitching La Victoria Salsa and the talks were proceeding at a good pace. Mike came over to Wyckoff from his Pennsylvania home and I sat in as he and Bill went over the package and the sales pitch. They weren't agreeing about all of it, but I mostly kept out of the discussion.

Over the next week or so Mike took the reins more directly and he sealed the deal with La Victoria. I'm not sure it would've happened if he hadn't done that.

That fall Bill was working several days each week at the Nobody Beats The Wiz headquarters, and each time he'd return to the office he'd complain in no uncertain terms that those people were bad guys. So he got to work replacing them as a sponsor.

Soon thereafter, he landed a multi-faceted deal with Kendall Motor Oil. Etchells would be the most important part and he'd have Kendall as his new primary sponsor. Top Alcohol Funny Car driver Frank "Ace" Manzo would get a smaller deal. Pro Stock Motorcycle rider John Mafaro would get the smallest piece of the pie. Both Manzo and Mafaro were from New Jersey. They had a guy. His name was Griffith and he got them a deal.

While that was going on, Bill was also in discussions with Kendall to get them into NASCAR. The comparison was so stark I was amazed.

For about the same money Etchells was getting from Kendall, NASCAR team owner Felix Sabates would happily provide a small space for a Kendall decal behind the rear wheel well on Kyle Petty's car. It was, maybe, two feet by two feet. It seemed ridiculous but it's what Kendall wanted.

We flew to Atlanta for the final race of the NASCAR season to make the announcement and show off the decal on Petty's car. I couldn't believe how small it looked. Everyone on the team treated us like big shots for the day and we watched the race from the infield before ducking out early. All I could think about was how much more Chuck Etchells could do for Kendall with even just a fraction of that money.

That winter three important events occurred. Bill bought me one of the first Apple Macintosh laptops and a small portable printer so I could produce actual pit notes at the races.

Also, one of the executives at Kendall happened to be friends with a guy who drove a car in endurance races. Kendall would be sponsoring the car at the 24 Hours of Daytona and NASCAR driver Kenny Wallace would be brought in to help with the driving.

Finally, Bill walked away from Nobody Beats The Wiz and put all his eggs in the MMI basket. He even thought we maybe, possibly, should get a real office.

As January brought us into 1993 it also brought me the news that I'd be headed to Daytona twice in the coming weeks, first for the 24-hour race in late January and then again a few weeks later for the Daytona 500. Both trips would be in support of Kendall, which had retained us to do their PR.

I made the first trip by myself and was under no illusion that the Kendall Chevy Camaro, running in the GTS class, would have much success while sharing the track with so many well-funded teams running in much faster classes. I did some press releases for the race and planned to put out pit notes if the group managed to do anything spectacular, but mostly I marveled at the concept of racing non-stop (hopefully) for 24 hours.

The race started in the middle of the afternoon and the Kendall car had only three drivers while most other teams had four or five. Owner Paul Mazzacane would start the race and share the driving with Chester Edwards and Kenny Wallace. When I met Wallace, and I asked him how the car looked, he just rolled his eyes and shook his head.

As day turned to night, and the six-hour mark approached, Wallace was in the car. We watched as he drove past the pit and headed out into the road course section on the infield, but he didn't come back when he should have. He hadn't wrecked. The car simply quit on him in the darkness.

I was told by the crew chief that if a driver accepted assistance from a safety vehicle or another car, a penalty could be instituted or the car could be expelled from the race. Finally, after many long minutes of uncertainty and waiting, someone in the Kendall pit yelled, "Here he comes!" as he pointed down pit lane. Kenny Wallace was outside the car with the driver's door open, pushing.

The crew ran to meet him and by the time they got back Kenny looked exhausted. A few minutes later I asked him how far he'd pushed the car. He smiled, winked, and said, "From right before the start of the pit lane. The car behind me pushed me to there, in the dark. I don't think anyone saw us."

As midnight approached I was amazed that I'd been at the track for 12 hours, and yet the race wasn't even half over. I drove back to my hotel on the beach and slept for six hours then headed back to the track. It was roughly 7 a.m. when I arrived in the pits. There were still approximately eight hours of racing left.

For the Kendall team, though, there was very little racing left. The car was balky and the motor was dying. By mid-morning they were done and Kenny Wallace didn't look too sad to hear Mazzacane say so. They finished 48th overall, and 16th in the GTS class.

Two weeks later I was back in Daytona with Bill for NASCAR's biggest race. Whereas the 24-hour race takes place in front of a few thousand fans at the enormous Daytona International Speedway, the Daytona 500 nearly fills the place.

We left the hotel at dawn to fight the traffic and, since we were hosting the Kendall people in an elevated tent on the infield portion of the famous tri-oval, once we were in there we were basically there for good.

Kyle Petty did great during qualifying, putting his Mello Yello Pontiac with its small Kendall decals, on the pole. The decals weren't any bigger but they were die-cut and much nicer looking.

They were still located behind the rear wheel wells, though, meaning they'd often be obscured by streaks of rubber as the race went on.

We wined and dined the Kendall folks and I enjoyed watching all the pomp and circumstance as the huge race track filled with fans. Our tent was between the start-finish line and the first turn, so we had a good vantage point for the race.

Petty did lead for a few laps but a wreck on lap 170 ended his day 30 laps before the finish. That didn't end our day. Five hours later we were still stuck in the tent as the traffic gridlock prevented anyone in our part of the infield from moving. My thoughts on the Daytona 500 were centered on the difficulty in seeing much more than the cars streaking by in front of us and the fact we were there for nearly 12 hours just to watch a race that lasted less than three. I wasn't that impressed with the entertainment return for the effort we invested.

By the time we got back to New Jersey it was time to get out on the NHRA tour with Etchells' new Kendall car and Dunn's La Victoria Salsa dragster.

I was finally getting to be somewhat known to the other PR reps and the NHRA Media Relations staff. With my new laptop and portable printer I enjoyed coming up with witty or unusual things to put in pit-notes I would distribute in the media center. Before long, I had a nickname — "Pit Note Bob" — and it wasn't necessarily meant as a compliment.

Laptops and portable printers were still rare, meaning little actual work went on in the media center during a race. The vast majority of the effort was verbal, with reps whispering quotes or ideas to reporters. The rest of the time the place was little more than a social scene. When I showed up with my laptop, putting out notes multiple times each day, a few of the established PR people saw that as a shift in the way things were going to be done. My nickname came from comments like, "There he goes, putting out another pit note."

I'd also been following the exploits of an underfunded Funny Car driver from Essex, England, named Norman Wilding.

Norm had been the best Funny Car racer in Europe for a few years and he came to America to see if he could make it on the NHRA tour. The fact he often qualified for eliminations was a testament to his tuning and driving abilities as well as his budgetary discipline.

I introduced myself to him at a race early that year and found him to be charming and witty, with a very thick accent that made even normal conversation sound hilarious, in an authentic Monty Python sort of way.

Norm's strategy to stay on the tour was to qualify in as few runs as possible. It didn't matter to him if he got in 16th, he just wanted to get in the show to get a check. His austere budget allowed him to make the next race if he got that check. He'd usually have to sit out a race or two if he failed to qualify.

In addition, he'd figured out one thing about racing on Sunday. If he were to somehow win in round one it would cost him more to race in round two than the correlating increase in purse money. It was, for a guy like him, a losing proposition to win the opening round. So like any good entertainer he decided to make the fans happy before running the round and most likely losing. He was the master of the monster burnout.

I saw him carry most of those smoky burnouts well past half-track. I saw him take one to near the finish line. And, although he gave it a game effort from time to time, I never saw him win a round. It didn't matter to me. I thought he was fantastic and more than just a little marketable.

I brought him up to Bill, who made it abundantly clear he disliked the idea that we'd even consider adding him to our portfolio. He wanted no part of it.

By that time I'd finally gotten to the point where I had doubts regarding our business relationship, but I've never put that all on Bill. We just couldn't work together and were equally to blame for it. I probably needed thicker skin.

He needed my PR work, though, including the near constant flow of NHRA stuff as well as the NASCAR race recaps I was doing for the Kendall executives. For Kendall, I watched every race on TV, following along to write reports on Kyle Petty. So we found a way to work it out.

I would work from Harriman and whenever I finished my PR assignments I'd call Bill and we'd meet at a Dunkin' Donuts for a cup of coffee. I'd give him the work on a floppy disk and he'd head back to the office. I think it's safe to say we both liked it better that way.

The days seemed to pass slowly that spring. It wasn't a great way to work and it seemed to stretch out forever, but in reality we only did that routine for about two months. Finally, I told Bill I was going back to St. Louis to start my own agency. If he didn't want to work with Norm Wilding, I did and I'd represent him. He actually took it well, immediately hiring me back as a consultant. I'd work from St. Louis and FAX him what I wrote. If it was really important and time-sensitive, I'd FedEx a floppy to him. We hadn't heard of email yet.

One more time, I packed up a truck and headed home. At least Bill and I were up-front and honest about it. We were oil and water from the first day but he did a great job as a marketer and I felt I'd done a great job as a PR rep. In that regard, we were a good team. By working as a contractor for him, we both got what we needed.

I found an apartment a mile or so from Woodleaf Court. I figured it was going to be a rough go initially, in terms of income and expenses, and it would be nice to eat Skip's pot roast and his legendary chili.

Taffy supported me by taking her PR efforts to a new level. She bought a Mac Classic desktop, the little one-piece Macintosh computer with a nine-inch black & white screen. I would give her lessons on how to use it and I could come over every day and use it myself. That worked out great for both of us.

I took a huge chance and took out a big $12,000 loan in order to start RJW Marketing. My first client was Norm Wilding, who would receive the benefit of my hard work for no retainer. If I could put a sponsor deal together he agreed to pay me 20 percent of it. That's two or three times more than marketing people typically got. The pressure to succeed, however, was clearly on me.

I also talked with a Pro Stock driver named Lewis Worden. He lived south of St. Louis, about 30 minutes from me, and after one meeting he and his team owner, Steve Ash, agreed to put me on a monthly retainer. I'd do sponsor searches and pitches, and would help them generate more publicity by doing their PR work. My monthly fee was $600.

To supplement that, Bill was paying me $50 for every press release I wrote for his NHRA teams and another $50 for each Kendall update. The checks arrived in the mail right on time.

It was still a money-losing proposition but I was betting on myself. And boy, that was a bet with some seriously long odds.

Around this time, Norm had moved in with a lovely British girl he'd met down in Florida. I headed to Kissimmee for a week so my driver and I could work together on proposals, marketing materials, and creative ideas when we weren't sitting around a pool somewhere. That wasn't a bad thing for a guy coming from St. Louis during the winter.

The trip turned into two weeks and we came up with a lot of solid materials and landed some good meetings. We earned a 30-minute presentation with the head of marketing for Olive Garden, who liked both Norm and our concepts. The one thing that killed the idea was their inability to secure the rights to actually serve their delicious food at the races.

We had a few more meetings, but Norm's luck was running out. What parts he had left were getting pretty old. When things like crankshafts and cams get old they tend to break. Instead of making the show on one or two runs and then laying down a big smoky burnout on Sunday, he was tearing up a lot of parts and failing to qualify. He was so low on cash there were times when I gave him my Shell credit card so that he could tow his trailer to the next race.

My Pro Stock guys were doing a lot better but the sponsorship side of it was as hard as it ever was. We'd get a nibble, have some meetings, and something would always come up to dash the deal. They were in a tough spot, as well, because both Lewie and Steve worked full-time jobs. In order to provide a sponsor a full season's worth of racing against elite competition they'd both have to become full-time racers, so there was a bare minimum they could accept to make that work. It was always more than the prospective sponsors wanted to pay.

In late March I was sitting at my desk in my home office, staring at my bank statement. Almost all of the $12,000 loan had been spent getting up and running. My credit cards were maxed. My income was just enough to pay the rent. Skip was feeding me a lot and I still had the use of Taffy's new Mac, but I was running out of time and I was almost out of money.

Once again, the phone rang.

I'd gotten to know Doug Greenwalt when I was at Heartland Park. He was a young go-getter from Nebraska who had won awards for the great work he provided the Kansas City Royals as an intern.

Doug said he was currently working as a sales and marketing rep for the Kansas City Attack indoor soccer team. The Attack had come to town after the MISL and the Comets had folded and were part of the National Professional Soccer League (NPSL). They played at Kemper Arena.

Doug sounded like he was in a hurry, as if he was afraid I wouldn't want to talk with him.

"I know you're loving the racing stuff and you probably won't have any interest in what I'm about to say, but hear me out," he said. "This franchise can be really good but one of the co-owners is trying to be the GM and he can't do it. We're bleeding cash. I talked to the principal owner about you and he hopes that you'll at least consider the job. Is there any way in the world you'd come over here for an interview?"

I was staring at my bank statement and a lot of red ink at the moment he called. It was another one of those moments in my life that blindsided me at just the right time. I hesitated for a second, as if I was mulling it over, and then told Doug I'd be happy to at least listen to what they had to say. As we say in Latin, "Forwardis Plowicum."

I drove to Kansas City and they put me up in a nice historic downtown hotel. The team's principal owner, a gentleman by the name of Don Kincaid who had made millions in the busing business, did not come to the hotel for the meeting. Instead, he sent Tom Lynch and Jerry Herbert, two of his minority owners. Both gentlemen joined me in the hotel restaurant for dinner and they came armed with reams of budget reports. I hadn't expected them to open their books for me but they clearly wanted me to see how much work had to be done.

They'd lost a lot of money in the seven months they'd owned the team. To do that, they had broken a sacred law of sports marketing that dozens of indoor soccer teams before them had also violated. They gave away more tickets than they sold. A lot more.

The grim numbers on the report included a total of just under 300 season tickets. That was astonishing in a town where the MISL team, the Comets, had regularly packed Kemper. In the season that had just ended, they'd averaged selling about 1,500 tickets per game (including those season tickets) while they gave away close to 4,000. So, their average attendance was around 5,500 in a 14,000-seat arena, but only about 1,500 poor souls had actually paid good money to get in. What they paid was another question altogether.

Kansas City is a hotbed of youth soccer. They should've been averaging 2,000 per game just in group sales to those kids and their teams. The season ticket base was almost non-existent. Walk-up sales were just as bad. It was a catastrophe.

As I looked at the numbers I recognized a couple things right away. Kansas City loved soccer but the fans were ignoring this team. Plus, people who get free tickets are not likely to buy them in the future. Fixing it was going to take a lot of hard work.

Two days later Don Kincaid called me and offered me the job. He'd pay me only $30,000 per year but he'd supply me with a free car and an apartment. I figured I could make it work. With the free car, I could sell the one I owned and come close to paying back my loan.

I accepted. I was going back to the world of indoor soccer.

I sang it out loud. "I'm going to … Kansas City. Kansas City here I come!"

More Soccer Balls

It was time to relocate yet again but this time a professional moving company handled all my household goods while I packed as many clothes and personal items as possible into my car. I'd already heard from the Attack that I'd be spending the first 30 days in a suite at the same charming downtown hotel, while they looked for an apartment for me.

When I arrived in early April my first meeting was a social one. Team owner Don Kincaid and his wife Patty hosted me at their beautiful home, not far from Country Club Plaza. How beautiful and upscale was the Kincaid manse? George Brett lived in the same neighborhood.

We only talked business for a short while. Don had an afternoon full of meetings with the entire ownership group set for the next day so our time at his house was meant as a casual gathering, in order for us to mutually get to know each other. After a couple of drinks and a long spirited conversation, which covered all sorts of topics, Don smiled broadly and said to Patty, "This is what we need," as he nodded toward me. "Patty, I just wanted to spend some time getting a feel for this guy and he passes the test with flying colors." That was nice to hear.

I awoke early on my first morning and headed for Kemper Arena, carrying my briefcase while wearing a suit and tie. I did not have to enter anyone's home or go to my mom's house to use the computer.

I walked into the employee entrance, strolled past the Kemper management office, and took a left down a long interior concourse that circled the building. Just a few yards ahead were the offices of the Kansas City Attack. The club's 1993 NPSL championship trophy was the first thing I saw as I walked through the door.

The receptionist showed me to my office and I was pleased with its executive look. A large desk, built-in cabinets, drawers, and a credenza filled the room but the dusty and disheveled look of the place indicated the possibility that no one really cared a new general manager was arriving. There was no getting around the obvious fact I'd have to energize and motivate whatever staff members I planned to keep.

That first morning was a "get-to-know-you" series of individual meetings with the staff. Within three hours, I got a feeling for our first big challenge. Everyone seemed excited and motivated to do the best possible job in a variety of roles but not one of them said, "I'm a born salesperson and I can't wait to sell tickets."

Doing in-game promotions is fun. Arranging and playing the game music is fun. Doing PR and promoting the team is fun. The team's successful summer youth-soccer camps were coming up soon, and managing those camps was certainly fun. Selling tickets, whether they're group blocks or individual season-tickets, is generally not fun unless your genetic makeup includes that rare strand of DNA that makes a person love the sales process. Nobody in the office really came across as a sales-oriented person. If we were going to survive, that would have to change.

That afternoon I headed to Shawnee, the suburb where Don and his ownership partners had their offices. He'd made a lot of money in the busing business and his story was a great example of entrepreneurial spirit and the rewards that can come from risk. While attending college, Don took a part-time job as a school bus driver. In the mid-70s, with just $400 in the bank, he took out a Small Business Association loan and bought the company. By the early '90s, School Services & Leasing was one of the largest school bus companies in America, with 4,000 employees. Don had also branched out with Kincaid Coach Lines, a luxury charter bus company.

When Don sold School Services for a bit over $200 million, he had the wherewithal to commit to projects that were important to him. And with seven children in the Kincaid household, soccer had become a central part of their lives. At the same time, the Atlanta Attack indoor team had relocated to Kansas City to replace the defunct Comets but ownership was shaky and the team's finances were a mess. Don saw it as his civic duty to purchase the Attack and keep indoor soccer in town. He did so in late 1993, a mere month before the season started and a year before my arrival. Of that eleventh-hour purchase he said, "Why did I buy a failing soccer team? Because my kids wanted me to. Seriously. This is for them and all the other soccer families in Kansas City."

Don was under no illusion the Attack would generate income and he had the financial resources to fund the operation for a good length of time, but the losses in his first year were staggering. They were a body blow even to a man who had just sold his private company for $200 million. He'd made it clear that it was my job to stem the bleeding, if not stop it completely.

At our first meeting in his Shawnee office we sat at the conference table with no agenda. I'd already met Tom Lynch and Jerry Herbert at my initial interview a few weeks earlier and at the Shawnee meeting I also got to know Dennis Shaw, who had been the de facto general manager prior to my hiring. Don kicked things off by asking, "Tell us your philosophy about running this franchise."

I spoke for the next hour. They asked a few questions, but mostly they listened.

I began by telling them I'd become a disciple of Jon Spoelstra, who was widely considered a genius when it came to turning failing sports franchises into models of success. With the Portland Trail Blazers and New Jersey Nets, he took organizations that were nearly laughingstocks and turned them into league leaders in attendance, promotions, and revenue.

His approach was simple although it ran contrary to what other general managers had been doing in the NBA (and some other sports) for years. He believed tickets must have consistent value. Period.

Franchise owners have egos. They also hate to be embarrassed by lousy attendance. Therefore, they'd instruct their staffs to lower prices at random times, create a variety of discount programs, or give the tickets away if they had to — all in the false hope those folks would later buy full-priced tickets. It was a fool's errand.

Spoelstra came to Portland and confronted just such a scenario. His first goal was value. To get there he had to clean up the ticket sales process. Tickets would range in price, of course, as they do in any arena, but the tickets at each level had to cost a specific amount. No longer would the poor soul who paid face value for an upper level seat be surrounded by people who had gotten in free, or found a "Buy One, Get One Free" coupon in the paper. Everyone would pay the same amount.

He then stunned the league by increasing the price of some of the best seats in the house, at floor level. The seats were already expensive and they had not be selling well in recent years. Instead of lowering the price of those courtside seats, he raised it by a considerable amount. Those seats now had a different perceived value, literally because they were so expensive.

He made sure the customer service for those prestige seats broke new ground as well, and before long they were sold out. Not long after that the entire arena would consistently be sold out. I gobbled up every bit of Jon Spoelstra advice I could find. It all made perfect sense to me.

And the best thing about Spoelstra's approach was that it wasn't a theory. It wasn't even subject to debate. It had been implemented with his teams and it was proven to work.

The next concept on which I attempted to sell the group was the theory of A, B, and C games. It was an important concept for a sport like indoor soccer. The Attack would play 20 home games at Kemper, and while some of them were on weekends they couldn't all be on those prime dates. The Attack shared the building with the Kansas City Blades of the International Hockey League and the Blades were considered the primary tenant at Kemper. They got first pick on the dates. The Attack was left with whatever the Blades (or concert promoters) left them.

Indoor soccer had always been a game that appealed to a young demographic. So young, in fact, a big percentage of the sport's most avid and loyal fans could not drive themselves to the arena nor could they afford to buy tickets for themselves. They were kids. Who played soccer.

With that in mind, Friday and Saturday night games were the team's best options. They were the A games. Sundays or holidays weren't nearly as good, because there would likely be school the next morning. They were typically B games. Weeknights were C games. They would always be a tough sell.

As I explained to Don and his associates, "With the staff we have, we need to concentrate at least 75 percent of our group sales focus and advertising spending on those A games. With that kind of effort we can take a crowd of 4,500 and turn it into 6,500 or more. Twenty percent of our effort can be aimed at the B games. We might be able to increase group sales enough to turn 3,500 into 4,500. You have to be willing, though, to bite the bullet on the C games. If you put the same sales effort into a C game as you did an A game, you'll be lucky to go from 2,500 to 2,800 fans. It will be ugly on those Tuesday nights in January but we just have to maximize the better dates. When that buzz gets going in town, that the Attack put 8,000 into Kemper last Friday, the other games will increase as well."

They all nodded. They all thought it was a bold approach. Time would tell if they could keep biting the bullet if the weeknights looked atrocious. They were, after all, owners and investors. It was real money — their real money. And, during the prior season, they'd already established a track record of padding the gate by giving a lot of tickets away.

During the upcoming 1994-95 season, stretching from late October to mid-March, we'd have seven weeknight games. We'd also play at home on eight Sundays. That meant 15 of our 20 home games were either C or B games. We played a grand total of five games on either a Friday or Saturday night. This was clearly not going to be easy.

To make the team's schedule even more of a challenge there was this thing called the American Royal, one of the largest livestock shows in the country. It took over Kemper and its support buildings for nearly a month, forcing the Attack and the Blades to stay on the road while the cows, horses, and sheep were in town.

We would open the season on the road, in Milwaukee on Friday, October 28. The next night, we'd open at home against St. Louis, on October 29. Our next home game would be on a Sunday. As in Sunday, November 27. From just before Halloween to just after Thanksgiving, we'd be gone. And with luck, not forgotten.

After the home opener, the players would have to deal with games in Wichita, Detroit, Chicago, Detroit again, and Cleveland, before coming back to Kemper to play Dayton. I'd never seen anything like it.

After those initial rounds of meetings it was time to get to work. Back at the arena, I called a staff meeting and laid out my vision, including the A, B, and C games, the need for professionalism, and the absolute necessity of actively selling tickets. We'd dress the part, act the part, and work like pros. There was no other path to success.

The sales room within the Attack's office featured five cubicles and a large white dry-erase board. On that board we would write each sales person's name and track the tickets they had sold, on a daily basis. On the far right side of the board we drew a tall thermometer, marked off by increments of 100 season tickets. The goal was to get the red ink in that thermometer all the way up past 1,000. They had sold just under 300 the year before.

We couldn't start group sales until we had the full official league schedule but I wanted everyone in the sales room to start pitching season tickets immediately. At the time, we didn't know the dates for our complete schedule, but we knew we had 20 games to sell as a package.

I also instituted a variation on the season ticket. Instead of buying a set number of seats to all 20 home games, fans could buy a 20-coupon "Flex Plan" and have the option to use those coupons in any way they wanted. They could bring a group of 20 to one game or go to all 20 games by themselves. The Flex Plan was popular right out of the gate.

My PR director was a smart guy named Tyler Cundith. He'd come from Johnson County Community College and I could tell in our first meeting he knew what he was doing. I already knew Doug Greenwalt was sharp but the rest of the men and women in the sales room were mysteries to me. They mostly shared a soccer background, which would be a good thing for networking when it came to group sales with local soccer clubs, but none of them had shown much in terms of results in their first year.

Don had let me know that he would allow me to fire the whole staff if I wanted to, or as he put it, "Blow it up and start over." I had considered that but I decided to give this group a chance. They might just need better leadership. I actually had to fight him on the subject, just a bit, but he deferred to my judgment.

My game operations guy, Jacques Tournoy, was by all accounts really good at putting on "the show" that every home game had to be. He showed me his game scripts, in which every detail of the behind-the-scenes operation was spelled out, minute by minute, and they were terrific. He'd never been pushed to sell, though, and I felt it was a waste of intelligent resources to have him not pitching in while everyone else teamed up on the phones. He agreed to make his share of the sales calls, and I appreciated that. People were going to have to get out of their comfort zones to make it work. The entire staff knew I was evaluating them on a daily basis and changes would be made if results were not what we were looking for.

As the GM I only was responsible for the business operation. Our head coach, a great guy named Zoran Savic, would be in charge of player personnel, contracts, scouting, and the playing of the actual sport. It was key for Zoran and me have to have a tight relationship, and we soon had that.

Among the sales reps it was clear we had a wide variety of talent and dedication in the room, but just by looking at the numbers I could see we had one rep who was, by far, the most successful. He sold nearly as many group tickets as the rest of the staff combined, but he did it working at his own pace, working his own hours. His peers in the room just didn't have his contacts or his soccer relationships. Such a thing can create a bit of conflict in the office.

"Look," I told Don, "he's by far the best sales guy, and it's not even close. It's going to be on me to work with him on his style but I'm not going to say goodbye to thousands of group tickets just to make the rest of the staff feel better. I want them to be jealous. I want them to compete with his numbers. I'm keeping him."

While we waited for the schedule from the league office it was time to leap into action with our summer camps. Each camp took place for a week, at different parks and fields all around the area. Each day featured a full six hours of coaching and training, all done by the Attack players themselves. It was a terrific program and very successful. It gave me a sense that there really was a fan base out there. We just had to reach them.

And our players were the greatest bunch of ambassadors a GM could want. In total, as a group, they'd make more than 300 personal appearances per year, all free of charge. Every Monday, they'd get a packet outlining every place they had to go, when they had to be there, and what to take. All of them pitched in and they were fantastic when they got to their destinations.

Our mascot was popular, as well. Fuzzy the Attack Cat was a big smiling feline wearing an oversized Attack uniform. Kids absolutely adored him and for good reason. The guy inside the suit was hilarious, and Fuzzy could put any crowd into stitches. He made many of the appearances with the players.

My determination to have the entire organization act and look first-class was tested early in the summer. Four of our guys were supposed to hold a quick clinic and autograph session in a soccer-crazy suburb. Somehow, signals got crossed and they missed it.

When the youth league director called and told me about it, he was fairly apoplectic. I did my best to calm him down, apologizing profusely and repeatedly, then finally I said, "I'm going to bring the entire team down to your field next Saturday, in full uniform. They'll put on a two-hour clinic and sign autographs for every kid. We'll stay until the last family goes home." He thought that sounded good.

I told Don about it, and he agreed the whole team should go. He said, "I'll just grab one of the school buses and we'll all go together." I said, "Don, get us one of the luxury charter buses. I want us to look like big leaguers when we arrive. Big-league athletes don't ride on a school bus." Despite the fact Don was involved in the ownership of Kincaid Coach Lines he would have to pay to rent that bus. He could've borrowed a school bus for free. He agreed to do it and we made a splash when we showed up in the big bus. The kids mobbed the players as they stepped off the coach.

In addition to the camps, as well as my own appearances at local business meetings, Rotary Clubs, and banquets, I also dove into the deep end on the sponsor front. I tried to pitch at least six new deals each week and we were successful in landing a bunch of them. Our biggest sponsor was Thriftway, a local grocery chain, but we also had promotional deals and signage sponsorships with the likes of Budweiser, Sprint, Wendy's, Olive Garden, Western Auto, Boatman's Bank, Mr. Goodcents Subs, Eagle Snacks, and many more. On top of those, we secured a large number of trade agreements with radio stations, cleaners, medical clinics, dentists, and yes, apartment complexes. We finally landed that just as my 30 days at the hotel were coming to an end. Zoran got a free apartment on the north side of town and I landed one south of downtown, in Roeland Park.

Just when I finally had an apartment I also finally had my company car. It was a new, bright white Toyota Camry. Within an hour, it was festooned with Attack decals on each door.

As for my weekly schedule of business meetings, speaking engagements, and other social gatherings, I lost track of how many people at those events came up to me after I had spoken, and said, "Thanks for coming. That was great. I can't tell you how many times my kids have begged me to take them to an Attack game."

I'd look them right in the eye and say, "Well. I think it's time that you did." I built that into my typical speech, telling each group that story hoping they could relate to it.

The work wasn't as manic as it had been when we started the St. Louis Storm right before the season started but I tried to treat each day as something precious, and instill that philosophy in my staff. With our home opener set for October 29 we only had so many days to sell, pitch, promote, and get ready. Every day wasted was a day lost.

As part of the NPSL we enjoyed a league-wide sponsorship from adidas, which supplied us with home and away uniforms, travel bags, sweat suits, and practice gear. The adidas director of soccer promotions called to welcome me not long after I started and he treated me with such class and generosity while I was with the team I wore nothing but adidas for many years after.

In terms of our uniforms, we had the Attack logo on the front of our home whites but I wanted to take a page out of the baseball book by having the words KANSAS CITY in arched block print, on the front of our blue road uniforms. That went over big with everyone and the Kansas City Chamber of Commerce commended us for it. I felt a little sense of pride every time I'd accompany the team on road trips to Wichita and St. Louis, which were bus trips, and I'd see them take the field in those road jerseys.

With all of that going on I had another promotional target in my sights. The person I had to pitch it to was Don Kincaid.

I called on him at his office and laid it out. "Look," I said. "I was working for this professional drag racing team in the Pro Stock class, with a driver named Lewis Worden. They don't have a primary sponsor, so it just says 'Ash & Worden' on the side of their car. I want the Attack to sponsor them when the NHRA tour comes to Topeka next month. Our logo will replace their names on the doors."

Don loved the idea. We agreed on a price and I called Lewie. The answer was an instantaneous "You bet!"

For the Topeka race, Lewis Worden would drive the Kansas City Attack Pro Stock Oldsmobile. We got the biggest rock radio station in town to join in as an associate sponsor and earned more positive publicity out of that than any other promotion we did that summer.

On the day before the Ash & Worden team had to be in Topeka, they stopped at Kemper and we invited season-ticket holders and a bunch of youth soccer league-directors to stop by and see the Pro Stock car. It all went fabulously and in the end I had finally delivered a sponsorship to Lewis Worden and Steve Ash. It was just one race and it wasn't a huge check, but it was a check. It was my thank-you to them for standing by me so loyally when I represented the team.

At the race we set up a sales booth by the team's pit area, had staff members take turns putting on the Fuzzy mascot suit (it was brutally hot all weekend) and had a few players in uniform, signing autographs and mingling with NHRA fans. We even purchased a 10-foot-wide sign on the drag strip barrier wall right in front of the main grandstand, with our home-opener date and our phone number in big bold print.

The event in Topeka was terrific. The fans loved Fuzzy and lined up for player autographs and Zoran and his guys enjoyed the racing. I was interviewed by two television stations and two radio outlets. It was a heck of a way spend a midsummer weekend, as we continued to get ready for the season.

We were all working hard, putting in long hours and dealing with all the stress of not only being ready but also being successful by the opener. One evening, after I'd moved into my apartment (seeing my furniture again for the first time in a month) I returned home after a long day at the arena and sat down on my sofa to relax for a minute. I still had on my suit and tie. Seven hours later, I woke up. It was 2 a.m. and I hadn't moved.

One ongoing item on my pressing agenda was the hiring of a new radio voice for the Attack. There were some gentle suggestions from the ownership group that I should hire a very high-profile guy to do the play-by-play, to gain us some extra credibility in the market.

My feelings on that had changed since I hired Kevin Slaten in St. Louis, to do the P.A. announcing. I said, "I want a good announcer, but I want a guy who lives, eats, and breathes this team. I want him to be absolutely passionate and hungry. We'll get more good out of that than we would out of a high-priced celebrity."

We put the word out that we were looking for audition tapes and they began to arrive shortly thereafter. I listened dutifully to the first few tapes but nothing was getting me very excited. I then popped in a cassette that sounded exactly like what I was after. The announcer's name was Bob Rennison, and on the tape he was calling a Kansas City Blades hockey game. He was nearly flawless, his voice was clear, he enunciated well during a fast-paced game (not an easy thing to do) and his call clearly indicated his own excitement.

I figured if he could call a hockey game he could certainly call indoor soccer. The two sports were nearly identical in terms of flow. And, if he was calling a Blades game he must already be fairly accomplished.

I called Bob in for an interview and was pleased to see he was just a normal suburban husband and father, not a local celebrity or a sparkling TV personality. I told him I liked his tape and was impressed that he had done a Blades game. He said, "I have to be honest. I sat up in the top rows of the arena and taped that myself. If you hire me here, it will be my first professional announcing job and I'll do anything to be the best announcer in the league."

I stopped listening to tapes. I had my man. Bob Rennison would be the play-by-play announcer for the Kansas City Attack. On top of that, he'd be a tireless promoter and ambassador for the team and his everyman personality would resonate with our fans.

As the summer concluded our whiteboard in the sales room showed some solid progress. We had just cleared 900 full season tickets, our group sales for the opener were coming along well, and it felt like there was a buzz beginning to build in town.

Group sales can be handled a lot of different ways but we concentrated on making it as easy as possible for soccer teams, Boy Scout troops, and other organizations. Our sales reps would meet with the heads of the groups and discuss how many tickets they thought they could buy, at the group price. Rather than forcing them to buy that number we would consign a slightly larger amount of tickets to them, with no firm obligation.

Sometimes they'd call back and indicate they needed more. Sometimes they returned a percentage of the tickets if they couldn't sell them all. They'd have to do that a number of days before the game so that we could put the tickets back into the system.

Another way indoor soccer teams sell group tickets is to allow youth teams to play on the arena floor before the game, even before the gates opened. All they had to do was apply for a slot and buy their own tickets. We were booking those slots heavily and the home opener was filled within a day after the positions were offered.

We had a ticketing room in the office as well, with a glass window fans could approach to buy individual game tickets. In that room was the main ticketing computer and I would check it regularly to see how many individual tickets we were selling for the October 29 opener. There was a nice flow to it.

We anticipated having a good walk-up sale for the opener and with that in mind I hired a troupe of clowns, stilt walkers, and jugglers to entertain the fans who might have to wait in a long line outside, in the elements, at the main Kemper Arena box office.

We also needed a dance team and when local choreographer Alisa Clevenger came to my office with an offer to put such a group together, I said yes but I had a request. I'd agree to let her have a small dance group made up of girls her age who had been dancing together for years, but only if our main dance group was different. I wanted our main team to be full of cute, adorable, little girls. Eight to 12 years old would be the target.

I felt an adult group might not appeal to some of our younger fans and our older fans would expect them to dance as well as the Laker girls. If the young group made a few mistakes, they'd still be adorable. Maybe even more adorable.

Alisa set up a cattle-call audition at a local banquet hall and Doug Greenwalt and I acted as two of the four judges. The girls stole our hearts and so many of them could really dance I was instantly optimistic about it. Within days we had our dance team, made up of 18 precious little dancers. They were fantastic. I nearly tore my rotator cuff patting myself on the back for that idea.

Alisa's older group, it turned out, was also terrific. We had one-two punch of pure awesome when it came to dancers, and no other team in the league had the level of talent we had.

Back at the arena we had a new Astroturf floor, thanks to the Great Flood of '93, which inundated Kemper along with a lot of other parts of Kansas City. Having a brand-spanking-new floor allowed us the luxury of selling major ad space on the Astroturf, and Thriftway, Western Auto, and The Kansas City Star newspaper all stepped up. We were looking more big league by the day.

Indoor soccer is played on Astroturf that's laid over the hockey ice while the boards and glass stay in place everywhere but in the goal area. Indoor soccer goals are placed flush into the boards as opposed to hockey goals which are on the playing surface, out in front of the boards. That required the Kemper staff to remove a few sections of the hockey boards and glass to install our 14 x 8-foot goals and nets.

With one goal being right in front of the access tunnel that led to the offices and locker rooms under the stands, and which the Zamboni used during hockey games, we had a large open area there. I knew the promotion for which I wanted to utilize that space.

I contacted our favorite hard-rock radio station and we put together our "Couch Potato" promotion, sponsored by The Rock, 98.9 FM. We obtained a gaudy overstuffed sofa and placed it next to a lamp on a riser right behind the goal. The radio station would select the winners with a call-in promotion and those couch seats would end up being prized possessions. The campaign was a huge success and I'll admit I encouraged the winners to razz the opposing goalkeeper, who was just a few feet away and separated by only a net. When Victor Nogueira of the Milwaukee Wave got so rattled he threw his water bottle into the net right in front of them, I knew I had a real asset.

I also copied an intermission promotion I'd seen at another indoor game. We bought eight small parachutes, the kind of pilot chute that jumpers use to pull the main chute out of the pack, and anchored them with mini-soccer balls. We then tied them to the metal catwalk that spanned the playing surface just under the ceiling, high above the field. During the intermission after the first quarter one lucky fan would get a chance to push a Thriftway grocery cart around the floor in an effort to catch all eight parachutes as they fell. And yes, we randomly alternated which chutes we untied to keep them running back and forth. It never failed to get the crowd roaring. And to make it rock a little more, Jacques played The Gap Band's hit "You Dropped A Bomb On Me" while the contestants were running around.

On the boards, all around the field, the Blades had affixed decals for their advertisers and sponsors. We'd have to create our signs on vinyl and velcro them to the boards, covering the Blades sponsors. I'd been told they would look fine at the start of a game but as players would collide or passes would ricochet off the signs, they'd sometimes come loose and flop on the floor. We made sure we had staffers at the ready, to run out there and fix them after the whistle stopped play.

In terms of the game on the field, I was fully conversant in indoor soccer and still loved it. The game had a flow just like hockey with the five field players playing short shifts before jumping over the boards to be replaced. That allowed them to sprint the entire time they were on the field, which kept the action going nonstop.

There was no offsides rule in the indoor game, so players could cherry pick at the offensive end if they wanted but most guys were solid two-way players. They had to be with only five field players out there at once. Those who were adept at passing knew there was actually a sixth field player available. That player was everywhere but never moved. That player was the boards. Players could pass the ball to themselves or a teammate by deking a defender one way while hitting the ball off the boards the other way. The game had constant flow and with the goals flush against the glass most missed shots rebounded right back out. I'm not sure you could've convinced me to be a goalkeeper. Those guys were always under siege.

Over the years, the MISL and the NPSL had messed around with the scoring system many times. In the beginning, the indoor game used standard soccer scoring with each goal being worth one point. By 1994 the NPSL was using a system more like basketball, and the fans seemed to like it. A standard goal was worth two points but a three-point arc was painted on the floor, 45 feet from the goal. Just like in hoops, if you buried one from "downtown" you put three points on the board.

As the end of October came into sight, I felt really good about all of it. The team flew out, with Bob Rennison in tow, for their opener in Milwaukee. That night, I grabbed a beer and flopped on the sofa in my living room to listen to the game on the radio.

Bob went on the air right on time, at 7 p.m. The Milwaukee Wave then proceeded to stretch their pregame introductions and pyrotechnics out for 20 solid, interminably painful minutes. That forced my rookie play-by-play guy to stretch and ad-lib to fill the void while the home team tossed any semblance of an on-time start out the window. Bob did an admirable job, but I was none too pleased with the Wave's lack of sportsmanship and punctuality. They'd introduced the Attack first, which was standard procedure, and that meant their big show and long delay did two things. It left Bob struggling to fill the gap on the radio while it also left our players standing on the field, cooling off after they'd just gotten warmed up. I would not forget this.

We lost a tough one in Milwaukee that night, falling to the Wave 9-7. It was time for our home opener.

The following day I arrived at the arena before 8 a.m., excited to open the doors that night to see if anyone would walk in. We put our velcro signs on the boards and we watched the Kemper crew put down the floor and insert the goals. I peeked at the ticket computer on an hourly basis, and helped answer the phones in the box office, taking credit card numbers and stuffing the tickets into envelopes for the will-call window.

My clowns and jugglers arrived. The players nervously got dressed and kicked a ball around the hallway outside the locker room. The St. Louis Ambush (who had replaced the defunct Storm) arrived and did their pregame routines in the visitors' locker room.

The attending media and my staff enjoyed our pre-game dinner provided by Olive Garden, a team sponsor. Finally, at 6 we opened the gates. There were fans already waiting in line.

Around 6:30, as I nervously paced around the arena to fix problems and keep an eye on things, Don and Patty Kincaid approached me in the concourse with wide smiles on their faces. At the same time the head of operations for Kemper joined us. She said, "Congratulations to all of you. This is the real deal. And traffic is backed up for a mile getting into the parking lots."

When it was time to introduce the teams, we brought out the Ambush first and I'd made it clear to our game operations people that we needed to start on time. I wasn't going to do to St. Louis what Milwaukee had done to us.

Before we introduced the Attack we dimmed the lights and showed a brief video Jacques and I had created. The scoreboard at Kemper had rudimentary video capability but we took advantage of it by creating a very funny piece featuring all sorts and types of attacks. We had clips of the Marx Brothers, the Three Stooges, a shot of elephants stampeding, and various old black & white films of troops or animals sprinting across open fields. Then, a static shot of an upturned thumbtack. And my voice, calmly saying "A tack." I was glad to hear that get a laugh. Finally, we cut to one of a number of different closing videos we'd accumulated. This one was a clip of the Attack Pro Stock Oldsmobile doing its burnout in Topeka with the team logo clearly visible on the doors. Then it cut to a close-up of Lewis Worden in his pit saying, "Aw, enough of all that. Let's bring out the Attack!" The crowd went nuts.

One by one, the players ran past me in the tunnel as they dashed out onto the field to start the home season. Brian Haynes, Goran Hunjak, Jeff Rogers, Kevin Koetters, Eddie Carmean, Nate Houser, Warren Westcoat, Wes Wade, with his long flowing locks of curly blond hair, and the rest of the team. We introduced every player on the 16-man roster, and the trainer, and head coach Zoran Savic. Then a singer performed the national anthem. Finally, the referee blew his whistle and play began. We were officially a soccer team playing in front of 9,000 screaming fans.

And we started the game right on time. 7:05 p.m. on the dot.

We lost that night, in a 10-9 heartbreaker, but we'd drawn a great crowd and everyone paid a fair price to get in. Our paid attendance was over 8,000. In addition to what we sold, we'd given away fewer than 1,000 tickets.

After the game I was exhausted but pleased. From the players to my staff, everyone gave it a 100 percent effort. I was proud of everyone, including myself.

Zoran then took the team out on their American Royal-induced road trip while we worked diligently in an office that began to smell more and more like a barn as the animals overtook the Kemper complex. The team managed to go 3-2 during the month of road games and we returned to Kemper on the Sunday night after Thanksgiving. That may have been listed as a B game on my schedule, but the combination of the holiday a few days earlier and the restart of school on Monday, kept our group sales low. We only drew about 3,200 that night.

As the season went on we got into our routines and pretty much had all of it down pat. Some nights were great, others were painful. It was exactly what I'd predicted when I presented the concept to Don, about the A, B, and C games. We had eight games on Sunday nights and I quickly learned those were barely better than the Tuesdays, especially in the dead of winter.

On Sunday, December 18, it was cold and snowy. The Cleveland Crunch were in town to play us, and we admitted exactly 2,672 hardy souls into the building. We won the game, in a 17-4 rout, but after the game Don came into our office and stood in the reception area so I could hear him ask my PR guy Tyler a question. He said, "Tyler, just hypothetically, if a bomb had blown up in the arena tonight, how many people would it have killed?"

Tyler said, "Are you including the players and vendors?"

"No, just fans," Don replied.

Tyler said, "About 2,600."

The bullet was already getting hard for him to bite.

Those weeknights were tough. But, the win over Cleveland launched the team on a 10-game winning streak and by the time it ended in mid-January the crowds were getting incrementally bigger. When we beat Wichita 19-4 on January 15, another Sunday night game, we put 4,400 in the place. That still wasn't what we wanted but it was way better than 2,600. And we were still charging consistent prices and giving away as few tickets as possible.

During one of the many weeknight games I inadvertently learned a customer service lesson I'd never forget. There were plenty of empty seats but one married couple found themselves stuck in a full row, with groups of four on either side of them. So, they decided to move back one row, into a row of completely empty seats. The Kemper Arena usher came down and told them they couldn't do that. They'd have to sit in their assigned seats.

After a few minutes of trying to talk common sense with the usher the wife basically blew up at him. She and her husband stormed up the steps and demanded to see someone from the team. I was called, on the walkie-talkie, and I met them in the concourse.

The woman began to calm down but she and her husband were still very upset and incredulous about the ridiculous demands the usher had made. I handed them tickets to my personal seats, right on the glass, and asked for their phone number so that I could call them the next day to see how they enjoyed it.

Before I did that on Monday, I talked to the head of Kemper operations and she told me, "Well, we tried to empower the ushers to make common sense decisions but they didn't seem to have any common sense. We had nothing but problems. So, we made it simple. We told them to follow a set of rules and nothing else. I promise we'll hold another meeting and try to keep this from happening again."

I called the couple and they were very happy with that news. They also loved watching the game from my seats. They asked if I'd come to their office for a meeting, because they wanted to be involved with the team. Once I got there, I discovered what they did for a living.

They owned a computer consulting business, but before that venture they had developed some other popular software and had sold that company for a lot of money. They said, "Can we give the team $45,000? We'd just like to help in some way." I said they certainly could, but maybe we could come up with something better. And that we did, for the following season.

They sponsored a new "Student Honor Roll" program we quickly devised. We'd do all the leg work meeting with all the Kansas City school districts, and each school would give their best students two tickets to a preselected "Student Honor Roll Night" game during the '95-'96 season. The couple bought every ticket. At full price.

I told this story to my staff, in great detail. The lesson was this: Treat every fan as if they're a millionaire. You never know which ones might actually be just that.

On February 10, we finally got to play another Friday night game. We beat Harrisburg 21-13 to improve our record to 21-9 and 6,854 fans showed up to cheer for us. It was getting better, but we really needed more of those Friday dates. Unfortunately, we only had one left. We beat the Chicago Power 21-4 in front of 4,865 fans to improve our record to 27-10.

On March 4 we actually got to play on a Saturday night. It was one of only two Saturday nights we had all year, with the other having been the home opener, and it was one for the ages.

We had a nice crowd of 6,182 in the house, but we were trailing the Baltimore Spirit with just a couple of minutes left to play. The score was 10-6, and the clock was ticking. Zoran pulled his goalie and put Jim Schwab on the floor as the sixth attacker. Right after that we scored a standard goal, worth two points, with 45 seconds left. It was 10-8.

As the clock ticked down under 15 seconds, and the crowd stood, Schwab left the goal empty and moved forward to position himself just outside the 3-point arc, where Wes Wade found him with a masterful pass. Schwabbie never hesitated. He one-timed it with a slicing blast past the diving Baltimore keeper into the lower right corner, and the crowd went ballistic. A five-point comeback in the final 45 seconds gave us an 11-10 win. Outside the locker room after the game, Zoran spotted me and we shared a hug. I congratulated him and he gave the compliment right back to me, saying, "Bob, that crowd won us the game. They were amazing. This thing is really turning into something big."

We were headed to the playoffs with a 29-11 mark. The year before the Attack had finished 14-26. It was the biggest turnaround in league history. Zoran and the players earned the credit for that.

Before we opened round one against Milwaukee, Jacques and I huddled with a TV producer to create a new intro video. It would turn out to be epic, and a bit of payback. Just a bit.

We took Van Halen's song "Right Now" and edited a highlight video to it in the same style as the one Van Halen had made for MTV. Various highlights would be interspersed with large block-print cut-aways, with phrases like "RIGHT NOW, would be a good time to stand up" or "RIGHT NOW, would be a good time to yell."

The song, and our video, clocked in at just about five and a half minutes. Can you tell where I'm going with this?

Before game one, P.A. announcer Ed Bishop introduced the Wave at the normal time. Then we turned the arena lights off.

The opening piano notes of the song filled the arena. The video played and the fans began to stand and cheer. It grew to a crescendo when the final highlight clip featured the two-point and three-point goals, in succession, from our huge comeback over Baltimore. By then, the crowd was going bananas.

We beat Milwaukee, and swept them out of the playoffs in three games. On the morning after the first win, however, I got a call from the commissioner's office. It was the league's director of operations.

He never uttered a calm word. He simply commenced with a tirade and he never let up for a full minute. I could sense how red in the face he must've been over the phone.

He lit into me, sputtering, "Coach Tozer, from the Wave, called me from the arena last night. He woke me up. He said you played a 15-minute video after you introduced his team and they had to stand around in the dark. I'm telling you right now, if you play that video again I'm personally assessing you a fine of $5,000. Do you hear me? I will not tolerate this. You can never do that again, and I'll never forget you did it."

Finally, when he either ran out of words or ran out of steam, I got a chance to reply. I said, "First of all, calm down. You're a raving lunatic. Secondly, the video was five and a half minutes long, not 15. Thirdly, on opening night back in October, the Wave left us standing on the field for 20 full minutes, and that left my rookie play-by-play guy on the air with no action to call. You can fine me $5,000 if you want. You can fine me $50,000 for all I care. Hell, you can fine me $500,000, but you won't get a penny out of me. You call Coach Tozer back and tell him they can stay in their locker room and walk out without any introductions, if they want. We're playing the video in game two."

I never got another call from the league office and I never got fined.

We then stretched our semifinal round, against St. Louis, to the final game. Don was even gracious enough to bring the whole front-office staff to St. Louis for all the road games, putting us up in the Marriott along with the team.

In the final game we were ahead through much of it, but the Ambush came back to win at the end in dramatic fashion. We were five minutes of good soccer away from playing for the championship. It was over, but it had been a great run. And it had been a lot of fun. We rode the bus back to Kansas City and took a few days off.

By advancing that far in the playoffs we shortened our off-season by close to a month. It was almost time for our 1995 summer camp season and when we returned to the office we diligently got to work on that. For the first time, we scheduled a one-week camp in Topeka and Don was nice enough to offer the six players assigned to that camp a chance to stay in a hotel. That extra hour of sleep would help them get through the week.

We changed radio stations for the next season, going from a hard-to-hear small station to one with a much bigger and better signal. Bob Rennison's voice would be resonating over multiple states. During that first year, when we'd played in St. Louis or Wichita, I rode the bus with the team and did color analysis next to Bob in the radio booth. It was great fun, and we had a fantastic rapport on the air.

For home games, when I'd be kept busy helping with game operations, we had a young man by the name of Sean Wheelock doing the color with Bob. He did a good job and right after the final playoff game he approached me about a different subject.

"Some friends of mine and I want to start a baseball team in the Kansas City Men's League," he said. "We're pretty good, and I know a couple of ex-Royals who said they might play. Maybe some other guys in the front office can play, too. Would you be willing to be the player-manager?"

I hadn't played in a couple of years and I was closing in on 40, but I said I'd think about it. When Sean told me that he and his buddies were getting together at a local park to "practice" I said I'd tag along.

To put it kindly, they were relatively terrible. They had a hard time just playing catch. Their idea of practice was throwing the ball up and hitting fly balls to each other since none of them could throw BP. Sean did say he had two other friends who were "awesome" but what I saw that day was a mess. And no, there were no ex-Royals interested in playing for us.

One of my sales guys, who knew the local Budweiser distributor, said he didn't want to play but he could get us free uniforms. Sean had a backer who would pay our league fee and the nightly umpire costs. Well, heck. If it was all free, maybe I could make something happen.

I went into Tyler's office and said, "Who do you still know with the baseball program at Johnson County Community College?" He said he knew everybody.

"Well, I need some help," I told him. I asked him if he could make a call to see if the coach knew of six or seven guys who would play on this summer team with me. I was desperate.

The next day Tyler handed me a slip of paper with the name Marc Venneman on it, along with a phone number. Marc had played at JCCC and then gone on to Avila College and played there. I called him and he was really friendly on the phone. He also sounded interested in playing. We decided to meet at a local batting cage to size each other up.

Marc was a great guy. And he was also a great player. We both committed to it and he went to work rounding up some ex-teammates from JCCC and Avila. When we all got together for a real practice I was happy to discover they were also great guys, and they could all play. And those other two guys Sean had, who were "awesome" were pretty good, too. We had about 12 guys and that was enough to play three games a week for a couple of months.

We gathered for our first game on a Saturday afternoon at Kansas City, Kansas Community College. Our team, officially known as the Kansas City Attack — even though our white uniforms with red pinstripes had "Budweiser" stitched on the front — was pretty good. Not as good as the Wizards, but close. It was real baseball.

I managed and played center field. Sean's buddies, with whom I'd "practiced" that first day, were not happy to see all of these strange guys with real skills. I put Sean in as the DH that first game and he went 0-for-4 with four strikeouts. The other guys watched. In good conscience, I couldn't play them. I honestly don't believe it would've been safe for them out there. If they watched and kept taking batting practice with us, there would come a day when we'd have some guys not show up and then they'd get their chance. And, no doubt, the ball would find them. It always does.

We were down a run in the bottom of the ninth when I came up with a man on. I felt pretty rusty in all facets of the game and hadn't put many good swings on the ball to that point, but I got lucky and crushed one that cleared the left-field fence by 20 feet. It was opening day for the Attack baseball team, and it was a walk-off winner. Doug Greenwalt played third admirably for a guy who had only played softball to that point. Marc Venneman played second and was, clearly, the best player on the field. Sean Wheelock never made contact, but he smiled all day. He just desperately wanted to play real baseball for the first time in his adult life.

We played all over the metro area that summer, night games during the week and broiling day games on Saturdays, and as we melded together as a team we got better and better. Sean and his buddies got in a few games but after a couple weeks one of them confronted me in the dugout and said, "This was our idea, and you're not letting us play. We want to play."

I told him I understood, but this wasn't Little League and they were completely over their heads at this level. I added that I'd totally understand if they wanted to quit. Two of them did. Sean stuck it out and finally had an at-bat in which he did not strike out, after 22 consecutive ones in which he did. I give him a lot of credit. He had the idea and he had the tenacity to give it everything he had. He loved wearing the uniform and he never grumbled. He just enjoyed being there and experiencing it. The guys on the team gave him a nickname. They called him "The Natural."

Marc could just flat hit. He batted from the left side and was a classic "slash" hitter who could spray line-drives all over the park and pop one deep when they came in on him. He was absolutely one of the best hitters I'd ever played with. I don't remember the exact numbers but I know he hit close to .450 that summer. I had the second-best average on the team, hitting around .330 with 10 home runs.

I also admired Marc's intellect and sense of humor. Before the season ended I asked him what his plans were after he graduated from Avila. He wasn't sure, so I offered him a job. During the 1995-96 season Marc would be my director of ticket operations. He was a real asset to the organization.

In the end, my game came back almost totally. My hamstrings were an issue, so I could rarely run as fast as I wanted, but my outfield play was good and I hit a lot of bombs. It was fun.

And we wrapped it up by winning the Kansas City Men's League Championship. We played a really good team from Olathe in the finals, squeaking out a win in Game 1. The next night we'd either win Game 2 for the trophy or have to play a doubleheader to decide it. The Olathe team was made up of guys still in college or just out and the pitcher in Game 2 was incredible. He had the nastiest slider I'd ever seen, and I had no chance against him. It was odd though, that none of us were worried about it. We knew we would beat them in the final game.

We did, and we were champs. It had been a fantastic and unexpected summer of baseball. It had also been my final summer of baseball. I would never play again.

Back at Kemper, we had some turnover in the front office. A couple of sales reps left to take, as they put it, "real jobs with actual salaries." In addition Jacques and our receptionist departed. Jacques admitted he really didn't like selling tickets, to which I replied, "I understand. I don't like it either." Tyler left, as well, to head back to JCCC to head up the Sports Information Department.

I held a string of interviews and added some outstanding new talent to the front office. Natalie Lutz was a fantastic PR pro and Elizabeth Ouseley hit the ground running as my game ops director. I promoted Doug to sales manager and he helped train what was nearly a full new staff. I could tell we were in great shape, in terms of the group, but we still had to sell those pesky tickets.

As the season approached, my top sales guy continued to be an enigma. He rarely worked the same number of hours as the rest of the group but he was again lapping them on the sales track. The rest of the group, by then, also included Bob Rennison. Being the ultimate team player, Bob offered to work in the sales room for the same commission as the rest of the group and he was my most dedicated rep.

Just two weeks before our opener it looked like we might end up with a sell-out on our hands because our group sales appeared to be amazing. Appearances can be deceiving, though, and this time they were. Kemper's capacity for soccer was about 14,800 and we'd been hinting to the media that we might sell out. At one point we actually had very few tickets left. Then four or five large groups brought back about 80 percent of the tickets we'd consigned to them, just days before the game.

We'd shot ourselves a bit in the foot. By telling the media we were close to a sell-out, we damaged our walk-up because fans didn't think tickets would be available. We still ended up with more than 10,000 folks in the building but we missed the sellout and that was a disappointment.

Zoran had once again assembled a great team and it was obvious we'd have a chance to go far in '95-'96. Bob was doing a terrific job on the radio, our promotions were rocking it, and we even had a few big crowds on some giveaway nights.

Our professionalism and look improved greatly when we hired a graphic artist named Carl Fowler to design our game program, media guide, and sales materials. We looked absolutely first-class.

Back at Kemper, Zoran had also signed a new goalkeeper, Bret Phillips. He was outstanding, and in tandem with Warren Westcoat it gave us a one-two punch in terms of keepers. No other team in the league had a pair of guys as good as ours, which was a very good thing considering the beating those guys took in goal.

I had an idea for our new keeper. I asked him if he'd consider changing his number if it would help me bring a big new sponsor to the team. He said he'd worn No. 1 his entire career but if it would help the organization he'd certainly consider it.

I then called the regional marketing office for Phillips 66 gas stations and asked for a meeting. My plan was to have Bret wear number 66. His last name would be right above the number on his back. If I could package that with a big promotion, a giveaway, and some advertising, I thought I might get $25,000 for the package. If it worked, I'd give Bret some of it for doing it. Goalkeepers can be as superstitious as any athlete, so changing numbers for a sponsorship was a big deal. I totally got that.

On the day of the meeting, I was walking out of the office when our receptionist took a call for me. I shook my head at her, and she said to the caller, "I'm sorry. Mr. Wilber is out of the office. Can I have him call you when he returns?"

She hung up and said, "Some guy named Whit Bazemore? Is that right? It was a bit of a strange name." I told her she got it right, and asked her to put his number on my desk.

On the way to Overland Park for the meeting, I was taken aback, flustered, confused, and surprised at myself. It was as if I was playing a role in a movie and now the script called for my character to make a rash, and possibly really odd, decision. It was surreal. I felt I had no control over what was about to happen.

I had a job I loved. I had taken the team to an entirely new level. I was respected in the business community and a popular guest speaker all around town. I was even a pretty good color analyst on the radio. And yet, in my head, I was nothing more than an actor with a script while some writer in another place was about to radically change my life. It was a complete out-of-body experience.

I don't even remember the meeting. My mind was elsewhere. I know, in the end, Bret didn't have to change numbers so the sponsorship never happened.

When I returned to the office, I went straight to my desk and called Funny Car driver Whit Bazemore. I'd gotten to know him when I was working for Bill Griffith, and then after I left Bill's company Whit had me come to a few races to help him with management and PR on a contract basis. I knew he wasn't calling me to ask for soccer tickets.

He told me that he'd just landed his first big sponsor, after years of pinching pennies and piecing smaller deals together. There was no denying Whit was a bulldog when it came to chasing sponsors. He was good at it but what made him better was his tenacity. He worked at it for years. He was on fire from Columbus to Dallas, crashing and burning with so much regularity his nickname was Whit Blazemore. But he never quit. And now he'd finally landed RJ Reynolds Tobacco Company. He'd be driving the Smokin' Joe's Funny Car, beginning in 1996.

He said all the right things. He praised my work and said he'd love to talk to me about it but he also said he was talking to some other people. He offered to fly me to Indianapolis in the coming days, where we'd have dinner together to discuss it over some fine food and a bottle of wine. I took him up on the offer.

I flew to Indy late one Friday afternoon, right in the middle of the NPSL season. Whit put me up at an airport hotel and the next day he picked me up and took me to the team's shop, where crew chief Rob Flynn was busy organizing everything with no time to spare. Dickie Venables, Kurt Elliott, Lew Arrington and a few other guys were hard at work as well.

That night, at a nice bistro in the Broad Ripple section of Indy, we talked about the job. I knew I could do it, and do it well. I also knew that Whit and I shared one common thing. We both had dreamed of this. I'd dreamed of having a full-time gig as a team PR rep since the day I left Heartland Park. And this would be a big-time gig. We talked title (general manager) and compensation (matching my Attack numbers) as well as a free car (courtesy of a Ford dealership). I told him I'd call him soon, and I headed back to Kansas City.

I was tormented, but I didn't have much time to stew on it. The Smokin' Joe's team was leaving for a preseason test session in days and after that the Winternationals in Pomona. Whit needed my decision.

I called Tom Lynch and Jerry Herbert and asked them to meet me for lunch. I figured talking to Don about this could end up spiraling off topic and out of control and I trusted those two guys to listen and give me a fair opinion. Over appetizers, I said, "Guys, I love it here. I love what we're doing. I know we can do better, and we will. But, I got a job offer the other day that has me confused. I'll stay here if you can get Don to make it worth my while. Even with the free car and apartment, I'm still hardly making any money. As a general manager, I think I should be compensated as well as Zoran is, or at least close to that. He's making twice what I am, and he deserves every bit of it. He's the best coach in the league, and I think I'm the best GM."

They were both great about it. Tom, in particular, had taken a real liking to me the first day I arrived, and I'd often drive down to the Shawnee office to chat with him for hours. Jerry was a much more serious guy and he was the team's treasurer, so he was tuned in to the money situation.

Jerry said, "Well of course we want to keep you, but I have to be honest. Don's losing a lot of money and the rest of us are tapped out. To keep the lights on, Don's having to put more of his own cash into the team's account. If you can wait until the season is over that would be a much better time to ask for a raise. He's not in the right mood for that question now."

I didn't have time to wait until the season ended. I needed to make a decision right then.

I called Whit and took the job. I then went and saw Don and explained it to him. NHRA was calling and I had to be true to that. I loved the Attack, but I loved drag racing as well.

Don accepted my resignation and the Kansas City Star ran a story about my departure the next day. In it, I had nothing but honest praise for the organization and for the opportunity I'd been given.

Don and his minority owners also decided to put off hiring a new GM until the season ended. Natalie and Elizabeth would have to step in to cover everything I'd been doing.

I met with both of them and saw the terror in their eyes. They were already very busy and now they were taking on my responsibilities as well, with their first game at the helm coming in just two days. Over the next few weeks we'd be in near constant contact on the phone, as I did all I could to get them through it.

I hadn't realized, ahead of my decision, that I might be abandoning respected colleagues but I had such admiration and respect for both of them I couldn't escape the thought. I'd be as helpful as I could possibly be.

Whit agreed to cover my moving expenses, so just days later yet another Mayflower truck arrived at my apartment. When it was loaded, I headed for the airport and got on a plane. I needed to get to Indy, find an apartment, and call the moving company to tell them where to deliver my stuff.

Whit left a van for me at the shop, on Gasoline Alley in Indy. I had to take a cab there, ask the woman at the shop next door for the keys, and get the van out of a jigsaw-puzzle squeeze of the crew guys' personal cars. The team was out west, testing.

I asked the woman who had handed me the keys, "If you were me and you were looking for an apartment, where would you look?"

She said to stick to the west and northwest sides of town, outside the interstate loop that circled the city. The best cross-streets to start with would be 38th and 56th, near Eagle Creek.

It was a wet, dank, bone-chilling day in late January. I had less than 24 hours to find a place to live.

I looked at three or four complexes near 38th but didn't see anything I liked. Then I found The Oaks of Eagle Creek on 56th. I toured a really nice end-unit townhome, with a master bedroom upstairs, a nice home office downstairs, and a large living room. The Indianapolis Colts training facility was right next door. I signed on the dotted line.

Whit flew back to Indy after the test session, and a few days later I was on my way to Pomona, in my official capacity as general manager and public relations representative for Whit Bazemore and the Smokin' Joe's team.

Plow forward? Sometimes you do that out of instinct. Sometimes it's planned. Sometimes it's all of the above. Or maybe it's none of the above. It just is.

A Most Interesting Indy Experience

The team's shop on Gasoline Alley was small by professional racing standards, so Whit had also leased a larger space a few units down and used it mostly for storage. The problem for me was that neither space included an office. I'd be working from home until that could be rectified.

Whit loaded me down with Smokin' Joe's polo shirts and a very bright jacket boldly featuring a mix of purple, yellow, and green and the copyrighted camel with a scarf around his neck. I had the photo for my NHRA "hard card" permanent credential taken while wearing it. I still have that credential and the jacket still looks so very 1996. It nearly glowed in the dark.

In just a few days, we were headed for Pomona. The media center in the new tower behind the Pomona starting line was a huge step up from the typical standard at the time but it was still populated by many of the same PR reps who had been on the tour for years. This time I wasn't the newest of the new guys but I was still standing on the bottom rung of a ladder inhabited by some veteran talent. I'd have to earn some stripes before I was fully admitted to the fraternity. Fortunately, the only "hazing" that was done consisted of things like giving me the worst seat in the room.

In terms of the actual work, I discovered one challenge immediately. With our team's primary sponsor being a tobacco company there were a lot of people in charge who were very interested in how they might be portrayed by a PR hack at a drag race. Those folks made it clear that I couldn't simply blast out anything I wanted in the media room or in a press release. And if we had any really big announcements to make, they'd want to see it and approve it before we did.

Looking back, that was a good thing. I was too inexperienced to be given the freedom to spout whatever came into my mind and, had we not had those guidelines clearly laid in front of us, the chances were good I might eventually screw up Whit's deal. I certainly did not want that to happen.

I was forging new ground in my own career while, typical of me, rarely stopping to analyze anything or do more than simply plow forward. The train was moving and I was aboard, wherever it was going to take me.

One place it would take me was a string of grocery stores and sandwich shops. With no social media in play at the time, 95 percent of any PR work I would do at the track would happen after each lap the Smokin' Joe's car would make. That left me with all sorts of free time, while I was surrounded by hard-working crew guys who were often hungry. Recognizing my availability Whit would send me out for lunch on a daily basis, and he'd also ask me to bring him bananas. It wasn't that he loved bananas, he only liked them as much as anyone else, but he felt it was critical to eat them regularly for the potassium and other nutrients they contained.

In Pomona, I learned the ropes. Whit sent me out to get good sandwiches for the guys, into an area with which, one could say, I wasn't totally familiar. I think I was six or seven miles from the track when I finally found a sub shop and a grocery store. Then I had to plow my way back to the track and park again. At some venues, including Pomona, that was no big deal. At others, as I'd learn, if you gave up your parking spot in the middle of the day you might return to find the whole place full. It was something I'd have to sweat out each time.

After Pomona we got into our routines fairly quickly. I'd work from home during the week and I'd make regular drives over to the shop, but the place was so crowded and so busy I felt I was mostly just in the way. Finally, Whit made the decision to build a pair of offices in the second unit and he and I took on the role of general contractors, working with construction people who could turn it into a professional space. The only problem was, the progress was painfully slow. For many weeks there was no progress at all. The construction guy had a full-time job and our work had to happen during his free time so the completion of work could be measured in snail-like terms. Until it was done, I'd remain in my office at my apartment.

In the meantime Whit and I took an afternoon to browse around an office supply company in the suburbs north of Indy. We both picked out large executive desks and comfortable office chairs. We didn't technically have offices yet, but we had the desks and chairs! It was a start. And what a relief it was to know I wouldn't have to sit on a wooden kitchen chair while working.

The woman who sold us the furniture was attractive and she seemed plenty smart. Those were two key elements for me so I then took it upon myself to send her thank-you note. In addition to saying thank you, I also asked her out on a date.

Unbelievably, she called me and said she'd love to and we made plans to meet at Champp's (a popular bar and restaurant) on Indy's north side. She also brought along a bodyguard, in the form of a male friend named Mike. That didn't bother me at all.

Champp's, it turned out, was also a gathering spot for a lot of IndyCar drivers, crew members, and owners. The place was full of racing jackets and I recognized a lot of the faces. I also recognized my date didn't seem to be having a totally wonderful time. That might have been because her buddy Mike and I hit it off so well we spent most of the time cracking each other up while she stared at us with a blank look of disbelief. I think her plan for protection backfired, just a little.

Finally, she said, "I think I'm going to go home. You two can stay and have fun." And we did just that. Mike and I became pretty good buddies, meeting regularly in the Broad Ripple area on weekend nights. He was a funny character and my first real friend in Indy. It wasn't feeling like home yet, but it was getting better.

The third race on the schedule was Gainesville, in March, and Whit and I drove down to Florida together. The fact we did that says a lot about Whit. He had pinched the life out of every penny for years, as an independent racer, and just because he had a big new sponsorship with a world-famous company didn't mean he'd shake off that instinct to save money. The only things he splurged on were shiny new parts for the race car.

On the long drive, I got to know Whit a lot better. He was a fabulously interesting guy with a backstory that reminded me of myself. He'd been a photographer and shot a lot of drag racing action. He'd gotten to know a lot of people in important places, but he was young and inexperienced at anything other than clicking photos. Still, he followed his heart and put it all on the line to become a Funny Car driver.

He had no rich philanthropist who could finance his dream. He had only that dream. And he had an enormous capacity to work ceaselessly to make it happen. More often than not, at more races than he'd care to acknowledge, his inexperience and that of his crew chief conspired with worn-out parts to create mayhem, often of the inferno variety. I'd seen Whit on fire so many times I feared for his life.

But he never quit. He worked at it like a madman, and he kept networking and pitching new sponsors with an obvious and admirable sense of desperation.

On the trip to Florida he was just like he was when he interviewed me over dinner and a bottle of wine. We had marvelous conversations about a wide variety of subjects including the news that his favorite musician was Jimi Hendrix and the policy, when riding with him, was that the driver could pick the radio station or CD but the passenger controlled the volume.

We were from different worlds but our methods for finding ourselves there in the same spot, in the same car, at the same time, were similar. We had both just kept plowing forward, trying to attain our dreams.

When we got to Gainesville I began to understand something else about Whit. He had another personality and it was the one that manifested itself when he drove through the gate and into the pit area.

The jovial, intellectual, interesting guy from dinner was replaced by the single most focused racer I'd ever met. He put mental blinders on when he got to the track. He wasn't there to be anyone's best friend. He wasn't there to have a good time and yuck it up with his buddies. He was there for one reason and one reason only.

He was there to win.

The shift to his track persona was jarring at first. I'd never been anyone's full-time PR rep before and I'd never met anyone quite like Whit, so I wasn't ready for it. His laser focus was unlike anything I'd seen out of any other racer I'd met. I was there to help him, as one of his assets, and I was expected to pull my weight and stay out of the way.

When the race was over and we hit the road to drive back to Indy, stopping in Atlanta so I could meet his father, the more jovial Whit resurfaced. The dichotomy between the two personalities was stark, and it was something to which I was going to need to adjust.

The Ford Aerostar van we had been driving was my company car but when we got back from Gainesville Whit got some unexpected news. The dealership that had supplied the car had only expected it to be driven locally, around Indy. They also expected it to be returned with less than 10,000 miles on it. That would've been good information for Whit to have but they had not been clear about it when delivering the car.

They wanted the van back to put it on their lot and when they heard it had more like 20,000 miles on it they were none too excited. It took all of Whit's enormous negotiating skills to get them to agree to provide us a new car and to increase the number of miles we could put on it.

I drove the van up to the dealership in Chicago and apologized profusely for our oversight. The dealer grumbled a bit and never smiled. Then he handed me the keys to a new Crown Victoria. The reason that large sedan was given to me was apparent at first sight. It had some heavy hail damage. It basically looked like it had been left in the middle of a golf driving range. I didn't care about that, though, and the dealer didn't seem to care how many miles I'd put on it.

The next race after Gainesville was Houston. Once again I drove, although Whit chose to fly. On Sunday night at the end of a long hot weekend I stopped at the diner outside the La Quinta Inn at which we were staying, for a dinner of bacon and eggs.

At 3 a.m. I woke up, knowing things were drastically wrong. I had food poisoning of the worst variety. The team was sticking around a few days to do some testing at the Houston track, and I managed to get word to Whit that I was sick and staying in my room. I stayed there until Wednesday.

I was still feeling awful, but at least my system was completely cleared out and I could focus enough to walk. I went down to the lobby and spotted Whit and Kurt Elliott. Kurt said, "You don't look too good," and Whit added, "As a matter of fact, you look green." It had been a rough few days.

I made up my mind to go ahead and hit the road and got as far as Jackson, Mississippi about seven hours later. I checked into a Holiday Inn and spotted a grocery store across the street. I wasn't hungry for any substantive food, but I was happy to notice that fruit sounded good. I bought some grapes, a banana, and a nectarine. It was the first food I had ingested since that fateful dinner three nights earlier.

The next day I made it all the way back to Indy in 11 hours and in Effingham, Illinois I actually had a hankering for a ham sandwich. Arby's was the only place I could find that offered one at that hour, but it sure tasted good.

After Houston, we were racing most of the time. That's probably a good thing because the construction of our new office space had not just slowed, it had ground to a complete stop. We had a few walls in, a couple of windows framed, and not much else. I was still working from home.

At the Atlanta race I checked into the motel in Commerce and saw a shiny and very racey-looking Ducati motorcycle parked by the lobby door, under the portico. It was Whit's, and he loved to ride that bike. He also loved to ride it fast. It only looked scary to me. I worried about him on that thing. A lot.

As spring turned to summer my typical race-week workload consisted of writing a press release making sure to follow the rules established by RJ Reynolds, which meant I had to write banal stories. I didn't have email yet but we had a FAX machine modern enough to allow group transmissions, so about 20 key sponsors and media members got each one.

I'd then travel to the race via air or road. In 1996, NHRA events were four days long so I'd spend four days going to grocery stores, finding sandwich shops, and getting into, out of, and back into the track. In the media center I'd put out a few printed notes called "Whit Bits" but frankly I was so hamstrung with what I could say they were mostly uninteresting. And then I'd travel back to Indy.

To be completely blunt, it was all fairly dull and I never really felt like I was a part of the team. I was strictly a behind-the-scenes support guy. The one crew guy who seemed to take a liking to me was Lew Arrington, who was quite young. He and I would actually go out to lunch at least once a week. Rob Flynn treated me with respect but the rest of the guys barely noticed I was around. It wasn't everything of which I had dreamed.

By the time we got to the Memphis race, expertly placed on the schedule at the end of June, it was broiling under the Mid-South sun and I was on the losing side of the "living your dream" sweepstakes. Did I mention it was broiling in Memphis?

It was as hot as I'd ever been. It was well up into the 90s with humidity that nearly matched the temperature. And Del Worsham, still every bit a kid, rode by me a few times doing wheelies on his BMX bike, saying hello.

Later in the weekend Del came over to the Bazemore pit and he introduced himself to me, as if I needed to know who he was. He said, "My grandmother is here and she can't handle this heat. Do you think there's any way you could get her into the Winston suite? It's kind of important."

I told him I'd do whatever I could, and within minutes we had Grandma Worsham in the air-conditioned comfort of the Winston suite.

The next race was Topeka and I could tell my heart wasn't in it. I went through the motions, at least happy to realize I knew where the grocery stores and sandwich shops were in that town.

Then, when I got back to Indy, I received yet another life-altering phone call. It was David Goins, the owner of the Indianapolis Twisters indoor soccer team.

It was a story I'd heard too many times. They'd been playing in a new league, the Continental Indoor Soccer League (CISL) for a month or two and were bleeding money as if the team's jugular vein had been severed. He was desperate. Would I care to come downtown to talk about being the GM?

It was all a bit surreal. At the Topeka race I think I'd gotten my head wrapped around the idea that this particular job wasn't exactly the dream I'd been trying to attain. And then a soccer owner I'd never met called me the next day. I told David I'd be at his office the following morning.

The Twisters played at Market Square Arena, which was also the home of the Indiana Pacers, but there was no office space for them there. They rented a floor in an old office building two blocks away. After I was ushered in, I met Goins in his office and he introduced me to his brother Rodney, a former soccer player who was acting as a sort of general manager. Not a wholly interested one, but he had the title.

We talked about the team, about the market, and about public interest in the Twisters and the sport itself. The consensus was Indianapolis could be a good soccer market but the Goins brothers hadn't figured out how to tap into it, and they were running out of money.

We toured the office and I was introduced to the staff. The first gentleman I met was the PR director. The second person, a young lady, was also a PR director. The third person, a woman, was in charge of merchandise. The fourth, a guy slightly younger than me, was involved with hospitality of some sort. The final staff member, an eager young man who stood out from the rest, was charged with game operations. Not one single person was selling tickets. Not one.

We talked it over and when David asked what it would take for me to come aboard and save the sinking ship, I shot high. I asked for $90,000 and I demanded a contract. It wouldn't be a handshake deal, and it wouldn't be a contract with the Twisters. I asked for a personal-services contract with David Goins himself. For three years.

He stood up and shook my hand, smiling as he said "You've got a deal!" Maybe I should have asked for more.

I paced around my home office the next morning. I finally built up enough courage and called Whit, saying, "Hey man, we need to talk. I don't think this job is right for me. With all the restrictions on what I can and can't write, it's almost an administrative job. There's no real space for creativity and our sponsor is already one of the most recognizable brands in the world. You're wasting money on a guy like me. You could hire a 19-year-old out of junior college to do this."

He wanted to discuss how we could make things better and how much more improved it would all be once we got into the new offices and new shop, forcing me to get to the next point.

"Well, I got an offer yesterday to take over the Indianapolis Twisters indoor soccer team," I said. "They're going to pay me a lot more than I've ever made and I'll have free rein to do whatever I want to make it a success. I've decided to do that."

There was a pause on the line and then Whit said, "You know what, that's very cool. I can't stand in the way of you doing that. I wish you all the best, and let's get together for lunch to talk about how we map out whatever the transition is that we'll have to make."

Within a week I was no longer a part of Bazemore Racing and the team was out on the NHRA Western Swing. It was a trip I had looked forward to, since I'd never made the Western Swing before, but I resigned just days before I was due to leave.

I was, instead, the general manager of the Indianapolis Twisters and with the CISL being a summer league, we had a home game the night of my first day on the job.

I'd also taken the time to buy a car, since the Crown Vic went back to Whit. I went straight to the local Saab dealership and bought a new 900SE Turbo. To get the loan, I brought a letter from David Goins stating that I had just become the new GM of the Twisters. I was instantly approved.

At my first game, I noticed quite a few things. There might have been just 2,500 people in the place but the ones who were there were having a great time. There was definitely energy in the building. Plus, the fans had to have all been part of the walk-up because there were no sales reps to pitch group sales. The team was good, and the action on the floor was nearly as fast-paced as the NPSL had been. And, the game production was well done. It kept the "crowd" jazzed up and excited from start to finish.

The next day, I sat in David's office and was very blunt.

"We have no sales people," I said. "Were you expecting to announce the formation of the team and then have the place sell out all by itself?"

He said he had no idea how to run the team, and he'd relied on Rodney for that. I told him we needed to make a boatload of changes.

We certainly didn't need two PR people. The woman in the corner office, who often had her door locked while she was in there "working" on merchandise that had already been produced, had to go. The guy doing hospitality had a great outgoing personality. He should add ticket sales to his job description. The guy who did game ops was fantastic at that job, but his personality was also terrific and he was the one person on the staff who seemed eager to do more. He should sell tickets, as well.

I asked David how the relationship was with the local youth soccer kingpins. He scrunched up his face and said it wasn't good. Apparently, just after the team was launched, the single most important youth soccer administrator in the Indy area called on them to talk about what they could do to help the Twisters. He offered all sorts of plans to get discounted tickets to the thousands of kids playing in the area. According to David, they demanded the moon and told the man they wouldn't provide any discounted tickets. Those had been the last words spoken before the gentleman stormed out. They were no longer on speaking terms, at all.

Boy, oh boy. I had taken this job knowing it was a mess. I had no idea the level of messiness could even approach what was going on there.

We held a press conference at the arena, to introduce me, and the media descended on me like ants at a summer picnic. What I could tell by their questions, and by the way they were phrased, was that the media wanted the Twisters to succeed. Every TV station, the main newspaper, and a bunch of radio stations were there. They treated me like a savior.

We had a staff meeting the next morning where I laid out my vision for the organization, and it wasn't pretty. Everyone on the staff would have to pitch in with group sales and I'd attempt to mend the fences with the local youth soccer administrators. We needed some more manpower, as well. We were already halfway through the season, though, so I had to admit that we were realistically working toward 1997. We'd just have to survive that long. I'd keep most of the staff around but everyone was being evaluated on a daily basis.

At my second home game I got the first inkling that things were worse than I'd thought. The Market Square Arena staff informed me they would not open the gates that night unless they got the rent money up-front. And, our media and sponsor dining room, where the team hosted a reception prior to every game, would not be allowed to open without payment up-front.

I got David to hand me a check for the rent. I handed the arena management person my American Express card for the reception. David promised to pay me back.

There was a common description for a certain type of indoor soccer team owner back then. People would say "He acts like a millionaire, but only has about $50,000 to his name. He just moves that pile around to make it look like more."

I was already seeing that. The rent issue, with the Arena, would be a constant battle.

Attendance ticked up a little after all the media publicity surrounding my hiring, but group sales never got off the ground after the preseason kerfuffle with youth soccer kingpin.

I got my paycheck and deposited it, so it was at least a good thing to have some money in my hands. My first Saab payment was coming up soon.

Two weeks later, I got my next check and deposited that. I then paid all my bills.

Within days I was getting calls from the bank that checks I had written were bouncing right and left. I drove over there and met with the manager, saying, "I've deposited checks for $2,900 twice in the last two weeks, and I've written checks for a total of about $3,000. How is that possible?"

He clicked a few key on his computer and said, "Well, there's the problem. Your second paycheck came back due to insufficient funds. It bounced."

They gave me 24 hours to straighten it out and if I could do that they'd refund all the fees for the checks I'd bounced. I made that happen, and David did an Oscar-worthy job of acting completely stunned that he'd bounced my paycheck.

Then, just a few weeks into my job with the Twisters, I was surprised to get a call from Whit. I said, "Hey man, what's up with you?"

His reply startled me, and he sounded really out of it. He said, "I'm in California. I was riding the Ducati up the freeway, on my way to Sonoma, and one of my bags got caught up in the rear wheel. I went down hard, man. I'm lucky I'm alive, to be honest."

I asked him how badly he was hurt, and what his plan was, and he said, "I can walk, but I'm about skinned alive. I'm planning on driving in Sonoma, though. The hard part will be getting in and out of the car."

He did drive, despite enormous pain. And it was made worse when his parachutes didn't come out on one run because the handles broke off in his hand when he reached for them. With the parachute handles being on the same side of the roll cage as the brake handle he had established a routine where he could reach across with his left hand to pull on the wires if something like that happened, but he'd seriously strained the rotator cuff in his left shoulder in the wreck and he couldn't do that. He rode the Smokin' Joe's Funny Car into the sand, adding another insult to his many injuries. I had a strange internal sense of "I knew this would happen" about that Ducati, but I kept it to myself.

Back in Indy, where my new job and old one would share the sports stage over Labor Day, the U.S. Nationals were coming up in just a few weeks. And I had another idea about how we could get the Twisters better known in the area. We would sponsor a race car. A Nitro Funny Car. And I knew just the team owner and driver who would do it. Norm Wilding.

I had to bring David up to speed on NHRA, Norm, and what a Funny Car was but he was really excited. We decided on $10,000 and I presented the concept to Norm on the phone. He graciously accepted the offer and we designed some decals to go on his beautiful blue Funny Car.

As a make-good to a number of Twisters sponsors who were unhappy with attendance at the games, we put their logos on the car as well. All of them appreciated that.

When race week arrived Norm came north from Florida with the car ready to go, fully adorned with all the big decals. He also included a list of names on the rear quarter panel. It was a list of the four people who had helped him the most. Mine was one of them. It was the first time my name had ever been on a race car and it was so large Whit came over to me when he saw it, laughing as he said, "Wow. Are you sponsoring Norm yourself?"

We did a display at a local Kroger store, since they were one of the Twisters' sponsors, and that went well. It was also time to pay Norm the $10,000 we promised him. When David approached me he said, "We don't have the money."

The look on my face must have created a little fear in him because he then smiled broadly and said, "I'm just kidding. I have it right here in cash," as he pulled out an envelope. Then he added, "Except it's $9,000. That's all I could afford." At that point, Norm nodded and the Twisters officially only shorted him a grand.

Norm didn't qualify for the race but he signed lots of specially printed Twisters handout cards and a lot of people came by to see the car and grab a pocket schedule.

Also, from that point forward when I'd get my paycheck every other Friday I would march straight downstairs to the bank in the building next door, where the Twisters had their account. I would cash my check (holding my breath) and walk out with an envelope containing about $2,900, then I'd deposit that at my bank. I was never going to take that chance again.

The league office was clearly concerned about the fate of the franchise and the head of the league, Roy Turner, came to Indy to spend a few days with us.

Roy was an indoor legend, having coached the Wichita Wings in their MISL heyday when the "Orange Army" filled the coliseum for every game. It was a pleasure for me to meet him.

His only goal was saving the franchise. If he could bring a consultant in, to help me with the turnaround, he would do that. We played golf together one day and had long sincere conversations about it in the cart. He was an indoor soccer man. He loved the game.

David and Rodney were sure he had ulterior motives. They saw it as a palace coup and they bluntly told him to go back to home and not bother them. I was left shaking my head.

Turner then began discussions with the Indianapolis Ice of the International Hockey League. He convinced them to buy the Twisters, since the two leagues' seasons didn't overlap and the talented Ice staff could run both franchises. The Goins brothers would get a payback, although just quarters on the dollar compared to what they'd lost, and I would be kept on as the GM.

I was all for it. The Ice staff was all for it. Roy Turner was all for it. Lawyers were involved, and for days the meetings dragged on as both sides tried to get as much out of the deal as they could. I was simply an observer.

Finally, a verbal agreement was struck and I think most of us (perhaps not David and Rodney) felt a huge sense of relief. We called a press conference for the next day, in my spacious corner office two blocks from Market Square Arena.

I stood behind my desk as crews from every television station in town set up their cameras. Roy Turner arrived, the owner of the Ice arrived, and finally David Goins came into the room.

I stood behind him as he approached the podium. He greeted the assembled media and held up the contract with the Ice. He then said that he'd changed his mind and he was folding the franchise, effective immediately. He dropped the contract onto the podium, just for effect. You could've heard a feather hit the floor.

I, of course, was as completely blindsided as everyone in the room. I'd never been part of anything like it. With the Storm, Milan Mandaric could be hard to work for but he had plenty of money. With the Attack, Don Kincaid could be irascible as well but he had more than enough money. Folding the franchise without telling the staff was never a worry there. Getting fired was a worry, but nothing like this ever crossed my beleaguered mind.

After David went back to his office and the media picked their jaws up off the floor, I went in to see the Goins brothers while all the other pale and sweaty Twisters employees sat shell-shocked at their desks.

I asked him what had just happened and he insisted said he'd simply changed his mind that morning. He'd rather walk away with the losses than accept defeat and "give the team away." He still saw Roy Turner as a nefarious interloper who was trying to run them out of town so he could ride in on a white stallion and save the day. I knew, for a fact, Roy had no desire to run a franchise. But my opinion was disputed, and it was too late.

David wished me well in my future endeavors and I calmly reminded him that I had a three-year personal services contract and with such a thing he was obligated to pay me. I even allowed that I'd rework the contract to one year which only left him responsible for another eight or so months. He nodded, and said, "You're right. And I'll honor that."

The next day David said he'd talked to his lawyer and he was told that the only way he was on the hook for my pay was if I came to work from 8:00 to 5:00, Monday through Friday. If I didn't show up the contract could be broken.

I told him we ought to at least find something we could do together in the sports world, so we could be productive while I sat down the hall from him five days a week. I had no intention of not showing up.

We finally settled on NHRA Drag Racing. Our goal would be to find a way to be heavily involved with a Funny Car team, in some nebulous way we hadn't quite yet figured out. I didn't want to be involved if David was going to own the team, thanks to the soccer fiasco, but I got to work on some big ideas.

The one we settled on was unique. We'd find a solid but unsponsored Funny Car team and offer them $100,000 for the sponsor rights to their car. Then, since we would own the space on the sides and hood, we'd get to keep 100 percent of any sponsor income we could generate.

We ran it past Norm Wilding first and I was actually a bit surprised that he turned it down. His equipment was really getting old and he not only didn't think he could make the whole tour on $100,000 he knew he couldn't do it if he spent what was necessary to get his car up to date.

I then called a PR friend who knew everyone, and I asked for Del Worsham's phone number. I called Del and reminded him who I was, relating the Grandma Worsham story from Memphis the prior summer, and he said, "Oh, yeah. How are you, man?"

We chatted for a while and I told him our plan. He said, "Well, we run a really tight ship here but we plan to run the whole tour without a primary sponsor. We have a bunch of guys who help us out, like Texas Stagecoach, and Auburn Foundry, and NLM Electrical, and together we think we can compete and run every race. Let me talk to my dad."

For a week we went back and forth, faxing outlines of the car and negotiating who controlled what space, and finally we all agreed to do it. David would pay them $10,000 a month for 10 months. If we didn't cover that in new sponsors, that would be on us. If we found $500,000 in sponsor money, we'd get it all and net $400,000. The Worshams would simply take David's $10,000 a month and make it work. It was found money for them. We didn't agree to it with a contract. We didn't agree with a handshake. We agreed over the phone.

My job was going to be the search for sponsorship while I also raised the Worsham & Fink Racing profile by doing a lot of really aggressive PR work and media relations.

Just a few days later Del called me sounding very confused. He said, "We've been hearing from some guys at CSK Auto. They're the parent company for Checker, Schuck's, and Kragen Auto Parts, based out of Phoenix. They want to sponsor us and they want to give us a little more than $200,000 to be the primary. I don't know what to do."

I said, as quickly as I could, "You should hang up with me and call them. Take the deal before they change their minds."

That was basically all I said. I didn't know what that would mean for me or David. Most racers would take the deal and then tell guys like us, "Hey we appreciate it, but we don't need you now. See ya later."

The next day Del called again and said they'd taken the deal. He then added, "They wanted to start talking about how to implement all this crazy stuff and I said, 'I have a marketing guy. His name is Bob Wilber. You'll have to talk to him about all of this.' So you should be hearing from a Joe Spica or Ron Chisler within 24 hours."

Del and Chuck Worsham had no contractual reason to do that. In many ways, it was an odd thing to do. They could've kept all the money, but with our agreement they owed us about half of it while we now didn't owe them anything.

It was, however, the single most loyal and "right" thing I'd seen in any sport, from any individual, in a very long time. Maybe ever.

Del and I would talk daily as they got the team together, ordered uniforms, and got things up and rolling. He told me, "My dad and I will run the car. We want you to run the sponsorship, do the PR, and take us to a new level. If you have to replace CSK, that's OK. You do your work, and we'll do ours. Do you think we can be successful?"

I told him I had no doubt. The dream was alive.

Meanwhile, the Ducati had struck Whit once again and this time it was much worse. He was riding on the Blue Ridge Parkway when he swerved to give a truck more room in a curve, but he lost control of the bike and was seriously injured. He had a compound fracture in his left leg, torn ligaments in both knees, and a lot of tissue damage. His season was over so he put his childhood idol, Dale Pulde, in the Smokin' Joe's car. Pulde then went on to win the Dallas race, with Rob Flynn and the crew. They went to the Winner's Circle without their wounded driver.

As I was plowing forward to go to work for the Worshams, Whit was deciding to put the motorcycle away until he was done racing. As he said, "I love riding Ducatis but it can be pretty costly, both physically and emotionally. I'm not going to ride anymore, as long as I'm racing."

I was fortunate to be heading to a fantastic opportunity. It was one that looked exactly like my dream job.

Whit was fortunate to be alive. As were both of our dreams.

The Dream Comes True

In terms of my contracted salary with David Goins, I at least had a real reason to go to work every day. I was putting together marketing materials, creating a media guide, and talking to Del on near-daily basis. At the same time, I also got to know Joe Spica at CSK very well during our phone conversations as we nailed down a lengthy to-do list before Pomona.

And things were getting incrementally better in terms of responsibilities and how the work was getting done. David ran another company called Executive Sports Management, and by the time the Worsham deal happened he was happy to spend all of his time with it while I handled the racing stuff by myself. I did make sure, as part of our deal, that we had an ESM decal on the car. There might have been no more than six people in the racing world who knew what ESM stood for but it was on there.

What many people don't remember is that there would also be another CSK car on the NHRA tour in 1997. In the Pro Stock class, the car owned by Bill Orndorff and driven by Jerry Eckman would sport the same paint scheme as the Worsham Funny Car. It was a smaller deal but they had been a successful team for many years and they'd be our pseudo teammates, although the two operations were separate.

I made the trip to Pomona for the Winternationals and walked straight to the Worsham pit area. In front of it was an old Oldsmobile Funny Car body painted in some funky flat colors with a Checker, Schuck's, Kragen decal on each side and the hood. The rest of the associate sponsors were on there was well, but in black vinyl and in block letters.

Del saw me as I approached the pit and a big smile spread across his face. He loudly said, "There he is! Come on in, dude."

He introduced me to his dad and to his lovely sister, Susan. Then Grandma Worsham, who was already a legend in the sport. She followed her grandson around by car on the whole tour and sat in the stands watching every run he made, meticulously keeping stats and notes. The crew included three associate sponsors who did more than just write checks. They also worked on the car. There was John Fink, who owned Auburn Foundry, in Indiana; Frank Gilchrist, who owned Texas Stagecoach, in Houston; and Nick Puglisi, who owned NLM Electrical in New Jersey. The remainder of the crew featured only three full-time employees. The first was a kid so skinny I thought his pants would fall off at any moment. His name was Marc Denner, and he was from Wichita. I mentioned the Wichita Wings indoor soccer team and he said, "Oh, yeah. I was part of the Orange Army when I was a kid." He then looked at my feet, upon which were my adidas SAMBA indoor soccer shoes, and he said, "I probably had a dozen pairs of those."

As a member of Worsham Racing, Marc started just a few days before I did. He never let me forget his seniority.

Steve Brown, who was known to everyone as Fuel Boy, was a South Carolina country boy who would look you right in the eye with respect while he treated everyone around him the same, no matter their status or position. And Dave Janse, who had worked for Del and Chuck for a few years, looked enough like Del I had originally thought, in 1996, that they might have been brothers, or at least cousins.

Larry Liu, who lived in Minnesota and who had worked previously for Al Hoffman, was a fly-in guy, commuting to the races while he maintained his own repair shop in the Twin Cities suburb of Shoreview. Wayne Smothers, another talented guy who flew in to work on the car, was one of the nicest and funniest guys I had ever met. He felt like a lifelong friend by the end of my first day and he coined the nickname Bobinator, which some people still use when addressing me.

Halfway through my first day I'd had more one-on-one interaction with my teammates than I had since I left Heartland Park. I was truly part of the team. The dream wasn't just alive, it was happening in front of me.

On that first day, I was handed my crew uniform shirts. To save money, Del and Chuck just bought dark blue short sleeve button-down shirts, and had a few logos embroidered on them. We each got three.

On the track, we qualified well with the first Checker, Schuck's, Kragen Funny Car ever to hit the track. Del's time of 5.035 put him third on the ladder but when the CSK car smoked the tires in round one on Sunday against Gary Bolger, our initial foray was over.

Before I had flown out to Pomona, I'd followed my conscience and had a conversation with David. Since our planned payments had all been covered by CSK and the sponsorship put us ridiculously "in the money" on our deal, I managed to convince David that we should lower the amount of money the team owed us. It was the right thing to do, and if Del was going to show me such loyalty by having me interact with CSK then we should show some loyalty in return. We'd accept $3,000 per race as our part of the deal. There were 22 points races. That meant we'd accept just $66,000 of the $100,000 the deal would've provided.

Of course, that $66,000 still wouldn't cover what David would be paying me, so we needed to find some more sponsor income if it was going to work out.

Fortunately for David, ESM was doing very well. He'd let all of the Twisters staff go except for the eager young game-operations kid, who then moved in to share my spacious soccer office with me. His name was Mike Roan, and he was a fantastic guy.

The model for ESM was simple. David and Mike would pitch corporations to hire ESM as the host for hospitality gatherings at huge sports events. That year, at the end of March, the NCAA Final Four basketball tournament would be held at the RCA Dome in downtown Indy. It was a perfect event for ESM.

David and Mike successfully sold a large number of corporate packages. They reserved a private hotel banquet hall within walking distance of the RCA Dome. They ordered fancy catering. They bought authentic leather NCAA basketballs to give to the guests. And finally, David worked with local ticket resellers (more often referred to as scalpers) to buy the number of tickets he needed for the companies that had bought the entertainment packages. Even with all that spending, they'd still make a lot of money after paying for the individual elements.

As the Final Four approached I was heading off to the rest of the races to represent the Worshams, who by then had taken delivery of their new Dodge bodies and had them painted in much more vibrant colors although Del's car was still blue. An ESM decal was in each side-window.

At the season's second race, in Phoenix, CSK persuaded NHRA to break with precedent and allow the CSK Pro Stock car to park next to us in the Funny Car pits. When an engine mishap caught their awning on fire and the Funny Car crew sprinted around to help them put out the flames, I was far too naive to have any idea that such a thing would roundly be considered suspicious in the Pro Stock world. As far as I knew, they caught their awnings on fire all the time.

With everyone from CEO Maynard Jenkins to a slew of vice presidents and regional managers watching us in CSK's hometown, we managed to qualify eighth at a race in which 23 Funny Cars were competing for 16 spots. In round one Sunday, we got our revenge on Bolger when he smoked the tires while Del went end-to-end. In round two, we faced Kenji Okazaki and made another clean lap. We were going rounds with the company watching, and we had Dean Skuza in the semifinal. It was a good race, side-by-side for much of it, but Skuza edged Del at the stripe to end our day.

We put on a good show for the people at CSK. Still, I remember thinking to myself, "I sure hope they don't expect this every week. This isn't as easy as we made it look today."

When I got to Gainesville in mid-March my name had been added to a hand-painted list on the rear of the car, under the heading "Special Thanks." I had my photo taken next to it.

The NCAA Final Four was fast approaching and David and Mike were working maniacally back in Indy to make sure all the details were in place. Even though we all worked in the same office space, they were so busy I rarely interacted with them.

I was back from the Gainesville and Houston races, at my apartment on the day of their big corporate event downtown, and late that night I got a phone call from David.

"I got arrested," were the first words he spoke. "I ended up with no tickets, and the guests blocked the doors and called the police. I totally screwed up. I'm out on bail, but this is really serious. I think they're going to charge me with fraud. If you want to, you should take the motorsports division and do it yourself. That's the best thing for you and the Worshams. I'll just give it to you."

According to David, he had made a play to earn a little additional profit and it cost him dearly. The amount scalpers were asking had been dropping on the final day of the tournament and David thought he could "flip" his tickets for those with a lower price tag. He sold his allotment and called the reseller he had always used. The guy was tapped out. David had no tickets.

He scrambled for an hour to find what he needed but the only tickets left on the street were singles or pairs and there weren't nearly enough of them. He had to face his guests and break the news to them. Then the police came.

I immediately called Del.

The Winston Invitational in Rockingham, North Carolina, was coming up the next weekend. The event was an NHRA-sanctioned race but it was for cash only (no Winston points could be earned) with the winner taking home a cool $100,000. That was a huge amount of money for Del and Chuck, but with no NHRA points being awarded I had not made plans to go to Rockingham.

"Hey man, something big just happened and I'm going to pack a bag and drive down there to Rockingham," I said. "David got arrested, and he's in trouble. I'm taking over the motorsports segment of ESM. We'll talk about it when we all get there."

I was on the road the next Thursday and in Rockingham that night. I went out to the track at first light the next morning and filled Del and Chuck in on the gory details, with all of the background leading up to the fact I hoped they'd be good with the concept of me taking over the effort personally. They both shook my hand and Chuck said, "Sounds fine to us."

The agreement was altered to become a simple contractor position. They'd pay me a gross fee of $1,000 per race, because I didn't have much overhead and I wanted every possible dollar to go to the team. I was now officially a member of Worsham Racing.

To cap off the monumental weekend, Del drove his way to the final round of the big-money event but he lost to John Force just before a downpour. My head was spinning.

When I got back to Indy, I cleaned out my downtown office and wished Mike Roan well. He was bewildered over what he'd just gone through with David and he'd decided to move to Hilton Head, South Carolina. That was a good move. It was time for both of us to make a clean break.

I took a long and serious look at my bank balance and credit card debt, and thought to myself, "I sure hope I can make it through this year. If I can somehow survive on a thousand bucks a race, it will all get better next year. I know we can get a jump in the sponsor fee. I just have to get there."

At roughly the same time, my college roomie Lance McCord and I had been talking about a get-together with some of our former teammates. SIUE didn't have formal reunions but we thought it might be fun to have a dozen or so of us meet up in Edwardsville for a weekend.

That concept morphed into a full reunion and it was something Lance and I developed, managed, and organized by ourselves. We ended up with nearly 30 guys on the invite list, we had an official reunion hotel, and we scheduled dinners for two nights, followed by a cookout at Radar's house on the final day.

A lot of the guys still lived near Edwardsville but a number of us were going to have to travel. I hadn't seen most of the guys for 19 or 20 years, and we had a fantastic time for three days and vowed to do it again.

A couple of days later, Lance called me.

"Hey, I have something to throw at you," he said. "We were all talking about our wives at the reunion and it struck me that I know someone you should meet. Her name is Barbara Doyle, and she works here at IBM, but in a different division than me. I met her at a meeting and I thought about you. I know you better than anyone, and you two are perfect for each other. I gave her your email address, and I'll give you hers. Now I'm out of it. It's up to you two."

Barbara and I emailed each other tentatively, at first. Then the emails became more frequent and more personal, as we divulged our likes and dislikes, our pet peeves and our passions. Then we traded handwritten letters in the mail. We finally graduated to photos, and I sent her a package that represented my life. In it were a baseball, a batting glove, a spark plug, a signed handout card from Del, and a long letter from me, telling her how smitten I was. Lance had clearly done a great thing.

Finally, after nearly a month, we progressed all the way to a phone call. Talk about taking it one baby step at a time! As we've always told people, the key was taking it step by step and getting to know each other from the inside out. Meeting in person was the final stage in the process.

We were both falling in love, despite the fact we hadn't been in the same room yet. All we needed to do was get together and then we could confirm what we both already knew. Barbara lived in Chapel Hill, North Carolina. I took out an atlas to find a spot halfway between Indy and Chapel Hill, and my finger landed on Knoxville.

I have nothing against Knoxville, but it didn't seem like the appropriate place for the two of us to meet. I then noticed the Great Smoky Mountains on the map and I had an idea. On my new desktop computer (another Mac, of course) I used my Earthlink dial-up connection to get on this thing called the internet. I searched Yahoo for cabins in the Smokies and found a charming little place called the Honey Bear Hideaway on the top of a lush forest hill. And I rented it for a weekend.

On the scheduled day, I arrived right on time and got checked in and unpacked. I had brought along a portable CD player and a six-pack of beer. I also lit some candles and put on some music, as I waited for my future wife to arrive. The CD was by the Gin Blossoms. I still think of that day every time I hear "Hey Jealousy" on the radio.

And I waited. Unbeknownst to me, Barbara was equal parts excited and petrified and she talked herself out of the trip a dozen times that day. She finally built up enough courage to make the drive over and arrived only a few hours late. The candles had long since melted away but the Heineken was cold and I kept my promise to meet her out in front of the cabin with a freshly opened bottle.

I remember it as if it were yesterday. She got out of her Mazda Miata and smiled. We looked each other directly in the eye and hugged. I knew at that precise moment that I would marry this woman. If she'd have me.

We spent a couple of glorious days there, and even went so far as to have "the conversation." We knew each other like best friends, thanks to the way we'd been going about things, and we knew we'd get married.

My only caveat was then spoken.

"People are going to think we're nuts and ridiculous if we even talk about this now," I said. "So, let's wait until the end of the summer to make it official. I won't even ask you until after Labor Day." Barbara agreed. We then extended our time together when she asked me to follow her back to Chapel Hill to see her house there.

1997 was rapidly becoming the most important year in my life. I turned 41 in June, but it was as if all the stars in the universe were aligning to provide me a new beginning. Barbara felt the same way, as her life turned a corner following a messy divorce.

As I drove back to Indy, I also knew I'd be leaving there. I'd be moving to Chapel Hill to live with Barbara. It was just a matter of when.

We talked daily and got together as often as possible. We met at Disney World for a couple of days and when she had a conference in St. Louis, I drove down for a quick overnight trip. We decided Shasta and I would move to her house right after the U.S. Nationals, over Labor Day.

Meanwhile, I was talking to Joe Spica at CSK on a daily basis. It was not unusual for us to talk three or four times a day. Joe was a detail-oriented guy, which is a good thing when you have as many moving promotional parts as a Funny Car program. What was better, though, was his sense of humor. We could make each other laugh with ease. He also quickly began calling me "Professor" while I dubbed him "Doctor." I deeply believe that, over the years, our relationship was a key to the longevity of the CSK program.

Ron Chisler was also assigned to the motorsports program at CSK, and we would also talk often. Ron was a good man, with a ton of integrity, and I respected him enormously from the first conversation. Still, it was Joe who became such a regular caller he soon felt almost like family.

On one fateful day, during the early part of the season, I did a small job well and it changed my job responsibilities for the next 19 years. Chuck asked me to put a new decal on each spill plate. When I put them on straight, he said, "Nice work. That's your job now. You're in charge of decals." Had I put that first one on a little crooked I wouldn't have spent the rest of my career sticking decals on every race car with which I had an association.

At around the same time, I made another new inroad in terms of my career. I talked Del into launching DelWorsham.com and I managed the fledgling website. Being on the internet was changing every aspect of the sport. Our site took off and quickly became one of the most popular in the NHRA realm and the "Photo Gallery" page was the main reason for that. Little did I know, at the time, that my approach to the selection of website photos was an indicator of how I'd approach blogging eight years later.

Pictures of the race car doing a burnout were fine but they were everywhere. As I told Del, "I want fans to look at the photos from each race and feel like they were right there behind the ropes with us. And I can take them there in photos." I would later write my blog with the exact same intent.

Initially, we hired a guy in central California to host the site and make updates for us. I'd actually shoot the photos on 35mm film and send him the prints. Hey, it was still the Dark Ages. Within a month of its launch the site was going great and the photos were the most popular feature.

Del helped me out by providing me with a used Compaq laptop he'd found. It ran Windows, of course, and that drove me a little crazy but at least I could do pit notes at the track. Pit Note Bob was alive and well.

I also started developing my master email list so I could write pre-race and post-race stories and send them out to sponsors, members of the media, and anyone else who wanted to get them. Everything was changing — fast.

As that first season progressed the race car was good and Del was brilliant, but our tight budget kept us from winning a lot of rounds. It was tough out there, against some formidable competition, and we were still underdogs. And, I figured, the people at CSK still thought it was easy. My stock statement, to Joe Spica and Ron Chisler after any question about our performance, was: "If this stuff was easy, we'd all be tied for first place."

By the time we got to Columbus, Ohio, in the middle of June, Del had amassed a grand total of six round wins to go with 10 losses and one inglorious DNQ. Unfortunately, two of those round wins came in Rockingham so they provided no points and we were sitting outside the Top 10, in 11th place.

In the first round at Columbus, Del (who had qualified 12th) faced some cat named Chuck Etchells. Chuck's car went up in tire smoke at the hit of the throttle, handing Del his seventh round on the season, but at the finish line the Checker, Schuck's, Kragen car burst into flames. It was a major fire but Del got it stopped and clambered out. Back in the pits I got my first whiff of a smell I'd always hate. It's the smell of burnt carbon fiber. It smells like death.

The crew somehow got the car cleaned up and back together but the second round was deja vu all over again. Dean Skuza smoked the tires at the hit and the CSK car tore away to another round win, and another inferno both under the hood and inside the cockpit. This one was even bigger and it singed Del's hands a little before he got out.

Del was still a young driver, but having started in the Funny Car class at age 21 he was already a veteran and he'd been on fire enough times to know the drill. In 1994, at Englishtown, he blew up a motor and caught his car on fire in a very big way. The burns to his hands were significant, requiring skin grafts, and he spent many weeks in the hospital and then a couple of months in rehab. This time, three years later in Columbus, he knew when to say "uncle." He wanted no more of the explosions until they figured out the problem and they chose not to compete in the semifinal. The fact the CSK body was badly charred to the point of being crispy helped them make that decision.

The two fires, however, were not the biggest news at the Columbus race. Just before the first qualifying session, as Eckman and Orndorff warmed up the CSK Pro Stock car, an explosion rang out and crew members ducked for cover.

On the ground, a pressurized metal bottle was spewing vapor. It was nitrous oxide, a horsepower booster that was, and still is, strictly illegal in the Pro Stock class. The team quickly put their car away, locked the trailer, and left the track. Within days, both Eckman and Orndorff were fined and suspended indefinitely. The Checker, Schuck's, Kragen Pro Stock car was never seen again.

The next race on the docket in '97 was St. Louis, and Barbara coincidentally needed to be there for some IBM meetings. On her one free afternoon I drove her over to the track to meet Del and the team.

It was the day before racing was set to start, though, so with it being "set-up day" the teams and crew members were all in a casual mode. Her one comment about that was, "I thought it would be more formal. Don't you guys wear uniforms?" I'm not sure she believed me when I replied that we did, indeed, all dress alike when actual fans were in attendance.

Right after the St. Louis race came the Western Swing and that three-in-a-row segment of the tour came with a benefit and a challenge. The benefit was the fact I'd get $1,000 each Sunday for three straight weeks. The challenge was actually making it to all three races. I was nearly broke and most of my credit cards were maxed.

When I flew to San Francisco for the Sonoma race, I rented a car from Budget with my Sears card. Sears owned Budget Rent-A-Car then and the rental company accepted the parent company's charge card. It was the only card in my wallet that had enough credit left to pay for a car.

At the end of the race Del brought me up to the tiny lounge in the Worsham Racing trailer and he looked me right in the eye.

He asked me, "How are you doing financially?"

"Not very well," I replied.

"I kind of figured that," he said in return. "I know how much it costs to come to all these races and I know what we're paying you. I also know you have rent for your apartment, a car payment, and lots of other things you have to pay for. Unless you're independently wealthy, you've got to be broke."

I admitted as such, and he said, "How much do you need to get healthy again?"

I really didn't know what to say, but the first figure that popped into my head was $5,000. That wouldn't erase my debt but it would put me in a much better position than I was currently in.

"No problem," Del said as he wrote me a check for five grand, calling it a "midseason bonus."

I thought Del was a great guy when all we'd do was say hello in the pits. I learned about his integrity when the CSK deal came up and he insisted they talk to me, when most others would've taken the money and waved goodbye. On that day in Sonoma, it became clear that I'd never met anyone like him. And he valued what I brought to the team. It was a defining moment in my life and career. The dream was happening, and I was right in the middle of it.

When the Western Swing was over, I put Shasta in my car and drove him to Chapel Hill. He'd get to move in with Barbara before I would and she welcomed my furry little buddy with open arms.

As Indy approached, I put "Moving Sale" notices in every building at my apartment complex and within a day I'd sold my big sectional sofa, along with my washer/dryer combo, my desk, and my bed. I'd be moving right after the U.S. Nationals, and by the time that day arrived all I needed was a rental van. I didn't come close to filling it.

I took off in the van while Barbara followed in my Saab on the Tuesday following the Labor Day race. We spent the night in Charleston, West Virginia, at a Red Roof Inn. The same Charleston where I'd spent the summer as a three-year-old son of a baseball manager. It was also after Labor Day, and that was a key date in our life as a couple. At one minute before midnight I turned to Barbara and said, "Oh by the way, it's after Labor Day. Will you marry me?"

Luckily for me, she said yes. She also punched me in the arm for waiting all day to ask.

Barbara needed to get back to Chapel Hill in a hurry the next day, so I followed at a more leisurely pace in the van. When I got to the convenience store near her house, I called her from a pay phone and made one request.

"Please don't be offended, but when I get there in a couple of minutes I'd really like to see Shasta and spend some time with him," I said. She was fine with that. He was, after all, my little boy.

He was also adapting not only to Barbara's house, but to my racing schedule. Since he was a kitten he'd shown many fabulous traits but one bordered on sheer talent. I knew I could leave him enough food to last through any race weekend and I never once came home to an empty bowl. As if he could read a racing schedule, he seemed to know how long he needed the food to last and he'd ration it perfectly.

In addition, he made no secret out of the fact he adored Barbara and that was important because, until he had met her, he had shown no inclination to like anyone but me.

For an office, I settled into what would've been the dining room at Barbara's lovely home. She was only using that room to store wine, though, so I pushed some cases out of the way and put my computer on an antique table. And, as the weeks flew by we began finalizing our wedding plans. With both of us having been married before we each felt the common urge to run off and get married alone, because we didn't want our friends and families to feel obligated to spend a bunch of money to be there. With that settled, we picked Hawaii as the location. We'd get married on New Year's Eve on the beach in Maui. We'd cash in some airline miles to get there but we wouldn't scrimp on lodging or dining. If we had to borrow money for our wedding, then so be it.

On the track, 1997 ended on a series of down notes. Starting at Indy, we won exactly one round of racing at the final seven races. We needed to get on a roll if we wanted to catch Gary Densham, who was 10th in points, but our parts and our luck ran out. We ended the season 12-22 with one DNQ. We finished 11th in the standings.

But we also concluded the year with a very engaged and loyal sponsor. When we had attended their convention in Phoenix that fall we began discussions on how to restructure the deal. They would raise our payments in 1998, which was a good thing, while they also asked if we could come up with an "incentive bonus plan" of some sort, so that we'd get paid more if we did well on the track. Del and I discussed that for a few days and I then fired off the proposal to Spica.

Our goal was to be a top 10 team and to guarantee that beyond doubt it would be wise if you averaged getting to the second round at all the races. You didn't have to actually get to the second round at all 22 points races, but for each first-round loss you'd have to get to the semifinal at another to keep the average going. If you could do that you'd probably end up sixth or seventh in points, and that was our goal.

We devised a bonus plan that would pay us a little for every second round appearance, and much more for each incremental round thereafter. We also would get a $5,000 bonus for winning the awards for either Best Appearing Car or Best Appearing Crew. If we raced well enough to be 10th or better in 1998, the bonus plan would kick in close to six figures.

On top of that, we asked them to change the payment plan in one way. Clutch discs were then as they are now, in that they were usually inconsistent from one production batch to another. The bigger teams had an edge because they could buy their discs in one large batch. We had never had that the financial wherewithal to earn that privilege. We asked CSK to lower our monthly checks from February to November, but to significantly increase our January check. We could then invest that money in new discs that would all be from the same batch.

Shortly thereafter they presented us with the formal multi-year contract. It wasn't for as much as we'd asked, but it locked us in for two more seasons and it was a substantial step up from the first year's sponsor fee. And, it included every element of the bonus plan we had pitched.

Chuck Worsham had asked me a number of times during the season if I was out there finding a new sponsor. He didn't think CSK was paying anything close to what the program was worth and he thought I should be beating the bushes to find us a better deal. My answer to each of those questions was the same.

I said, "We already have a sponsor, and I see it as my job and my responsibility to grow this into the exact deal you want. Developing CSK into a bigger sponsor is way easier, and way better, than trying to find a replacement for them."

After the Worshams signed the new deal, Del understood completely what I'd been talking about. As he put it, "The best things about these guys are that they're for real, they're really passionate, and the check comes each month right on time. Someday, I want to be able to pay you $100,000. If you handle your end, and we get better with the car, we can develop this thing into something big." I was honored to be trusted to handle my part of the program.

Chuck had begun to hear from the CSK guys about how good my PR work was. They said, "He paints some really good pictures with his writing. Heck, you guys can DNQ and he makes us feel like you did great!"

From that point forward, if we'd stumble in qualifying or on race day Chuck would say to me, "How are you going to sugarcoat this one, you silver-tongued devil?" I'm not sure that was a compliment, but even if it wasn't I appreciated the fact that he knew I brought some real value to the team.

Finally, on the Sunday night after the 1997 Finals in Pomona I was introduced to a new concept. It was very informal in those days but it was something all the pro teams knew about. It was the end-of-season pit party.

When the race was over, and our season ended with it, I was preparing to head back to the hotel in West Covina when Del said, "Hang out. After all the fans are gone, we have a big party. It's a lot of fun."

An hour or so after the final car had raced down the Pomona track, teams started to circulate and socialize. At Jim Head's pit there was a stereo playing and a disco ball spinning under the awning. Red Solo cups were everywhere, filled with a variety of adult beverages. It was, indeed, a lot of fun. Nearing midnight, I headed back to my room. I was already looking forward to the 1998 rendition.

After I got back to Chapel Hill, where I was feeling more and more at home, we finalized our wedding plans. Barbara found a private residence on Keawakapu Beach in Maui, where the woman who owned the multi-million dollar house would allow us to be married on her lawn, just steps from the sand. We'd also be heading over to the islands a few days before our wedding day to spend some time in Honolulu before shifting over to Maui.

To wrap up my work, I decided I wanted to give the team and the sponsor an easy-to-read compilation of the season, so I spent the early part of December assembling a coil-bound booklet aptly entitled "1997 — The Season In Review." It was the first such document I had ever put together but it established a precedent. I'd compile one after every season going forward, for the rest of my career.

For Christmas, Barbara and I drove to Pittsburgh to spend the holiday with her brother Tim, the only Doyle sibling still residing in her hometown. It was a great way to get to know Tim, his wife Kelly, and their boys Colin and Sean, who were just little kids at the time. Christmas is made for kids and being around them is the best possible treat.

After the holiday, we were off but we almost didn't make it. To get to Honolulu in one long day, we had to take a 6 a.m. flight out of Raleigh. We arranged for a taxi to pick us up at 4:30. At 4:35 the taxi's honking horn woke us up! We'd arranged so much, and Barbara had done the brunt of it, but both of us forgot to set an alarm.

I've never brushed my teeth, combed my hair, and gotten dressed so quickly. We made the flight with minutes to spare.

On the second leg, from Dallas to Honolulu, we were seated in the coach section of an American Airlines wide-body jumbo. We shared that space with the Vanderbilt University basketball team. The young man who sat behind Barb's seat was about 6-foot-10. The guy behind me was an inch taller. Neither one of us could recline our seat backs at all, since the players were wedged in with their knees against our seats. It was an inconvenience for us but it must have been miserable for those big guys.

Our first few days were spent at the New Otani Hotel, near Waikiki. Rather than being directly on Waikiki Beach the New Otani sits further east, almost at the foot of Diamond Head. It was gorgeous and we loved the place. We snorkeled in a protected lagoon, we walked on the beach, we hiked to the top of Diamond Head, and we sampled the nightlife in the more bustling part of the city, enjoying the Mai Tais all the way.

We also discovered the restaurant at the New Otani. The Hau Tree Lanai featured outdoor dining with beachside views of the Pacific and the peppercorn Filet Mignon was, and still is, one of the best steaks I've ever eaten.

After a few days we jetted over to Maui and checked into a condo Barbara had found online. It was right on Keawakapu Beach and only 200 yards from the tropical backyard where we'd be getting married on New Year's Eve.

The condo came complete with a couple of boogie boards, as well, and I quickly discovered how much I liked that. There was a storm out at sea, so we had some nice four to six-foot waves, and I rode so many I about tore all the hair off my chest. What a riotous time we had.

I had never snorkeled before we arrived on Oahu so, of course, we took it to a whole different level on Maui. We took a snorkeling cruise on a catamaran, in deep water, and had the privilege of swimming next to giant sea turtles who apparently have an appetite for frozen peas because that's how we attracted them. Then the boat took us out to Molokini, the crescent-shaped and partially submerged volcanic crater offshore. They dropped us off inside the protected lagoon, where the sea life was teeming with all sizes and colors of fabulous fish.

Then, they told us they'd move the catamaran outside the crater and we'd need to swim out to them when it was time to go.

When our time was up I started kicking my way out toward the boat, looking down and around at all the brilliantly-colored fish, and then as I was looking straight down I passed over the edge of the crater. What had been bright and brilliant and full of fish, instantly became an absolute abyss.

I'd never seen nor experienced anything like it. I was swimming along in water no more than 20 feet deep, where I could clearly see the bottom, and then there was nothing. It was impossible to tell how far down I could see because it all just disappeared into an endless descent featuring the darkest navy-blue water I'd ever seen. Considering I'd just snorkeled for the first time a few days earlier in front of the New Otani, in water no more than eight feet deep and often less than five, it was an imposing thing to experience. Swimming along in that incomprehensibly deep water has a way of making your tiny human existence seem inconsequential. Fortunately, I kept the panic at bay and got back to the boat.

When New Year's Eve arrived, the weather threatened to ruin all our plans. The storm at sea had spawned rain showers in paradise but just before the sunset ceremony was to begin, it finally stopped raining.

Barbara looked enchanting. I was aiming for handsome. We exchanged vows under a bank of palm trees with the Pacific surf serenading us. We popped a bottle of champagne and enjoyed two glasses out on the beach. The wedding planner drew a large heart in the sand with the words "Just Mauied" written within.

We'd met, via email, roughly nine months earlier. We'd met, in person, about six months prior to this moment. We were standing on the beach at sunset, me in my tux and her in her beautiful dress, wearing wedding rings and toasting ourselves with bubbly. We were husband and wife.

From the beach, we headed to the Grand Wailea Resort for a private wedding-night dinner. The hotel had arranged for us to eat our celebratory meal on a private balcony in front of the Grand Dining Room. When we approached the desk and gave them our names, the Maitre 'd seemed nervous.

His eyes shifted back and forth as he rocked on one foot and then the other, before he finally said, "We have a bit of a small problem and I hope you are not too inconvenienced. We have another very important guest who also requested the private balcony. She is very recognizable, and likes the privacy very much. I'm not even supposed to reveal her name, but if you'd be so kind as to share the balcony with Halle Berry and her boyfriend we would very much appreciate it."

Well... OK!

We just smiled and said hello when we were seated, and soon thereafter a small cat wandered onto the balcony between our two tables. Halle Berry gave the kitty a pat on the head and said to us, "Did you just get married?" We then chatted with her throughout dinner, and her boyfriend looked none too pleased to have us invading his New Year's Eve date with one of the most beautiful women on Earth. He ignored us. Halle was wonderful.

After dinner, as we passed through the incredible lobby to get in a taxi, our new buddy Halle shouted from across the room, "Congratulations again, you two. And Happy New Year!"

From that night forward, whenever Halle Berry would appear on TV or in a movie, I would nudge Barbara and say, "There's your friend." And yes, for the record, she is absolutely as gracious as she is beautiful.

Before our trip was over we departed the condo and spent a couple of days on the other side of the island, in Hana. The road to Hana is well known as a challenging route full of curves and bridges, all on narrow pavement carved into the side of the hills above the Pacific Ocean. Barbara could never have made the trip in the back seat, but being on the passenger's side up front allowed her to only feel queasy. Motion sickness is no fun.

We rented a hillside condo in Hana, atop a long open field that stretched to the ocean. Horses looked back at us while we enjoyed the view. It had been a heck of a trip. And we were going back home as husband and wife.

When we returned from Hawaii it was time to crank up the processes for the 1998 season. 1997 had been a momentous year for me and it was great to have some continuity for the next season.

I'd entered 1997 working for a guy who had folded a soccer team out from under me. I persuaded him to make a generous offer to Del and Chuck Worsham and that got me in the game again. Then, David's legal issues opened the door for me to work directly for the Worsham/CSK team, although it came with a cut in pay. And, I met a girl and got to know her. We were married on the final day of the year. Sometimes you only figure out enormous moments in hindsight. I know I realized, in real time, that it had been one of the most important years of my life.

Not too far into 1998, Barbara got her first indication at work that IBM might be wanting to promote her again and that such a promotion would entail another relocation. If she got the position, as a company controller, we'd be moving to Austin, Texas.

She got the promotion, and we started to put the wheels into motion. We'd be moving. We also sold Barb's Miata and she began to drive the Saab, while I bought a used BMW 325i and drove that.

Del and Chuck gave me a nice raise for 1998, allowing me to not only pay all my bills but also contribute to the bottom line in my new household. My theory about just getting through 1997, knowing that if we did survive it would all start to become better in a big way, turned out to be true.

As an organization, we were improving rapidly in every way. Del and Chuck bought Joe Amato's transporter and the old cramped home-built rig was put out to pasture. We retired the button-down blue shirts and ordered custom crew uniforms from Simpson. Yes, they originally showed up with the words "Checker Schuck's Kragen" only half the size they were supposed to be, but Simpson remade them for us. We were certainly looking a lot more big-league.

We also signed a deal with General Motors and switched to Pontiac Firebird bodies with a new red and white paint scheme, designed by Guy Tilden, a graphic artist at CSK.

At the same time, I made a call to the marketing people at Mac Tools and landed our first tool sponsorship, allowing the team to hit the ground running with all new power tools to go with drawers full of shiny new wrenches and screwdrivers, all put away in fancy new red boxes.

And then the season started in February. It mostly did not go well. We lost heartbreakers, we lost blow-outs, and we demolished our fair share of parts.

We did manage to get a round in the bank at Pomona, but lost in front of our sponsors in Phoenix in the first round. By comparison, the Phoenix first-round loss seemed highly preferable to the DNQ we hung around our necks in Florida. To make it worse, the entire event was postponed for a week when torrential showers swamped the track after Friday qualifying. We had to go back to Gainesville the following weekend in order to officially screw up and miss the show.

We did, however, earn $5,000 by being named the winners of the "Best Appearing Car" award.

We then reeled off three more first-round losses in Houston, Atlanta (on Monday, after rain), and Richmond. Del and Chuck didn't seem to have much luck, and the car was being a brat. We needed some good news.

For me, the upcoming move to Austin was a bit of personal good news. The Houston race had given me a chance to drive over and spend a day in the state's capital city, to get a feel for where we might want to live and how much it would cost. I'd heard the area west of town, near Lake Travis, was a great spot. Upon my inspection, I concurred. We'd have to go house hunting together but I felt confident I'd at least found the part of town that would suit us the best.

After the race in Houston my fun meter hit another new mark on the gauge. CSK had invited us to their national convention at the Las Vegas Hilton and we needed to get there as soon as possible after the event. They wanted to display the race car, as well, so we needed to drive the transporter across half of America to do that. Marc Denner and I joined Del and Chuck for the long haul. We left Houston Raceway Park as soon as we could get packed up, and hit the road heading west on I-10.

I enjoyed riding in the front passenger seat for a shift, while Marc and Del snoozed in the sleeper's two bunks. It was my first time in a big rig and I was enjoying the view from way up there.

Later, Chuck and Del swapped the driver's seat and Marc and I took over the bunks. In the middle of the night, Del planned to fill up the tanks with diesel at a truck stop in El Paso. I woke up in the top bunk when he stopped at the top of the ramp. As he pulled in, to fuel up, I thought he shut the diesel motor off. I was wrong.

"Oh, crap," Del said. "I think I ran us out of fuel."

Diesel motors do not like running out of fuel. When the tanks do go dry, diesels can be notoriously hard to start. Our rig had run out of fuel at the exact moment Del pulled up to the pumps. After filling both tanks, Del hit the starter. No go. He tried again. No go, again.

Finally, they primed the motor with WD-40 and that got the pumps going fast enough for it to kick over. Apparently, that's an old trucker's trick. It was balky at first, but at 3 a.m. we were rolling again.

After roughly 26 hours of driving, after sunset on Monday night, we pulled in at the Hilton and parked the big rig on the edge of the lot. Riding along had been a real adventure but just like those long bus rides in the minor leagues I found it almost impossible to sleep.

The next morning we pulled the rig around to the freight entrance to unload the car. Las Vegas is a heavily unionized town and we'd already been told that the union convention workers would insist upon moving the car into the hallway where it would be displayed. So, we got it down on the ground with the transporter's liftgate and stood back. The workers walked around it for a while, discussed what to do, and finally said, "Why don't you guys move this thing. We'll escort you in."

For two days, we displayed the car and Del signed autographs. A lot of autographs. With thousands of CSK employees and executives on-site the autograph signing basically never ended. On the final night, the big send-off banquet was scheduled and we were the guests of honor.

It was a big hullaballoo, unlike anything I'd ever seen. After a massive banquet the musical guests took the stage. Brooks & Dunn rocked the house with all their country hits and I'm sure they didn't do it for pennies. We all had a blast, and we bonded a little more with our CSK counterparts.

But the team still desperately needed some good news, and it came three races later in the form of a 4.983 run in Dallas during the third qualifying session. It was Del's first trip down the track in the 4-second range and it made him the 14th member of the Castrol 4-Second Club. We celebrated with cigars after the fourth qualifying run and when another team sent over a bottle of Dom Perignon, we consumed it. Only, of course, because it would've been rude not to. It's a cultural thing.

A photo taken of us under the awning with our cigars and red Solo cups of Dom, included Del's new girlfriend. She was a lovely young lady by the name of Connie Medina. Del had met her not long after he made a huge change to his life by moving out of Chuck's house (where the race car "shop" was actually the garage) and into an apartment after the '97 season. By the time Dallas rolled around it was getting serious, and we all approved. It was great to have Connie with us for such a big moment.

We also won a round on Sunday, in Dallas, but managed to follow that up with another DNQ in Englishtown. I remember thinking it was a good thing we'd run the 4.98 at the Texas Motorplex. Had we not had that to smile about, we might've been losing our minds by the time we left New Jersey. Del got a huge ring for making the Castrol 4-Second Club, and a bunch of us ordered them as well, paying for them ourselves. I still wear mine from time to time.

I learned another lesson from Del after that DNQ in Englishtown. When we smoked the tires in Q4 I took off my ear muffs and threw them to the ground, shattering them into pieces. I was standing at the fence, in front of the top-end of the grandstand. When I told Del I'd done that he calmly said, "Hey man, you can't do that. You have to let it roll off your back. Never let this stuff get you too down. It all comes around, so even during the bad times we have to look professional and act like we've been here before."

I felt a little (a lot) embarrassed and I took those wise words seriously. I would never again publicly show any signs of anger.

We then had another bounce-back moment, in Chicago at the brand-new and incredibly impressive Route 66 Raceway. Until Route 66 was opened, tracks like the Texas Motorplex in Dallas or Houston Raceway Park were touted as "supertracks" in the world of drag racing. Route 66 took things to an entirely new level and we marveled at its size when we arrived. From the pits, it was easy to imagine we were parked next to a major college football stadium.

At that inaugural race we managed to get past Cory Lee in round one. Then we put Cruz Pedregon on the trailer. In the semifinal, we sent Jim Epler packing. We had a date in the final with one Whit Bazemore. I had to watch from the grandstand.

In 1997 and 1998, PR reps were not granted "Restricted Area Access" credentials. Our options were to watch the races from the media center or from the stands, unless our team provided a crew pass for us. Those crew credentials were precious, so they were rarely "wasted" on a PR person.

I had stood at the fence in Dallas watching my team make its first 4-second run. I was in a similar location at Englishtown when we failed to qualify. Now I was at the fence again as Del and Whit faced off in the final. I was pacing and nervous, frustrated I couldn't be down there with my team. We lost, but we were feeling better about ourselves. It was the first final round I'd been to as a full-time PR rep, on my own.

Barbara and I had taken one weekend off to travel to Austin on a serious house-hunting trip. After cruising through a westside development called Steiner Ranch we were about to settle on a modest two-story home there. And then the agent we had retained mentioned a development just to the east, on the other side of a huge ravine, called River Place.

It was a big step up, almost to the point of being intimidating. River Place had its own golf course and country club. It had some magnificent homes. It had canyons and ravines and views for miles. It was far more upscale than anything Barbara and I had ever dreamed of. We saw one house we liked which had just been completed, and because it backed to trees and had no view, it was priced to sell. We were stunned it was in our range and we put a contract on it immediately. It would be the nicest home either of us had ever inhabited, much less owned.

The next day we drove by the house again and noticed five cars in the driveway of the home across the street. Maybe they were having a party. On a Monday morning. Maybe.

We took a walk and peered around the backside of that house, peeking over the fence. We could see beds in every window, including the kitchen and living room. Apparently, a dozen people lived in the house right across the street from the one we had just bought.

We got back in the car and drove around River Place some more, debating whether or not we should cancel the contract. And when we turned right onto Love Bird Lane we saw a "For Sale" sign. The little brick house was tucked into the side of a canyon down a steep winding driveway, looking like only a small ranch-style home from the front. In back, though, you could see that the front of the house was only the upper level. An entire lower level was below it. The back of the house featured massive windows with spectacular canyon views.

We called the seller's agent and got a showing an hour later. By that evening we were breaking the news to our original agent, explaining the gaggle of residents in the home across the street. We then worked with the listing agent alone and within a couple of days we had bought ourselves a home. On Love Bird Lane in River Place.

People asked us, "Did you buy it because it was on Love Bird Lane?" The truth was, we nearly didn't buy it because of the street name but the house was too cool to pass up. By early summer, we were moving in.

At the same time, on the track things pretty much going south again. We went winless in Columbus, St. Louis, and Denver (where we won Best Appearing Crew for another $5,000).

And speaking of my hometown of St. Louis and its addition to the NHRA tour, it bears a mention that I never understood the original scheduling of that race. For the first decade of its existence Gateway International Raceway hosted its NHRA national event right smack dab in the middle of summer. In St. Louis. It made no sense.

I always said, "I would've loved to have been in the boardroom the day NHRA added St. Louis to the schedule, and someone thought late June would be a great time for the race. Did no one raise any questions about that?"

We raced in St. Louis when it was well over 100 degrees. We raced there when they had the local fire department flood the track in an effort to cool it off. We raced there entirely at night and still sweltered.

Finally, in 2006, they moved the race to early May. For 10 years, I shook my head at the June date and prepared to roast alive.

After losing in Denver, we did manage to pick up round wins in Sonoma and Seattle before making it to the semifinal at both Brainerd and Indy. The semifinal finish in Brainerd was of the heartbreaker variety, when we couldn't fire the car to even face Ron Capps. But, the wins in rounds one and two moved us into 10th place. We were getting there, in terms of our goals.

We picked up our 12th round win in Reading, Pennsylvania, then went winless at Topeka and Memphis before winning round number 13 back in Dallas. A first-round loss in Houston led us back to Pomona, where we promptly ended the year on the sourest of notes. We failed to qualify.

We finished the season with a 13-19 record, with three ugly DNQs, but we got to a final and did some good things, including the fact we'd earned our gaudy Castrol 4-Second Club rings. It seemed like there was a light at the end of the tunnel. We just hoped it wasn't a train coming in our direction.

To cap it off, we all got to attend the NHRA Awards Ceremony as the 10th-place team. We rented a stretch limo, put on our best formal attire, and rode in style to the Cerritos Center for the Performing Arts. Did I mention we were getting there and seeing the light? We'd attained our first goal. We were a Top-10 team.

In the weeks leading up to the banquet Denny Darnell, the head of media relations for NHRA, asked me if Del, Chuck, and Grandma Worsham would all be attending. He said it was important for all three of them to be there. Finally, he confided in me and asked for my secrecy on some big news.

During the banquet, the Worshams were going to be surprised. World-class tuner Alan Johnson took the stage to award the 1998 Blaine Johnson award, presented in honor of his late brother. The award would regularly be presented to a person or group who best exemplified all of the admirable qualities for which Blaine had been known.

When Alan began talking about a family who never hesitated to help when he and Blaine were first starting out in the sport, Del and Chuck began to fidget. They knew he was talking about them. When Alan called all three Worshams to the stage, I think Del was more than a little terrified.

It was well known that while Del was cool as a snow cone in the car, he was uncomfortable with a camera in his face or when he had to speak in public. Because I was sworn to secrecy, I couldn't tip him off. He had to simply get up on stage and say something. He did a fabulous job and I think that surprise speech helped him turn a corner when it came to those sorts of things.

As we wrapped up '98 and began to look forward to 1999, Barbara and I were discovering just how much we loved Austin. The food was amazing, especially at our favorite Tex-Mex stop, Chuy's in Barton Springs. The margaritas weren't bad either, and as the "Live Music Capital" of the United States, there was plenty of fun to be had downtown around 6th Street.

Our home on Love Bird Lane took shape quickly, and it was very comfortable. It wasn't ostentatious or over-the-top like some of the McMansions in River Place and it was perfect for us. Its design was basically upside down. When you walked in the front door my office was immediately to the right, the living room to the left, and the kitchen just ahead. Downstairs, in the lower level, was the master bedroom, two guest rooms, and a second living room. In the master bath was the biggest Jacuzzi tub either of us had ever seen. We called it Mega-Tub and we used it almost every night.

The house sat on nearly an acre, although the lot was shaped like a piece of pie as it ran down the steep side of the ravine, eventually coming to a point. We picked our way through the brush and trees one day just to "see our land," as it were. There wasn't much we could do to use most of it, and there were plenty of critters to deal with, but at least we knew no one would build behind us and block our amazing view, which stretched across the big ravine all the way to Steiner Ranch.

Not long after we moved in I opened the back door to walk out onto the patio and deck and a scorpion calmly walked right in the house, with his tail curled perilously over his head. It was as if he'd been waiting to be let in and once he was in the door he just stopped and looked around. Having almost no experience with scorpions (other than those I saw in James Bond movies) I wasn't sure what to do but I knew better than to try to pick him up with my hand. So I grabbed a magazine and thrust it under him just long enough to toss him back outside. We decided we probably wouldn't go "see our land" too much more after that. You never know what you'll find in the Hill Country of Texas, but scorpions, black widow spiders, large snakes, and lots of other living beings were almost always around. We once opened a drawer in the bathroom to see a creature sitting on Barb's makeup. It was hideous, and all we could call it was a "gazzillopede" due to all its squirmy legs. You'd be wise to shake out your shoes before putting them on each morning.

One day, as I drove up River Place Boulevard to go to the local H-E-B grocery store, I saw something large and black crossing the road ahead of me. I wasn't sure what it was but I saw it from a good tenth of a mile away. I thought it might be a kitten and if it was I was going to stop and save it. As I got closer I figured it out. It was tarantula and it was huge. As in gigantic. And I don't care how many people tell me tarantulas are cool and make good pets. No, thank you.

Not long after the '98 season ended, Joe Spica called with an idea. At CSK they were thinking of expanding their marketing footprint again and that meant a couple of things. The first was their intention to sponsor the Phoenix race itself, making it the Checker, Schuck's, Kragen Nationals. The second was a plan to add a Top Fuel car to the stable.

A few of their original thoughts about who we should team up with only made it clear they still had some learning to do about the sport. In turn, Del made it clear we weren't interested, at all, to race with some of the teams they were thinking about. He said, "Look, there's one Top Fuel team out there that's a lot like us. The owner tunes the car and drives it, and he has no primary sponsor. I'm sure he'll do it for what you're giving us. His name is Jim Head."

Del then called Jim and explained the deal to him. The gist of what he said was, "Jim, it's not a ton of money but it's their money, not yours. And the check comes on exactly the right day each month. They're still learning the sport, but they're already passionate about it and all they really want to do is win. You should take this deal. Just take the money and do what they ask."

Jim did just that, and we made plans to share a pit space with him and his team in 1999. He'd park his motorhome across the back of the pit, and we'd set up some tables, umbrellas, and chairs in the middle of the "U" shaped area with his team on the right side and ours on the left. We had a teammate.

While all the planning for '99 was taking place Del's personal life was changing. Right around Christmas he called to tell me that he'd asked Connie to marry him. The second part of that conversation included, "And I want you to be my best man." I was stunned.

Del had been racing on a big stage for eight years. He had friends who had been with him since the first day. Heck, he was famous! And I had just completed my second season as his team manager and PR rep. Yet somehow he asked me to be his best man. The honor was — and always will be — all mine.

They set a date for February, and they chose the MGM Grand in Las Vegas as the spot. CSK also had chosen the MGM Grand as the spot for their annual convention in 1999, so we were going to be getting plenty comfortable at that fabulous resort.

We were all plowing forward.

Winning Is Good

The winter prior to the 1999 season was filled with details ranging from paint schemes, to uniforms, to new associate sponsors, in addition to the regular PR work I was becoming so much more comfortable with and adept at. We also had to find the time to do some preseason testing before we headed for Pomona the first week of February, then had to carve out the time for Del and Connie's wedding, in Las Vegas, on February 21, just days before the Phoenix race.

The aforementioned associate sponsors would be a key piece of the puzzle going forward, as CSK discovered that working with vendors and having them support the race team was a valuable asset for both the team and the sponsor. Although the sponsorship payments were growing the Worsham organization was still lagging well behind the big hitters in the class in terms of budget, so having CSK arrange to have spark plugs, filters, oil, solvents, and other "bottom line" items donated to the team was a big step forward.

In an interview at the time Del summed it up nicely when he said, "I guess if our first primary sponsor had been a beer company we just would've gotten the checks each month and some free beer. I've got nothing against free beer, but having CSK as our sponsor means we get free oil, solvents, filters, bearings, and a whole bunch of other stuff we would've had to buy. Right down to things like shop towels and Pepsi. It was just like having CSK write us a check for all of that stuff. It goes right to the bottom line."

Things were getting better and our red CSK car was being adorned with a bunch of new decals to support the vendors who were donating product to us. In addition, we kept building our direct relationships with General Motors and Mac Tools. Since tools typically have a long lifespan we were able to branch out each year and order more optional stuff, knowing we had a large enough inventory of basic wrenches and ratchets. As our tool boxes grew the amount of time-saving power and air tools increased right along with the sponsorship. Again, relationships were the key. Earning the trust and support of Tony Merritt and Roger Spee, the key marketing people at Mac Tools, was important to Del and me.

Establishing ourselves with GM and the Pontiac brand was also a critical component in our growth. We did all we could to maximize the value we were providing for Pontiac and we worked hard at those relationships, as well. Fred Simmonds, who managed the GM Racing program, believed in us and went to bat for us on numerous occasions.

Early in the year, during a test session in Phoenix, we helped Cristen Powell get started on her Funny Car license. I'd known Cristen enough to say hello to her in the pits but we got to know each other a lot better as she learned the ropes in a Funny Car. She was a terrifically talented racer, who had a passion for going fast, but as I got to know her better I learned what her best attribute was. She was as good a person as anyone I'd ever met in the sport. She still is.

And while she was making laps I got to be the guy who guided her back from her burnouts. There's a first time for everything, and that was big fun.

In terms of relationships with NHRA, there were some new people in the Media Relations Department and I took that as an opportunity to make a big request. I asked them why PR reps weren't given "Restricted Area Access" hard-card credentials.

The answer, from a new NHRA guy, was, "I have no idea. It would be smart for you to have that. Can't your team provide you with one?"

I explained that our crew passes were usually outnumbered by the total number of actual crew people we had at a race, so they were almost never given to me. I'd had one of those only two or three times in two years. I also mentioned how valuable it would be to have instant starting-line access to Chuck and the crew, to get comments and explanations right after things happened. One week later my PR colleagues and I each got a letter inviting us to apply for (and pay for) a Restricted Area hard card. Sometimes you just have to ask.

As Pomona approached I had a feeling our profile at the track was going to elevate a bit with the Head Racing partnership and Jim's Top Fuel car. With a much bigger pit area, the visual impact of the two CSK teams would likely be greater than the simple sum of the two parts. What I didn't know was that such a likelihood actually made Del a little nervous.

When Del and I drove out to the track for the first time, after the teams were set up, we drove in the pits and came around the corner to see it all. He got quiet, then said, "Oh, my gosh."

By then, entering his ninth year of professional racing, most people knew Del was shy around the media and in front of big groups. Among his teammates and peers he was a completely different guy and extraordinarily popular but he didn't do well with public speaking or media work. What I discovered on that first day in 1999 was that the root of it was Del being slightly uncomfortable as the center of attention. Up until then the Worshams' pit area blended in amidst a long row of big rigs. With another transporter parked next to them they were insulated from the glare of standing out in a crowd. Del loved signing autographs, and would do that as often as possible, but he was never comfortable being the focus of attention. He was a bit intimidated when we got out of the car and saw the full two-team set-up.

Del was also smart enough to know that he was going to have to get used to it. The CSK program showed no signs of doing anything but getting bigger. There was no going back to the good old days. These were the newest version of the good old days.

He still wasn't comfortable making speeches or being interviewed but he was getting incrementally better at it. Spica had asked me if I could give Del some "media training" and we had done a bit of that sort of thing, even with NHRA's help, but I never was much of a believer in it. Being uncomfortable on camera is something that is induced by stress. Practicing it was doing it without the stress. Just like I always hit a ton when the baseball games didn't count, it was hard to fabricate the stress level to make the training seem real.

Then, one day early in 1999, we were going to be involved in a promotion and I was asked to introduce Del in front of a large crowd. That sort of thing was right in my sweet spot so I had no problem ad-libbing it, even getting a few laughs from the group. Del did his bit, and afterward he said, "You make that look easy. How can you make it look so easy? Don't you get nervous?"

All I said was, "Why get nervous? It's just talking. You and I do it all day, and that doesn't make you nervous. Why should talking to a group make you nervous?"

Maybe it was my imagination but I swore I could see the figurative light bulb go on over Del's head. He had a kind of wry smile, and he nodded. It is, after all, just talking. He got better and better in all of those situations and he improved on them almost daily. He had finally turned that corner.

One major retail promotion involving our team, our driver, and our car was also about to happen. Somehow, some way, for some reason, Hot Wheels and McDonald's had asked me if we would agree to have the CSK Funny Car involved in a huge Happy Meal promotion.

A very professional executive-looking guy had approached me at our pit during the Finals at the end of '98 and he briefly pitched me the concept, adding that he could only have one NHRA team and he was talking to some others as well. My initial thought was that he was either kidding or a complete imposter. When he handed me his card, I knew he was neither. I said yes immediately and made a pitch for just how much we'd do to help promote it. We would run Hot Wheels decals in a prominent location on the car, we'd help with PR, and I'd be the point person from the first day, helping Hot Wheels with the design. I understood there would be no financial compensation for the promotion but the exposure would be priceless.

One day later he returned with a colleague and let me know they'd selected us. We had a lot of work to do in a limited amount of time.

A series of Hot Wheels cars would be packaged in Happy Meals for months and we were chosen to be the only drag racing representatives, alongside some NASCAR, IndyCar, and Formula 1 teams.

Roughly eight million Del Worsham Hot Wheels cars would be given away. I worked closely with the Hot Wheels guys on the design of our little car and because our sponsor was an auto parts retailer there were no restrictions on what logos we could show. If we'd been sponsored by a beer or tobacco company we wouldn't have been able to be a part of it without taking the logos off, but I hit it off really well with the guy who was making the promotion happen and he agreed to everything I asked for.

I wanted the car to look like Del's real car, right down to having his name above the windows and the CSK logos on the sides and hood. We also managed to get a small Mac Tools decal included as well as the Auburn Foundry logo. John Fink and his family owned Auburn Foundry, in northeast Indiana and he had been supporting Del and Chuck for many years, often stepping up when times were financially tough. Because of that, the team was still almost universally known as Worsham & Fink Racing.

And there were actually two versions of the CSK Funny Car. One was the current version and a second car was the "future" version, in a science-fiction sort of way. It featured 12 cylinders and a rear-engine design and it looked like something from well into the next century. Both cars also came as interactive kits. The kids would receive them in the correct colors but a sheet of decals would also be in the packaging, along with instructions as to how to apply them and where to put them. I imagine there were more than a few creative applications of those decals by eight-year-olds all across America.

I also managed to make our car the only one to appear on the actual paper bags that would be used for the Happy Meals, in those days before Happy Meal boxes, and Del's Firebird was on the promotional signs next to the drive-thru ordering system.

We were in Arizona when the promotion kicked off and as a group we all headed for the nearest McDonald's. It was surreal to stand there, with Del Worsham himself, and stare at all the promotional stuff that featured our car and our driver.

I'd like to be able to say the entire McDonald's promotion came about because of some amazing legwork done by the PR guy but that wouldn't necessarily be true. I think luck played the biggest role in landing it. I'll take credit for giving our driver and our sponsors more exposure than any of the other stock cars or open-wheel cars in the promotion, though, and again that was further proof that relationships, honesty, and integrity will get you a long way. Even new relationships.

On the track, to kick off the season, we came out of the blocks really well in Pomona. We qualified fourth on a new personal best time for Del, of 4.96 seconds. We faced Dale Creasy in round one Sunday.

I like Dale Creasy. I always have. He's a great guy who has persevered through a lot of adversity. That being said, there was no way we should lose to him in round one.

We knew Dale would make a conservative pass just to keep us honest, but we also knew we could slow down a tenth of a second and still win by a good margin.

And then the CSK car smoked the tires. When Del pedaled it the car decided (in its own evil and possessed way) to instead shake the tires. We lost to Dale's 5.22 and Pomona was over.

On the other side of the CSK pit Jim Head won his first round in the red and white colors but then lost in the second. Our new pseudo-teammate already had one more round in the bank than we did.

I headed back to Austin for a week and a half and then it was time to head to Vegas. Del and Connie had decided to get married in style, at the MGM Grand's wedding chapel in front of a gathering of close friends and family.

As the best man it was my responsibility to arrange a bachelor party on the night before the wedding. We were in Las Vegas so it was an obvious choice to do something racy, along the lines of "what happens in Vegas, stays in Vegas." That would've been obvious. I chose, instead, to rent a private section of a room at Dave & Buster's, the adult version of a gaming arcade. We could drink all the beer we wanted and still have fun playing pinball and other arcade games.

And we could walk back to the hotel. I'm not sure about the other guys but Del had a great time. So did I.

The next day it was my job to help the groom put on his tux. For guys who don't do it often, that can be difficult. My next responsibility was to get him to the chapel on time, while avoiding any contact with Connie until she walked down the aisle. I wouldn't say he had cold feet but he was as nervous as I'd ever seen him and I had the solution. In their luxurious suite they had a few adult beverages to choose from. I took the bottle of Skyy vodka out of the freezer and poured him a shot. That "liquid courage" broke the ice and we headed downstairs.

The ceremony was short but also heartfelt, emotional, and just plain wonderful. Afterward, Barbara and I joined the Worsham family, the Medina family, and other close friends for a celebration. I was thrilled for my boss and honored to have stood next to him on what was one of the biggest days of his life. After the party, they only had two days for a honeymoon before we needed to be in Phoenix for the Checker, Schuck's, Kragen Nationals.

With it being the first year of CSK's sponsorship of the race our promotional and appearance schedule took a big turn for the busier. We came into town on Tuesday night, did displays around town on Wednesday and Thursday, got up before dawn to be on the morning news shows, did a tour of the area TV stations for interviews, and generally ran like crazy for two days. I'd gotten Spica's assurance that once we were done on Thursday night the rest of the weekend would strictly be about racing. He kept his word.

We then had nothing but trouble during qualifying thanks to a gaggle of gremlins that nibbled at our performance every session. We even broke an oil line during a warm-up, spraying 70-weight synthetic oil all over the side of the transporter and most of the crew. Both literally and figuratively, it wasn't pretty.

We managed to sneak in 12th and somehow earned back a little luck by getting past Dean Skuza in the opener. Another oil leak ended our day in round two. We'd survived the first CSK Nationals but we hadn't owned it.

A few weeks later we needed to head to Las Vegas again, for the CSK convention and banquet. This time it would be at the MGM Grand and after Del and Connie's wedding we were familiar with the place.

We'd ordered more than a thousand T-shirts and Del and Jim spent almost an entire day signing every one of them for the attendees. I'd never seen so many boxes of T-shirts in my life.

To cap off the weekend we had another banquet and concert. This time it was Huey Lewis and the News and we all had a sensational time dancing and jamming to their hits. Barbara had even made it from Austin and we had a marvelous time at the show.

After the concert Jim's son Chad Head (who is never shy) sought out Huey and asked him to come with us to the upstairs club at MGM. Much to our surprise, he said he'd love to.

While a group of about 15 of us walked through the resort and the massive MGM casino it was difficult for us to keep up with Huey, who kept his head down while moving fast through the crowd. At one point a totally panicked Joe Spica turned to us with desperation in his eyes, yelling, "Come on everyone. We're LOSING HUEY!" We managed to catch up despite our laughter and had a good couple of hours with Huey at the club. He was kind, gracious, and very inquisitive about our sport.

Back on the tour, after qualifying 16th and losing in the first round at Gainesville we stayed around to test on Monday. We'd added Grant Downing to the crew midway through the season in '97 and Del had taken notice of his chassis-building skills. Under his company name of Paralax, Grant had built Del and Chuck a new car and they hauled it to Gainesville as the spare.

On Monday, we tested it. On Monday, a few crew guys had to return home, so they couldn't be there. On Monday, I worked on the car. You read that right.

I'm a pretty observant guy and I'd been watching intently for a couple of years to see what each guy on the crew did. OK, I couldn't see much of what the bottom-end guy was doing, on his back under a dripping motor, but I'd already surmised I would never do that job anyway.

On Monday, Chuck asked me if I'd pull the right-side head off the car after it made its first lap. I jumped at the chance. I was slow but I knew how to get the spark plugs out take the valve covers off, and disassemble the valve train. I needed some pointers from Chuck and Del as I went along but I managed.

At one point, Bazemore passed the end of our pit and he saw me straddling the header pipes as I pulled push rods out of the head. He just smiled and said, loudly, "Are you kidding me?" All I could do was laugh and keep paying attention.

When it came time to put the motor back together, I was instantly petrified. Now, my best friend's life was potentially in my hands. Brute strength and attention to detail are what you need to take the motor apart. Finesse and a lot of experience were needed to put it back together.

When Chuck's instructions, with regards to torquing the heads were, "Tighten those nuts until they're just short of being too tight" you know you're in trouble. I put it back together, listening to Chuck the whole time as he worked on the other side of the motor, and when we were finally done and towing the car back to the line I almost couldn't watch.

It went down the track. It didn't blow up. And, the chassis worked so well Del decided it would become our new car at the next race, in Houston.

After that lap I told Del, "Hey, man. I promise I'll never ask you to write a press release in 15 minutes. I don't think you should ever ask me to work on the motor again. I was scared to death. I'll clean the body and help pack the parachutes, but please keep me away from the motor." He smiled and said that was OK. My career as a crew guy lasted one service and one run. I'd had enough.

We went to Houston with our new Paralax chassis and won two rounds but then managed only a 2-8 round record as we slogged through Dallas, Richmond, Atlanta, Englishtown, Chicago, Columbus, St. Louis, and Denver. We were struggling. Our record, heading into Seattle and the second leg of the Western Swing was just 5-12. On the other side of the CSK pit, Jim Head was in exactly the same shape. He was 5-12, as well.

We were in our third year of the sponsorship and we weren't really getting any better. We'd added a Top Fuel car to the mix and we still weren't getting any better. On top of that, we weren't really using the pit area for CSK corporate hospitality, since we had nothing but a few umbrellas and tables while Chef Chad Head made Saturday night dinners for us on the grill. And, we couldn't really trade much tuning info with our teammates, since Top Fuelers and Funny Cars have to approach their tune-ups from different angles.

When we got to Seattle and did yet another display at a Schuck's Auto Supply store, we were testy, frustrated, and irritated. That night I walked over to a restaurant next to the motel with Chuck, Marc Denner, and rookie crew guy Eric Scheumann. I wasn't really paying close attention to the conversation the others were having (I sometimes tuned those out when they'd get too technical) but when Chuck made one last comment and both Marc and Eric stood up, threw their napkins down, and stormed out, I realize things were worse than I'd thought.

I looked at Chuck wide-eyed and said, "What just happened?"

He just said, "I guess they didn't like my comment about doing a better job of keeping the pit area clean."

I was totally blindsided and at that point I was very much worried about our team being able to survive the season intact. It felt like we were coming apart at the seams with no sewing kit that could stitch us back together.

The next day at the track I saw Chad Head talking with a guy as they pointed to a spot on the dragster. A few minutes later, the gentleman returned with a fresh decal for that place on the car.

Chad introduced me to John Chindemi, saying, "This guy will save your butt someday. He has a full decal & vinyl shop in his truck and he goes on the tour with us. He can fix anything."

As fate would dictate, I needed a new die-cut decal the next day. I searched out Chindemi, in his white box truck, and asked him if he could help me. Thirty minutes later he showed up in our pit with exactly what I needed. He also brought us some karma.

We had qualified a strong fifth and on Sunday we drew Dale Creasy again in the first round. Dale was still the same nice guy and we still should've beaten him. This time we did. We made a nice clean run and took the win.

A week earlier in Denver, Del had bought a new piece of equipment that changed my role on every run we made. He purchased a second-hand video camera and it became my job to shoot every run. Del wanted to see an angle that showed the sides of the rear tires so I knelt next to the retaining wall about five feet behind the car. In Denver I was nothing short of terrified each time I did it, and that weekend was about getting a feel for it.

In Seattle I was getting more and more comfortable but it was still a challenge to get the shot right and not be startled by the launch.

In round two, with Al Hofmann in the other lane, I got my first lesson in what little peripheral vision there was peering through the tiny viewfinder. I saw the amber lights flash and saw the CSK car tear away, then I saw an orange timing block skitter across the lane behind our car. Hofmann had hit the block. We were going to the semifinals

No worries there, of course. All we had to do was beat John Force to go to the final. Del had not beaten Force in a round of racing since — get this — 1992. So, 1999 seemed like a perfectly good time to do it. Del made another clean lap and Force smoked the tires. We sprinted back to the pit area, hearts racing, as we headed to the final round.

It was at that point I was introduced to another new thing. An NHRA official came by with a sheet of paper for us to fill out. It was a "contingency award" form and we'd need to check every box next to an official NHRA contingency-sponsor whose decal we had on the car. Del handed it to me and said, "Can you take care of this?" I was happy to do it. A few minutes later the same official returned and I not only handed him the sheet, I made his job easier by walking around the Firebird body with him pointing out all the decals I'd checked off.

The minutes ticked by. The energy level in the pit was unlike anything I'd ever experienced. Then, it was time to head to the staging lanes. The year before, when we ran Whit in the final at Route 66, I had to watch from the railing. With my new hard card and camera I'd be kneeling right next to the CSK Pontiac for this final, and it would once again be against Whit.

Just 5.283 seconds after the bulbs flashed, Del Worsham was crossing the finish line with Bazemore far behind him. A half-season's worth of frustration, anger, disappointment, and irritation all instantaneously vanished. We celebrated like maniacs. Del hadn't won a race in eight years.

I hopped on the scooter and tore down the return road, pumping my fist at the crowd. They were standing, cheering, and waving at me. I was a perfect stranger to them but I worked for Del Worsham and we'd just won the race. I had tears in my eyes.

I beat the team to the top end — we didn't send the tow vehicle down before the run back then — and he ran toward me when I pulled up on the scooter. When he jumped into my arms my lower back took instant notice of the strain but I didn't care. We had just won the race.

That sticker from John Chindemi must have been the secret. Or maybe the blow-up at dinner on Thursday night. Either way, I'd take it and all of those horrible feelings were gone. We were winners.

Spica was there for the race and after we got done in the winner's circle he proclaimed that we were all going to dinner. And, it was on him.

At that dinner he ordered every appetizer on the menu for our huge table of grimy racing guys. And we each ordered an entree to go with it. In addition, more than a few drinks were consumed. During the dinner, Joe clinked his glass to say a word to the group. He raised his glass and said, "Something occurred to me tonight. Winning is good. Winning is really good. We need to do this some more." We agreed and our roaring cheer indicated that.

As it neared 10 p.m. we headed back to the hotel and I still had work to do. I needed to write my post-event report and send it to my email list, which had by then grown to nearly 500 people. It would be the first one I'd ever written about a race win.

I sat at the desk and composed myself for a minute and then I began to write. I wasn't the polished writer I am today and I wrote most of my stuff in a very personal "insider's view" sort of way. I didn't know much about PR yet and I most certainly didn't know much about AP style and the correct format for such things. I just wrote from the heart.

The next morning I pinched myself to make sure it had really happened. Then I checked my email. I'd never before logged on for email and seen more than 10 or 12 new notes. On this morning I had nearly 100. It was the dawn of a new internet age and it introduced itself to me that morning. Every note seemed to be as "from the heart" as the story I'd written.

We hadn't graduated to the level of world-beaters but we did pull off another amazing thing in Brainerd, where we needed to out-qualify Al Hofmann by three spots on the ladder to take the eighth and final Big Bud Shootout berth from him. Throughout three sessions of qualifying Hofmann was keeping pace and we weren't able to seal the deal. In Q4 we put our best run on the board and moved ahead of him, by exactly those three precious spots. Hofmann was behind us in line, though, and he clearly had the performance to take back at least one spot and cement his berth. He ran great. But not great enough. We were in the Big Bud Shootout at Indy. We even won a round there.

During the driver introductions for the eight-car Shootout, announcer Bob Frey interviewed each driver briefly and Dean Skuza reset the national record for funniest interview. Bob asked him what he thought his odds were to win the event. With a very serious face, Dean said, "Well, Bob, it's funny you should ask, because I've thought about this a lot. I stayed up late last night analyzing it from all angles while looking at the ladder and thinking of all the other teams in this event. I'm pretty sure our odds are one in eight." Brought the house down.

The biggest news about the second half of the season had little to do with our performance on the track. By late summer, Spica and the other executives at CSK were talking to us about the future. Spica said, "We're not really getting our money's worth with this two-car team. Neither one of you are running all that well and frankly Del is doing a majority of the promotional work. Would you guys consider running two Funny Cars next year?"

We said we would and the first thing on our agenda was finding a driver. Richard Hartman was our first choice because of his longtime relationship with Del and Del's great respect for Richard's driving ability. The CSK response to that was along the lines of, "We don't need two versions of Del."

Frankie Pedregon was driving for Big Jim Dunn then and Del instructed me to find him and ask him what he thought. I did that and Frankie said, "I'm your guy."

When we told Spica we could land the the third Pedregon brother the deal was sealed. It was still top-secret in the pit area and all of us were sworn to keep it that way.

I called Gary Graves, the reporter who covered NHRA for USA Today, and pitched him an exclusive story. He said he'd think about it. I called him again and pitched it again. He'd get it first, even before NHRA and National Dragster. He agreed and told me to get him a full press release. How much he could run in the paper and where it would be in the sports section were things we wouldn't know until it was published.

With CSK's blessing we tagged the Topeka race as the time for making the announcement. I called Gary Graves at USA Today and he gave me the good news. The story would run on September 30, the first day of the Topeka event.

On that Thursday morning I awoke at the Days Inn in Topeka and tip-toed to the lobby. I bought a copy of USA Today from the machine and flipped to the sports section. I was relatively certain we'd be buried on the last page. Instead we were at the top of page three. The story was huge.

I was actually nervous when I saw it. My hands were shaking as I read my words and Del's quotes in the nation's biggest newspaper. An hour later we learned that nobody at CSK had been able to contact Jim Head about it before the story ran. He was not pleased. In Jim's defense there were a few things working against him. He'd always been an independent racer, doing things his way and doing it for the love of racing. He also owned a large company and that kept him extraordinarily busy. Doing a lot of promotional stuff for CSK was very difficult for such a busy businessman and with his team's performance pretty much mirroring ours it wasn't meant to be. CSK came to the conclusion that running two Funny Cars as a true team would be a much more efficient way to work, and potentially be more successful.

At the final few races, especially at Pomona for the Finals, Del and Chuck talked to a variety of mechanics and crew chiefs to assemble what would be the new "blue team." In Pomona we announced David Fletcher would be the crew chief and that the blue team would be based out of John Fink's shop in Auburn, Indiana. We hired the crew guys we needed and let the racing world know that we'd be hitting the ground running in 2000, right back there at Pomona Raceway. We finished the year 12-20.

We had a massive list of things to do during that short off-season and one of them involved a wedding. Marc Denner had been dating a beautiful, smart, and funny girl named Krysta and when they got married in December we all got to dress up and have a heck of a hullabaloo. Krysta fit right in. I'll never forget Marc's line after the first time I met Krysta and I told him how pretty she was. He said, "Yeah, I know. I can't believe she's dating me!"

On the racing side there was an enormous amount of equipment to buy because the Worsham organization had to effectively double in size in just a couple of months. On the PR side I had to create a lot of new materials, featuring information about guys I really didn't know that well. To get a head start on that, on the day after Pomona I drove out to Frankie's house near Chino Hills and we sat in his living room for a couple of hours with me interviewing him and taking copious notes.

In terms of corporate and sponsor work we had to create many things from scratch. Once CSK settled on two Worsham Funny Cars the next logical step was to make the pit area a true hospitality venue.

Our red and blue transporters would be lined up parallel, with a space between them. Now we needed to complete the horseshoe.

We didn't have a suitable third rig to place across the back of the pit and we didn't own a motorcoach that would be a viable anchor for hospitality, either. We decided to go with a tent and we discussed renting one at every venue. The quality of those rentals can be all over the board, though, so we opted instead to buy one and set it up at every race.

We also decided to buy plastic flooring and stanchions with retractable-belt barriers, to outline where people could and couldn't go.

When it all arrived at Chuck's house before the start of the season we figured the best thing was for us to do a full test run, setting it all up in his driveway. The flooring came in one-foot squares so it all had to be snapped together to make the floor. It was mostly black but we bought enough red and blue to jazz it up a bit. It was tedious work, on hands and knees, snapping it all together. Once it was down, we broke it up into much larger squares and stacked them in the back of the transporter. We weren't smart enough to think of rolling up long strips of flooring. Once we saw another team doing that, we adapted.

As for the tent, it was kind of an engineering marvel. It was 20 feet by 20 feet and it had four upright posts in the corners and a large peaked roof. The sidewalls had clear sections that acted as windows. And to put it up, no nuts or bolts were involved. Using tension, and two strong cables that crossed in the middle to connect the tops of the four uprights, it all held itself together.

That would be fine as long as the wind didn't blow. We needed a way to secure the whole thing to the ground so we figured we'd just drive spikes into the pit area asphalt and be done with it.

At CSK, graphic designer Guy Tilden got to work on a new car design. Our two Funny Cars would be identical, in terms of paint and sponsor logos, but Del's would be red and white while Frankie's would be blue and white. There would be some debate about the scheme Tilden finally came up with.

Joe Spica and Ron Chisler were both car guys. They loved going to car shows to see the neat paint schemes and fancy graphics and they made no secret about it. When it came time to take our team to the next level, with two Funny Cars, they directed Tilden to create a design that looked as if one layer of paint was peeling off to reveal another below. It required an awful lot of airbrush work to pull it off.

Our response, as a team, was along the lines of, "OK, this is a neat design. But, this isn't a car show. It's a race, and this is a Funny Car. Things break, bodies get damaged. We won't have a way of repairing this on the road. Let's come up with something more basic."

They were adamant. We were going to have to do it their way, and somehow figure out how to fix things when they broke. The initial design had a free flow to it, as it should have. After all, if the illusion was to be that of paint peeling off it should be random.

As we were putting the flooring and tent together for the first time, an airbrush guy came over and applied the "peeling" sections to an older body Chuck had painted to be our first mock-up. The airbrush guy did a great job, free-flowing to make it look real. We thought it looked fantastic, and we took it with us to Phoenix for approval.

When Spica and Chisler saw it, they hated it. They pulled out the official "final" design from Tilden and said, "It has to look just like this." Oddly, what they had come up with, via committee, was a body that didn't look real in terms of the illusion. It was perfectly symmetrical, exactly the same on both sides of the car. It didn't look real because it didn't look random and considering the man-hours it was going to take to create these masterpieces we felt it should look real. We were overruled, and we would paint it exactly as seen on the artwork.

Pontiac had stepped up its program with us and we had new bodies being mounted while we were testing in Phoenix. We would not have time to get them done for Pomona, though, so two 1999 red cars would be used there. We'd just put Frankie's name and number on the sides of his. That was fine anyway because the new bodies would debut at the season's second race — the Checker, Schuck's, Kragen Nationals in Phoenix. There'd be no better time to show off the new cars.

When Pomona rolled around I flew west from Austin to join the team and once again drove to the track with Del on set-up day. If he was nervous seeing the '99 pit set-up for the first time he was a little overwhelmed by what he saw in 2000. The tent was up, the flooring was down, and both teams were getting ready to get after it, side-by-side with hospitality space in the middle. It looked big-league to both of us.

The guys had used large steel spikes to anchor the four legs of the tent, which by then they had dubbed "Camp Snoopy." When they did that an NHRA official came over and told them, "We'll let you go this weekend, but don't ever do that again. Find a better way to anchor this deal without putting holes in our asphalt." When the guys pointed out that nearly every display in the Midway was being anchored by identical spikes, the official said, "I don't care. You heard what I said," and walked away.

Camp Snoopy also attracted the attention of some of the more high-dollar teams, who had many thousands of dollars invested in fully customized hospitality centers. They weren't shy about going to NHRA to complain about our tent. Poor Camp Snoopy couldn't get through its first day on the tour without causing trouble. Spica himself talked to NHRA about the tent and that issue was never raised again.

We had a lot of new crew guys, wearing new crew shirts, at that first race. With a bigger budget we could afford to hire some additional guys as well, and assign more full-time people to each car. Tom Abbett, who had worked for Al Hofmann, and longtime wrench Brooks Brown joined the red team, while the crew on the blue side included new crew chief David "Fletch" Fletcher, who had been Wes Cerny's right-hand man on the Joe Gibbs' Funny Car for years. We also welcomed Jason Davis, who had spent a year on a Top Fuel car; Beau Maile, who had been with Tom Hoover and Cory Lee; Steve Boggs, a longtime crew member for Eddie Hill and Jim Head; and Roger Rayburn, who had spent a season with Paul Romine.

And I finally had a place to work in the pit area. I'd share the lounge in the blue transporter with Frankie. I could set up my laptop, bring along a printer, and have an office. And, I'd be working in there with a truly hilarious guy.

We got both cars qualified at that first race and considering there were 24 Funny Cars attempting to make the show the blue team's No. 16 spot didn't seem so bad. Especially in comparison to Cruz Pedregon, Cristen Powell, and Scotty Cannon who joined the list of eight drivers who did not make the field.

Del won a round, but lost in the second. Frankie never got to run. On the burnout, his throttle-stop got twisted and he couldn't get the car in reverse. He had to idle down the track.

All in all, it had been a whirlwind transition to a two-car team and we'd at least had a solid test-run in Pomona. Phoenix, for the CSK race, would be a whole new ball game.

The new bodies arrived with the elaborate paint schemes that would no doubt drive us nuts. Chuck had filled four five-gallon buckets with concrete, which would be used to hold Camp Snoopy in place. And when we got to Phoenix on Tuesday night we knew we had a long haul ahead of us, in terms of the "dog and pony" stuff we'd be doing until Friday.

We started off with a big display at the Checker Auto Parts store just up the street from CSK headquarters. We followed that up with early morning TV appearances and a tour of the local stations to do afternoon interviews. On Thursday morning, we had a photo shoot scheduled and we arrived before sunrise to grab that "morning light" photographers love so much. That evening we took part in a race with all the of the CSK staffers, driving Pontiac courtesy cars.

Friday, we rolled the new airbrushed cars to the line for more photos, side by side, and then the hoopla was over. It was time to race. We got both cars in again, but this time it was Del in the No. 5 spot and Frankie in the No. 12 position on the ladder. Those two run each other in round one. Del took the win.

Here's a trick with which you can amaze your friends at your next drag race. Do you know how to instantly tell which qualifying spots face each other in round one? The total always adds up to 17. Try it. That day it was 12 vs 5, with 5 moving on. Del lost to Tony Pedregon in the second round. We were all exhausted.

Before we could even get to Gainesville, three weeks later, we had to venture back to Vegas for another CSK convention, this time with Frankie joining us. Autographs were signed, hands were shaken, and smiles were evident all around. Our musical treat, on the final night, was a concert by Earth, Wind, & Fire. It was all good.

We got into the swing of things in a hurry but there seemed to be one continuing problem as the season got rolling. The teams were not always on the same page. They got along fine and when one team would go out early they would jump in to help the other guys, but there was some obvious tension between the two groups. It didn't take long to figure out it had a lot to do with the blue team being based in Indiana. They were out of sight and out of mind during the downtime and it was hard for either team to arrive at the track for set-up at exactly the same time. Disagreements were not uncommon but we'd have to find a way to make it work. We didn't have room for two teams at Chuck's house.

We raced in Vegas for the first time and marveled at the enormity of The Strip at Las Vegas Motor Speedway. It was one more chance to stand back and soak in how fast the sport was growing and changing.

After 12 races Del was 8-12, which was a nice improvement over 1999 when he won only 12 rounds all year. Frankie, Fletch, and the blue crew were 4-12. The learning curve was steep.

Prior to the season, Del made one key decision regarding Team CSK's income and activity level. He decided to not just accept exhibition match-racing invitations but to go out and solicit them as well. If we had an open weekend, he wanted to be match racing. The extra income would be important.

We'd already done one early in the season, in Montgomery, Alabama. At that event it became clear to me that my usefulness at an exhibition race would come in a new way. I'd still videotape our runs but since there was no PR to do, the best thing I could do to help the team was sell t-shirts. And every sale added to the bottom line.

After the Chicago race we headed to a place called Walters, Oklahoma. I couldn't find it on a map. It was actually just a bit north of Wichita Falls, Texas and there was indeed a tiny little dragstrip there, called the Texhoma Motorplex. It was an eighth-mile track with seating for maybe 500 people on rickety wooden bleachers. The lights were actual street lamps. When we arrived to stare at the place, after having just raced at Route 66, we stood at the starting line and Del said, "I'm not sure two Funny Cars can actually fit on this track." Everything about it was miniature.

I knew what we were getting paid for the one-night show and I knew what the track operator was charging for tickets. He'd need to put 2,000 people in the place to make any money and that was roughly four times the amount of seats he had. I decided it wasn't my responsibility to worry about that.

We set up and got ready and the fans started to show. Before long, out on the big dusty Oklahoma plain where you could see for miles, it began to look like the final scene from "Field of Dreams" with headlights lining up as far as we could see.

There were probably three thousand people there. And we sold more T-shirts and souvenirs in one night, to that crowd, than we had at any other match race. It was pretty cool and they crowded around us soaking it all in.

When Del and Frankie went up to make their first run, after sunset, Del was his typical self. He was always game for anything. Frankie looked a little worried.

To give the cars some traction the operator had applied an entire drum of VHT compound to the track. It was green, but it was sticky.

Amazingly, when the two CSK cars lined up and took the green light their flames crossed. I'd never seen anything like it in my life.

In the gloomy darkness of the pit area we sold some more T-shirts and went back up there for the final run. The track had hired an "emergency crew" made up of off-duty volunteer firefighters but we discovered during the first run that they'd showed up in street clothes and they'd never seen a Funny Car on fire. They didn't even know how to lift the body but that really didn't matter. In street clothes they couldn't be of any use. So, Del put Brooks Brown in a full fire suit and sent him to the top end with an extinguisher. He'd be our emergency crew.

Both guys did big long burnouts and the crowd went nuts. They both smoked the tires but Del pedaled his car numerous times to make the show as good as possible. We were done for the night but the fans didn't want to leave. They hung around our pits until we sold the last shirt and piston. I think we departed the track around 1:30 a.m.

Over the Fourth of July weekend we were part of the gigantic "Night Under Fire" match race at Norwalk, Ohio, which was an IHRA track at the time. Most of us had never been there and were impressed with its enormity. Compared to the Texhoma Motorplex it seemed like the L.A. Coliseum.

Earlier that week I had begun ghost-writing a daily diary for Del on NHRA.com and here for the first time I'll admit I wrote every word of it. We called it "Del's Diary" and we purported that it was him actually writing the thing but I wrote it all in his "voice," which I had down pat. Things were "rad" when he was "stoked" especially if it was going down "for reals." I wrote it every day for more than a week, bringing the readers behind the scenes as we traveled and raced. Only later, when I started my NHRA.com blog in 2005, did I realize I had actually been blogging five years earlier with "Del's Diary" in 2000. We just didn't know the term "blog" yet. I had included photos of the rigs driving through Norwalk and the guys setting up and getting ready. I had to write about some other stuff later that night and the next morning.

As they always did the Bader family put on a great show and we pushed the festivities out until the last souvenir was sold. On our final lap Frankie would run in the left lane and Del in the right. It was dark in Norwalk, especially past the finish line a quarter-mile away. The track appeared to disappear into nothingness down there.

When our drivers did their epic burnouts I made a decision to shoot the video while standing, instead of kneeling down, and I'd locate myself between the two cars to shoot it. It was too dark to worry about getting valid video for any tuning purposes. I was just shooting it to have something to do.

They launched and shot flames well over each car's roof but Frankie's car smoked the tires early. Del kept on flying, with the flames up until past half-track, where it was difficult for us to see him in the gloom.

All we saw were sparks and smoke on the right side of the track. And then more sparks on the left side. Marc Denner yelled "He crashed!" and before I could turn around or digest that the guys were in the tow vehicle heading right down the lane, chasing after him.

I walked back to the pit listening for some good word on the P.A., and finally after two interminable minutes the announcer said, "Del Worsham has gotten out of the car under his own power."

Tony Pedregon had actually been the first person on the scene, since he'd just raced in the pair before us and was still at the top end. He said Del was out cold when the car finally came to a stop. Our crew was there just seconds later and Del came to when they arrived. The emergency crew mostly just watched but they were ready to overreact and cut the chassis apart if given the chance. Marc and Chuck pretty much took over the leadership roles down there and within a minute they had Del in the tow vehicle, headed back to the pits.

I quickly roped off an area where we could safely put the chassis and body. We were on the west side of the Norwalk track, where the sportsmen pits are now, and our area was two patches of asphalt with a strip of grass between them. I'd been selling T-shirts in that grassy area all night. I roped it off and waited for the flatbed. When the body arrived I couldn't believe what I saw. From the front edge of the right-side window all the way to the back, the entire side of the body was gone. And the vultures descended.

Fans will do odd things when fueled by beer. They came right through the rope I'd put up and tried to pry pieces off the body for souvenirs. I came unglued.

After much shouting I got them all back and put up new ropes. Chuck took a position right in front of the body to dissuade the fans from trying to get back for more bits and pieces.

There was a good reason for that. The body was a total loss but it still had quite a few struts, pads, nuts, and bolts that could be salvaged. The guys would do that back in the shop. We'd at least been smart enough to run two old 1999 bodies for the event.

When Del got back he was still a bit dazed. I showed him the video I'd shot and when the sparks appeared on the screen he looked at me and asked, "Did I just crash? It looks like I crashed." He had no memory of it.

Chuck made a quick decision right then. He and I were going to drive Del back to Auburn immediately. We were afraid someone might take him to a Norwalk or Sandusky hospital and keep him there. In Auburn, we'd have John Fink and his resources to get the best medical care.

We left the track after midnight with Del in the back seat of my rental car. Chuck and I had both heard that you should never let a person with a concussion fall asleep so we talked to Del the whole way. It seemed to take forever to get there. It was a 150-mile trip. We got back to Auburn around 3 a.m.

I dropped Del and Chuck off at the shop, where they were staying, and headed back to my room at the Comfort Inn. I was still stunned. I couldn't stop seeing the sparks flying whenever I'd close my eyes.

I learned in the morning that Del had then driven himself to the Auburn hospital, where he asked for a CAT scan. They cleared him and let him go. I assume he had a concussion. It's hard to get knocked out by an impact and not have one but the CAT scan gave us all some reassurance.

When he got back to his California home the next day, he called me with a complete report.

"I am sore and bruised all over," he said. "But the worst thing is my tongue. I bit the hell out of it and it's swollen. It hurts really bad. You should see these bruises, dude. I'm a mess."

He also told me that after we had left the track another Funny Car team came over with an adjustable wrench they'd found. They had discovered it on the track. They had also found it in the right lane. Marc Denner said it was the exact shape of a big dent in the wheelie bar. We'll never know for 100 percent sure but all signs seemed to point debris on the track causing a blown right rear tire, causing the wreck. Norwalk didn't have a return road then. Support vehicles would run down the track to get to the other end, often with tool boxes bouncing and rear hatches open. It all seemed to add up but we'd never know who might have let a wrench fall off the back of their tow car or if that was even the cause of it.

And we had the Winston Showdown, at the fabulous new Bristol Dragway, the next weekend.

It was a hit-or-miss proposition if Del would run in the exhibition event, where Top Fuel dragsters and Funny Cars would race each other. We got to the track Friday and Del looked pretty good. Then he showed me the bruises. He was covered in them.

His tongue was still sore and he was speaking with a lisp, but other than that I was amazed at how much he'd recovered in just a few days. He said Larry Dixon had called him and urged him to start driving with a football mouthpiece. Larry had experienced a few Top Fuel mishaps and he knew all about how sore a driver's tongue could be. He said he was lucky to not have bitten a big hunk of his tongue off one time. Del had one with him by the time he got to Bristol.

The team skipped the first session to make sure the car and the driver were both ready to get back on the strip. When Del staged for the second session, I wasn't sure I wanted to watch. As soon as I put my eye to the viewfinder I couldn't help but see the sparks again. I was still seeing them in my sleep. I honestly think I was more nervous than he was.

Sure enough, he calmly ran it all the way and jumped into the No. 2 spot. That's Del Worsham, for you.

Del faced David Grubnic and his dragster in round one on Sunday. I can't say I was crestfallen when we lost. Frankie lost as well. I couldn't wait to get home. We had the Western Swing staring us in the face.

In Denver, kicking off the Swing, Del made another big move in terms of personnel. He hired Rob Flynn to come aboard as co-crew chief. As Del put it, "We need another set of eyes and Rob has some seriously talented eyes when it comes to tuning these cars. He's smart, he's experienced, and he can help me oversee all of this stuff so that I don't get caught in the weeds and lose sight of what we're trying to accomplish."

When we got to Seattle at the end of July, we arrived with the defending champ driving the red car. And on his final qualifying pass an engine detonation blew the Firebird shell clear off the car. The repairs and airbrush work weren't enormous but they were expensive and time-consuming.

In round one something happened that the world had never seen before. Two Checker, Schuck's, Kragen Funny Cars advanced to the second round at the same race. Del beat Scotty Cannon and Frankie beat Dean Skuza. It had only taken 14 races to do that. And, while Del went out in the second round, losing to Jim Epler, Frankie powered past Tommy Johnson and Epler to advance to the final. For the second consecutive year, a CSK Funny Car would have a chance to earn the Wally trophy amidst the evergreens.

Frankie lost, smoking the tires against John Force, but after a semifinal finish for Del at Denver and a runner-up for Frankie in Seattle, things felt better. Plus, and it was a big plus, Del was fine.

Just a week later, in Sonoma, Del lost in the first round and Frankie suffered a DNQ. The phrase "hero to zero" isn't a cliche for no reason. Drag racing is a humbling sport.

We won a few more rounds in the late stages of the season and the red team managed to DNQ in Houston. Both teams would finish the season with one failure to qualify.

In Pomona, to wrap it up, we quite literally ended the season with a bang.

During Friday's qualifying session Frankie lined up next to Scotty Cannon, who was driving his Oakley-sponsored car. Both cars looked to be making strong laps but Frankie's blue CSK Pontiac dropped three cylinders at once, all on the right side, causing it to make a vicious move to the right and then it crossed the centerline. Despite his best efforts to steer it back he crashed into Scotty's car and the two became entangled as carbon fiber and parts flew through the air and littered the asphalt. Both drivers were OK but both cars were destroyed. As the saying goes, among racing PR types, "If you can't be good, be spectacular."

An hour later Jim Jannard (the founder and owner of Oakley) came over to our pit with his ubiquitous cigar and fancy sunglasses. He stared directly at Chuck with a stern look on his face. Then he said, "Chuck, shouldn't we be exchanging insurance information, or driver's licenses, or something like that?"

That broke the tension.

On Monday Fletch, Rob, Del, and I met at Del's home. Our goal was simple. We wanted to discuss how to make the two teams work better together and how to be more efficient. The answer was clear and it was a project for me. I'd be writing a crew member handbook.

One of the guys had one from a prior team and I used that as my template, but I expanded upon it greatly. We would put rules in place for setting up and tearing down Camp Snoopy, including the specific guideline that both teams would do it together and neither team could set up their pit area until it was done. We'd have specific guidelines for dress, both at the track and at the hotel. There would be a rule stating both cars had to be serviced and "on the ground" before the red Solo cups could make an appearance. There would even be rules for the transporter drivers who would thereafter be required to take the most direct route from one destination to the next, with no side-trips or diversions unless Del or Chuck authorized them.

Every rule in the book addressed a point of grievance that had been brought up in our organization at some point, and those grievances had begun to infect the atmosphere. We were going to become one big team not two groups working side-by-side, even if it took a book to lay it all out. Each member would have to sign a form that stated he had read the entire book and agreed to abide by all the rules.

In addition, another change was also mine to make. On the last day of each race I'd post, in both transporters, a memo entitled "Next Hotel" with information on where we'd be staying for the following race. If communications were a problem we were determined to fix that problem. If cooperation had been an issue we were going to make it clear just how much the two teams would cooperate. We were growing up as an organization.

In early December when Barbara and I were vacationing in Hawaii, I went to a bookstore in the Ala Moana Shopping Center to buy the newest edition of "ESPN — The Magazine" which had come out that day. In it was a full-page photo of Frankie's crash. It was a vivid photo and it clearly illustrated just how lucky we were to still have Frankie and Scotty Cannon around.

At around the same time, Barbara and I faced a challenge. She was a rising star at IBM and had been on the fast track toward executive status for many years. We loved living in Austin and could easily imagine staying there until Barb retired. IBM wanted to give her a new promotion, however, and it was a big one. She'd be a director, reporting to the vice president of investor relations for IBM. She'd sit in an office on the same floor as her boss, as well as CEO

Lou Gerstner and CFO John Joyce. That meant the job was located in Armonk, New York. They wanted us to move.

We had no choice but to think about it. When IBM invests so much money and time to groom an up-and-comer you absolutely should feel obligated to do what they want. You should, but we really didn't.

She stalled, finally telling them, "My husband and I aren't ready to move to New York or Connecticut. I can't do it now."

So they came back with Option B. She could move there on a six-month temporary assignment and they'd provide a furnished corporate apartment. We could then take some time to look around and get a feel for the area. Maybe look at some houses. Maybe talk ourselves into it.

The apartment was in Ridgefield, Connecticut. Barbara accepted the offer and we pulled the trigger. I'd go there as often as I could, she'd come to the races as often as she could get away, and I'd look after the house in Austin. It was not going to be easy.

After she moved we figured it might make it better for her if Shasta was up there. I had to fly him from Austin to La Guardia and I was stressed out just thinking about it, but he was a perfect little passenger under the seat in front of me. When we landed I pulled his carrier up onto my lap and unzipped it enough for him to poke his head out. The guy sitting in front of me looked back and said, "Wow. I had no idea there was a cat under my seat. What a good kitty!" Yeah, he really was.

It was terrifically hard to have two homes and it was made harder by having one we loved, in an area we adored, while being pressured to move to a place for which we really had no affinity. Austin was relaxed and laid back. It was fun. It was a happy place with good weather and great Tex-Mex food. New York and Connecticut can be hard places to live. They're stressful, they're crowded, and nothing much comes easy there. The weather can be depressing. And on top of all that, you get to spend two or three times as much for a house.

We went on multiple house-hunting trips and managed to say no to everything we saw. I did see one home, on a day when I was out looking with our agent, and I thought, "OK, I could live here." It was a modern open-concept house, much like all the houses in River Place down in Austin. Barbara was out of town so I couldn't pull the trigger, but I liked it. I was willing to take this one for the team if she wanted to move. When she got back the next day, the house had already sold. I took that as a sign.

We looked around some more and again didn't like anything we could afford and couldn't afford anything we liked. It was going to be hard for a while.

At the same time the vacant lot that sat next to our Austin house was turning into a beautiful home. The McCarley family came over often to inspect the construction, and we were thrilled to have such fun people moving in as neighbors. Interestingly, our neighbors shared our first names but he was Robert and she was Barb. I was Bob, and my wife was Barbara. Their little boy, who would walk out of the house naked from time to time, was Colin. Baby Cate came soon thereafter.

Robert and Barb were fabulous. Despite my Barbara being stuck in Connecticut so much, we all got to be great friends and the McCarleys would often take me out to dinner when I was home alone. Robert was an insurance agent and Barb was a reporter for the biggest radio station in town. Just as our lives were in turmoil, with IBM continuing to pressure us to move, we had met some of the best friends we'd ever have.

2001 was coming, though. It was going to be a big year for our team, a big year for Barbara, and a huge year for the three of us (Shasta included).

A Watershed Year

As we entered 2001 I knew it was going to be a challenging year in myriad ways. We were entering the fifth year of the CSK sponsorship and it felt like we were balancing on the fulcrum of either losing the deal or making it one of the best programs in the sport. Entering the season Del's overall round record with CSK as our sponsor was 54-83, including the two round wins at Rockingham which did not count toward NHRA points. He'd been to two finals and won one of them. He had also DNQ'd six times over the course of the four years. His best points finish was seventh.

In one year with the program Frankie and the blue team had gone 12-22 with one final-round appearance and one DNQ. That all adds up to a 66-105 overall record. If you managed a baseball team that went 66-105, you'd lose your job.

So, we needed to start winning. As in "more often" not just "every now and then." Our sponsorship income was still lagging behind the big hitters in the class but it was getting to a point where a lack of wins could add up to a lack of return-on-investment for CSK.

CSK put together a plan to make special-edition bodies a regular part of our program. The marketing department had a total of six one-race bodies on the docket for 2001, so we'd be swapping out Firebirds at a rapid rate. At least, by then, the vinyl technology had improved considerably, so while none of the special bodies would be full vinyl wraps they all would feature basic paint schemes with large printed vinyl applications on the sides and hood.

With each special body CSK would be able to further leverage the vendors involved, and that would aid their business model. And they'd have die-cast cars made of each special body as well, hoping to sell those in their Checker, Schuck's, and Kragen stores. All of that was good. Winning would make it even better.

On my own personal front 2001 was going to be a challenge as well. Barbara was still in Connecticut, in her spartan corporate apartment. Shasta was there with her. I'd be minding the fort on Love Bird Lane, in Austin, and we'd try to all be together as often as possible. The problem was that "as often as possible" wasn't nearly often enough.

The best news for me was that 2001 would also be my fifth year with the Worshams. I would turn 45 right in the middle of the season and I had never held one job for five consecutive years. Did it feel exactly like the dream job I'd been hoping to land for so long? No. It felt better. Much better. I was valued, trusted, and by then I was well compensated. The risk had produced a reward beyond any dream I'd ever had.

And I was truly part of the team. My relationship with the crew was terrific. Del and Frankie were great friends. David Fletcher and I found out early that we would be great friends, as well. His race computer in the blue rig was at the bottom of the stairs that led up to the lounge. To get to my post I'd squeeze past him to climb those stairs. When he'd come back from a great run I'd pass by and say, "You're my hero, David." When things didn't go so well, I'd pass by and Fletch, in his charming British accent, would ask, "Am I still your hero, Bob?" I'd reply, "You are and you always will be."

After Del, my best friend on the team was possibly the most unlikely one. John Fink and I were more different than we were the same. We came from starkly different backgrounds; we were both well educated, but in completely different fields. We shared very few similarities in terms of social strata, politics, or wealth. But — and it was the biggest of all buts — we shared the same sense of humor. From the day we met the traits we didn't share took a backseat to the ones we did. Laughter was the common denominator that bound us together.

Delivered with a slow almost-country style, John's one-liners and observations left a lot of people scratching their heads but they consistently left me laughing out loud. I made him giggle a bit, as well.

In short order we were riding to the track together, eating dinner with each other, and packing the parachutes as a duo. When John and I made the Western Swing together, for the first of many such trips, Chuck Worsham said, "I've never seen Fink do that before. He's always been a loner. You're the first person he's ever asked to travel with him." It was my pleasure.

Frank Gilchrist, his wife Barbara, and their sons Kent and Craig, also became extended family. The first time I traveled the Swing without flying, I rode along with Frank and Barbara in their Prevost motor coach. To make it even more thrilling, after Frank stopped for fuel the first time, still in Texas, he got back onboard and said, "You take the wheel."

I was more than a little uneasy about it. I'd never driven a bus before and wasn't totally sure how to start it. I knew for a fact, though, it was the first time I'd ever driven anything with an enclosed trailer attached to it. After a 10-second tutorial, Frank sat in the front passenger's seat.

"Now remember, this thing is wider than you think," he said. "Compared to a car, you're going to need to adjust. Just make it seem like you're riding right on the center stripe and you'll be OK."

I drove for the next six hours. Frank had gone to the bedroom in the rear, where Barbara was also sleeping. I was getting tired too and just before midnight I pulled into a rest area. I had no chance of being able to back up with the trailer attached so I needed to find a pull-through parking spot. They were all full. I got back on the highway and kept going. An hour later I finally saw a Wal-Mart and I pulled into the lot, parking out on the edge.

Later in the trip, on our way from Seattle back to Texas, we stopped by the side of the interstate in the middle of Montana. I got out to stretch my legs and happened to look up.

"Frank, look up there," I said, as I pointed skyward. "Just look at that. It's amazing."

Frank looked up and simply said, "Wow."

We were both city boys. We'd seen Orion and the Big Dipper all of our lives but neither of us had seen a night sky like that. With no light pollution or moon that night, it bore almost no resemblance to anything we'd ever seen. It looked like a science fiction movie. The Milky Way wasn't just visible, it was a clearly obvious stripe of limitless stars stretching from horizon to horizon.

Somewhere in Wyoming, I went back to take a nap in the bedroom while Barbara drove the bus. Like me, she'd never driven one before. After a few hours I got up and went to the front, where I asked Frank how we were doing. He said, "We're doing great. Barb's been driving 85 miles an hour for three hours." He said it with a gleam in his eye.

Team CSK was made up of a great bunch of people and with our new handbooks it was a much more tightly knit group. Most important, it was rewarding and fun. For me, the rewards and the fun also came in the form of a free car. A very powerful and fast car.

Fred Simmonds, at GM Racing, had continued to increase Pontiac's support of Team CSK. By 2001 we were getting free bodies, free wind tunnel time, free heavy-duty GM SUVs, and a lot of other backing. For the '01 season they added two Pontiac Trans Ams to the program. When Fred let us know about that, prior to the start of the season, Del called me and said, "I'm taking one of them. I want you to have the other." Shortly thereafter, I was test-driving a gold Trans Am WS6 at an Austin dealership. The next day I went to pick it up. When I got there the dealer had bad news.

"I can't let you have this car in the condition it's in," he said. "We prepped it for delivery and ran all our diagnostics and there's something wrong with the motor, in the valve train. It actually needs a new motor."

Oddly, he wouldn't let me have the car I picked out and he wouldn't let me pick out another one. It was a strange situation in all regards. The disappointment was huge. The next day I called Fred and told him about it. He was not very happy, and he said, "I'll take care of this."

The following morning, the dealer called me.

"Well, you must be someone really important," he said. "A truck just dropped off a new motor for your car. It was flown in here from the plant. And, we have instructions to have it in the car and have the car in your hands by the end of the week."

I told the guy I wasn't important at all, but I knew a guy at General Motors who was. I got the car that Friday.

At the Phoenix race we once again went through our now-familiar "dog and pony show" routine for three straight days. The pre-dawn television appearances on the local morning news never got much easier.

The CSK convention was still happening annually in Vegas, although they had moved it to the Paris Resort by then. We didn't have a musical act to enjoy but they did hire a hypnotist.

He brought a dozen CSK people up on stage and had them doing all sorts of funny stuff. Barbara swears I was doing it too, at our table. I think she was the one who was hypnotized.

We were, by then, an integral part of the company and their national meetings. It was nothing short of phenomenal to think how far we'd come, but we still needed to win.

By the time we'd wrapped up Gainesville Del and Frankie were each 2-3. The next stop was Houston.

We began the weekend by doing something important. We ate. We had already established the tradition of a pre-Houston team meal at Lupe Tortilla, Frank and Barbara Gilchrist's favorite Tex-Mex place, and we all looked forward to it with Pavlovian responses. It was that good. Remember, always (ALWAYS!) order the "Steak Lupe" entree after you enjoy the queso dip. Or, just get anything you want.

At the track out in Baytown, after one qualifying session Del was in the No. 8 spot while Frankie was 14th. After the second session, Del was sitting atop the leaderboard with a strong 4.810 while Frankie sat 17th. On Saturday, Del ran 4.888 in Q3 before smoking the tires in Q4. Frankie improved to the No. 11 spot. Del's earlier time held easily. It was his first No. 1 since 1991.

Del and I rode to the track together in my Trans Am early Sunday morning. As we walked in a member of another team stopped us and shook Del's hand. He said, "Today is your day. Remember I said that. Today is your day."

We had Tony Bartone in round one. Our 4.910 sent him home.

We had Dean Skuza in round two. Skuza ran 4.941 and probably deserved a better fate. Our 4.854 sent him home.

In the semifinal Gary Densham was the opponent. At the time, Densham was driving for John Force and he had a fast race car. We "slowed" to a 4.967 but he smoked the tires. Del and the red team were going to our third final as a group. That John Force character would be waiting for us.

Del did his burnout. I knelt down by the retaining wall on the right side of the track. The lights flashed.

Del was away first, by two and a half hundredths. Force had gotten to the final running 4.884, 4.829 (winning over Frankie and the blue team), and 4.822. He'd been dominant all day. He ran 4.859 in the final. It wasn't enough.

When 4.852 flashed on the board and the win lights came on in our lane, it was bedlam. Seattle in 1999 had been incredible but we were masters of finesse on a slow hot track that day, running 5-teens all afternoon while everyone else was smoking the tires. In Houston conditions were stout and all the big hitters were swinging their home-run bats. We qualified on top and never looked back. It was a totally different sort of win and it felt good. It felt wonderful, actually.

After the winner's circle festivities ended and all the photos were taken, the guys put the car away while I wrote my report. Then we all went to Outback for dinner.

At dinner, I started a new tradition. With Spica not in attendance, I clinked my glass with my spoon and I gave an off-the-cuff speech. I have no memory of what I said but like that first decal that went on straight it changed my career. For the next 14 years, on two different teams, I would be in charge of the speech after a win.

And, our round-record moved to 6-3. Frankie sat at 3-4.

It had, indeed, been our day.

As is so often the befuddling case, Del went on to lose in the first round at the next two events, while Frankie went 2-2 by getting to the second round at both. Things were looking up for the blue team. David Fletcher was still my hero.

In Atlanta, Del was No. 6 after the first day of qualifying while Frankie was No. 7, and both teams worried about ending up in the dreaded No. 8 vs. No. 9 situation.

On Saturday, we ended up No. 9 and No. 12 with Del in the better spot. On the ladder, the two CSK cars couldn't face each other until the semifinal.

Frankie had the privilege of running Force in the opening round at Atlanta Dragway. Force's 4.967 was strong but it wasn't strong enough to outrun Frankie and his 4.857. It was his quickest run of the event.

Del got by Densham easily, in the first round. He then blasted past Johnny Gray in round two, while Frankie took out Whit Bazemore.

For the first time, the two CSK teams would be facing off in a semifinal to see who would carry the Checker, Schuck's, Kragen banner to the final round.

Del ran 4.897 for his quickest run of the day. My hero, David Fletcher, sent Frankie down the track to a 4.871 and a trip to the final. It was one of the best, and closest, races of the day. Ron Capps would be Frankie's opponent in the money round.

They left the line almost as one, with Frankie earning a two-thousandths edge. The two cars were in lockstep for 330 feet. When the big Goodyear slicks on Capps' car spun shortly thereafter and the blue CSK car stayed planted, the 4.902 that came up on the scoreboard was more than enough for the win.

The red team had gone to the line to support their teammates but they stayed respectfully back during the lap. When Frankie won they dashed forward to celebrate with the blue guys.

For my hero, David Fletcher, it was his first win as a crew chief.

Talking to the media, Frankie said, "I woke up this morning and knew we had Force in the first round, but I had this weird sense of calm about me. I figured, hey you have to beat the guy at some point. It seems like you always have to beat Force to win a race, so why not beat him early and get on a roll."

Del was quoted as saying, "I told Frankie that I've won four of these and never gotten choked up. But when he crossed the finish line and TV cameras were on me, I had to wipe away tears. I'm so proud of him, and so proud of David, and I'm so proud of the blue team. This was a team win. We all won this and the blue team earned every bit of it. They dominated this event."

We doused Fletch with a cooler of water, just to cap it off.

As we moved forward I was also adding a new skill set to my repertoire. I wasn't a T-shirt designer, because I have no artistic genes whatsoever, but I was becoming a pretty talented T-shirt design "concept guy."

We'd been introduced to Boris Podtetenieff, who owned a company called T-Shirts Unlimited in Redding, California. He was a great guy with a passion for racing and he had some fantastic designers on his team. He'd never made inroads with the NHRA crowd, though, so he was excited to work with us. We started off with your basic drag racing tees, featuring drawings of the car doing smoky burnouts on the back and a logo on the front, but not long after we began working together I started to have some fresh ideas. Usually, they came out of nowhere.

The first one came to me after Del began surfing again. I called Boris and said, "Here's a new idea. Del's Funny Car, on the beach, under a palm tree, at sunset."

Boris said, "OK, sounds pretty cool. But why on a beach?"

I said, "Because we're going to put a surfboard on the roof and the tagline under the artwork will be 'A Perfect Summer'."

We sold a lot of those but then in 2000 I had another idea. We'd just expanded to a two-car team so I gave Boris the concept and his artists nailed it. The back of the shirt featured a drawing of a typical suburban American home. In the driveway sat the red and blue CSK Funny Cars. The tagline said "Just Your Typical Two-Car Family."

I hit my biggest home run not long after that. Sitting in our house in Austin watching David Letterman, I laughed at his latest "Top 10 List" bit. I walked to my office, grabbed a sheet of paper, and within five minutes I had written it down. The ideas came as fast as I could write them.

We made a simple black T-shirt out of it, with white ink. On the back it read as follows, and keep in mind Jerry Toliver was sponsored by the World Wrestling Federation at the time, while Scotty Cannon had a mohawk:

TOP 10 REASONS I'M A DEL WORSHAM FAN
10. He fixed my skateboard
9. Autograph lines too long over at Force's trailer
8. I like saying "Checker-Schuck's-Kragen" 3 times really fast
7. I can't grow a mohawk
6. No crybabies allowed in CSK pit area
5. His teammate is the "cool" Pedregon
4. He's been driving a Funny Car since he was 4
3. Only driver I've met who called me "Dude"
2. Two words: Chuck and Grandma
And, the No, 1 reason I'm a Del Worsham fan...
1. I never liked pro wrestling anyway!

When they were printed I took one to Bob Frey in the announcer's booth and presented it to him. He took it and simply said, "OK, thanks."

A few minutes later I was walking back to our pit when I heard Bob on the P.A.

"Hey everybody, I was just handed one of the newest Del Worsham T-shirts. Now I gotta admit, I'm usually not a fan of T-shirts that try to be funny because usually they're not funny at all. Comedy, as they say, is hard work. But this one cracked me up."

He then read the whole thing and told the crowd where to buy them. We were printing more by the next day.

After Frankie's big win in Atlanta the blue team readied for the first special edition body, at the following race in Englishtown. 3A Racing was the company that would take over the primary spot for one weekend, and the design of the car was a wild combination of squares and bold colors. We had to ask Spica what 3A Racing actually made. It turned out they were a manufacturer of "dress-up parts" for street cars. Chrome exhaust tips were their most widely recognized piece. CSK sold a lot of their parts.

They had an office in New Jersey, which explained why CSK worked with them to have Frankie in a 3A car for the E-Town event and as the weekend went on and we got to know their executives better, the decision was made to give them the body after the race. It was our oldest body at the time and had been repaired so often it was overly heavy. It would be a nice gesture to give it to them so they could put it in the lobby of their building.

That was a great plan. Right up until the semifinal.

Frankie had pounded his way past Ron Capps and Whit Bazemore in the first two rounds, simply outrunning them. He'd had a small backfire in round one, knocking the burst panel off the car, but the damage was minor. In the semifinal, against John Force, he had a big boomer.

When the motor let go it shredded the 3A body to bits and Force coasted around Frankie to advance. It was a lousy way to end a great weekend and Frankie had won six rounds in a row before the car blew itself to smithereens. His record improved to 11-7.

Del had qualified seventh for the race and in round one he astounded all of us. Running Tony Bartone, he posted not just a win but an otherworldly elapsed time. His 4.779 tied the quickest run ever made in a Funny Car and it was the quickest run ever in the new 90-percent nitro age. If he could run a 4.826 before the day was over, he'd leave with the record.

Instead, he smoked the tires in round two. Still, there was no getting around the fact that Team CSK was beginning to look like real contenders.

Then we went to Topeka and Del lost in the first round while Frankie failed to qualify. And the blue team didn't just barely miss the cut. With 23 cars on the grounds at Heartland Park, they qualified 23rd. It's a humbling sport.

The next race was in Joliet and Del was about to join in the special edition body lottery. The sponsor would be Mountain Dew. Coca-Cola would begin its sponsorship of the NHRA series in 2002 but CSK's longtime association with Pepsi was grandfathered and they were allowed to remain in our associate sponsor mix. The Mountain Dew car would be a memorable one, for more than one reason.

First of all, it was painted a bright yellowish green. The car looked sensational — impossible to miss. The driver was equally as impossible to miss, and for a guy who didn't like a lot of extra attention that was a bit nerve-wracking for Del. His one-race fire suit was the same bright color as the car. The first time he put it on Marc Denner said, "He looks like a human Hi-Liter pen!"

During the first session, on Friday, Del streaked to the No. 1 spot with a 4.831 at 315 mph. On Saturday, he smoked the tires early on the first run, so the team approached Q4 as a run that would give Chuck, Del, and Rob their baseline back. It was overcast and very chilly, with the temperature struggling to make it up to 60 during the afternoon.

Del launched hard in the "Do The Dew" car and was running fast early. Then, the engine let go. The concussion from the bang launched the gorgeous body high in the air where it did a couple of gymnastic backflips before gravity took over and brought it back to earth. As Del said later, "It wasn't hurt too bad by the explosion. It was crunched up pretty badly though, when it came back down."

The body was indeed "crunched up" when the guys got the car back to the pit. It would eventually be fixed but that wasn't going to happen at the track overnight so a Plan B had to be hatched. I raced over to Chindemi's truck and asked him what he thought. He said, "Let's do all we can to make your red CSK car a Mountain Dew car." If he was up for the effort, I was all in too.

John didn't have the capability of printing new Dew logos for the sides and it was too late to have new ones shipped in. So he said we should put the Dew body inside Camp Snoopy and run some heaters on it to warm it up as the sun set on a cold Chicago Saturday. Cold vinyl is brittle and it can be almost impossible to work with. Warm vinyl is flexible. We had to find a way to heat the whole body up and if we could do that John felt like we might be able to transplant them onto the red body. I'd never seen that done before.

We got it as warm as possible inside the tent and John went to work while the crew put the red CSK body in there with us. Somehow, he worked pure magic. He took the big Mountain Dew logos off the green car and put them in place on the red car. The Checker, Schuck's, Kragen logos were wider than the Dew ones, though, so he then put white vinyl over the letters that showed and he added "Do The Dew" in black vinyl on top of that.

The CSK logo on the hood was too big to cover and we were out of time. Still, John Chindemi had worked a vinyl miracle.

When he was done, late that evening, we all stood around and marveled at it. I said, "I didn't even know it was possible to do something like that."

John replied, "I didn't either. But it was worth a try and it worked out."

On Sunday, Del drove the hybrid CSK-Dew car past Bruce Sarver in round one, Frankie in round two, and Jim Epler in the semifinals. We were going back to another final round and Force would again be the opponent.

Del got away first, and that was critical. He and Force were side-by-side the whole way. At the stripe, Del's scoreboard read 4.811 while Force's showed 4.805. Del's reaction time got him there first. Victory was ours, with a modified CSK body made to promote Mountain Dew, and Del did it against the champ on a holeshot. It was, basically, incredible.

With those four consecutive round wins in the bank we moved on to Columbus. Both cars qualified well but Frankie went out in round one. Del, however, got by Densham, Tommy Johnson, and Tony Pedregon to have yet another rematch with Force in the final. So far, in 2001, we were 2-0 against the champ when the Wally trophy was on the line. After the final in Columbus we were 2-1, but Del's record on the year improved to 16-9. And the season wasn't half over. It was quite an improvement for a guy who had gone 10-21, 13-19, 12-20, and 17-22 during his first four years as the CSK driver.

Then, through St. Louis, Pomona, Denver, and Seattle Del went 5-4 to push his record to 21-13. Frankie, meanwhile, checked in at 12-14 with a DNQ on his report card.

For the Western Swing that year I drove my Trans Am to Denver by myself. After the Mile-High Nationals, John Fink joined me for the ride up to Seattle and then down the coast to Sonoma. Barbara managed to meet me there for the final race of the Swing.

Before that, though, we had to produce and race two more special-edition bodies just for the Denver race. Oddly, they were Jurassic Park bodies. I have no idea why. Del's body was painted metallic red while Frankie's was metallic green. Chindemi would adorn them with various dinosaurs and claw marks at the track.

We got to Bandimere Speedway a full day early which meant we couldn't park in the pits. So we set up the rigs down the hill in the gravel parking lot. Chindemi arrived in his truck, and over the course of the day he concentrated on the big decals while I applied all the little ones. I'd done enough of that, by then, to have a bit of a routine when it came to getting started. Like a lot of things in life, there's a moment before you start when you realize, "OK. Here we go. There won't be any stopping until I'm done." To get started I always put Del's name on the car first.

By late in the afternoon both cars were done and back in the trailers. We'd park in the pits the next day. The cars looked really cool and the fans went nuts over them. CSK had die-casts made of these cars as well, and they sold great in the stores. There was a built-in market of people who collected Jurassic Park stuff. The Mountain Dew car flew off the shelves as well, to race fans and Pepsi collectors. Within a year, the Dew die-casts were selling for well over $100 on eBay.

At Denver we discovered that dinosaurs don't make race cars go fast. Del qualified 16th, barely avoiding his own Denver extinction, while Frankie got in 11th. Both lost in the first round. Final score: Bandimere 2, Dinosaurs 0.

After the ride up to Seattle and the scenic trip down the coast and through the redwoods, it was time for Sonoma. There, Frankie would run a special-edition Fram Filters car, at the Fram Autolite Nationals. The attractive orange and black car qualified ninth but won only the first round on Sunday. And another die-cast was born.

Before Sonoma, though, Del did something odd. Instead of traveling down the coast with us he flew home. None of us could figure that out, until he delivered the big news. Connie was pregnant. With twins! She'd be due in February. I wrote a press release and NHRA.com ran it as the banner news bit on their Race Notebook page.

Del flew in Thursday and we were ready to go. Known as Sears Point Raceway at the time, the track in Sonoma still featured the dual-purpose drag strip which doubled as part of the road course. That arc of NASCAR rubber across the drag strip made it one of the most difficult right lanes to negotiate on the entire tour. One might not think a thin band of rubber could upset the tuning of a heavy and powerful Funny Car but if the sun was out and the track was hot it could be nearly impossible to negotiate the right lane without tire smoke.

Without lane choice on Sunday, Del was saddled with the right lane against Ron Capps. Somehow he managed to make a full run without tire spin and his 5.04 edged Capps' 5.059 in an absolute thriller. The solid run gave him lane choice in round two, where he'd face Bruce Sarver. Sarver smoked the tires at the trouble spot and Del's 5.100 earned lane choice over Whit Bazemore in the semifinal, by just 5-thousandths of a second.

As it turned out, Bazemore gave it a great effort in the semi by cleanly getting by the bump and running a solid 5.019 in the right lane. Del grabbed four hundredths at the line and then outran Whit, taking the win with a 5.008 to move on to his third final of the year. He'd have lane choice over Jim Epler.

When Del blasted to a 5.044 while Epler — you guessed it — smoked the tires in the right lane, we celebrated vociferously at the starting line. It was the first time I had experienced the challenge of keeping my composure while shooting the video despite hearing my teammates cheering behind me. I managed to do that and when I stood up Tom Abbett was leaping into my arms. We were laughing as much as we were cheering. For so long, for so many years and so many races, round wins were incredibly hard to come by. Now, in the span of 13 events, Del had won three races and Frankie had won one. Four wins in 13 races? Incredible. It seemed surreal.

And about Tom Abbett. As a Missouri boy he was a lot like me in that classic Midwestern sort of way. We hit it off fairly well, although early in 2001 we did hit a bit of a rough spot when Del granted the use of the second Trans Am to the PR guy. I'm not sure why that bothered Tom but it did and I refused to let it fester. After a pointed comment or two I looked him right in the eyes and said, "Let's talk about this."

We sorted through it and a fine lasting friendship was born. Once again, honesty had been the best solution. We talked it out.

Tom was the guy who backed Del up from the burnout. To get a head start on that, once the body was lowered after the motor was fired, Tom would jump over the retaining wall and run downtrack to be in position when Del stopped after the burnout. Back in '99 when we won Seattle, I just happened to be standing near the starting line for the burnout. After we won round one I knew where to stand for the rest of them. I stood in that exact spot for years because racers and baseball players are superstitious. I was all of the above.

Eventually, as Tom would run by me we started pointing at each other. We did that every lap after doing it the first time. Finally, and I don't remember which race win it was, I was a little extra nervous in round one and I was subconsciously patting the outside of my right leg with my right hand before pointing at Tom. He saw that, and when we won the round and moved on to the next one, Tom was patting his leg when he ran by. By the final round it had rapidly evolved into a thing. Two slaps on the leg, then point and pull the trigger as if our hands were pistols. We called it "Slap, slap, bang!"

In Sonoma, after we beat Epler in the final, we began to show our veteran knowledge about post-race festivities. As the final pair down the track, Kenny Bernstein beat David Grubnic to win the Top Fuel Wally. We already knew this drill and were instantly saying to each other, "Let's go. We've got to beat Bernstein to the winner's circle."

NHRA has it much more efficiently organized now but back then there was only one winner's circle location for all the pro classes. In Chicago, Bernstein had won in Top Fuel and while we took our time celebrating at the top end, they beat us to the winner's circle. No one in the sport had a better sponsor-marketing effort than Kenny. And that meant no one in the sport had more photos taken, with a wider variety of sponsor hats being worn, than the Bernstein team. We had to wait for close to 45 minutes to push the CSK/Dew car into place to have our photos taken. In Sonoma we hustled and got there first. Call it a double-win for the CSK guys.

Moments after the winner's circle fun had ended John Force and Gary Scelzi showed up on a pair of huge bulldozers. They then began to tear up the drag strip. Sears Point was undergoing an enormous renovation, one that would bring with it the new 15,000-seat main grandstand and would finally separate the drag strip from the road course. Many of us grabbed asphalt souvenirs.

The CSK executives then announced we'd all be having dinner at an exclusive restaurant in Napa. They had reserved a private dining room for our big group. At the end of the night the wine bill alone was more expensive than anything I'd ever seen. There were bottles of Silver Oak being opened almost non-stop. We were becoming solid pros at celebrating.

On Monday Barbara and I headed east in my Trans Am, stopping in Lake Tahoe for a night. She then had to fly back to New York for work so I dropped her at the Reno airport and began the long drive home — 1,700 miles, to be exact.

On the first day, after leaving the airport I was only going to drive as far as Las Vegas. It's just a seven-hour drive but it's seven hours of near nothing in the Nevada desert. I got to Vegas in time for dinner.

The next day I was aiming for El Paso, 700 miles away. Down through Phoenix and Tucson, then east on I-10 through a sliver of New Mexico before arriving in El Paso, tired after 12 more hours of driving. Of course, I was in Texas by then so the last day would be a piece of cake, right? It was, if by "piece of cake" you mean 575 miles. The house on Love Bird Lane never looked so good as it did when I pulled in after that long trip.

After a trip to Brainerd where Del won a round and then lost a close one to Force, and where the blue team failed to qualify, it was time for the Mac Tools U.S. Nationals in Indy. Both Del and Frankie had also earned spots in the Budweiser Shootout, the big-money "race-within-a-race" set for Sunday, before the U.S. Nationals final eliminations on Labor Day.

The key for any team participating in both the race and the Shootout is to get solidly qualified for the U.S. Nationals as quickly as possible. That allows the team to focus on going fast in the Shootout without having to worry about the real race on Monday. With Del's 4.83 and Frankie's 4.87 on Friday, that mission was accomplished.

Winning three rounds would earn a team $100,000. Frankie won in the first round but Del was beaten by that pesky Force guy. Frankie then powered past Jim Epler in round two. He would face Bazemore in the final for a hundred grand.

When Bazemore smoked the tires on the hot track and the blue CSK car kept on trucking to the finish line, we had a winner. Frankie was handed the oversized check for $100,000 then was put on the iconic Budweiser beer wagon, pulled by a team of Clydesdales. They paraded in front of the grandstand with Frankie waving and the majestic horses prancing.

The winner's circle for the Shootout is in front of the tower. And while the festivities happen and photos are taken the Top Fuel class is running their final qualifying session, just a couple hundred feet away. It's the only winner's circle celebration where most of the participants have their earmuffs on.

If Frankie could win the race on Monday he'd earn another $125,000 for the team. He made it to the semifinals, but the mountain was too steep.

Indy is the the biggest and most prestigious race of the year and it also acted as the unofficial beginning of the championship homestretch. Del's round record was 23-15. The most rounds he'd ever won in a season was 25, in his rookie year. He also had three event wins. He had never before won more than two events in a season and that also happened a decade earlier, in 1991. Frankie's record was 15-15, with one race victory and the Budweiser Shootout trophy. The blue team was making progress and David Fletcher was still my hero, but they knew they had to clean up the DNQ problem. They'd already suffered two of those.

Del was plenty excited after Indy and he knew he had his best-ever points finish out there as a target. We'd have to finish strong to make that happen but we were running great and both teams were finding a stride I'd never seen in my five years with the organization.

Del gave a lot of credit to Rob Flynn. Rob had come in with those fresh "talented eyes" and had quickly brought in some new tuning ideas. His fingerprints were, by then, all over the success of both CSK cars. The master plan was coming together.

After the Indy race I went back to Austin for a few days and then headed up to Ridgefield to spend a week with Barbara before the Reading event. Reading was set for the weekend of September 14-16 at historic Maple Grove Raceway. I could easily drive there from Ridgefield.

We all know why that didn't happen. We all know exactly where we were on Tuesday, September 11.

Barbara was at IBM working. Shasta and I were lazily spending the morning over cat treats and cereal, respectively. At around 9 a.m. Barbara called me.

"Hey, can you turn on the TV?" she asked. "We just heard the World Trade Center is on fire. Check it out for me."

I did that. I saw what really happened. I saw the second plane hit. I called her back.

"Just come home, right now," I said. She, by then, knew what was happening.

IBM is one of the biggest companies in the world. She was the No. 2 person in their investor relations department, working for a vice president, the CFO, and CEO.

You didn't just pack up your stuff and leave work at IBM. They had a detailed disaster plan on how to shut down systems, safeguard information, and transition into a time of crisis. She didn't get home until late that afternoon.

And it had been such a glorious day. The sky was as blue as I'd ever seen it. The temperature was beyond comfortable. It ended up being the worst day of most Americans' lives.

Ridgefield was roughly 60 miles from the World Trade Center. On a good day, you could drive there in two hours. Just before noon I heard the sad wail of the Ridgefield Fire Department's sirens as their trucks and their brave men headed for the catastrophe.

Once Barbara did get home and we could pull our eyes away from the television, we assessed our own personal situation. It was difficult to get calls to go through on cell phones but I managed to reach Del. I finally spoke to my parents as well. Barbara did the same.

At the time we didn't know how long financial markets would be closed. We decided we should go to the bank and get what we could out of an ATM. The limit was $300 each so that's what we took out.

As we were doing that a gentlemen in a sedan pulled up in front of the bank, which was already closed. He walked over to the flagpole and slowly brought the flag down to half-staff. He then got in his car and drove away.

We decided to go to the grocery store to stock up on supplies. The streets were nearly deserted. At the store there were only a few cars in the parking lot. Inside, maybe a dozen other folks were walking silently, pushing their carts like zombies, up and down the aisles. No one spoke. No one even looked up.

Del managed to reach the teams, both of which had been at the Auburn shop after Indy. They had been loading up and were ready to leave for Reading. He told them to hold tight.

It took a few hours, maybe even a day, but NHRA did the only thing they could do. They postponed Reading until early October. The next race on the schedule would then be Memphis, on September 21-23. We had no idea if we'd be racing there but we had to plan for it.

As the days passed and the new normal of a shattered world set in, NHRA made the bold choice to hold the Memphis race as scheduled. On September 18, the Yankees played baseball. Three days later we'd be drag racing.

Before the first round in Memphis, the pro drivers went out on the track and unfurled a huge American flag. Just standing there, for the national anthem, was one of the most difficult and emotional things I'd ever had to do. All around me, tough, daring men and women who put their lives on the line to go fast had tears streaming down their faces. Holding the giant flag with both hands, they had no way to wipe those tears away.

We raced in Memphis and Chicago before going back to Reading. Nothing in the world seemed to get any less surreal. In the meantime, Del was having some private conversations with a man who could help take us to the next level.

Johnny Gray had been racing a Funny Car out of his own pocket. His pockets, by the way, were quite deep. But like John Fink, Johnny didn't become prosperous by wasting money. He was in the oil business and he was doing very well, but his Funny Car was eating more cash than he'd imagined possible.

The conversations between Del and Johnny were about the blue car. Johnny offered to bring a solid amount of money to Worsham & Fink Racing. He'd get a few associate spots on the blue car in exchange, to bring along some companies he did business with, and he'd get to drive a fast car. And it would cost him a mere fraction of what he was spending to do it on his own.

It was a tough decision to make and it couldn't be made without CSK's buy-in. For a few weeks the discussions continued and the biggest stumbling block was the fact Spica and Chisler knew almost nothing about Johnny Gray. Finally, Del made it clear that the change would be huge for both the team and CSK. If CSK kept signing us to extensions and increases, we could quickly be in a position where the championship might be attainable.

"We all like Frankie and he's done a great job," Del said to Spica. "But, this isn't about having a friend drive the car. This about all of us taking a big step. We think we should do it."

Eventually, the executive team at CSK agreed. They also planned to meet Johnny and his wife Terry over dinner in Pomona. In the meantime, we had to race in Dallas. Del planned to meet with Frankie there and tell him the news.

I was in the reserved parking lot behind the pits at the Motorplex that Friday morning. Frankie pulled in a few minutes after I did. He'd stopped to chat with another racer for a bit and then saw me. He looked stunned.

"Hey, Bobby, am I fired?" he asked. Del had wanted to be the one to talk to him first, but I wasn't about to lie to my friend's face.

"Hey, man, Del wanted to talk to you first, but we are making a change," I said. "You've done a great job Frankie. It's been a privilege to work with you, but you know how this sport works as well as anyone. We're all on day-to-day contracts."

He went and spoke with Del and everyone came out of that meeting understanding it. Frankie was very professional about it. The blue team even won five rounds at the final six races. He finished the season No. 7 in the standings.

Del went into Pomona fighting hard for third place. Prior to the race, we put out a press release and announced Frankie had resigned to pursue other options. It was the least we could do for him and it allowed him to circulate at Pomona and meet with other teams.

On Thursday night we had our dinner with Spica, Chisler, and the Grays, and I could tell the CSK guys liked Johnny's demeanor and his honesty. They liked his resume, as well. He was a fantastic businessman and he'd driven just about everything with wheels. He was going to be a big asset.

The following night NHRA and Winston held their annual dinner for PR representatives at a fine restaurant in Ontario. In my first four years with the Worshams, I'd managed to find a lame excuse to miss it three times. I don't know why, exactly, but I do know that I still felt very much like an outsider and still "the new guy" compared to many of my PR colleagues who had been doing it for a long time.

I was staying at Del and Connie's house for the weekend and as Friday night rolled around I was hemming and hawing and certainly acting like I didn't want to go. Both Del and Connie insisted that I should and that I'd regret it if I didn't. I went.

After we gathered in a small private room and as we sat down around a long table one of the veteran PR people said to me, "Bob, you should give a speech on all of our behalf, especially thanking Winston for all their years of sponsorship."

Susie Arnold, who did PR for Kenny Bernstein, uttered a key line. She said, "Hey, you're the most loquacious one here. We want you to do it." We all thought loquacious meant "well-spoken" and I took it as a compliment. Later, we discovered it meant you simply talk a lot. That applied, too.

I gave a nice little speech, everyone clapped, and I thought we were going to eat. Then the Winston rep began to speak. He was announcing the recipient of the 2001 Winston PR Rep of the Year Award. I didn't know there was such a thing. And as he spoke, it started to feel like a lot of people were staring at me.

When I heard my name announced I was utterly stunned. Even though I was a loquacious guy, I was stunned enough to be at a loss for words, other than "wow" and "thank you." They handed me a glass plaque with my name etched on it to commemorate the presentation, as well as a special bottle of wine.

To this day there are still PR reps who call me Mr. Loquacious from time to time. Not many, because we're all getting old, but there are a few. And I'm still completely stunned they gave me that award. We toss around the word "honor" too freely. When I was presented that plaque, it was truly an honor. It still is.

When I got back to Del and Connie's house they acted surprised when I showed the plaque to them. I've never asked if they knew it was going to happen. It seemed a bit odd that they would push so hard for me to go.

As the race unfolded Del got on a roll again. Qualified 11th, he got his lucky round out of the way immediately, smoking the tires but still beating Ron Capps in the opener. He then powered past Tony Pedregon in round two, winning with a 4.823. Then in the semifinal he won another nail-biter, this time taking out Dean Skuza by a foot with a 4.827. In the final round, Del's fifth of the year, he'd face Whit.

It was dark when the final round was contested. Abbett and I did our "Slap, slap, bang" routine as he ran past me. As I always did, I knelt by the wall and turned on the camera.

At the flash of amber, Del hit the throttle and his CSK Pontiac went into immediate tire spin. I was crestfallen. It wasn't like us to smoke the tires at the hit like that, so something mechanical must have befallen us. And then I heard the guys behind me screaming and yelling. I hadn't noticed the bright red light staring at us from Bazemore's side of the tree. He'd fouled at the start and the race win was ours.

They say there are no ugly wins and no good losses. I guess that's true. It seemed odd to be celebrating but it was a heartfelt bunch of hugs we all shared.

By the time the guys towed the car back to the winner's circle from the top end they'd taken a razor blade and cut off the left half of the number 8 on the side of Del's car. He'd finished eighth in 2000 and we ran the number all year. By cutting it in half, they had already managed to put the first 3 on the CSK Pontiac.

We celebrated, took our photos, and headed back to the pit and Camp Snoopy where Del's favorite band, The Tijuana Dogs, were getting ready to play. Later that night, the world's most famous margarita machine would make an appearance.

Mega-Rita was a former Worsham nitro motor. It powered three five-gallon mixers and it made a lot of noise and a lot of flames when it did that.

Our pit party had grown beyond the informal parties from years before. We took it up a notch and brought in a band. When Del had the idea for Mega-Rita it gave him another project to tackle. The man does like projects.

When it came time to make the blades, he was going to just fabricate something that looked like blades when he realized the technology was already proven and readily available. So, much to Connie's dismay, he took apart the kitchen blender and copied those blades, only five times bigger.

2001's party was big and almost out of control, at times. We realized we'd need to add some beefy security and we'd make it invitation-only the next year.

We were thrilled with what we'd done in 2001. Five events wins and one Budweiser Shootout trophy between the two teams. Del had finished 35-20, with four event wins. It was, by far, the best year of his career. Frankie had finished 20-21. We had a third-place car and a seventh-place car in the final standings.

We had 2002 to look forward to. And we couldn't wait. But first, Barbara and I treated ourselves to another Hawaiian trip.

In late November we started out at the New Otani in Honolulu because we'd enjoyed it so much the first time. Then we shifted over to Maui and spent a few days at the absolutely fabulous Fairmont Kea Lani Resort. Beyond any doubt, it was the single nicest hotel I'd ever been in. Our suite overlooked the ocean at Wailea and the private beach was just a short walk from the majestic open-air lobby. The Kea Lani also featured two pools connected by a water slide. Barbara and I became 12 again, and we'd race the actual 12-year olds back up the steps to slide back down, over and over. In the upper pool, a swim-up bar beckoned after a dozen trips down the slide. Mai Tais were consumed.

Finally, we headed back to Hana again but Barbara wanted nothing to do with the winding churning road to the little village. We'd done some research for alternative transportation, and had discovered Paragon Air.

Paragon Air featured one airplane. It was a six-seater, if you counted the two seats in front for a captain and first officer. For not much more than a typical flight between islands, Captain Ron flew us over to the tiny airstrip in Hana, where a vintage open-air bus from the Hotel Hana Maui was waiting for us.

Sept. 11 had been just two months earlier and all forms of tourism in the United States were suffering. Hawaii, though, was really hard hit. When we got to the Hotel Hana Maui, a wonderful resort with individual luxury bungalows spread out over the property just off the beach, it was nearly empty.

One group of guests was made up of Victoria's Secret models, and their crew. They shot swimsuit photos at the pool one day while we were sunning nearby. Later, when their new catalog came out, we scoured the photographs to see if we were in the background. Sadly, we had been PhotoShopped out.

On our final day, as we sat in the open-air bus to be taken back to the airstrip, the driver pointed out a scruffy young man with stringy hair and a beard standing at the concierge desk. Our driver said, "Watch this guy. You'll recognize him."

It was Leonardo DiCaprio. There weren't many guests staying at the Hotel Hana Maui, but those we had been hanging out with represented some prestigious company.

On our Paragon flight back, our captain flew us over George Harrison's estate. George had passed away just days earlier. Once we were at the Maui airport, we checked in and then passed Prince and his entourage on the concourse. Then we flew home on an historic flight. It was the last flight from Hawaii to St. Louis TWA would ever make. The crew was emotional throughout the flight and they gave away every ounce of liquor en route, making the "red eye" overnight flight incrementally more of a red-eye. My former favorite airline would be fully absorbed by American on December 1.

It had been an incredibly eventful 2001.

The Hits Keep On Comin'

As 2001 came to a conclusion Barbara's six-month temporary assignment with IBM had eclipsed the 18-month mark. It showed no sign of ending.

I went up to be with her and Shasta for New Year's Eve. As we toasted the new year, still vividly remembering Sept. 11, we wondered aloud how this was all going to end. Should we make a new effort to find a home in Ridgefield? Could we possibly continue to live in two different places? It was all a depressing mystery.

Shortly after I returned to Austin, Barbara phoned and said, "A headhunter just called me about a job as the head of investor relations for a company called Lawson Software. They're not very big and I'm not sure I want to go there. They're in St. Paul, Minnesota."

I don't think she expected my response. I told her I'd love to move to Minnesota. For a chance to do that I'd happily sell the house in Austin and we could all, once again, be together. She was confused and asked me why I'd want to move to such a place.

"I've wanted to live in Minnesota my whole life," I said. "When I was a kid, my dad worked for the Twins. When I was a scout, Minnesota was my favorite state in any region I ever covered. The people are so nice and it's a beautiful place. For years, I've thought that I'd like to get back to having four distinct seasons but if we're going to have winter I want it to be a real winter. Let's go!"

She pulled the reins in a little, saying she'd think about it. At the very least, she reasoned, going through the interview would be good experience for someone who had been with IBM for 18 years and thought she'd never leave.

A few days later she went to an office in New York and conducted a video-conference interview. Not long after that, Lawson Software offered her a job. She would be vice president for investor relations. The company had just recently gone public and they needed an expert to help them shore up their investor base.

Lawson offered to bring us both up to St. Paul for a visit. We could check out the area and even look at a few houses to see what we could get for our money. We accepted. It was February.

We took all the warm clothes we could find and flew to the Minneapolis-St. Paul Airport then grabbed a cab to our assigned destination, the St. Paul Hotel in downtown St. Paul. It was diagonally across the street from Lawson's headquarters.

As the taxi pulled up to the hotel, I realized something.

"I've been here," I said, to Barbara. "I've been in this hotel. I remember it. I was just a kid and my folks brought me up here for some sort of winter banquet with the Twins. It was the first time I ever flew on a plane, and we stayed here. I remember ice carvings in a park across the street. I could see them from our window."

Indeed, the park was still across the street. And, in an uncanny sort of coincidence, it was filled with ice carvings.

At the front desk we asked about the park and the sculptures and the clerk told us it was Winter Carnival in St. Paul. We were there for the final weekend of the annual event.

We quickly did some online research to find out what Winter Carnival was all about. Basically, it's a way for Minnesotans to show how tough they are in the winter, and how much they embrace it. Who puts on a full outdoor carnival, complete with a massive parade, when it's 5-below zero? St. Paul.

To make it more campy and a lot more fun, the final act in the weeklong carnival is the Torchlight Parade. The story told that night is the battle waged by King Boreas and his royal court of the north wind. They were clad in white and represented winter.

Their sworn enemies were the Vulcans, who wore red and streaked their faces with soot. Vulcanus Rex was their leader. They worshipped fire and would bring summer back to St. Paul.

Citizens in the area had to choose a rooting interest in the annual tussle. We figured summer sounded like a good thing. We still root for the Vulcans. Hail the Vulc!

Over the course of a couple of days Barbara met with the executive team at Lawson and we spent an afternoon looking at homes around the area. We could get a lot for our money, compared to Austin. We could live a lifestyle we'd never before known, compared to New York or Connecticut. I was sold. Barbara was intrigued, but she was coming around.

On our final night, the Torchlight Parade wandered right by the hotel. It was well below zero, so we bundled up as best we could and joined the huge crowd. Many were shouting "Hail the Vulc!" and we joined in, also making a V with two fingers.

Each year the parade passes in front of Boreas and his royal family, as they watch and wave from a viewing stand. It ends with the Vulcans bringing up the rear of the parade, with torches and flame throwers lighting the sky. They attack Boreas and his north wind brigade, but are repelled once, and then again. On the third try, the Vulcans overthrow Boreas and his group and summer is once again guaranteed to return. The Vulcans were on a long winning streak. They were roughly 75-0 on the night we saw this spectacle.

Within a week Barbara made up her mind. She'd be joining Lawson and we'd be moving to Minnesota. The first step was for her to resign from IBM. The next step was for her and Shasta to head back to Austin; we needed to get the house on the market.

We hired a real estate agent and spiffed the place up as well as we could. Barbara then had to get to work, so Lawson provided a corporate apartment in St. Paul in a high-rise building. The apartment was in a section of downtown called Lowertown, which is an apt name since that part of the city is situated downhill from the area where Lawson and the St. Paul Hotel are found. Shasta went with Barbara to keep her company.

Meanwhile, I was busy getting ready for the 2002 season. We'd finally convinced CSK to abandon the airbrush artwork for the red and blue cars. It was too complicated, too expensive, and frankly it wasn't even that attractive. What we got in return was a perfect case study for proof that "design by committee" can cause a disaster.

Seemingly everyone in marketing at CSK had their input and their fingers on the design. What they ended up with was a fairly simple concept and it looked fine on paper. The red and blue colors would each be offset by black and silver. As a team, we were just happy to see base colors and simple graphics.

The red would be a dark candy apple. The blue would be a dark royal. The silver would be used as a way to separate the red and blue from the black, which surrounded the two cars around the bottom edge, with slashes and points on the hood, and solid black on the roof, the rear deck, and the spoiler. The CSK logos would be in white, with a slight silver edge to the letters. It looked OK to us. We were ready for a change.

When we saw them in person, it didn't look so OK. The red and blue we'd been told to use were both slightly darker than regular red and blue. Being surrounded by so much black they looked even darker. The silver stripes were attractive but the silver edge around the logo and wording made it all look blurry.

Dave Kommel, a veteran drag racing photographer who had seen enough paint schemes to have valued input, minced no words. On the day we rolled them out he said, "They're going to look awful in photos. The black around the bottom will blend in with the track. The red and the blue are both too dark. The silver around Checker, Schuck's, and Kragen is a mess."

I didn't know enough to have an opinion. But the next day, when I saw the first photos online, I knew he was right. We'd have to let CSK come to that opinion themselves, though. We'd fought them for a year over the airbrush design. We didn't want to look like brats and complain about the replacement look.

Before we made our first qualifying run in Pomona I convinced Del to let me pull a little prank. We'd finished in third place in 2001, so we were running the number 3 in 2002. Instead of a normal digit I had Chindemi make us up a set of Roman numeral threes and I put those on the sides of the car just behind the side windows.

When we made the turn in front of the tower for our first run Bob Frey said, over the P.A. system, "You can always count on those wacky Worshams. Check it out folks, they have their number on Del's car in Roman numerals. I've never seen that before."

We figured NHRA would tell us that day to put a regular number on the car and I had them at the ready. Or maybe the next day. Or maybe when Pomona ended. They never said a word and we ran the Roman numerals all year. Because we were wacky.

Del got off to a strong start. He made it to the final round before losing to John Force. Johnny Gray made his debut as the blue team driver a good one. He advanced to the semifinals where he faced off against Del and lost.

We went to Phoenix and, of course, partook in all things promotional for a string of early mornings and late nights, until the race itself mercifully started on Friday.

On Sunday, coming out of the 10th spot, Del beat Gary Scelzi in round one. Johnny, who had qualified 11th, lost to Force's teammate, Tony Pedregon.

Then Del disposed of the third Force driver, Gary Densham, in round two. Scotty Cannon tried but failed to beat the red team in the semi. Force, who had beaten Del in the final at Pomona, would be in the other lane for the Phoenix final. The champ was going for his 100th Funny Car win. The champagne and special hats were ready.

The Pomona final had been a pedalfest, with each driver hitting the throttle numerous times before Force crossed the win stripe first. At Phoenix there would be no such drama. Del powered cleanly to a 4.940 while Force smoked the tires. At the starting line the team and a huge throng of CSK executives went collectively bonkers. Force's champagne had to be put away.

After all the hoopla, Spica made a call to Fleming's restaurant in nearby Chandler, and we all went out for a world-class dinner. The red team, the blue team, and a dozen CSK people had a whale of a good time. And yes, I gave a speech.

Del had won his sponsor's race, and the cover of National Dragster magazine would be a keeper. It showed Del's car with a bold headline that read "Not In Our House!"

Even with all that success, though, Del had far more important things on his mind. Connie was due with their twins any day. He rushed home to her and a little more than a week later they welcomed Katelyn and Madelyn Worsham to the world. Kate and Maddy were gorgeous and even in the earliest photos of them, just after they were born, it was clear that Kate looked like Del while Maddy looked like Connie. Our driver and friend, for years known as "The Kid from the Coast" who was stoked when things were rad, was growing up fast. And he was a dad, twice over.

Gainesville was next but I needed to get down to Florida a little early. My mom and dad were, by then, both in an assisted-living facility in St. Petersburg. I hadn't seen them more than a couple of times per year once I moved away to Indy, Chapel Hill, and Austin. Taffy was showing clear signs of Alzheimer's although physically she was fit. Skip was just the opposite. His mind remained clear but cancer was consuming his body. I needed to see them.

Skip was mostly bedridden by then. His eyes grew a little brighter and a lot bigger when I walked in the room. Taffy nearly cried and she called me Bobby the entire time. Looking at my dad, I knew the end was not far away. I just hoped my mom could hold off the dementia enough to be there with him.

With that visit weighing on me, I made my way back up to Gainesville and watched as Del failed to qualify. What a crazy sport drag racing is. He was 7-1 and fighting for the points lead with John Force. And he failed to make the show at the third race. Johnny and the blue team made it a little better by advancing to the semifinal. Fletch was still my hero.

At the next six races, Del went 5-6, running his record to 12-7. Johnny went 3-5 with a DNQ in Las Vegas. He was 7-8 on the year.

In the tuning room, as that so-so period of racing unfolded, tension seemed to be rising. Del and Chuck were not always agreeing with Rob, who had done so much to make us as competitive as we were. Rob, in return, seemed to be digging in his heels. I felt like it was my responsibility to mend this mess.

I brought all three of them into the red team's lounge after we'd lost in the first round at Englishtown. I acted as a bit of a mediator, just trying to get it all out in the open and start fresh. I wasn't being pushy but I was steering the conversation and it felt like we were making headway. No one was really comfortable in the room, but at least they were talking.

And then Top Fuel driver David Baca walked in. Without knocking. Baca is an outspoken guy. When he came in the room not only did the conversation stop, but he never let it get going again. Finally, Rob left and nothing was accomplished. We were due in Topeka the next weekend, but before we got there Rob left the team.

With all that drama surrounding me, I still had a wife (and cat) in St. Paul and we needed to find a place to live. Our real estate agent was from the south-side suburbs and he was intent upon showing us homes in Burnsville, Prior Lake, Lakeville, Eagan, and Savage. We'd seen close to 40 homes when we found a beautiful new house in Savage, not far from MSP airport. The area seemed nice, the commute wouldn't be terrible for Barb, and we'd both have quick access to MSP. We put an offer on it and it was accepted.

With a closing date of a month later we readied ourselves for the move. We also had an offer for our house in Austin. It was all coming together until we discovered the seller of the home in Savage, who had also built it but never moved in, was in the middle of a contentious divorce. The house was caught up in the settlement negotiations. We cancelled the contract. Now, we had to find a home in a hurry.

I'd been doing all sorts of online research and to me it seemed like the eastern suburb of Woodbury was the right fit for us. We hadn't been there because our agent was showing us the part of town he knew best. We finally talked him into showing us homes in Woodbury.

Over the course of two more weekends we had finally seen somewhere close to 90 homes. I'm sure we were driving the agent nuts, but none of them felt right to us. Many of them were gorgeous, some were stunning, but none of them felt right. Finally, on the verge of exhaustion, he took us to a house in a development called Marsh Creek. When we pulled into the driveway, I whispered to Barbara, "This is the place."

When we went inside we knew it was the place. It faced a large pond with an unobstructed view. What we didn't know until we entered was that there was another smaller pond directly behind the house. The living room was two stories tall, and all windows. It was a million-dollar view. We'd found our home, and it was bigger than any home either of us had ever lived in. It was three levels, although the lower level was not yet finished, and it had three bedrooms, a dedicated office, a formal dining room, a beautiful kitchen with a large center island, and a sunroom. It was about 3,900 square feet, with another 1,000 square feet of lower level left to be completed.

We'd be closing in early May. The movers would be leaving Austin right on time.

Once we were moved in and settled, we met the neighbors. On one side, a woman named Patty lived by herself in a large home. She worked for Target, in its corporate headquarters, and traveled almost constantly. On the other side, Dave and Nichol Jacobsen lived with their two kids, Justin and Alexa, who were 12 and 10. Within days, we were becoming friends. And it's a good thing for Barbara that we did.

We hadn't gotten to know the Jacobsens all that well yet when on one windy day Barbara opened the front door and two birds flew in. More precisely, two birds got blown in. I was at a race. Barb had no idea what to do so she called the Jacobsens next door. Originally, when Nichol answered, Barbara asked to talk to Dave. Nichol said he was on a conference call and it would be some time. She asked Barbara if everything was OK. Barb told her about the birds, one of which had flown back out, and Nichol came running over.

The second bird was panicked and trapped in the sunroom. Nichol was willing to grab it, so Barbara gave her a pair of oven mitts.

Somehow the two of them got the bird to safety, then they laughed hysterically and a bond was formed. They were best friends in no time. Dave and I, being guys, followed along. That's just how we roll.

Our real estate agent, who was thrilled to have finally found a home for us but probably more thrilled to get rid of us, gave us his Twins tickets for an upcoming game. We'd be heading to the Metrodome to see the Twins play the Indians from the seventh row right above the visitors' dugout. Neither one of us had ever set foot in the bland 80s-style inflated stadium with the big baggy for a right-field fence.

I don't recall if the Twins won or lost but I cheered lustily and had a great time. After the game, in the car, Barbara said, "Why were you acting like such a big Twins fan?" Her tone of voice was one of confusion and skepticism.

"You don't understand," I said. "I've been a Twins fan all my life. I grew up in St. Louis with a TC hat on my head. I've been waiting to live here since I was five. I really am a Twins fan!" I'm still not sure she got that, but before long she was a Twins fan too. We'd be season ticket holders for the next decade.

Before the NHRA tour got to Chicago, CSK came up with a new design for our cars. It was bright, swoopy, and gorgeous. When they sheepishly told us, "This first design we came up with didn't look as good as we thought it would. Would you be willing to change it to this?" as they showed us the new design, we collectively said, "Well, if you really want us to then that's what we'll do." In private, we shared high-fives.

By then, we'd also brought in Chris Cunningham to assist David Fletcher with a fresh set of eyes. Chris fit in nicely, and his experience could clearly help both teams.

At the Chicago race, Del qualified in the No. 5 spot while Johnny was No. 11. On Sunday, Johnny lost to Tony Pedregon in the opening round. Del would be carrying the ball.

In round one, Del beat Tommy Johnson, with a 4.858 pulling away from TJ at the stripe.

In round two, Del faced John Force yet again, and his 4.875 was just enough to edge Force in a thriller.

In the semifinal, Del faced Force's teammate Gary Densham, and the stylish new CSK Pontiac outran Densham by a car length.

Scotty Cannon was the opponent in the final. It was Del's third final in the first 10 races of the '02 season. 4.878 seconds later, it was also his second win. Cannon smoked the tires early, and we all levitated in celebration back at the starting line. All of a sudden, we were working our way back into the points battle.

That win meant we'd also won the spring Chicago race in back-to-back years. The gaggle of photographers in the winner's circle posed father and son standing in front of the car, back to back. Life was becoming pretty good in Worshamville.

We had races in Columbus and St. Louis to round out June. Barbara and I used every spare second to get fully settled in our home.

With the Western Swing upon us, I prepared for the grind of Denver, Seattle, and Sonoma on consecutive weekends in July.

On the Thursday morning before the Denver race, I figured I'd pack early for my afternoon flight. Just as I finished zipping up my suitcase my sister Mary, who was living with her husband Lonnie and their kids near Orlando, called.

"Skip's not doing well," she said. "They don't think he'll make it through the day. We're heading over to St. Pete right now. I'll keep you posted."

I sat nervously in my office for an hour. She finally called.

"He passed before we got here," she said. "They said he died peacefully."

How is it that your father can be so gravely ill for so long, and yet … How could he battle against that cancer until it got him at 83, and yet … When the moment comes, you're still stunned.

I told Barbara but I stayed stoic about it. I also told her I was still going to Denver. The team needed me. It was my job. I then called Del and told him the news, and that I planned to be there.

An hour later, still stunned and processing it, I finally got it. My dad, my hero, was gone. I cried for 30 minutes, and then composed myself before calling Del again.

"I don't know what I was thinking," I said. "I won't be there. I need to be home."

Del said, "I'm glad to hear that. I thought you were crazy to come to this race. I'll call you constantly. Stay home and deal with everything you have to deal with."

When I told Barbara, she had much the same sort of response. She knew I was in denial when I said I was going. Staying home was the only way to approach the grieving process.

It would be the first race I'd ever missed with Team CSK.

I then called Jeff Romack, who did PR for GM Racing. I asked Jeff if there was any way he could help me by putting out some pit notes in Denver, over the weekend.

Jeff was one of the classiest and most professional guys I knew in the sport. He was also really good at what he did. I had a sense he'd be happy to help me, and he was.

On Friday and Saturday, I followed along as well as I could in that era before live-streaming or NHRA apps on our phones. Jeff stayed in touch, and Del called me after every run. He ended up qualified in the No. 9 spot. Johnny was No. 6.

I created a big bold memo on my computer, using the largest font I could find that would fit on a sheet of paper. It simply said "Kick Some Ass!"

I called the team hotel and got their fax number. I asked the desk agent to give the memo to Tom Abbett.

On Sunday morning, he hung it inside the transporter.

Johnny lost in the first round, to Force.

Del beat Tommy Johnson in the opener, running a 5.086 up on the mountain.

In round two, Del beat Scotty Cannon with a 5.122, pulling away.

In the semifinal, Del faced our old buddy and former teammate Frankie Pedregon, barely edging him with a 5.363 in a side-by-side battle.

Tony Pedregon would be the opponent in the final. NHRA.com did have a scrolling eliminations update on its main page then and, as each pro final would be run, it would refresh and update with the results. Minutes felt like hours. I stared at the screen as it finally showed me that Matt Hines had won in Pro Stock Motorcycle.

Then, an eon later, the scroll refreshed and I saw that Mike Edwards had beaten Allen Johnson in Pro Stock.

Time was moving impossibly slow. Perhaps Albert Einstein could have explained it to me, but in my mind it was like a bad kind of magic. The second hand on my watch was barely moving.

I was behind my desk in my office, which was just off the living room. Barbara was out there, on the sofa, watching TV.

I waited. And waited. I was barely breathing.

Finally, it refreshed and began to scroll. I almost couldn't watch.

And there it was. The Funny Car final. Del Worsham (5.160) defeated Tony Pedregon (5.193). I yelled, loudly, "YES!" and Barbara came running. And then the tears started flowing again. It's a process, and my team was part of helping me get through it.

Not long after, John Fink called from the Winner's Circle. He passed the phone around to a bunch of the guys, and when my hero, David Fletcher, came on the line he got through about three words before he started crying. We were a mess, but in the bigger picture we were a tight family and their support was absolutely priceless.

The day was special for everyone, but especially for Del. He and Connie had Kate and Maddy with them. It was their first race, and a win was a great way to initiate two little girls into the drag racing world. Winning the race in my father's memory was Del's priority as well.

In his post-race interview with the media, he talked about the challenge of running up on the mountain, at Bandimere. But he wrapped it up with this quote:

"There were all sorts of motivations for us this weekend," he said. "I had my baby girls at the track for the first time, which was a happy thrill. On the flip side, our team manager Bob Wilber was not here this weekend, missing his first race since he joined us in 1997. Bob's dad, Del Wilber, passed away early Thursday and we all dedicated this race to Bob and the memory of his dad. When we got to the final, I was hoping more than anything that we could pull this off for Bob and the Wilber family.

"It says, right there on each side window, 'In Memory, Del Wilber' and this one is dedicated to Bob Wilber and his late father. We put all this pressure on ourselves and we wanted to see what we're made of. I guess we're not too bad."

Yeah, not too bad at all.

For what the Wilber family had been through, and for me being in Woodbury at home instead of with my team on the mountain, it was beyond special. I shared Del's quote with my brother Del, and he couldn't believe it.

"That's the greatest thing I've ever read," he replied in an email. "Now I know why you love this guy so much. I can't wait to meet him." Del and his wife Kay made plans to do just that, later in the season at the Las Vegas race.

The loss of our father brought all of us back together, and brother Del and I repaired the ding my resignation from DW+A had inflicted. We became very close from that point forward and Del began to formulate a plan for a family charity, called The Perfect Game Foundation. I would be a Founding Advisor and a key contributor.

Statistically, the win at Denver made Del 21-9. Prior to our emergence in 2001, when we picked up 35 rounds, Del hadn't won more than 17 in an entire season since 1992. Even in those great early years of 1991 and 1992, he won just 25 and 24 rounds. We'd won 21, and we still had 10 races left to go.

A week later, it was time for Seattle. And for me, it was time to get back out there. It is widely known that the NHRA community is like a family. Teams that want to rip their opponents' hearts out on the track will step up immediately to help when the chips are down. I still, to some degree, felt like the new guy and an outsider. That feeling would be forever erased once I got to Seattle.

From the moment I arrived at the track it was one long series of hugs, handshakes, and sincere well wishes. From good friends to people who were barely acquaintances, it seemed like everyone in the pit area stopped to see how I was doing. It was overwhelming. It was also wonderful. I realized I had two homes. One was a beautiful house between two ponds with my incredible wife and crazy cat. The other was the race track. It felt great to be there.

Del made a strategic decision during that period. He was not out of the hunt for the championship but he knew he'd not only have to keep winning races and rounds, he'd also need Force to start losing before the finals. He decided to bring out a third car to aid in that mission.

Cory Lee would drive a black Checker, Schuck's, Kragen car in Brainerd and Indy. After that, a decision would be made whether or not to keep running it. We were a three-car team, and Cory put the nickname "Mustang Hunter" on his car, targeting Force's Ford.

Cory made the field in Brainerd, qualifying No. 14, but he spun the tires against Whit Bazemore in the opening round and hit a timing block. Meanwhile, Del managed to pick up one round win but Force went on to win the race.

They call the U.S. Nationals the Big Go. But since we were sponsored by Mac Tools, the Mac Tools U.S. Nationals was even bigger. In the final qualifying session, Cory went from outside the field into the No. 16 spot. When he did that he bumped out Whit, who drove a car sponsored by Mac's competitor, Matco Tools. The CEO from Mac Tools high-fived me so hard my hand stung for an hour.

During a seven-race stretch, Del had gone 9-7 to raise his round wins to 30 on the year. We'd gone 35-20 in 2001, so to match that we'd need to win five rounds in the final three races.

When those final three were upon us it was clear Del wasn't going to win the championship, so we parked Cory's car. Our new goal was to finish third again, still Del's best. The initial race of the final three was Dallas. On the points sheet we entered in fourth place, nine points behind Gary Densham.

After four rounds on Sunday, we were in third. We also were in the winner's circle. I won't say it was becoming routine, and I know we never took any win for granted, but we were absolutely getting used to it. We weren't surprise winners any longer. It wasn't an upset to see a CSK car being photographed with the Wally trophy after a race. We were contenders.

When Del picked up one more round in Vegas we had our 35 rounds and we'd locked up third place in the standings. Johnny ended up 12-21 and he held on to earn the number 10 for his blue CSK car in 2003.

In Pomona, Del kept a promise to Cory and brought the third car back out. Cory managed to pick up a round win then he faced Force in round two. The existence of the third car was based on hunting Mustangs. The Mustang won the round, the race, and the championship.

We'd given it our best shot, and maybe we bit off more than we could chew, but it was exhilarating to be in the thick of a title hunt for as long as we were. And the number 3 would be on the car again in 2003, although it would be a regular number, not a Roman numeral. That gag had survived all season.

After the cars were put away the pit party began. With Johnny Gray being part of the team, and with his extensive oil industry business relationship with Halliburton, he arranged to have a custom trailer delivered right to our pit after the race was over. It was, in effect, a giant rolling steak grill and the Halliburton guys fed us like royalty that night. It was such a big deal that for the first time we had to make the pit party an invitation-only affair. We arranged for temporary fencing, had hulking security guards in bright yellow t-shirts, and gave entry tickets to those we'd invited. With the Tijuana Dogs rocking the house, we bid 2002 adieu in style.

We attended the NHRA Awards Ceremony the next night and all applauded in earnest when Johnny and Del took the stage. We had a few drinks at the after-party and then piled back into our rented limo for the ride back to Del's house. Within minutes, every person in the limo was asleep. When the season is underway you suck it up and keep going. When the banquet is over you realize just how tired you are.

The upcoming off-season would be the first Minnesota winter for Barbara and me. To get ready for that we needed some warm clothes. We went to Kohl's department store and roamed the aisles with a large cart. When we checked out and paid for our purchases we looked like the transplants we were. We had coats, sweaters, boots, hats, gloves, and anything that looked warm piled in the cart. Clearly, the upcoming winter had us a little worried.

We also made a different major purchase. We bought a hot tub.

We had a deck off our sunroom, and the area below it was a perfect location for the tub. I spent two days leveling it and putting heavy concrete tiles down. When the tub arrived, we filled it up and tried it out for the first time. It was incredible. The hot tub instantly became a central part of our lives, especially in the dead of winter. It was only a few steps from the lower level door so the cold would never deter us from enjoying the 102-degree bubbling water.

Once winter arrived for real we realized we had already become Minnesotans. We loved it. The ponds both froze, the snow came down, and the temperature dropped. The best thing about Minnesota winter, though, is that it's often sunny. Growing up in St. Louis I was used to months of gray depression, and we looked forward to spring as much for the sun as we did for the warmth.

In Minnesota, the snowstorms would arrive, we'd scrape the white stuff off the driveway, and the sun would come back out for days on end. When the thermometer dipped below zero, sometimes staying there for a week or more, we'd just bundle up a bit more seriously.

In the bubbling spa, I set a personal best for coldest temp in the tub. It was -17 outside. It was 102 in the water. For that one I wore a stocking cap.

The Twin Cities are built for cold. In downtown St. Paul and downtown Minneapolis, most of the buildings are connected by skyways and tunnels. During our first winter we became diehard fans of the Minnesota Wild hockey team. When we went to games, we could park for free in the garage at Barbara's office and leave our coats in the car, no matter how cold it was. By using the skyways and tunnels that zig-zagged all over downtown, we could walk to Xcel Energy Arena in 15 minutes without ever stepping outside.

Friends from warmer climates would ask us how we could stand it. We'd both say, "It's not that bad. The sun is out most of the time, and you dress for it."

When our friends from Austin would call and ask us how we were surviving in what they assumed to be Siberia, they'd say, "How do you do it? You can't even go outside for four or five months." I'd remind them that they, also, couldn't do much outside for four or five months and then I'd add, "When it's hot in Austin, you can only stay so cool. When it's cold here, we just add more layers."

And when the ponds were frozen, we discovered the joy of watching Justin and Alexa Jacobsen play hockey.

Dave was meticulous about carving a rink on the back pond. Once the ice was thick enough, he'd drive his four-wheeler out onto the surface with a blade on the front. He'd make a perfect hockey rink, piling the snow up to act as boards all around the skating surface. Then, with great patience no matter how cold it was, he'd haul a hose out onto the new rink and flood it. That fresh water would soon freeze into a perfectly smooth rink. Dave was a human Zamboni.

The kids were both great hockey players, and Dave and Nichol were every bit the standard description of hockey parents. They had bought the equipment and hauled those kids to practices and games since they were old enough to lace up skates. When they'd bring their friends over for weekend afternoons full of hockey it was a joy to watch from our living room as they skated, passed, and shot the puck. Dave often set up lights for them and they'd play into the night. We would assist by turning on our rear spot lights. The joy of those afternoons and evenings, watching those kids have so much outdoor fun even when it was below zero, was the magic of Minnesota. We loved it.

When our first Thanksgiving arrived and the Jacobsens added us to their large extended family, we knew we were home.

I'd also seen a well-built guy walking his dog almost every day that winter. No matter how snowy or cold it got, he and his golden retriever would make daily trips up and down the street. We didn't know who he was until Nichol told us. He was Andrew Brunette, a star player for our new favorite NHL hockey team, the Wild. He lived six houses down the road.

2002 had been a landmark year. Barbara and I had moved from Austin to Woodbury. We'd finally escaped the pain of her temporary assignment in Connecticut and we realized we'd most likely never found the right house up there because, deep inside, we knew it wasn't right for us. Within days of our arrival in Minnesota we knew we were home.

With the racing team we'd reached a new level. On the tour, I was no longer the new guy. I was a trusted and respected member of a very good team. I was surrounded by the racing family.

The dream job was all mine.

As we moved forward into 2003 I was caught in a mental crossroads thinking about our performance. Had '01 and '02 been a mirage? Were we really this good? If I acknowledged that we just might be, would that be the jinx that would bring us back to earth? I had no real idea but in my heart I knew we'd come a long way from that ragtag group in 1997 who wore button-down shirts embroidered with a few logos.

There was one big alteration in our camp as we moved into 2003. Chuck and Del decided to make a change with the blue team. They made Marc Denner and Chris Cunningham co-crew chiefs and released my hero, David Fletcher. Like a baseball team firing the manager to create a spark, it was done to jump-start the team. The best year the blue team had ever had was Frankie's 20-20 mark in 2001. They won 12 rounds in both 2000 and 2002. '03 would be an important year.

Another big change was the move of the blue team to Southern California. Jerry Toliver's shop in Riverside was big enough to house everyone and for the first time since its inception the blue team would share work space with the red squad.

The new blue team came out with flourish, making it to the final round at Pomona before losing to Tony Pedregon. Del and the red team started slowly, going 1-2 at the first two races before making it to the Gainesville final, where Gary Densham ended Del's day.

Del came close again in Houston but lost by inches in the final round to Tony Pedregon. We'd been on the good side of so many tight final rounds over the prior two years, it felt quite disappointing to run 4.969 and come up short to a 4.963.

At the next race, in Bristol, Del only qualified 10th but ran Ron Capps, John Force, teammate Johnny Gray, and Whit Bazemore out of the building to earn the Wally. Between the two teams, we'd been runner-up three times, and a winner once, in the first six races. It was good to finally seal the deal at Thunder Valley.

One race later, in Atlanta, the blue team almost did it again. They came up just short in the final, against Tony Pedregon, whom we seemed to be running a lot. You know you've reached a different level when runner-up finishes are so disappointing.

Back at home, our Minnesota Wild were in the playoffs for the first time and the "State of Hockey" was collectively going crazy. The Wild were quickly down three games to one against the Colorado Avalanche but managed to come back to make it a 3-3 series. We'd been lucky enough to have seats on the glass for Game Six, when Richard Park buried a shot in overtime to send the series to its final game.

In Game Seven the Wild beat the Colorado Avalanche in overtime, stunning the Denver crowd into disbelief. We were watching on TV and went outside after the goal to scream and yell to the heavens. I could hear car horns honking from miles away. It was our neighbor Andrew Brunette who scored the game winner on Patrick Roy and it's still considered one of the greatest moments in Wild history. The next day, the neighborhood kids descended on his driveway with chalk, decorating every square foot of it. We had a hero in our Marsh Creek midst.

Back out on tour things were quiet for the next four races, as Del went 3-4 and Johnny went 0-3 with a DNQ at Columbus. During that set of events, we added a de facto teammate.

Del had met Michael Karp over the winter. Michael's dad, Arnie Karp, was a Top Alcohol Funny Car legend on the east coast and at one point he was even represented by my former boss, Bill Griffith. Kidney disease had ended his career, but when a longtime crew member, Pat Murphy, donated one of his kidneys Arnie found himself on the road to recovery.

By 2003 he felt good enough to drive again but he wanted to complete the dream and run a nitro car. Michael, a phenomenal businessman in Los Angeles, approached Del and Chuck. He was working at Staples Center, in charge of upscale dining there, and he hosted us at a Lakers game before the Pomona race, to discuss his plan. We ate a sumptuous dinner in a private dining area and then watched the game from a suite. As Michael explained, he aimed to land a big sponsorship utilizing his numerous high-level contacts in L.A., and if he could do that he'd want the Worshams to be involved, putting the team together and running the car.

It sounded like an overly ambitious plan. It also sounded like a lot of work, and possibly a distraction, but I think our consensus was that Michael didn't realize how hard it would be to put the deal together. If he did, it would be a financial benefit to us, but we weren't holding our breath.

Within a month, Michael had worked his magic. He landed a movie company, Artisan Entertainment, and the plan was to use the race car to promote the retail sale of DVDs featuring movies in their catalog. The first one would be Terminator 2. The team would debut at Chicago. Gary "Skippy" Kennedy was brought in as the crew chief and a full team was put together. They DNQ'd at their first race, but it had all happened so fast we all felt it was a good first baby-step.

They qualified at the next race, in Columbus, and were awarded "Best Appearing Car."

Our next race was in St. Louis.

I'd had an idea about a fun TV feature and pitched it to ESPN2's producer. He loved it and we scheduled it for Thursday afternoon and evening. The theme was "Worsham Racing Tours St. Louis."

As a group, all three teams visited the Gateway Arch and went to the top in the tiny pods that run up and down each leg. Matt Ilas, a talented and popular camera operator and producer, came with us to document our tour.

From the Arch, we went to Rigazzi's Italian Restaurant on The Hill in south St. Louis just a couple of miles from my high school. A former classmate of mine, Mark Aiazzi, owned and ran the place. He took Del and Matt into the kitchen and had Del make his own pizza.

From Rigazzi's we went to another St. Louis institution for dessert. Ted Drewe's Frozen Custard is a landmark in the Gateway City. On any spring, summer, or fall night, especially after a ball game or some other big event, the sidewalk around Ted Drewe's will be packed with eager customers, all ready to dive into the frozen custard treat called a "concrete." We ate, happily, in front of Matt's lens.

It was a fun afternoon and evening and it made for a great bit on the ESPN2 St. Louis telecast.

The race at Gateway International Raceway was still peculiarly scheduled in June. In '03, we would at least try to escape the St. Louis summer blast-furnace by running the entire event at night. That was the theory, at least, and the schedule did show us running qualifying sessions on Friday and Saturday at 6 and 9 p.m. Sunday's eliminations kicked off at 4:30.

Someone, apparently, forgot to factor in the date. At the end of June the sun is up in St. Louis until after 9.

For once, we got lucky. It was only 85 degrees on Friday afternoon and into the high 70s by the second session. On Saturday, it was equally as comfortable. When the first round went off on Sunday it had heated up to 92, but we'd raced many times in St. Louis when 92 was just a dream.

Johnny had qualified No. 9 but he lost to Scotty Cannon in the first round.

Del had sneaked into the field in the 16th position with a 5.08.

When he lined up next to Gary Densham in round one TV commentator Mike Dunn said, "If anyone has a chance to win a race from the No. 16 spot, it's Del Worsham."

We beat Densham.

We beat Scotty Cannon in round two.

We beat Ron Capps in the semis, moving Del's all-time record against Capps to 4-15.

In the final, we gave up lane choice to John Force.

You learn a lot when you start to win races regularly. If you're getting to the final round on a consistent basis, you're going to run Force a lot. He's always around.

This time we got by him by a car length. We'd gone from the 16th spot to the winner's circle, and during the final it was actually dark.

We did all the post-race stuff and headed back to the pits. By then, it was closing in on midnight. There was no rush to head to a restaurant for a celebratory dinner, though, because everything near the track was closed.

With the win Del improved to 20-12 on the season and the red team moved into the No. 3 spot in points. The past two seasons we'd finished third. The goal in '03 was to match or improve on that position.

The Western Swing didn't go particularly well for any of us. Del went 2-3, Johnny went 2-3, and Arnie 1-2 with a DNQ. He won his first round of racing by beating Gary Densham in Seattle.

With a week off before Brainerd we all headed home to recharge the batteries, but I had a special occasion up my sleeve.

With the extra time off and with me now being in Minnesota, we arranged for all three teams to descend on our Marsh Creek home on the Wednesday of Brainerd week. We had a huge cookout, enjoyed some cold beverages, and had a great time. And then my phone rang.

It was Arnie. He had news.

He'd slipped and fallen on a wet sidewalk and had injured his knee substantially. He couldn't drive. We needed a new driver and we needed one fast.

Del called Phil Burkart.

Twenty-four hours later I was picking Phil up at MSP and we headed straight for Brainerd, two and a half hours away. The next day Phil was in the Terminator car.

When qualifying was over, Del was in the No. 9 spot, Johnny was No. 13, and Phil was No. 16. Between the three of them we won nary a single round. We were all pretty exhausted, mentally and physically, but there was no time to rest. We had to get ready for Indy.

By the time eliminations rolled around at another epic Mac Tools U.S. Nationals, Del had barely qualified in the 16th spot and he'd won a round in the Budweiser Shootout. Phil and the Terminator team had out-qualified Johnny and the blue crew, but only by one spot and the two teams were in the dreaded 8 and 9 slots. They'd race each other in round one.

Del lost to Force in the first round while Johnny beat Phil to move on and face Force in round two. The blue team was victorious there, as well, and moved to the semifinal to face Gary Densham. With a win against Densham, the blue crew and Johnny were going to their third final of the season.

In that final Johnny lost a heartbreaker to Tim Wilkerson in a side-by-side contest. So close, yet again, but no payoff.

That race did impress upon me just how important the U.S. Nationals can be. Yes, it's just another race but it's more than that. It's The Big Go. It's the flashiest feather a driver can put in his or her hat.

Many drivers have put it perfectly with the line, "Even if I never win a championship, I want to be able to win Indy."

For the entire next year every time Tim Wilkerson would pull his car to the line, Bob Frey would announce his name by saying, "And here's your reigning Mac Tools U.S. Nationals champion, Tim Wilkerson."

Hearing that for a year was what finally pounded into my head how big a deal it was.

We all felt pretty good about what we'd done. The red team was in a bit of a slump, having gone 2-5 since Denver, but the blue team had just come off a runner-up at Indy. Even the black Terminator team was feeling better about their chances and Phil was doing a great job driving that car.

And then Johnny Gray informed Del and Chuck that he was stepping out of the car, effective immediately.

Johnny had never won a race in a Nitro Funny Car. He'd been to three finals and had won 26 rounds of racing, but he was clearly frustrated that he hadn't won. He'd had enough.

And so another shuffle was on our hands. Del moved Phil into the blue car and hired Cory Lee to drive the Artisan car.

At first, Phil balked a little at the idea. He liked the guys on the Artisan team and he felt they were onto something there.

Del and I both said, "Dude, that's a temporary deal. Arnie is probably out for the year and it's pretty likely that the deal will go away after that. The blue car wins races and you can win in it. Plus, it's not going anywhere for the foreseeable future."

Phil agreed and Cory was thrilled to take over for him in the Artisan car. He even managed to win rounds at Memphis and Chicago.

Arnie, who had been pushing hard with his physical therapy, made it back to race again in Las Vegas. On the final qualifying run he crossed the centerline and nearly collided with the car in the other lane, missing it by inches. That car just happened to be driven by Del.

After the lap, and the DNQ it brought with it, Arnie came over to Del's lounge quite shaken. He told Del he was done. He'd never quite caught up to the car while driving it, and he'd never before driven anything nearly as fast as this nitro car. Almost hitting Del was the final piece to a puzzle he'd not been able to solve. Del called Cory Lee and put him back in the Artisan car for the final race, in Pomona. We were all disappointed for Arnie, who ranks as one of the all-time best guys I've ever met in the sport, but I had an enormous amount of respect for him after he acknowledged that he'd never caught up to the car.

The blue team did well as the season wound down. They went 7-6 and were, yet again, runners-up at a race losing to Tony Pedregon (that guy, again) when a small oil line broke after the burnout in Chicago.

Del had gone 5-6 heading into Pomona. He qualified No. 6 at his home track in So Cal, and he beat Scotty Cannon in round one.

He then faced Whit in round two and beat him with a 4.834, running 314 mph

In the semifinal he edged Wilkerson by three thousandths of a second. Del was on his way to his fifth final of the year, looking for his third win.

It's likely no one would've realistically envisioned who he would race in that final. His opponent would be a guy who had beaten Tommy Johnson, Tony Pedregon, and Gary Scelzi.

His opponent would be Cory Lee.

Cory had never won a race as a professional Nitro Funny Car driver. Del was looking for his 14th career win and 11th in the last three seasons.

When the amber lights flashed Del jumped the gun. He was 46-thousandths of a second too quick, and the red light was staring at all of us.

We were turning to walk across the track to congratulate our stablemates when Cory's car dropped a cylinder on the left side. It drifted toward the center of the track and kept drifting. Not knowing that Del had fouled, he kept his foot down trying to earn that elusive first win. It was a first win he'd technically already earned.

But then his car appeared to cross the centerline.

Chief Starter Rick Stewart held his hand in the air as he listened for the final call from race control on his radio.

When he heard the call, he became something like an NFL referee after a replay. He didn't say, "Upon further review" but he did hold both hands up to get our attention. Then he pointed to Del's lane and yelled, "This side. This side is the winner."

The "first or worst" rule had been instituted. Del's foul was first. At that point Cory could've coasted to his first victory. Crossing the centerline activated the "worst" part of the scenario. Cory had handed it back. Del had his third win of the year.

Del got NHRA's permission to bring both cars to the Winner's Circle. We positioned them nose-to-nose, with both teams in all the photos.

Cory seemed more frustrated than angry. That's the way he is. Nothing much fazes him. He wanted to win badly but once it was over, it was over.

And after another pit party and another banquet, the season was also over. We had just missed our third consecutive No. 3 finish in the points but with three wins and 31 rounds we'd be proud enough to run a No. 4 on Del's car in 2004.

It was going to be a busy winter at the Wilber-Doyle home. We'd hired a contractor to finish the lower level, creating a home theater setting for us while also adding a mother-in-law suite for Barb's mom, who loved to come up from Florida to visit. Neither of us had ever had so much space in which to live. Minnesota was our home and our home in Minnesota was a dream house.

Still, I couldn't help but wonder — would we be able to keep this performance up in 2004?

The Highest Highs

2004 dawned with many changes afoot. We'd eventually be making the switch from the old Pontiac Firebird bodies to a new Chevy Monte Carlo and those new bodies would carry yet another new paint scheme. Beyond any doubt, the renderings were the nicest we'd ever seen. Our Monte Carlos were going to look racy and fast. It was just going to be a matter of when we had them. We'd start the year with the Firebirds.

We had a few new crew members and quite a few holdovers. The returning guys, like Terry Snyder, Jason Davis, Isaac Bese, Ed Boytim, John Fink, Marc Denner, Chris Cunningham and a few other part-time guys, gave us continuity and that's a thing that can't be overstated in terms of performance. When the crew becomes a well-oiled machine, just like the parts within the motor, things go better.

After three straight years of solid performance it was time to see if we could step it up.

Since the start of 2001, when I'd felt the gnawing sense that we were at a tipping point with CSK and that we really needed to start winning regularly, we'd done just that. Del won 101 rounds and 11 races in three years. Between Frankie Pedregon, Johnny Gray, and Phil Burkart, the blue team won 53 rounds, the Bud Shootout, and a race. It was a three-year stretch of success just when we needed it most and our Checker, Schuck's, Kragen sponsorship was not only rock-solid, it was also getting to the point where we could spend the necessary dollars to run up front.

We had slipped a spot in the standings in '03, after two consecutive finishes in third place. We'd be carrying a big 4 on Del's car in 2004 and we not only wanted to get off to a good start we also knew we could. It would just be a matter of execution. And some luck. Drag racing is like that. It's more like golf than football. You can't play defense and all you can do is put up your best score. If that's good enough to win, you move on. Sometimes you birdie the hole and feel great but the other guy holes an eagle from 120 yards out. It's not supposed to be fair. It's supposed to be hard.

Still running the Firebirds, Del came out of Pomona at 2-1 while Phil and the blue team lost in the first round.

Back at the CSK Nationals, in Phoenix, we once again exhausted ourselves for a week before getting down to racing. One of the items on our agenda was another photo shoot and the staff photographer again wanted to do it right at dawn, to get that lovely light.

I said, "Wouldn't it be just as good doing it at sunset?" while I also wondered how stupid I was. I figured there must be something special about sunrise. The photographer thought about it for a second then said, "Well the sun comes up over here and sets over there, on the other side of the track. Our pit is over here."

"Well, then we'll drag the cars over there and shoot the photos facing the setting sun," I said.

Photographer guy thought about it some more and said, "Yeah, that'll work."

I was a popular member of Team CSK right about then.

On Sunday Phil made it to the semifinal, beating that John Force character in round one and Gary Scelzi in round two. Del was having a fine day as well having beaten Tim Wilkerson and Whit Bazemore before squaring off against Phil in the semis. Del won a close race.

In the final Del lined up next to Tony Pedregon, trying to win his sponsor's race for the second time in three years. Del left first by a wide margin and then pulled away for an easy win on Kate and Maddy Worsham's birthday.

Yes, it was just the second race of the season but for the first time in his career Del Worsham was in the Funny Car points lead.

Two weeks later the NHRA POWERade tour landed in Gainesville. It could be said Del's feet never landed on the ground. He aced his Gatornationals exam with round wins over Gary Densham, Jerry Toliver, Cory Lee, and John Force. To add a dollop of sweetness to the win he beat Force on a holeshot, with his 4.979 beating Force's quicker 4.977.

Three races. 10 round wins. Two race wins. It sure felt like we were stepping it up. It was the first time Del had ever won two races in a row.

But, of course, drag racing has a way of keeping you humble, if not grounded. The next race was in Las Vegas and Del lost in the first round.

Phil did OK there, though, if by "OK" you mean he managed to win the race to make it three races in a row with a CSK car in the winner's circle. And he did it with the first new Monte Carlo body on a Worsham Racing car. Out of concern or superstition, Del decided to run one of the Firebirds in Vegas so the blue car was the only Monte Carlo we were running.

Things calmed down over the course of the next five races, with Del going 6-5 and Phil going 4-5 in Houston, Bristol, Atlanta, Chicago, and Topeka. The next stop on the tour was Columbus.

Phil made it as far as the semifinal and in doing so he beat Force again (in round two). In 10 races he was 4-2 against the winningest driver in Funny Car history. In a repeat of the Phoenix scenario he lost to Del in the semifinal.

Del's path to the semifinal had been an odd one, illustrating the "luck component" of the winning equation. He'd run very well (4.900) in round one against a tire-smoking Tony Pedregon. In round two he smoked the tires early while Jerry Toliver built a lead of nearly 300 feet. Toliver then smoked his tires late in the lap. Showing his expert pedaling ability, Del eased back into the throttle and got his Monte Carlo to hook up. He passed Toliver in the lights to earn the win by mere inches.

After that round Chuck Worsham was quoted as saying, "We hear way too much that these races are won or lost in the tuning room and that the drivers can't do much to help you. This time the driver won the race. The kid is special, and he showed it right there. Del won that race himself."

Del then ran a 4.922 to beat Phil and move on to his third final on the year. Both Del and Gary Scelzi lost traction in that final round but Del pedaled his car twice and then he finally just put his foot down and kept it there. Jungle Jim Liberman would've been proud of that smoky 1970s-style ride to the finish line. Back at our end of the track all we could see was smoke. After an agonizing couple of seconds, we spotted the win lights on in Del's lane. The red team had their third win on the season and the driver was responsible for two of the four rounds.

As the season was settling in for a long slog through the summer I could tell I was taking my game to a new level, as well. Winning all those races meant I had a lot more to write about and my skills were being honed on a weekly basis.

PR work isn't usually thought of as a competition but all of us in the media center were expanding the methods we used to get the word out about our drivers. Some loved the "sales" side of PR, pitching stories and convincing editors to run them. I was never much for that although I was intent upon building relationships with those editors so that when I really needed to get a story in front of the public I could ask and get it done.

Mark Armijo, a newspaper reporter in CSK's hometown of Phoenix, was a guy I stayed in touch with. Louie Brewster, Steve Ramirez, and Damian Dottore all wrote for major papers in SoCal and were all great guys. Susan Wade, from Seattle, wrote for papers and freelanced a lot, and we had the kind of relationship where I could call or email her and say, "I need to get Del and CSK some ink up in the Great Northwest" and she'd follow up with a first-rate story. She still does a lot of work, much of it for Bobby Bennett at CompetitionPlus.com, and is one of the best motorsports writers I know.

The most important thing to me was making sure the stories I wrote were the best I could create and hopefully they'd be the best work coming out of the media center. My goal was creating compelling preview features, fully fleshed out at around 1,000 words. My daily updates would be concise but full of information. With my post-event reports I would try to paint the picture so well any reader could feel and see exactly what had happened. I couldn't do much of anything to make the car go fast but I could help our team and our sponsors by being the best PR person I could be. And I never allowed complacency to set in. To the contrary, each time I wrote something I really liked I made that the new benchmark going forward. I was always trying to get better. I had dreamed of this job for so many years but even the most optimistic version of that dream came up short of the reality I was living.

Winning rounds is like getting more at-bats. The more you win, the more you write, and the better you ought to get. And when your team wins four rounds there's a lot of celebrating and hoopla to take care of before the PR guy even has a chance to sit down and put it into words. I prided myself on being able to create an enjoyable and coherent story after all the fun, and I never once rushed through it just to be finished. I took the same amount of care every time I sat down to write.

After the win in Columbus, Del won two more rounds in Englishtown and he was right in the thick of the points race. All of that seemed irrelevant after the next race, in St. Louis.

Scheduled in the middle of the summer, yet again, the '04 St. Louis event was again a night race. On Thursday, after the teams set up at the track we brought ESPN camera operator Matt Ilas along with us for a special afternoon. Both CSK teams headed to my alma mater, SIUE, for an afternoon of batting practice with the Cougars coaching staff.

We all took turns in the cage until our hands were bleeding then had the coaches hit us fly balls in the outfield for another 30 minutes. It was great fun and we figured it would make for some good television on Sunday.

Early Friday, as I was relaxing in my hotel room waiting for an afternoon trip to the track my phone rang. It was Rob Geiger, a well-known PR pro who represented Top Fuel driver Darrell Russell. Rob and Darrell had just landed at the St. Louis airport and Rob said, "Hey man, what's the name of the Italian restaurant you always talk about, on The Hill?"

I told him it was Rigazzi's and that a high school classmate of mine still owned it.

"Why don't you pick us up at our hotel in downtown St. Louis and join us for lunch?" Rob said. My immediate thought was to come up with a valid excuse to say no but I couldn't fabricate one. So I said yes.

When we got to Rigazzi's and started our meal Darrell looked me right in the eye and asked about my background and my story. He said Rob had told him I had lived a very interesting life.

Darrell Russell was as handsome as any Hollywood star. His eyes and his teeth seemed to sparkle every time he'd smile as if they'd been enhanced by a special effects in a movie. And he smiled almost constantly.

He asked me questions — and took great interest in the answers — for a full hour. Then he asked me to tell him more St. Louis stories as we drove around Forest Park and other parts of my historic hometown, before I dropped them back at their hotel. I called Barbara and told her what we'd done, and I added, "The reason I went was because I couldn't come up with a good excuse after Rob asked me. I'm so glad I went with them. Darrell is one of the most interesting and most engaging people I've ever met. I feel like we're friends now and that was the first time I'd ever said more than hello to him."

On Sunday night, during eliminations in round two, Darrell's car crashed heavily as it crossed the finish line behind Scott Kalitta. We all knew it was a bad one and when no word was passed along over the P.A. system we feared the worst. It's standard protocol to say, "The driver is OK and out of the car" as soon as that happens. When no word comes, we all worry.

Darrell was airlifted to the best trauma center in St. Louis. And we waited. Lots of rumors were swirling but I tried to ignore them until something, anything, was announced officially. The word came after the final rounds were run. Darrell had succumbed to his injuries.

It was late but I called Barbara, fighting back the tears in my car. I told her the news with the simple line, "We lost him." It was all I could utter.

It was awful. It was brutal. It made no sense to me. I was completely shattered. Barbara said, "You were meant to meet him and have lunch. That's why you couldn't come up with an excuse. You were meant to know each other and be friends. It was fate. Your life is better because you met him and talked. You have to think of it that way."

I knew she was right, but my mind could make no sense out of what had happened.

Our baseball bit for ESPN2 never aired. The jovial video, full of us laughing it up, was inappropriate. How I wish it would've fit into a happy television show.

We somehow had to regroup as a racing family and head for the Western Swing. Phil and the blue crew did their part to bring us back to earth.

At Denver, up on the mountain, Del lost in the first round but Phil outran Wilkerson to move on. In round two, he hazed the tires at the top end but left Tony Pedregon behind. In the semifinal, Tommy Johnson gave Phil a run for his money but the blue CSK Chevy pulled away. In the final, Cruz Pedregon would be waiting.

Phil got off the line first, by a good margin, and he never looked back. It was Team CSK's fifth win of the season. It certainly felt like we were playing at a whole new level and with the wins came more confidence. With the confidence came more luck. What I quickly discovered was the notion that winning begets more winning. When you establish that you're capable of taking out anyone people start to press against you. And they make mistakes. And the wins keep on coming.

At Indy, we ran a special red, white, and blue patriotic body for our friends at Mac Tools. It was a beautiful car but it was out of competition too early, losing in round one. Phil managed a round win over Ron Capps, before falling to Gary Densham.

After Indy, the Reading race preceded Dallas by a week in mid-September. But when the remnants of hurricane Ivan swamped Maple Grove Raceway and the tour needed to get to Texas, the Reading race was rescheduled for early October.

In Dallas, Del beat Wilkerson, Bazemore, Force, and Cruz Pedregon to win his fourth race on the year. Oddly, both Wilkerson and Force red-lit away their chances at stopping the red CSK car. Winning begets more winning. Even John Force was pressing against us.

We then headed straight to Route 66 Raceway in Chicago and stayed on the same incredible roll. Del qualified No. 2 in Q4. He'd been sitting on top but slipped a spot when Force obliterated the national record. He got his revenge in the final. And to get there, no easy rounds would be had. Del raced Tommy Johnson, Jerry Toliver, and Eric Medlen in three incredibly tight races, beating Medlin on a big holeshot. Del's win over Eric was by just .0087 of a second with his 4.807 beating Medlen's much quicker 4.783.

In the final round, against Force, Del and the champ left nearly together but Del never trailed. It was his fifth win of the year, and it moved him back into second place.

After the return trip to Reading, where Del won two more rounds, it was off to Vegas and Pomona to end the 2004 season. In Vegas, Del beat Frankie and Wilk but Gary Scelzi got him in the semifinal and went on to win the race. Unbelievably, after nine months, 22 races, 38 round wins, and five Wally trophies, Del and Scelzi would arrive in Pomona in a dead-even tie for second place. It was nearly inconceivable. Every single point was going to be huge.

But it only got better. Going into the final qualifying session in Pomona Del was sitting in the top spot with a 4.737 while Scelzi sat ninth.

In Q4, Scelzi ran 4.728 to move ahead of Del. A few pairs later, in his final qualifying effort of 2004, Del matched Scelzi exactly with his own 4.728 and our brains desperately tried to make that all compute. And then we heard Bob Frey on the P.A.

"Del Worsham matches Gary Scelzi exactly but on the basis of speed, it's Del Worsham into the top spot and that puts him one point ahead of Scelzi for second place. Unbelievable."

Force ended up going around both of us, but we'd take that one point lead into race day. All we had to do was advance as far as Gary did and we'd finish No. 2 for the season. Being No. 2 probably disappoints John Force. We were thrilled to have the chance.

In round one Del elected to be the first pair, to press the issue. He beat Johnny Gray, who was then driving for Don Schumacher. Scelzi went much later in the session and he kept pace with a win over Bob Bode.

In round two Del again would be part of the first pair and he was lined up next to Phil. There would be more drama.

The left lane was clearly the dominant one that day in Pomona and Phil's team had lane choice. In a private meeting, before the round, Phil, Chris, and Marc sat behind closed doors and made a decision. They would put an aggressive tune-up in the car but they would choose the inferior right lane.

"I don't care what other teams say when something like this comes up, because that's their business," Chris was quoted as saying. "There's no spin coming out of here. We decided to do it and we let Del know. The only question he had for us was, 'Are you sure?' and we said we were. We were still going to run as fast as we could but the lane was important. It was the right thing for our team."

Del ran 4.785 to take the win. Scelzi beat Tony Pedregon to push the battle for second place into the semifinals.

Both Del and Scelzi had lost lane choice so both would run in the right lane. Scelzi went first, racing against Force. I made it clear to all the crew guys that should Scelzi lose we were to remain composed and calm. No celebrating someone else's loss.

When Scelzi smoked the tires right in front of us, as we waited in the water box, we all simply exchanged nods and winks. We acted like professionals and then we went out and ran 4.786 in the "bad lane" while Gary Densham smoked the tires. The high-fives felt good after that.

In the final, against Force and again without lane choice, Del gave it a game effort but came up a car-length shy of his sixth win. Still, it had been nothing short of a remarkable season.

Del's 41-18 record was a new career best by six rounds.

His five wins were a career best for any one season.

He entered the season never having won back-to-back races, and he did it twice.

In 2005, the numeral on the side of his car would be a 2.

Phil went 21-21 to give Team CSK 62 round wins on the year.

His two race victories meant a CSK car won seven of the 23 races contested.

His 10th place finish meant both CSK drivers would be on stage at the banquet.

This ragtag group had come an awfully long way. My gosh, we had come so far. A large number of people's lives had been completely altered for the better. Mine was one of them.

On the home front during 2004 Barbara and I were deep into the process of finishing the lower level and we learned a few lessons along the way. We invited a number of contractors to bid on the project and we took the lowest bid. We regretted that until the day we moved out of the house. To this day, our mantra with home furnishings or home improvements remains "Do it right the first time" instead of "Do it cheap and regret it."

It was nice but everything about the lower level was a step down from the quality in the rest of the house. The project did add about another 1,000 square feet to our total and much of that was in one big living space. There was also the mother-in-law suite, and it actually was designed specifically for my mother-in-law. Barb's mom, Jean, was coming up to see us regularly during the summers, so we put in a spare bedroom with its own full bath and a sitting area, just as she wanted it.

Out in the main living space we put in a huge HD television and a surround-sound audio system. Back then the biggest of the big screens were giant rear-projection sets and ours sat in the front of the room like a small submarine. It was the first time I'd seen HD, though, and it blew me away, especially when watching sports. For all those years as a kid I never knew what color TV looked like. Once that became commonplace we thought the picture was as good as a screen could look. When HD hit the market we realized just how bad television had been up until then.

As the race team prepared for 2005 we had no reason to think we would be any less successful on the track. We retained most of our crew guys and had integrated a new transporter into the mix, which allowed us to use the old blue rig as an anchor for a new hospitality center that more than doubled our capacity in terms of CSK guests while it also provided a dedicated office space for me. The lounge was transformed into a full office by Terry Snyder and the guys and it had the best air-conditioning in the pit. I became a very popular person on hot weekends. We also announced, early on, that we'd be making a body switch with the blue team. Phil would be driving a Toyota Celica.

GM Racing was cutting back support across the board by then and the offer to run the Celica bodies for the blue team was too good to pass up. I did, though, learn just how loyally some people can be attached to their favorite make and model. We got a bit more than just a little backlash switching the blue car over to a Toyota.

We also added a key associate sponsor to the team. Walery's Pizza, in Salem, Oregon, would have a logo on each car. Why would a pizza shop in Oregon help sponsor a Funny Car? Because Dave Walery was very close to Terry Snyder and Dave loved drag racing. We'd been to the restaurant on the Western Swing and had seen the wall of Team CSK memorabilia in the back room. It was a perfect fit for us.

When Dave then installed a pizza oven in the hospitality rig, we were taking it to a new level. And when he asked me what my favorite toppings were and I told him pepperoni and black olives, Dave dubbed that the "Wilber Special." The pizza was incredible. We were living large.

Also, at CSK a man by the name of Jim Schoenberger was taking on more and more responsibility for the racing program. Jim was one of the most interesting and gregarious men I'd met in the sport and we connected on an intellectual level almost instantly. He was smart, deep, and truly a man of the world who regaled me with stories of trips to places I'd never been. He was also a joy to work with. Our relationship went from professional to personal in a hurry.

As the season kicked off I was experiencing an evolution in another way. Tom Abbett and I had been doing our "slap, slap, bang" schtick for years. And now, other guys on the crew started coming up with special handshakes or fist bumps with me and we'd do them before every lap. It was easy for them because they only had to remember one such routine. I had to remember them all and eventually would be dashing around during every burnout, doing things as simple as a double fist bump all the way to routines that including high-fives, low-fives, back slaps, and jumps. It was fun but it was hard to keep straight, and if we screwed one up it seemed the car would always smoke the tires. The burden was real.

Out of the gate the red team struggled at the first two races, going 1-1 at Pomona and 0-1 in Phoenix. The loss in Phoenix, in the first round to Whit, was a hint of things to come. We ran great and lost by inches. Whit's 4.870 beat Del's 4.876.

We had won so many of those ultra-tight races in '04 it was stunning to see one go the other way in front of all the CSK people. It wouldn't be the last time we would lose a nail-biter.

Meanwhile the blue team went to the final round at Pomona before smoking the tires against Tommy Johnson. They also advanced to the semifinals in Phoenix, losing by inches to Ron Capps. The five round wins in two races, though, put Phil Burkart in the points lead.

The points lead lasted one race. At the third race of the season, in Gainesville, the blue team never got untracked. They ended up No. 20 with a DNQ. Del did better, qualifying fourth and winning a round, but his season was not off to the start we wanted.

We brought out the blue Toyota at the next race, in Houston, and it was adorned with a large Lupe Tortilla decal on the rear quarter panel and spill plate. The "Steak Lupe" entree was great, but it didn't help the blue team overcome Tony Pedregon in round one. His 4.849 beat Phil's 4.865 in another close one that went the wrong way.

Things got frustratingly worse for both teams over the next six races, in Las Vegas, Bristol, Atlanta, Columbus, Topeka, and Chicago.

Del went 1-6 over the stretch, including more tight losses. In Bristol, Columbus, and Topeka the total margin of all three losses didn't add up to a car length. It was getting very frustrating, race after race.

Phil and the blue team fared even worse during that six-race stretch. They went 0-5, with a DNQ in Bristol when only one session was run due to rain and Ron Capps was the driver inserted into the Top 16 because of his points.

Heading to Englishtown, we were a collective 10-18 with two DNQs.

Del seemed to right the red team's ship there in New Jersey. He qualified fourth and took out Tony Bartone, John Force, Robert Hight, and Ron Capps to earn the win. The feeling was more one of relief than joy. It had been a rough go of it at the first 11 races.

The next race was in St. Louis. It was, again, a night race but when the national anthem was sung on Sunday evening it was 98 degrees. And both our cars lost in the first round.

Things got incrementally better on the Western Swing. Phil went to his second final of the year, in Denver, and then won the opening round at Seattle and Sonoma. Del went 2-3 during the Swing. Still, in all, we weren't winning enough rounds.

When we raced in Brainerd in mid-August, National Dragster editor Phil Burgess sent me an email. I called him about the subject that day.

These new things called "blogs" were just starting to be all the rage on the internet. During the Western Swing, my PR buddy Ted Yerzyk had done a daily diary for Schumacher Racing, on NHRA.com, and it was very popular.

Phil had reached out to about a dozen of us, asking if we could help our drivers write a blog, or even ghostwrite it for them. But here was the kicker: It would be for an entire month!

I'd done "Del's Diary" for a little more than a week, a few years before. I had no idea how in the world I could come up with enough material to fill an entire month. It seemed too daunting to consider.

And, I realized, I couldn't write it as Del. The blog theory was to give the readers behind-the-scenes stories to which they would otherwise have no access. It was not supposed to be about the race car or our elapsed times. That information was already all over the internet.

I lived in Minnesota. Del lived in SoCal. The blog would need a steady flow of photos and words about what he was doing at home, or on vacation, or at the shop. I had no access to that and I knew Del was too busy to give me material or take photos.

I told Burgess I didn't think I could do it. He said, "Well, you can host it then, as yourself. It can be about your job and your life on the tour. We'll see if a guy nobody ever heard of can write about stuff they don't care about, and still entertain them."

Consider the gauntlet thrown.

I started writing in earnest during the Brainerd race. At first I tried too hard to make every installment have a theme, or to include two or three crew guys as a main focus. I didn't have the confidence that anyone would want to read about me.

And then when we stayed at a hotel in Memphis that shared a parking lot with a Steak 'N Shake, I took a picture of my favorite burger place and put it on the blog, along with words about growing up in St. Louis and how much I loved Steakburgers. People reacted to that in a very positive way. I was feeling a bit more confident. The Mac Tools U.S. Nationals were next. I figured that would give me plenty to write about.

When we headed for Indy, Hurricane Katrina was heading for Louisiana and New Orleans. We were stunned by what we were seeing on TV. It was an enormous disaster.

Everyone's thoughts were with the people on the Gulf Coast, but we had two races to run. The Skoal Showdown (the special event previously known as the Bud Shootout) and the Mac Tools U.S. Nationals.

During qualifying, on Sunday, Del competed in the Skoal event and he beat Tony Pedregon in the first round. As I walked back to the pit from the starting line John Force's assistant crew chief Bernie Fedderly said, "This could shape up to be your day, Bob." I had no idea Bernie Fedderly knew my name. Maybe it was only because our names were stitched on our shirts.

In round two, we beat Robert Hight.

Running for the $100,000 prize in the final, we raced Eric Medlen. When he smoked the tires while Del ran 4.866, we won the Skoal money and a parachutist floated down from the sky to deliver the mock briefcase supposedly full of dough. As a team we were $100,000 richer. If we could "double up" and win the race, on Monday, our payday would exceed $225,000. It seemed nearly impossible to even consider.

In eliminations for the race itself Del started from the No. 4 spot and he beat Jim Head handily in round one. I went back to my office and put Eminem's "Lose it" on the iPod speaker deck atop my desk. The lyrics spoke to me.

"Listen, if you had one shot, one opportunity, to seize everything you ever wanted in one moment. Would you capture it, or just let it slip?"

In round two, we faced Bob Gilbertson, who had upset Tommy Johnson in round one. Gilby gave us a great fight but Del beat him by a bit more than a car length.

Back in my office, Eminem again blared out of the speakers.

In the semifinal the pressure and the nervousness were palpable. We raced Whit Bazemore. He smoked the tires. Del ran 4.893.

We had won the Skoal Showdown. We were going to the final round at the Mac Tools U.S. Nationals. So much money and prestige was on the line I couldn't fathom it. None of it seemed real.

Eminem again filled the air.

"Listen, if you had one shot, one opportunity, to seize everything you ever wanted in one moment. Would you capture it, or just let it slip?"

We were facing Frankie Pedregon in the final. He had a fast car, tuned by Brian Corradi. They'd beaten Gary Densham, Eric Medlen, and Gary Scelzi to get there. We knew it wouldn't be easy.

Before I left the pit I thought about it deeply. We'd had a string of great years, but never were in a position to do something like this. In 2005 we were struggling to get back to our form of the previous years. And yet here we were, at the season's biggest race and on its greatest stage, on the cusp of history.

If we lost, no one would remember this. We'd take home roughly $125,000, which was still great money, but well short of what we'd collect if we won.

I had never been so nervous at a drag race. Time seemed to be standing still.

When we finally went to the line I felt extremely light-headed as we walked forward to the water box. I was momentarily concerned about my health. Then I realized I wasn't breathing. I was so nervous I had forgotten to breathe. I had to silently remind myself, "Inhale. Exhale. Take deep breaths."

As the two cars staged, it all seemed so massively overwhelming I was afraid the video camera might be shaking in my hands. And the incredible unknown that is a final round was never on better display. As Del and Frankie staged, I realized that in a little over four seconds one team would be U.S. Nationals champions and the other would walk away. No one knew, as the staging bulbs illuminated, who would win. In other sports that's sudden-death overtime. But every single drag race ends with sudden-death overtime. Every final round is a walk-off winner.

Through my viewfinder, which was often the worst view in the house, I saw Del's CSK car tear away. Almost immediately Frankie's car appeared in the other lane. I couldn't tell who was ahead, I almost never could from that angle, but I knew for certain it was close.

When the win lights came on in Del's lane, I felt a primal rush of joy, excitement, and happiness all trying to escape my body at once. Our celebration was intense and it was 100 percent emotional and utterly real. It was completely unfiltered. We had done the unthinkable. The crowd knew the importance of it. They cheered for us almost as hard as we celebrated with each other.

Del had beaten Frankie by about three feet.

Our bonus plan in 2005 paid us each $1,000 for a win. We had nothing in the plan for the Skoal Showdown and we had no plan for doubling-up and triggering the NHRA $50,000 bonus for having done so.

Basically, Del owed us each $1,000 just like any other win. A couple of weeks later our paychecks appeared in our accounts and $5,000 had been deposited in addition to our regular pay. Have I ever mentioned that Del Worsham is a class act? Yeah, I thought so.

The double-up win gave me some great material for the blog. My audience was growing.

After Indy, Phil Burgess informed us all that the blogs were going over so well on the website we'd be continuing them indefinitely. That news weeded out a few who hadn't been contributing much, but it motivated me to do even more.

Realizing much of my rapidly growing readership base were from places that did not have four distinct seasons, like we did in Minnesota, I took it upon myself to make my home environment a key part of the blog. I'd take a photo of the back pond, from the same spot in the living room, and share that regularly calling it Pond Cam. Shasta became a major part of the blog as well. Twins games in the summer and Minnesota Wild hockey games in the winter were all part of the story, too. Instead of turning off drag racing fans those elements all became so popular I was beginning to receive fan mail. And, in terms of where the blog would eventually go, it was only just beginning.

Before the season ended we battled another hurricane. As the Dallas race was approaching, Hurricane Rita was churning in the Gulf of Mexico and she seemed intent upon targeting Houston. Rita was so big, and Katrina was so fresh in everyone's memory, the population took heed when evacuation orders were given along the coast. Much of our team had been in Houston, with Frank Gilchrist, and they all hit the road north. It took them many hours just to get out of the city. It was gridlock.

Just before the Dallas race NHRA made the right move. They postponed the event until October.

When Rita later had no impact on the Texas Motorplex those who so often like to hear themselves pontificate on the internet ridiculed the decision. What they were thinking about was the weather. What they weren't thinking about was the impact the hurricane did have on the state. Thousands had fled Houston. Many of them filled hotels in Dallas and even further north, and they were not yet cleared to return home. No one wanted to kick anybody out of a hotel so a bunch of drag racers could stay there. There was no room at the inn. Any inn. The NHRA made the only choice it could. We'd let things settle down and come back in a month.

When we wrapped up things in Pomona, Del ended the year with a 22-21 record. He also had wins in Englishtown and Indy, with the Showdown added to the fun. It felt like a huge disappointment, to us and to CSK. We officially admitted we'd had a "down year" on the track.

That wasn't lost on me. We'd improved so much, through '01, '02, '03, and then we'd had such a magnificent '04. To slide back to 22 rounds after having won 41 in '04 felt like a huge step back. We finished eighth in the standings.

Barbara and I managed only a quick getaway to Miami that winter. She's a Penn State alum, and the Nittany Lions were playing Florida State in the Orange Bowl on January 3. We headed down for that and got a chance to walk on the beach in Fort Lauderdale for a day before the game.

When we returned from Florida, it was time to crank it up for 2006. After the ups and downs of 2005 I had no idea where we were headed but we were all ready to plow forward.

End Of An Era

2005 may have included our sensational "double-up" win at Indy and another victory at Englishtown, but that 22-21 record ate at us. We entered 2006 determined to get back on the good side of the .500 mark and hopefully win three, four, or five races again.

We also had another new design for the cars and it was the best one yet. We'd been doing a lot of special-edition vinyl wraps on our cars over the prior couple of years and we'd discovered the sore spots with those applications. Vinyl is very susceptible to heat and cold so it doesn't like indentations in the body (where it can shrink and pull off the carbon fiber) and it really doesn't like going around sharp angles. Those locations were where almost all the bubbling and tearing would happen.

So we painted the Monte Carlos a base blue and red, with a white "fade" stripe across the nose. Then, all the primary CSK logos would be applied via three large decals which would only cover flat surfaces on the sides and hood. It was gorgeous.

Phil was back in the blue car, and we continued to have a lot of continuity when it came to our crew. Along the way, we had added some new guys who brought a lot of talent to the table. Seth Randall, Travis Nicholson, Larry Lush, Todd Blakley, Chris Cunningham's dad Mike, Tom Leskovan, Chase Steele, and Warren Bryning became key parts of the machine. Warren and I hit it off quickly, with him calling me Bobby Boucher ("Booshay") from Adam Sandler's movie "The Waterboy." With that challenge thrown down, I refused to ever call him just Warren. He was Warren Zevon, or Warren Buffet, or (my personal literary favorite) Warren Peace.

Others would come and go quickly, finding the life too hard and the job too demanding. When people would ask me about the path to a crew job, I'd always start with one caveat.

"Being on the crew looks glamorous, and for a few seconds each day it kind of is," I'd say. "But it's 99 percent knuckle-busting hard work. If you think of it as a job, you won't last a month. It's too hard, the hours are too long, and once you're on the tour the travel is too back-breaking. This has to be in your blood. It has to be your passion. It's not a job."

The shortest tenure in Worsham Racing history took place around this time, although the guy was there for such a short period I can't exactly recall the year. We were doing preseason testing and an eager young applicant spoke to Del and Chuck about working for us. He said all the right things and they offered him a probationary job. If he was good, and he liked it, he could possibly stay.

He worked hard all morning and then said he was going to get a burger at the concession stand. We never saw him again. He lasted four hours.

As the '06 season cranked up, we were optimistic. At the first eight races Del went 8-8 and Phil went 7-6, but the two missing numbers in Phil's loss column were DNQs. How tough was it getting to be out there? The DNQs came despite strong qualifying times of 4.876 and 4.849 in Atlanta and Columbus. There was no margin for error in the Funny Car class.

Another interesting trend that was starting to eat at us was the frequency of ridiculously close losses. From 2001 through 2005 we so often won those side-by-side battles it seemed like we owned them. Despite Del's eight round wins at the first eight races he lost in the second round with times ranging from 4.77 to 4.82, usually getting nicked by mere inches.

Still, at 8-8 it seemed like Del and the red team were going to have a solid year. At that pace we'd at least get back up somewhere near 25 round wins and if we could win a couple of events we might climb back to 30. The blue team seemed capable of doing the same.

And then came the middle third of the season. At the next eight races Del went 2-8 and both of those two rounds came at the same race, in Brainerd. We lost in the first round six straight times after a stunning DNQ in Topeka. Del had qualified at an impressive 97 consecutive races before that misstep. Phil also went 2-8.

With seven races left, Del was 10-15 while Phil checked in at 9-14. And we were still losing way too many rounds by inches, a foot, or a fender. It was getting to be enormously exasperating.

I took my job personally and let the frustrations get to me. Probably too much. The guys at CSK were, by then, giving us a good hunk of money as were some key associate sponsors and the same long list of CSK vendors, who gave us parts. I knew Spica and Schoenberger expected more out of us. They expected wins, not close losses, and we seemed stuck in a rut that always left us just short, race after race.

After each agonizing loss I'd sit at my laptop in the lounge and prepare to explain it. By the midpoint of 2006 it seemed like I'd used the same truthful explanations over and over again. We'd run quick enough to beat everyone in the field except the driver in the other lane. We'd step up two-hundredths from our qualifying time and lose by a thousandth. We'd qualify well up into the top half and draw names like Capps, Hight, Beckman, or Pedregon in round one.

I was pushed to the limit to keep my stories and updates positive, but always truthful. There were some PR reps who would basically write the same report every week no matter if their team did well or was blown out. You'd be hard pressed to know if their weekend had been good or bad.

I always tried to find the silver lining but if we just flat stunk I wouldn't be afraid to quote Del as saying exactly that. And I let him blow off some steam with quotes about how frustrated he was. I wanted the CSK guys to know how much we cared, how we took it personally, and how much it meant to all of us. Blowing smoke by pretending everything was peachy wasn't the way to do that.

Finishing strong was what we were after. We'd been aiming for 30 or more round wins and with just seven races left Del only had the 10 he'd managed to eke out. All but two of those came at the first eight races.

Down the stretch Del won just two more rounds. He finished the year a stunning 12-20. And we had thought 2005's 22-21 mark was a disappointment.

Phil and the blue team didn't do much better, despite a real pick-me-up of a win in Reading. Driving a special-edition Havoline car, Phil qualified 12th and then beat Capps, Scelzi, John Force, and Hight to take the trophy. The final round was a thriller, with each driver pedaling his tire-smoking car numerous times before Hight's finally sashayed across the centerline while Phil feathered his way to the finish. We needed that. We needed it quite badly.

We found a restaurant in nearby Morgantown and enjoyed a communal dinner, while continually thanking and congratulating Phil, Chris, Marc and the team. It had been a little more than a year since I'd last given a speech.

When we wrapped up the season in Pomona, Del needed a big race to get into the top 10 and earn a spot on the stage at the banquet. What he got was something completely different. He earned a trip to the hospital.

During qualifying, on Friday, I took my spot kneeling next to the red car and shot the video as it tore down the track. When it blew up just short of the finish line, buckling the body badly, I instinctively clicked off the camera. Then, we all watched a horror movie play out on the big screen.

Del couldn't reach the parachute levers with the body buckled and he was still traveling at a high rate of speed down Pomona's shutdown area. Right in front of me, Terry Snyder was pounding his feet into the ground while yelling at the car as if that might help. "No, no, no, NO!" he yelled with raw emotions, but the car didn't listen.

It hit the sand-trap going fast, and when it did that the nose of the car dug in. I had never seen a Funny Car do a somersault. I'd prefer to never see it again.

Del's car flipped tail over nose and initially landed on its roof. It then launched again and cleared the actual catch fence with room to spare. When it landed hard, on its wheels, it was just a few feet shy of the chain-link fence that separates the track property from Fairplex Drive.

There was an awful lot of dust in the air, and the big screen was shut off immediately, so we all sprinted toward the tow vehicle. As I neared the return road, a crew member from another team pulled up with a golf cart and shouted, "Get on, Bob. I'll take you down there."

Golf carts are not exactly speedy. This one, at this moment, seemed to be stuck in molasses. The drive to the top end took forever, although the leisurely pace did allow us to hear Bob Frey say on the P.A. that Del was out of the car under his own power. At the same time, Robert Hight came toward us on a different cart and when he saw me he yelled, "He's OK."

Once we did get down there Del was already sitting in the ambulance. When I poked my head in, he said, "Bob, glad you're here, man. My butt hurts. I hit pretty hard." He also had a few lacerations on his shins, but mostly he was bothered by his posterior.

They took him over to Pomona Valley Hospital and I headed back to the pit to find Connie. Once I got there Connie and I hopped in my car and drove the couple of miles to the hospital. We were ushered into Del's area in the emergency room and he gave Connie a hug. He told us he had a broken tailbone.

After a while, he said to me, "Go back out there and see what you can do about making me a cushion for the seat. Like, take some towels and roll them up into a donut I can sit on. I don't think I can drive if my tailbone is hitting the seat real hard. It really hurts."

Connie stayed with Del and I headed back to the track.

Fink and I took the fluffiest white towels we could find and got after it. Within 20 minutes, with the help of a roll of tape, we had fashioned a U-shaped pad around the bottom edges of his driver's seat, in the backup chassis the team already had out. If he could bear to sit on that he could drive.

He returned to the track a few minutes later and we watched as our friend, who had crashed in a horrific incident just a couple of hours earlier, gingerly got into his race car. He made it clear he'd be racing. About 13 hours later he'd be strapped in for Q3. He drove it to just short of the finish line.

On Sunday, Del faced Gary Densham and smoked the tires early. Densham smoked them late. Our talented leader got his car to hook up and was tracking Densham down but he simply ran out of real estate. And so it ended.

I'd only given one post-victory speech all year but I'd have a chance to make another kind of speech during the pit party that night. The Tijuana Dogs singer, Matt Mauser, handed me the mic and I verbally pointed out all of the hard work and perseverance our guys had shown. I thanked CSK for their loyal support and reminded everyone in the room how far we'd come since 1997 and our off-the-rack crew shirts. Then, more music and more dancing until we were totally spent.

Del had won just 12 rounds and he'd also missed the top 10 by a couple of rounds. More important, he survived one of the scariest crashes I'd ever seen. Phil and I would attend the banquet together on Monday night, joined by Seth and his mom and sister. There would be no Worsham entourage at all.

Barbara and I had two key things we were thinking about. We'd booked a cruise for December and we'd been taking our wonderful Shasta boy to see the vet fairly often. He was about to turn 16 and he'd really been slowing down. That's pretty old for a cat, even one as spoiled as he was, but the doctor prescribed some special food and he perked back up. It was just old age and we wanted to make the rest of his life as comfortable and happy as possible.

The cruise was going to be a real adventure. We'd be sailing for 15 days, but 10 of those days would be long stretches at sea. The round-trip itinerary began and ended in San Diego. The destination was Hawaii. It was five days at sea, five days island-hopping, and five days back. I wasn't sure if it was going to be a dream trip, or a horribly boring one.

Neighbor Alexa signed on to be Shasta's cat sitter, and off we went. I had no idea if I could even handle five days at sea, but I was excited to find out. And the blog was only getting bigger and more popular so I figured it would be a key part of the trip as well.

As it turned out, the five days at sea were idyllic. Five glorious days of nothing but water in all directions, aboard the ms Rotterdam of the Holland America line. We relished every minute of it. There were wonderful meals, some great wine, and time to relax, work out, and just completely decompress. I was confident I could do much more than just five straight days at sea. It's a skill that can't be coached. I'm a natural at it.

We first made landfall at Hilo, on the Big Island. Our next stop was Oahu. When we got to Honolulu, we were honored to meet a very special man. Adam Vincent had sent me a note a few years earlier, looking for a diecast car. He let me know then that he'd been struggling with cancer for some time and his thirst for NHRA Drag Racing would never be quenched again, in person. He wasn't allowed to fly.

We got off the ship and hailed a taxi, taking it to a comfortable little home in Pearl City. We then spent two glorious hours with Adam and his wonderful wife Francine. When it was time to go, they insisted on driving us back to the ship. The hugs we shared were completely heartfelt and sincere. It was one of those experiences that changes a person. I knew I'd always have a place in my heart for Adam and Francine. We were connected.

Back on the ship, a PR secret I'd been working on and carrying with me was coming to a tipping point. While I was on Maui I talked to Del. A press release I'd had saved on my laptop for a couple of weeks was going to need to go out soon. Probably from the ship.

We were changing drivers on the blue team.

Jeff Arend had come to us with a program that would aid the bottom line. That would've meant nothing to us if Jeff couldn't drive but Del had a huge amount of respect for his abilities.

When we were at our last port, in Kona back on the Big Island, Del let me know it was time to do it. The timing of it was like threading a needle while running full speed. We were actually strolling around the quaint little town when my phone rang and Del and I managed to just barely keep enough battery life in our phones to make the decision to put the release out. In an hour, we'd be departing Kona for the long trip back to San Diego. I'd be out of touch for the next five days, in terms of phone calls. So, if it had to happen, it had to happen right then. I told Barb to stay in Kona and have some more fun. I ran back to the pier to get on the tender boat that would take me out to the ship, anchored offshore.

I was more than a little nervous. Phil was popular, and I liked him a lot as well, but this was a deal that gave us a little added budget and Del didn't think we were giving up anything in terms of the blue team driver. We were replacing one good driver with another.

From the aft lounge on our deck, where I could pick up a Wi-Fi signal, I hit "Send" and sent it out to the world.

It caused quite a stir and I wrote about it on the blog at length the next day, out on the ocean as we cruised to the northeast. I was as honest as I could be, and I think fans appreciated the honesty. My email didn't blow up nearly as much as I feared. I got far more "thank you" notes than any sort of hate mail, as readers and fans let it be known that while they loved Phil they trusted us to do the right thing and they'd be onboard with Jeff in 2007.

It was time to move on.

That winter, back at home in Minnesota, we were fitting in very well in our neighborhood. Beyond the Jacobsens next door, we'd become fast friends with a number of couples and families all around our Marsh Creek development. A New Year's Eve party, hosted by either Scott and Barb Meehan or Terry and Lynn Blake, became an annual event we always looked forward to and Barbara and I made sure to thank our assembled friends for once again celebrating our anniversary. We never did understand why they made us wait until midnight to celebrate but we appreciated the gesture.

We'd also hired a talented contractor, Jeff Russell, to replace our small deck with a spacious screened porch and had enjoyed our first year with that new living space. Below, on the patio next to the hot tub, we had a stone wall and a fire pit installed under a new pergola, while we also installed a more attractive cinder-block wall that separated our small yard from the pond. It was a year of big projects at what was no longer a house. It was home.

The blog was going great and as 2007 arrived and we made the trek back out to Pomona to fire up the Funny Cars for another season, it was becoming clear that the blog was also changing my life.

I'd been a relative unknown to fans, up until then. But as the readership numbers for the blog increased, to many thousands of readers per week, what started as a shout or a handshake here or there began to develop into a steady stream of greetings. It was a little startling. When Del and I walked through the pits together that day, and as many people said hello to me as they did to him, he said, "This is cool. You're getting kind of famous."

A year and a half earlier, when I'd made the commitment to write the blog as myself and about myself, I was nervous. Barbara was slightly incredulous, and she was convinced I was going to embarrass myself and fail. Her point was a good one. Who would want to read about me?

By 2007, Pond Cam, Shasta, and Minnesota were subjects many NHRA fans were not only familiar with, but avidly enjoying. Month by month the readership numbers increased and the fan mail arrived with regularity. Before long my blog was drawing more readers per week than all the rest of them combined. It was a revelation that made me quite proud and quite surprised.

Prior to the season NHRA announced their new playoff system, called the Countdown to the Championship. In its initial season the Countdown would feature the top eight cars in the pro classes who would have their points reset and then battle it out for the big trophies, starting at Indy.

Once we reconvened in Pomona to start our 11th season with CSK, we also began to hear some rumblings about our sponsor. They were a target for a takeover and we'd have to be paying close attention to that. We figured a solid rebound of a season, with Jeff now driving the blue car, would help us in many ways.

It didn't turn out that way.

Del ran 4.797 in the final qualifying session, at Pomona. That only got him in the field in the 16th position. Two pairs later, when Tim Wilkerson ran 4.723, we were bumped out. Starting the year with a DNQ was exactly the wrong thing. Jeff did get in, 11th, and he managed to win two rounds but 2007 was not erasing the depression of 2006.

At Phoenix we did our annual "dog and pony" stuff for three days. On Thursday, Jeff was scheduled to do the pre-dawn interviews at the track so he and I met in the hotel lobby at around 5 a.m. As we walked to my car my phone rang. It was Spica.

"Hey, the TV station cancelled on us so you don't have to go," he said. "You've got to like that news. You can keep sleeping."

I didn't have the heart to tell him we were already in the car. Jeff and I did go back to our rooms, though, and I got a little rest before we left again at 7:30.

On Friday Del smoked the tires on both qualifying runs. Fortunately for us, the entire field was struggling and our 5.296 was good enough for 14th overnight.

Saturday's sessions weren't any better. Del smoked the hoops at the hit in Q3 but with nearly everyone having trouble on a tricky track, our earlier 5.29 was 16th.

By the time Del ran in Q4 he was 20th. His 4.932 wasn't good enough. It only moved him up to 17th and it came complete with a major engine explosion in the lights. Two races and two DNQs to start the season.

Jeff did manage to squeak in 16th, but he lost in round one. So much for a rebound.

Martin Fraser, who had risen through the ranks at CSK and was by then president of the company, was a larger-than-life man. He was huge in stature and his outgoing personality owned whatever room he was in.

After the DNQ, he approached Del and put one of his massive arms around him.

"Listen, I need you to understand one thing," he said. "This doesn't matter. It's great when you win, and you've done that more than we ever imagined, but this doesn't matter. Spica would cringe if he knew I was telling you this, but listen to me. This. Doesn't. Matter. Everyone in this company loves you. The race car helps us do business. It raises our profile. Don't worry about this. I've got your back."

That meant the world to Del and when Martin removed that big beefy arm from his shoulder it took a lot of weight with it.

After Gainesville, where we failed to win a round with either team, I headed back up to Jacksonville to catch my flight home. Both teams had stayed behind to test on Monday.

I was sitting at the gate at the Jacksonville airport when Del called. He sounded a little shaken.

"Hey, Eric Medlen is testing today and he just had a bad crash. It really doesn't look very good," he said. "I'm worried about him. No one is saying a word but they're having a really hard time even getting him out of the car."

When I got back to Minneapolis, I called Del and heard the rest of the story. Eric had crashed heavily and had been airlifted to the hospital. Del had already heard that he had severe head injuries.

Over the next four days we held out hope that Eric would recover, or at the very least survive. Emergency surgery and an induced coma were keeping Eric going but the life-support systems were really what were keeping him alive. By Friday, that week, the family requested the systems be turned off. Eric Medlen died shortly thereafter.

I didn't know Eric well but he always took the time to say hello to me in the pits and the lanes. He had a smile that lit up his whole face and just a quick "hello" made the recipient of that greeting feel better.

Eric's death was not in vain. The research into his wreck caused immediate improvements to the rest of the cars in the class, including better padding around the drivers' heads. People are alive today who might not be had those improvements never been made.

The loss of Eric was tough on everyone but once again racers showed the mettle that makes them so competitive, and they got back on the track.

Things got a little better for us. Despite the two DNQs, Del went 7-6 at the first eight races, even making it to the final round at St. Louis, a race which mercifully was finally moved out of June and into May. In that final Del ran a strong 4.918 but Ron Capps edged him with a 4.882. Jeff went 3-8 during that opening one-third of the season.

During that stretch we brought out our first new Chevy Impala bodies and they not only looked fast they also looked beautiful. The new design we'd been running on the Monte Carlos looked even better on the Impalas.

During the summer, Del went 4-8 while the blue team picked it up a notch. Jeff won five rounds in those eight races.

In late June, we made the trip back to Norwalk for its inaugural NHRA national event. For the first time since I'd joined the team, we would not be racing at Columbus. The great fans from Ohio would instead get to enjoy the massive stadium at Norwalk.

On the red team Ryan McGilvry had joined the crew at the start of the season. In Norwalk, a young man named Matt Madden arrived to begin work as a rookie in the pro ranks. Matt had quite an introduction to Funny Car racing.

After smoking the tires in Q1, Del kept his foot down during the night session in Q2 despite the fact the motor sounded like it was nosing over after half-track. At 900 feet, it exploded.

When they towed the mess back to the pits, all eight rods were out of the block and the chassis was bent. Matt Madden's first day at the drags featured one very long night.

On Saturday Del was not yet in the field when he made his first pass. Running strong, the red CSK car crossed the finish line with a 4.873 to land 16th. It also crossed the line without its Impala body. An explosion cracked the hood of the car and at 300 mph that crack quickly turned into a carbon-fiber cataclysm. The beautiful body was shredded into dozens of pieces.

Although Gary Scelzi, Jerry Toliver, and Scott Kalitta were all outside the field going into the final session, Del and Chuck knew they had no choice but to work on the car and sort out the problems. If they were bumped, then so be it.

Somehow all three of those big hitters failed to bump into the show. Del lost to Robert Hight in the first round on Sunday, but the engine held together.

I flew home the next day, from Cleveland, and when my plane landed at MSP I turned on my phone and saw that I had a voice message from Barbara.

When I called her, she was in tears.

"I was out on the porch with Shasta, and he was just sitting by my feet watching the birds," she said. "And then he tried to stand up but he fell over. He died, Sweetie. I rushed him to the vet but he was already gone."

I made it home as fast as I could and the tears flowed. I'd had my little buddy for 16 years. He was our child. And he was gone. The sadness was so enormous. We held each other for hours and I felt terrible that I hadn't been there for him. I also felt so bad for Barb, who had to be the one who dealt with it. There was a hole in our home but it wasn't the right time to fill it. We knew that, and as hard as it was we had to get back to work. I needed to be in Bristol in just a few days.

I took the time to carefully write a heartfelt blog about my fuzzy little boy. It was hard to see the laptop clearly throughout much of the process but I told his story as well as I could. I just wasn't sure how my reading public would accept it. I shouldn't have worried.

Emails flooded in within an hour of the blog's posting. The reaction was the same as it would've been had I been blogging about a relative or a best friend. He was, after all, "my little guy" and one of my best friends.

One of the notes was from a gentleman who introduced himself as a reader since the first blog. He let me know how much the Shasta installment had touched him and wanted me to understand that he was thinking about me, despite the fact we'd never met. That was kind of the beauty of the blog. The way I wrote it made readers feel like they knew me. The common comment was, "When I read your blog, I feel like you're in the room talking to me." I considered that the ultimate compliment.

The guy's name was Buck Hujabre. I had no idea how to pronounce his last name but figured (incorrectly) it must be something like "Hoo-JAB-ray." He told me he was an aspiring stage actor living in New York. My internal mental response to that was, "Yeah. You and every other bartender in Manhattan!"

Buck and I began to correspond regularly once we realized we were connected at some primal level when it came to being funny and forward-thinking. We could be sophomoric or five levels deep into sarcasm, but we cracked each other up with regularity.

And just a few months later he landed a role in the national touring company for the Broadway hit "Jersey Boys." So, he really was an actor. And a musician. And a singer!

After Bristol we were off on yet another Western Swing. Del made it to the final round at Sonoma but lost there to John Force, 4.831 to our 4.851. Another heartbreaker.

At Brainerd, the most noteworthy thing was an unexpected introduction. I was out in front of our hospitality center when a gentleman and a woman approached me. He said, "We came here last year and our tickets weren't waiting for us. I was pretty mad about it, but we decided to give it another shot this year."

I then proceeded to stand there and talk to the two of them for 40 minutes, wanting to make sure they had a good time. He was from Winnipeg and he told me how he'd been a starter at the local drag strip back in the day, when they used flags to signal the drivers when it was time to go.

His stories were rich, and I really enjoyed speaking to both of them. Finally, I said, "So what's your connection to CSK?"

He said, "I know a guy named Carl who works there. He's a fan of a band I used to be in."

I thought to myself, "OK, I'll bite" and I said, "What was the name of your band?"

"Bachman-Turner Overdrive. I'm Fred Turner."

You never know who you're going to meet at a drag race. Fred and I still email regularly.

After Brainerd came Reading. Heading into Maple Grove Del was sitting in the No. 9 spot in points. To catch Jim Head, in order to get in the Countdown, a specific list of things had to happen. Del would need to win the race, Head would have to lose in round one, and somehow Del would still need to tack on four additional points during qualifying.

He got the qualifying points. He was due to race Jeff in the opening round. And then the rains came.

On Monday, Head lost his race in round one. When Del and Jeff pulled to the line and the tree flashed its amber bulbs, Del hit the pedal and streaked to the win.

When Del then beat Tony Bartone in round two, the miracle of catching Jim Head was still possible. And then it rained again.

We came back out on Tuesday and it rained. All day.

By then, we'd been kicked out of our original hotel because a Jehovah's Witnesses convention was moving in. We found rooms south of Reading and we were all completely out of clean dry clothes. We didn't have the time, nor did we have the inclination, to sit in a laundromat so a few of us just went out and bought new socks, t-shirts, and underwear. We weren't lazy. We were exhausted.

Finally, on Wednesday, we ran the semifinals. Del lost to Tony Pedregon. It had been a long race featuring days full of rain and multiple hotels, and we'd come up just short of making the playoffs.

While we battled it out on the track O'Reilly Auto Parts was making a push to buy CSK. No one was totally certain when that might happen but with the merger-wheels in motion CSK made the decision to continue to back Del in 2008, but only as a single-car team. It was actually a contract extension, since our deal ran out at the end of 2007, and it was a very gracious thing for the company to do.

They could have just killed the program and saved the money but their loyalty to us was too great. They wanted to keep us out on the road while the potential merger moved to a conclusion and that would help keep us relevant while we also searched for a new sponsor. We'd probably need to do that, because O'Reilly had no history of partnering with NHRA teams at the primary sponsor level. Although CSK would push for a change in that policy there was no guarantee they could make it happen. They weren't exactly playing from a position of strength.

When all of these rumblings had begun, my neighbor Dave Jacobsen was looking for something new to do. He'd done very well with a successful optical business and finally had sold his company, but retirement wasn't suiting him much and he'd become a big fan of our team.

Being a smart guy, I put two and two together and asked him to have lunch with me one day. Over a Caesar salad I pitched him an idea. We didn't have the budget to put him on a salary but Del had agreed to pay him an oversized commission if he could land us a new primary sponsor. Dave eagerly agreed to do that.

Dave started coming to all the races and joined in to get his hands dirty quite a bit, while in-between events he pounded the phones pitching deals. He discovered it was a lot harder than selling eyeglass frames but he kept after it with a bulldog's tenacity.

At the same time, our house had been a very quiet place for a few months after we had lost our fuzzy little boy. We had needed to go through the grieving process to get over our loss, and to limit the reminders I had put his bed and toys away. That was a hard thing for me to do.

As summer faded into fall we both started to feel the need for more feline companionship. We talked about it at length and came to the conclusion that we'd adopt kittens, and there would need to be two of them. Littermates of the same gender would be the ideal option.

One day, I decided to stop at the Humane Society in Woodbury. I walked through a number of the rooms and checked out a bunch of cute kittens. In the final room I saw two nearly identical black kittens sharing a cage. They were a couple of months old but still small. When I opened the cage they came out and jumped on me. I had, at that moment, been adopted.

I had to leave for the Richmond race, though, and Barbara wasn't with me. I called her and said, "You have to go adopt these kittens while I'm gone. You just have to. They're incredible, and they already adopted me."

She wasn't sure if I was serious or not. I made it quite clear that I was very serious.

A day or two later she went up there herself and found them still there. It was meant to be. She got them, and brought them home. We'd already settled on the names Boofus and Buster but Barbara had to figure out which one was which. From the day they came home, one of them was about 20 percent smaller than the other. It just seemed right that the little guy would be Boofus.

I couldn't wait to see them. I even got on an earlier flight and made it home Sunday night. I wondered if they'd be afraid of me, or even just a little standoffish, but they met me at the door and immediately began rubbing on my legs. And when I picked up the little guy, he sneezed right in my face. Welcome home!

Like many animals who are adopted from a shelter, they came complete with "kitty colds" and Boofus had his first. As soon as he got better, Buster caught the cold. Finally, when everyone was better, we had the two most hilarious little brothers in our midst.

Originally, our nickname for the two of them was going to be "Da Boyce" because that's how Minnesota hockey players and coaches talk. "Here we go, boyce" could be heard on any bench at just about any level, throughout the state. It didn't take but a few weeks for that to morph into "the boyz" though, because that just seemed to fit them better.

Back out on the track, as we pushed hard down the stretch, the red team got it together a little better, going 7-7 at the final seven races. Del finished 18-21. It wasn't what we were after, but it was an improvement over the 12-20 record one year earlier.

Jeff finished the season 12-23. Shortly after the Finals at Pomona his driving tenure with Worsham Racing would end, as well, as we transitioned to a single-car team.

Dave had a number of potential programs in various stages of development. We also really enjoyed working together, and we developed a lot of great marketing and background materials to take our pitches to a new level of professionalism. I was the creative guy and he was the salesman. We made a great team but I was under no illusion that it would be easy.

By the time the season had ended, with yet another pit party, it was mind boggling to think how much had happened in one year. But it was a long way from being over.

In early December I got an email from Francine, the wife of my friend Adam in Hawaii. She was writing to me confidentially because Adam would've been upset if he knew what she was up to. Things were really bad for them, and about to get a lot worse.

She'd been laid off from her job and they'd been burning through whatever savings they had. By the time she wrote to me, their situation was dire. They could barely put food on the table and they were no more than a week away from being evicted from their home.

Francine knew that being homeless would be the end for Adam. His cancer was worse than ever and he'd never survive that. So, she reached out to me.

I was stunned, but I was also eager to help. I just had to figure out the best way to do it. I talked it over with Barbara and we both agreed that I should FedEx a check to them for delivery the next morning. It needed to be enough to keep them in their home. The cost to us was irrelevant. It needed to be enough.

We thought of establishing a charity but that would take too long. I knew exactly what to do.

I sat down to write my blog on December 19, 2007. The first part was about our night at the Wild hockey game the previous evening. Minnesota Wild fans are known as "The Team of

18,000" and I explained, in the blog, the wonderful communal feeling at the games. And then I used that as a point of comparison for all of my blog readers.

I knew it was a risk. I wasn't sure if it would work. I wasn't even sure if I'd lose some readers just for asking, but I had to ask.

I wrote about Adam and Francine's situation. I spelled it out clearly. I apologized for doing it. But I finished the plea with the words, "This is not just some guy. It's not a late-night commercial about feeding hungry children. This is a friend. I've been in his house. I've hugged him myself. He needs our help" and then, with Francine's permission, I listed their home address.

Within five minutes, and I'm not exaggerating in the least, I got the first email from a reader, who wrote, "My check is in the mail."

By that evening, I'd gotten hundreds of them.

The next day, when my FedEx envelope arrived at the Vincent home, Francine called me in tears. She was overwhelmed, but I had to tell her about the blog. She hadn't logged onto Adam's computer yet, to see it.

I told her about my plea and about the overwhelming response I was getting. The emails were still pouring in 24 hours later.

"I don't know what will show up in your mailbox, Francine, but if these emails are any indication I think it will help," I said.

The next day she called again. When the mailman left their house, the box was overflowing with envelopes. Some sent cash, others sent checks, most included a Christmas card for two people they'd never met.

She had me in tears too, just listening to it. By the end of the week they had all the food they needed and had kept their home. There was no danger of ever losing it. Adam wrote back to every person who pitched in, with handwritten notes of thanks. That's the kind of guy he was. Many readers made a vow to continue to send the Vincents "a little something" every Christmas, and they did just that. Jeff Arend and his wife Windy often sent personal notes, just to say hello and help out a little more.

I'd known the NHRA was a big family. They'd been there for me. Nothing felt as good as this, though. Everyone came through, in many ways. They saved a man's life that week. Adam survived until March 24, 2013. May he rest in peace.

As we moved into 2008, it was quickly obvious that we'd need to put "sponsorship sales" on the front burner. The talks between O'Reilly and CSK were growing more serious.

Del had worked out a deal with Top Fuel owner Dexter Tuttle for our two teams to pit together for the sake of hospitality. As a one-car team we couldn't set up our hospitality center, but with Dexter and his team on the other side we had our "U-shaped" pit back again.

The loss of the blue team also had all of those guys looking for jobs, and a number of them were hired by Bob Tasca, including Chris Cunningham. On Del's team, we welcomed Carl Boyd and Kevin Maddux to the fold.

Dave was working hard on the sponsor front, but our timing wasn't good. The economy was just starting to tip over in the early part of the year and we'd already missed out on 2008 budgets by not being out there pushing hard, a full year earlier.

Before the season kicked off we went to Vegas for some testing and that's where I got to meet the new guys as we all had a beer in the casino at The Cannery hotel, near the track. At one point I got up and said, "I'm going to go play some slots. Maybe I'll see you guys after a while."

I only play slots when I gamble in Vegas, because I don't want my bad decisions to cost me money while playing blackjack, poker, or roulette. The way I see it, the biggest bad decision you can make with a slot machine is to play it in the first place. And, over the years I'd graduated from quarter slots, to dollars, and finally to five-dollar machines. I'd heard, from some savvy slot players, that the bigger the bet the better the odds of winning and the bigger the payout.

I also pick my machines on a "feeling" I get when I walk by. I like machines that have special bonus wheels, so that if you activate the bonus thing you know for sure that you're going to win something. It's just a matter of how much.

That night I saw a machine I liked, with a spinning bonus wheel, and I sat down. I put in two $100 bills and hit "Max Bet" because that's the only effective way to play slots. At a different casino I once sat next to a woman who hit the ultimate result, with three "Wild" emblems lining up across the line. Her machine's bells went off and I knew that "Wild" line would pay $25,000. Except she only played $1 instead of the maximum bet of $3 and that oversight cost her $23,800. And then she just sat there and kept playing, betting just $1 with each spin.

After two spins, I didn't hit the bonus wheel but I did have a line that went "Double Bonus - 7 - Double Bonus." As I tried to do the math to figure out what three sevens paid and then double that and double it again, the bells just kept going off. Before I could finish the equation the machine payout screen read $1,250. I printed the ticket.

You should always walk away after a machine hits a big winner, so I stood up with my pay slip. And the machine right next to the one I'd been playing called to me. It was an identical machine and I still had a few additional $100 bills burning a hole in my wallet so I sat down and put $300 into it. At that point, I was playing with house money.

On the second spin, just like on the first machine, it hit a winner and it was the bonus wheel. I pressed the button to activate it and I ended up doing OK. It landed on the $2,000 prize. I took my slip and walked back to the bar. I'd been gone exactly two minutes.

When I showed the guys my pay slips they refused to believe it. They pored over them to ascertain they were real and had actually just been printed. Then they shook their heads in amazement. When they asked me what I was going to do with the money, I told them I had already formulated a plan.

When Barbara and I had gotten married I didn't have enough money to buy her any kind of decent diamond, so we had an older diamond from her family mounted on a new ring. With my winnings of $3,250 I would be buying her a very real diamond.

A few weeks later we arrived at Pomona and parked next to Dexter's pit. Alan Bradshaw would be driving his Top Fueler with upstart energy drink "Vis Viva" on the sides. Across the back of the pit, our hospitality rig in its full set-up design sat.

Under our awning sat a brand new Impala Funny Car body adorned with the same paint/vinyl hybrid design. It was sparkling and gorgeous.

And then Del finished qualifying in the 23rd spot, starting the season off with a DNQ for the second straight year.

In 2007, NHRA had instituted the "Top 12" rule for qualifying and with that in place only the top 12 qualifiers on Friday had their times carry over. On Saturday, everyone from 13th on down would start with no time on the board. With Pomona having a unique 1-1-2 qualifying schedule for Thursday, Friday, and Saturday, the rule would be in effect through the Friday run.

In 2008, at the first race, the Top 12 rule bit the CSK team like a rabid dog. Del ran 4.967 to land in the top half of the field in Q1. In Q2, Del ran a 4.974 so he'd made two consistent quality runs, but the 4.96 from Thursday slipped to the 13th spot. That meant he'd go into Saturday with nothing on the board. In effect, the two nice runs never happened.

On Saturday, the red CSK car smoked the tires early in Q3. Del would go into Q4 in the No. 22 spot. When he smoked the tires again, he was toast. It was not a pretty way to start the year.

And it got worse. We went to Phoenix and did it again. We lost the Friday runs due to rain, so the Top 12 rule had no effect. We just smoked the tires twice and never had a chance.

2008 was starting off poorly, and while we were in Phoenix we got the latest updates from the company executives. It was looking almost certain that O'Reilly would complete the purchase. Jim Schoenberger vowed to keep the pressure on for O'Reilly to pick up our deal, but ultimately it would be their decision.

At Gainesville, we won a round. Considering we hadn't made the show at the first two a round felt pretty good.

And then we headed to Houston, where we'd be running a special-edition K&N Filters Impala at the ironically named O'Reilly Spring Nationals. We qualified better, landing in the No. 4 spot, and then beat Jerry Toliver in round one with a 4.922 that was one of the better runs in the opener. Tim Wilkerson posted a huge 4.870 to earn the right to race us next. We'd noticed that Wilk and his Levi, Ray, & Shoup team looked legit early in the season.

Del ran 4.917 to send Wilk back to the trailer. Then he ran another 4.917 to oust John Force. In the final it would be us against another Force, but this time it would be daughter Ashley.

She made a solid lap, putting a 4.971 on the board. Del left first by a huge margin, though, and then compounded that with a 4.933 to win going away.

Pomona and Phoenix had been horrible. Gainesville got us back on track. In Houston, we thought we had our mojo back.

With so many new guys on the team, we made our first mistake of the day while towing the car to the Winner's Circle. Instead of going down the return road and then into the pits the guys pulled it under the tower, where we were quickly surrounded by a sea of fans and unable to get it into place for a solid 15 minutes. We finally got it in front of the banner and the new guys, including Matt Madden who had not tasted a win in 2007, had their photos taken with the driver and the Wally.

And then we were once again terrible. At the next six races we won one solitary round. And we suffered two more DNQs, failing to make the show at Topeka and Chicago on back-to-back weekends.

As a diversion from the depression at the race track, I'd been staying in touch regularly with my actor buddy Buck who attempted to teach me the pronunciation of his Afghan name via email. It was something along the lines of "Hoo-ZHA-bear" but it was hard to figure out in print. We soon realized we'd have a chance to do it in person. "Jersey Boys" was coming to Minneapolis for an extended stay.

Buck left tickets for us at the theater and we were thrilled by the show. It moves at such a fast pace, and there's so much live playing and singing of Four Seasons' songs that anyone can sing along with, it simply rocks along under its own momentum. Buck was, at that time, a "swing" actor in the show, playing multiple roles and changing costumes almost constantly. We played "Where's Buck?" from our fifth-row seats all night long.

After the show he met us at the stage door. It was the oddest thing to meet a man for the first time yet feel as if I'd known him for years. Hugs were exchanged all around, then he gave us a fabulous backstage tour and I figured that was a good way to cap off the evening.

Barbara had other ideas. She asked him if he'd like to join us for a beer and then we could drop him off at the corporate apartment the show had provided. I winced a little, not wanting to impose on him in any way, but he quickly said, "That would be awesome! There's a little bar right next door."

We sat and talked over a few beers for more than an hour and it was instantly apparent to me that he was as interested in hearing about the NHRA and my job as I was about his gig. He'd been going to races since he was a little kid in Baton Rouge and his eyes would get big when I'd mention Kenny Bernstein or Don Prudhomme. Those guys were his childhood idols, and I worked around them nearly every weekend.

When the night concluded, and we dropped him off, I knew I'd made a friend for life. And a very interesting friend with an amazing skill set he was.

The next race was Englishtown.

Leaving the Newark airport in my rental car, I got a call from Jim Schoenberger. He got straight to the point. Martin Fraser had called Del to let him know the sale was going through. They were still going to bat for us, trying to convince O'Reilly to at least give us one year to help them with the transition and rebranding, but they weren't getting much of an indication that O'Reilly would do it.

We weren't stunned. It had felt, for months, like this was going to be it. We, at least, wanted to go out strong. We qualified OK, in the No. 5 spot.

During Q4, Scott Kalitta entered the last session in the 20th and final qualifying spot. I was in the Media Center in the tower behind the starting line standing next to Todd Myers, the PR rep for Kalitta Motorsports. I was there to offer support for my buddy.

When it was Scott's turn to run in his yellow DHL car, I was patting Todd on the back as the Kalitta machine tore down the track on an obviously solid run. And then it blew up, in a very big way.

It crossed the finish line still doing 300 mph and the 4.974 moved Scott all the way up to the 13th spot. The Toyota body had buckled, though, and the DHL Solara was bearing down fast on the sand trap at the end of the racing surface. Scott was just along for the ride, because the buckled body kept him from reaching the parachute levers. From my perspective, Scott's car seemed to hit the sand much faster than Del's had in Pomona before the somersault.

When Scott's car hit the sand we all lost sight of it due to the amount of debris it kicked up. The big screen feed was shut off immediately. It had clearly been a big wreck. I told Todd, "Go. Go down there and be with your team," and he took off running.

Time stood still. For 40 minutes, we heard nothing. Then the NHRA announced it would take another hour, at least, to fix the fence and the trap. They told the remaining Funny Car teams to head back to their trailers. It was too late for that. Almost all of them had already turned around and gone back on their own.

I walked out of the tower toward the lanes and the first person I saw was Tim Wilkerson. Wilk looked at me with a very somber face, shaking his head slightly. He said, "I'm hearing that he died. I don't know if it's official yet, but some people who would know have already passed the word to all the teams here. It's terrible if it's true."

It was true. And it was terrible. We were all crushed. Del was very upset about it, and angry that it had happened to a friend and a colleague he'd always loved and respected.

Nobody wanted to race on Sunday but in this case what is usually a cliche was quite true: If there was any one person in the sport who would have demanded that we race, it would've been Scott Kalitta.

Robert Hight lined up with an empty lane next to him as the first Funny Car to run in the opening round. Scott's team, and the other two Kalitta teams, lined up behind the starting line in the empty lane, with their arms draped around each other's shoulders.

When Hight came back from his burnout and staged the only sound at the track was the rumble of Hight's motor. The capacity crowd was silent.

When the bulbs flashed Hight simply let go of the brake and idled down the full length of the track. The most noticeable and overwhelming sound, at that time, was the sound of sobbing. It seemed as if everyone was in tears. I'd never seen anything quite like it, and I hope I never see anything like it again.

We won two rounds, losing to Wilk eventually in the semifinal. He went on to win the race. He, of course, dedicated it to Scott. He also invited every member of the DHL team to the Winner's Circle.

Tim Wilkerson had three wins and a strong grip on the points lead. When we'd gotten that early impression that the LRS car was pretty good we were kind of right, but not exactly. It was way better than we'd thought.

At that point our lousy performance was only made worse by our grief over Scott's passing. There was no fun in it, and it seemed we'd lost whatever magic we'd had since 2001.

At the next six races, ranging from Norwalk through the Western Swing and then Brainerd and Reading, we posted a not-so-stellar 2-6 record. At Denver, NHRA instituted the 1,000-foot length of track for the nitro classes. Nearly every driver I knew supported it. Most vowed they would never race 1,320 again.

Also after Denver I made another new friend thanks to NHRA Drag Racing. Dave Jacobsen and I were flying back to MSP on a night flight and we were both upgraded to First Class. Across the aisle from me was a young man who was clearly an athlete. Having been around them my entire life, I have pretty good radar for sports guys.

When we arrived and went to baggage claim the same guy was there with us and he spotted my Worsham Racing polo shirt. He came over and asked me if I'd been at the race, and if I worked for Del. He told me he'd been there for the day and was on his way home.

I introduced him to Dave and we all talked for a bit. The guy seemed really excited to meet some dudes from the NHRA and he was pelting us, rapid fire, with questions. I finally asked him what he did for a living and he said, "I play hockey" just as a Colorado Avalanche bag slid down the carousel.

"You play for the Avs?" I asked.

"I did, but I was a free agent and just a couple of weeks ago I signed with Toronto," he replied.

I asked him his name and he told me it was Jeff Finger. The Avs play the Wild a lot. I knew exactly who he was. He was a great defenseman and he used to shut down the Wild's offense regularly.

We exchanged info and vowed to stay in touch. To make sure that happened, he texted me a few days later and told me, again, what a pleasure it was to talk racing with us. Yet another new friendship was born. Cool dude, that Finger. Unfortunately, many injuries (including a string of concussions) ended his career just a couple of years after we met.

After the Swing was complete, and Brainerd and Reading were in the books, we headed to Indianapolis. We were headed there with a 10-12 mark and with an astounding four DNQs

At Indy, we were in the Skoal Showdown and we managed to beat Robert Hight in the first round. During the race that Wilkerson cat beat us in the opener, 4.167 edging our 4.176 in a dyslexic scoreboard finish. It seemed sadly fitting, after all we'd been through.

It was at Indy when Del came up to my office and said, "Can you and Dave guarantee that we'll have a sponsor next year?"

"I can't guarantee anything, and we're not really that close with anyone," I replied.

He then told me about Alan Johnson's new team for 2009. It would feature a Top Fuel car driven by Larry Dixon and it would also include a Funny Car. The entire team would be financed, substantially, by the country of Qatar. Alan had offered Del the seat in the Funny Car.

I never hesitated. I said, "Take it. Go right over there and take it before he offers it to someone else. We'll all land on our feet. Go over there and say yes."

He mentioned that he could probably get me an interview for the PR position but he knew Alan had worked with a guy named Rob Goodman for many of the Winston years, and Rob would be the natural to take that spot. I told him not to worry about it.

He took the job. It was all coming to an end.

We went to Charlotte next, winning a round at the incredibly impressive zMAX Dragway. We marveled at its size and majesty. The main grandstand, on the pit side, had more seats than almost any other track did in total, counting both sides of those venues. And yet, in Charlotte there was another massive grandstand on the right side. There were also four lanes although lanes three and four would not be used in 2008.

When we moved on to Dallas, just a few days later, I included official word of the CSK acquisition in our pre-race feature story. It was real and now the NHRA world knew it.

Barbara was really worried about me finding a job. She asked almost every day if I'd been sending out resumes or applying with various teams. I always had the same reply. I told her I had a feeling that the offers would come as soon as we announced the folding of the team. I wasn't worried about it. That was pretty classic me. Just plow forward.

I was right. I hadn't been at the track for more than two hours when the number of people who asked me if I'd consider working for them reached six. Some I knew wouldn't be a good fit for me; some I thought would be fantastic. None of them would quite be like the prior 12 years with Del, but life moves on and I needed a good job.

During qualifying Tim Wilkerson's wife Krista approached me under the tower. We'd been getting to know each other better that year, after she admitted how much she enjoyed my blog, and I was happy to see her approaching me that day.

She said, "Please don't accept anything until you talk to us. Tim's only focused on racing right now but he wants to talk with you."

I said I'd be honored to talk to him whenever he was ready. I'd hold off on everyone else.

Wilk had a lot to focus on. He'd been in the points lead since he won the St. Louis race in May. At Charlotte, he entered the Countdown playoffs in first place. By the time he had gotten to Dallas he had won four times. He would then go on to win in Dallas and win again in Memphis.

For us, and a lot of other teams, the final few races of the season would certainly be about doing well in our own rights but very few racers could deny being Tim Wilkerson fans. As a single-car guy who owned the team, tuned the car, and drove it, he was a rare breed. Being from Springfield, Illinois, with his race shop located in the back portion of Wilkerson's Service Center, he was every bit a small-town guy with a Midwestern sensibility.

He'd shown plenty of signs of success over the years, but in 2008 it all came together to make him the top story of the entire tour. Everyone was watching Wilk. Almost all of us were cheering for him.

A few days after the Dallas race, he gave me a call. He asked me how much Del was paying me. When I told him, he said, "Well, OK. At least I know."

Two days later, he called me again.

"OK," he said.

I asked him what he meant.

"I'll pay you what Del paid you. You can start Dec. 1."

I asked him what he was doing the next day. When he said he'd just be working in the shop, I told him I would be flying down and we'd do this face to face, over lunch. It was important to me to put all of our wants, needs, and desires on the table to make sure we were compatible. I also wanted to make sure he understood what I did and how I did it. He seemed amused that I'd spend the money to fly to Peoria, rent a car, have lunch, and then fly back home.

For a number of years Tim had employed a husband-and-wife team to handle his PR and the Levi, Ray & Shoup hospitality. I was honored, deeply, that Tim would offer me a job but I knew the couple and knew they worked very hard at it. These career changes can sometimes be messy.

I took a morning flight from Minneapolis to Peoria then drove down to Springfield, an hour away.

When I walked into the shop every head in the place turned to look at me. They smiled and nodded but I don't think they were totally up to speed as to why Del Worsham's PR guy was walking into their work space.

Over lunch, at Panera Bread across Stevenson Drive, I spelled out all of the things I thought we should discuss and Tim agreed with all of it. We were definitely on the same page.

As for starting Dec. 1, I told him that Barbara and I had already booked a Caribbean cruise for the first two weeks of the month but he said, "Don't worry about it. You'll start on payroll Dec. 1."

His goal was to step up the PR effort and I was pleased to hear him say, "I'm not really sure what's important and what's not, but everyone I talked to said you're as good as anyone and better than most."

I was also pleased to tell him that I thought he'd be getting a three-for-one deal, because I'd ask both Dave Jacobsen and John Fink if they would join me at Team Wilkerson Racing.

As for hospitality, he told me he'd be stepping it up in that regard, as well. He was hiring Annette Schendel who had been working for Don Schumacher. Don Schumacher Racing was widely considered to have the most professional corporate set-up in the sport. If Annette worked for DSR, she was first-class. That's the only way they knew how to do it.

In addition, Tim had been renting tents at each race where LRS wanted to entertain and he was tired of how tacky most of them looked. It was time to go big.

Bob Tasca was completing his first year in the Funny Car class and he'd made an offer to Tim. Team Wilkerson would make the switch to the Shelby Mustang body and would be teammates with the Tasca organization. The creative part of the agreement was the hospitality.

With NHRA's help, the two teams would always park next to each other in the pro pits but both teams had right-side doors on their transporters. That was good, because Tasca agreed to put hooks on the left side of his rig, and Tim's guys would set up a full first-class hospitality center off that side of Tasca's trailer. Nobody had ever thought to do that before. With a large awning hung off Tasca's rig, and our giant vinyl LRS banner covering the left side of it, it looked like a free-standing hospitality center.

We decided to wait until Pomona to make all the news public. Dave agreed to join me at once, and John said he'd want to think about it but he was heavily leaning toward doing it. One day later, he committed.

I had every reason to think it would be a very big Pomona weekend. Tim was in the hunt for the championship, Del wanted to finish strong with all the CSK guys there, and it would be the last time Team CSK raced. Ever.

We had clanked another DNQ in Vegas, our fifth of the year, and we came into Pomona limping like a quarterback with a torn knee ligament. We were willing and eager to gut it out, but there wasn't much left in the tank.

I had put out a quick press release for Wilk, announcing the new staff for the LRS team in 2009, and I'd written about it in my blog on Thursday. I had a lot of things to write about then, as we combined the sadness of the end of the CSK era with the exciting start of a new LRS adventure. People seemed genuinely happy for me when they heard the news. I think they knew Wilk and I would be a good fit.

Annette, whose husband Rich was already working on Tim's car as a fly-in guy, came over to meet Dave and me in the Worsham pit. It was then we discovered that we all lived in Minnesota. Dave and I lived next door to each other, in Woodbury, and Rich and Annette lived and worked just a couple of hours south, in Janesville. They actually lived only about 80 miles from where Dave grew up. All of us would be flying into and out of MSP to get to the races.

Then we got down to racing. And, we did it again. Tire smoke and a backfired blower left us with no time on the board going into Q4. Over the 12 years, we'd made our fair share of heroic last-ditch runs to go from outside the field right into the show on the final pass. This one seemed as huge as all of the prior ones combined.

The script had us making the quickest run of the weekend and going right to the top. Nobody read the script, though, and we smoked the tires at the hit of the throttle. I could only stand there and stare as the CSK Impala idled across the finish line. I didn't know what to think. It was over. There were 20 Funny Cars on the property. We finished qualifying in the

No. 20 position. It was an inglorious conclusion to a sad and frustrating year. It didn't seem right that this group would go out that way.

We didn't even get to race on the final day of our final event.

We did show up, and the guys began the process of putting everything away for the last time. When it was time for the opening round I went to the line to see if Wilk could close the deal and win the NHRA Funny Car Championship. He faced John Force in round one.

At the final few races, Cruz Pedregon had gotten hot. He entered Pomona with a small lead in the points but Wilk and Hight were within close range. The big trophy could easily go to any of the three of them.

When Pedregon won his opener, the window grew a little more narrow.

Tim Wilkerson and John Force were the next pair.

When the amber lights flashed, Wilk and Force left the line nearly identically. Wilk left first by only two thousandths of a second. But something was wrong. The red light in Wilk's lane was on.

I let things settle for quite a while but when I saw Tim walking in the pits a couple of hours later, I approached him. He was dumbfounded.

"I know for a fact I didn't red-light," he said. "I don't know what happened, but I saw all sorts of yellow and actually thought I might be a little late. Something screwy happened and it happened at the worst possible time. Force got out his car and said the same thing. He said there was no possible way we were both red and I was just red by an inch more. No possible way."

Later, Tim and his son Daniel came over to the CSK pit and they brought along a crew shirt for me to wear. Inside the hospitality center we took individual head-shot photos and shots of us in pairs and as a trio. My teammates on the CSK squad stood and watched, then offered a mock golf clap.

Once the race ended, and Cruz won the title, we waited a bit for the crowd to leave and then our pit party started. Without a doubt, it was the saddest pit party of them all.

I had felt, for months, that I needed to commemorate all of this in some way. I finally settled on a t-shirt and sweatshirt design and Boris at T-Shirts Unlimited brought it to life. Within the first hour at the party, he sold every one he had printed.

On the back, each of the 12 years was represented. Tiny Wally trophies, in the appropriate quantity, were included over the appropriate years. Each year had a caption. I wrote it all in mere minutes. It went something like this:

1997 - CSK era begins. First car is blue (nice color!) Not much else to report.
1998 - Red becomes Del's color. Welcome to the 4-Second Club. Runner-up in Chicago.
1999 - Hello Wally! Hello Seattle! Del's car in 8 million McDonald's Happy Meals.
2000 - The 2-car era begins. Frankie joins the team. Comedy level rises.
2001 - 4 wins for Del. 1 win for Frankie. Drinks all around!
2002 - 4 more wins. Hey, this is fun! Johnny Gray drops in.
2003 - 3 more wins for Del. Phil Burkart and Cory Lee show up. Cory crosses center line. Oops.
2004 - Del wins 5! Phil wins 2! Earth spins off its axis.
2005 - Can you say double-up? $100,000 drops from the sky. '05 officially declared "off year"

2006 - Phil wins Reading! Thank you, blue team. Del somersaults in Pomona.

2007 - 2 runner-ups. Lots of explosions. Anything else?

2008 - Del's 22nd Wally in Houston. CSK goes away. Many people cry.

Below all of that, it read: "The Future… Whatever it holds, we are richer for having been part of this."

During the party, when the Tijuana Dogs took a break I grabbed the microphone to say a few things. I wanted to do it and get it all out before I became too emotional, and with every passing minute we were all descending into that abyss.

I was as sincere as I could be. I recalled our humble beginnings, back in 1997. I talked about how we grew this great program from next to nothing into a model organization. I spoke honestly and earnestly about how we always felt like friends and partners with the entire CSK staff. Then I wrapped it up.

"These last 12 years have meant more to me than any of you will ever know," I said. "This is my family, right here in this room. I will never forget that. It has been a privilege and a real honor to work alongside all of you. We created more than a few miracles here, but now we have to move on. I love every one of you."

There was not a dry eye in the house, and that included my own. The rest of the night as all about hugs.

It was all very surreal.

I never anticipated having to plow forward like this but I was going to the right place. For all 12 years, whenever Barbara would ask me what other teams I might want to work for if I couldn't work for Del, my answer was always, "It's a short list, and I think that Wilkerson guy is at the top of it."

I allowed myself to understand and appreciate that my own hard work and dedication had created this chance to keep doing what I loved for a team that would instantly make me feel at home. I was leaving one family to join another.

A Fresh New Challenge

Before I could even think about starting my new job with Team Wilkerson I had to finish up all my PR "Season in Review" work for Del. And, I had to go on vacation. A guy needs priorities.

Our cruise was departing from Fort Lauderdale so we went down a day early and I texted Krista Wilkerson a photo I'd promised to send her. It was of my feet, in the sand, on the beach.

The next morning we headed for the cruise port and boarded the ms Zuiderdam. There's a thrill involved in walking across the bridge from the pier to a ship, and then finding your way around the various decks, lounges, restaurants, and communal spaces. The possibilities seem limitless.

I had never been on a cruise before I met Barbara. The only thing I knew, and the only thing I expected, was what I'd seen watching "The Love Boat" on TV. Soon after we got married we sailed the Caribbean on the Wind Surf, a small ship with a capacity of only 300 passengers. We later took another Wind Surf cruise, marveling at the ship's computer-controlled sails that assisted the diesel motors, before we "stepped up" to the Holland America Line and its big ships.

We also started out with small quarters, gradually working our way up to larger staterooms with each ensuing cruise. Each time we'd book something better, that became the new baseline. There would be no downsizing on any later cruise. This time, aboard the ms Zuiderdam, we took it all the way to a full suite with a large veranda.

As the ship's horn sounded and we left the port we headed southeast toward Half Moon Cay, a private island owned by Holland America. Unfortunately, upon arrival the captain informed us that the water was too rough and the tender boats would be unable to take us ashore. With the skipper's assurances that he'd "make it up" to us we then headed further south to Aruba and Curacao, just a few miles north of the Venezuelan coast. To get there we cruised for two full days while eating spectacular food and sipping incredible wine. Our only goal, in terms of consumption, was to get off the ship without having gained any weight. To do that we'd walk at least two miles around the decks each day and hit the gym every afternoon. We had done that on the longer Hawaiian cruise and it worked like a charm. With the walks and the workouts, you could earn your decadence.

We enjoyed a submarine ride in Aruba and marveled at the quaint village of Willemstad on Curacao, with its Dutch architecture and brilliantly colored buildings. From Curacao we'd head west. We were going to the Panama Canal.

After another day at sea, we arrived at the canal before sunrise. We awoke at 5 a.m. and walked to a forward viewing area on Deck 6, where the staff had croissants and orange juice waiting for us.

We staked out a spot at the railing, staring off into the distance as the running lights from dozens of freighter ships sparkled all around us. They were waiting to make their passage, lined up and anchored in some sort of prearranged queue. Another large cruise ship was directly ahead of us and we'd get the "express lane" trip. As the sun began to rise, it all came into focus.

We could see the entrance to the canal in the distance as we slowly approached. The first set of locks, which would raise our ship 85 feet, would get us to Gatun Lake.

There are two "lanes" in the canal, and multiple locks to raise and lower ships, but the canal is not necessarily a strict two-way street. Ships are raised or lowered as the traffic demands and we were going in with the other cruise ship right next to us. To see the giant vessel rise so quickly as the locks were flooded was astonishing. Within an hour after arriving at the canal we were sailing into Gatun Lake. We stayed there a couple of hours and then returned to the Atlantic Ocean by heading back down the locks to once again be at sea level. It was one of the most fascinating things I'd ever experienced.

The next day we docked at Limon in Costa Rica, where there was a pier big enough for two large cruise ships to tie up at the same time. The luxury of simply walking off the ship, without having to be shuttled to shore on a bobbing tender boat, was very much appreciated.

We'd be docked there for the full day and while other passengers headed off on zip-line adventures, we'd booked a combination boat and train excursion that would take us deep into the jungle. Aboard the boat we passed tiny riverside villages where local children waved at us from the shore. We got within feet of Howler Monkeys, who hung from low branches to vocally illustrate how they got their name. We rode an ancient train to the beach, seeing sloths for the first time. It felt like Disney World but it was all very real. Like the trip into the Panama Canal, our Costa Rican adventure was enthralling.

Two days later we docked at Fort Lauderdale and the cruise was over. For a guy who only began cruising after his 40th birthday, I'm well versed in the sadness of that last day. If only we could find a way to make each hour of a cruise pass as slowly as they did in high school math class, instead of sprinting by at warp speed, the whole experience would be even better.

We disembarked on a warm sunny morning and took a taxi straight to the airport. We boarded our plane and flew north. When we landed at MSP it was roughly 80 degrees colder than it had been when we took off. Welcome home.

It was time to get to work.

As an outsider, prior to joining Team Wilkerson Racing, I'd had mostly favorable opinions about the organization. I was happy Tim had made the commitment to step up the pit area and hospitality center, while also bringing in a pro like Annette. I wanted to make an impact as well and the first part of doing that entailed the establishment of a TWR brand.

With the help of Boris at T-Shirts Unlimited, I came up with a very collegiate-looking "stacked" TWR logo. I'd make the pitch to Tim and the folks at LRS that the new logo should be on everything. It has been the official mark of TWR ever since.

I'd also been messing around in rudimentary ways regarding a design for the hospitality center. Having been the go-to guy for just about everything that wasn't a race car, a tool, or a shiny motor part, for 12 years, I figured I'd need to be that guy for TWR as well.

In early January, Annette and I met at a gate on the C concourse at MSP and boarded a flight to St. Louis. We'd be driving up to Springfield after we landed and then heading to the Hampton Inn across the road from the shop. The next morning Tim picked us up at our hotel and drove us over to the Levi, Ray & Shoup world headquarters to meet with the LRS marketing team, including the senior manager of marketing, Shannon Heisler, and her assistant Shelley Williams. Dick Levi even took time out of his busy schedule to meet us and welcome us aboard.

The things I learned that day were profound in many ways. Immediately upon entering the lobby of the headquarters I could tell the Funny Car was a focal point for the entire company. There's a huge framed photo of it right as you walk in. Everyone we met admitted to adoring Tim Wilkerson. LRS sales and marketing reps use the car, the hospitality center, and the races to generate considerable business. They were excited about the fresh direction Tim had taken and eager to hear our plans. And finally, I discovered what a huge asset we had in the person of Annette Schendel.

I had assumed she'd be a top-notch pro, thanks to her experience at DSR, but even with that as a baseline I was enormously impressed by her attention to detail, her passion for doing things the right way, and her complete understanding of how hospitality should work. I quickly realized how little I knew about how it all had to happen. She had answers to questions I'd never even pondered.

After that day of meetings, I knew how fortunate we were to have Annette on the team. And because she had it all nailed down expertly, I knew I could focus even more on PR and sponsor relations. She had hospitality covered.

At that first meeting I also made it a priority to better understand what LRS did. I knew, as an outsider, that not many fans or racers really had a good grasp on the company. Some thought it was a law firm.

LRS is an information technology company, which is a fancy way of saying they're a tech firm. The company has multiple divisions but the bread-and-butter was the division upon which Dick Levi founded the company. It's called Enterprise Output Management (EOM), which again is fancy wording for something pretty simple. Back when computers were first starting to show up on office desks Dick Levi was working in tech for the state of Illinois. They asked him to write the code to allow these various computers to communicate with each other and with printers. Things were that rudimentary at the time.

When he did that, he recommended they patent the code. They declined, so he patented it. It's the technology gift that keeps on giving. When the majority of people who own computers hit the "Print" button, that command is going through a licensed piece of LRS software.

As the company grew, Dick wasn't hesitant to branch out. Today, LRS has multiple divisions, each producing products that help streamline processes in a wide range of ways. In addition to the EOM branch, they provide tech solutions for retirement planning, network support, education services, web services, and more. If it's tech, they can handle it. Their world headquarters are in Springfield, Illinois, just a few miles from Team Wilkerson.

Another key part of my job would be the team's website. As part of the sponsorship LRS had its web services division maintain and host the site, and as the PR guy I'd be submitting my materials to a great guy named Andy Krug, who would "make it happen" when photos, bios, or press releases needed to be added. The only problem was the site was several years old and it needed a makeover. That would happen but everyone agreed we had our hands full getting ready for the 2009 season and it therefore made sense to postpone the makeover, and the corresponding training I would be receiving in order to be more self-reliant, until later.

What wasn't being postponed was a new paint scheme. With the move to the Mustang bodies there was a blank slate to work with and Tim had already shown Shannon and Dick a few renderings from the best Funny Car graphics designer in the business. If it could be dreamt, Greg Ozubko could bring it to life. And then some.

Dick Levi had a thing for flames in the paint scheme. He loved flames. The painted ones, not the real ones. No one much likes the real ones. As 2009 neared and he settled on the Ozubko design he liked the best, he said, "OK, this time no flames." Tim was shocked.

A few days later, after Greg adjusted the artwork, Dick took another look and said, "Nah. I think we need the flames, but just small ones down the lower part of the sides."

That was, at least, a step in the flameless direction.

Cars were painted, uniforms ordered, business cards printed, and in mid-January it was time to hit the track. Before heading to Pomona we'd make a quick trip to West Palm Beach for a test session attended by a large number of teams. It would be my first official trip to a track as the team manager and public relations rep for Team Wilkerson Racing.

To get to West Palm I'd have to make a connection in Atlanta. Anyone who has changed planes in Atlanta will know where I'm going with this.

I had a 90-minute layover, so it shouldn't have been any sort of problem. And then we were delayed an hour getting out of MSP. The pilot said we'd make much of it up while in the air and he thought everyone's connections would be fine. Air Traffic Control had other ideas.

ATC slowed us down and put us in a holding pattern and the minutes ticked by. Finally, we touched down exactly 25 minutes before my West Palm flight was due to leave. We seemed to taxi forever and do so very slowly. We pulled up to a gate. And we waited. There was no ground crew to guide us in.

The minutes were flying by. The pilot then came on the P.A. and said, "Well, they don't have a crew here so they've changed our gate. We have to move over to the B concourse." We had originally been going to the A concourse.

More taxiing. More minutes flying by. Less time for me to make it. After we did, mercifully, park at our gate on B, I dashed off the plane and found a monitor to see where I needed to go. I had to get back to the A concourse, just two gates away from where we were supposed to have parked. I ran to the escalator to get down to the underground train and waited for one to arrive. When it did I boarded the train and tapped my foot nervously as I rode it to the A concourse. Off the train I sprinted to another escalator and took it up to the gate level. As I turned the corner to arrive at my next flight, it was being pushed back by the ground crew. And, it was the last flight of the day to West Palm Beach.

Had we not been late from MSP, had ATC not slowed us down, and had we not wasted time sitting at an A gate until we moved to B, I would have been bored waiting for my connection. Instead, I was stranded.

Ever since we'd moved to Minnesota, Barbara and I had been Northwest Airlines fliers almost exclusively. No airlines are perfect but we were generally quite happy with how well they got us where we were going and how they treated us. In early 2008 we heard rumors we didn't necessarily like. Delta was in talks to merge with Northwest, if by "merge" you mean Delta was buying Northwest and integrating its people and planes into a new and bigger Delta. We hoped the rumors were untrue, but they not only were true they were actually happening. In late '08 the deal was approved. In 2009 the difficult merger began, although at first it was all behind-the-scenes and we continued to book our tickets on Northwest.com and fly on Northwest planes with Northwest crews.

The difficulty of turning two completely different airlines into one larger operation was monumental and there were plenty of growing pains. This day, and my missed connection, were a prime example.

I found a service desk and waited in line. In just a few minutes an agent called me forward and I explained my situation. A woman was next to me, working with another agent, and I could overhear them talking about the airline providing a hotel room for the night. The room would be at a Baymont Inn.

After I explained my missed connection the agent I was working with said, "Thank you for your loyalty and status Mr. Wilber. I'm reserving a king room for you at the Hilton and a voucher for dinner and breakfast. You'll be on an 8 o'clock flight tomorrow morning. We'll have your bag sent to baggage claim so you can have it with you tonight."

In the morning I checked my bag and flew down to West Palm. When I got off the plane, my bag did not. Apparently, at ATL they're really good about getting bags from one connecting flight to another but not so hot at making sure a bag checked 90 minutes before a flight actually gets on the plane with its owner.

I got in my rental car and headed to the racetrack, hoping my bag would be at the hotel by the time I got there that evening.

As I walked into the pits the first team I saw was Del's new group. Al-Anabi Racing was making its first appearance as an organization and I'd never seen so many shiny new things all in one place. Everything from the tool boxes to the transporters, the race cars to the scooters, and the tow vehicles to the uniforms looked 100 percent brand new. It was quite a sight.

Tim's transporter still had the same design it had sported for many years and many of the decals were either faded, torn, or peeling off altogether. The first new Mustang body was there, though, and it looked fantastic. Even with the small flames running down the sides. It still needed almost every possible decal, since all it had were the Levi, Ray, & Shoup logos on the sides and hood and a decal for Diversified Yacht Services (another one of Dick Levi's companies) on the spill plates, so I'd have plenty of work to keep me busy.

A few minutes later I saw Del in the lanes and after a hearty handshake he said, "Hey, that rock-and-roll guy you met once is here at the track. I can't remember his name, but I just saw him and he asked about you. He's probably still here."

I pieced that together and figured it out. The "rock-and-roll guy" was Fred Turner. I spotted him just a minute later.

In a most amazing coincidence, Fred and Donna were driving through Florida in his motorhome and they just happened to be on the small road that ran by the West Palm race track. As they approached Fred saw the big transporters and he pulled in. When he saw Del he asked about me. And there we were, in the same place at the same time. What, precisely, were the odds of that?

We had a great conversation and Fred hung out with us for a few hours. Fred was on that road, in his motorhome, because he detests flying. He told me that his flying issue was part of why he quit touring completely, because driving between all the shows in his bus created a never-ending schedule of gigs and highways and it was exhausting. Still, even then, if he was going to Florida he'd be doing it at the wheel of his motorhome. And he passed a race track he didn't even know was there.

Over the course of the next couple of days the guys got themselves in race shape and I took over the video responsibilities from Krista. Tim liked the view to be from directly behind the car so I'd be standing instead of kneeling, and I'd once again be the closest person to the race car every time it ran.

I also utilized the weekend to get to know my new teammates. Jeff Jacobs was Tim's "car chief" (although none of the guys technically had titles) and as such he was in charge of the service between runs, allowing Tim to focus on the tune-up. Kevin Wilkerson was Tim and Krista's youngest son. Rich Schendel, Annette's husband, was the most talented fabricator I'd ever been around. Brandon Lavely was a former soccer player and a hard-working clutch guy. Jon Gimmy was the closest to my age and since he lived just 90 minutes from St. Louis and we both loved a lot of the same classic rock, we figured we'd attended a few of the same concerts over the years. Nick Shaff was a bundle of energy and I quickly discovered why the team considered him "the Energizer Bunny." Sam Mattox was the newest and youngest crew guy.

Yes, my bag did finally arrive and our testing was mostly OK. I headed back home to Minnesota with Pomona looming just a few weeks away.

I'd not just joined the team by myself, though. I had indeed come as part of a package deal. Neighbor Dave would come to the races and work the marketing phones when we were home. John Fink didn't just come along, he was also kicking in some money as he'd usually done for the Worshams. With John came his buddies from home, Rick Strang and Jerry Muzzillo, who were always referred to, collectively, as Rick and Muzz. They were volunteers who cleaned parts and helped out wherever possible, typically attending about a dozen races a year.

Rick had a unique look. His nickname was and still is "Hippie Rick" thanks to his long, flowing locks of wavy blond hair. He perpetually kept it at shoulder length and he's still easy to spot on television when he and Muzz attend a race.

Eric Buttermore was also a friend of John's who would be attending a number of races on his own dime. He was a great guy who didn't mind getting his hands dirty or mixing fuel.

When we flew out to Pomona to kick off the 2009 season, hopes were high. After all, Wilk had not been knocked off the championship perch until the final day of 2008. We were all excited to get going but Mother Nature had another plan.

Rain washed out Thursday. More rain won the day on Friday. We were scheduled to make two passes Saturday to set the field.

On the first run, my first official lap with TWR, we had glitch after glitch. An air line that runs the timer system failed at the step of the throttle and the car shook the tires. Tim then pedaled it once and got it going again but by then his visor had fogged up and he really couldn't see very well. He limped it across the line with a 5.14 and was 17th.

It had been a nice day up until that point, with blue skies featuring a few puffy white clouds. But as the guys serviced the car for the second run, a large black cloud approached and it then parked itself right on top of the track. There was blue sky all around, but one large ominous cloud right over us.

It held off for a while but then opened up and washed out the rest of the day. NHRA set the field. At the first race on the heels of only one badly botched run, we had "earned" a DNQ. It was a heck of a way to kick things off.

I have, of course, been a part of a number of season-opening DNQs and as a PR guy I know the drill. If you're ever going to DNQ doing it at the Winternationals in Pomona is the best option. You will leave there only a round (plus qualifying points) behind eight teams. And you have the rest of the season to make that up.

In addition, Tim was genuinely not that worried about it. He said, "Hey, if we would've run all four sessions and smoked the tires all four times, looking like knuckleheads, then I'd be a little concerned. We got one run in and had some glitches. We'll be fine."

A couple of weeks later the luck reversed. In Phoenix Wilk made only one full under-power run Sunday but ended up with a semifinal finish by out-pedaling John Force and Jack Beckman in the first two rounds before losing a close one to Mike Neff in the semis. Despite the Pomona DNQ Wilk was actually ahead of his pace from 2008 when he started the season 0-2.

Our team's performance picked up a bit going forward but it was mostly a string of second- or third-round endings, with no trips to the finals. From Gainesville in March through Denver in July, Wilk went 12-11 making him 14-12 heading into Seattle.

One of the highlights in that stretch of events happened in Topeka when a second LRS Funny Car and a second Wilkerson competed in the race. Daniel Wilkerson made his highly anticipated debut as a professional at my original stomping grounds. Not only did "D Wilk" make the field, he out-qualified his dad while doing so, landing in the No. 8 spot to Tim's No. 12. It was a stressful weekend for everyone involved but it got Daniel's feet wet and we were all really proud of him.

As for me there was definitely an adjustment and a learning curve during the first half of the campaign. While Tim and Del are both extraordinarily great people they have distinct personalities and approaches to the operation. Del is still very much "the kid from the coast" and Tim is every bit "Springfield's own" with his Midwestern down-home values.

When people would ask me what it was like, after 12 years with Del, I'd say, "It's great, and I'm thrilled I'm here. I'm just adjusting to being much more of a PR guy and less of a manager. Del was extremely low maintenance. Tim, in a lot of ways, is no maintenance at all."

Tim was so hands-on I didn't have as much managing to do. I did bring my decal skills to the team and I think that took some work off of a few people's plates but in terms of getting him where he needed to be to sign autographs or walk on the stage for driver introductions, at the specific time he was supposed to be there, I just let him do his normal thing. He was used to doing it all himself.

What I liked the most about Tim and Krista from the first day I joined them was the laughter. He takes his racing absolutely seriously but Tim loves to laugh and he's a very funny guy. I could crack him up, he had me in stitches often, and we both kept Krista laughing almost constantly. That's a good thing because she's a worrier and gets stressed out fairly easily. In short order I became her best friend at the track and I took it upon myself to keep her loose and as stress-free as possible. Our friendship blossomed into something truly special.

As we rolled into Seattle, still looking for that first final round of the year, we were one crew member short. Sam had left the team the day before racing began in Denver, needing to attend to some family issues back home. He would never return.

To get through that race Neighbor Dave and Annette pitched in with parts, tires, and support while I did all I could to make sure our heavily attended hospitality weekend went smoothly. Denver features a massive Saturday hospitality crowd as Dick Levi hosts family and friends. Somehow, we all managed.

In Seattle we got off to a decent start in qualifying and that's always a good thing. Getting down the track in Q1 gives the team confidence and it also gives the tuner a chance to stretch things out, knowing a spot in the field is assured. By the end of Friday we were sitting No. 3.

On Saturday we found the edge and stepped over it in Q3, smoking the tires. With a more conservative "just get down the track" approach in Q4 we ended up going into race day from the No. 7 spot.

On Sunday, we faced the always-tough Robert Hight in round one as the first pair. Tim left on Robert by a little then made his best run of the weekend with a 4.180 to take the win. We were all pretty charged up as a we left the starting line.

In round two, again running as the first pair, we needed to get by Mike Neff who along with Robert Hight and John Force made up the three-headed JFR Funny Car juggernaut, to advance to the semifinals. Wilk got a slight advantage off the line but Neff stayed with him the length of the track. Tim won by a couple of feet. It was getting interesting. Something about it felt like it was our day, but Ron Capps was our next opponent so it only got tougher as we went.

Running as the first pair for the third straight round, Wilk again got a little edge at the tree and held on for another round win, running strong on a tough track. We were going to our first final round of the year and we'd face Tony Pedregon there.

Pedregon would not be the only challenge in the final. The sun was beginning to be a real issue as it can be anytime the Pacific Northwest clouds aren't around to block it. During Friday qualifying NHRA often stops the Funny Car session to let the sun set during Q2 because the track runs east to west and the drivers can be blinded.

427

In the Sunday final the sun was just beginning to become a nuisance but things went off as scheduled. Wilk was a little late off the line this time but his 4.211 was enough for him to drive around Pedregon for the race win. We celebrated at the line with some serious gusto and complete sincerity. It was a big win for all of us.

Afterward Tim was quoted as saying, "It was getting pretty late in the day and the sun was becoming a problem. I guess that would sound pretty dumb to anyone who lives in Seattle, that the sun would ever be a problem, but when you can barely see the tree and barely see the lane you're running in it's a bit of a worry, let me tell you. I just pointed it straight and went on instinct."

His instincts were clearly right on point.

After the winner's circle festivities, the guys put the car away and Tim asked Dave and me to go scout out a restaurant for dinner. We drove up the hill to I-5 and found a nice steakhouse then called our winning driver with directions.

As we were wrapping up dinner the tape-delayed race was airing on ESPN2 and the bartender was kind enough to put it on the TV behind the bar. It was more than just a little surreal to watch Tim stand there with his eyes glued to a television that was showing him at work. We got to cheer again, all over, when our car crossed the finish line first.

Having become part of TWR just in time for a season-opening DNQ I can assure you that it felt fantastic for me to join the team in a celebration like that one. Yes, I clinked my glass and said a few words. We were getting on a roll and I could feel it.

After a quick flight home it was back on the road to Sonoma just three days later, flying into Sacramento for the first time as part of a travel experiment. Most people fly into San Francisco and some fly into Oakland but neither option is all that good in terms of freeway traffic. From San Francisco you also have to actually drive through the city on surface streets for a few miles just to get to the Golden Gate Bridge. To me, Sacramento looked like it might be worth a try. I was happy to see it work like a charm. No fuss, no muss, and at the hotel in just over 90 minutes.

Finkster and I would also be staying at a different hotel than the team. Tim knew a hotel owner who ran a place in Fairfield, east of Sonoma on I-80. The owner offered nice rooms for a very good rate, especially when compared to any of the places near Sonoma, Napa, Novato, or San Rafael. The downside was the fact Fairfield is 45 minutes from the track, on a good day. There just aren't that many good days in terms of traffic, in that part of the world. Plus, coming in from the east requires a trip across Route 37, a two-lane bridge/causeway across the North Bay that backs up easily and all too often. John and I wanted nothing to do with that drama so we booked rooms at the Sheraton Four-Points in San Rafael. We'd stayed there a few times with the Worsham team and were comfortable with the drive.

We picked up right where we'd left off in qualifying, landing No. 8 after Q1 and No. 4 after Q2 which is always the Sonoma "home run" session as the sun sets and the track cools rapidly. Under much hotter conditions on Saturday we smoked the tires both times but still entered the race No. 4. We'd face Jeff Arend, who was driving the former Scott Kalitta DHL car for Connie Kalitta, in round one.

The marine layer cloud-deck is always tricky in Sonoma. It's tricky all over the Bay Area and it can roll in or dissipate almost without warning, changing the temperature by as much as 10 degrees in mere minutes.

It usually burns off by mid-morning at the track but it hung on long enough to keep the temperature at just 68 degrees for round one.

Tim and Del had many things in common when it came to racing, and one of those was related to pairings. If given the choice they'd both take the first pair in round one. Going first negated the advantage the multi-car teams normally held, because they'd have no chance to watch teammates run. Wilk and Jeff Arend would be the first pair in Sonoma. Both drivers left nearly identically and Jeff made a strong lap but Wilk's 4.176 was a full car length better. We'd won five consecutive rounds.

By round two the marine layer was retreating and things were heating up fast. Air temperature was up to 76 and the track temp was up to 114 degrees. We faced our teammate Bob Tasca.

Wilk again got a tiny edge at the tree, leaving maybe one inch in front of Tasca. Both cars ran extremely well locked in a side-by-side race the length of the track. Margin of victory at the stripe: 0.0066-seconds. Winner: Tim Wilkerson. Streak: Six straight rounds.

The air temp was up to 80 for the semifinals with the track up to 119. We faced Gary Densham, who was running as an independent, and Gary had gotten by John Force and Cruz Pedregon to earn his way there.

He wouldn't get any further. Wilk got away with a substantial reaction time edge of more than four-hundredths and Densham was never a threat to catch him. Our 4.204 was easily enough to advance to our second consecutive final. Streak: Seven straight rounds.

The final would be a repeat of Seattle. Tony Pedregon, who had qualified 10th and beaten Del, Mike Neff, and Robert Hight to advance, would line up in the other lane.

I wasn't nervous. I wasn't worried, either. I was more inquisitive as to how this would all work out. Could we win two races in a row after not having been to a final at the first 13? Could we make another clean and competitive lap, in tricky conditions on a 121-degree track? Could we beat Tony Pedregon in two straight finals?

The answers were: Yes, Yes, and Yes.

Tim was behind off the line and still behind at 660 feet, but the LRS car stayed planted while Tony's car began to spin the tires. We took the stripe with a 4.249. We'd done it again.

There are so many different kinds of emotions when you win a race. There's the literal explosion of happiness when you win that first one. When you get on a roll, and they start to come regularly, it shifts into pride and satisfaction although you never get over the instant of pure excitement when the win lights come on. When it's something epic, like winning Indy and doubling up with a Showdown win, it's almost inconceivable how much emotion can pour out of you in just seconds. In Sonoma it was mostly along the lines of a quick and emotional celebration at the starting line followed by a winner's circle deal that was full of the warm satisfaction of a job well done. We were in fourth place in the standings and we were proud to be there.

So, because drag racing is like this, we then went 0-4 at Brainerd, Reading, Indy, and Charlotte. Heroes to zeroes in no time flat.

We managed to pick up a round win in Dallas and then headed to Memphis, where Daniel would once more be racing a second Levi, Ray & Shoup Mustang.

Daniel again out-qualified his dad, landing eighth to Tim's 11th. He'd be racing Ron Capps in round one on Sunday. Tim would race Tasca. Except nobody faced anybody on Sunday. We were rained out.

On Monday, Daniel and Capps squared off as the first pair. It was only Daniel's second round as a pro but he showed that natural Wilkerson talent by leaving first and getting a 2-hundredths edge at the tree.

His LRS car left cleanly and Daniel was pulling away from Capps. It appeared a huge upset was in the making. I was standing behind the starting line shooting the video. I couldn't fathom what I saw next.

As Daniel's car kept driving away I was just beginning to feel a glimmer of hope that he'd get his first round win when, in an instant, I saw the entire left side of Daniel's car while I also caught a peripheral view of a tire and wheel assembly leaving the car and bouncing down the track.

I have that bad habit of clicking the camera off whenever I see something totally wrong happen. I never had an explanation for that when Del would ask why I couldn't keep taping. My thumb just did it. My thumb did it again that Monday in Memphis. By the time Daniel's car crossed the track at full speed, narrowly (and fortunately) missing Capps' car by mere inches and then crashing head-on into the far-side guardwall, the camera was off. I was sickened by what I'd seen and horribly worried about him. He'd hit the wall nose-first, and hard.

The impact tore the body off the car but Daniel wrestled with the wheel to straighten it out. As he scraped down the guardwall he had no rear wheels on the car at all.

Seconds became an eternity. We waited for word on the radio. Finally, one of the guys on Daniel's crew said, "He's OK. He says he's OK, and he's getting out of the car." The relief was enormous.

As I turned to walk back to the pit Chris Cunningham's wife Sheila stopped me and said, "Bob, go get Krista! She's walking down the track."

Yes she was. With her hands over her mouth she was walking slowly toward the wreck, almost sleepwalking. I ran to her and put my arm around her shoulder saying, "He's OK. He's fine. He's out of the car."

She leaned into me, with my arm around her shoulders, and we walked back to the lanes in silence.

Tim had been two pairs back, already strapped in his car and around the corner a bit, so he never saw the wreck. When he heard about it he unbuckled and got out of his car. I know he was disappointed I'd turned the camera off but my instinct had again overruled any conscious plan at that point.

Tim got on a scooter and went down to Daniel while the rest of us waited. It was going to take a while to clean the track.

Finally, when Daniel came back to the starting line I immediately hooked him up with Dave Rieff to do an ESPN segment on what had just transpired. Then we went up to the P.A. booth so that Bob Frey could talk to him and so Daniel could talk to the fans.

Somehow, some way, Tim had to get back in his car and race after coming too close to losing his son. None of us were too keen to do it.

He managed to hold his routines together well enough to beat Tasca, but we then lost to Ashley Force-Hood in round two. It was time to investigate.

Daniel said he'd watched a crew member torque the lug nuts on both rear wheels. He was certain they were tight. The only remaining sensible answer would likely be wheel stud breakage, and that was indeed what happened. If the studs shear it doesn't matter how well the nuts are torqued, and once one wheel was off the force on the other took it off as well. It was a horrific accident, but all of the safety equipment worked. Eric Medlen and Scott Kalitta each had a hand in saving Daniel's life.

Back in the pit I knew the kid was OK when he recounted the lap. He said, "It was just truckin' man, and going dead straight. Then all of a sudden I felt a bump and I was sideways. I saw Capps fly by and I was thinking 'I got this, I got this' as I tried to steer it to the right. Then I realized, 'I don't got this' and it hit the wall."

I looked at the chassis in the trailer and couldn't believe it. Everything on the front of the car was smashed all the way back to the blower and block. The top pulley on the blower was the most forward thing left. And he walked away.

Tim was quoted as saying, "I'm not going to sit here and tell you that I was able to turn off the switch and not think about it but you have to give these cars 100 percent of your attention, so I was able to get back into my race mode and we did OK."

Amazing.

At the next race, in Richmond, two cool things happened. We went to our third final of the year, beating Cruz, Hight, and Neff to get there, which was great, but we lost to Del in the final. The other totally cool thing also happened on Sunday, when we had a special visitor.

Former Top Fuel driver Bob Vandergriff is an outstanding golfer, and a fine all-around athlete. At a celebrity golf tournament somewhere he'd met Detroit Tigers pitcher Justin Verlander, who is from Virginia. With us racing there right after the conclusion of the MLB regular season, and with the Tigers just missing the playoffs, Justin had called Bob to see if he could hang out with him and experience the race. The only problem with that idea was the fact Bob had already decided to not compete in Richmond. So Bob called me.

"Hey, do you know who Justin Verlander is?" he asked.

"Are you kidding me, of course I do. He's incredible," I replied.

So we set it up for us to host Justin, his parents, and his brother on Sunday in our hospitality center. I kept an eye on the area out front and recognized Justin as soon as I saw him.

We had a great time and Bob had already filled him in that I had played some minor league ball, so I think Justin and his family felt right at home. The entire Verlander family could not have been more gracious and they all enjoyed themselves enormously.

Just five days earlier, at the Metrodome in Minneapolis, Barbara and I witnessed the single greatest baseball game either one of us had ever seen and as I've documented here I've seen more than a few. It involved the Twins and Verlander's Tigers, although he did not pitch in the game.

The Tigers had been in first place for much of the season and held a seven-game lead over the Twins as late as September 6. They put together a decent September, going 16-12, but the Twins picked up a couple of games in the standings. When the Tigers lost two of their final three games while the Twins were winning their final three games, the two teams ended up in a tie. They would have to play Game 163, a one-game tiebreaker, to settle it.

The Metrodome was packed, despite the Twins having only two days to sell tickets. Barbara and I felt lucky to get seats out in center field.

The game itself was an intense rollercoaster.

It was scoreless through two innings but the Tigers quieted the raucous crowd by scoring three in the top of the third, with the big shot being a two-run homer by Miguel Cabrera.

The Twins got the crowd back into it with a run in the bottom of the inning then scored one more in the sixth to make it 3-2. When Orlando Cabrera hit a two-run bomb in the bottom of the seventh, the Twins took a 4-3 lead. The Metrodome was rocking.

But Magglio Ordonez went deep in the top of the eighth, and we had a 4-4 tie on our hands. The ups and downs were relentless.

The 162-game regular season had needed a 163rd game. The 163rd game of the season needed extra innings. And the Tigers struck first, scoring a run in the 10th. With the season on the line the Twins got the run back in the bottom of the inning, after Michael Cuddyer led off with a triple and later scored on a base hit.

Alexi Casilla was on third as the potential winning run and when Nick Punto hit a line drive to left I think everyone in the ballpark thought the game was over. We were cheering hard, but the Tigers left-fielder made a strong play to catch the ball and Casilla hesitated before tagging up and leaving third. He was barely tagged out at the plate. We were going to the 11th. I was hoarse.

Both teams were held scoreless in the tense 11th.

In the top of the 12th the Tigers loaded the bases with just one out and when pitcher Bobby Keppel threw an inside pitch to Tigers' hitter Brandon Inge it appeared it might have grazed his jersey. Had home-plate umpire Randy Marsh felt that way the Tigers would've taken the lead, once again. He called it a ball.

Inge then hit a slow roller to Nick Punto at second, who had to make a split-second decision. Inge ran well and Punto was in front of second base by the time he caught the grounder. A double-play would get the Twins off the field, but Punto knew it would be hard to double-up Inge on a ball hit that slowly. He instinctively fired the ball home and got the force out by a step. Keppel struck out the next batter and we went to the bottom of the 12th, still tied.

With Carlos Gomez at second after a lead-off single and a ground out, Casilla made up for his earlier miscue on the bases by hitting a single to right. Gomez could fly, and he dove home safe to score the winning run. 5-4, in 12 innings. I thought the inflated Metrodome roof might just blow right off. It was the most exciting game I'd ever witnessed, considering the lead changes, the big plays, the clutch performances, and what was at stake.

In Richmond with Verlander, just those few days later, I concentrated the baseball talk on the fact I'd played in the Tigers' organization, as well. I didn't mention Game 163. Justin had gone 18-9 that year. It was his breakout season as a pitcher. He was about to reap the significant monetary rewards of pitching that well in the big leagues. That offseason, he signed a 10-year contract worth $219 million.

Two years later, in 2011, he went 24-5 with a 2.40 ERA and 250 strikeouts in 251 innings. He won the Cy Young Award unanimously. Days later he also won the American League Most Valuable Player Award. He'd had a great time with Team Wilk in '09 but I'm guessing those events ranked slightly higher on his favorites list.

Back on the tour, the last two races were in Vegas and Pomona. We went 2-1 at each race, concluding my first season with Team Wilkerson at 31-21. We had finished fourth in the points.

When Pomona was over I left the track and headed back to the hotel. Clearly, Wilk was not going to host a pit party like the raucous one we'd held each year with Del and I didn't really feel like cruising around looking to see which teams were going to step into the void. I was just tired.

As I walked toward the media parking area north of the staging lanes, I heard someone shout out my name in the way only blog readers did. I signed off each blog with the line, "Wilber, out!" so entire legions of readers only shouted what this particular guy yelled, as he jogged toward me. He said, "Hey, Wilber."

He looked like a cool dude and he was excited to tell me he'd been reading the blog forever and he loved it. He said he was in a band, called The Asphalt, and he handed me their new CD as a gift.

"I was hoping I'd see you tonight, and I want you to have this," he said. "I'm the drummer, and reading in the blog what kind of music you like I thought you might like some of this. Let me know what you think." His name was Nick Turner.

That was pretty cool. When I got home I downloaded it to my phone so I could listen at the gym while I worked out. It was fantastic. They were a regional band, hooking up on bigger tours for sets of dates, and I could tell Nick was fine percussionist. Another interesting friendship formed thanks to the blog. Thanks, blog!

We all headed home. My first year with Team Wilk was in the books.

The prior year, after the heartbreaking loss of the championship on the final day, the unofficial group that called themselves Wilk's Warriors had held a banquet for Tim and the team in Springfield. It was a big deal and got plenty of news coverage in the Springfield press.

Dan "Dozer" Hough was the man behind it all, and he had a lot of help from others to pull it off. By all accounts, it was a roaring success. He wanted to do it again in 2009.

Dozer was also the man behind the Warriors. A local funeral director, he had been a fan and a friend of Wilk's since the beginning. He was passionate and well-connected in the community and he should always get the credit for spreading the word and bringing hundreds of people into the Warriors group. There's no better fan base in the sport. None.

The banquet for '09 actually happened just after the new year, and Barbara and I made the trip. It was spectacular. The hotel ballroom was packed, a great band rocked the house, and then Dozer said a few words, I said a few, and Tim thanked everyone for coming. I'd never seen anything like it. A totally unofficial fan-driven banquet that was as nice as anything I'd ever been a part of.

That night, I became a Warrior and a true member of the family. What a year it had been and I was already counting the days to get back out there and do it again in 2010.

I'd noticed, throughout the year, that a lot of Worsham fans had followed me over to Wilk's team when I made the transition. They'd typically ask me, "So how do I become one of Wilk's Warriors?"

I'd say, "It's easy. You just believe that you are one. After that, you're in."

New Races, New Places

Barbara and I were wrapping up a bunch of big projects by the time 2010 arrived. We had decided to hire Jeff Russell again, after the great work he did on our screened porch and patio.

Everything he'd done for us was gorgeous and it made our house incrementally a little bit more of a home. Our home. The next big deal was our master bath. Jeff and his talented guys basically gutted the place then replaced the rickety shower door with a thick seamless glass enclosure, new tile, and multiple shower jets. The original builder's-grade floor was replaced with custom tile, painstakingly cut and installed at a creative diagonal, while the original and practically useless triangular jetted tub was ripped out to make room for a fabulous deep soaker with forced-air bubbles. By the time I was ready to leave for Pomona Jeff and his guys were finishing up, and it felt as though our entire house had been upgraded. A remodeled master bath will do that.

Another benefit of getting to know Jeff was our mutual appreciation of Minnesota Wild hockey. Jeff owned two season-tickets in the second row behind one of the goals and he was thrilled to sell us 10 games. We loved those seats. Being that close to the glass in a location where big, burly NHL hockey players often crashed and collided at full speed was a rush, and we cheered for our Wild with vigor.

We had officially become Minnesota sports fans of the highest order. We had the 10 Wild games from Jeff, we'd had a 20-game plan with the Twins with lower level seats down the right-field line at the Metrodome and were excited to be moving outside at Target Field in April. We'd also been given Timberwolves basketball tickets when Barb bought a new 2010 Lexus.

When I saw the marketing materials in the showroom, boldly offering Timberwolves tickets to new-car buyers during that particular month, I also spotted the small type at the bottom of the poster. It read "While Supplies Last." I could see that coming a mile away.

We were buying the car anyway — we hadn't even discovered the promotion until the deal was done — but when she signed the papers to close the sale I asked about the promotion and the general manager said, "Oh yeah. We're a major sponsor of the Timberwolves. They'll be in touch with you within a matter of days." I was still skeptical.

Less than a week later I got a call from a young man who introduced himself as Conor Noonan, a Wolves sales rep. He welcomed me to the Wolves family and said he had my ticket order processed and they were great seats. He then offered to meet me outside Target Center to hand-deliver them if I had time to drive over to Minneapolis that afternoon. I did, but I was still skeptical. One man's great seats can be another man's nosebleeds.

I pulled up to the main entrance on 1st Avenue, diagonally across the street from the music club of the same name. First Avenue, the club, was made famous in the Prince movie "Purple Rain."

Conor approached my car and introduced himself. He was a really young guy but he could not have been more professional. When he handed me a pair of tickets he said, "Here are your tickets for this weekend. The rest of your full-season tickets will be mailed to you tomorrow in a special welcome packet. I just wanted to make sure you had these."

Full-season tickets. I was flabbergasted. And then I looked at the pair of tickets he'd handed me. They were in the "Lexus Courtside" section. Row 7. Unbelievable.

With 41 games worth of seventh-row tickets there was no way Barbara and I could make even half of those games, but we were successful in sharing them with friends and neighbors. Conor's professionalism, treating us like his most prized customers despite the fact we had not spent a penny on the tickets, was one of the most outstanding examples of customer service I'd ever seen. In the future I'd buy 10-game packages of center-court tickets just to show my appreciation, and twice Conor upgraded us to seats directly on the floor. It really doesn't get any better than that.

In addition to the new living spaces at home and the new basketball tickets, one additional major change was afoot as I prepared to head for Pomona to kick off the 2010 NHRA season. Dave Jacobsen would not be making the tour with me after more than two years as a teammate.

Dave had done a marvelous job for us and was highly respected, but landing big sponsorships is one of the most challenging sales endeavors I've ever been a part of and he'd been doing it on a commission basis. I knew firsthand how expensive it was to travel the full tour, since I'd always worked as a contractor who paid his own way. The difference between us was that this was my full-time job and I was therefore paid a salary to help offset those tax-deductible expenses, but he was not. He decided to go back into the optical business full-time. A nice steady income is a good thing.

When we convened at the racetrack in Pomona the guys all posed around the Funny Car and had me take a photo of them. They were holding a sign that said "We Miss Dave." I did too. We'd shared too many priceless moments on the tour to count. He was still my favorite neighbor but he was no longer my sidekick on the road.

When I arrived at the hotel that first night I heard my phone chime to alert me to a text message. It was from my hockey buddy Jeff Finger.

Normally, the NHL season would have been in full swing in early February but 2010 was a Winter Olympics year and almost all the NHL's biggest stars were playing in the games, up in Vancouver. The NHL schedule included an unusual two-week break to allow those players to participate.

Jeff thought that was as good a reason as any to head to L.A. for the drags. He spent a full day with us and it was a great way to further cement our friendship.

Tim made a couple of decent passes during qualifying but ended up 11th. On Sunday, we smoked the tires just past half-track and Ashley Force Hood sent us home. Not the start we were hoping for, but better than the DNQ from 2009.

Just five days later we were back on the track in Phoenix but the results were the same. We qualified in the bottom half and then lost in the first round, although Robert Hight edged Wilk by only 32 thousandths of a second. We were pretty adept at the whole "losing by inches" thing.

Maybe Gainesville, three weeks later, would be the catalyst to get us going.

My pre-race feature story for the Gatornationals was based on the theory of "hitting the reset button" on our young season. All along, Wilk had planned to use Gainesville as the event where we would bring out our first 2010 Shelby Mustang body while also putting it atop a reworked Murf McKinney chassis. It was actually Tim's chassis from 2008 but Murf had put a new front half on it and Wilk was eager to run it again. It was a fresh start, and as such it entailed a full day of decal applications. I had them spread all over the hospitality area while I dodged the raindrops that plagued the first two days of racing.

The new car was fantastic. With one session rained out we made just three runs prior to eliminations but all three showed great promise, as Tim sorted out all the new stuff. We qualified ninth with Dick Levi and many of his guests from Fort Myers-based Diversified Yacht Services in attendance.

On Sunday we practiced another Gainesville necessity by leaving the hotel well before dawn in order to beat the traffic. On another cool and overcast day we faced Jeff Arend in round one as the final pair. It wasn't close, as Wilk put a 4.188 on the board while Jeff smoked the big Goodyear slicks.

In round two we faced Matt Hagan. Wilk got away first (albeit by just two thousandths) and when Hagan had to pedal his mount, Wilk's new Ford powered to a clean 4.094. That put us in the semifinals with lane choice over Tony Pedregon.

The other semifinal featured our teammates from next door. After soundly defeating Jack Beckman and Robert Hight in the first two rounds Bob Tasca would face Ron Capps in his semi.

We both won. Wilk took out Tony P with another strong run while Tasca also made a clean lap to beat Capps. There would be a Shelby Mustang going to the winner's circle. It was just a matter of which one. Pomona and Phoenix already felt like ancient history.

In the final, Wilk grabbed a substantial edge at the tree, leaving more than two hundredths quicker than Bob. He never trailed.

Our 4.097 was too quick to catch and we leapt into each other's arms as we bounced in joy at the starting line. From 0-2 to 4-2 in just one day. We scrambled to get to the top end as quickly as we could to congratulate the boss. The new car had done OK. We'd reset our young season.

It felt great to go through all the post-race hoopla again and we relished posing for every photo. Once we got back to the pit Wilk told the guys to put the car away. We were going out to dinner.

It had already been a long day with a 5:00 a.m. alarm, and it was going to be a long night for me. I would stay with my team until dinner was over at the restaurant, imbibing in nothing more than iced tea, but then I had a 200-mile drive ahead of me.

I'd been getting updates on Taffy from my sister Mary, who lived in Sarasota. She kept me apprised of Taffy's ups and downs and made it clear the dementia was now in full dastardly bloom. Taffy didn't recognize her when she'd visit and with her mind so clouded our mother was also in a steep physical decline. I knew she'd likely not know who I was but I wanted to see her. I figured it might be my final chance.

Once dinner was over I hit the interstate and headed south, finally pulling into the parking lot at the Holiday Inn in Sarasota around 1 a.m. It wasn't until I walked in my room and set my bag down that I realized how completely exhausted I was.

In the morning, Mary picked me up and we headed for the assisted living facility. It was the fourth different version of such a place Taffy had been in, as Mary moved her into more and more secure locations. We found her curled up in a big floppy chair in the main communal living area. When I said hello I wondered if it was my imagination telling me that she seemed to recognize me.

After spending 20 minutes with her, we let her go back to sleep. As we walked out Mary said, "My gosh, she was locked on you like a laser beam. I think she knew you were her son. She hasn't looked at me like that in months."

I was overcome with sadness but still felt better knowing I'd seen her. She clearly didn't have much time left and her quality of life was miserable. I left knowing, deep in my heart, that she'd be going to a much better place in the near future. We could only hope she'd go peacefully.

Two weeks after Gainesville the NHRA tour arrived in Charlotte to try something very different. It was the inaugural 4-Wide Nationals and nobody really knew what to expect. Actually, I think we all did expect one particular thing: A lot of confusion. But we were also eager to check it out.

The 4-Wide race brought with it all sorts of things the drivers, tuners, crew members, and PR reps had never dealt with before. The most glaring, obviously, was the presence of four lanes at zMAX Dragway, with race cars in all four.

The first thing the drivers had to cope with was the Christmas Tree. The tree now had to help four different drivers stage their cars and then go. The process had a pretty good chance of being a mess.

The first tree for the 4-Wides was the same style as the current tree at the time but it had four sets of yellow incandescent Pre-Stage and Stage bulbs representing the four lanes. It was amazingly confusing and completely counterintuitive for drivers who had never before gotten out of their starting-line routines.

The crew chiefs had to figure out a way to make sure everyone was ready to go after the burnouts. At every race up until that weekend the two crew chiefs would make eye contact and nod at each other when they were ready. In Charlotte, there were two more crew chiefs and nodding would be too confusing. So, they got together and agreed each crew chief would raise his hand when his car was ready. When the fourth hand went up, they all walked away.

For the crew guys at the starting line there was then the confusion of figuring out who had won a lap and who had come in second, because two cars would advance in each round of eliminations. All of us had spent our entire careers looking for just one set of win lights, hopefully in our lane. Now we had to find two sets, out of four options, on two gigantic scoreboards. It was really hard to keep it all straight. It was hard to even know what lane we were in.

For the PR reps who kept team stats there was the problem of figuring out who you had won or lost against. Many of us kept detailed stats for our team, including annual head-to-head statistics against all the other drivers in the class. Elon Werner and Dave Densmore of John Force Racing, the most powerful 1-2 punch in all of NHRA public relations, did it by not doing it. They didn't include any head-to-head marks but counted the rounds.

I thought it made sense to do it this way: If you finished first, you beat the third-place driver. If you finished second, you beat the fourth-place driver.

We agreed, though, that there was no way to effectively track head-to-head at the 4-Wides in a way that would always allow the numbers to jive. The key was the final round which was also effectively the semifinal. If you lost there, you finished with a semifinal in your stats. If you finished second, you were the runner up. If your driver won the race, he or she would've technically beaten two drivers in that round. Elon thought it was just fine for me to do it my way while they did it their way, because neither of our numbers were official NHRA stats.

Somehow we all managed to get somewhat accustomed to the whole enormous deal, and we did manage to pull it off. As Tim put it, "It's a bit of a spectacle."

It was chilly on race day and everyone was bundled up when Tim appeared on the "NHRA Race Day" show on ESPN2, with Dave Rieff and Mike Dunn. I went up to the stage with him and in the background I saw a couple I vaguely recognized. The woman was holding up a large "Got Wilk" sign she'd made, hoping to get it on TV.

I didn't know them but I'd been seeing them at more and more races and they hung around our pit quite a bit. They also looked like really nice people.

After the show I approached them to introduce myself. Jim and Nancy Butler were from the northern part of Illinois and they considered themselves big Wilk fans because of their shared home state. Once those introductions were over and we all got to know them a little, they were adopted into our inner circle. Within a few years they would even volunteer to mix fuel and clean parts. Terrific people.

We qualified pretty well in Charlotte, then raced in a group that included Ron Capps, Melanie Troxel and Jeff Diehl. To advance we'd need to be quicker than at least two of those three drivers. Diehl was up in smoke instantly but Melanie made it a three-way race. It was amazing how difficult it was for our brains to remember the number of the lane we were in and then figure out if the corresponding number on the scoreboard was illuminated. We all hesitated to cheer, because we couldn't instantly grasp it. But we had come in second, trailing only Capps, and would be moving on.

In the second round, racing John Force, Jack Beckman, and Capps, Tim did something I imagine no other driver had done to that point and maybe none have done since. He had low e.t. of the round, outrunning all three of them, but did not advance and he did not foul. If round one confused us, round two had our heads spinning. The math looked like this:

Lane 1: Ron Capps - 4.064 seconds
Lane 2: Tim Wilkerson - 4.061 seconds
Lane 3: Jack Beckman - 4.505 seconds
Lane 4: John Force - 4.064 seconds

We lost on a double hole-shot. At the line, a .000 reaction to the tree is perfect. If a Funny Car driver is "perfect" he's just lucky. It can't be done. Anything between .040 and .050 is outstanding. Tim never pushed it. The risk of red-lighting was too great. He was consistently in the .070 to .090 range. On this lap, Tim had cut his standard everyday-of-the-week .080 light. Force was .041 and Capps was .068, and they both won with identical slower times. It's a weird sport to begin with but when four drivers are going after it at once it's like the weirdness factor isn't just doubled, it's squared.

The other thing that seemed squared instead of doubled was the sound at the starting line. The first time four cars launched at once, during an exhibition the year before, I went up to the line wearing my standard Mac Tools earmuffs. It felt like I had no ear protection at all. For the 4-Wide race I put in the best pair of earplugs I could find first, then my ear-muffs over them. It was still incredibly loud, and shooting the video was made more of a challenge by the enormity of the concussion made by 40,000 collective horsepower.

When we got to Houston two weeks later it seemed absolutely quaint and miniature. No gigantic stadium grandstand with suites along the top, just regular old bleachers. Only two lanes, known as "left" and "right" instead of 1-2-3-4. Only two cars at a time, running in standard pairs instead of quads. Going back to normal was nearly as big an adjustment as the 4-Wide thing had been.

From Charlotte through Englishtown (a span of eight races) we were a nice and consistent 6-8, which ran our record to 10-10 on the year. That was OK, but we new we needed some more wins.

Barbara and I also needed a quick getaway. We had a mutual weekend off after the Vegas race, so we decided to use it for a visit to Austin. We'd only been back once since we moved to Minnesota and the allure of seeing the McCarley family and having at least one dinner at Chuy's was an enormous pull.

We had a terrific time, and it struck me just how easily Robert and I slid right back into being dear friends. When they invited us to their house for a few hours we got to spy on our old house next door. It looked pretty nice.

The McCarleys were clearly friends of the highest order, and the kids were getting huge. It was a weekend well spent.

We were off to Bristol after Englishtown and that race ended up being a win that got away. We qualified in the No. 8 spot and got by Melanie Troxel in the first round. In round two, No. 1 qualifier Ashley Force Hood was a game competitor in a side-by-side race featuring late tire spin, but she ran out of real estate and Wilk took the win. In the semis, it was another chance to see the vast majority of my PR career on the track at the same time as Wilk beat Del in another fishtailing side-by-side thriller on a 138-degree track.

In the finals, it was Wilk against John Force and when the amber bulbs flashed it appeared we banged the blower at the hit of the throttle. Except, back in the pit it was discovered that the new safety cut-off system, which kills the engine, shuts off the fuel and puts out the parachutes if the manifold burst-panel opens, simply malfunctioned. What a bitter thing to swallow on such a good day.

Our next stop was Norwalk and once again it felt like we were about to break out. That feeling, the sensation that the next great thing is about to happen, wasn't rare. It also wasn't always accurate. There were plenty of times when I thought my team was the class of the field and on our way, but then we'd stumble.

At Norwalk we qualified 10th after being right around the middle of the pack for all four sessions. We faced Tasca in round one.

On a 114-degree track Wilk pulled away from Tasca with a solid lap. In round two, against Jeff Arend, another solid A-to-B run on a hot track. Wilk clearly had a handle on it.

In the semis, it was a replay of Bristol when we lined up next to Del in his Al-Anabi car. Tim was amped up. His .059 reaction time gave him a head-start against Del, who was just a bit tardy with a .098 at the tree. Head-starts against Del, by anyone, were hard to come by. At the other end it was Wilk across the stripe first but the scoreboards were startling. Wilk's 4.277 beat Del's quicker 4.251. Hole-shot city.

A summer storm was brewing and ominous black clouds were building rapidly just west of the track. NHRA made a rare call and let us know that they would run the pro classes in whatever order they arrived in the lanes. They also told us to hurry up. We had a date with John Force as soon as we could get there.

Given that Force had three teams to help him prepare he beat us to the lanes. With Tasca's guys helping us, we barely made it. You could smell the approaching rain as we pulled up to the water box.

Force and Wilk did quick burnouts and slammed their cars into the staging beams. Just 4.191 seconds later Wilk was leaving Force in his clutch dust to win his second race of the year.

After a celebration at the line and another at the top end, the skies opened. It was pouring as the guys towed the car straight back to the pit, figuring there would be no winner's circle activities in an absolute downpour. We had completed the race with mere minutes to spare.

When the rain did then abate, NHRA told us to tow the car back to the lanes for post-race festivities. It was really odd to do the winner's circle routines so late after the round at an empty track, but we loved it just as much. The best part, though, had come just a few minutes earlier.

It was still raining at the time but I wanted to get Tim up to the media center to do his interviews. I had my hands full with my camera, my phone, and a notepad, so Wilk grabbed an umbrella and carried it over our heads as we splashed across the track in full view of the media center, which sat on the top floor of a building next to the starting line.

When we walked in, Elon Werner stood up and said, loudly, "Wait just a minute, Wilkerson. And you too, Wilber. The winning driver, who just beat my driver who is the best in the history of the class, just carried an umbrella for his PR guy? Were my eyes deceiving me? One of you two should lose your man card. Maybe both." That got big laughs all around and kicked off the interviews on a high note.

After we were done and ready to head back to the winner's circle, Wilk stopped me just before we walked in front of the media center again. He said, "Hop on my back."

I told him I weighed 215 pounds and I sure as hell didn't want to be the guy who helped the winning driver throw his back out, but he insisted. So I jumped on, and felt him sag a little.

But there we went, across the track with me riding on Wilk piggyback style, waving at Elon and the other PR reps in the media center. I could see that Elon had his head down, typing away, but someone else spotted us and pointed us out. I saw Elon look up and then put both hands to his face as he laid his head on the table. It was nothing short of epic.

In 2010 the classic Western Swing was basically inverted for one year. Instead of starting in Denver we finished there, possibly due to a fruitless hope that a two-week move might help avoid the daily afternoon thunderstorms that always seem to come over the mountain to plague the race. Our first stop this time around would be Seattle, where we were the defending champs.

We won again, beating Tasca, Cruz, Hagan, and Capps. The only round that was even close was the final against Capps, where it was Wilk's 4.221 over a 4.246. Our celebration, however, was muted.

Mark Niver had driven in the Top Alcohol Dragster class for many years. He was one of those guys seemingly everyone knew and absolutely everyone loved and respected. During eliminations on Sunday he died in an innocuous-looking wreck in the shutdown area. It seemed harmless but it was far from that. After a long delay with no official word, as the medical personnel worked on him, we began to expect the worst. When the horribly sad news was announced, we were in shock. Tim had known Mark for many years and I could tell he was taking it hard.

But because racers race, the day went on. It's what we do. The pall that hung over the event was palpable, almost suffocating, and all those who hoisted Wally trophies at the end of the day paid their respects to their fallen comrade. Our winner's circle festivities were quick and to the point, and the stage was never set up for speeches, fireworks, or cheering crowds. NHRA just rolled out a backdrop and we took a few photos. I made sure to have a photo taken of me, Tim, and some special guests.

By 2010 I'd forged a bond with a large number of fans from all over the country because of the blog, which was in its fifth year. What was notable though was a few groups of folks who made the Seattle race an annual outing and who were all blog readers. Jane and Chris Gorny were from Vancouver and they were big fans of the Canucks hockey team. When Jane began to email me, it was mostly good-natured ribbing about the Wild's heated rivalry with her favorite NHL team. Both Chris and Jane are outgoing and funny people but since she was a little more "out there" I introduced her to the rest of the blog world as "Crazy Jane."

Kim Campbell's first email to me came early in the blog era after I posted a photo of Dealey Plaza in Dallas, where President Kennedy was shot. Kim is also from Vancouver and he's a brilliant attorney. I dubbed him Kim the Lawyer in the blog. He is one of the most fascinating and literate people I've ever met and his son Andrew quickly became one of my favorite young men ever. Like me, Andrew was lucky enough to be born to two incredible parents.

Scott Burris was a regular reader who lived in Gig Harbor, Washington. He's a commercial airline pilot, so blog readers soon got to know him as STP (Scott The Pilot.) When he'd send me emails he addressed me as BTPRG (Bob The PR Guy.) When he was laid off by United for a while he actually flew 747s for Kalitta Air, hauling freight instead of people for NHRA legend Connie Kalitta.

Tom Miller and his son Doug were regular readers from West Linn, Oregon, a suburb of Portland. Tom wrote to me often, signing his notes TomFWL (Tom From West Linn). He would address his emails to BobFW (Bob From Woodbury).

Because of the common bond of the blog, and because this varied group all came to Seattle annually, they met each other and soon became close friends, making their annual adventure even better. I made sure to have a photo taken of all of us in the Winner's Circle. The blog remained a marvelous thing.

There were other fans and readers from Seattle I got to know a little better as well, thanks to their devoted readership. Terry Mattis was a diehard NHRA fan who would always make a poster to bring to the Seattle race. Throughout the course of each weekend he'd get it signed by every pro driver he could meet, illustrating not just his love for the sport but also the accessibility of its stars.

Jeff Eason was a rock star in a popular regional band and I loved hearing his stories about the road when they toured with the likes of Sevendust and other internationally popular groups.

Early in the Worsham years, Del and I met a young kid by the name of Tristan Slezak. He was just a little guy at the time and very precocious, with thick glasses and a funny way of speaking to us. It didn't take long for us to adopt him as our favorite Seattle "mascot" and we got to know his father a little, as well. Really good people who were not well off. Race tickets can be expensive, so Del and I started leaving tickets for them. Tristan and I still communicate on social media to this day and I almost always end my notes by asking him to say hi to his dad.

Also early in the Worsham years, I had my photo taken in our Seattle pit next to a cute little girl with curly blond hair. She told me her name was Juliet and she lived in Santa Barbara. Her family loved the NHRA and came to as many races as they could in the western U.S. At the end of that year she found me in Pomona and handed me a print of that photo. We then took another one with her entire family. Other than little Juliet, I was shorter than all of them. By a lot. That family photo started a tradition and every time I'd see the Evans family at a race they'd give me a print of the last one, have me sign a second one, and we'd take a new one. We did that for nearly 20 years. In all the photos but one I stay shorter than everyone but Juliet. I stood on a chair one year to even things out. Flipping through the prints, I can also watch that little girl grow into a beautiful woman. And it all started in Seattle. A lot of great things happened there beyond just the stirring race wins.

And then we didn't win a round at either Sonoma or Denver.

My sister Mary was keeping in near constant contact and the latest news was the switch to hospice care for Taffy. The end was near. To complicate things, Barbara and I had made plans to meet her brothers Jim and Tim, and their families, at Yellowstone National Park right after the Denver race. I told Mary I'd cancel the trip but she insisted I go. Taffy was comfortable and basically unaware of her surroundings. Mary was sure I could go to Yellowstone and get back home to Minnesota before we lost our mom.

Barb's brother Jim works for the National Park Service so we'd have a tour guide of the highest order. That was good, because I'd never been to Yellowstone and the size and scope of the place would've intimidated me if I'd been on my own.

When Denver was over I flew to Salt Lake and then up to Jackson Hole, where I rented a car and drove to the park by passing the Grand Tetons. Once in the park I had directions on how to get to the lodge where we'd be staying but I kept the map open on my lap and kept my head on a swivel. There were bison everywhere, including the middle of the road, and plenty of traffic jams as people stopped their cars to take photos. Steaming hot water pits, geysers, mountains, rivers, lakes — it felt like I was on a different planet.

We spent three days there. It's one of the most incredible places I've ever visited. Plus, our tour guide was the absolute best.

And Mary was right. I was back home in Minnesota for a couple of days before I got the call that Taffy had died peacefully in her sleep. I offered to come down immediately.

"No, let's just all catch our breath for a bit," Mary said. "This has been a long drawn-out thing and we're not in a hurry to do a service or anything like that yet. We'll take our time and do something in a month or so after we get her urn buried next to Skip's at the cemetery."

I could tell Mary very much needed to decompress and get away from it for a while. She'd done an amazing job with both Mom and Dad down there and we all owed her the time and space to have a bit of a normal life again.

I wrote an obituary about my wonderful mother for the St. Louis Post-Dispatch, crying most of the way through it. The woman who had raised me, inspired me, nursed me through endless illnesses, driven me to school, given me confidence, and watched me play baseball, was gone.

But the truth is, she'll never be gone. The words in this book are only possible because of the DNA she gave me, and all these memories bring her back to life. I choose to remember that vibrant personality, that brilliant woman, as the mother I was lucky to have. But I still miss her. Every single day.

But it was time to get to Brainerd.

A year earlier, at an autograph session in Pomona, we'd met Tom "Shorty" Shannon and his wife Cheri. As it turned out they lived just a few minutes from Barbara and me, in Cottage Grove, where they owned and operated the American Motorsports Bar & Grill.

In 2010, we established a new Brainerd routine. Shorty would feed us all weekend, including a classic "Minnesota hot dish" breakfast on Sunday, and we'd run a small decal for his "car bar" as he called it. Good people, good food, good times!

We managed a semifinal finish in Brainerd, where we lost in that third round to independent racer Bob Bode. When Bode went on to win the race I knew Tim was happy. Bob Bode certainly had to remind Tim Wilkerson of himself, out there taking on the big boys and girls for the love of the sport.

We entered the Countdown in the No. 6 spot in points.

We lost in the first round at Indy, which was in the Countdown then, and we followed that with a clunker of a DNQ at Charlotte. Dallas would be next, and Jeff Arend had managed to get something really special on our mutual agendas.

He had been playing golf one day with Alan Johnson and one of Alan's buddies, Bryn Smith. Bryn had pitched 13 successful years in the big leagues, mostly for the Expos and Cardinals. Somehow, during that round of golf it came up that Jeff and a few other guys at Kalitta Motorsports were big fans of the band Rush, a trio that's also my favorite.

"Well, I'm friends with Geddy Lee," Bryn said. "Check out the tour they're on and maybe I can get you backstage to meet him."

Jeff, being a polite Canadian boy who always follows instructions, did just that. Rush would be at a big amphitheater in Dallas the same weekend we were racing there. Bryn then decided to come to the race on Alan's plane, to join us and see his old rockstar buddy. Todd Myers and Jon Oberhofer of Kalitta Motorsports were also big fans and I was invited to tag along with the group. We had backstage passes waiting for us at the performers' entrance.

To say we were all giddy about Geddy would be an understatement. When we got there it felt like we were floating instead of walking, as we were escorted past drummer Neil Peart's tour bus and the BMW motorcycle he rode between shows. Then we passed guitarist Alex Lifeson, who was having a casual conversation just like normal people do. We were nudging each other a little to make sure we weren't dreaming. We were ushered into a back room and offered beer and chips as we nervously waited. An assistant came in the room, shook Bryn's hand, and said, "I'll go grab Geddy." I turned to Todd at the exact second he turned to look at me, and I said, "'I'll go grab Geddy.' I believe that's a sentence I've never heard before."

Seconds later, Geddy Lee, the best bass player in the world, walked into the room. He looked exactly like Geddy Lee.

He and Bryn chatted for a bit while we all tried not to look too starstruck, then Geddy worked the room and shook all of our hands. I was worried that was the end of it so I spoke up and said, "Can we get a group photo with you?" He was happy to do it.

The show was amazing, of course, but we did have a little screw-up with our tickets. Eventually, most of us were moved over one section to the left of where we were initially told we'd be sitting, but for some reason Jeff's ticket was fine. He stayed there.

We all met backstage again during the intermission and then went back out to scream, sing, and play air-drums for the second set. When the show ended 11,500 people all began streaming out of the amphitheater at once. What were the odds that we'd immediately bump into Jeff in that sea of humanity? They were 1:1 actually. We literally bumped into him almost immediately.

Having grown up as a Wilber, I am rarely starstruck. Meeting Geddy Lee was an exception to that rule. And, of course, I still have my backstage pass.

We won a round at Reading, lost in the opening round at Las Vegas, and then went to Pomona to wrap up the season. We put a bow on 2010 with a DNQ. It was possibly the ugliest bow in the history of decorations. It was a resounding thud at the end of what had been a pretty nice season and we punctuated the clank by also blowing up the motor and cooking the body in a big fire on Friday.

The only backup body we had with us was a Summit Racing Equipment special-edition car we'd run at the Las Vegas race, in support of our important associate sponsor. It featured a stunning blue chain-lightning paint scheme with a lot of incredible airbrush work, but fortunately the Summit logos on the sides and hood were not painted. They were large decals. If I could find a vinyl shop open on Friday night (John Chindemi was no longer on tour with his shop on wheels) I thought I might be able to create a new LRS car with a beautiful blue paint job.

I found a shop out in Ontario and called. Once they heard who we were and what we needed, they offered to stay late and print some die-cut LRS decals for me. But first, I needed to have the correctly formatted artwork emailed to them. Tim called his vinyl guy in Springfield, reaching him at home, and he sent the vectorized version of the LRS logos.

Fink and I then drove to Ontario, found the vinyl shop in an industrial park, and pulled up to the rear door. The owner and a few of his workers had all the lights on with the overhead door open, and were lounging around waiting for the race car guys to show up. We thanked them profusely and headed back to the track. We had a lot of work to do, installing decals that were so big they were two-man jobs.

On Saturday we took to the track with the hybrid Summit/Levi, Ray, & Shoup Shelby Mustang, but the rescue effort didn't help us run very well and we failed to make the field. Kerplunk.

We finished 25-18 on the season, with two wins, but the late season slump and the pair of DNQs left us in 10th place. My 14th full season as a PR guy and manager was in the books.

After quickly wrapping up my "Season In Review" documents, Barbara and I took off on another eagerly anticipated vacation.

On one of our earlier trips to Hawaii we'd spent some time on The Big Island of Hawaii at the Kona Village Resort, a spectacular place on the water that featured a world class restaurant, impeccable service, and unique accommodations. There was no standard hotel there. Instead, you got your own private Tahitian "hale" (HA-lay) with a peaked thatch roof. You were not allowed to bring the outside world with you. There was no television, no internet, no phone, and no air-conditioning. The trade winds and a ceiling fan kept you perfectly comfortable. The sound of crashing waves just a few yards away would lull you to sleep. I left my laptop at home.

The resort was divided into distinct villages with one part perched on old lava flows, while another surrounded a secluded lagoon, and a third sat beneath swaying palms within sight of the pristine beach. All the sections were connected by sandy trails lit at night by tiki torches. It was an amazing place.

On our first trip we'd stayed in a hale on the lava, which was fascinating all by itself. How many times do you even get to walk on lava flows much less stay in a private hale out there on the black rocks? At sunset we would walk out to the point where the lava sank into the sea, and wait for the green flash when the sun finally dipped below the horizon. For years I thought the quick green flash was nothing more than a rumor. I saw it every night at Kona Village.

Going back in 2010 we made the call to reserve a beachside hale and it would feature one of my favorite extras at the resort: A rope hammock strung between two majestic palm trees. I had learned the first time that I have an amazing ability to lay there for hours, sinking into a relaxation mode I rarely ever find. It was another one of those things that can't be coached. You must have the innate ability. I was a natural.

We flew over after Pomona and I was more excited than an eight-year-old at Christmas. It was truly paradise — a place where you had no choice but to let it all go and turn it all off. One of the resort's regular visitors was Steve Jobs. That's the kind of place it was.

For the first day we adjusted and slowed our tempo. By the morning we were fully immersed in Kona Village. We swam, ate three magnificent meals a day, and attended a fabulous luau one night. There were Mai Tais involved, as well.

That second morning, as we strolled in our flip-flops down the sandy trail to the restaurant, we could feel the relaxation sinking in. There's a real sense of panic when you turn it all off but we loved the sensation when we finally realized how wonderful it was to be there unplugged and purely enjoying the tropical paradise. It was a sort of awakening.

We did book an excursion for one day of the trip. We signed up to take a guided tour to the top of Mauna Kea, a dormant volcano rising 13,800 feet above the ocean. Some of the world's biggest observatories are located at the top. With no smog, almost no light pollution, and that elevation, Mauna Kea was a perfect place for astronomers. I couldn't wait to see it.

The excursion company was taking a bus full of us from various Kona resorts and we were the last to be picked up. On the way up the winding roads we climbed slowly at first then rapidly as we hit the steep part of the mountain. About halfway up we stopped for a meal at an abandoned plantation. The meal was typical picnic fare, but what we were also doing was acclimating to the altitude. We spent 45 minutes there, at about 8,000 feet.

Then, when we were above the clouds and nearing 11,000 feet, we stopped again to "take photos by the roadside" as our driver put it. After 20 more minutes of acclimating we made the final climb.

Most people don't realize there are places on Hawaii that aren't tropical and warm. At the top of Mauna Kea it's downright cold. We were given heavy winter parkas and gloves and then told by the driver to be cautious as we stepped off the bus. There wasn't any real danger of falling off the volcano but at nearly 14,000 feet your equilibrium feels terribly "off" and you tend to walk like you're tip-toeing on ice. It's easy to be pretty light-headed, as well.

The observatories were unbelievable. They looked as if they were massive props from a science fiction movie. There are about a dozen large telescopes up there, independently run and funded by numerous countries, with budgets well up into the billions of dollars to help the scientists perform important astronomic missions.

We couldn't go inside any of them but we were there for sunset and that was a "pinch me" moment as we watched the sun go down while the observatories began coming to life, with their enormous domes spinning into place. It must be strange and wonderful to work there.

On the long dark ride back to Kona we had one more stop to make. About halfway down the mountain there was a small park where amateur astronomers set up their own powerful portable telescopes. Unfortunately, Saturn was not in the sky that night. I would've loved to have seen that but Jupiter was above us and after my right eye acclimated to the viewing lens, I gasped out loud. There was Jupiter with its orange bands and large spot clearly visible. Amazing.

On our last day we drove around the southern tip of the island to Mount Kilauea and Hawaii Volcanoes National Park. Another phenomenal trip with grand vistas of centuries-old lava and hissing vents of fresh new steam. It was like a Hawaiian version of Yellowstone.

It was time to leave and that made us sad, but not as sad as we'd be in just a few short months.

In March, after the huge earthquake struck Japan and spawned massive tsunamis that reached as far as Oregon and California, Kona was right in the crosshairs. When the tsunami reached Kona Village it effectively destroyed it. Scores of hale were ripped off their foundations, the lagoon filled with furniture and wreckage, and the waterline inside the main restaurant was a stunning seven feet above the floor. Kona Village was gone. I'm still saddened by it, but so happy we made that trip after the 2010 season.

My 2010 Thanksgiving, however, was going to be quite different.

I'd been having some chronic issues with my left ankle for a number of years. At first, it would flare up and be enormously painful, like there was a knife stuck in it, maybe once a year. Then twice a year. By 2010 it seemed to be sore more than pain-free.

I'd seen a score of doctors for it and had gone in for an MRI around 2006. That doctor diagnosed a partially torn tendon just under the knobby "ankle bone" on the inside of my foot. At the time, we didn't schedule surgery.

By the fall of 2010, I was over it. I finally found a sports-injury surgeon who specialized in ankles and feet and got in to see him. We did another MRI and he agreed with the first doctor's diagnosis but on one frame he saw what the root cause was. There was a bone chip floating in there.

Many of the worst flare-ups over the years had come after prolonged periods of sitting or laying in awkward positions. I'd self-diagnosed a bone chip many years before because it truly felt like I was being stabbed, but then it would go away almost as fast as it flared up. And I still remembered the at-bat at the Valmeyer Tournament like it had just happened. Foul ball off the ankle. Bone chip.

The next step was a bone scan, although I had no idea what such a thing was. As I laid uncomfortably on the table I could see a shadowy version of my left foot and ankle on a monitor the nurse was staring at. When she pressed the button to start the scan tiny points of light began to pop up around my ankle bone. Soon, the whole area was lit up by those pinpoints of light.

A few days later, back at the surgeon's office, he brought up the scan on his monitor and his eyes widened. He said, "How in the world are you even walking?" We scheduled the surgery right away and it would happen the day before Thanksgiving.

On this particular Thanksgiving we had family coming. Barbara's sister Kitty and her son Todd traveled from Orlando while her niece Erin flew in from Denver. At least Barb would have some extra hands around the house after I came home on crutches.

The surgery was at 8 a.m. on Wednesday. We got up at 5 and drove the five miles to the surgery center. When they wheeled me in and began the anesthesia it marked the first time in my life I'd ever been put under. The next time I opened my eyes I was in the recovery room.

When the doctor came in he gave us the update. He'd removed the bone chip and also found a number of bone spurs, which he cleaned up. He also stitched the tendon back together and then sewed me back up. On top of that he reported the presence of some crystals in the joint. He wasn't completely sure what that was about, but his guess was arthritis.

I spent the next week with my foot and ankle in a splint, heavily wrapped. Within days, the crutches were an extension of me.

It was a wonderful Thanksgiving but it brought with it a massive blizzard while I was stuck on the couch. It was awful to not be out there helping although Kitty and Todd did get to play in it and unsuccessfully attempt to shovel some of it.

When the bandages came off a week later I saw the new scar for the first time and it looked pretty substantial. There was also the word "YES" I'd written on my skin with a Sharpie before the surgery, to make sure they worked on the correct ankle.

The good news was I had no pain whatsoever, which of course led me to cheating a bit (just a bit) on the "no weight on it at all for the first week" rule. Then the surgeon disappointed me greatly when he said, "The nurse will be in here in just a minute and she'll put the cast on."

There are first times for everything. I'd also never had a cast before, and I be wearing this one for weeks. I chose blue.

Three weeks later when the same nurse expertly sawed the cast off my leg, I was free. First time fully under, first major surgery, first cast, first time on crutches. Yay for me.

And I've not had one day of ankle pain since.

2011 would be my third season with Wilk and the LRS team, but a lot of other things were happening at home.

The worst of it was the passing of Barbara's mother, Jean. She had made a habit of coming up to Woodbury during the summers and we loved having her there with us. In August of the prior year, while I was on the road, she fell attempting to climb the stairs to our upper level. She was rushed to the hospital in Woodbury and by the time I got home the next day the doctors had made the decision to transfer her to a major medical center in downtown St. Paul.

Once they stabilized her it was clear that she'd need to move to an assisted living center. Barbara's sister-in-law Deb flew in right away, from Denver, to help us and then Barb's sister Kitty dropped everything to drive up from Orlando to help, and she stayed with us throughout the difficult process. The fall and winter were a blur of nursing facilities and ups and downs with Jean but the general direction of her health was a steady decline.

During the first week of January she really began to slip. She was rushed to the same medical center in St. Paul on January 7, and Barbara's brothers flew in to be there. The end was clearly near and as sad as that was it was also a relief to know she'd finally be done suffering. With family by her bedside, she passed away Sunday afternoon. It's the only time I've ever been in the room with someone as they died. Jean was strong-willed, stubborn, and very much in charge. She lived two days after the life-support systems were removed. She wasn't letting anyone else call her shots. That's how she was. In death she was surrounded by her children and some of her grandkids. It was really tough and I don't know how Barbara and I could've coped with it had Kitty not come up and quarterbacked everything for months.

Barbara's job was about to be thrown into flux as well. Lawson Software, the company that recruited her and brought us to the Twin Cities, was going through a lot of turmoil with private equity firms looking to buy the public company and take it private. Since Barbara was the vice president in charge of investor relations her job would be eliminated if the takeover happened. We had no control over any of this, other than Barbara doing her best to keep the company moving forward. We knew we were in for a rocky ride.

The 2011 NHRA schedule was an odd one, in a few ways. The Phoenix race, traditionally the second race of the year for as long as I could remember, was moved to the middle of October. In St. Louis, Gateway International Raceway had been shut down after its parent company encountered serious financial problems. We had only 22 races on the calendar and it started with some heavy-duty travel for the guys driving the transporters. The first five races were in this order: Pomona, Gainesville, Las Vegas, Charlotte, and Houston. NHRA teams and their brightly decorated rigs would be crisscrossing the country almost nonstop.

Another huge change on the NHRA landscape involved my friend Del Worsham. In 2011 Al-Anabi Racing would field two Top Fuel Dragsters and no Funny Cars. Del would be in one of the "long cars" tuned by Alan Johnson.

On Team Wilk, we added Chase Steele to the crew. Chase had worked for the Worsham team a few years earlier but at the time he was fresh out of college and still young. He liked the job and his teammates but by the end of his first season he was homesick. We all thought he'd done a great job and were sad to see him go.

When Chase came to a race in 2010 he told me that he'd made a mistake, and that his first stint was something he never should've ended. He asked me to keep him in mind if we were thinking of adding anyone. I took him right inside to see Tim.

Chase was a character, but his name was just as unique. His mother had been a big-time fan of a certain television series starring Pierce Brosnan and she named him after that show. His full name was Chase Remington Steele. Once we learned that, his new official nickname alternated between Remmie and Rem Dog.

Chase and I had gotten along great the first time and we picked right up when he joined Team Wilkerson. We'd also had some complicated pre-lap handshakes, so those were brought back out as well.

As for me, I was adding a new piece to my responsibilities and it was one no other PR persons had in their job descriptions. I started to help the guys push the Funny Car into the water box for the burnout. Of course, because I'm a man of routines, I developed a bunch of those for every lap.

I'd carry the video camera until just before we started the car. Then, I'd hand it to Krista. I was positioned on the right side of the car with my left hand on the fender corner just below the spoiler. I'd wait for the car to be started with my right hand on the side of the fender. As soon as the fuel came on and the tone of the motor changed, I'd slap the fender with my right hand. That usually stung a bit.

Three of us would then push the car forward and as it reached the water box I'd peel off to the right. Krista would be waiting for me with the camera. Time after time, month after month, and then year after year, always the same routine.

At the starting line, I'd become good friends with two of the ESPN camera operators who were down there with us. Nelson Jones was from Winnipeg and we often flew together because he would almost always connect in Minneapolis. Nellie, as we all called him, was a great guy and he'd often put the camera on me to get me some air time. Like I needed that ego boost.

Dana Sherman was a former college football player and he looked the part. He was big and burly and he was always around at the starting line, as well. As soon as the car would do its burnout, Dana would almost invariably walk toward me with his heavy camera on his shoulder, and he'd put his left fist out in front of him, while shooting. A large number of our fist bumps made it on TV and one made it onto the highlight video NHRA would play on the big screen before every Funny Car session.

They were great guys, but they were also true professionals and outstanding at what they did. It was backbreaking work lugging those heavy cameras around in the heat of the summer, standing just inches from the race cars during burnouts then ducking under the bodies when they were lifted. They had eyes in the back of their heads to keep from bumping into us and we always had an eye out for them, to help keep them safe.

In addition to the camera guys, I had also gotten to be good friends with TV personalities Dave Rieff and Gary Gerould. I'd met Dave when he started in the sport as a pit reporter. Luckily, the CSK team was pretty good then so he had plenty of opportunity to interview Del. I helped set a lot of those up.

Getting to know each other, it didn't take long for Rieff and I to find out we had a mutual appreciation for the NHL. His favorite team was the Tampa Bay Lightning, and at one point Dave even drove up to Woodbury from his home in Omaha to go see the Wild take on his "Bolts" at the Xcel Energy Arena. Then he spent the night at our house, but not before putting on a one-hour solo performance as a John Force impersonator. He has him down perfectly and

Barbara and I couldn't stop laughing. It's been great to watch Dave develop into such a great lead announcer on the TV shows. He's a really good guy who is passionate about his craft.

Most drag racing fans know that Gary Gerould had a long and illustrious career in motorsports television and he ranks as one of the most professional interviewers who ever worked the NHRA telecasts. Many don't know, however, that Gary has been the radio play-by-play voice of the Sacramento Kings since 1985. When the Kings came to town to play the Timberwolves in 2010 we visited with him at his radio perch at the top of the lower bowl before the game and on their next road trip through Minneapolis we took him to dinner at Murray's, one of the best steakhouses in the country. Gary Gerould is a true gentleman and a pro. He's one of those people who make you think, "It's an honor to know that guy."

When we got to Pomona to kick off the 2011 campaign we had a new vinyl wrap on the transporter and everything looked two or three levels better. We were getting there.

And then it rained. Bizarrely, it was a brief little shower that turned into a hail storm. In Pomona, California. Maybe that was an omen of some sort.

Basically, the highlight package for our 2011 season consisted of winning Seattle for the third straight year after qualifying No. 1 there. That was really about it. As a secondary highlight, we were the runners-up in Sonoma, but frankly losing in the final round was no longer that big of a highlight for us. We were there to win.

Throughout the 22 races we lost in the first round 14 times and were eliminated in the second round 5 times. We went to three semifinals and won two of them. Of our two final rounds, there was the Seattle win and the Sonoma runner-up. We finished 14-21 and felt fortunate to finish 10th.

Daniel Wilkerson made it out for a few more races, competing at Atlanta, Norwalk, and Indy in a Summit Racing Equipment car. The kid did great all three times, picking up his first career round-win in Norwalk and then winning a round at Indy. The Indy round-win came over Johnny Gray, who was breathing down Tim's neck to get into the Countdown. The kid delivered for his dad and that locked up Tim's spot in the playoffs

Norwalk was also memorable because Buck Hujabre showed up. The "Jersey Boys" tour was in Cleveland at the time and he brought along another cast member on Friday and then came back by himself on Sunday. This was no late-in-life infatuation for Buck. He'd been a drag racing fan since childhood in Baton Rouge, so I was thrilled to continue to introduce him to the stars of the sport and provide that "behind the ropes" experience. By this time we were the best of friends.

The "Jersey Boys" tour also made another three-week stop in Minneapolis, in 2011. When Buck excitedly told me about that, I had an idea but I was almost too timid to present to him. First, I cleared it with Barbara who excitedly said "Yes!" when I ran it by her. Then, I called Buck and said, "Hey, man. Would you and the family like to live at our place while you're here? You can have the whole lower level. That's gotta be better than another corporate apartment, right?"

I was hoping I wouldn't hear any hesitation as he searched for an excuse but I shouldn't have worried. He immediately said, "What an offer. Are you sure? Are you absolutely sure?"

Not much later, Buck, his wonderful wife Mary, and their son Gibson arrived at our Woodbury home. We spent three great weeks with them and while they were there something happened that will forever be remembered and will forever tie us all together. Gibson took his first steps. And, of course, we got to go see the show again. The first time we saw it Buck was a "swing" actor and musician, popping up on stage in background roles almost constantly. The second time, he was still playing various instruments but he also had a full-time role.

Another major milestone for the Wilber/Doyle household was a career change for Barbara. Lawson was, indeed, acquired by an equity firm and taken private. On the day the deal was signed, the CEO, CFO, and Barbara were out of work.

As part of her executive-level contract Barbara had a "change of control" agreement in place. Should the company change hands, she'd be compensated with a generous severance package.

"Do you think I can retire now?" she wondered aloud to me.

"Yes, I think you can," I replied. "But we'd have to develop a pretty strict budget. No more flying off to Hawaii on a whim or going to Austin just to eat at Chuy's. Why don't you take a month or two off and see what you think."

She agreed to do that and it marked the first time since the day she graduated from Penn State that she wasn't working eight to 15 hours a day. She'd earned it.

As summer turned to fall a headhunter called. Barb told me that a firm in Spokane was seeking an executive-level finance person to take over investor relations and they wanted to meet her. I could only smile and laugh a little. When Lawson had come calling we moved to Minnesota, where I'd very much wanted to go. Her next stop could be Spokane, where I'd spent two wonderful summers with my dad and his Indians ballclub.

She took the job.

The company was Itron and their world headquarters was located in Liberty Lake, Washington. Liberty Lake is a small suburb of Spokane, on the east side just a mile from the Idaho border. Since we'd both be traveling a lot the location of the airport was important. Although Liberty Lake was on the opposite side of town from the airport it was still only 20 minutes away. It's a compact place.

It was going to be a big change of scenery for us, both in terms of the mountains, the weather, and the fact Liberty Lake was inhabited by fewer than 7,000 people.

Itron is in the metering business. If you look at the gas or electric meter on the side of your house there's a good chance it will be an Itron meter. It's a high-tech business now, featuring smart meters that communicate with the utility companies, and Barbara was brought in specifically to tell the company's story to investors. She's the best in the world at such a thing.

We made a few house-hunting trips but hadn't decided what to do when it occurred to us that we should wait until spring to put the Woodbury house on the market and move. Barbara would be so busy when she started her new job, and she'd also be flying all over half the globe to meet investors and learn more about the company, it didn't make sense to rush off and relocate right away. The company would put her in a furnished corporate apartment at the Big Trout Lodge just a few blocks from the office, and we'd get together as often as time and travel allowed. With the memories of the IBM experience and its endless "temporary assignment" still vivid, we vowed to get our house sold in the spring and then find a place to live.

For the record, the Big Trout Lodge was neither big, nor were there any trout, and it wasn't a lodge. It was an apartment complex.

While she got to work in Spokane the NHRA season wrapped up in Pomona. Wilk finished the year in 10th place, with that less-than-sterling 14-21 round record.

Del Worsham did better. My former boss and close friend won the Top Fuel championship. From our first days together in 1997 I knew Del had what it would take to win the big trophy. All he needed was a car as good as he was. With Alan Johnson tuning his Top Fuel Dragster, he had the whole combination.

Del had entered the Countdown in good shape but the Al-Anabi team stumbled a bit at the first few playoff races. Del told me later that Johnson informed him before Vegas that he was bringing out a new chassis for the final two races and he planned to win them both to grab the championship. They did just that and it was Del's win in the semifinals at Pomona that clinched it. He then went on to win the race.

To see Chuck Worsham jumping around behind the starting line with tears in his eyes brought tears to a lot of other people's eyes as well. And that included me. I could not have been prouder.

Del confided in me after it was over. He said, "This has really been stressful. I'm thrilled we won this deal, but it was an emotional grind all year. I have the best tuner in the business, the best equipment, the best support, the best of everything. If we were ever going to lose a round or lose a race, it almost always had to be the driver's fault and the other drivers in this class are just cold-blooded at the line. My car and my tuner were flawless. That's a lot to live up to, but we did it."

Once things quieted down after the season ended, Del announced that he was retiring from driving. He'd be joining the Kalitta Motorsports team as crew chief on Alexis DeJoria's Patron-sponsored Funny Car. It was time to move on. I thought it was an amazingly bold move but I knew he could succeed.

By the time I returned to Woodbury, we were nearing Thanksgiving which was our favorite holiday of the year. The Jacobsens had, by then, completely adopted us as part of their extended family and they did Thanksgiving right. In addition, the turkey fairy came to our house every Thanksgiving morning.

With a house full of family, Dave and Nichol always made two turkeys but they only had a single oven. So, bright and early when Barbara and I were still in bed with our boyz, Nichol would tiptoe in and stick the second turkey in our oven. We'd arise to Thanksgiving aromas wafting up from the kitchen. It was marvelous. Their hospitality was so much like family it was heartwarming. It was home.

Finally, over the Christmas holiday, Barbara and I took off for Florida. We'd only be staying a few days but we'd be doing so at Disney's Animal Kingdom. It was fabulous. It was also not cheap but it really did feel like a 4-star safari and our room overlooked a courtyard where giraffes and gazelles calmly walked by our balcony.

We're both Disney fans, and whether it's the Magic Kingdom, EPCOT, Animal Kingdom, or even Disneyland in California, I'm always up for the next visit. This particular trip was a terrific way to wrap up the year.

2012 needed to be better on the race track, but life was pretty good off it.

Aches And Pains

My 2012 started out with a new problem. Barbara was in town during early January but she needed to fly to New York for a day of meetings. She didn't really have time to come back to the house before heading to the airport so we met at a McDonald's for a cup of coffee before she left.

When I hopped down off the stool I felt a little twinge in my left knee. Barb noticed, and asked me if I was OK. I didn't think it was any big deal.

When Barbara called that night I told her it was pretty sore and maybe a little swollen. I kept ice on it until I went to bed.

The next morning I awoke thinking, "Man, it's a drag to have this cast on my leg." It was a drag, but I didn't have a cast on my leg. The knee was swollen and seriously painful. Throughout the day I kept looking for glimmers of hope that it was magically getting better all by itself. I'm usually pretty good at that but this time the knee was winning the battle despite me resting, elevating, and icing it.

When Barbara got home that night, I said words she rarely ever hears from me.

"If this isn't better in the morning, we should go to the emergency room," I said. "I don't want to mess around with a GP who can't get me into a specialist for a week. We ought to just go to the hospital."

I absolutely never want to go to the hospital.

The next morning it was not any better. Just before noon we drove over to Woodwinds Medical Center in Woodbury, a state-of-the-art new hospital on the west side of town.

The ER was pretty quiet and when I told the nurse what the problem was she got me into a room quickly. When the doctor came in he took one look at my knee and just said, "Whoa."

A nurse followed him in, and she said, "Well, that's a quite a knee ya got there."

They quickly drained 60 cc's of fluid out of it, filling numerous syringes. The fluid was cloudy. I was stunned to hear, "We're admitting you right now. We can't run the risk of infection."

I was starving and thirsty but there was talk of having me in surgery later that day so I wasn't allowed anything more than a couple of ice chips and even those were slipped to me as if they were contraband. As afternoon turned to night I was sure we'd be putting it off until the next day. At 9 p.m. I got the word the surgeon was finishing a procedure and as soon as he was done they would have me on the table next.

The surgery room was in the basement of the hospital and it was kept so cold the surgeons had winter jackets on over their scrubs when we met in the hall before we went into the room. I kissed Barbara goodbye and less than a minute later I was under. For the second time in my life.

When I awoke, I was so cold I was shivering uncontrollably. They finally gave me some blankets and we rolled out to a recovery room.

There, the surgeon filled us in on how it had gone. There didn't appear to be any infection, so that was good. They'd gone in arthroscopically, through small incisions on both sides of the knee, and he showed me some photos from the camera they stuck in the joint. All of my bones, ligaments, and meniscus were fine. The worrying thing was the evidence of tiny crystals attached to the bones. I instantly remembered my ankle specialist telling me the same thing.

The knee doctor had tried to blast them with a laser, he tried scraping them off, and he tried prying them off. The crystals didn't cooperate.

By about 1 a.m. I was in my room attempting to sleep with a very sore knee. As the surgeon said, "If you ever saw how we move this around when you're under, you'd pass out. To get the scope where we need it we make your knee do some very unnatural things."

I sent Barb home and went to sleep. Then, like ghost images in the dark, the rest of my night featured nurses and specialists popping into the room.

The next day I started developing a fever, although I was also walking up and down the halls. That night, the fever broke but instead of discharging me the next morning they decided to keep me two more nights. After three nights in the hospital I was ready to go home.

Within days, the knee swelled up again. Instead of the hospital, I went directly to the surgeon's office and he drained another 40 cc's. And again, two days later. Finally, after a third trip to his office, the swelling went away.

That, as we say, is a tough way to start a year.

I was back at it 100 percent by the time Pomona rolled around and we did at least win a round there. We also debuted two new crew members. Travis Wirth was a really nice young guy who had been the chief starter at Cordova Dragway where Wilk match-raced each summer. Nick Casertano, who had worked on the CSK blue car for a bit before joining John Force's organization, would be a fly-in guy who would take over the unofficial title of "car chief" by overseeing the service between rounds. It was great to meet Travis and really nice to be working with Nicky again.

Sadly, John Fink had decided to stay at home. He and his wife Tammy wanted a more normal life and I couldn't fault him for that. He loves drag racing a lot but he loves Tammy more than anything or anyone in the world. John knew he'd have to make a clean break and not come to any races. My original 3-for-1 deal for Wilk when I arrived in 2009 (not counting Rick, Muzzy, and Eric, who kept coming to races) was now down to just me.

We were taking on a new look in a lot of ways and the crew was certainly one of them. Cole Nance had joined us in 2011 but by 2012 he'd had enough and was gone. Chase was gone as well, coming to the conclusion once again that life on the road was not for him. I was sorry to see both those guys go. Travis and Nicky were back, as were Nick Shaff, Brandon Lavely, and Jon Gimmy, and we also added a new guy by the name of Brandon Burgess. Since we already had a Brandon, the Burgess lad was dubbed B2. The guys meshed well, though, and I didn't think we'd be missing a beat.

We followed Pomona up, however, with a DNQ in Phoenix.

At the same time, Barbara and I were getting ready to put our house on the market and find a new place out in Spokane. There was a lot going on if by "a lot" you mean it was almost overwhelming. The thing about moving, though, is that you can't ignore it. It all has to happen, and you have to be confident you'll get through it.

When considering where we'd live in Washington our initial thought was to try something different. After all, we were moving to a part of the country that was new to to both of us. We started looking at condos and lofts in the city. Neither one of us had ever done the urban living thing and this seemed like a good time to try it.

We found a gorgeous place atop The South Hill, an elevated area directly south of downtown, and it was immediately the one we wanted. It had views for miles, including the downtown skyline, and we could walk to restaurants, coffee shops, parks, and stores. It was exciting to even think about it. It was nearly new and still owned by the builder of the four-story structure, where each condo filled a complete floor in a building that resembled a pagoda. We made an offer. They accepted.

The condo was much smaller than any home Barbara and I had lived in together and there was no room for my office. So, once again trying something I'd never before done I spent a day looking at rental office space in downtown. The plan was for each of us to get up each morning and drive to work. Maybe I could take the boyz with me every now and then.

But then the deal fell apart. Only one of the four condos in the building was occupied by its owner. The builder was renting out the other three. The woman in the unit we put a contract on had another year on her lease and she refused to go. We made her an offer we figured she couldn't refuse, including free rent and a rebate, but she said no. We had to back out of the contract.

That problem, though, became the catalyst for our solution. We were seeing, firsthand, that the Spokane housing market was a long way from the rebound we were leaving in Minnesota and we also admitted that we wouldn't be putting down any roots out there. At some point, whether it was two years or more, we'd be wanting to move back to Woodbury.

We then focused on homes for rent and we also decided to make it the ultimate easy commute to work for Barbara. We'd find a place in Liberty Lake. So much for the urban living thing. It was back to the comforts of suburbia for us.

We saw a few that were pretty nice and one that was gorgeous, with sweeping views of the peaks and the lake after which the town was named. It was everything we could've wanted, except for one thing. The real estate agent showing it was also going to be the property manager for the owners and she was an absolute certifiable kook. And I don't mean that in a funny, zany, wacky way. Every question we asked was answered with a loud obnoxious rant, as if we were just plain stupid to ask if the pool table stayed or if the owners would fix that broken gate on the deck.

When we left — or rather, fled — I said to Barb, "I love everything about the house. It's perfect for us. But there is no way in the world I can ever again be in the same room with that woman. She's insane."

Barb replied, "I'm glad you feel that way, because that's exactly how I felt. I was really uncomfortable just being near her. It felt like she was trying to intimidate me. But now we have to find a home. In a hurry."

We had mere days until the movers came to Marsh Creek. Once the house was empty we had agreed with our agent to have it professionally "staged" in order for it to look its most appealing.

I flew back there to get ready for Gainesville, and when I got home I logged on to a couple of real estate websites to continue the Liberty Lake search. I saw an adorable house on the second green of Meadowwood Golf Course, one of three championship courses in the little town of 7,000 people.

The house was a detached townhome in a gated community, which meant it was a standalone home but the HOA would cut the grass and plow the snow on the streets. We'd be in charge of plowing the short driveway but the street plowing was a big benefit. The city of Liberty Lake did not own a plow. They used the L.I.M. method for clearing the streets. Let It Melt.

The house wasn't for rent but I could see online that it had been on the market for a long time. I called Barbara and asked her to check it out. If the owners were underwater with it, and losing money, maybe they'd consider renting it to us.

She called me the next day, after having seen it, and said, "They jumped at the chance to rent it to us. They're a military couple and he's been transferred to a base over by Tacoma so they have to go. They want $1,900 a month and they want us to sign a two-year lease. What do you want to do?"

I told her to sign on the dotted line. I trusted her instincts and tastes. I'd be happy to move in, sight unseen.

I needed to get to Gainesville. The movers would be packing us up as soon as I got back.

To get to Gainesville, though, I would not be flying. I would be driving my car, a Volkswagen Touareg crossover SUV, 1,500 miles to Orlando. I had decided to give the Touareg, which I owned free and clear, to Barbara's nephew Todd.

Todd had been having a tough time in terms of employment, cars, and relationships and all of that leads to a tough time in the happiness department. The fact he drove an old beater of a car didn't help with the dating part and that was pretty depressing for him. It was a rough cycle to break, and he needed a hand. He needed a lift. He also needed a nicer car.

The first day I drove to Iowa City. The next day was a long haul, all the way to Dalton, Georgia. The third day, I was exhausted but I got to Orlando that night. In the morning, I picked up Todd in his new SUV.

"I want you to have this car, but don't feel in any way obligated to keep it," I told him. "It doesn't get very good mileage but it's worth a lot of money with the low miles I have on it, so you should probably sell it and buy something you really like. Something new, with a full warranty."

It felt really good. It still does. It helped change his life. I think it might've been the first step in a fantastic turnaround he then undertook on his own. I love the guy.

I grabbed a rental car at the Orlando airport and headed up to Gainesville. When we lost I headed back down to Orlando and caught a flight in the morning. After I got home, our world was starting to spin faster and faster.

It took the movers one full day to pack us up. And that was after a massive downsizing campaign we'd done. Too many trips to Goodwill to count, too many things given away to friends, and too much junk were all part of the equation. At one point, we'd had the trash company drop a 10-yard dumpster in our driveway. We filled it.

The Marsh Creek house was about 4,500 square feet. The rental home in Liberty Lake was about 3,400. We decided to rent a storage unit in Woodbury to leave some furniture and a lot of other stuff behind, including more than 20 Wally trophies. I took just three to Liberty Lake. That storage unit was our anchor to guarantee we would, indeed, return home. We just didn't know when.

The next day, all the boxes, sofas, chairs, and tables went on a United Van Lines truck. We filled two-thirds of it. Barbara's car, the Lexus hybrid that had earned us those Timberwolves tickets, was picked up by a transport company. We were flying out the next morning and Boofus and Buster were coming with us.

We were in first class, but the boyz were none too happy to have seen their only home go away before they were carted off to a big noisy airport full of strangers. They were howling up a racket and we hadn't even gotten through security. Our vet had told us he ethically could not prescribe any tranquilizers because he didn't believe in them and thought they were too dangerous, but he insisted the boyz would be fine if we covered their carriers with blankets. He clearly didn't know them that well.

We'd made the decision, before heading to the airport, that we would apologize to everyone around us right away. We also brought numerous sets of earplugs to hand out if needed. I had hoped the boyz might surprise me and be good. Unfortunately, it didn't quite go that way.

Actually, Buster did pretty well after we finally got up in the air. Barbara was seated at the window and she brought his carrier up onto her lap. It had a mesh end-panel on it, and he mostly just sat there and looked outside as long as Barbara would keep petting him.

Boofie was far less agreeable. I put his carrier on my lap and kept the blanket over him. I then had to squeeze my hand in through the zipper at a very odd angle and had to pet him on the head nonstop. If I paused even for a second the long growling meows would start right back up. It was nearly a three-hour flight. It was exhausting.

When we landed we got our bags and each picked up a rental car. Barbara still had her place at the Big Trout Lodge and since the movers weren't scheduled to arrive for a few more days we headed there, each with a cat in the car. Boofie, who normally hated riding in cars because it always meant he was going to the vet, fell asleep on the back seat before I pulled out of the lot.

We made a decision that day. For the sake of the boyz, for our own sake, and for the sake of all the other passengers, we would never again put those guys on a plane.

Itron had arranged the move and paid for it, and just a few days later the truck arrived in Liberty Lake. We had a new home. And, surprisingly, we sold our old one directly from the Open House our agent Angela hosted right after we left. We had five offers, and the best one was $12,500 over asking.

The Liberty Lake home was a two-level house but the lower level had only window wells below grade so there were no views down there. From the front porch, though, we had majestic views of Mica Peak and the surrounding mountains. Out the back door, the patio was no more than 20 feet from the cart path around the second green. It wasn't a pond, but it was beautiful.

The highlights of the house were both in the lower level. The first was a phenomenal home theater the owners had left behind for us, including blue theater-style light sconces on the walls, a huge screen, a seven-speaker surround system, and a set of four electrically operated reclining theater seats. We'd never had anything like it. I was allowed to decorate it as my man cave.

The other highlight was a real honest-to-goodness steam room. It was huge, with a bench that could easily hold four people, and it was tiled from floor to ceiling. We were eager to try it out, but first we had to get settled.

Having given my VW to Todd, I also needed a car. Barbara had owned an Audi A6 for a long time, and she loved that car. She thought I should drive an Audi as well, but her one request was for me to get their crossover SUV so we'd have the space in the back to make gardening runs to Home Depot. I bought a Q5 within days and joined the club of folks driving vehicles with the four interlocking rings on the grill.

We were getting to know the little neighborhood a bit better each day and it was exactly what we'd expected. It was peaceful and quiet. The town itself was also really nice, which was not surprising because basically the whole place was brand new. For a century, Liberty Lake had been an outpost by the lake of the same name. It was a place where Spokane residents could have a cabin and spend weekends. It had only recently sprung up as a master development and was finally incorporated in 2001. Oh, and the names of the lake and the town are not related to the concept of liberty. It's named after a French pioneer who settled there in 1871, who had Americanized his name to Stephen Liberty.

It was a lovely little town but its size was hard for me to get used to after living in Woodbury and the Twin Cities. Liberty Lake Road gave us access to I-90, and it bisected the main business area of the town. On either side of it, duplicates of each style of retail seemed to be uncannily located. A McDonald's on one side, Carl's Jr. on the other. Albertson's on one side, Safeway on the other. Subway on one side, Quizno's on the other. Pizza Hut on one side, Dominos on the other. Gas stations, banks, taco stands, you name it. Competing companies on either side of the street. The one dry cleaner in town had the rare monopoly. It was bizarre, and it was all contained in just one long block.

We'd already been told about the quirky nature of the three best restaurants in town, so we checked them out quickly. Hay J's Bistro was wonderful. It was a cozy little place with world-class cuisine, fresh salmon, and seasonal dishes regionally sourced and prepared by a real chef. It was in a small building attached to a gas station and convenience store on the north side of I-90. Palenque was the one authentic Mexican restaurant in Liberty Lake, and it was pretty good. It was, at the least, as good or better than anything we had in the Twin Cities. It was located in the pro shop at Trailhead Golf Club. And finally, Ding How was a highly rated Asian restaurant and sushi bar. It, too, was tiny and always packed. It was in strip mall on the east side of Liberty Lake Road, tucked between Pizza Hut and the UPS Store.

With the town being so golf-centric, carts were street-legal. Kids could drive them, as well, but only on the sidewalks, and that made summer walks pretty interesting. There was a lot to get used to, but we'd also made another unofficial promise to ourselves. We weren't going to exactly be antisocial but we had come to grips with how sad it was to leave all of our friends in Woodbury and we didn't want to go through that again. In Liberty Lake we'd mostly just keep to ourselves.

And, while all that was on our plate, we both had jobs. My first race after the move was Las Vegas and I quickly experienced something I was going to have to get accustomed to — I'd be connecting to get almost anywhere, mostly in Salt Lake City but sometimes in Minneapolis. In addition, Spokane is a long way from almost everywhere. From Minneapolis I had flown to almost every race nonstop. Simply by being based out in Spokane I'd immediately go from Platinum to Diamond Elite, Delta's highest level of frequent flyer, due to the added miles and flight segments.

I also quickly came to appreciate the Spokane airport. After flying out of the behemoth that is MSP for a decade it was fantastic to park right across the street from the small terminal, rarely be in lines longer than 10 people at TSA, and always know that the number of optional Delta gates for my departure was exactly three. It wasn't long before I knew all the gate and desk agents by name.

We lost in the opening round at Vegas, then managed to go 3-8 through Bristol, although I watched that one on TV.

I didn't go to Bristol because we weren't doing hospitality there and it's an expensive race in terms of travel. Our team budget was fairly static and as each year passed, with the cost of racing going up, things got tougher. A month earlier I'd agreed to take a 5 percent pay cut to help out, and in return Tim offered to let me skip a race or two and do the PR work from home. Bristol represented the first time I'd ever voluntarily skipped a race I was otherwise able to attend. It felt enormously odd.

Afterward, I talked to Elon Werner on the phone and when he asked me what it was like I said, "It was really weird. The first thing I worried about was that no one would even miss me. It was just weird as heck to not be there, but it's a real pain of a race to get to and it saved me a lot of money. Then, when Tim went out in the first round I looked around and realized I was home. That part was pretty good."

By the time the season was half over Barbara and I were both getting comfortable in our new town. We'd even ventured down to the Spokane Arena to watch the Chiefs, a junior team in the Western Hockey League, play a home game. The center on the third line was named Liam Stewart, and he seemed pretty good for a 20-year old who grew up Hermosa Beach, Calif.

Liam's mother spent much of the hockey season in Spokane to watch her boy play. Her name was Rachel Hunter. She was divorced from his father. His name was Rod Stewart. We had a celebrity in our midst!

One commitment we had made was to not allow ourselves to be total homebodies. We were in a part of the country with which we were unfamiliar but it was also gorgeous. We needed to explore. Being wine lovers, the first such trip would be to Walla Walla, on the weekend between the Atlanta and Topeka races in early May.

We'd both been to Sonoma and Napa quite a bit but it was no secret that the area around Walla Walla and the Columbia River was becoming one of the best emerging wine regions in the world. We also timed our trip with the annual hot-air balloon festival. The wine was spectacular, with the L'Ecole Winery ranking at the top of our list. The balloon festival was mind-boggling, and a first for both of us. As an added bit of fun, when we left to go back up to Spokane we drove past the Walla Walla ballpark where I'd played in 1979, as a member of the Medford A's. New and old, all mixed into one fun weekend. We arrived home late on Sunday, with six cases of Walla Walla wine in the back of my new Audi.

Our next trip was coming up quickly. We had a weekend off between Bristol and Joliet and we used it to continue doing exactly what we'd sworn to do. We drove up to Glacier National Park.

Even the drive was magnificent as we crossed through Idaho and into Montana, then drove north up to Kalispell before arriving at the southwest entrance to the park. Barb had done her standard massive research and reserved a room at the rustic park-operated motel right at the shore of Lake McDonald in Apgar Village. When we walked into our room, after parking by the door, we couldn't believe what we saw. If real life was like cartoons, our eyes would've popped out of our heads. The front of the room was nearly all windows and it looked like our room was actually in the water, not near it. Waves were splashing on rocks no more than 10 feet away, and the majestic lake was ringed with snow-capped mountains.

We quickly took a boat tour of the lake, then had a wonderful dinner that night before ending it with a couple of glasses of wine as we sat on the sidewalk outside our room and marveled at the scenery.

The next day, we accomplished the must-do item for any trip to Glacier. For just a few months each summer, Going To The Sun Road was cleared of snow and open for traffic. It had just been opened to cars a few days before we got there.

If the incredible view of Lake McDonald was stunning, driving Going To The Sun Road was both awe-inspiring and somewhat terrifying. It's a two-lane road that bisects the park, and that means it clings to the side of some seriously high and stunningly steep mountains. I kept my eyes on the road while Barbara handled camera duty from the passenger side. The mountain goats stared at us as we slowly passed while the ongoing snow melt caused absolute rivers of water to crash down the mountainside just inches from the car, and sometimes actually on the car.

At the peak, we were in the clouds when we stopped at the Logan Pass Visitor's Center. In Minnesota I was well versed in the art of pounding "snow sticks" into the edge of the yard to give the plow drivers an idea where your grass was hidden under the white stuff. Mine were always the tall ones, about 36 inches high. The snow sticks at Logan Pass were roughly

30 FEET high. The snow that was still there was easily 10 feet deep. To get to the visitor's center from the parking lot, we walked on a fully plowed sidewalk with the remaining snow towering over us.

We then headed to the east side of the park and stayed that night in a cabin overlooking the St. Mary entrance. It was all otherworldly. We were both mesmerized, and both very happy we'd kept our promise to do some exploring.

Work beckoned, however, and we made the long drive back to Liberty Lake the next day, going around the south side of the park to see more sights before we hit the road.

We were getting into the brunt of the racing season but still not doing as well as we'd hoped. By the time we got to Norwalk, we only had five round-wins in the bank. Then we went to the final round there, and we beat some big hitters to do that. All four of our rounds were Ford vs. Ford.

We beat John Force in the opener, in a race where both cars smoked the tires. We then beat Robert Hight in round two, with a 4.19 that was low e.t. of the round. We raced Tasca in the semifinal and won on a hole-shot.

In the final, we raced Mike Neff. Before the run, Tim said, "We don't really have a handle on it yet, and I sure don't want to give this thing away by smoking the tires. I plan to just go down the track and make him beat me, fair and square."

That's exactly how it played out. Wilk left the line first and led at the 330 block and at the 660 timer. Neff drove around him at the stripe. Fair and square.

Tim had entered Norwalk in 11th place, a full 90 points behind John Force in 10th. He left only 30 points behind, with five races left in the regular season.

Dan Wilkerson had driven his Summit car in Atlanta, earlier in the year, and he was also in Norwalk that weekend. Unfortunately, his motor let go during qualifying and he got his first taste of a Funny Car fire. It was a pretty big one and the body was toast, but Dan was OK.

Tim left Norwalk in 11th place, and he hadn't been in the top 10 since Pomona. Heading straight to Denver, we lost in the first round and were 12th in the standings. We had four races to make up a considerable amount of ground.

On the friendship side of life, my buddy Buck was at a crossroads. Mary had been pregnant with their second son and in late March little Hudson Hujabre was born. With two boys, Buck knew he couldn't stay in the touring show and he informed the producers that he was going to have to leave the cast. He would've been thrilled to move back to New York to be in the Broadway show, but there were no openings in that cast. They asked if he'd stay in "Jersey Boys" if they put him in the permanent show in Las Vegas. I was thrilled they gave him the opportunity. He and Mary were thrilled to move to Vegas. Now, he was guaranteed the chance to see at least two races a year.

Back on our tour, by the time we got to Brainerd it was your standard backs-against-the-wall moment for the LRS team. We had to make a move. We got to the semifinal at that race but still left in 12th.

At Indy, there were four drivers vying for the final two spots in the Countdown, with Jeff Arend and Bob Tasca in 9th and 10th respectively. Matt Hagan, the defending world champion, was in 11th. Wilk was 12th. We needed to pick up two rounds on at least two of those other drivers to make the playoffs.

We stepped it up. Wilk qualified No. 4, with a strong 4.060 and then the rains came. Eventually, eliminations had to be held a week later, as if we needed to build the drama a bit more.

Wilk faced Bob Tasca in round one, in a matchup that would represent the first leg of the mission. Tasca ran 4.125 against Wilk's 4.131, but the win lights illuminated in our lane. Hole shot.

Arend and Hagan both won in round one as well. There was still work to do.

In round two it was Wilk against Jeff. When Arend spun the hoops and Tim ran a clean 4.135, we were on the cusp of making it. Hagan also won his second-round race.

In the semifinals Neff took out Hagan. Wilk beat Johnny Gray. We were going to the final round at the Mac Tools U.S. Nationals and had accomplished our goal. Arend clung to the No. 9 spot in the standings and Wilk entered the playoffs No. 10. Tasca and Hagan missed the cut. It's a cutthroat sport, even for the world champ.

In the final round, Neff again got the better of us. His 4.079 beat our 4.152, and we had our second runner-up on the season with both coming at the hands of the guy everyone called Zippy.

We started the Countdown strong, going to the second round in Charlotte where I had a special visitor. My former SIUE baseball teammate Fernando Aguirre, the man who taught us all to say "Me gusto los legumbres" at the lunch table, had just retired as CEO of Chiquita Brands. He and his wife came out for some drag racing fun and they went bananas (rim shot). It was great to see him.

We then won a round in Dallas before heading to St. Louis. I'd have another special guest there.

Barbara's nephew Colin was about to graduate from Slippery Rock University and he was looking to fulfill a two-week internship requirement he would need in order to graduate. He asked me for some advice and my reply was, "Why don't you come to St. Louis and Reading and intern for me?" He thought that was a heck of a good idea, and his advisers approved it.

He flew into town with a free Delta ticket I had obtained with miles and spent three days with me at Gateway. He learned the ropes in the media center, and helped Annette and the LRS folks during our annual "big show" with Dick Levi and what seemed like most of the company. Overall, he got a good taste for what sports marketing and PR are all about.

He also got a feel for winning and losing on the NHRA tour. Tim beat Robert Hight and Dale Creasy in the first two rounds before losing a close one to Hagan in the semifinals. We were suddenly in 5th place, with visions of a championship in our heads.

The next weekend we reconvened in Reading. Colin attended that race without having to get on an airplane. He drove over from Slippery Rock, also in Pennsylvania, on Friday night and roomed with one of the guys.

We promptly failed to qualify, after just missing the top 12 on Friday and then being unable to crack the top 16 on Saturday. We had slipped back to No. 9 in the standings. The good news, for us, was that we could actually leave Reading. Once again, rain plagued the event and eliminations had to wait until Monday to be completed.

We then went to Vegas and lost in the first round. I was able to make it a personally better weekend by hanging out at the Hujabre home on Monday before catching my flight home. It was my first chance to meet little Hudson and it was remarkable to see how fast Gibson was growing up. A year and a half earlier, he'd taken his first tentative steps at our Woodbury home. During my visit to their place, he was sprinting around the house at full speed.

At Pomona we picked up a win in the opening round and officially ended the season in eighth place, with a 21-24 record despite not winning a race. Not bad for a team that had to make a minor miracle happen in Indy just to make the playoffs.

A week later, Barbara and I were headed back to SoCal for a concert.

Rush was on tour in support of its latest album, "Clockwork Angels." There wasn't going to be a chance to see them in Spokane but on the tour schedule I saw a show at the Honda Center in Anaheim one week after Pomona. I spent the extra cash to buy VIP seats, knowing it might be my last chance to see them. We ended up in the third row. Jeff and Windy Arend were going to the show, as well, sitting in a suite. We made plans to stop in there and see them before going down to the floor.

Before heading to the show, though, we dropped by Del and Connie's new house in Villa Park, just a few miles away. The house was lovely, the backyard was idyllic, and the chance to get up close to Del's World Championship trophy gave me goosebumps. But Del was acting a bit weird.

"Just tell them, Del," Connie finally said.

He took a deep breath and told me how, just that day, he'd been asked to take over the driving duties in the DHL Funny Car, the same DHL Funny Car Jeff had been driving since Scott died. Kalitta Motorsports had hired Tommy DeLago and he would take over the tuning on the Patron car. Del agreed to do it. He was kind of excited to get back in the car.

He said he'd talked to Jeff and they were cool, but he really felt bad about it. He also added, "Don't say anything. Word hasn't gotten out yet."

Yeah, great. I was on my way to a Rush concert where, just minutes later, I'd be in the same room with Jeff.

When we got there everybody in the suite seemed in fine spirits, but Jeff grabbed my arm and said, "Follow me for a sec."

We went out front of the suite and he asked me, "Did Del tell you?"

My artful (and not untruthful) answer was, "Did Del tell me what?"

He then told me all about it. What a thing to be in the middle of.

The show was amazing. I still marvel that those three guys were writing and playing some of their best music ever, after 40 years together. When they played the entire new album after the intermission with a string section backing them up, the crowd went crazy.

We bumped into Jeff and Windy as we left the arena, and all he could say was, "Best concert ever. Wow." Wow, indeed.

By the time we got home from Anaheim we were getting our first taste of winter in Liberty Lake. We'd been there enough prior to moving in to have an idea of what winter was like in the part of the country known as the Inland Northwest. It wasn't necessarily pretty.

When most people think of Washington they think of Seattle, Puget Sound, and the Cascade Range of volcanic mountains. I'm never surprised when even my geographically intelligent friends admit they thought the whole state was like that and are completely unaware that the entire middle of Washington is more like a desert. The Cascades block the humid coastal air and a lot of storms from coming into the center of the state, where the ground is brown and flat. It stays flat until just after Spokane, where the hills quickly grow into mountains. Liberty Lake sits directly at the foot of the first tall peaks.

During the winter, we discovered, it's typically in the low 30s or high 20s and the depressing days of overcast or fog can stretch for weeks at a time. The air that hovers over Liberty Lake often gets caught in temperature inversions where warmer air rides up over the cooler stuff on the ground, trapping it there against the mountains. Having moved to Liberty Lake from a much colder place I could state without reservation I liked Minnesota winters better. It might be 10 below outside, but the sun was usually shining. We rarely saw the sun that winter in Liberty Lake.

With the moderate winter temperatures, when it did snow in Spokane it tended to be wet and heavy. The homeowners had left their snowblower behind and that winter marked the first time I'd ever operated one. In Minnesota, the snow tends to be powdery, at least until March. It was easy to scrape off. The Spokane snow could throw your back out.

In November, we had a wedding to celebrate as Daniel Wilkerson and his lovely, sweet, girlfriend Brianna tied a knot we all saw coming 10 miles away. A better matched couple you'd be hard pressed to find. Everyone was growing up.

As we looked forward to the 2013 racing season I got a phone call from Phil Burgess, the editor in chief of *National Dragster* magazine. He asked if I'd be interested in writing a regular column. My compensation would be a free subscription.

I was a little nervous, but I agreed at once. We settled on "Behind The Ropes" as the title and I would write it seven or eight times a year. The theme would be my view of the sport, from my vantage point. I would call on my many years of sports marketing and PR experience to illustrate where I thought the sport was going.

I was anxious because column writing is a completely different approach from anything I'd been doing. The blog, obviously, was conversational and stream-of-consciousness writing while PR work is a different technique, and much more structured but still quite creative. Column writing was more formal. I was excited to add this new format to my palette.

It was also time for a new paint design for Wilk's Ford and with the help of Greg Ozubko we came up with a fun gimmick. Dick and Shannon at LRS helped us narrow it down to four possible designs and we had the fans pick the one they liked the best.

It was a neat idea but we didn't take the time to make it an online vote. We just put the designs out there, on my blog and NHRA.com, and had fans send the name of the design they liked the best to a new email address I set up on my laptop. I didn't know how many responses I would get, but two things happened. 1) The fans picked a design we called "Swoops" and it won by a landslide. 2) The amount of email was so overwhelming it crashed my computer. Thousands of emails in just a little more than a week can apparently do that.

I bought a new MacBook Pro, killed off that email address, and salvaged as much data as I could from the old laptop. And I bought an external hard drive for backup. Never again would I risk losing everything if my laptop threw the rods out.

With the new design selected and the first body painted, we gathered in Vegas to do some testing and I flew down for a day. While there, I got to meet two new crew guys and they were both brothers of current members of the team. Ryan Wirth joined his brother Travis and Dave

Shaff joined his brother Nick. I wondered, at the time, what the over/under was on the date of the first time we'd see two brothers rolling in the dirt fighting. It turned out everyone was mature enough to not let that happen.

We managed to lose in round one at Pomona, kicking off my fifth year with Team Wilkerson, but then earned a semifinal finish in Phoenix where a new friend of the team became part of the family. Tim had met young Gerald Meux at a race, along with his girlfriend (and soon to be wife) Kari. Gerald had been recruited out of college by Hormel, as a sales and management rep, and after the first time I'd met him I told Tim, "That guy is going to be on the fast track. He'll be at their headquarters in Minnesota in no time." Tim agreed, and we were both right. And we thought Gerald and Kari were a hoot. The fact they'd always bring a variety of sandwiches and hot lunch entrees when they'd come to the races was a bonus.

Winning two rounds at Phoenix was great but my mind was elsewhere and it was in a terrible place. The McCarley family was on my email distribution list for all the updates I sent out, and the address they used was Barb's home email. After I sent out one of my daily updates from Phoenix I was pleased to quickly see a response from that address. The note was written by Robert.

I could not have been more stunned or devastated. Just a few days earlier, Barb had been killed in a horrible accident on the main four-lane road we had all traveled on a daily basis to get to the grocery store or to downtown Austin. I read the words over and over and couldn't process them. It was impossible.

Robert said the kids, who were 13 and 11 at the time, were handling it pretty well. He said he was a total mess. I couldn't even fathom it. This wonderful woman, this fantastic mom, this incredible friend and neighbor, was gone. A car had crossed the centerline right in front of her.

Robert asked me to tell Barbara and he asked for a little time before he and I talked. He had a long way to go with his grieving process. It took me a full 12 hours before I could even call Barb to tell her. I was absolutely sick.

I'd lost my parents, I'd lost other friends, and I'd watched too many professional drag racers lose their lives, but for some reason this one hurt very deeply in a slightly different way. It was truly and honestly the last thing I ever anticipated, and Robert's email utterly crushed me. My heart ached for Robert and the kids. I have no idea how I could even come close to handling that. The world lost a shining light that day. Rest in peace, neighbor. We miss you.

The next race was Gainesville and I had made plans to fly to Minneapolis a day before I needed to fly down to Jacksonville. Just getting to spend the night back in Woodbury would not only be good for my soul, it would also make a long trip more manageable.

There was just one problem. Leading up to my departure day, I was having a ton of pain and swelling in my left foot. It wasn't in the spot where I'd had the surgery, it was on the outside part of my ankle and foot and it really hurt.

I had a walking boot from the surgery days so I put it on and screwed up my courage before heading to the Spokane airport. The boot did a good job of relieving the pain and as I boarded the aircraft I was feeling pretty confident I'd be OK. But when it was time to get off the plane at MSP, I could barely walk. I slowly limped to baggage claim and then to the rental car.

I knew I was in bad shape, and didn't think I could even get on a plane the next day. I talked to Wilk and we went over some options. First of all, I'd see how I felt the next morning.

If I could travel I could stay at the team hotel on Friday and rest. Or, I could just change my flight to Friday and have another 24 hours to be off my feet before I went down there. I told him I'd call in the morning.

I was distraught when I woke up the next day. It wasn't better. It was worse. I was pretty much in agony. I had to call Wilk and tell him I couldn't make it. There was just no way I could get through two airports and a long flight like that.

"We'll be OK," he said. "You get better and I'll keep you posted as we go. Give Annette a call, too, so that you two can talk about hospitality. We have a big group of Diversified Yacht people coming on Saturday."

I called Annette and we talked it over. She'd run a streamlined program for the guests and let everyone know I was sorry I couldn't be there. Then I limped to the car and drove myself to an urgent care center.

The doctor who saw me couldn't believe I'd walked in there. She wasn't sure what the problem was but when I told her my history of inflammation she prescribed Prednisone, a strong steroid. I wish she had told me to take Prilosec with it.

Prednisone is strong stuff. Within two days my foot was feeling a lot better. My stomach, on the other hand, was a complete mess. It hurt like a punch to the solar plexus. I was drinking Gaviscon like it was a milkshake.

I stayed off my feet throughout the weekend and during that time I got a call from Top Fuel owner/driver Bob Vandergriff.

He and NASCAR's Kurt Busch were planning a softball game. Not just any softball game, mind you, but a NASCAR vs. NHRA charity softball game in conjunction with our Charlotte race in just a couple of weeks. He asked if I'd help them out with some PR.

I was thrilled to do it. The game would be played at the home stadium of the Class-A Kannapolis Intimidators. The late Dale Earnhardt was from Kannapolis. Get it?

The NHRA team was going to consist of Tony Schumacher, Brandon Bernstein, Antron Brown, J.R. Todd, Shawn Langdon, Clay Millican, Del Worsham, Chad Head, Matt Hagan, Morgan Lucas, and Vandergriff. The coaches would be Alan Johnson and Bryn Smith. I would be the manager, making out the lineup and getting everyone in the game.

On the NASCAR side, they had Kurt Busch, Martin Truex Jr., Clint Bowyer, Kasey Kahne, Matt Kenseth, Michael Waltrip, Darrell Waltrip, David Ragan, Brad Sweet, and Parker Kligerman.

I wrote a press release and shared it with Bob, Kurt, and Kurt's PR rep. It was pretty cool to be asked to do it and a little nerve-wracking to be involved with the NASCAR people, who clearly worked at a different media level than we did.

I also got to know the front office staff of the Intimidators since we'd be playing in their ballpark on the Wednesday night before the Charlotte race.

When I put out the release there was that familiar sense of excitement, knowing it was a big one. We got everyone fired up on social media and the tickets began to sell. That was fun, too. I hadn't worried about ticket sales since my abbreviated stint with the Indianapolis Twisters in 1996.

When the day arrived I was a little nervous. I got to the ballpark early, met up with Bob and Bryn and got a jersey to wear, then waited. An hour before the gates were set to open, the fans were lined up more than 200 deep.

We had a huge autograph session set for the hour before the game and that was great opportunity for all those fans in stock car country to meet some drag racers.

During the game, those drag racers showed the stock car boys how it's done. Final score: NHRA 19 - NASCAR 5. And it wasn't that close.

We had definitely wanted Courtney Force to be there, but she had made it clear she didn't want to play. I was fine with that. I just wanted her there for PR purposes and for the autograph session.

She was with us in the dugout during the game and once the score was out of reach Vandergriff and a few other guys were working on her pretty hard, to get her to pinch hit. The peer pressure finally got to her, and we sent her up there.

She hit a single and the hilarity ensued. As she went from base to base on other NHRA hits, the NASCAR players stopped her each time to have their photos taken with her. By the time she scored the entire NASCAR team was running to the plate to take one of the funniest group shots ever. It was all good.

When I got back to Liberty Lake I'd totally had enough of the knee and ankle problems. I talked to an orthopedist I knew, who recommended an arthritis center downtown. It took me a few weeks to get in, and by then it was sore again. They gave me a cortisone shot in the ankle and that helped, but I needed extensive blood work to get to the bottom of the issue.

We started a few new drugs while they studied the blood and when I went back in a few weeks the doctor said, "I was thinking gout at first but your symptoms aren't like gout. There's a broad class of inflammations we call pseudo-gout, and I think that's what you have. It's just a matter of narrowing it down."

He gave me some more Prednisone and told me to hit it hard the next time anything flared up. Even better, he gave me the tip about Prilosec. It counteracts the stomach problems and makes the Prednisone bearable. At least we were making some progress. He also told me to contact him as soon as another flare-up occurred. He thought they had a better shot of diagnosing the problem if they could look at me when I had some swelling and talk about what I'd done immediately before it happened.

I also was going to have Dave back with me at the track for the Houston and Dallas races. Annette couldn't be there for those events, and Dave volunteered to fill in. It was great to have my former neighbor and road warrior with me again once Houston rolled around. By then, Neighbor Dave had become a well-known character in the blog and in the pits.

I also was developing a great friendship with a guy in Texas I'd be seeing at the Houston race. Dennis Peek lived in New Braunfels, between Austin and San Antonio. He was a big fan of the NHRA and read my blog regularly. I often wrote about the music I liked and he reached out to let me know he was a musician who liked a bunch of the same stuff.

When he introduced himself to me at a race in Dallas, I found him to be fascinating. He was a cool guy and much like Buck and Jeff Finger, what made it click was that we were each eager to hear all about the other guy's job and lifestyle. All the conversations were two-way and a lot of fun. I peppered Dennis with questions about the bands he played in and the music he liked and he was thrilled to get an up-close experience at the track when I'd bring him into the hospitality area.

In 2013, in Houston, he brought his lovely wife Keena with him. Another blog-created friendship was blossoming. NHRA Drag Racing was clearly a conduit to a large number of memorable people.

We had just come off a semifinal at the 4-Wides in Charlotte before we went to Houston. That semifinal had moved us back into the top 10, in the No. 9 spot. Houston was also going to be our first race with the semifinals and finals televised on "live" TV and NHRA had warned us about the quick turnaround times. They'd been pushing us at the races leading up to it, to get us used to it.

Before the race, Tim said, "With these short turn-arounds, I can pretty much guarantee you that we'll be in the final, because I don't think my guys can do it."

At Houston, we qualified No. 2, then faced Del in round one. We beat him. Then we beat John Force in round two. Tim's prediction still looked good.

When we got past Ron Capps in the semifinals, the racing on the track was replaced by the race to service the car in the pits. Tasca's team came over and in a couple of instances where our new guys weren't totally up to speed, Team Tasca members took over.

NHRA had an official literally pacing in front of our pit, pointing to his watch. With just seconds to spare we pushed back. Cruz Pedregon would be our opponent in the final and it was obvious as we passed his pit that they were in trouble. They were way behind in their service.

We pulled around to the staging lanes but stayed way back. Pro Stock was already running, and Funny Car was next, but we stayed back.

An NHRA official came over to tell us to pull under the tower, but Wilk asked, "Tell me about Cruz first."

The official said they were just then buttoning up their car but we needed to get up to the line and if they didn't make it we would run alone.

When he walked away, Tim said, "Not a chance we're running without Cruz. We'll pull up, but we won't start it. If they think a solo on live TV is better than waiting a minute, they're not thinking clearly."

We pulled up to the line and everyone acted busy. Guys were testing this and adjusting that. I was basically just pacing. Then, on the big screen we saw a shot of Cruz's car being towed to the lanes. We were nearing the top of the hour and NHRA wanted us to start. Nicky passed the word back to them. We were waiting.

Cruz's car got to the line and his guys looked exhausted. We let them gather themselves a little, and then we started the LRS Ford. We had a drag race to run.

We smoked the tires. Cruz won. No one on our team would've done it any other way. There was never a discussion. We didn't want a freebie.

The runner-up moved us to 6th place. Another semifinal in Atlanta, the next weekend, moved us into 5th. It was our high water mark on the year.

In Topeka, I had a chance to reconnect with Bob Rennison, my former play-by-play guy from the Kansas City Attack. I hadn't seen Bob in quite some time, possibly as long as 16 years, and I was eager to catch up on his career as the play-by-play announcer for the Missouri Mavericks hockey team. I was very proud of the career he'd built over the years. It was his first drag race, and another fan was created. It only takes one visit.

Chicago marked the halfway point in the year, and after it was over we were 13-12, in 8th place. I, though, had not been to all 12 races. I'd agreed to take another pay cut in 2013 to help the bottom line, and Tim upped the number of races I could work from home.

To that point, I'd already skipped Bristol and Epping. We weren't doing hospitality at either and by skipping them both I probably saved myself at least $2,000. Later, I'd be skipping Norwalk, Sonoma, Seattle, and Charlotte. I was doing my part to help Tim with the team's finances, but we clearly needed to land some new associate sponsors.

Dick Levi loved our race team but he was successful because he took care of his business. He had formulated the exact amount he could afford to pay us and still get a return on his investment. Any dollar spent beyond that would be wasted. We'd been at or near that number all five years I'd been with the team. Over the same period, the cost of racing had gone up considerably. We started pushing hard, even right in the middle of the season, to land some new associates. And if someone had interest in a full primary deal, we'd have to consider that, too. We didn't have any choice but to start looking.

LRS was also going to finally update our website and just like we'd done with the car design we would be putting it to a vote. This time, they saved my laptop by making it a full online click-to-vote election.

We loved the one the fans picked and I flew down to Springfield to spend a day with Andy Krug and the other guys from LRS Web Services, getting a full tutorial on how to go in and make all the changes myself. It would open up a whole new vein of social media for us, to go with our burgeoning Facebook and Twitter accounts.

They made it so I could be pretty autonomous with any changes, but Andy loved being involved and I enjoyed working with him, so we agreed he would continue to post my preview feature stories before every race and he'd make sure our new photos were placed correctly on that page.

We were pretty hot-and-cold the rest of the season, never really getting on a huge roll and never getting to another final. We also had to take it all the way to Indy to clinch our Countdown spot. Gosh, what a surprise. Through it all, from the day I arrived, I don't think Wilk's demeanor wavered more than a degree in either direction. He had an absolutely uncanny ability to stay calm and focused. It was amazing.

In addition, having not won a race in more than two years we would need to win a fan vote, and then a lottery, to become the eighth team in the Traxxas Shootout. The year before, we were proud to get eight percent of the vote because Courtney Force (who drove the Traxxas car) got more than 50 percent. In 2013, Courtney was already in. We thought we might be able to win the fan vote ourselves.

At Brainerd, the pursuit of a Countdown playoff spot was tight. We came into the race in eighth place but Bob Tasca was only three points behind. In 10th, Robert Hight trailed us by only 33 points. Outside the top 10, my buddy Del was just four points behind Hight. There were too many optional ways for it to happen, and a lot of those options wouldn't be good for us.

We qualified in the No. 5 spot. We'd race Jeff Arend in round one, while Tasca would race Courtney Force, Hight would face off against Chad Head, and Del would face Ron Capps.

At 9 on Sunday morning, Tim took an important call from NHRA. Jeff Arend had hopped a fence the night before and had broken some bones in his foot. He couldn't drive and we'd have a solo in round one.

And, of course, we smoked the tires but got the win. When Tasca lost to Courtney and Del lost to Capps, our playoff spot was all but secured. We ended up beating Robert in the second round before losing to Capps in the semis.

We would go to Indy in eighth, with a 46-point lead on Tasca, a 50-point lead on Hight, and an 81-point lead on Del. The math was definitely on our side, but math doesn't play favorites. We'd need to secure the spot ourselves.

The voting for the Traxxas Shootout began right after Brainerd. My campaign strategy was simple. I'd energize Wilk's Warriors with an all-out social media blitz, creating a series of funny online posters to implore our fans to vote, putting out a new one each day. We ended up with 41 percent of the vote, giving us 41 pingpong balls in the lottery hopper. I was pretty proud of that.

The lottery was held Wednesday of Indy week, so I would not be there. Krista would act as my eyes and ears and she'd be totally in charge of nervousness. She's a natural in that department.

Tim dumped his 41 pingpong balls in the hopper, followed by Del, Jeff, Alexis DeJoria, Tony Pedregon, Robert Hight, and Bob Tasca, who all split the other 59 percent.

One of Tim's pingpong balls popped out of the hopper to put us in the Shootout. Too bad it's not that easy to win the actual lottery.

In the Shootout, Wilk beat No. 1 seed Matt Hagan in round one and outran Cruz Pedregon in the semifinals, but we lost on a holeshot. During the race itself another semifinal finish removed any drama for the Countdown and Tim entered the playoffs from the No. 8 spot.

We were definitely running better, but while we qualified No. 3 in Charlotte and No. 9 in Dallas we came away with no round wins. It's a hard sport.

In St. Louis, for our annual hullabaloo with Dick Levi and LRS, we qualified No. 7 and picked up a round win. Unfortunately, it was our only round win of the playoffs. After coming into the Countdown 8th, we finished the season 10th.

I finished the season with more arthritis issues.

At Reading, not only did I feel great but the weather was (gasp!) outstanding for all three days. It all seemed perfect, and Barbara was there with me. On Sunday her brother Tim and his son Colin (my former intern) came over from Pittsburgh.

When we lost in the first round we hung out for a little while but decided to take off before the race ended. We were all going to Pittsburgh and the plan was for Tim, Barbara, and me to attend Monday's Pirates-Cardinals playoff game at beautiful PNC Park. When it was time to leave the track, Barb decided to ride with her brother and Colin rode with me.

I was tired, but other than that I felt pretty good. When Colin and I stopped at a turnpike rest area for a break I could tell my left knee was sore but I didn't think it was anything major.

Once we got to Tim's house and had dinner with extended family, my knee was getting a little tight.

Tim had cans of his favorite craft beer in the fridge and he offered me one. It was good, although I'm not a big fan of thick "hoppy" beers, but by the time we were going to bed I drank two of them with him to be sociable. Barbara and I then retired to a dark little corner room in the basement.

When we woke up in the morning, I knew it was bad. My knee was swollen and very sore. I'd been to this rodeo before and the bull always inflicted pain.

I tried to explain to Barb how bad it was but frankly by that time I think she was getting exasperated by the frequency of these episodes. I know I was.

I had to tell her there was no way I could go to the game. I'd watch it on TV from the sofa with a pack of ice on my knee.

By the time the two of them got back, I was seriously hurting. And, we were supposed to fly home the next day. I couldn't walk without excruciating pain.

I called Delta and Hertz and both companies showed fine customer service by waiving all fees and allowing me to keep my flight and my rental car open-ended until I was fit enough to fly.

Tim, who is a medical device professional, knew a lot of doctors. That's a good thing when a guy like me is in a town where he knows almost no one. He cut through all the red tape and got me in to see an orthopedic guy.

Like the other doctors before him he initially thought of infection and he was talking about admitting me to the hospital. As best I could, in the state I was in, I explained my history. Fortunately, he got it. By the time I left the doctor's office I'd had nearly 100 cc's of fluid removed (that would, technically, be considered "a lot") and I was in a wheelchair with a set of crutches on my lap. Getting into and out of the front passenger seat of the rental car was extraordinarily awful.

I was back on the Prednisone. And once I negotiated the steep stairs to the basement I was nearly a captive down there.

The next day I hobbled to the car and went back to the doctor's office. A different doctor, who didn't take nearly the time or care, painfully drained some more fluid. And I took some more pills.

By Thursday, after three days of dark depressing pain, I went back to the doctor one more time but at least I had graduated back to crutches. I got a small round of applause from the staff when I "walked" in.

On Friday we headed home. Delta arranged for a wheelchair to meet me at the curb, which was a good thing but I hated it. I detested being wheeled around inside the airport and I seriously hated being moved to the front of the TSA line. I felt like an invalid, but I knew I wasn't. I was just hurting.

By the time we got to the gate I gave the wheelchair pusher a tip and sent her on her way. It would be me and the crutches from that point forward.

We changed planes in Minneapolis and headed straight back home to Spokane. I'd already called my arthritis specialist and had an appointment for Monday.

When I went in they immediately drew blood. I was feeling a lot better thanks to the Prednisone, and they sent me home. The next morning, I got a call from the doctor himself and he said, "We've got it now. We've figured this out. We're going to make your life a lot better. Come see me tomorrow. I'll squeeze you in."

They'd finally nailed down the exact type of arthritis it was and he told me I'd immediately be going on Allopurinol, taking 300 mg per day. He thought it might take a year or two but the drug should help totally get rid of these problems. He also handed me a list of triggers that could cause flare-ups. Shellfish, overly processed foods — like white bread or white rice — and beer were on the list. When mentioning the beer, he said, "Especially those really grainy craft brews. You could probably drink all the Coors Light you want, but those thick craft brews that are full of hops and barley can instantly trigger this stuff."

Imagine that.

I have not had a beer since that day. The shellfish thing was only tough in two ways. I did like shrimp cocktail and I love a good crab cake. Other than that, I was never a lobster tail or crab leg guy so that was easy.

I also made up my mind that I was done with soda. I'd been a Diet Coke guy for a long time but upon reflection I thought it would just be better to never have another soda. I have not had one. If I get a craving for carbonation I drink a Pellegrino water.

Quite honestly, it had been a very tough year. I needed a break.

Got Wilk? Know The Man

I'd known Tim Wilkerson for roughly 12 years before I went to work for him in 2009. I met him, briefly, in 1993 when he was driving his Top Alcohol Funny Car at the Columbus NHRA national event and my Pro Stock driver, Lewis Worden, said, "You need to go meet that guy who drives the NAPA alcohol Funny Car. He's pitted over there in the mud."

I trudged over to his pit, stuck out my hand, and said, "Lewis Worden said I should come over and introduce myself."

His response was, "Well, that's cool. I'm Tim Wilkerson."

I still had a couple of additional forays through the world of indoor soccer in my future when we met and I really didn't get to know him well until I worked for Del, but there was always a connection there. An almost eerie connection.

In 2005 his mother passed away just as the St. Louis race was getting underway, but he followed her dying wishes by competing.

Conditions in St. Louis that summer were brutal. 2005 was the year the Safety Safari flooded the track a couple of hours prior to the 4 p.m. start of eliminations on Sunday, in a desperate attempt to cool it off. It was hard on everyone.

Wilk's pit was located diagonally across the aisle from the Worsham spot. Although both Del and Phil Burkart went out in the first round, and the conditions were awful, I stuck around to see if the grieving driver of the Levi, Ray & Shoup car could do any good. He made it all the way to the final round.

While his team was preparing his car for the final, under the glare of lights at nearly 10 o'clock on Sunday night, I walked to the end of Del's pit in the darkness and looked over at them, about 30 yards away. The split second I spotted Tim, standing in the door of his trailer watching his guys work, he immediately looked up and made direct eye contact with me. Then he gave that patented Wilkerson closed-mouth determined nod of the head and pointed at me. There was a connection there.

In the time I'd worked for him, going into the 2014 season, I'd learned a lot more about the guy everyone called Wilk.

Tim has zero pretense. He puts on no airs and he never tries to be anything he's not. He was born and raised a Midwesterner with a philosophy that says you work hard for everything you want. You put your family first. You are honest. You have integrity. Your word is your iron-clad bond.

With those qualities he might be the most unique "famous driver" in all of racing. There's a certain ego that most racers not only have, but also need. It's the mental approach of having to at least appear certain that you are the best. Wilk is missing that gene in his DNA strand.

Instead, he's humble, he's respectful, he's straightforward. He doesn't drink, smoke, or do much of anything other than love on his family and respect his opponents. He handpicks his crew guys to be reflections of him. I'm not sure how I fit in on that landscape, because I'm quite different than he is, but we always got along well.

I might be the suburban boy from St. Louis who went to private schools and then off to college on a baseball scholarship, but we had more connections than differences. I knew Springfield well. I knew all of central and southern Illinois well. I'd gone to school there, I'd worked as a baseball scout there, and I worked for Converse in that very region. I knew as many two-lane backroads and small Illinois towns as Wilk did. Maybe more.

We didn't know a lot of people in common, but we knew a lot of places. Had I been from California or New York, we would've had very little to talk about other than the race car. Being from St. Louis, we had plenty to talk about.

And we had plenty to talk about that had nothing at all to do with the race car. Many of the crew guys and drivers I had worked alongside, or had gotten to know, had a hard time talking about anything other than cars, whether the discussion was about Funny Cars or the hot rods they were working on at home. With Wilk, just as with Del, if I asked a question about the car he would expertly answer it in terms I could understand. But we talked about many things, and we were rarely at a loss for conversation, whether it was television, movies, or any other subject.

Wilk is also hilarious. He's one of the most serious guys I know when it comes to his car, his team and his driving, but he can be silly and funny at any moment. He knows when to break the tension. Away from the track he can have everyone around him in stitches, and he can recite lines from all of his favorite comedy movies. He has too many favorite comedy movies for me to count. He values laughter.

You had also better be ready to take some ribbing around him, especially if you're a suburban St. Louis boy who went to private schools. At one point, in 2014, he actually called me a "preppy." I hadn't heard that word in three decades. And, for the record, it's obvious Wilk never saw me in high school. I was a lot of things but I was never a preppy. If anything, I was more of a hippie.

I could dish it out just as well, though, and it was always good-natured. When I joined the team Tim had a Blackberry and he loved that thing. When the rest of the world transitioned to Apple or Samsung he clung to that ancient Blackberry as if it were a family member.

After he ribbed me once, in front of the crew, I said, "This, from the guy who attends Blackberry Owners Conventions where he says hello to the other four Blackberry users in the country. Do you guys have some sort of bet as to who will be the last Blackberry standing?" He laughed and said, "You got me."

He can also be pretty emotional. More than once I saw him take the stage in the winner's circle with tears in his eyes. It's all about that honesty.

He's very perceptive when it comes to other people's personality traits, and that included mine. He spotted my outgoing "confidence" (the kinder/gentler synonym for cockiness) early on and he would hardly ever give me a direct compliment because he probably felt like that was handing a dollar to a rich guy. Every now and then, though, he'd get the positive points across by quoting someone else.

"Dick and Shannon think you do a fantastic job, so keep it up and know that I appreciate it," he'd say. "They rave about you, and that's a good thing."

When I got more heavily involved in our LRS hospitality, I recommended we buy a small P.A. system so I could speak to the group on Saturday. He looked at me a little skeptically, and said, "Yeah, that would be great. You would actually want to do that?"

Of course I would, for two main reasons. 1) I've never been afraid of the sound of my own voice. Heck, I wanted to be a play-by-play announcer, so a little banter and stand-up comedy in the hospitality area were right in my strike zone. 2) I wanted the hospitality experience, for Dick, Shannon, and every LRS person and their guests, to be the best it could be.

By 2014, I'd perfected my spiel and it really was like stand-up. Comedians often talk about "good crowds" and "bad crowds" and for years I assumed that was bogus. A crowd was a crowd, right? Not right. Within a minute of saying hello to a group I could tell if it was a good crowd or a bad one. Most of the time they were good crowds, who laughed at my jokes and paid rapt attention. Every now and then I'd get a group that ignored me from the outset, kept talking, and never even turned around to look at me. But it was a great experience and Wilk appreciated it.

"You do a great job with that stuff," he said. "I don't know if it's necessary, but I can always hear them laughing and clapping. They eat it up, so keep doing it."

I always finished my emcee schtick by doing my favorite bit. I'd ask for the crowd's attention, because I had something important to say and a favor to ask. I'd then look out at their faces and tell them how hard the crew worked.

"Yes, it's a little bit glamorous if you're in the background of a shot on TV for 1.5 seconds, but the rest of it is nothing by knuckle-busting hard work," I'd say.

I'd then explain that drag racing isn't like the stick-and-ball sports. At the starting line, we can't hear the crowd. And then I'd say, "These guys are the best in the business, and this is your chance to be heard. So, let 'em hear how much you appreciate their work!" And the crowd, as they say, would go wild. I loved doing that.

The bottom line is that Tim Wilkerson is one of the most unique and unpretentious racers I've ever met. To that end, whenever I'd have friends or family at the track, he'd always take the time to come over and meet them. And then he'd treat them like members of his racing family from that point forward.

People like Buck Hujabre and his family, Jeff Finger, Dennis Peek, Kim the Lawyer, Crazy Jane, Gerald and Kari Meux, Shorty Shannon, TomFWL, and Scott The Pilot can attest to that.

And, of course, there could be no better person to be married to him than Krista. She's a saint. And, she's the best friend I've ever had at the track. The word "gem" isn't good enough. She's a mother figure to the crew, but she's a dear friend and confidant to me.

Over the course of my entire career with Wilk rarely a week went by, at any time during the calendar year, when I didn't get a phone call from Krista. I still get them. And I feel a wave of happiness wash over me every time I see her name on my phone.

As we entered 2014, I could sense something different in myself. I was getting tired of certain parts of it.

I'm a guy who can't help but stress over travel. I got that from my father. Every week, when it was time to leave, I'd worry about how busy the airport and the TSA lines would be. I'd worry about my flight being on time. I'd worry about being upgraded. I'd worry about who might sit beside me. I'd worry about my bag making it. I'd worry about my rental car being available, and even when it was I worried about it being a smelly clunker. I'd worry about my hotel reservation being right. And just to cap it off, I would worry every day about traffic getting into and out of the track. After the race, I had to worry about all the same stuff in reverse.

Do all that worrying for more than 18 years, 10 months a year, and it begins to wear you down.

I still loved my job, and relished the creativity demanded by the writing. I loved hosting hospitality and getting people to laugh, and then have them shake my hand to thank me for what I'd just done. I loved winning rounds, and winning races ranked among the greatest thrills of my entire sports career. Those hugs and high-fives are as real as it gets. But the travel was always hard and it got incrementally harder being way out there in the upper lefthand corner of the country, in Spokane.

It helped that we were still implementing the "no-travel" rule if there was no hospitality — although there were a few races where we didn't have it but I opted to attend anyway. I paid my own way, in terms of travel expenses, so that was on me. I would skip four races in 2014.

Heading into Pomona it was the same old first-day-of-school feeling. Here we go again. Counting the half-year with Whit in 1996, it would be my 19th season in the PR driver's seat.

After the season was but two races old Barbara and I took a weekend to do something marvelous. In the middle of February, we went to the north shore of Lake Superior.

Our close friends from Marsh Creek, Joe and Mary Beth Gillis, had bought a quarter-share of a beautiful condo about 23 miles beyond Duluth. In total, it was about 175 miles from Woodbury.

The condos at the development, called Larsmont Cottages, were spectacular. Going there in the dead of winter was otherworldly. The snow was high and crunchy. The thermometer rarely rose above zero. The ice was alive on the lake as it buckled and groaned, punctuated by what sounded like rifle shots as it cracked. All of that, combined with the beauty of the condo, the warmth of the fireplace, and the incredible hospitality of our dear friends, made it unforgettable.

People think I'm exaggerating when I tell them Minnesotans don't let the cold get them down and they don't allow it to force them inside. We were there three days and never once hesitated to see the sights. We made it as far as Grand Marais, nearly 100 miles east. We stopped and saw the historic Split Rock Lighthouse, high on a craggy cliff above Lake Superior. We hit every T-shirt shop on Highway 61 and sampled most of the food. It was invigorating. We were sad when our time ended but also wary of our own desires. We didn't trust ourselves to be there much longer without giving in to the urge of buying a portion of a condo of our own, making sure to match it up with Mary Beth and Joe's quarter so we could all be there together. We're still tempted and now Scott and Barb Meehan have done just that, to make the gravitational pull even more intense

And speaking of Woodbury, we were really missing the place and our friends. We began to seriously contemplate when we could move back and where we might live.

After the north shore trip we got back to the real world and I returned to racing. At Gainesville, I was thrilled to be joined by John Fink. The Finkster came strictly as a spectator but it was great to see him. The next day I was joined by Barb's sister Kitty, her nephew Todd, and Todd's beautiful girlfriend (and future wife) Angie. What a doll. I was over-the-moon happy for him. I was happy for both of them.

In the media center I was finally understanding something that had been coalescing in my brain. During all my time in NHRA there had never been a better group of team PR reps in the room. Never.

They were energetic, creative, hard-working, and fun. It energized me to be around them, so for the first time in my career I started to work out of the media center rather than cloister myself in the pit.

Elon Werner was one of the most talented PR people I'd ever met. He played at a completely different level than I did, and with his client being John Force he also played at a much faster pace. The man was in the big leagues. And there are few people I've ever known who are funnier than Elon. Whenever my phone rings and his name is on the screen, I prepare myself to laugh. Deeply.

Kelly Topolinski, Sadie Floyd, Leah Vaughn, Scott Woodruff, Cody Poor, Allison McCormick, Pat Caporali, Laz Denes, Ted Yerzyk, Lee Montgomery, Jeff Wolf, Sarah Adams, Caleb Cox, Nicole Clark, Rob Geiger, and a few more who worked part-time, including Brandon Mudd, were hard to keep up with. I'd had a sort of mild disdain for the media center for a long time. Now it was strictly admiration.

On the track, an ongoing problem we'd been witnessing was the instant destruction of Funny Car bodies during engine explosions. We'd seen detonations in the sport since its birth but with lighter carbon-fiber bodies, more horsepower, and big speed, these fireballs made confetti out of Funny Cars.

The prior season, in the interest of safety, NHRA had mandated that tethers would hold the body on in the event of a big boomer. Some of the teams thought that was a grand idea. Most did not. The fear was for the drivers. Holding the body to the chassis might keep parts from flying but in most cases it would keep the body over the driver, which could make the problem worse. At Sonoma, those fears became reality when Johnny Gray's car blew up and the tethers held the body. Nearly pinned inside the car, he was fortunate there hadn't been a big fire. The tethers were then made optional but the problem remained. In 2014, a couple of teams had different ideas about how to release the concussion of an explosion, at least enough to keep the body from shredding.

Tim's concept was to build tunnels along the sides of the firewall that separated the motor from the cockpit, and those tunnels would lead to openings along the bottom edge of the side windows. If the motor were to let go, all of that force would have a way out. Of course, there was no way to test the idea without actually blowing up a motor. We hoped it remained nothing more than a theory.

NHRA did ask him to alter the side windows a little. Tim figured the openings along the bottom edge would probably create drag and slow him down, so there was no advantage, but the Tech department didn't want him running windows so significantly different than everyone else's. His next step was to put a flap over each opening, with a hinge at the top and plastic screws to hold it in place. In the event of an explosion, the plastic screws would shear and the flaps would lift up. In theory.

At Atlanta, we got to try them out. Tim's LRS car was running strong when it suffered a major engine failure. The force of the explosion tore off most of the right side of the body. It was just gone. On the big screen, as it coasted to a stop, it looked like a movie scene in which he'd opened the passenger door on his coupe and a passing car had taken it off.

Later, a photographer showed us a series of rapid-fire shots he'd taken. In one, we could see the left-side window vent open, and flames were shooting out of the opening totally horizontally. On that side of the car, the theory worked! On the right side, not so much. At least we tried something new.

And it was that explosion that told me I was nearing the end. After the run, I called Barbara and all I could say was, "I think I've had enough. I don't want to see these anymore."

I got over it, and got past it, but the feeling was impossible to ignore.

As we always did, we got into the magic of the grind in which weeks are a blur and months fly by at incomprehensible speed. The season became one of the more unique ones of my career, which to that point had seemed to be punctuated by roller-coaster rides that provided either great success or frustrating failure. This time, we were "good" all year but never quite great.

On only two occasions did we lose in the first round at consecutive races. We lost three in a row in the opening round at Epping, Chicago, and Norwalk, and lost two in a row at Brainerd and Indy. Other than that, we won rounds.

Mostly, we went to the second round. We lost there 11 times, but we did earn three semifinal finishes and we got to the final round at Bristol. I wasn't there, but I watched on my laptop.

Wilk came into that Bristol event with a 64-race winless streak. He beat Bob Tasca in round one, Alexis DeJoria in round two, and Tony Pedregon in the semifinals. Tommy Johnson then edged him in the finals. The streak was 65 races without a Wally.

After Bristol, it was more of the same. First round, second round, or semifinal. And once again, both the Countdown and the Traxxas Shootout hung in the balance. Both goals were attainable, but we'd have to step up when it counted.

Tim moved around Jack Beckman into 10th place at Denver. It was precisely a three-point lead. "Fast Jack" would pick up four points during Sonoma qualifying, taking 10th back again. But, because fate serves up delicious entrees, the two matched up in round one.

When Wilk ran 4.094 while Jack spun the tires, we moved back into 10th place. We lost in the next round but the potential Countdown spot was ours to lose.

Meanwhile, at home, there was talk at Itron about setting up a new executive-level office in Oakland, since most of the chief officers in the company did not live in Spokane. The company already had an office there and the theory was it would cut travel costs and keep the key executives in the same place more often. They suggested that Barbara and I should consider moving there.

We were not opposed to leaving Liberty Lake. We weren't thrilled about moving to Oakland, though, and I was far more opposed to it than Barbara. I did a cost analysis spreadsheet to figure out how much money it would cost me to do my job from there and it was fairly enormous. The increase in airfare alone would cost me a significant portion of my income.

Finally, after much cajoling we agreed to spend a couple of days down there to see it for ourselves. We reserved a hotel room in Emeryville and flew down in late summer.

On our first day we took some real estate listings we'd gathered and drove over the hill and through the tunnel to Orinda, Walnut Grove, Pleasant Hill, and even as far northeast as Concord, which was the last stop on the commuter train from Oakland. Barbara had lived in the Bay Area before she was transferred to Chapel Hill by IBM, and I'd spent quite a bit of time there when I was scouting for the Blue Jays, based out of Fresno. We didn't think we'd like living directly in Oakland or Berkeley and we assumed we couldn't afford it. So we looked at the northeast suburbs first.

None of it felt right. None of it was "us" and we knew it. It can be a fantastic place to visit and frankly we were having fun while we were there but we couldn't see ourselves living there. It was the same challenge we faced when we evaluated IBM's request for us to move to New York or Connecticut. Why would we spend so much more money, to live in a smaller home, in a place where we didn't feel comfortable?

We did a quick tour with a real estate agent the next day and we saw a number of condos in the Oakland/Berkeley area. The one place we liked, on Alameda Island with views of downtown San Francisco across the bay, cost roughly three times as much as our Marsh Creek home had sold for. And it was a 1,200 square-foot upstairs condo with 1980s appliances.

Ultimately, the trip served two important purposes. It allowed us to say, "OK, we looked, but we're sorry. We have no interest in moving there" and it allowed me to see a dear old friend for the first time since 1978.

I'd connected with my former Paintsville teammate Vince "The Bronze Fox" Bienek on Facebook. He and his wife Mary, whom he'd met in Paintsville, were real estate agents in Sonoma. We'd purposefully kept our second evening free and asked them to meet us in their adopted hometown for dinner.

Vince made reservations at El Dorado Kitchen, right on Sonoma Square, and we drove up to meet them. We arrived first, by a minute, and when Mary walked in the bar area I recognized her immediately. Vince soon followed, and the hugs were as heartfelt as they should have been after 36 years.

Dinner was wonderful, the conversations were nostalgic and hilarious, and once we'd paid the check we went outside on a typically delicious Sonoma evening to re-enact a photo. I had brought along an old faded Polaroid taken of Vince and me in the Paintsville clubhouse. We held it up to repeat the poses and managed to do a good job of creating a "before and after" comparison. We both looked pretty good for old guys.

We had not seen or spoken to each other since the last day of the season in 1978 but the conversation flowed as if we'd never lost track of each other. Another fine friendship rekindled by social media.

When we got back to Liberty Lake Barbara did inform the CFO at Itron that we would not be moving. It's a good thing, too, because the new executive office idea was soon thereafter tabled.

Back in the racing world we stumbled along for the next couple of races and left Brainerd still in 10th place. We'd go to Indy ahead of Beckman by 16 points. We also needed to once again win the fan vote and lottery in order to be a part of the Traxxas Shootout.

On the Monday after Brainerd I began my third consecutive campaign to earn Tim a spot in the Shootout. My concept of funny posters on social media had worked so well before I saw no reason to reinvent the wheel, so I came up with new funny photos and new captions to keep the public's attention and to get those valuable retweets and shares.

I also knew I had a huge decision to make. I'd allowed the first thoughts of, "Am I done with this?" creep into my head. The Atlanta explosion made me feel different and although I got over it I never forgot it. Maybe it was time to do something different. Maybe it was time to write a book. I didn't know, but I realized it was the first time I'd legitimately had these thoughts since the first day I arrived in Pomona to go to work for Del and Chuck in 1997.

I finally decided. I would run it past Tim at Indy, but first I had to get those Traxxas votes.

This time around we had some serious competition, from some big-hitters with talented PR people. When voting concluded, Wilk had 38 percent of the vote. Fast Jack had 29 percent. My buddy Del had 13 percent. Matt Hagan finished with 10 percent.

With Krista again acting as my eyes and ears for the lottery in downtown Indy, I waited patiently for the word. For the second year in a row it was one of Tim's pingpong balls that popped out of the lottery machine. Bam!

When I got to the track Friday and saw Del in the lanes, he was all smiles. His crew chief, Nicky Boninfante, walked over to me and said, "Hey, if I ever run for office, I want you to be my campaign manager." That was the ultimate compliment.

Before the first qualifying run, I went up into the lounge with Tim and said, "Hey look, I've been thinking about something. I was back and forth on this for a few weeks, but if you want me back I'll commit to another year. I might want to skip a few more races, though."

Tim quickly said that would be fine. At one point, he'd even told me I could skip all the races, except for Gainesville, Chicago, Denver, and St. Louis.

My reply was along the lines of, "Yeah, but I'll always want to come to both Pomona races, at least one Vegas race, Brainerd for sure, and right now I can drive to Seattle, so there you are, already up to nine of them and I'm sure I'd add a few more to that. I don't want to disappear completely."

He was fine with that. And I felt relieved to have it behind me.

We lost to John Force in the opening round of the Shootout, but our work was not done. We still needed to secure our Countdown spot by finishing at least 10th.

Beckman had put even more pressure on by qualifying in the No. 2 spot. He had young Blake Alexander in round one on Monday. Wilk had gotten into the field in the No. 6 position, and he would face Tommy Johnson. The sole mission was to, at least, advance as far as Fast Jack.

Beckman and Alexander were the second pair. On paper, this was a mismatch of large proportions but as P.A. announcing greats Bob Frey and Alan Reinhart like to say, "That's why we don't run 'em on paper." Alexander went end-to-end with a 4.133. Beckman smoked the tires at the hit of the throttle. We were in the Countdown. And then we smoked the tires against Tommy Johnson. Big thanks went out to Blake and his legendary tuner, Paul Smith.

To open the playoffs we won a round at Charlotte and two at Dallas. Those rounds, added to the first-round wins we'd later pick up at Reading, Vegas, and Pomona, allowed us to finish the season in 9th place.

In Vegas, a close friend and colleague received an incredible honor. It was well earned.

In the media center during qualifying, Elon Werner was presented with the Jim Chapman Award, which recognizes a lifetime of excellence in motorsports PR. Not just drag racing PR. Motorsports PR. I told you he played at a different level. Elon is not just a big-leaguer, he's Hall of Fame material. When you're a PR guy and people like Ron Capps, Antron Brown, Robert Hight, and your boss John Force pack the room to be there for the presentation of such a lofty award, you've made your mark.

As it usually did, the Vegas race lined up with Halloween and many racers and fans brought their kids to the track in costume. The pro teams always had candy available. For the adults who wore costumes, and some of them were epic, candy wasn't necessarily the goal. Getting on TV was something to which a Las Vegas Halloween participant could aspire. The guy who painted himself gold and came as a lifesize Wally trophy usually got on TV. His costume was pretty stout.

In our pit, two adorable little Teenage Mutant Ninja Turtles came calling. With masks on it was hard to tell who they were, but when the slightly larger Turtle gave me a hug on the leg I knew I'd spot his parents somewhere nearby. Buck and Mary were giggling just a few feet away. Gibson and Hudson were priceless.

After the season wrapped up, Barbara and I returned to our standard Liberty Lake routines. But we had major plans for late December.

The year before, when December rolled around it became clear that both Barbara and I would come up just a bit short of Diamond Status on Delta. To make Diamond you have to earn 125,000 qualifying miles. Not miles you earn from hotel stays or car rentals. Not bonus miles from promotions or credit card use. Medallion Qualifying Miles, or MQMs as they're known, are the miles flown on actual flights. The minimum is 500 per segment, so even a quick trip to Chicago will earn you 500.

The only way to get more MQMs than miles flown was to buy a First Class ticket. If you did that, you'd generally earn 1.5 miles per mile flown, depending on the fare class. 125,000 miles is a lot of flying. Too much, actually. No wonder I was getting tired of the grind.

The prior year, Barbara and I had each needed a "boondoggle" trip to get to that lofty 125,000 mark. She flew first class to Atlanta on a red-eye then got right back on the same plane and returned to Spokane. That sounded exhausting to me. My boondoggle was more creative.

I bought a first-class ticket that took me from Spokane to MSP. I spent the night there, then flew the next morning to Fort Lauderdale. I walked on the beach, had a steak dinner, and got up early the next morning. I then flew from Fort Lauderdale to Atlanta, where I changed planes and flew to Salt Lake City, where I changed planes and flew to Ontario, California.

It took me all day to do it and I only made it with the help of a great desk agent inside one of the Delta Sky Clubs at the Atlanta airport. My flight was delayed, and it looked like I might miss my connection in Salt Lake. He double-booked me to make sure I had a seat on two optional flights and in the end I made it but I didn't get to Ontario until nearly 10 p.m.

I slept at the Holiday Inn near the airport and caught an 8 a.m. flight back to Spokane, again connecting in Salt Lake. When the flight crew arrived at the gate I had to chuckle and so did they. It was the same crew I'd flown with less than 12 hours earlier. It was late December. 2014's status was on the line. A flight attendant did a double-take and then said, "I know what you're doing. Are you making Platinum or Diamond?"

I ended up with 129,000 miles. Diamond it was.

In 2014, Barbara and I again needed an extra big trip, in first class, to retain our Diamond status. This time we figured we might as well get a fine vacation out of it. We booked first class tickets to Hawaii and the MQMs would come in bunches. Delta had just started nonstop service between Spokane and Seattle and a holiday promotion would double your MQMs if your flight connected in Seattle from GEG. I think we hauled in something like 14,500 medallion miles for the trip.

The year before, my sister Mary and her husband Lonnie admitted they'd had enough of the real estate business in Sarasota. Their kids were all grown and out of the house, the business was cutthroat, and as they approached retirement they weren't having much fun.

They owned and rented out a cozy condo on Kauai. They had bought it, sight unseen, a year or so earlier and fixed it up enough to be a rental. They figured someday they'd live there themselves.

When their tenant called and informed them that he had to move out, the decision was made. They would sell their home, quit their jobs, renovate the condo, and live on the island.

The ground-floor condo is about 750 square feet. To downsize that much they sold or gave away almost everything they owned. When they left for Kauai, they each had two suitcases. That was it. They both landed 20-hour a week jobs in order to get benefits, with Mary working at Pier 1 while Lonnie worked at Home Depot. They were clearly among the most overqualified employees on the island, but then again it's not uncommon for talented people to chuck it all away and head for a place like Kauai. With the rest of their time, they hiked, walked on the beach, and got to know just about everyone in Kapaa, on the eastern shore of Kauai. We were going to see them.

Just being able to leave the boyz behind was a fortunate thing. At the gym, Barbara had met a nice woman by the name of Nancy Brubaker. As they got to know each other Barb discovered Nancy did a lot more than just lead yoga classes. She was also a pet sitter.

When Barbara brought Nancy over to the house, I knew we'd found our girl. Boofus and Buster were generally shy around anyone new. Sometimes they'd even go so far as to hide under the bed. When Nancy walked in the house and folded herself down onto the floor both boyz walked right up to her and put their front paws on her lap. She was a cat whisperer. She'd be coming over every day while we were gone to do yoga with Boofus and Buster.

With that freedom to be gone for more than just a couple of days Barb and I decided to make it a three-stop trip, to maximize our time in Hawaii. We'd both done the heart of Waikiki tourist scene a number of times before we met but we'd never really done it together. So, we booked two nights at the Hilton Hawaiian Village Resort and did all things Honolulu and Waikiki for a couple of days. We even went back to the New Otani and had our favorite dinner of peppercorn Filet Mignon at the Hau Tree Lanai. It was still incredible.

Our Wilk Warrior friends, Jim and Nancy Butler, were in Waikiki just before us. We missed them by mere hours when they flew home just before we arrived. Jim, though, took the time to pass along a tip about a place called Aloha Kitchen. It was a tiny little restaurant about two blocks from the beach and the resort. If you didn't know it was there you'd almost certainly never spot it. Jim sent me an email raving about the breakfast they served and the next day we confirmed the opinion. And as we walked there, we passed a line of tourists that was out the door and down the sidewalk at a place approximating a Denny's. Aloha Kitchen was a block away, and 100 times better.

We then flew over to Maui for two nights at the Fairmont Kea Lani. The first thing we did was walk back up the beach to find the house and backyard where we had gotten married 17 years earlier. We got a heck of a workout on the long hike there and back.

We had a big adventure planned for the next day. We were going whale watching!

We drove over to another resort the next afternoon and met the rest of our whale watching group at the sign-in desk. There would be a gaggle of about 20 of us, plus five crew members, on a fairly large catamaran. It had a main cabin and bridge, with a small bar in the lower level and some deck chairs above, but it also had a few large cargo nets we could lie on while cruising. It's awfully sweet to rest in something like a giant mesh hammock as the Pacific Ocean races by just a few feet below you.

Getting on the boat was the first adventure. When it arrived from its previous trip the captain backed it to within about 20 feet of the beach. After everyone got off, it was our turn to get on. It wasn't easy. The boat was bobbing up and down about three feet with every wave that arrived on-shore and it would rock backward and forward at the same time. A ladder-style gangplank was lowered into the water but you had to time it just right to catch the boat when it was at the correct height and moving the right way. Watching the others, I could tell it was quite a step up even if you did it just right, and you had to duck your head to keep from bonking it on a cross strut. It was a bit of a thrill, but we both managed to somewhat gracefully board the boat.

The crew was great and they gave us the broad points as we headed off shore. It was just the beginning of the whale migration season so they couldn't guarantee what we'd see but they had spotted a few on the previous trip, so they were optimistic.

It then became our jobs to scan the sea and the horizon looking for telltale signs of whales, including splashes from their tail fins and mist from their blowholes. We learned how to point them out, as well — 12 o'clock was straight ahead and 6 o'clock was straight behind. When the first passenger yelled, "Whale, 9 o'clock!" it was a massive thrill. Then another, and another. The crew were as excited as we were, maybe more so. It was clear this was much more than just their job. It was their passion.

The cruise was supposed to be 90 minutes and after about an hour we'd seen probably a dozen whales, ranging from specks in the distance to as close as 200 feet. Then one of the crew spotted a whole pod of whales about a half mile away. The throttle went down and off we went. We followed those incredible mammals until we were supposed to be back at the beach. It's a good thing, apparently, to be on the last cruise of the day.

Just as we turned to head back one of the crew excitedly yelled, "Oh, my, a mother with her young calf at 1 o'clock. Look!"

We were only about 125 feet away. The same crew person yelled, "This calf might have been born today but if not it was yesterday. That's as small as they get."

Mama was swimming along gently, rising and falling as the calf stayed by her side, learning to swim in the ocean. He was tiny. As in tiny like a large SUV tiny. That was a real thrill.

We had to get off the boat in the same exciting way we got on but Barbara and I both managed to do so without completely dunking ourselves in the water. Then we stood on the beach mesmerized by what we'd just done and seen. Another bucket list trip I never knew should be on my list.

The next day, we were off to Kauai. We had plans to drive our rental car to the Marriott Courtyard Hotel, which was on the beach and only about 200 yards from Mary and Lonnie's place, but were surprised to be greeted by them when we got to baggage claim. We still got the car to give the four of us more space to tour the island together, but it was great to see the two of them waiting for us. It was the first time I'd been on Kauai, but seeing Mary's smiling face when I got off the airplane made it feel like home.

Having grown up together, Mary and I always had that bond. As we got older, became adults, and took on all the things grownups need to address, we saw less of each other. But whenever we did get together it was as if we were still on Woodleaf Court. A sibling bond like that is impossible to break.

Kauai was spectacular although our visit started with a bit of a mystery. We checked in at the Marriott, got the keys to our "Ocean View" room and headed up to it. Mary and Lonnie were on their way over from the condo.

When we entered the room, at first it looked fine and it did have a nice ocean view. Then I noticed a book on the nightstand. And the ice bucket atop the armoire. And some clothes in the closet. Not good.

We took our bags back to the desk and told the clerk what we'd found. She had a look on her face that indicated she didn't believe us. She stared at her computer screen shaking her head. Finally, she said, "Well, the room is clean and shows it's reserved for you tonight. I'll have someone go get those things."

I said, "No, I don't think so. This room was straightened, it wasn't turned for a new guest. I wouldn't even want to pull the covers back to confirm that. We need a different room."

It took a while but they got us a new one, on the other side of the U-shaped hotel. It, too, had an ocean view if by "ocean view" you mean it was possible to see small slivers of the ocean between the palm trees and the wall. We weren't going to be spending a lot of time in there anyway.

Mary and Lonnie had three days full of adventures planned for us. We would cover the island from Princeville, Hanalei, and Haena at the top, all the way around to Waimea and Kekaha on the southwestern corner. All the time, on the roads that ring the outer edges of the island, the lush mountains soared above us with so many waterfalls crashing down their steep sides it became commonplace to see them.

It rains a lot on Kauai but it also stops raining and becomes paradise numerous times a day. It has a small-town and "old Hawaii" vibe to it that is in stark contrast to the cosmopolitan buzz of Oahu and Maui. About the only things we'd ever experienced on the islands that even came close to the entire feel of Kauai were Hana, on Maui, and Kona Village, on the big island. Those were remote spots. All of Kauai was like that.

I'd told Barbara, before we got there, that even though Mary and Lonnie hadn't been living there long they would already know every waiter and bartender, on a first-name basis, within a 20-mile radius of their condo. The first of their favorite haunts we hit was Oasis on the Beach, a bar and bistro located, not surprisingly, right on the beach. It was walking distance from the hotel.

As we entered Oasis it was like a scene from the TV hit "Cheers."

"Mary and Lonnie!" multiple people yelled. The bartender already knew my name and I'd never stepped foot in the place. Barbara just shook her head and laughed. It was the same everywhere we went.

It's not that often you go on a vacation and see most of it from the car but Kauai is kind of like that. You head for destinations and get out and explore when you're there, but just the rides between targets are beyond belief. It's the most beautiful and wonderful island I've ever visited. Yes, I could live there.

We saw things we'd never imagined. We went to the top of Wai'Ale'Ale, at 5,148 feet, and had our photo taken next to the sign that reads "One Of The Wettest Spots On Earth." You have to consider yourself extremely fortunate to get up there and see the canyon views featuring too many waterfalls to count. We just made it. Minutes after arriving and gawking at the scene the clouds quickly returned and we were within them. It's the price you have to pay for all those waterfalls.

Our last stop on the trip was Poipu Beach, one of a few standard-issue tropical sandy beaches on the island. It was a great way to unwind and let the sun soak in. We even spotted a few whales, far offshore.

On Christmas night we flew back home. On the plane we relived the trip and mentioned our favorite parts. Finally, Barbara said, "I think my favorite part was really just you and Mary. You finish each other's sentences like you're actual twins."

I give Barbara and myself some credit for how we do this sort of thing. We both work hard and have for a long time. We earn every dollar we are paid and then some. We have saved or invested substantial amounts of our incomes for many years but we don't squirrel it all away in fear of someday being broke. We live in the moment a lot and we take advantage of all of that hard work and business travel to do things like jetting off to Hawaii for a week. We have done some amazing things together. And we're in no mood to stop doing them.

We had one more trip on our agenda because who doesn't want to get on another airplane? We headed back to Woodbury for our annual anniversary party, hosted by dear friends and neighbors. We allowed them to celebrate that New Year's Eve thing, too.

A Life-Altering Decision

It was time to get to work for the 2015 season. The first big news was a transition on our team. We had four new crew members.

Richard Hartman would be joining the team to take over the so-called "car chief" position and that made me smile. I'd been following Richard since my first national event at Heartland Park, way back in 1991 when I seemed fixated on his car as I shot photos. I'd been a big proponent of hiring him to drive the first CSK blue car, before Frank Pedregon got the gig. And now, in 2015, we'd finally be on the same team. It took a while but I knew Richard would bring something to our group that would be invaluable.

He knows these cars. He knows how to tune them. He knows how to assemble them. He knows how to lead a team. And — this is important — he's driven them.

We also added Joe Serena, Mark Dritt, and Daniel Grinnell. In addition, Rich Schendel would be attending far fewer races and Annette had made the decision to get off the road as well. It was going to be a much different look in 2015.

I headed to Phoenix for a couple of days when the team was testing there, feeling it was important to get to know these new guys and see the team begin to mesh. It takes a while for a team to get back in the flow if even one important guy leaves. Dealing with four new guys and the loss of some veterans who departed for other teams or ventures meant almost starting from scratch.

I liked what Tim said, though, after the first day.

"Richard is going to make a huge difference," he stated. "The fact that he's worked on these cars all his life is great, and he's a very smart guy, but his driving experience is going to be important. After my first test lap the first thing he asked me was, 'How did it feel?'

"That stunned me for a second, and then I realized why it did," Tim continued. "He knows what it feels like to drive one of these. First day, and we were already talking at a different level than I've had with any of the talented guys who have worked here. You watch, he's going to make a big difference here."

We reconvened in Pomona a couple weeks later. It was time to start the grind one more time.

By this point I'd established a lot of great friendships in the sport. Whether it was drivers, crew chiefs, crew members, PR people, NHRA staffers, National Dragster writers and photographers, or any of the other people who populated this circus that toured from town to town, these were some of the most valuable friendships I'd ever formed. And that didn't even count all the fans and blog readers. Buck Hujabre is a man I'll always consider a dear friend of an entirely different sort, at a completely different level. I feel enormously fortunate to have done these things and met these people.

In the PR realm, though, I realized two of my colleagues had risen to a special place in my heart. Elon Werner and Kelly Topolinski connected with me in a different way. Like best friends we shared our hopes, our dreams, our ideas, and our idiocy with such honesty, and with such a direct mental connection much of it could go unspoken. The spoken parts, whether in public with the bigger group, or tucked in a corner, on the phone, or via email and text, were so valuable I wasn't really sure how to imagine the job without them.

We shared thoughts among us that few other people, other than our spouses, knew. We motivated each other, we bounced ideas, we had each others' backs, and we pushed each other to find a way to get just a little better at this thing, every single day.

And the ribbing in the media center could be merciless. Kelly specialized in Pro Stock media relations although she also had some Funny Car clients under the umbrella company she dubbed WinLight Communications. Elon loved to egg her on about Pro Stock. If I'd ever join in his chorus of lines like, "Kelly, are Pro Stock cars technically even race cars?" she'd tilt her head and stare at me with a stern look and say, "Stop it, Wilber. You're just making him worse."

Working alongside this group of young pros kept me going. Being friends with Elon and Kelly was one of the biggest highlights of my entire sports career. That is not an overstatement.

On the track Team Wilk got off to a slow start, going winless at Pomona and Phoenix, although Phoenix was the first of eight scheduled non-travel races on my 2015 docket. I realized I was settling into those stay-at-home events and I made it a point to stay in touch with Elon and Kelly despite not being in the press box with them.

I did make the trip to Gainesville and we advanced to the semis to at least break the seal on the win column for 2015.

I worked Charlotte and Las Vegas from home and without me the team picked up just one round. By then, it was mid-April and spring had finally arrived in the Inland Northwest after another dreary winter. I had gotten through it without having to fire up the snowblower but the long stretches of overcast, fog, and cold were pretty typical of what we'd come to expect.

With spring being officially sprung and with an off-weekend ahead of us, Barbara and I booked a return trip to Walla Walla. She found a remarkable Bed & Breakfast online and we reserved a room there. It was a large converted house called "Vine & Roses" and the photos she showed me were spectacular.

When we checked in I realized the photos hadn't even done the place justice. It was phenomenal. It was also the first time I'd ever stayed in a B&B, so once again we were breaking new ground and doing so at a very high level.

For our first day we booked a limo to take us on a wine-tasting tour. That's always the way to go, if you can do it. We visited large high-tech wineries, small boutique places, and all sorts of vineyards of varying scope. And when the limo dropped us off we unloaded six cases of wine. We marked the boxes with our names, and put them in the dedicated wine cellar at the B&B.

We walked to downtown Walla Walla and had a great dinner, then enjoyed the stroll back to our room at dusk. I doubt many people realize what a cool town Walla Walla is. We didn't until we moved to Washington.

On our second day we had quite an event planned, but first we enjoyed a sumptuous breakfast the proprietor provided, sharing the room with our fellow guests. There were 12 of us, total, meaning all six rooms at Vine & Roses were occupied.

We planned to stop at one more boutique winery around noon and then head to Northstar, a premier vintner located on the south side of Walla Walla near the Oregon border. We'd sample a few of their best but then we'd cap off our trip with a unique hands-on blending experience.

A group of 12 of us gathered in a beautifully appointed room, where we each would sample a number of wines they had in barrels on the wall. Taking copious notes, we then put together what we thought would be a great blend of the wines we'd tasted. Using measuring cups and funnels, we did just that. When our bottles were full they gave us labels to write on with Sharpies of various colors.

My label said, "The Wilber Blend"

It was 50 percent Walla Walla Merlot, 45 percent Red Mountain Merlot, and 5 percent Petite Verdot.

I was happy to hear the host tell us that since our wines weren't "gassed" with nitrogen to give them a long shelf life, we should drink them within a few months. A few weeks later, we had friends over to do just that.

We stacked a few more cases in the wine cellar at the B&B and when we got up the next morning to eat breakfast before we drove home the other guests who were in the dining room applauded. They said, "You win!" They were referring to the amount of vino we had purchased.

And those friends we had over to drink our wine were another story. Barbara had accepted a seat on the board of directors for the United Way in Spokane. One of the other members was a woman named Carla and she and Barb got along famously from the start. Carla was the president and CEO of Numerica Credit Union, the largest of its type in Spokane.

When they got to the point of learning each other's backgrounds, Carla told Barb her husband was from St. Louis. Barbara said, "My husband is, too. He always tells me that the first question any St. Louisan asks another when they meet, is 'Where'd you go to school?' meaning high school. Where did your husband go?"

Carla said, "St. Louis University High."

"Wow," Barbara replied. "What year did he graduate?"

"I think it was 1974," Carla said.

Barbara couldn't wait to get home to tell me. She confirmed that I had, indeed, graduated in 1974. She told me about Carla and that her last name was Altepeter. Then she asked if I knew a guy named Tom Altepeter.

Of course I did. We were classmates. What, exactly, were the odds of something like that? I don't have a clue, but similar things seemed to happen to us all the time.

Tom and I weren't tight friends at SLUH but we were classmates and liked each other. A few nights later we met for dinner at our mutually favorite Liberty Lake spot, Hay J's Bistro. When we walked in I recognized Tom right away. After a handshake and a hug, both of our wives asked, "When was the last time you guys saw each other?"

In unison, as if we'd rehearsed it, we said, "Graduation."

A few weeks later we learned they had a 10 a.m. tee time on Meadowwood, the golf course upon which we lived. At about 10:10 we walked out to our backyard and waited for them. As they approached the green we gave them an earnest golf clap and presented them with mimosas. It's the little things.

Not long after that they invited us to dinner at their house in the south part of Spokane Valley (the suburb between Spokane and Liberty Lake.) When we walked in, Barbara and I had the same thought. If we had lived in a house like the Altepeters' our entire Spokane experience would have been much different. The home was stunning. It was as if we'd taken something as fantastic as our Marsh Creek home and dropped it right on top of a large foothill. It had views for miles including a great vista that included Mount Spokane, the 5,800-foot peak that watches over the area from 30 miles away. Again, what were the odds of the wives of two SLUH classmates meeting each other in Spokane, Washington?

Back at work I actually did attend the Houston race. We lost in the first round. After six races, a quarter of the schedule, we were 4-6.

At Atlanta, we ran 4.041 to qualify in the No. 6 spot. Tim felt pretty good about things heading into Sunday. He would face Del in round one.

Conditions were great on Sunday and that's not a common thing to say about the race that takes place closer to South Carolina than Atlanta itself. Commerce, Georgia, home of Atlanta Dragway, is about 90 miles from the Atlanta airport. It is roughly 40 miles from the South Carolina border.

When Tim posted a 4.035 he beat Del by two car lengths. It not only gave us our fifth round-win on the year, it was also low E.T. of the round.

In round two we beat Jack Beckman with a 4.085 that was, again, low of the round and the only 4.0 posted in round two. Tim's hunch about feeling pretty good looked like a valid one.

We faced John Force in the semis and again ran low of the round. Tim's 4.163 left Force several car lengths behind. We were heading to the finals, where we'd race Ron Capps.

I wasn't nervous. We'd been to our share of final rounds since that last win, 85 races ago. I was excited but I was mentally prepared to appreciate the great day we'd had if Capps beat us.

Wilk left first and never trailed. Capps smoked the tires pretty hard around half-track and

I could hear the guys behind me starting to yell and celebrate. But then I saw Tim's tires hazing a bit. I kept the camera on him, and had time to think "Oh, geez — don't let Capps pedal it and drive back around us." He didn't. Tim kept his foot down and we got the win. Four of our guys had never celebrated a national event win on the NHRA tour before, including Richard. I hadn't celebrated one since Seattle in 2011. That was a span of nearly four years. Did it feel good to jump around, high five, and hug on the starting line? Yes it did. It very much did.

There were more hugs and high fives at the top end and then the tow back to the tower for the winner's circle photographs. When the photographers were about done I spotted our guys all digging bottles of Mello Yello out of a cooler. I took a step back and just got my camera to my eye to catch them all simultaneously drenching the boss with Mello Yello goodness. It's nice to let loose every now and then. You know, like every 85 races, whether you need to or not.

Sadly, for me, I had a doctor's appointment coming up early the next week in Spokane and had made a reservation for a flight out of Greenville-Spartanburg at first light the next day. I had to skip the team dinner but after I finished my P.R. work and post-event report I celebrated with the guys a little more in the pit, before heading out.

Maybe that was an indicator of where my career and head both were. In earlier years I would've rescheduled the doctor's appointment and changed my flight, no matter what it cost me. I didn't even consider that in 2015. I just wished everyone well and drove to my next hotel.

At the next race, in Topeka, we finally crossed a threshold others had been obliterating before us. For the last calendar year elapsed-time records in the Funny Car class were being surpassed at a rate no one could fathom. What had taken a decade to accomplish, throughout my career and before it, was being done in a single weekend as world records fell at an astonishing rate. After Matt Hagan broke the 3-second barrier in Charlotte back in 2011, driver after driver had inched closer to the line and then crossed it. But in late 2014 and early 2015 the leaps in performance were off the charts.

It took a while for the explanation to come out. Some smart guys on big-budget teams started laying the angle of the header pipes further to the rear of the car instead of mostly up like they'd been forever.

Tuners had always used the headers to provide downforce with the exhaust from all that horsepower pushing down on the car as it raced down the track. By laying the headers back more the pipes actually supplied quite a bit of thrust. It was revolutionary. With the loss of some of the downforce it also made the front end of the car a little light and for months we were seeing brilliant drivers plow into timing blocks or scrape the wall. It's hard to steer when the front tires are dancing off the racing surface.

At Topeka, Wilk ran 4.061 in Q1. On Saturday, when rain only allowed one session, Wilk broke into the threes. Not a 3.99. Not a 3.98. No, he jumped all the way up to a 3.971. That's how fast times were changing (pun intended).

On Sunday, Tim posted a 3.984 in round one. He'd waited his whole career to break into the threes and he did it twice at Topeka. When he ran a losing 4.005 in round two, a run that would've been his career best just two days earlier, it looked positively slow.

I skipped the travel for the next three, in Englishtown, Epping, and Bristol, where the team went out in the opening round at the first two and then the second round at Bristol. That got us all the way into July. The year 2015 was half over. Once Norwalk was complete on July 5, the season would be half over as well.

At that juncture a lot of thoughts were spinning in my head. More than ever before I was questioning my desire to keep doing this. I really didn't know what I wanted to do and I would consider the option of switching it up again and joining another team if the fit was perfect, but mostly I was just confused. It wasn't wholly pleasant.

I was talking to Elon a lot and we were comparing notes about the things that challenged us the most, mentally as well as physically. He was a great sounding board and really good at knowing what I needed to hear as opposed to what I might have wanted to hear. Our conversations were pretty priceless.

After Norwalk was complete, with a semifinal finish, we moved into the third quarter of the season and I hit most of them. In Chicago, another semifinal and we were solidly in eighth place in the Mello Yello points standings.

Earlier in the year I'd been sharing ideas about a reunion with my college buddies Lance McCord, James "Oscar" Noffke, and Bob "Radar" Ricker. We chose to meet up the weekend after the Chicago race and spend two days in Cooperstown, at the Baseball Hall of Fame, followed by a day in Washington, D.C., where we'd attend a Washington Nationals game and tour the monuments.

After my wonderful experience at the B&B in Walla Walla, I booked rooms for us at an equally charming bed & breakfast in Cooperstown. The entire reunion, including the trip down to D.C. on the Acela high-speed train, was more than just fun. It was valuable. Before we all returned to our various homes we shook hands on a promise. We would do this every year until we couldn't do it any more. It wasn't a suggestion or a "good idea." It was a pact.

Back from that terrific trip it was again time for Denver with another huge crowd in our hospitality center for Dick Levi's big day on Saturday, and we made it to round two. I worked the Sonoma race from home, and we lost in the first round. Maybe there was something to that?

Right around this time I was thinking about a new car. I'd only had the Audi since we arrived in Spokane three years earlier and it had just 29,000 miles on it. Then I got a marketing outreach letter from the general sales manager at the dealership in Spokane, saying "We're looking for a Q5 just like yours. If you want to bring it in we'll take a look and tell you what we'd give you for it."

Normally, that stuff goes in the trash. This time it piqued my interest because it made me realize my Audi was right in the sweet spot for a trade-in. It was in perfect shape. It was a highly desirable car. And for a car its age it had low miles. I went ahead and took it in. They offered me $29,000 for it. I'd just paid it off the prior month so 100 percent of anything someone would give me for it could go toward a new ride. I considered it, but didn't see myself going right back into another Q5. So, I told the guy I'd think about it and I told Barb what I was thinking.

She and I are from two distinctly different schools of thought when it comes to new cars. I like to put a new one under me every few years. She'll keep each of her cars six years, or longer. When I explained my theory using dollars, she got it. My car was at the absolute peak of its used-car value. If I waited another two years it might be worth $20,000 or less. Then, the transition to a new vehicle could require a hefty loan. I wanted to see if I could get into something really cool, and really solid, for next to nothing. She was skeptical.

I dropped in at an Acura dealership and drove their coolest crossover SUV (yes, the rules were still that I'd have a car with which we could haul mulch.) The problem was, it was at the end of that model's cycle and it would be updated in 2016. I didn't like the sound of that but the dealer offered me $31,500 for my Q5. Now we were talking.

I then drove to downtown Spokane and drove the Lexus NX200t. It felt like a race car. It even looked like a race car, as much as a small SUV can.

The sales guy, D.J., already had a buyer for my Audi. He had a standing order for a "low miles, great condition, Q5" from a customer in Montana. He offered me $33,000. When I got him to drop the price on the Lexus by $3,000, we were getting close. I went home for the night to let D.J. think about it. After all, I was the one with the leverage. The worst that could happen to me was that I'd continue to drive an incredible Audi.

The next day DJ came up to right around $35,000 for my car. Then I played the ace I had hidden up my sleeve.

We'd bought a Subaru Legacy in the Twin Cities to use when we'd be in town. It was nothing spectacular, just a nice little grocery-getter, it had about 39,000 miles on it, and it was a 2009. It was also low to the ground and hard for me to get in and out of. We had paid a bit over $12,000 for it and owned it free and clear.

When I started to add up how many times we paid $60 each way for a taxi, just to get from MSP to Woodbury where the Subaru was sitting, it didn't make much sense. And when both of us would be in town, we'd have to rent a car anyway. During most of our stays there a rental car for one night was cheaper than the two cab rides by quite a bit.

"We're close," I told D.J. "Look, I've got an '09 Subaru Legacy that it's in good shape. The only trick is, it's in Minnesota."

"I'll take it," he said. "We constantly have used-car demand for Subarus here. I'll give you $10,500 but it will probably cost you a thousand bucks to ship it here."

He made that offer sight unseen. When I said, "OK, for all you've done I'm going to buy you three tickets to the Seattle NHRA race, and a chance to be behind the ropes with us." He thought that was awesome.

The next day I wrote a check for $4,200 and I owned my new Lexus free and clear. I considered it a win for everyone. D.J. sold the Audi the next day and emailed me a few days after the Subaru was delivered to proudly tell me he'd sold it, too.

He and his two kids attended their first NHRA event a few weeks later. It was all good.

With the consistent number of rounds we were winning our spot in the standings was pretty good. We were still eighth after Seattle but that wasn't the single most important thing that happened that week.

Tim had put together an associate sponsorship with Rottler Manufacturing the year before. They make big industrial machines that we needed for engine block and cylinder head work. They were based in Seattle so in 2015 we hosted them at the track while we ran a special edition Rottler car, with Dick Levi's permission.

On top of that Tim had also put together an associate deal with Curry's Transportation, out of Muscatine, Iowa. Jason Curry loved drag racing.

He owned a huge truck stop, service center, and sales dealership right in the heart of America. He was very successful at it, and he was thrilled to see his logo on Tim's car. After his first year, he saw the value and he stepped up the program.

He was a dealer for Western Star trucks and began to discuss providing an elite custom-built truck for Team Wilk. We really needed it. The Volvo Tim had been running forever was on its last legs. Jason came through in a big way and we took delivery of candy-apple Western Star with every conceivable option. We were in the big time thanks to a new sponsor who understood the value of the sport.

In 2015, the team would visit the Western Star assembly plant in Portland on the way up to Seattle from Sonoma.

I didn't travel to Sonoma but I had a new Lexus that wanted to be on the open road. So, I met the team in Portland on the Wednesday before Seattle.

This may come as a shock, but I've never really been a truck guy. Despite the fact Lance, Radar, and Oscar all worked at a truck stop during college, when they regaled me with stories of Freightliners, Macks, and "cab-over Petes," I knew hardly anything about big trucks. I certainly didn't know the many levels of luxury and performance. To me, Western Star made trucks. That was all I knew.

When we got there, early Wednesday morning, I learned I knew nothing. Western Star trucks are among the most elite vehicles on the road. We were loaded up with hard hats, yellow vests, and foot protection and got a guided tour of places only the workers normally go. We watched bare chassis come in one end and fully finished gorgeous trucks leave the other. It was fascinating to watch.

When we left there the guys headed for Seattle but I had other plans. I drove to the coast and checked in at the RiverTides Suites Hotel, in Seaside, Oregon. I read the literature upon arrival and learned why the hotel had its name. The Necanicum River empties into the Pacific Ocean there and when the ocean tides come in, the river backs up and rises. You don't often see a river have a tide. It was a great way to relax and get ready for the weekend.

Driving up the coast the next day I learned another lesson. Because I'm always learning lessons. When you drive up the winding coast roads by yourself, you don't see much. My eyes were on the curves and the hills but it was still a great drive in my new car.

The key thing about my Seattle trip, though, wasn't the car, or the truck plant, or the great folks from Rottler, or D.J. and his kids. It was a conversation I had with Kelly Topolinski, tucked in a corner behind the media center.

Kelly worked really hard. She juggled numerous clients and had established a well-earned stellar reputation in the sport. I wasn't sure how she managed to pull it all off.

When I asked her if we could talk she dropped what she was doing immediately. That's Kelly.

When I told her I wasn't sure what I wanted to be when I grew up, and I wanted her advice, she had an odd sad look on her face.

"Oh, my," she said. "I was going to talk to you about the same thing. I've crossed the bridge and I've decided this is my last year."

She loved her job. She loved her teams. But she loved her husband Patrick more than all of it combined. He'd been on the tour as a Pro Stock crew member when they had met and fallen in love but now he was working at a shop and no longer on the tour. She was the one leaving him every week, and she'd had enough of that.

"I want to write a book," she continued. "I want to be home and be a great wife for my unbelievable husband. I love everyone out here but I want normalcy, a chance to sell things at flea markets, and I want a warm, wonderful home in Tennessee."

I was stunned but I was unabashedly smiling broadly. I wanted all of that for her. She deserved it. She'd earned it. And her words lit the fire in me. I almost had tears in my eyes.

"Well, that settles it," I said. "This is it for me. I not only want to write a book, I *have* to write my book. These stories go back to my early childhood and I want to tell them all while I still can. There's no way I can keep doing this job and write a book. That's too many words to process every week. I needed someone to inspire me and to motivate me. Thank you, my friend. You've done it."

My head was spinning, but as I always could feel when it was time to plow forward. The door had opened and I'd already walked through. I was going to do this.

I had made a reservation in Ellensburg, Washington, about halfway across the state, for Sunday night after the race. If I got out of the track OK (we went to the second round and I bailed out), I'd make it there before dark. When I got there, I rolled the dice and cancelled the room. I got home before 11 p.m.

Barbara and I talked about it. She could not have been more supportive. To be frank, I had accepted a number of pay cuts to help the team and I was happy to do that. I'm a team player. It's why I've been in sports my whole life. But, despite skipping a bunch of races I wasn't making much compared to the final years with Del. It wouldn't be as financially hard to walk away from as it would've been a few years earlier. Barbara told me to go for it.

I wanted to take the next few weeks, while we were racing in Brainerd and then heading to Indy, to process it all and put my plan into place. I would tell Tim and Krista my plans at Indy.

In another bit of good news we entered the Countdown without too much drama — there's always *some* drama — in eighth place. And, this was big, because of the Atlanta victory we were automatically in the Traxxas Shootout. That was great because I was hardly up for another campaign to get in on the fan vote. I wasn't sure I could make that happen three years in a row.

When I got to Indy and headed for the track I didn't mess around. Within minutes on Friday, I went up to the lounge to see Tim and Krista. I told them it had been a tough decision but I was not going to be coming back in 2016. I was going to write my book — the book friends, drivers, and crew guys had been telling me to write for years. I was glad I waited because right there and right then I knew it was finally the right time. It was absolutely the right time.

I know Krista had an inkling. And if she did Tim probably did as well. They are married, after all. Neither of them was shocked or speechless although the official "for real" nature of what I'd just said made Krista's lower lip quiver quite a bit.

We talked about it for 15 minutes and they were so supportive I was uplifted. If I'd been motivated and raring to go since Seattle I was a racehorse in the starting gate after that meeting in Indy, but we had a lot of details to work out.

I'd keep working as if nothing had changed and I would do all of my normal post-season wrap-up stuff after Pomona. Tim generously agreed to pay me through November. There were a lot of emotions in the room but it was all good stuff and it felt terrific to know they were both behind me so much.

And, the St. Louis race was still to come. That always entailed a lot of work but the most important thing for me was that I'd get a chance to talk to Dick Levi face-to-face. Tim had no problem with me breaking the news to Dick, Shannon, and Shelley via email after Indy. All three of them were sincere and gracious in their responses. I like heartwarming. It's a good feeling. I was experiencing it at all new levels.

That Friday night in Indy when rain finally halted the proceedings, I dashed to my rental car, a nice brand-new Kia Optima, and drove out the back gate. Traffic was already backing up and the state troopers wouldn't allow cars on that back road to turn left on Raceway Road, which would've been my preferred way back to the hotel. Instead, I had to go straight and cut through a residential neighborhood. I'm sure the residents were thrilled with that traffic-flow plan.

I then turned left to get over to Route 136, Crawfordsville Road, which would take me to the intersection with Dandy Trail where a gas station/convenience store sits on the right side of the intersection while a CVS pharmacy is on the left. After a left turn there I'd be back on one of my patented "secret back-way routes" to the hotel utilizing my local knowledge from the days when I lived in that part of Indy.

The traffic was a little backed up at the light. The road was still wet but it was only misting at the time.

Most of the cars and trucks were either going straight or turning right. As I inched forward, the dedicated left-turn lane began and I swung out to get in it. I had clear sailing to the light where only one other car was waiting to turn left. The light was initially still red so I wasn't in a hurry, but then it turned green with an arrow so I sped up to maybe 10 miles an hour. I was no more than 15 yards from the turn and the roads were wet, so I was being cautious.

A large black pickup was still sitting in the lane to go straight, blocking my view of what was in front or beside it. As I passed the truck it felt like my car exploded. The driver of the truck never looked in his sideview mirror to see if I was there. He did, however, flash his lights and wave through a young girl in an old car. She'd been waiting to turn left, from the convenience store onto Crawfordsville Road, for a long time and had been unable to get through the nonstop line of cars leaving the track. She floored it. And hit me right in the front fender before her car spun around and hit me again, on the passenger door and the rear quarter panel. All I heard was the awful sound of impact and the rattle of parts as they hit the ground. All I saw was a wall of white to my right. For the first time in my life I'd been in a car when the airbags went off. Fortunately, it was just the ones on the right side. The one in the steering wheel can break fingers, wrists, and noses.

I knew what had happened and I wasn't worried. I was furious. I yelled "damn it!" at the top of my lungs. Why would anyone hit me? What the hell just happened?

I also knew I was sitting in the middle of a busy road and most of the departing race fans were still behind me. I couldn't see a thing to my right but I was determined to get that Kia into the convenience store parking lot. I hit the gas and everything sounded worse than awful. The grinding sounds were matched by fierce front-end vibrations, but like a mad man I kept my foot down and hoped everyone else was out of my way. Somehow, I got that car into the lot and actually parked it in a spot. When I got out I could see the right front wheel assembly was broken. The wheel itself was at a grotesque angle. The flattened tire had been rubbing against the road sideways as I drove it and parked. The headlight was busted out and the front bumper and quarter panel were mashed. In the back, huge damage to the quarter panel, and another flat tire. This one had a hole in it the size of a grapefruit.

I wasn't hurt but I was surely dazed as I tried to process it all. The first thing I did was call 911.

While waiting for the police officer I got a better handle on what had happened. A nice woman pulled in next to me and said she seen the whole deal with the truck driver waving the girl through. She said the girl stood on the gas, apparently not wanting to wait any longer to get out of there. The black truck was, of course, long gone.

The woman I was talking to was an insurance agent, coincidentally. She gave me all of her info so that I could get her statement later and ask her about anything else she knew. She said, "None of this was your fault but you're going to have to prove it and I'll sign a statement." That was a good thing.

Then, I called the National Car Rental emergency line to report the accident. I sat on "hold" for an exasperating 20 minutes, pulse still pounding.

While I was waiting, Top Alcohol Funny Car racer (and Wilkerson family friend) Andy Bohl pulled in for gas with his crew. He came over to see what happened and to check on me. Then he said, "How in the world did you get this car from up there to right here? You even parked it in a spot!"

I said I probably could've picked it up and carried it at the time. Adrenaline is a powerful thing.

The police officer came and listened as I explained it all. The girl who had hit me had pulled her car off the road, too, and was in the lot at the CVS. As the officer and I were talking a woman ran up and shouted at the policeman, "Why are you here? My daughter is UP THERE. She was in a wreck."

In a moment of incredulity, I pointed at the Kia and said, "Your daughter DID THIS!" Mom looked a little shocked.

I called Barb to gave her the basics and promised to call again from the hotel.

It took hours but finally the police officer left and National informed me they couldn't find a wrecker. I said, "No problem. I'll leave it here in the lot with the keys on the floor, driver's side. Nobody can drive it. It will be here in the morning."

I called a cab, went back to the hotel, and phoned Barb. It hit me then how unlucky I was that night, but how very lucky I was in other ways. Had the girl pulled out a second sooner I would've broadsided her instead of the other way around, except I would've hit her in the driver's door. It was all a matter of split seconds.

I was a little sore the next day, but nothing too bad. I picked up a new rental at the airport and headed to the track. I had posted about the crash on Facebook, so just about everyone knew about it when I got there. What a wild deal.

Over the course of the next month or so, the girl admitted fault 100 percent and my State Farm agent worked with Allstate to get National repaid. They had officially declared the car to be a total loss and recouped some of their money from a salvage yard. It didn't cost me a penny but it dragged on for quite a while and still affects me when I'm driving. I trust no one. I never assume any other driver will be smart or drive safely. I'm constantly alert. I approach every intersection assuming someone will do something stupid. I guess I'm now the exact definition of a defensive driver.

I didn't attend the Charlotte race, which was the first stop on the six-race Countdown. Considering we lost in the opening round I was happy to not have flown more than 2,500 miles each way to be there. St. Louis was next.

It was a deeply important race for me. With it being the team and the sponsor's home race (the track is about 95 miles south of Springfield) it had always been important. Even in the CSK days it was special because it was my hometown. In 2015 I was wrapping it up and I wanted everything to go smoothly.

One annual part of my St. Louis experience was escorting Dick and his guests into the track. They would fly down on the LRS jet, landing at a small airport about 10 miles from Gateway Motorsports Park. When they were in their limo, Dick would call me. I'd hop on the golf cart and drive out to the front gate. We did the same drill at Gainesville, Chicago, and Denver. I was used to it.

My first stop would be the state troopers who were directing traffic. I would tell them my primary sponsor was on his way, in a limo, and that I'd be escorting them in. The limo would then leave and not come back until it was time for Dick and his guests to drive back to the jet. Not once did I ever get any pushback from the troopers.

When Dick and his guests arrived, this time in a party bus, they followed me to the ticket takers who went onboard the bus to scan everyone's tickets, and then the driver slowly followed me into the beehive of the pit area. I'm sure it's jarring for folks who have never been to a drag race to discover they are driving around amidst loud race cars that are on their way to the staging lanes.

In St. Louis, NHRA would always put our pit at the end of an aisle. They knew we needed access for Dick. When we arrived and everyone disembarked, Dick was all smiles. He shook my hand and then gave me a hug.

"I'm so sorry to see you leave, Bob, but I'm really excited for you," he said. "You've just been so good for us. You're the best."

As I wrote that quote I realized how few people have ever known Dick said things like that to me. I told Barbara and a few other people but I never thought it was appropriate to tell Tim. I may be confident but I try not to be arrogant. Dick's words meant the world to me.

We had a great day and a good race. Doing my bit on the P.A. in the hospitality center, I performed all the normal schtick but then got a little serious. Most of the guests were regulars for this race and they knew me. I informed them it was my last St. Louis race and told them what I was going to do. I capped it off by asking the crowd to gather around me. I then held my iPhone up and took an epic selfie of all of us.

When it was time for Dick and his group to head back to the party bus I followed on the golf cart. As Dick was about to board the bus he stopped, looked me right in the eye, shook my hand, and wished me luck. He told me he wanted an autographed copy when the book was done. He then turned to get onboard but stopped. He turned around again and gave me an enormous hug.

"All the best to you, Bob," he said. "I'm really proud of what you're doing and really excited for you. Thanks again for all you've done for me and LRS. It's been a privilege."

Maybe he had something in his eye or his allergies kicked in right at that moment. If so, I had the same problem. The word "touching" doesn't come close to describing it. Dick Levi is an important man. On that day he made me feel like the most important man in world.

Reading was next, and no one found it hard to believe that major Atlantic storms were scheduled to completely blanket the area with rain. All weekend.

As the race approached we kept an eye on the forecasts. They never got any less dire.

When Tim and I talked on Tuesday, my comment was, "NHRA should just postpone this now and give everyone a chance to regroup. It's not like this is a line of thunderstorms, it's a huge disturbance from a tropical storm. This is crazy."

Tim agreed, and later that day he called me back.

"Listen, why don't you do Reading from home," he said. "Our Saturday guest list is as low as it's ever been and with the weather it's doubtful a dozen of them will show up. There's no reason for you to fly across the country just to get rained on. Save the money."

It took me exactly half a second to say, "Are you sure?"

Reading made it nine races I would skip in 2015.

The savings weren't all that great for me, though. I couldn't get a refund on the Delta ticket, but I could cancel my rental car and hotel room.

Since I had to eat the airfare I instead got Delta to alter the ticket to just be a round trip to MSP. I'd cover the race from there.

Friday was a complete washout. As I followed the Twitter feeds of my PR colleagues and many racers I can't say I was sorry I missed out on the gully-washer fun.

On Saturday one session actually happened. In it, Tim ran 7.717. That's not a typo. That's how green the track was. His 7.717 landed him in the No. 4 spot. Again, not a typo. And everyone stayed very cold and wet.

Sunday was dry, but cool and overcast. Tim called and said, "There's a groove out there where you can set a national record but it's really narrow. You can't get one inch out of it."

He ran 3.985 to win in round one. Nearly four seconds better than his qualifying time. A round later, Tim was done and I was in Woodbury. The first part of that sentence was disappointing. The second part of that sentence wasn't a bad thing.

Dallas came and went and I got to see my buddy Dennis Peek. It was time for Vegas and then Pomona. My final season was winding down. We had something special lined up for Vegas.

Tim had been dragged to one stage-production musical in his life, a more classical opera-style show. He hated it. Krista and I had been trying to get him to "Jersey Boys" since I joined the team. This time, we succeeded. I played the "It's your last chance and it would mean a lot to both Buck and me" card. It worked. He agreed. We'd go on Thursday night.

Richard Hartman had also asked me if he could take me to dinner that night. I told him we had plans and that he should come along as well. He was thrilled to say yes.

Knowing Las Vegas traffic at rush hour, we gave ourselves an enormous amount of time to get down to the Paris Resort on The Strip. We figured if we got there early we'd get a bite to eat before the show. We did pay for our tickets but Buck got us a huge "cast member discount" and had us placed in the "show seats" just a few rows from the stage.

And, of course, the traffic never materialized and we were there 90 minutes before the curtain. We sat at a Paris bistro and ordered dinner.

We had barely been seated when my phone rang. It was Buck, who told me he, Mary, and the boys were all at the resort because the show had planned a Halloween extravaganza for cast and families. They were done with that and wanted to come see us. A minute later, Team Hujabre walked up to our table.

Buck was playing a much more substantial role in the show, by then. In addition to that he'd taken on the understudy position for the Bob Gaudio character. Bob Gaudio was Frankie Valli's close collaborator on The Four Seasons. His role is the second most important in the show.

Buck had a devilish grin on his face when he and the family arrived at our table.

"I'm so glad you're all here, and Tim I know you're going to love the show," he said. "And you'll be seeing quite a bit more of me than you normally would. I'm going on as Bob Gaudio tonight."

Earlier in the week Buck and I had kidded around about hiring a hit man to bust the regular Gaudio's kneecaps. He didn't go quite that far, but he did ask the producers and the standard Gaudio cast member if there was any way he could go on in that role on Thursday. They said yes.

The show was fabulous, as it always is. Krista was to my right and Tim was on the other side of her. Every time Buck would do something amazing and Tim would clap, she'd elbow me. I think I had bruises. Maybe a fractured rib.

Tim, Krista, and Richard were blown away. It felt great to have gotten them there so that they could see the enormous talent on display.

After the show Buck came out of the actor's door to see us. Tim gave him a hug. Oh, what a night (that would be a Four Seasons reference.)

We had something special cooked up for Friday qualifying as well. I needed a cover shot for this book. I wanted a real artist to shoot it. Fortunately for all of us in the NHRA world, we had a world-class artist shooting photos on the tour. He'd shot Super Bowls, World Cups, and all kinds of sports for the likes of Sports Illustrated and USA Today. Mark Rebilas made art with a camera.

I'd asked him if he'd be willing to shoot the cover shot and a few other photos of me at a race, and I held my breath when I asked him what it would cost. We knew each other and liked each other, but away from the track we were no more than social media friends.

He looked me right in the eye and said, "I know how important this is, what you're doing. I'll get all the shots in Vegas, and it will be an honor to do it." The price he offered me was a fraction of what I'd expected.

I had the staging of the shot in mind so I brought an indoor soccer ball and a Minnesota Twins hat with me to Vegas. I ordered a wooden baseball bat online I had it sent to Buck's house. He brought that to the track Friday morning.

The plan was to do the shoot in the lanes prior to Q2 on Friday evening, when the warm light from sunset would be just perfect. Tim and the guys were gracious enough to service the car quickly and get it to the lanes early. Everyone was accommodating and gracious beyond belief.

In a completely coincidental moment of pure luck, Del's DHL team pulled up right next to ours. Mark said, "We can have them move that," and I replied, "No way. This is basically my whole career right here in one shot."

I was really quite self-conscious as Mark and his assistant got ready to shoot. I grabbed the bat and ball out of the tow vehicle and could sense that crew guys on other teams were watching. We shot at least a dozen sets of photos in different poses and on various sides and locations around the car. What you see on the cover of this book is the phenomenal work of Mark Rebilas as a photographer and Todd Myers as a graphic artist.

After the photo session we qualified 10th and lost in the first round. My season and my career had but one more race to go.

Barbara would be flying down to Pomona to be with me. And we'd both make the trek up to Hollywood for the NHRA Awards Ceremony on Monday night. I was feeling a little (a lot) melancholy as I prepared to travel. My friends in the media center and in the NHRA Media Relations Department had a few things up their sleeves.

We had our annual P.R. reps dinner on Friday night at a wonderful restaurant in nearby La Verne. Barb flew in that night and got there just in time for the dinner. We filled parts of two rooms at a pair of long tables and the stories and laughs were flowing even before the appetizers and first round of drinks arrived. This group had really become close and nights like that Friday were priceless.

We enjoyed a marvelous dinner, with Barbara by my side. When it was over, there were speeches. And awards. And thanks. And dedications.

Joanne Knapp was also celebrating her final race. She'd been doing P.R. with her husband Jon for years, representing Summit Racing Equipment for many of them. When Jon tragically lost his battle with illness just a couple of years earlier Joanne honored his legacy by continuing to work. Her career was celebrated that night, along with Kelly's and mine. It got a little emotional.

My colleagues had a heartfelt gift for me and they'd kept it a secret for a couple of races. Elon had purchased a baseball and over the course of the Dallas and Vegas races, plus Friday at the track in Pomona, he'd gotten it autographed by nearly every P.R. person, photographer, writer, and editor I knew. They presented it to me that night. Elon said the number of times I walked in a room and someone had to hide the ball was too great to keep track of.

Did I mention it got a little emotional? I'll never lose that ball.

To cap it off the head of media relations at NHRA, Terry Blount, stood up with another baseball. He'd gotten it during his long and illustrious newspaper career, much of which was with the Houston Chronicle. It was autographed by a Cardinal Hall of Famer, the great Bob Gibson. With a tear in his eye, he presented it to me and said, "I couldn't think of a better place for this ball to go."

It was one of the most memorable dinners of my entire life. I'll never forget it.

The next day, longtime friend and blog reader Kim the Lawyer flew down from Vancouver. He had some lame excuse about cheap airfare and having Pomona on his NHRA bucket list. I'm pretty sure I know why he came. Barbara and I met him for a drink at the Sheraton on Saturday night. His gift of a pewter two-handled Scottish drinking cup, known as a Quaich, stunned me. The quaich allowed friends or rivals to share a drink across a table from both sides of the cup. It's a great way to remove poison from the list of things that might be in the cup.

During one of the final qualifying sessions we pulled up to the line to make our lap. There was nothing on the track, no oil being cleaned up, and no reason not to fire the car.

Except Mark Lyle, the Chief Starter, told us to wait. I was standing in position at the right rear of the car when a television camera operator appeared next to me. Something was clearly up.

I heard Alan Reinhart say, "I want to take a minute to tell all of you about a special person who is retiring after this race." He then went on to say some of the most humbling and complimentary things I've ever heard, while the camera put my image on the big screen. Yeah, a little something must've gotten in my eyes. The fans actually clapped when Alan was done. It was not lost on me that NHRA had helped coordinate that. They held up the race so Alan could say something. Jim Head walked over with a broad smile on his face and shook my hand, as did all the crew guys and other racers nearby.

We qualified 11th and when the LRS car smoked the tires in round one on Sunday, all I could do was wistfully watch it idle down the track just like I had when the CSK car did the same thing on its final lap. Maybe such a slow-motion ending was the most appropriate. I just stared down the Pomona track, remembering it all. I put my arm around my wife and we walked back to the pits.

I was done but we weren't about to leave. The Funny Car world championship was on the line and my friend Del was in contention. Barbara and I were staying until the end. Plus, Chuck Worsham's wife Lou had instructed me, in no uncertain terms, that I was not allowed to leave the track until I came over to their pit. Rule No. 1: Always do what Lou Worsham asks.

When Del raced Jack Beckman in the semifinal, a win would earn him the championship. It would also make him one of just three drivers to ever win it in both Top Fuel and Funny Car, along with Kenny Bernstein and Gary Scelzi. Barbara and I respectfully stayed behind the viewing fence, allowing the DHL team and the Worsham family to watch this as an unobstructed group. When the win light came on in Del's lane, everyone went nuts, including Barbara and me. I yelled, "I have to go" and she understood. I let the DHL guys do their thing. I wanted to congratulate Chuck. With tears in his eyes, all he could say, over and over, was, "How 'bout that!"

Barbara and I then rushed over to the DHL pit at the Kalitta camp. Del was doing interviews at the top end and was driven down the return road with his trophy and jacket. Connie, Kate, and Maddy were there. Chuck and Lou were there. They handed me a packet of heartfelt presents, including a number of photos from back in the day. The entire extended group of Worsham family and friends were there, including Frank Gilchrist. When Del arrived, I didn't want to intrude but he spotted me and yelled my name. If I think about it hard enough, I can still feel that handshake and hug. There were a lot of people crying.

Del, of course, still had a final round to run. Of course he beat Tommy Johnson to win Pomona after having won the championship. Considering all we'd been through, and how far both of us had come, it was a perfect ending to my final day of racing.

I was more than a little exhausted when we got back to the Sheraton, but the glow of everything that had been happening to me was irrepressible. I couldn't stop thinking about all of it.

The next day we headed to Hollywood for the big dress-up party. I'd spent the money to upgrade to a corner suite on a high floor at the Loew's Hotel just off Hollywood Blvd.

We looked spectacular. Everybody looked spectacular. The meal was great, and Tim Wilkerson actually said to Barbara, "Which one do you think I would like better, the red wine or the white wine?" I never thought I'd hear those words. I think it was a genuine nod to both of us, for the very real commitment we'd both made to the cause over the last seven years. He enjoyed a glass of both!

The speeches were great, the show was great, and as opposed to many of the banquets from back in the early days, it moved right along at a good clip. We stood and cheered for Del, who illustrated how much time had passed since that first year with CSK when he took out his glasses in order to read his speech.

When the show was over, it was time for the after-party at a club across the complex from the ballroom. I hadn't made much of an effort to attend the after-parties in recent years. I was too old and tired to be racing the clock to midnight. This night was different.

I wanted to spend it with my wife. I wanted to spend it with my best friends. I wanted to spend it with my colleagues.

For the first 30 minutes Barbara and I tucked ourselves into a booth with two very real friends who were attending their first banquet. Over the blaring music while dealing with the flashing lights we held a fun conversation with Lewis Worden and his wonderful wife Donna. In terms of the real roots of my own personal PR career, there were no better people to sit with.

When they headed off to bed we circulated among my PR colleagues. We managed to pass our phones around to have a number of grainy group photos taken. At no other time could you find us all in one spot looking that fine.

When we ducked out, quietly and without fanfare, we returned to our room and I slept like a brick. It was over.

We had time the next day to have lunch with one of Barbara's cousins, Bonnie, who lived in North Hollywood. That was a terrific way to end the weekend. With family.

After we traveled back to Liberty Lake I quickly wrapped up all of my Season in Review binders and shipped them off to Tim, Dick and Shannon. I kept one for myself, of course.

We spent a cozy and wonderful Thanksgiving in Berthoud, Colorado, with Barbara's brother Jim, his wife Deb, and their incredible kids James, Erin, and Leah. Erin, who had recently moved into her first house with her fiance Eric, hosted our meal. It was over-the-top fantastic, and the company could not have been better. I enjoyed every second of it.

It was December by the time all of that was complete, and we had a couple of monumental things up our sleeves. The first one would happen online.

Barbara had been gracious and supportive enough to allow me to write this book. To do that, she let me quit my career and focus on it full-time. That would be a hit to our finances, and as much as I appreciated that I also felt bad about it.

I had thought I would never do any sort of crowdfunding for the book. It's not like we were broke and I couldn't write it without other people's money. It felt like it would be asking for a handout.

But then I realized a key thing. We would be losing my income in 2016 and it wouldn't be fair to Barb for me to also cover the cost of self-publishing with money from our savings account or retirement funds. That's what I needed to get my head wrapped around in order to eagerly start a Kickstarter campaign.

I set up the page, wrote all the copy, and was ready to launch it by the middle of December. All I needed to do was pick the amount of money I was trying to raise. On Kickstarter, it's an all-or-nothing deal. People make pledges in various amounts but nobody gets charged a nickel, and you don't receive a penny, unless you hit your target. I had to be realistic.

When I told Barb I thought I could raise $25,000 she shook her head. I could almost hear the cartoon cowbell sound effect.

"There is absolutely no way," she said. "The whole theory of crowdfunding is to get a lot of people to give you a little money. I say you shoot for $2,500 at the most."

We "compromised." I set the target at $20,000. We had 45 days to raise the funds. If we made it, the funds wouldn't cover everything I needed to do to make the book a success but the financial burden would be significantly lessened. I let a bit of doubt creep into my head, wondering who on earth would pledge enough to get me there but I reminded myself of one thought: The NHRA family. They'd always been there for me.

As rewards, I offered crew shirts, jackets, and Wally trophies. A person would have to pledge $500 for a Wally. I'd be cleaning out a lot of closets and shelves, at the same time.

Considering the average pledge across all of Kickstarter is around $25, my campaign seemed quite aggressive. I had to have confidence to flip the switch and launch it. I was nervous when I did it.

I had already selected Outskirts Press as my publisher for one very good reason. Instead of taking a hefty fee to produce, publish, and sell a book, they partner with the writer. The upfront fee was much smaller but they would then split the profit on every sale. That made it in their best interest to promote and market the book. I liked that approach.

We went live with the Kickstarter on December 14. Within minutes the first pledge came in. It was from one of my PR colleagues, Pat Caporali. The NHRA family was at work.

The campaign would run for 45 days, with it coming to a close on February 1, 2016. I'd watch it every day and had a special chime added to my in-box on my laptop. Every time I'd get an email from Kickstarter telling me I had another backer, I could hear it from almost anywhere in the house.

At the same time I was due to write my final blog at NHRA.com, and it was posted on the same day as the Kickstarter launch: December 14.

In the blog, I reminisced about many of the memories I'd created over the 10 years and four months I'd written it. It was an emotional installment to write but I was incredibly excited about what lay ahead.

Within days I'd be moving my blog to our family's website in support of The Perfect Game Foundation, our charity my brother Del spearheaded. The only goal of TPGF was to give a boost to young women and men who needed a "contact" in the sports world in order to get through the door. We would be that contact. We were paying it forward for all the great fortune we'd had to be born the children of Del and Taffy Wilber.

I'd been writing a blog called "Bob On Baseball" there for a few years but only adding to it four or five times a year. Brother Del was happy to let me transition it to "Bob's Blog" and I brought the same "view into my life" approach that had been so successful at NHRA.com. Many of my loyal readers made the move with me.

I'd have to leave the Kickstarter and blog deals behind for a while, though. Barbara and I were heading back to Kauai and this time that's the only island we were visiting. We'd stay at the same Marriott, arriving December 22 and returning December 26. We'd get to spend Christmas with not just Lonnie and Mary, but also their daughter Leigh who had packed up and headed to the island as well.

Every day was magical — I think even more so than the trip a year earlier because we focused totally on Kauai and family. If there was a spot we loved the first time, we went back. If there were places we didn't have time to see the year before, we made time. It was sublime.

And we ate pretty well, if by "pretty well" you mean we ate like royalty all five days we were there. We met more restaurant owners, bartenders, waiters, and coffee servers who all knew Mary and Lonnie by name and had no problem envisioning ourselves living there. Maybe some day.

When I'd posted on Facebook that we were going I got a message from Tony Evans. The Evans family was the group that always had a photo taken with me in Pomona, while they towered over my shrimpy 6' 1" frame. They were going to be on Kauai at the same time, at their beach house at "the end of the road" on the north side of the island. Tony, his parents, and family friend Molly wanted to get together for lunch on our final day. Our flight out of Kauai didn't take off until around 8 p.m. so we had the time. I assumed we'd meet at a restaurant after Barbara and I made the drive around the island. They insisted we come to their beach house.

I figured they rented it seasonally. They did not. They owned it. And most of the land around it. When we arrived we couldn't believe the place. It was overwhelmingly cool, with vast beach and ocean views and a design that clung to the side of steep Kauai mountain.

I started asking about it and it turned out the home had been in the family for generations. They were descendants of what was really Kauai royalty. Again, it proved you never really know who you're talking to when you agree to have a photo taken, year after year.

And the spaghetti lunch was awesome. The views were worth millions. The company was priceless.

We headed back to the airport and flew, overnight, back to Seattle and then to Spokane. The trip was everything we'd hoped it would be and much more. Plus, it put both of us back over the Diamond threshold.

A few days later, we headed back to Woodbury for New Year's Eve and our anniversary. Barbara's sister Kitty flew up to meet us for that. 2015 was officially over.

I was a little nervous.

I was taking on something blindly, with no real clue as to how to do it. I made a promise to myself about taking this on as my job. I'd work at it every day and since I'd already transitioned my blog to our family charity website, I'd work at that every week as well.

I'd also keep close tabs on the Kickstarter campaign. When we cleared $10,000 by early January I thought we had a chance. Then there was a bit of a lull, where we went from 10 or 12 new backers per week to more like five or six. When I mentioned that to a Kickstarter veteran he said, "That's normal. Now, your biggest backers will keep an eye on it and get you over the hump. Just watch."

Dick Levi stepped in, with an enormous pledge. Shannon Heisler did as well. Smaller pledges began to pick up steam. The number of people who chose the $500 Wally reward stunned me. The total reached 12. Two of them wrote me to say, "Keep the Wally. I just wanted to help."

As February 1 approached, the writing was going OK but not great. I was trying to find my rhythm. I'd selected a fabulous editor, in Greg Halling. He'd be working with me weekly to establish the pace and the style. I was learning from him on a daily basis. He was teaching this old dog some great new tricks.

During the last week of the Kickstarter deal the pledges ramped up. Del Worsham, Antron Brown, many crew members, many blog readers, and many strangers from as far away as Australia backed the project. Even better, guys like Antron, Del, and Ron Capps took it upon themselves to retweet my Twitter posts often, to their vast audiences. Every time they'd do that, I'd get another pledge from a complete stranger.

On the morning before the deadline I was stunned to see an email from Kickstarter with the subject line, "YOU MADE IT!" I had gone to bed still more than $2,500 short but I had until midnight that last day to make it. Overnight, four more big pledges came in, including very generous ones from Del and Buck. The one that put me over the top came from a totally unexpected source. It was Bob Vandergriff.

I emailed Bob to express my enormous thanks and his response was, "Happy to do it. I think what you're doing is bitchin' and I want you to succeed."

When the final bell rang, we'd surpassed $22,500 on the pledges from 99 total backers.

That average Kickstarter pledge of $25? Our average pledge was about $225. That's a stunning number.

The NHRA family. What a group. The emotions associated with making that happen were just a little overwhelming. They still are.

I had made myself a self-employed writer. Nearly 100 people had helped me do that and many more offered checks and other support. I owed it to each and every one of them to do this right. I'd go to my office and sit at my desk every day, writing, editing, and conceptualizing. There was also a ton of research to do, to get the timelines and the facts straight.

When I started, I was clueless how to do it.

I sat down for the first time on January 6 and I began to write. I didn't know how long it would take. I didn't know how long the book would be. I didn't know if I was even capable of the project.

I let none of that stop me.

On October 20, I wrote these last few pages. In December, Greg and I finished the last "once over" in terms of editing. In January, it was shipped off to Outskirts Press.

You are holding the result in your hand. It has been the most amazing thing I've ever experienced.

Now let's see what comes next.

Plow forward!

Epilogue

I've always been a writer. I initially figured I was a pretty good one as early as sixth grade when I won an essay contest that drew thousands of entries from all over St. Louis. By high school, I knew I was onto something. College confirmed that.

For the last 20 years I've been effectively writing for a living. Public relations reps do that and I took great pride in trying to get better every year, and get more creative every week. I didn't always succeed but I never stopped trying.

When I sat at my desk to begin this book, on January 6, 2016, I started writing. I had no idea how to do this, but had a decent "best guess" plan in place. The first thing I wrote was an outline.

I didn't follow the outline precisely but I used it as the road map to the finish line, or the mountaintop as I described it. It gave me a rough idea of all the subjects I wanted to cover and it alerted me to the fact the book would be long and full of details. The way I saw it, there was no real reason to write it if the details were skipped. The joy is in the details.

It was another new style of writing I was trying to conquer, at a new pace. After 20 years in the NHRA it felt like I could write feature stories and press releases in my sleep. This was a much bigger deal. I don't think, looking back, I really knew how big it was. I just plowed forward.

Plowing forward ended up being the theme that runs through the entire book but it wasn't in the outline or on my radar when I started. Instead, as story after story came to life I recognized it as an ongoing theme and built it in from that point forward. It's the story of my life. Plow forward.

When I approached Greg Halling to be my editor I knew I was asking the right guy. As a highly respected journalist with a deep appreciation for drag racing, baseball, and the best words to describe them, he knows how to maximize impact and keep a short and concise flow going.

When we started working together there was no denying my propensity for long parentheses-laden compound sentences. Greg worked with me on a more economical style from the first day. It was my mission to "go to school" each week and analyze his input, hoping to deliver exactly what he wanted the next week. It worked. I got an A.

It's remarkable how much I grew as a writer during this process. I turned 60 halfway through it, and yet I was still getting better on a daily basis. If I'm now considered a professional writer, even an author, it's clear to me that I was every bit an amateur when we started.

I suspect it's possible I could've done this without Greg. It's completely impossible, however, to think I could have done it nearly as well. As the executive editor of the Standard-Examiner in Ogden, Utah, he has a very stressful full-time job. And yet, he finished initial editing just two weeks after I finished writing.

When we started, I asked him, "How much should I pay you?" and he told me his compensation would come in two ways. First, he'd have a hand in creating a book out of thin air. Secondly, he wanted an autographed copy. That was it. We were both in it for the same reason. Not to get rich, but to make it happen. I disregarded his compensation plan, though. I sent him a Wally, because he's a champion.

I also could not have written this book without the support of my wonderful wife, Barbara Doyle.

She knew how much I wanted to do this and she understood it couldn't happen if I kept working by writing 8,000 words a week between the PR stuff, my column at National Dragster, and my blog. There wouldn't be enough words in my head or energy in my hands.

So I quit my job. I certainly didn't quit working, I just walked away from the job that provided an income. And I focused solely on this book.

The only week I took completely off was the week we finally moved back to Minnesota, from Spokane, in early June. Even with professional movers handling most of it, such a thing is stressful and overwhelming. It all demanded my full-time attention. And then there was the nearly 1,400-mile drive "home" with Barbara and the cats, Boofus and Buster. Other than that, I got up every Monday morning and went to work for another week, churning out roughly four chapters per month.

I adapted quickly to new routines. I found my pace and my best approach and most of that was built around a technique of getting my brain up and running each morning by doing research and reading. Between baseball and drag racing, where stats are very much the glue that holds both sports together, there was a lot of research to do. A lot. But that was good. I'd crunch the numbers all morning and be ready to put it into words every afternoon.

I can't count how many times I'd get so deeply involved in the writing I would be absorbed right into it. I'd think, "Man, it must be getting to be 3 o'clock" and I'd look at my watch and see that it was more like 6:30. It just happened.

An old worn-out saying tells us that ignorance is bliss. I think I'm living proof. I had no idea what I was getting into and no idea how to get to the mountaintop. Had I attended a seminar about writing a book of this scope, I probably would've walked away. If my entire life has been a series of "plow forward" moments, this book may be the prime example.

I just kept plowing forward until I was done.

Throughout the process there were side trips. In all, I attended seven NHRA races in 2016, going to Gainesville, Joliet, Sonoma, Brainerd, St. Louis, Las Vegas, and Pomona. As one of my former PR colleagues, Lachelle Seymour, deftly pointed out on Facebook, I was doing a lousy job at being retired from racing. I couldn't stay away. I very much enjoyed the power and the majesty of the racing but it was the people that mattered most.

Going to those races gave me a bridge to this different life. I could stop in for a day or two, arrive at the track when I wanted, leave when I felt it was time, and recharge my batteries in terms of the incredible group of former colleagues I so very much valued. And I could spend valuable time with my best friend in racing, Krista Wilkerson.

In Sonoma, Barbara came along and we took my Paintsville "Bronze Fox" buddy Vince Bienek and his wife Mary to their first drag race. Elon Werner gave them a fantastic tour through the sprawling subdivision known as the John Force Racing pit area and two new fans were created.

In July, my college teammates Lance, Oscar, and Radar kept our new tradition of an annual reunion alive when they made a trip to Minneapolis and St. Paul. We spent two nights in Minneapolis at the Grand Hotel, sharing that luxurious place with the Cleveland Indians.

I'd reached out to Dave St. Peter, the president and CEO of the Twins and an adviser for our family charity and he arranged a mind-blowing behind-the-scenes tour of Target Field, including a trip to the actual playing field for batting practice. We then spent a night at the St. Paul Hotel and "crossed the beams" by having most of our Woodbury friends join us for dinner and drinks. I think almost everyone is still laughing. And my Woodbury friends now understand why I love these guys.

In September, Barbara and I made a trip to St. Louis but it wasn't for the race. Instead, we visited the campus of SIUE along with most of my teammates from our 1977 team. As a group we were inducted into the Athletic Department Hall of Fame. Stan Osterbur gave me the biggest man-hug in history, complete with a kiss on the cheek.

As the summer vanished I realized I was getting close. By October I could look ahead and actually count the number of chapters I had left.

On October 20, I finished the first draft of principal writing. I had not even contemplated how that would feel. Just plow forward until you write the last chapter, right? That's initially how it felt when I typed the last period on the end of the final sentence. Then I stood up to walk away, like I had on any other day for the prior 10 months.

The emotions completely surprised me. Before I took a step they swept over me like a tsunami. The enormity of the project finally hit home. I had never let it, up until that time, but on October 20 during the late afternoon, it nearly drowned me with emotion.

On January 5, 2017, I had finished writing and Greg and I both finished editing, each going back through the entire book three times to trim and fix problems. Some really good stuff ended up on the editing room floor, but it was clear we had no choice. In its initial form, the book was close to 1,000 pages. I started on January 6, 2016 and finished on January 5, 2017. That's slightly uncanny.

After a year of dedication and hard work, I had written a book. Me. I just did it.

What a wonderful process this has been. Writing these stories, remembering these characters, and stringing it all together in one lengthy lifetime of experiences, reinforces my belief that I'm still the luckiest kid in the world.

Photographic Evidence

Taffy and Del Wilber circa 1947

Christmas Eve 1958, with Mom and Mary

Where the heart is. Woodleaf Court

Hoops with my "Irish Twin" (I was always a ham)

Those lovely high school years

Rockin' the Spirits t-shirt as a college freshman

Summer after freshman year, with Bill Lee. Playing with the big boys!

SIUE Varsity (a line drive in the box score)

With Stan Osterbur and Dave Schaake. Snowed out.

The Hawk at his Paintsville locker

Another day, another road trip - Johnson City

The Count and The Hawk – 1978

The Count and The Hawk – 2016

With Alto in Medford - 1979

With Alto in Joliet - 2011

Skip and Taffy - Watching their boy at the Valmeyer Tournament

She did like fast cars!

1997 Winternationals in Pomona - Day 1 with this guy
The dream begins...

Just a couple of kids in Maui

8 million Del Worsham Hot Wheels cars!

Camp Snoopy in action

Visiting Francine and Adam Vincent in Hawaii

How it feels to win the $100,000 Showdown (Photo by Auto Imagery, Inc.)

It feels even better to "double up" (Photo by Auto Imagery, Inc.)

Pond Cam features Neighbor Dave's rink

A couple of crazy boyz!

A new era begins - NHRA Finals 2008

January 2009 - Fred Turner drops in at West Palm Beach

With Dick Levi and my buddy Krista Wilkerson

My "intern" Colin meets Shannon Heisler

The Hujabre family comes calling on Halloween in Las Vegas

We're still loyal Twins fans

Mary Bienek and "The Bronze Fox" get the guided Elon Werner tour of JFR

The G-Man, Gary Gerould. A pro's pro

Minnesota tough - The North Shore of Lake Superior at 10-below

"I know you're out there. I can hear you breathing…" (Photo by Mark J Rebilas)

Lee, Wilber, Arend, and Myers. Just hangin' with Geddy like it's nothin'...

Reunion time - Wilb, Oscar, Lance, and Radar

Just taking one last look… (Photo by Mark J. Rebilas)